HILL COUNTRY

COMPLETELY UPDATED 4TH EDITION

Discover the wonders of Texas with *Texas Monthly*® Guidebooks from Gulf Publishing Company:

Austin
Dallas
El Paso
Houston
New Mexico
San Antonio
Texas
Texas Bed & Breakfast
Texas Parks and Campgrounds
Texas Missions
West Texas and the Big Bend

HILL COUNTRY

COMPLETELY UPDATED 4TH EDITION

BY RICHARD ZELADE

Gulf Publishing Company
Houston, Texas

To
Erv and Florence, and Diana

Gulf Publishing Company
P.O. Box 2608
Houston, Texas □ 77252-2608

10 9 8 7 6 5 4 3 2 1

Library of Congress Cataloging-in-Publication Data

Zelade, Richard, 1953–
    Hill country / by Richard Zelade. —Completely updated 4th ed.
      p.   cm. — (The Texas Monthly guidebooks)
    Includes index.
    ISBN 0-87719-242-1
    1. Texas Hill Country (Tex.)—Tours.   2. Automobile travel—
Texas—Texas Hill Country—Guidebooks.   I. Title.   II. Series.
F392.T47.Z44   1997
917.6404′63—dc21   96-45588
                                              CIP

Printed in the United States of America.

Texas Monthly is a registered trademark of Mediatex
Communications Corporation.

CONTENTS

ACKNOWLEDGMENTS

In the more than twenty years spent putting together *Hill Country,* I've done a lot of listening, looking, and reading. Each experience—no matter how small—has increased in some way my understanding of the Hill Country and subsequently has enhanced this book. For this I am grateful. But I owe special thanks to a number of people.

I would particularly like to thank the staff of the Barker Texas History Center (now the Center for American History) at the University of Texas at Austin, who spent hours shagging down all the files and books I was forever requesting.

In putting together each trip, I found at least one book that proved to be a particularly valuable source of background information and/or quoted material. By trip, the books are as follows:

Take a Ride on the Fredericksburg & Northern Railroad: *Rails Through the Hill Country* by F. A. Schmidt; *Charcoal and Charcoal Burners* by Fritz Toepperwein; *Fredericksburg Self-Guiding Auto Tour* by Joan Jubbard.

Hermit of the Hills/Highland Lakes: *Pioneers in God's Hills* by the Gillespie County Historical Society; *History of Burnet County* by Darrell Debo; *Llano, Gem of the Hill Country* by Wilburn Oatman.

Mormon Trails: *The Lyman Wight Colony in Texas* by J. Marvin Hunter; *Evolution of a State* by Noah Smithwick; *100 Years in Bandera 1853–1953* by J. Marvin Hunter; *German Artist on the Texas Frontier: Friedrich Richard Petri* by William W. Newcomb, Jr.

Hill Country Rivers: *A Hundred Years of Comfort in Texas* by Guido Ransleben; *Mountains of the Mind* by Horace Morelock; *Unser Fortschritt; Our Progress* by the Comfort Heritage Foundation, Inc.

Enchanted Rock: *Blanco County History* by John Moursund.

Riding the Fault: *History of New Braunfels and Comal County, Texas 1844–1946* by Oscar Haas; *Texas, with Particular Reference to German Immigration and the Physical Appearance of the Country* by Ferdinand Roemer; *Tales from the Manchaca Hills* by Edna Turley Carpenter.

Williamson County: *Land of Clear Water* by Clara Scarbrough; *History of Burnet County* by Darrell Debo; *Williamson County Centennial 1848–1948* by the Williamson County Centennial Committee.

Shiner Pilgrimage: *The History of Lavaca County* by Paul Boethel; *Earth Has No Sorrow* by Dee Azadian; *On a Mexican Mustang Through Texas* by A. E. Sweet; *Historic Lockhart Then and Now* by Zona Mae Withers; *Historical Caldwell County: Where Roots Intertwine* by the Mark Withers Trail Drive Museum.

The Wild West: *A History of Lee County, Texas* by the Lee County Historical Survey Committee; *Evolution of a State* by Noah Smithwick; *Coronado's Children* by J. Frank Dobie.

Central Texas Stew: *Driving Tour of Industry, Texas* by Anne Lindemann; *Guide to New Ulm;* and *Flaming Feuds of Colorado County* by Lillian Reese.

And finally, thanks to Margaret Keidel, John and Edward Balcar, the Riskes, Gould Davis, Jimmy Nuckles, the Kliers, Mrs. Simek, Speedy, Emil, Joe, Cracker, Mr. Siems, Frank Wagner, C. W. Carlson, Clara Scarbrough, Max Theis, Red Casparis, Chuck Zelade, Susan and Jeff Reid, Brook Watts, Bill and Doris Bacon, Bob and Suzan Leggett, Kristin Brown, Anders Saustrup, Odies Schatte, Barbara, and Marianne. Thanks also to Emil Holtzer, Alton Koch, the Twin Sisters School Association, Rusty Vogt, Winnie Petty, and Walter Doebbler. Fourth Edition thanks go to Marvin Finger, Andrew Sansom, Robin Giles, Edith Giles, Bill Stein, Buddy Rau, Louis Polansky, Helen Mikus, Joe Nick Patoski, Walt Falk, Royce Nelson, and John Morthland.

Introduction

Texas, more than any other state, is the crossroads of America. Four major continental divisions come together here: the Rocky Mountains, the Great Western High and Lower Plains, and the Gulf Coastal Plains.

The farming woodland Caddoes, the cannibal coastal Karankawa, the roaming Apache hunters, and the desert cliff-dwelling Pueblos—all of them once called Texas home. The cultures of Old Mexico and the Old South, the Wild West, and the Great Plains met and sometimes clashed here. German, Czech, and Scandinavian emigres of the nineteenth century flocked to Texas in search of a new and better life, much like the northern snowbirds of today.

Birds from all corners of the North American continent meet here, more than 600 different species in all. Rocky Mountain and Eastern species of oak and pine converge uniquely in Texas which has at least 5,000 species of plant life.

All these "roads" have led ultimately to Central Texas—the heart of Texas—resulting in a singular cultural, geographical, and physiological potpourri which manifests itself in foods like chicken-fried jalapeños and wurst tacos; pronunciations like "Purd'nallez" (Pedernales), "Gwaddaloop"(Guadalupe), and "Manshack" (Manchaca); Texas-German words and phrases like "der Outlaw," "der Bollweevil," "die Fenz" (the fence), "das Stinktier" (the skunk), "der Mesquitebaum," and "die Kuh dehornen" (dehorn the cow); Czech-Texan words like "rencak" (rancher), "polkat" (skunk), "akr" (acre), and "barbekue" (barbecue). And only in the Hill Country of Central Texas will you see the sacred Enchanted Rock and the limestone fences, houses, barns, and Sunday houses of the old German Texans.

Then there is the Balcones Fault, that great crack in the earth which bisects the whole of Texas—separating the Rocky Mountain upland from the coastal lowland—but which manifests itself only in Central Texas, dividing the region yet ultimately binding it together.

The trips in this book are meant to reflect the one-of-a-kind diversity which is Central Texas and the Hill Country. They take you out of the big cities, off the freeways and super highways, away from the fast-food franchises and shopping malls, and introduce you to the small towns and ghost towns, mountains and valleys, rivers and creeks, cafes, beer joints, stores, and some of the fine folks of Central Texas and the Hill Country—the wonderful sweet cream that always rises to the top of a bottle of whole milk. But like good whole milk, that which is uniquely Central Texan gets a little harder to find every year.

Richard Zelade
Austin, Texas

How To Use
This Book

We deliberately take to the tasty backroads so as to treat you to the Hill Country's most vivid flavors. In *Hill Country,* getting there is always at least half the fun.

While *Hill Country* takes you far and wide across the heart of Texas, it is not a comprehensive guide to the area and does not pretend to be. There are other excellent books of the guidebook genre available, such as the *Texas Monthly Guidebook to Texas* (Gulf Publishing Co., Houston), which can be used in conjunction with this book.

Although Texas is becoming predominantly urban, small towns and the open country are still the state's bedrock and the strongest links to our traditional, unique Texas past. This all holds true in booming Central Texas as well.

There is still a distinctly different mentality in our backroads communities—an informal order of things in which roads and streets are often only casually marked and directions are given even less formally. Exact street numbers and street names may not exist or are not known. Hours and days of business, while usually reliable, are still left largely to the whim of the individual proprietor, who may just decide to take the day off, close early, or open late.

Directions given in this book are designed to make the traveler's progress on these trips as trouble-free as possible. These directions may seem unorthodox or obscure at times. But as one discovers when one comes to an unsigned four-way junction with no significant landmark except an old rock schoolhouse at one corner, the notation "Turn left at the intersection marked by the old rock school-house" makes perfect sense. The implementation of 911 emergency service across the state required that all urban and rural streets and roads be signed, which has made exploring easier (and getting lost harder), but sometimes the signs get knocked down or stolen.

Hours and days of operation given are designed to be as accurate and as up-to-date as possible, but should not be blindly relied upon. Not all places have phones, but wherever a phone number is listed, it's best to call ahead before driving out—places get sold, burn down, and close down; owners die and they take odd days off.

Several trips can easily be done in one day, others definitely take two days, some go either way. Distances are such that you should have to drive no more than 30 miles out of your way to find overnight accommodations, since some of these small towns and villages have none. Generally, any town with over 1,000 people does.

Each city's listing begins with the name of the county in which it is located, the best estimate of the city's current population, and (in parentheses) the telephone area code, when appropriate.

Restaurants are rated according to expense by dollar sign symbols. If two symbols are given in a listing, they indicate the price spread on the menu.

$	= Under $7
$$	= $7 to $17
$$$	= $17 to $25
$$$$	= Over $25

Accommodation listings include the following dollar codes indicating standard rates for a double room. Room tax is additional.

$	= Under $45
$$	= $45 to $60
$$$	= $60 to $80
$$$$	= $80 to $100
$$$$$	= Over $100

The following symbols indicate charge cards accepted at the various establishments:

AE	American Express
DC	Diners Club
MC	MasterCard
V	Visa
No Cr.	No credit cards accepted

Wheelchair accessibility is indicated by the letter "W," meaning that the facility is accessible by wheelchair—at least one entrance is wide enough for a wheelchair and there are no more than two steps. "W variable" indicates that the establishment is accessible only in part. Call ahead if you have any questions about a particular stop.

You should always carry a good state highway map with you. *The Roads of Texas* (Shearer Publishing) is an excellent travel companion; each road is identified by name or number. It is available at most Texas bookstores. Accurate, detailed maps of individual counties may be purchased from the Texas Department of Transportation. Address orders to: Texas Department of Transportation, Travel and Information Division, P.O. Box 5020, Austin, TX 78763-5020, (512) 465-7397. Or you can purchase the maps over the counter at 4000 Jackson, Building 2, main floor, in Austin, Monday through Friday, 8 a.m. to 5 p.m.

If you don't want to do a whole tour—just part of it—or if you just want to visit a specific place, remember that about half the towns and places in this book will be found on any good state highway map and are accessible by major highways. So you can save time by driving straight to the town or place you want to see, or to the spot where you wish to pick up a specific tour.

With only a few documented exceptions, all the road mileage in this book is over paved, reasonably good to excellent roads. Perhaps 20 out of nearly 2,000 miles are gravel, and these are well-graded, located in the arid uplift between Fredericksburg and Llano.

Be particularly careful when driving in rainy weather. Slow down on the winding roads and be wary of low-water crossings. Do not drive across any low-water bridge covered by more than one foot of water, and cross only after checking the depth and flow yourself. Days when bridges are uncrossable happen only a couple of dozen times a year.

Central Texas and the Hill Country are filled with interesting sights and sites: parks, museums, caves, swimming holes, rides, stores, dance halls and beer joints, and town and church festivals. Some are free; most charge admission or accept donations. At press time for this fourth edition of *Hill Country,* the Texas Parks and Wildlife Department was poised to revise its parks admission policies and fees for the second time in 12 months. With this in mind, the listings simply reflect whether admission is charged. Generally, adults will pay $5 or less to enter any site or festival listed. Many offer reduced prices for senior citizens and children. Notable exceptions are the Vanishing Texas River Cruise and the Hill Country Flyer.

One phenomenon of the 1990s has been the proliferation of bed-and-breakfast inns across Texas. Most of the towns in this book now have at least one B&B establishment. Many are so new that they have not yet had time to "prove" themselves. Future editions of *Hill Country* will contain more, firmly established B&Bs.

With the advent of the World Wide Web, it is now easier than ever to keep up with the latest in park and tourism information about Central Texas and the Hill Country. Here are some good sites, as of early 1997. All addresses must be prefaced by http://

www.tpwd.state.tx.us

The Texas Parks and Wildlife Department has complete, up-to-date information (fees, activities, history, flora/fauna, busy season, etc.) on all state parks, historic sites, and natural areas. You can make reservations on-line, subscribe to *Texas Parks and Wildlife Magazine*, visit the store, and more. Excellent site.

www.dot.state.tx.us

The Texas Department of Transportation Web site's Travel and Information Division Page offers comprehensive, timely town/city information (history, attractions, events, lodging, restaurants, etc.) for the entire state.

www.texasmonthly.com

The *Texas Monthly* Web site has information of interest to Hill Country explorers and links to many other Texas sites.

www.austin360.com

The *Austin American-Statesman's* Web site has information on the Hill Country and Central Texas.

www.auschron.com

Austin's alternative weekly, the *Austin Chronicle,* has a site that often has information about events and happenings in Central Texas and the Hill Country.

Good search engines to try (they will overlap considerably, but each will provide unique hits) are Yahoo, Lycos, Webcrawler, Altavista, Hotbot, and Dejanews.

In concocting *Hill Country,* I blended together history, personal observations, folklore, and trivia, then spiced it up with a little geology, geography, and humor. I hope you have as much fun exploring Central Texas with this book as I had writing it.

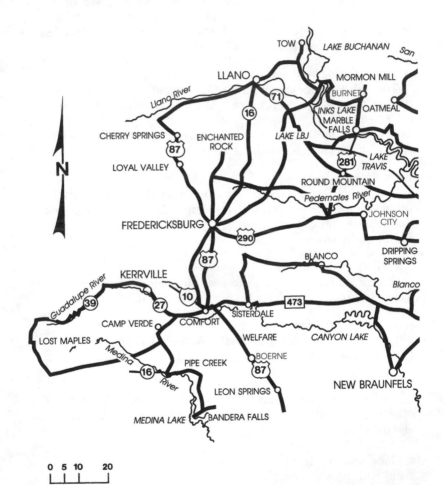

TOW

LAKE BUCHANAN   San

LLANO

MORMON MILL

BURNET

71

Llano River

16

INKS LAKE

OATMEAL

CHERRY SPRINGS

ENCHANTED
ROCK

MARBLE
FALLS

87

LAKE LBJ

LOYAL VALLEY

281

LAKE
TRAVIS

ROUND MOUNTAIN

Pedernales River

FREDERICKSBURG

JOHNSON
CITY

290

DRIPPING
SPRINGS

87

BLANCO

Blanco

KERRVILLE

Guadalupe River

10

39

27

473

SISTERDALE

CAMP VERDE

COMFORT

WELFARE

CANYON LAKE

LOST MAPLES

Medina

PIPE CREEK

BOERNE

NEW BRAUNFELS

16

River

87

LEON SPRINGS

MEDINA LAKE   BANDERA FALLS

N

0 5 10   20

MILES

HILL COUNTRY TOURS

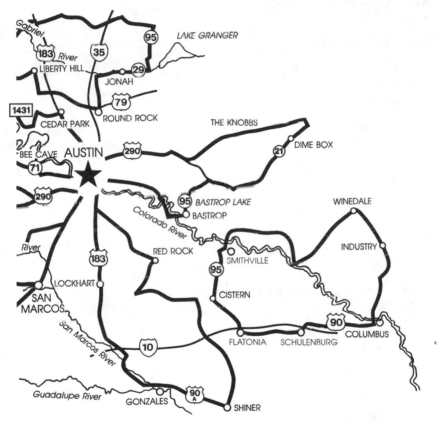

CENTRAL TEXAS CHAMBERS OF COMMERCE, VISITOR CENTERS, AND ASSOCIATIONS

All the Chambers of Commerce and Visitor Centers listed can provide up-to-date tourism information on the Hill Country area of Central Texas.

Austin Chamber of Commerce
512-478-9383

Austin Visitor Center
800-888-8287

Bandera Chamber of Commerce
800-364-3833

Bastrop Chamber of Commerce
512-321-2419

Blanco Chamber of Commerce
830-833-5101

Boerne Chamber of Commerce
830-249-8000

Burnet Chamber of Commerce
512-756-4297

Canyon Lake Chamber of Commerce
800-528-2104

Columbus Chamber of Commerce
409-732-8385

Comfort Chamber of Commerce
830-995-3131

Elgin Chamber of Commerce
512-285-4515

Festival Institute at Round Top
409-259-3129

Flatonia Chamber of Commerce
512-865-3920

Fredericksburg Convention and Visitors Bureau
830-997-6523

Georgetown Chamber of Commerce
512-930-3535; fax 512-930-3570

Georgetown Convention and Visitors Bureau
800-436-8696

Gonzales
830-672-6532

Gruene Visitor Information
830-629-5077

Hill Country Tourism Association
830-895-5505

Johnson City Chamber of Commerce
830-868-7684

Kerrville Convention and Visitors Bureau
800-221-7958

Kingsland/Lake LBJ Chamber of Commerce
915-388-6211

La Grange Chamber of Commerce
409-968-5756

Lago Vista Chamber of Commerce
512-267-7952

Lake Buchanan/Inks Lake Chamber of Commerce
512-793-2803

LBJ Heartland Network
830-833-2211

Llano Chamber of Commerce
915-247-5354

Lockhart Chamber of Commerce
512-398-2818

Luling Chamber of Commerce
830-875-3214

Marble Falls/Lake LBJ Chamber of Commerce
830-693-4449

New Braunfels Chamber of Commerce
800-572-2626

Round Rock Chamber of Commerce
800-747-3479

San Marcos Convention and Visitors Bureau
800-782-7653, ext. 177; 512-396-2495

Schulenburg Chamber of Commerce
409-743-4514

Shiner Chamber of Commerce
512-594-4180

Smithville Chamber of Commerce
512-237-2313

Stonewall Chamber of Commerce
210-644-2735

Taylor
512-352-6364

Weimar Chamber of Commerce
409-725-9511

West Kerr County Chamber of Commerce
800-257-4322

Winedale Historical Center
409-278-3530

TAKE A RIDE ON THE FREDERICKSBURG & NORTHERN RAILROAD

Approximately 70 miles

Few of us today can fully appreciate the trials and tribulations of pioneer travel through the Hill Country. Overland trips that once took weeks now take hours. Certainly there has been no more revolutionary change in the modern lifestyle than this reduction in time and space. The average Roman family would have needed about two weeks to make the ox wagon trip from San Antonio to Fredericksburg, the same amount of time needed by the Adelsverein wagon trains two millenia later.

Then the railroad came along, and it turned the two-week journey from San Antonio to Fredericksburg into a one-day ride. Small wonder that people viewed the railroads with a mix of apprehension, awe, and admiration. As it turns out, the iron horse was merely the vanguard in a transportation revolution, the magnitude of which few of us can fully grasp.

1

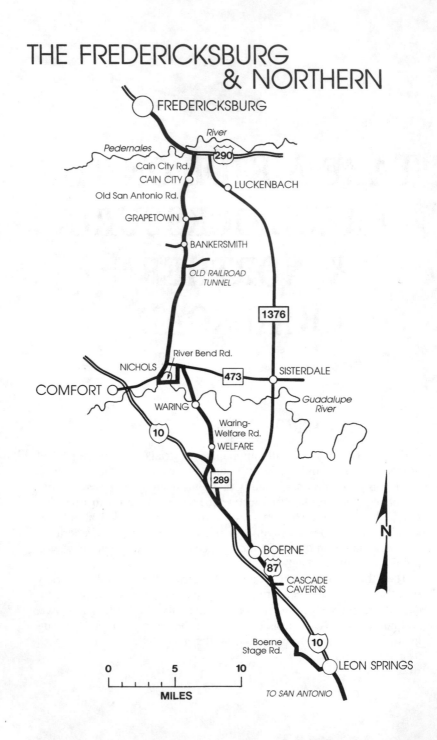

THE FREDERICKSBURG & NORTHERN

FREDERICKSBURG

Pedernales *River*

290

Cain City Rd.
CAIN CITY
LUCKENBACH

Old San Antonio Rd.

GRAPETOWN

BANKERSMITH

OLD RAILROAD TUNNEL

1376

River Bend Rd.

NICHOLS
473
SISTERDALE

COMFORT

WARING

Guadalupe River

10

Waring-
Welfare Rd.
WELFARE

289

BOERNE

87
CASCADE CAVERNS

N

Boerne
Stage Rd.
10
LEON SPRINGS

0   5   10

MILES

TO SAN ANTONIO

Wondrous mighty as it was, the railroad had its problems in the Hill Country. Most lines just avoided this part of Texas entirely and the few roads that dared enter the hills were arduously expensive to build. These railroads were highly coveted. Existing towns like Kerrville and Fredericksburg battled for routes, and developers looked forward to establishing new towns along the rights-of-way. In this southern section of the Hill Country, Kerrville won the first round for railroad service, becoming the western terminus of the area's first road, the San Antonio and Aransas Pass (SA&AP) railroad, in 1887. Owned by the Southern Pacific system, the road was later called the Texas and New Orleans (T&NO).

But progressive, persistent Fredericksburg was not to be denied, and although they had to wait nearly 30 years and ended up building it themselves, the townspeople of Fredericksburg finally got their railroad in 1913. The San Antonio and Fredericksburg Northern, as it was first incorporated (later the Fredericksburg and Northern, or F&N), came into the world amid much ballyhoo and high expectations.

It never lived up to its advance billing. Ditto for the Kerrville branch of the SA&AP. The highways soon took away what business they had. And so the tracks of both were pulled up years ago and are now just dimming memories among the thinning ranks of Hill Country old-timers. But the towns they created and nurtured still hang on, even as ghosts, and if you look in the right places you can still catch glimpses of the ghost tracks themselves.

This trip takes you along the length of the Fredericksburg and Northern, from Fredericksburg to the southern terminus at Fredericksburg Junction east of Comfort. Here you transfer over to the SA&AP for the last leg of the excursion to San Antonio. And the scenery is pretty nice, too.

FREDERICKSBURG

Gillespie County Seat • 7,745 • (830)

Unlike their free-thinking intellectual compatriots in the nearby German villages of Comfort, Sisterdale, and the "Dutch settlements" of Castell, Leiningen, and Bettina, Fredericksburg's early settlers tended to be practical-minded, God-fearing tradesmen and craftsmen, merchants and professional men, farmers and mechanics who saw a chance to improve their quality of life in Texas. Most had joined the Adelsverein back in Germany, finding the society's promises and terms irresistible. (The Adelsverein is further detailed in Mormon Trails—The Dutch Settlements; Riding the Fault—New Braunfels; and Central Texas Stew—Shelby.)

Full of hopes and expectations, thousands of these immigrants landed on the Gulf Coast at Carlshafen (Indianola) in Calhoun County during the years 1844 through 1847. Hundreds of them never left the beaches of Carlshafen, falling prey to a host of plagues that burned through the crude tent-and-shack city like wildfire.

Several thousand managed to reach New Braunfels, which was the first way station on the trail to the Adelsverein's intended settlement area, the desolate 3-million-plus-acre Fisher-Miller Grant. Prince Carl of Solms-Braunfels, the first commissioner general of the Adelsverein in Texas, founded New Braunfels in March 1845.

Less than three months later, Prince Carl was back in Germany and the Adelsverein in Texas had a new commissioner general, John O. Meusebach. Meusebach was one of the few practical thinkers in the Adelsverein leadership and a wise choice to succeed Prince Carl. Meusebach realized that to succeed in Texas, the Germans would have to assimilate the native culture rather than trying to remain distinctly German. Meusebach accordingly dropped his title of nobility on the very day he sailed for Texas; Baron Ottfried Hans von Meusebach declared himself John O. Meusebach, Texan. Upon his arrival in New Braunfels, Meusebach found the Adelsverein's books hopelessly entangled and the society even more hopelessly in debt than previously feared. Meusebach also soon realized that another way station north of New Braunfels would have to be set up before the society's final push into the distant Fisher-Miller Grant could begin.

Meusebach commenced his search for land in August 1845, and by that winter he had bought 10,000 acres of wilderness on credit, located 80 miles northwest of New Braunfels. The tract was well timbered and near the Pedernales River. Two strongly flowing creeks coursed through the acreage. Surveyors sent to lay out a route to the embryonic settlement reached here in January 1846.

By the end of April, some 120 men, women, and children borne by 20 wagons and two-wheeled Mexican carts had commenced the 16-day journey to this new outpost, named Friedrichburg (Fredericksburg) in honor of Prince Friedrich (Frederick) of Prussia, a patron of the Adelsverein. Arriving on May 8, 1846, the colonists were on their own three days later. After helping pitch the tents and then building a couple of huts, the teamsters, soldiers, and a few young able-bodied men returned to New Braunfels. Those who remained got to work laying out the new city and planting crops. Militia companies were formed to protect the settlers from Indian attacks. Talk about culture shock—most of these groundbreaking pioneers had stepped off the boats from Germany only a matter of weeks earlier. Waves of disease swept through Fredericksburg during that first year, but the survivors persevered, and with the subsequent wagonloads of reinforcements, their ranks had swelled to over 500 by early 1847.

Life became easier for the beleaguered Germans in 1847. That year, the breakaway Mormon leader Lyman Wight brought his flock from Austin to a spot near Fredericksburg on the Pedernales, where they established the community of Zodiac. The more experienced Mormons helped the Texas-green Germans learn many of the finer points of life on the frontier (See Mormon Trails).

And after several months of negotiation, Meusebach signed a peace treaty with the Comanches in May 1847 at Fredericksburg regarding the country between the waters of the Llano and San Saba rivers. The treaty relieved Fredericksburgers of one of the deadliest headaches of frontier life: attacks by Indians who did not wish to make way for the white interlopers. Elsewhere in Texas, the Comanches would resist the Anglo onslaught fiercely, more so than any other Texas tribe. But the peace signed by Meusebach, U.S. agent Robert Neighbors, and the Comanche war chiefs Santa Anna, Poch-An-Sanoch-Go, Moora-quitop, Matasane, et al., on the banks of the Pedernales was largely kept, at least around Fredericksburg. The treaty allowed each group to travel freely and unmolested in each other's territory. In addition, "In regard to the settlement on the Llano the Comanches promise not to disturb or in any way molest the German colonists, on the contrary to assist them, also to give notice, if they see bad Indians about the settlement who come to steal horses from or in any way molest the Germans—the Germans likewise promising to aid the Comanches against their enemies, should they be in danger of having their horses stolen or in any way to be injured. And both parties agree, that if there be any difficulties or any wrong done by single bad men, to bring the same before the chiefs to be finally settled and decided by the agent of our great father."

The Comanches further agreed to allow the Germans to survey the country as far north as the Concho River and perhaps the Colorado. In return, Meusebach was to give the Comanches presents to the amount of $1,000, along with additional provisions to be given to the Comanches during their stay in Fredericksburg to amount to about $2,000 worth or more. Fifteen commercial establishments were in operation here by the end of 1847.

The establishment of Fort Martin Scott by the U.S. Army in 1848 gave the people of Fredericksburg a chance to earn some desperately needed cash money. The town had previously subsisted on the barter system. The government paid in solid gold for its contracted supplies and services. Fredericksburg got an additional boost when the army established its primary military road west to California through the town. Fredericksburg was the last real outpost of civilization before El Paso, and most travelers bought supplies here before making the long push west. And things got even better when the waves of forty-niners began rolling through, bound for the goldfields of California. But while their purchases swelled the town's coffers, the cholera germs these transients left behind filled the city cemetery with hundreds of new graves.

Gillespie County was created in 1848 from parts of Travis County and Bexar County, and Fredericksburg became its first and only county seat. Gillespie County was named for Richard Gillespie, a Texas Ranger who was killed leading the American charge on the Bishop's Palace in Monterrey, Mexico, on September 21, 1846, during the Mexican War.

Besides serving as county seat, Fredericksburg became a regional trade center. Many of its industrious Germans became drovers, hauling in goods from San Antonio and the coast to supply the town and the string of army frontier forts just to the west, and hauling out locally produced cotton, grain, fresh fruits, and vegetables. The trip to San Antonio was at least a 10-day trudge for the lumbering ox wagons, and it often took a month to reach the coast.

In the spring of 1861, most Texas counties voted to secede, but 96 percent of Gillespie County's electorate voted against secession. No doubt there was strong Union sentiment in overwhelmingly German Gillespie County, but the final tally was also influenced by the voters' realization that secession meant war and war meant both the loss of a major market for local products and the removal of protection against Indian attacks. But the drovers managed to stay busy anyway. Many were conscripted to drive for the Confederate Army; others ran cotton down to Mexico, where the bales brought solid gold, not worthless Rebel paper money. The war actually spurred the Texas-Mexico cotton connection. At the height of the war, in 1863, the cotton wagons creaking through New Braunfels hauled the greatest volume in town history. Much of it was Gillespie County cotton. The payoff was good, but not without its dangers. Many Confederates regarded such border trade as treasonous and therefore punishable by death. Others with fewer scruples merely murdered the drovers for their money.

After the war, Fredericksburg again began to supply western-bound travelers and the reestablished frontier forts. As the iron horse crawled west across Texas after the war, Fredericksburg merchants began to hunger after some rails through their town. They hungered for about 40 years. Meanwhile, the big ox wagons continued to roll over the hills to and from San Antonio.

When Fredericksburgers got wind of the San Antonio and Aransas Pass railway's plan to build a new road northwest out of San Antonio to the High Plains, they immediately formed a committee to confer with SA&AP manager Uriah Lott to convince him to lay the rails through Fredericksburg. The committee was prepared to fork over right-of-way land and some fat cash bonuses to the SA&AP for that privilege.

But Fredericksburg had an even more determined competitor for the rails: Captain Charles Schreiner and his city of Kerrville. Schreiner had been heard to say that Kerrville wanted a railroad real bad and that it should be obtained at any cost. Schreiner pointed out to SA&AP manager Lott that the route to Kerrville did not include any high mountains; only easy grades would be encountered. The same could not be said of the route to Fredericksburg. Schreiner also guaranteed liberal cash bonuses and the promise of much tonnage in and out of the area.

Both towns were held in suspense until well after road construction commenced. As the rails approached Comfort, there was much speculation as to which way they would veer from there: sharply north to Fredericksburg or south to Kerrville. When the big day of decision came, it was one of consternation for Fredericksburgers. The rails headed south for Kerrville. The first train arrived at Kerrville on October 6, 1887, and was received with a great celebration.

Business looked great for a few years, but in the end the Kerrville branch proved to be a big disappointment, never shipping out enough tonnage to make the line profitable. The great High Plains route never made it past Kerrville.

In Fredericksburg, the Railroad Committee refused to be discouraged. One successive deal after another fell through, almost always because of the high costs to be incurred by building through the Divide, a line of but-grudgingly penetrable hills south of town that separated the Pedernales and Guadalupe river watersheds. One plan, however, called for a different, longer, sinewy route around the hills into Fredericksburg. But because the route passed at one point within eight miles of Kerrville, Charles Schreiner used his considerable influence to kill this proposal. In the meantime, mules had replaced oxen, but the big wagons continued to roll. They hauled in the big steam boiler for Fredericksburg's first electric light plant in 1896, and the bulky machinery for its first ice-making factory in 1907.

In desperation, the businessmen of Fredericksburg teamed up with their counterparts in San Antonio to build their railroad. The money came out of their own pockets, to the tune of $400,000. Grading started in January 1913 on a 23.9-mile line from Fredericksburg to a junction with the SA&AP line about three miles east of Comfort. The route closely paralleled the wagon road to San Antonio laid out 60 years earlier, which is the road you will be traveling on.

The iron horse finally reached Fredericksburg in November 1913 and the town celebrated with a three-day gala affair. Wagon-borne farm folks bumped and rattled into town from miles around just to catch a glimpse of a "live" locomotive. They watched in awe as the great mechanical beast chugged to a halt. One of the farmers, who had traveled many hours to bring his family to view the spectacle, was filled with compassion. Walking over to the locomotive, he patted the tender gently and said, "Poor thing, you must be very tired."

Fredericksburg businessmen welcomed the railroad enthusiastically. They could now ship and receive merchandise much more quickly and cheaply. There were great quantities of locally grown cotton to be shipped out, as well as produce, grain, and livestock.

Perhaps most happy was the Nagel Brothers Quarry on nearby Bear Mountain, which could now ship its beautiful red granite out to the rest of the world. Before the railroad's arrival, it cost $125 to ship a wagonload of granite to Gonzales. On the San Antonio and Fredericksburg Northern, it cost only $20 to ship the same load.

Travelers were also elated. Heretofore, voyagers to Fredericksburg anticipated a fatiguing trip. Detraining at Waring or Comfort, they boarded a stagecoach for the last 25 miles, rattling over large rocks, over steep hills, through dust and mud. When they reached Fredericksburg they were usually fit only for a long rest. Many weary travelers took their rest at the famous "steamboat" Nimitz Hotel.

It's time now to take a stroll down sprawling Main Street, Fredericksburg's traditional principal thoroughfare, which looks much as it did on that big day in 1913. Reflecting the town's heritage, Main Street now sports street signs that designate it as "Hauptstrasse." Start at Main Street's traditional anchor, the Nimitz Hotel, which is now the flagship of the Admiral Nimitz State Historical Park

ADMIRAL NIMITZ STATE HISTORICAL PARK
328 E. Main • 997-4379 • Open daily • Admission • W variable

The Nimitz Hotel is detailed at some length in the Mormon Trails trip, but much about the place and its founder remains to be said.

German-born Charles Nimitz put to sea at the tender age of 14 as a member of the German merchant marine. He and his family came to America four years later, in 1844. By May 1846, Nimitz was riding on that first wagon train to Fredericksburg. He opened a four-room hotel on this spot in 1852. By the advent of the Civil War, the Nimitz establishment enjoyed a far-flung reputation as the frontier's cleanest and most congenial lodgings. Weary travelers were drawn like flies to the inn's hot baths, cold beer and wine, and tables loaded down with white bread and fresh vegetables.

Nimitz's hustling drive was typical of the Fredericksburg business community; if it couldn't be made here it could always be wagoneered here. Despite the rugged journey to and from major market centers, Fredericksburgers and their guests enjoyed a standard of living unknown elsewhere on the frontier. The merchants' aggressive drive, plus the farmers' productivity, multiplied by the needs and appetites of travelers on the Upper Emigrant Road, were the reasons why.

Nimitz's reputation was not tarnished by the hard times of the Civil War, even though the coffee was really a blend of parched sweet potatoes and toasted barley, and the cellar brewery had to be turned into a cistern. During the war, Nimitz organized the Gillespie County Rifles (one of several local frontier guard units) and served as the local conscription officer for the Confederate Army. Nimitz was one of the few Gillespie County residents who had voted for secession. The unionist sentiments of the majority were to cause them much trouble during the war. Nimitz and his men were honorable and evenhanded in their dealings with these reluctant Confederates, but others were not.

Perhaps most unsavory was J. P. Waldrip, who claimed to hold some sort of commission as a Confederate officer. He gathered around him a band of men who were anxious to avoid frontline duty but eager to murder and loot for personal gain. Soon Waldrip and his men were known and feared as Die Haengebande (the Hangman's Band). Die Haengebande prowled the countryside raiding and pillaging outlying German farms and dragging prospective noose victims from their houses, all in the name of the Confederacy.

When Captain Nimitz sent conscription notices to some of Waldrip's men, the plunderers proved their patriotism by invading the Nimitz Hotel for the purpose of stringing up its proprietor. Nimitz evaded the noose by taking refuge in the dank brewery-cistern.

James Duff, late of San Antonio, was another thorn in the county's side. Commander of the irregular Confederate unit Duff's Partisan Rangers, Duff was sent to Kerr and Gillespie counties following the declaration of martial law here on the frontier in 1862. Duff conducted a reign of terror in the name of the Confederacy. Duff was probably responsible for the cold-blooded massacre called the Battle of Nueces. Duff's Rangers continued their depredations for some months thereafter, before being recalled to San Antonio.

With the end of the war, many members of Die Haengebande were indicted for their actions. J. P. Waldrip died in the shadow of the Nimitz Hotel, felled by an assassin's bullet in 1867. Life at the Nimitz Hotel then settled down to a more peaceful, though still lively, style.

Stroll west from the Nimitz on this, the north side of Main. A few doors west is the old Dietz Bakery.

OLD DIETZ BAKERY
312 E. Main

This building was constructed about 1876 by George Wahrmund and served as a millinery shop and boarding house before becoming the Dietz Bakery. The bakery eventually moved on down the street, and the building served a variety of purposes before being restored to its original lines. Its mansard roof, lacy porch balustrade, and spindly, delicate porch-posts bring a little French flavor to Main St.

STRIEGLING HOUSE
310 E. Main

Next door to the old bakery is the old Striegling house. When built in 1908, this two-story limestone block house was one of the real showplaces on Main St. An aggressive, progressive businessman, Robert Striegling was an officer of the committee that brought the railroad to Fredericksburg.

On to the 200 block of E. Main, where the Keidel family complex anchors the east end of the block.

KEIDEL PHARMACY AND FAMILY HOME
248 and 250 E. Main • W

First you encounter the limestone Keidel Memorial Hospital, then the old two-story limestone Keidel family home, then the vintage Keidel Drug Store. Built in 1909, the latter was definitely Fredericksburg's—and possibly the nation's—first medical arts complex. Keidel brothers Victor, physician, and Felix and Wernel, dentists, maintained offices upstairs, while Kurt, pharmacist, ran the drugstore downstairs. Three distinguished generations of Keidel physicians served Gillespie County. Kurt's daughter Margaret Keidel owns the Keidel family drugstore today. Her great-grandfather Dr. Wilhelm Keidel was Gillespie County's first doctor and county judge. Uncle Victor is credited with performing the first blood transfusion in Texas. Grandfather Albert was a schoolmate of X-ray pioneer W. C. Roentgen in Germany, and on a back shelf Miss Keidel kept a bottle of blue cobalt with which he treated patients at the turn of the century. Most of the display cases and fixtures in the drafty high-ceilinged room date to the pharmacy's founding, and samples of the store's early stock are displayed in several of the cases.

Wilhelm was trained in Germany and came to Texas in 1845 at age 20. He enlisted in the U.S. Army for six months when the Mexican War broke out. He came to Fredericksburg to serve as the Emigration Company's doctor, although Miss Keidel noted that he wasn't a member of the first wagon train. Family legend has it that the job was to be only temporary—he was supposed to go to Johns Hopkins University in Baltimore for additional training. But he loved it here so much he decided to stay and was elected county judge the next year. A branch of the family still lives in Baltimore.

"The spring of 1847 was a good one, probably," Miss Keidel once observed. "The Hill Country—that is Mason, Willow City, Fredericksburg—was the only place you found bluebonnets then." But a friend of hers has always maintained that her grandmother brought the first lupinus (bluebonnet) seeds with her from Germany and then planted them here. "I was in Germany in August one year walking with a forest ranger in a preserve and he showed me a patch of bluebonnets that were waist-high," Keidel said, adding a final twist.

Wilhelm and the rest of the Germans were probably entranced with the babbling seasonal creeks and bowers of flowers. "German people are romantic," she declared, disputing the notion that Germans are a cold, reserved people. "The German language is romantic in that it paints pretty pictures. The romantic books about Texas and the Republic were as strong a lure as political or religious oppression at home." Some of the more optimistic emigrants kept mistaking the gnarled, twisted oaks for olive trees as their emburdened wagons inched toward their new home at the southernmost edge of the Llano Uplift.

WHITE ELEPHANT SALOON
242 E. Main • Currently houses Haas Hand Weaving • 997-3175

Next door to Keidel Drug Store is one of Fredericksburg's most eye-catching buildings, the White Elephant Saloon, with its imported bas-relief-carved white elephant above the front door. J. W. Kleck built this saloon back in 1888, when moonshine sold for 15 cents a quart and 13 saloons stood ready to slake a dusty throat's thirst. Most of Fredericksburg's gingerbread is wood, but elaborate wrought-iron filigree traces the White Elephant's roofline. A touch of old New Orleans, *mais oui*? White Elephant saloons appeared in several other towns and cities in Texas, acclaimed as "places of resort for gentlemen" and featuring long mahogany or cherrywood bars with elaborately carved ornamental details, above which hung numerous mirrors.

DIETZ BAKERY
218 E. Main • 997-3250 • Tuesday through Saturday 8:00 a.m. until sold out • No Cr.
 A few doors west is the current incarnation of the Dietz Bakery, Fredericksburg's oldest bakery, legendary for its homemade bread. Fredericksburg housewives depend on Dietz's and the **Fredericksburg Bakery** across the street, so if you want a selection rather than just what's left, get here before noon because the hot fresh bread sells fast. Whole wheat, white, French, and rye are among the offerings, not to mention a variety of pastries and cookies, all reasonably priced and very tasty.

A. WALTER—JEWELLER BUILDING
128 E. Main • Currently houses Dorer Jewelers
 In the 100 block of E. Main you come to the old A. Walter—Jeweller building, now housing Dorer Jewelers. This common little structure is saved from anonymity by the exquisite centerstone of its Alamo cornice. The smooth-as-glass red Bear Mountain granite bears an etched Roman-numeraled clock face set at 10 o'clock and the surrounding words "A. Walter Jeweller." Alphonse Walter built the place in 1908. Dorer's specializes in antique watches and clocks.

OLD FREDERICKSBURG BANK
120 E. Main
 Next point of interest west is the delightful, romantic old Bank of Fredericksburg building. Alfred Giles (whom you will learn more about shortly) designed this turreted, castlelike bit of the Old World about 1889 and prominent local financier Temple Smith erected it that same year. Most folks were rather suspicious of banks back then—after all, this was long before the advent of the FDIC and other federal regulatory agencies. So most bankers, Temple Smith includ-

ed, erected miniature castles or cathedrals like this one to house their customers' money—"A mighty fortress is our bank," to parody Martin Luther. Giles and Smith played it doubly safe by incorporating an Alamo arch into the facade. It is a mint first-generation Texas bank building, rare and impressive these days. One of the most tireless railroad boosters in town, Smith took 25 years to get his rails, the quest for which he embarked upon almost as soon as he arrived in Fredericksburg.

At the end of this block, where it intersects Adams St., E. Main becomes W. Main. Cross Adams. A few feet north of the intersection is the Fredericksburg Chamber of Commerce and Fredericksburg Convention and Visitors Bureau.

FREDERICKSBURG CHAMBER OF COMMERCE/FREDERICKSBURG CONVENTION AND VISITORS BUREAU
106 N. Adams • 997-6523 • Open Monday through Friday 8–5; Saturday 9–12, 1–5; Sunday 1–5 • W

You can walk away from here with several armloads full of free information about things to see and do in and around Fredericksburg, including the *Fredericksburg Standard-Radio Post's* quarterly Visitors Guide. Both the guide and the Visitors Bureau are the best places to go for information on the area's burgeoning B&B industry. Dozens of places have detailed, descriptive pamphlets available. If the Visitors Bureau is closed, a points of interest map is posted outside, by the front door. Write to 106 N. Adams, Fredericksburg 78624.

Walk a few more feet west on Main and you see a reproduction of the old Vereinskirche on your right, and the Gillespie County courthouses on your left. You are now on the Marketplatz, or Market Square.

VEREINSKIRCHE AND ARCHIVES MUSEUM
100 block of N. Main, in the Marketplatz • 997-7832 • Open Monday through Saturday 10–4, Sunday 1–4 • Admission • W with assistance

Set back from Main, smack-dab in the middle of the old market square is the Vereinskirche, whose coffee mill/Old World lines epitomize—as nothing else does—Fredericksburg's essential Germanness. Built a year after the Germans' arrival, the Vereinskirche (Society's Church) was the first public building erected in the new town. It served as nondenominational church, school, and meeting hall. The Vereinskirche you see today is actually a faithfully rendered reproduction of the original (except the original had fachwerk, or "half-timber," walls), which stood in the center of Main, between the courthouse square and the market square. The first Vereinskirche was torn down shortly after Fredericksburg's Golden Anniversary Celebration in 1896. This reproduction was built in 1935–1936 in preparation for the great Texas Centennial Celebration. The coffee mill church now houses the Gillespie County Archives and local history collection, along with a collection of objects from early Gillespie County days and rotating special displays, such as a collection of early-day pioneer clothing.

Also in Market Square is a bust and plaque commemorating Jacob Brodbeck, early aviation pioneer. Born in Germany in 1821, he emigrated to Texas in 1846. He taught school in the Vereinskirche in 1847, and later served as Gillespie County surveyor and district school supervisor. In 1863, he and his family moved to San Antonio. Before leaving Germany, Brodbeck had attempted to invent a clock that would run without winding. Once in Texas, he adapted his ideas to manned flight. By 1863, he had constructed a miniature airplane with a rudder, wings, and a propeller, powered by coiled springs. The wings were partly movable and made use of wind resistance, just like the aircraft of today. He also added a propeller screw for water navigation. He calculated that the plane's motive power and the wind's direction would allow for a flight speed of between 30 and 100 mph. By 1865, he was offering "certificates of interest" to potential investors in San Antonio and Gillespie County to finance his trial flight. Supposedly, he built a prototype and flew it several hundred feet, at an altitude "several feet higher than a tall tree," but crashed to the ground when the springs wound down. Brodbeck still hadn't solved the rewinding problem. He toured the eastern United States speaking publicly and seeking financial support but was unsuccessful. Some of his papers were stolen in Michigan. He returned to Gillespie County in 1870 and bought a farm at Luckenbach. Although unable to obtain a patent on his invention, he lived to see the Wright brothers validate his belief in man's ability to fly. Brodbeck died on his farm in 1910.

PIONEER PLACE GARDEN
Behind the Vereinskirche • Free • W

Behind the Vereinskirche is the Pioneer Place Garden, a quiet little green spot whose most obvious feature is the old wooden waterwheel. Said wheel was dedicated by the people of Fredericksburg to Lyman Wight's long vanished Mormon colony at nearby Zodiac, in gratitude for the invaluable help given by the Mormons during the difficult early years here.

OLD SCHMIDT HOTEL
218 W. Main • Not open to the public
Old Charlie Nimitz was not without competition as a hosteler in early-day Fredericksburg. Located midway through the next block west is the double-porched two-story limestone building put up as a hotel in 1857 by Ludwig Schmidt. It served travelers for half a century. Since then, it has been a store, saloon, drugstore, and doctor's office.

On to the 300 block of W. Main, where you first see a state historical marker.

The historical marker tells the story of Englebert Krauskopf, gunsmith, and Adolph Lungkwitz, silversmith, who together invented a guncap-making machine. 'Twas midway into the Civil War and the Confederates were already desperate for supplies and munitions Little cottage industries were springing up all across Texas and the rest of the South. While Joseph Fubanks was building his cotton cards factory on the San Gabriel River down at Circleville, artisan Adolph Lungkwitz (brother of painter Hermann Lungkwitz) and mechanic Krauskopf were trying to conceptualize a method of mass-producing cheap and reliable firing caps. Their conception was sharpened by the leanness of frontier life, their execution equally hindered by it. But they persevered and were soon supplying the Rebs and their own Hill Country neighbors (not coincidentally) with thousands of caps marked with the factory's distinctive lone star. The old factory no longer stands, but other remnants of the Krauskopf family's business enterprises remain.

KRAUSKOPF STORE
312 W. Main • 997-8107
Englebert Krauskopf's boy Oscar ran a hardware store in this structure for years. All in all, four generations of Krauskopfs operated the hardware store and three generations tended the general store next door. The building sports an attractive cast-metal cornice.

RUDOLPH ITZ SALOON
320 W. Main • Private residence

Just a few feet farther west is the old Itz Saloon. Many early builders obscured their buildings' rocky origins by covering the rough rock surfaces with stucco, especially when the stone used was limestone rubble. Such was the case with Rudolph Itz, who built this place shortly after the Civil War. It was long a popular saloon; with the advent of Prohibition it became a meat market.

Cross Main now, over to its south side, where you encounter the Pioneer Museum complex.

PIONEER MEMORIAL MUSEUM
309 W. Main • 997-2835 • April 1 through mid-December: Wednesday through Monday 10–5 (except Sunday 1–5); mid-December through March: Saturday 10–5 and Sunday 1–5; Admission • W variable

The Pioneer Museum is actually a collection of buildings that includes the **Weber family Sunday house,** the **Fassel home,** the **Kammlah barn,** the **Kammlah store and home,** and the **Fire Department Museum.**

The Henry Kammlah family came to Texas in 1845 and to Fredericksburg in 1846. In 1849, Henry Kammlah the elder built the front four rooms and attic of this rambling family complex. Into this space were crowded both his growing family and mercantile store. Son Henry Kammlah was a freight driver and survivor of the Battle of Nueces before he stepped into his father's storekeeping shoes. In the meantime, the house-store continued to grow; eight more rooms and a smokehouse were added. The store remained open until 1924. The Gillespie County Historical Society bought the house in 1955 and turned it into a museum. Today the front two rooms are filled with much of the store's old inventory. Some of the back rooms are filled with Kammlah family articles. Other rooms contain displays depicting pioneer life, centering on the Meusebach and Nimitz families. A wine cellar and three open-hearth kitchens round out the Kammlah house.

The Fassel house is furnished with period furniture. Its builder, Mathias Fassel, was a skilled wheelwright who helped keep Fredericksburg's rolling stock in repair. He was a busy man.

The Weber Sunday house was built in 1904 by August Weber. The "Sunday house" is unique to Fredericksburg. Most Sunday houses date to a period between 1890 and 1920. German ranchers and farmers who lived far from town built them so that they might have a place to stay in town over the weekend, when they came in from the farm to shop and go to church, hence the name Sunday house. A typical Sunday house has one room with a lean-to kitchen out back and a sleeping loft up top, which is reached by an outside stairway or ladder. The boys in the family usually slept up here. Most Sunday houses were built of wood, but some were rock. It's important to remember that not every tiny house in Fredericksburg is a Sunday house; some people just had neither the money nor the inclination to build anything larger.

The Fire Department Museum houses the town's turn-of-the century hand pumper, hose cart, chemical tank, and steam pumper inside a replica of the town's original fire station. The equipment is still functional.

The Walton-Smith log cabin was originally located near the Gillespie-Llano county line. Only the 14-ft. by 14-ft. core of the cabin is original. The limestone chimney, front porch, and kitchen were added here to duplicate the cabin's original appearance. The one-room White Oak School was moved here a few years ago. Children's educational and entertainment workshops are often held here.

At the southwest corner of the Pioneer Museum complex is the old First Methodist Church, which now serves as Historical Society offices and meeting room. It has displays of barbed wire and early Fredericksburg furniture. This is the oldest Methodist church in the Hill Country, having been built in 1855 of native limestone. Subsequent remodelings in 1912, 1923, and 1948 brought it to its current size and appearance. The original congregation split after the Civil War. The First Methodist Church stayed here, while the dissenters moved to Edison Street and founded the Edison Street Methodist Church. It only took a century, but the two congregations patched up their differences and reunited in 1970 as the Fredericksburg United Methodist Church. The new church kept the Edison Street sanctuary, and in the true Fredericksburg fashion of recycling buildings instead of tearing them down and building new ones, the congregation sold the old church building to the Historical Society in 1978.

SCHWETTMANN'S EMPORIUM
**305 W. Main • 997-4448 • Open Monday through Saturday;
Sunday afternoons**

Schwettmann's is a stuffed zoo, with everything from ostriches to trophy jackalopes. Looking for deerskin shoes, a zebra skin, or a buffalo robe? You've come to the right place. How about a wild turkey, poised for flight, for your living room?

ALTDORF RESTAURANT
301 W. Main • 997-7774 • Open Wednesday through Monday, closed Tuesdays and the entire month of February • Lunch and dinner • $-$$ • MC, V • W
Located inside an 1860 limestone house, Altdorf's dining room is pleasant enough, but in nice weather take lunch or that afternoon break outside in the biergarten. American-Mexican-German menu, with lots of sandwiches and finger foods. Good beer selection.

ST. MARY'S CHURCHES
300 block of W. San Antonio
On the back side of the 300 block of San Antonio are located two of Fredericksburg's most imposing churches, the Marien Kirche (old St. Mary's) and the new St. Mary's Church. Work on the Marien Kirche started in 1860 and was finished during the early days of the Civil War. The church's most distinctive feature is its stone spire, a strong reflection of the homeland Gothic. It has recently been restored. "New" St. Mary's supplanted the Marien Kirche in 1906, more finely detailed and delicate in appearance but equally Gothic. They make a marvelous pair.

PIONEER MEMORIAL LIBRARY/OLD COURTHOUSE
Center of the courthouse square • 997-6513 • Monday through Thursday • Free • W
Fredericksburg has had three courthouses. The first stood where the post office is currently located. Of the two remaining, it is the second, limestone courthouse that catches the eye.
Alfred Giles designed this 1882 edifice in the Romanesque Revival style, as evidenced by its formal balance, heavy decorative consoles, and classical roof slopes. The cut stonework at the corners and around the openings contributes to its stateliness while providing a pleasing contrast to the rougher, pitchface stones that make up the main body. The roof ridges are topped with an intricate wrought-iron cresting. The limestone came from nearby quarries, which helped keep the building's final cost down to $23,000.
Restored in 1967, the building's first story houses the **Pioneer Memorial Library,** while the second story contains a community hall and a beautiful wall tapestry depicting the history of Fredericksburg.

OLD GILLESPIE COUNTY JAIL
100 block W. San Antonio, directly behind the courthouse square • Open by appointment and on special occasions Call 997-5381 or 997-7444 to arrange tour.

This two-story limestone fortress is the second of Gillespie County's four jails and was built in 1885. Abandoned as a jail in 1939, it stood various county duties until the late 1970s, when Fredericksburg Heritage Foundation funds, matched by Texas Historical Commission dollars, made its restoration possible. The sheriff's office and kitchen are authentically furnished, as are the sheriff's living quarters. Graffiti decades old still mars the cell walls upstairs. The building is locked, but the wrought iron gate to the jailyard is kept unlocked so that visitors may examine the building's exterior. You will shudder at the jagged glass shards sticking out along the top of the west rock wall, a crude but effective way to keep prisoners from scaling the wall, a security method often seen in Mexico.

BONN BUILDING
121 E. Main

The Nagel Brothers supplied much of the rich red granite used in Fredericksburg's buildings, as evidenced by Main St. cornerstones. The Nagels were not above the hard sell, as can be seen in several of the cornerstones. One of the best of these decorates the Bonn building, built by R. C. Bonn in 1913 and trimmed in Nagel red granite. An immaculately frocked lady and top-hatted gentleman flank the inscription "R. C. Bonn 1913 A Convincing Fact That The Nagel Bro's Have The Best Granite For Building And Monumental Work."

VAN DER STUCKEN BIRTHPLACE
123 E. Main

On down E. Main is the site where noted American composer and conductor Frank van der Stucken's birthplace once stood. Frank van der Stucken the younger was born on this spot in 1858. With the end of the Civil War, van der Stucken the elder sold out his business interests here and sailed his family to Belgium, where the gifted young Frank could receive the best musical instruction. He studied under the noted Austrian Franz Liszt, finally returning to America in 1884. He was promptly highly acclaimed here as both composer and conductor. Van der Stucken became the first musical director of the Cincinnati Symphony Orchestra in 1895. In the following years van der Stucken received many international awards. He died in 1929 in Hamburg, Germany.

FREDERICKSBURG BAKERY
141 E. Main • 997-3254 • Tuesday through Saturday 8–5:15 No Cr. • W

Next on this tour is the second of Fredericksburg's legendary bakeries. The building containing the Fredericksburg Bakery was erected by Louis Priess in 1889. Here he conducted his general store on the ground floor and raised his family on the second level. The two-story limestone structure is imposing yet coquettishly frilly with its rail-thin iron porch-posts and lacy brackets and porch balustrades.

Priess sold his building in 1923 to George Stucke, who turned the store into a bakery, which it has been ever since. The giant wood-stoked oven gave way in 1945 to more modern gas-fired ovens and the ownership has changed, but the baked goods haven't suffered one whit over the years. All the white, wheat, and dark breads are good; the iced cinnamon-nut and banana loaves do anyone's breakfast table proud. The bakery recently added ice cream to its offerings. As with Dietz's, you need to get here before noon for the best bread selection, for many Fredericksburgers will eat from no other loaf.

BAUER TOY MUSEUM
233 E. Main • Open most days, sometimes closed Monday and Tuesday • Donations • W

Antique toys line shelf after shelf of this private museum, which showcases the collection of Don Bauer. These are mostly boy toys (trucks, cars, planes, trains, soldiers, tools) as opposed to dollies, but everyone will enjoy the scenes from Dickens' *A Christmas Carol* that were once part of an elaborate Christmas display in a Galveston department store. A World War I battle is re-created with armies of sturdy tin soldiers, while elsewhere a small town is re-created.

NIMITZ BIRTHPLACE
247 E. Main • 997-8549 • Historical marker • B&B Inn

On to the 200 block, where toward the end of the block you encounter the little whitewashed stucco cottage that was the future Fleet Admiral Chester Nimitz's birthplace in 1885. Two of his uncles Henke operated meat markets on Main St., and the old downtown **Henke Meat Market** stands next door to the Nimitz cottage, on the corner. The Admiral's birth room contains old family photos. The cottage currently houses a bed-and-breakfast.

Another block and you're back across the street from the Nimitz Center. Residential Fredericksburg has just as much to see as Main St. Austin, Schubert, and Travis, running parallel to and north of Main, and San Antonio and Creek to the south are lined with an extensive variety of vintage homes and businesses. This tour of residential Fredericksburg, which is admittedly just a sampling of the whole, starts with the 100 block of E. Austin, which runs parallel to Main one block north.

SCHANDUA HOUSE
111 E. Austin • Next to Fredericksburg Bible Church

In the 100 block of E. Austin, you see the tiny rock Schandua house, Fredericksburg's only fully authentic house restoration, right down to the absence of electricity and indoor plumbing.

VAN DER STUCKEN HOME/FREDERICKSBURG INN ON THE SQUARE
102 W. Austin at Adams • 997-3656, 997-7083

The stately two-story van der Stucken home stands guard over the market square, at the corner of W. Austin and N. Adams. Alfred van der Stucken, cousin of Frank van der Stucken the conductor, started work on this house in the 1890s. The house was originally one-story, but van der Stucken added on a second story as his family grew. The white gingerbread porch trim and balustrades plus the heavy cornice provide a brilliant frosting contrast to the weathered gray limestone walls. Alfred was a prominent miller and backer of the railroad. Upon van der Stucken's move to San Antonio in 1912, the house and mill passed into the hands of others. The van der Stucken home is now a commercial inn, furnished with period antiques.

VAN DER STUCKEN HOME
114 W. Austin • Private residence

On down at the west end of this block is another van der Stucken house. Felix van der Stucken built the one-story section of this limestone house soon after he bought the lot in 1864. The two-story section was added later. Its peculiar combination of Victorian and Greek Revival styles, along with its broad double front porch and markedly shallow roof, makes it one of Fredericksburg's most distinctive homes. Felix built a steam roller mill here in Fredericksburg during the postwar years, and it became famous as the Reliance Roller Mills.

The 400 block of W. Austin has several homes of interest.

JOHN WALTER HOME
408 W. Austin • Private residence
First on your right is the John Walter home, a place that couldn't seem to stop growing once it got started. John Walter first built the little log cabin out front in 1867. Soon he added to the cabin a room behind and two on the side made of quarry-faced limestone blocks. Elected Gillespie County sheriff in 1876, Walter on occasion used his home as a jail, specifically the big one-room rock kitchen, which connected to the main house by a *Durchgang* (enclosed walkway). Its two windows are still barred. The latest addition, built in the late 1970s, is the imitation fachwerk section on the far side of the kitchen.

STRACKBEIN-ROEDER HOME
414 W. Austin • Private residence
This unassuming little house is typical of the second generation of Fredericksburg homes, the successors to fachwerk and log. The attic/sleeping gable is reached by an outside staircase, and two of the four original rooms lack windows. Simple, functional, and not much more.

BIERSCHWALE HOME
110 N. Bowie at Austin • B&B Inn
Alfred Giles designed this home for William Bierschwale in 1889. Its style is distinctively Giles. County official, legislator, and banker, Bierschwale was an unwavering railroad booster.

Turn right on Bowie. At the end of this first block, you see on your left the distinctive double-chimneyed limestone house designed and built in 1856 by Johan Peter Tatsch.

TATSCH HOME
Bowie and Schubert • Private residence • Historical marker
Tatsch's detailed blueprints for the house now reside in the Library of Congress and the house is listed on the Historic American Builders Survey. Most noteworthy is the huge offset fireplace, which is large enough to roast a whole ox. A master *Tischler* (furniture maker), Tatsch supervised the stonemasons' work and did the woodwork himself. Churns, buckets, barrels, bedsteads, wardrobes, rockers, even spinning wheels—with nary a nail or screw in the lot—were turned out by his skilled hands. Today his solid handcrafted works command premium prices from collectors.

Turn left on W. Schubert from the Tatsch house, then turn left again onto Acorn 1 block later. Cross Main.

KLINGELHOEFER HOUSE
701 W. Main at S. Acorn • Private residence
Just after you cross Main, on your right is the home begun by Johann Klingelhoefer soon after his arrival here from Germany in 1847. It began as a one-pen fachwerk cabin, expanding room by room as the family grew. Klingelhoefer was the other man in the county court judge controversy involving Mormon leader Lyman Wight. Final victor in their pitched battle for the office, Klingelhoefer served for many years thereafter.

Turn left on W. Creek, 2 blocks south of Main.

ST. BARNABAS EPISCOPAL CHURCH
S. Bowie and W. Creek • Historical marker
Peter Walter started work on this little fachwerk cottage soon after his arrival in 1846, making it one of the oldest houses in Fredericksburg still standing today. A wagoner, Walter farmed the surrounding land between supply runs to Fort McKavett. St. Barnabas Parish bought the little house in 1952, restoring and consecrating it as a mission in 1954. It sits in the churchyard, on your right.

KRIEGER HOUSE
512 W. Creek • Private residence
Over in the next block on your left is the old bachelor *Bude* (shanty) of Adam Krieger and George Geyer. An 1848 whitewashed fachwerk cottage, the handsomely restored little house has an even older one-room log cabin out back.

PAPE AND DANGERS HOUSES
200 block of W. Creek • Historical markers
In the middle of the 200 block of W. Creek stand the old Pape log cabin and the little Dangers stone house, both of which sport historical markers. The Pape cabin is the older of the pair, and is perhaps the oldest surviving structure in the town. The Friedrich Pape family arrived here in May 1846, one of Fredericksburg's first 40 families. It had been a rough trip from Germany for the Papes. Three of the children had died on the boat over, and by the time the surviving Papes reached Fredericksburg, Mother Pape was very ill. The settlers communally built this little cabin for the ailing woman shortly after

their arrival. They used post-oak logs cut nearby and probably topped it with a thatched grass roof until a shake roof could be constructed. Friedrich sold the lot and cabin to the Reverend Gottlieb Dangers a couple of years later, and Dangers then built the front section of this rock house, about 1851. He added two back rooms and a cellar in 1857.

JORDAN-TATSCH HOME
101 W. Creek • Private office
   This is another 1850s vintage rock house, with subsequent frame additions.

The remaining 3 blocks of Creek are lined with a nice variety of old and not-so-old homes. Turn left on S. Lincoln at Creek's dead end. Turn right on Main St./US 290.

KIEHNE HOME/COUNTRY COTTAGE INN
405 E. Main • Historical marker • 997-7439
   Friedrich Kiehne and wife Maria built this house in 1850, and it was Fredericksburg's first stone building, its first really permanent dwelling. Kiehne was a blacksmith and he made most of the window hardware used in his home. The double front porches with the connecting stairway give it a distinctive look. The Kiehne home is one of the most immaculately restored buildings in Fredericksburg. It is now a bed-and-breakfast inn.

DINING

Andy's Diner is 4 blocks south of Main/US 290 on Washington.

ANDY'S DINER
413 S. Washington/US 87 • 997-3744 • Open daily
Tuesday through Saturday breakfast, lunch, and dinner
Sunday and Monday breakfast and lunch • $ • No Cr. • W
   Andy's is a favorite down-home eating spot for many locals, serving up homestyle Anglo-German food in unpretentious, untourist surroundings.

ENGEL'S DELI
320 E. Main • 997-3176 • Open Monday through Saturday
Breakfast, lunch • V, MC • $
Engel's has good sandwiches, salads, soups, and pastries that are mostly made on the premises. Daily lunch specials are usually a good bet.

GEORGE'S OLD GERMAN BAKERY AND RESTAURANT
225 W. Main • 997-9084 • Closed Tuesday and Wednesday, open Thursday through Monday • Breakfast, lunch, and dinner $–$$ • W
They serve hearty German-Texas breakfasts, sandwiches and salads, and a variety of German main dishes. Good breads and pastries baked on the premises.

SHOPPING AND OTHER ATTRACTIONS

DUTCHMAN'S MARKET
US 290, 2 miles east of the courthouse, just past Fort Martin Scott • 997-5693 • W
A variety of sausages, bacon, ham, jerky, jams, and jellies are cured or made using traditional Hill Country German methods. There are also cheeses and gift packages.

FREDERICKSBURG BREWING COMPANY
245 E. Main • 997-1646 • Open daily, lunch and dinner
This brewpub is just a couple of years old, but fits in like an old-timer. A variety of German-style lagers, pilsners, ales, and wheat beers are brewed in the line of copper and stainless steel tanks. Enclosed beer garden out back. Lunch and dinner are served.

FREDERICKSBURG HERB FARM
402 Whitney, off Milam • 997-8615 • Open daily • W
German gardens were the envy of their Anglo neighbors, who often bought the Germans' excess produce. The Fredericksburg Herb Farm carries on this tradition of urban farming. Hundreds of varieties of flowering, culinary, and ornamental herbs are organically grown and harvested for gourmet vinegars, olive oils, seasonings, teas, blossom potpourris, wreaths, bath potions, and body fragrances. A variety of old log, stone, and frame buildings house a B&B, tea room, candle shop, and massage room.

FREDERICKSBURG LOCKERS
US 87, 1 mile south of Main • 997-3358 • Closed Sunday

Home of **Opa's Smoked Meats,** which include sausages, turkey, bacon, etc. In business since 1947.

GISH'S OLD WEST MUSEUM
502 N. Milam • 997-2794 • Open most afternoons, but call ahead

If it has anything to do with cowboys or lawmen, from the 1870s to the 1920s, Joe Gish has it or wants it. Badges, guns, hats, chaps, boots, saddles, clothes, movie posters, autographed photos, and more.

THE KAFFEE KLATSCH/FREDERICKSBURG FUDGE
138 E. Main • 997-6117 • Open daily • W

Espresso, cappuccino, caffe latte, etc., desserts, ice cream, and Fredericksburg Fudge. Fredericksburg Fudge makes several flavors of creamy fudge and various varieties of hand-dipped chocolates and novelty candies. Those who are allergic to chocolate can indulge in white chocolate.

THE MAIN BOOK SHOP
143 E. Main • 997-2375

The Main Book Shop has the best selection of books about Fredericksburg and the surrounding country (there are quite a few) and Texas in general.

SIDE TRIPS

LUCKENBACH
Take US 290 east about 6 miles to FM 1376, then south (right) to Luckenbach. About 13 miles from Fredericksburg
830-997-3224 • W variable

Luckenbach, Texas, made world-famous by Waylon Jennings and Willie Nelson in the song of the same name, began its slow ascent to fame in the early 1850s when brothers Albert, William, and August Luckenbach, along with other Germans from Fredericksburg, began to settle here in the hilly, blackland section of Gillespie County. William Luckenbach opened a post office in 1854, named "South Grape Creek," which operated for 11 years. August Engel opened a new post office in 1886 and named it Luckenbach. Engel and his descendants added a blacksmith shop, dance hall, general store, and cotton gin. In 1970, the Engel family sold the "town" to Hondo Crouch, Kathy Morgan, and Guich Koock. Hondo began to promote the town; Jerry Jeff Walker recorded his famous live 1973 *Viva Terlingua* album there. Then came "the song," and the highway department quit putting up "Luckenbach" highway signs because they were always immediately stolen. Ironically, Crouch was only briefly able to enjoy Luckenbach's international notoriety; he died of a heart attack in 1976. But the Luckenbach scene and lifestyle have persisted. The town is open daily, but the store is normally closed on Wednesdays. Dances take place occasionally, and weekend shadetree jam sessions often coalesce during peak season. Toss some washers or horseshoes, whittle, drink a beer. The store sells T-shirts, cassettes, prints, and pottery. Barbecue is available on weekends.

LODGING

Fredericksburg can no longer boast of a Nimitz-class hotel, but there is no shortage of clean, pleasant, reasonably priced accommodations. Bed and Breakfast services, unknown of here before 1980, have come on like Johnson grass or Kudzu in the last couple of years. There are more than 200 now. Collectively, they offer a wide variety of homey lodgings in and around Fredericksburg at prices generally starting at $60 a night, many located in historic old homes.

BE MY GUEST LODGING SERVICE
402 W. Main 78624 • 997-7227
Be My Guest advertises a variety of accommodations in town and out in the country, by the day, week, or month.

COUNTRY COTTAGE INN
405 E. Main 78624 • 997-8549 • MC, V
Located inside the historic Kiehne Home, the Inn offers three suites and two single rooms, all with private baths. Most have king-size beds and whirlpool tubs. Complimentary wine and continental breakfast.

BED AND BREAKFAST OF FREDERICKSBURG
997-4712 • MC, V
B&B of Fredericksburg provides overnight lodging and a full breakfast in a variety of local homes, old and new.

BARONS CREEK INN
110 E. Creek 78624 • 800-800-4082, 997-9398 • MC, V

Barons Creek Inn offers bed and breakfast service in a restored 1911 home in the historic district, two blocks off Main. Four suites, one Sunday House-styled guest house.

GASTEHAUS SCHMIDT
997-5612, fax 997-8282 • AE, MC, V

Gastehaus Schmidt can provide lodging in a wide variety of historic or modern homes and buildings in and around Fredericksburg, such as a rock house featured in the Willie Nelson movie, *Barbarosa*.

Nearly a dozen motels are within walking distance of downtown, most of them locally owned and operated. **Miller's Inn** (910 E. Main, 997-2244) have kitchenettes available and accept trained pets. Patrons may use the pool at **Deluxe Inn** (901 E. Main, 997-3344) next door, which also offers good accommodations. **Dietzl Motel** (US 290 W. and US 87 N., 997-3330) has a large pool and small dogs are allowed. Some rooms have good views of the Hill Country; none have phones.

ANNUAL EVENTS

Throughout the year many special events and festivals are held in and near Fredericksburg. Among the oldest, though not the ones that draw large crowds, are the *Schuetzenfest* (shooting festival) on the weekend nearest August 1, and the *Saengerfest* (song festival) held in the fall.

MARCH or APRIL • Easter Fires Pageant • Fair Grounds, SH 16 S • Saturday night before Easter • Admission • W

The pageant in front of the Fair Grounds grandstand depicts the history of the city's famed Easter Fires that burn every year on the hills around town. A cast of several hundred portray Easter Bunnies, settlers, Indians, and wildflowers in a modern version of a legend that tells how a pioneer mother told her frightened children that the Indian fires on nearby hills were really just the Easter Bunny boiling dye to color his eggs (honest). Food concessions.

MAY • Founders Day • Pioneer Museum Grounds, 309 W. Main • 997-2835 • Saturday nearest May 8 Free • Charge for tours • W

Sponsored by and for the benefit of the Gillespie County Historical Society. Activities include demonstration of pioneer crafts, cooking, baking, quilting, blacksmithing, musical entertainment, and food. A tour of old homes takes place in the afternoon.

JUNE • Stonewall Peach Jamboree • Stonewall • Take US 290 to Rodeo Grounds • Approximately 12 miles east of Fredericksburg 664-2412 • Third weekend in June • Admission to grounds free during the day; admission charged for rodeo • W

This annual salute to the famed Gillespie County peach features a parade, peach auction, various contests, a rodeo Friday and Saturday nights, and the crowning of the Peach Queen on Saturday night, followed by a dance.

JULY • Fourth of July Race Meet • Fair Grounds, SH 16 S 997-2359 or 997-4923 • Weekend nearest July 4 • Admission • W

Horse races, bands, food, and beer.

JULY • A Night in Old Fredericksburg • Fair Grounds, SH 16 997-3444 • Third weekend in July • Admission • W

Lots of beer, food, games, contests, music, and dances (indoor and outdoor) provide a full evening of entertainment in a mixed German and C&W atmosphere. The fun begins at 5 p.m.

AUGUST • Gillespie County Fair • Fair Grounds, SH 16 S 997-2359 • Fourth weekend in August • Admission • W

The oldest county fair in Texas features livestock, handwork, sewing, home canning, baked goods, quilts, arts, crafts, and agricultural exhibits. There are also horse races, a carnival, refreshments, beer, and dances on Friday and Saturday nights in an outdoor pavilion.

OCTOBER • Oktoberfest • Market square, 100 block of W. Main 997-6523 • First weekend in October • Admission • W

Crafts, quilts, collectibles, food, and entertainment, including a waltz contest and children's carnival.

DECEMBER • Kristkindl Market • Market square, 100 block of W. Main • 997-6523 • Second weekend in December Admission • W
  Patterned after German Christmas markets, this fair features gifts, imports, baked goods, food, and entertainment.

DECEMBER • Candlelight Homes Tour • Various locations 997-2835 • Second Saturday in December • Admission
  Private homes and historic buildings are adorned with candles and old-fashioned seasonal decorations. Tickets available at Pioneer Museum, 309 W. Main, and Vereinskirche, 100 block of W. Main. Afternoon through evening tour.

Leave Fredericksburg on US 290, which parallels the old Fredericksburg and Northern tracks, which ran out of town east-southeast a mile or so to the south of US 290. About 4 miles out, you'll cross the Pedernales, and less than a mile later, you'll see the "Cain City" sign. Follow the Cain City Rd. south to the first of several towns that the F&N spawned.

  The railroad took this initial diversion east before turning to the business at hand—getting over the high hills to Comfort—in order to take advantage of a natural cut in the hills immediately south of the Pedernales. Indians following the Pinto Trail used this pass for centuries and, more recently, the Fredericksburg teamsters plodded through, taking advantage of the range's easiest grades.

In 2 miles, Cain City Rd. dead-ends into the old road to Luckenbach. Turn right, and you enter what is left of downtown, ghost town Cain City.

CAIN CITY

Gillespie County • About 7 miles from Fredericksburg
  Cain City is located right on the cut in the hills, smack-dab on the Pinto Trail, the Old San Antonio Rd., and the Fredericksburg and Northern railroad. Cain City's location was not happenstance. It all started when J. C. Stinson moved from Kansas to San Antonio in 1913. Traveling west from the Alamo City, Stinson fell in love with the Hill Country. Knowing that the F&N was pushing through the hills towards Fredericksburg, Stinson bought 324 acres here at Inspi-

ration Point later that year. He immediately hired a surveyor to lay out lots, parks, and streets, streets with grandiose names like Main Street, Broadway, and Grapevine Terrace, in true *Babbit* style.

Stinson's home was the first built in Cain City. Although Stinson fathered the town, it was named in honor of Charlie Cain, a San Antonio businessman who baled out the railroad at a very critical time. An F&N depot was the second building in Cain City. Cain City was a boom town in 1914 and 1915. A warehouse, lumberyard, post office, the two-story Mountain Home Hotel, a school, and two general stores as well as a few dozen homes went up. For the town's convenience, men, mules, and a steam-powered grader scratched out the road to Luckenbach. A telephone system was installed, and a water system established. The water system—a rare convenience for a town this size—employed simple gravitational pressure. A well was drilled, and the pure fresh water was pumped into a big steel storage tank on the crest of the steep hill overlooking the town. Water pressure for most of Cain City was thus provided by the water's downhill run.

That graded "high speed" dirt road to Luckenbach (now paved) drew a lot of trade to Cain City. Farmers from the Blanco and Pedernales valleys brought their cotton, corn, oats, and wheat here to have it shipped out to the waiting markets. Cain City saw no great cattle drives, but it did see some great turkey drives. Turkey growers from the Johnson City area, some 25 miles to the east, drove their thousands-strong flocks along the dusty, muddy road to the Cain City depot, where they were crated and hauled to San Antonio. Folks from Fredericksburg would ride out here from town, just for the novelty of the train ride. Often they'd stay long enough for a bite to eat in the Mountain Home Hotel dining room.

Stinson organized and built the Cain City Bank in 1917. The bank shared the ground floor with a drugstore; offices occupied the second story. A blacksmith and doctor settled here and there was even talk of an electric light plant to serve the city. The cotton gin came in 1919.

But Cain City began a gradual decline starting in 1922, when Stinson moved his family back to San Antonio. Without his leadership, the bank sputtered along for another two or three years, then closed its doors forever. The Mountain Home Hotel changed hands and shipping tonnage began to drop; people were leaving the old family farms in droves and highway-borne trucks were commanding an increasingly larger share of the shipping that remained. Cain City died with the railroad. The hotel was torn down in 1942. The railroad shut down and all its tracks were pulled up in 1944.

Just after you turn right at the T intersection with the Luckenbach road (2 miles from US 290), you see all that's left of old Cain City. The bank was torn down in 1982. All traces of the railroad's path have been totally obliterated. The dance hall, the stores, the lumberyard, the gin, even the old water tower have disappeared, leaving only a few houses scattered along the potholed, graveled paths that were once Main, Broadway, and Grapevine Terrace.

The bank ruins stood on your left at the corner where the old Luckenbach Rd. is intersected by Broadway. All that's left of the bank today are some red bricks from the vault in the yard of the one-story frame ranch-style house which stands where the bank once stood. Turn left on Broadway, which leads you over the top of the pass and then winds down to a junction 0.9 mile later with the western branch of the Grapetown Rd., aka the Old San Antonio Rd. Turn left here, at the yield sign. In 0.5 mile, you will see a section of the rail bed in the field to your left. Two and a half sparsely settled miles after you turn onto the Old San Antonio Rd., you pass another turnoff (to your left) to Luckenbach, and you're in the Grapetown neighborhood.

GRAPETOWN

Gillespie and Kendall counties • About 4 miles from Cain City

You're in Grapetown now, at least the far north end of it, for Grapetown in the older, larger sense stretches for another 5 miles down the road. In a few hundred yards you pass on your right the entrance to the Doebbler Quarry, then on your left is downtown Grapetown, marked by the arching **"Grapetown Eintracht Schuetzenverein Est. 1887"** sign.

Grapetown's first resident was John Hemphill, who began carving out his niche here in 1848. Subsequent settlers were overwhelmingly German.

Other than in personal plots, not much farming was done in this rough country neighborhood. Most of the men were drovers or cattlemen. Actually, a man could be both drover and farmer without too much trouble. Since the roads were so poor, a trip to Indianola and back might take months. A man could plant his spring corn crop, make a trip to the coast, return in time to cultivate his waist-high corn, make another trip, and return in time to harvest the crop. Two months for a round trip that one of our trucks can make in a day seems incomprehensible, but not when you remember that in wet weather the roads would get so sloppy that the high-wheeled wagons would sink waist deep in mud. A wagon train might progress so short a distance in a day that a man could run back to the previous night's campsite for a bucketful of still-burning coals. Remember also that they didn't have matches back then, either.

Apache and Comanche attacks plagued the isolated settlement, then the Civil War pitted neighbor against neighbor. Some chose to fight or drive for the Confederacy; others hightailed it for Mexico or the thickets of the nearby High Hills.

Here at Grapetown, on the banks of **School Creek,** are the **little limestone schoolhouse** with its red tin roof, **the shooting hall,** and the **old Rausch ranch house,** down at the end of the little road past the school and shooting hall. The Rausches have been here from the beginning.

The schoolhouse was built in 1884. The Schuetzenverein (shooting club) was organized in 1887, along with a Liedertafel (singing club), but this rambling wooden hall was not built until 1893. The Liedertafel is now just a fading memory, but the Schuetzenverein remains active. Members still practice and compete here regularly in preparation for the annual 2-day Bundes Schuetzenfest, a nearly century-old Gillespie County tradition. The Schuetzenfest dates back to the days when good shooting kept meat on the table and thieves out of the livestock pens. Many of the men were proud of their marksmanship, and eventually they started getting together for shootin' matches so that they might determine to everyone's satisfaction just who was the best Scharfschuetze (sharpshooter). Shooting clubs like the Grapetown group were formed in almost all the little communities. Six clubs exist today, whose members compete for the title of Schuetzenkoenig much as their grandfathers and great-grandfathers did.

From the **Grapetown community center,** continue south on the old Fredericksburg-to-San Antonio road. The aging Rausch ranch house is not the only remnant of old Grapetown; the road south is littered with century-old impregnable limestone houses and outbuildings. Many of the names on the mailboxes— Doebbler, Kallenburg, Leyendecker—have been here even longer.

You pass the quiet **Grapetown cemetery** on your right, then the **Gillespie/Kendall county line** a few yards south of an intersection with a gravel road (on your left), and finally, 2 miles south of the Grapetown community center, **South Grape Creek.**

Here on the north banks by the old wagon road, Friedrich Doebbler opened in his home a grocery, dry goods store, hotel, post office, and stage stop and named the complex **Doebbler's Inn.** The year was 1860, and Doebbler's place became an area gathering place and amusement center. Grapetown's first school and shooting hall were built across the creek from Doebbler after the Civil War.

Very little of this rough country was fenced, and the settlers' cattle grazed on the wide open range of the High Hills as far east as Sisterdale and as far south as Comfort and the Guadalupe River. Each fall the men and boys would round up the beeves and sort them out. They would usually sell the excess to Kerrville's Charles Schreiner, who drove area cattle to San Angelo, San Antonio, and Abilene, Kansas, during the postwar cattle-drive years. The big market-bound herds churned up a sea of mud or raised huge clouds of dust on the road through Grapetown.

Then the center of the neighborhood shifted north to its present location. All that remains today of early Grapetown are **Doebbler's old stone stables** near the creek.

___

BANKERSMITH

Kendall County • About 2 miles from Grapetown community center

During the 31-year existence of the F&N, Grapetowners were served by a station named Bankersmith, after Fredericksburg's Temple D. "Banker" Smith. What used to be Bankersmith is off in the woods to your left, along the banks of **South Grape Creek.** Most of Grapetown's social life took place up the road at the school and shooting hall, but most of Grapetown's commercial activity remained down here around Doebbler's old establishment. A post office, dance hall, store, garage, and warehouse sprang up to keep the little depot company. The old wagon road eventually became the first paved road north into Fredericksburg, and for a while, Grapetown and Bankersmith enjoyed the best of these two transportation worlds. But just about the time that railroad traffic started dropping off, the main highway north (our present US 87) was rerouted a few miles west, through Comfort. Grapetown was left high and dry. All the buildings brought on by the railroad's advent were demolished following its demise.

Just after you leave what was once Bankersmith, you begin to catch glimpses of the old F&N roadbed, first on your left, then on your right. You parallel it for the next mile. An occasional tie litters the embankments and an antiquated string telephone wire traces its path. The roadbed and your own asphalt path cross each other nine times in the next 10 miles.

A mile or so south of South Grape Creek, you also notice that you are climbing a steady though unspectacular hill. You see on your right the prominent right-of-way embankment. You're about to crest the **Divide of the Pedernales and Guadalupe rivers,** the high hill the F&N chose to bore through rather than struggle over. For years it was the only railroad tunnel in Texas, not to mention a subject of local pride and thousands of picture postcards to boot. A state historical marker to your left atop this high hill marks the tunnel's crossing path, some 60 feet straight below. Actually, the marker has been stolen several times. The site is also marked by a sign for the "Alamo Springs" development and a private road leading to the east.

THE TUNNEL
About 4 miles from Grapetown

Construction of the road had already commenced when engineers informed construction boss Foster Crane that a tunnel would have to be bored through the hill. They had earlier hoped that a 40-foot cut through the hill would suffice. No such luck.

The tunnel was to be nearly 1,000 feet long, and the north portal of the tunnel was prefaced by a cut 500 feet long and 40 feet deep. It would require the removal of over 14,000 cubic yards of limestone, blown out by eight carloads of blasting powder. The clear-out work was done by men wielding shovels and picks and by mules hauling scrapers and dump cars. It would take 6 months and $134,000 to complete the 972-foot tunnel, making it the most expensive piece of railroad construction in the whole state of Texas. It would remain Texas' only tunnel for years to come.

Work had started at both ends of the tunnel. Few believed that engineers could dig at both ends and meet in the middle, so considerable wagers were made as to how far off the shafts would be. Well, when they met it turned out to be a matter of a few inches. Men working deep inside the tunnel got their breath of life via a small shaft drilled from above ground to the top of the bore.

Park up here by the marker, get out, and take a look at the south portal of this engineering feat. Standing at the upper edge of the cut, look down at the roadbed and opening 40 feet below. Then look down the wild Block Creek Gorge, which leads into Rafter Hollow and had to be crossed in order to gain entrance to the south portal. This devilish depression was traversed by two trestles, known respectively as the Big Bridge and Little Bridge. Big Bridge was 700 feet long, 60 feet high, and contained 372,000 feet of board lumber.

The gap between Little Bridge and the tunnel entrance was occupied by a dump constructed of waste rock (rubble from the tunnel blasting) 200 feet long. Men and mules built the trestles, just as they had carved out the tunnel. Only the overgrown roadbed remains today—the bridges were torn down 40 years ago—but you cannot help but be impressed with the job these swearing men and beasts did with the terrain they had to tame.

The tunnel's novelty was strong enough to attract developers, who laid out the mountaintop pleasure resort community of Mount Alamo just adjacent to the tunnel's northern entrance, atop the broad plateau that forms the top of the largest hill in the Guadalupe Range. At an elevation of 2,300 feet, Mount Alamo was to cover a minimum area of 300 acres, and up to 1,500 acres at its zenith.

Promoters promised to install an electric lighting plant and water and sewage systems. A 75-room clubhouse complete with bath houses and screened sleeping porches was planned, as well as an 18-hole golf course. Surveyors laid out an elaborate system of streets and boulevards, the main artery of which was the 200-foot-wide Berlin Boulevard. Special coaches ran from San Antonio to Mount Alamo, bringing out potential customers to see the sights. The F&N built a station here and hired the line's only female stationmaster, Alma Cowan, to staff it. The resort paradise of Mount Alamo folded in the aftermath of Wall Street's Black Friday in 1929. Mount Alamo, the train station, died with the railroad in 1944, and title to the land reverted back to its former owner, Alma Cowan's husband Otto.

Standing by the tunnel's historical marker, looking out and down the spectacular gorge to Rafter Hollow and beyond that to Block Creek, you can see why developers had such high hopes for Mount Alamo.

OLD TUNNEL WILDLIFE MANAGEMENT AREA
830-833-4333 • Open daily • W partial

After the railroad moved out, Mexican free-tailed bats moved in, and the tunnel's roadbed slowly deteriorated into a stew of dirt, limestone, water, and guano (the guano contains carnivorous beetles that strip the meat off the bones of a bat corpse in a matter of minutes) that is up to 6 feet deep in places. Up to 3 million bats roost in the tunnel from late spring to early fall. Pregnant bats arrive first, but then they leave the tunnel to give birth elsewhere in the Hill Country. Come mid-summer, the mothers and their nearly mature offspring begin returning to the tunnel. The tunnel's population peaks in August and September. Experts believe that the tunnel is too drafty to be a successful bat nursery, which must have consistent warmth.

In order to protect this important roost site, the Texas Parks and Wildlife Department acquired a 10.5 acre tract that included the tunnel in 1991. Local louts often came out at twilight to get drunk and fire their shotguns at the bats as they came out to feed. Naturalists and conservations believed the colony was in mortal danger from steadily increasing human activity on and around the site.

Around sunset each evening (the exact time varies depending on the time of sunset and other factors), the bats boil out of the tunnel entrance to spend the night feeding on the Hill Country's bounteous crop of bugs. You can watch this dramatic exodus from an observation deck located high above the entrance. A river of life flows out of the tunnel for half an hour in late summer when the population is at its peak. They may fly as far as 30 miles a night hunting dinner, mostly moths and little flying beetles. They may snag the odd mosquito, but mosquitos aren't a major part of their diet. They really like the moths that are the adult forms of farmers' traditional enemies: corn borers, cutworms, and webworms. The colony collectively consumes 12–15 tons of insects a night. Time spent dining nightly varies with the climate. During a drought, when insects are relatively scarce, they may hunt until dawn, or longer, until they're full. It's best to get here 45 minutes to an hour before sunset on the day you go. With the first cold front of the fall, the bats hightail it out of here for Mexico. While many of the old, traditional prejudices against bats are now being dispelled here in Texas and elsewhere in the United States, they still exist in Mexico, where people go to great lengths to drive the bats away, like burning old tires in bat caves. The bats' future in Texas is now somewhat more secure, but continued persecution in Mexico may yet doom the species.

The tunnel's upper observation deck is always open, and Parks and Wildlife biologists are present nightly during bat season to answer questions. A lower viewing level is reserved for special bat tours.

From the Tunnel, continue south on the Old San Antonio Road.

Despite its spectacular tunnel and bridges, the F&N was a tooth-and-nail railroad, rivaled only by the Bartlett-Western railroad in Williamson County. The F&N may not have been the butt of derisive nicknames, as was the poor Bartlett-Western, but it did enjoy the same haphazard reputation among its patrons.

The F&N, once funded, was plagued with problems from the start of construction. Six hundred tons of steel rails had to be returned to their manufacturer, floods washed away large portions of the roadbed, and worst of all, as the surrounding cotton fields neared maturity, many of the gandy dancers deserted the road for the cotton fields. That didn't say much for working conditions on the F&N. The road owned outright only two locomotives; the rest of the locomotives and all the rolling stock were borrowed or leased from other railroads.

The first official train into an anxiously awaiting Fredericksburg was an hour late; the soft, shifting roadbed had kept the train's speed down. It had also experienced extraordinary difficulty in climbing the 2-percent grade that led up the gorge to the tunnel.

Rain drowned out most of the town's three-day schedule of festivities. Once the party was over, the F&N set about to make a living. It soon snagged the local U.S. Mail contract, but less than a year after its completion, the F&N sat in the hands of a court-appointed receiver, pockets-out busted. Meanwhile, the trains kept running, or at least tried to. It was not always easy. The roadbed continued to settle, especially where the soft limestone rubble fills had been built up. At many of these soft spots the rails would sink completely out of sight. There was a time when the 24-mile trip from Fredericksburg Junction to Fredericksburg took 18 hours. As many as a dozen derailments might occur during the course of a trip. Or the locomotive might run out of water, whereupon the engineer would hightail it as best he could to the tunnel, where he could drop a hose into the ditch where water always stood because of the constant tunnel seepage. In the wood-burning days, if the locomotive ran out of fuel the crew would trudge into the woods with axes and cut enough wood to complete the trip. There was almost always a rifle or shotgun tucked away somewhere on the train, and when someone spotted a fat deer or turkey the train would come to a screeching halt to give Robin Hood his chance. Even jackrabbits were considered targets worth stopping for.

The F&N could not afford a wrecking crane, so whenever a car derailed it was brought back to bear with block and tackle, ropes, jacks, and cables, plus the pulling power of a locomotive. Floods often destroyed or damaged bridges. Once the daily mixed (freight and passenger cars) was trapped on the road. Having crossed a bridge that was washed away minutes later by a sudden raging torrent of flood water, the on-moving train soon encountered a similarly washed-out bridge, thus leaving it isolated. Crew and passengers were forced to hike to a nearby farmhouse and stay the night with those hospitable folk. Another time, during the early 1920s, Little Bridge, leading to the tunnel's south portal, caught fire. An alarm was sent to the fire departments at Comfort and Fredericksburg, but they refused to send any of their equipment or men to help combat the blaze. So all road employees from the general manager on down piled aboard the little motor cars and sped down to the site to quench the flames. Folks said that when riding the F&N the traveler had to begin his journey before the month of August in order to reach the end of the line by Christmas. A drummer who had to ride the F&N to reach clients in Fredericksburg complained about the slowness of the train to his first customer. "Well yes, that's one way to look at it," the German shopkeeper agreed, "but think how long you get to ride for a dollar." Actually, the train managed to maintain an average speed of close to 12 miles an hour.

It was also said that the road's financial grip was so precarious that it could not afford to have any of its trains hit a horse, cow, or goat. Crew members were warned to maintain a careful watch for live-stock on the tracks, to stop the train immediately when straying animals were sighted, and not to move again until the offenders were removed from the right-of-way. Passengers were warned to bring along plenty of food, because there was a possibility that they would be suffering from hunger before their trip was over. A turtle stood a good chance of taking the F&N to a photo finish, they joked.

When passenger trains started running through the tunnel, it was the crew's custom to stop outside the portal and then check to see that no rocks had fallen from the ceiling onto the tracks. The conductor would request that all windows be closed before the train entered the tunnel, so that the choking black smoke would not flood the coaches. While passing through the tunnel, the engine exhaust would sometimes loosen small rocks, which would pepper the tops of the cars. During the winter, large icicles would form on the roof, sometimes growing to as much as a foot in diameter, making it impossible for the train to pass through until they were removed.

The road operated in receivership until December 26, 1917, when a group of San Antonio capitalists purchased it for $80,000. They promised to make many improvements and announced hopes of extending the road west to San Angelo and north to Llano. But as paved highways grew in length and number, along with the numbers of cars using them, the F&N's passenger and shipping business dropped off. It was not even able to pay operating expenses, much less the interest due on its bonds. With another change of ownership in the 1930s, the road lost all hope of turning a year-end profit, for its seven directors soon voted themselves annual individual salaries of $3,000. Attempts to sell the line to a larger company, like the Southern Pacific, failed. But still the trains bumped on, even though the passenger cars had been yanked from the daily mixed train.

From the tunnel, you slowly descend into the Guadalupe River Valley, headed toward Fredericksburg Junction. You parallel the gorge; it's on your left. Just 1.8 miles past the tunnel marker, you cross paths again with the old railroad. In another half-mile, you come to a private dirt road running off to the west named Giles Ranch Rd. A mile later (a little over 3 miles south of the tunnel), you come to a low-water crossing over Rafter Hollow. On your left you see a gap in the railroad embankment, where a wooden bridge once stood.

The old Hillingdon Ranch flag station stood near this low-water bridge, a flag station created primarily for the convenience of Hillingdon's illustrious owner, the prominent architect Alfred Giles. Born in London, Giles emigrated to the United States in 1872, and by 1875 he was in business at San Antonio as Alfred Giles, architect, still barely 22 years old. By his early thirties, Giles had begun to design the dozens of courthouses, jails, banks, and homes that marked his career. Many of them still stand today across Texas and northern Mexico. The classically heavy second Gillespie County Courthouse is one of his early major works; the Italianate Kendall County Courthouse addition is one of his later works. But he was more than just a successful architect. Giles, together with father-in-law John James, owned this model 13,000-acre ranch called Hillingdon. Here Giles raised horses, mules, registered Aberdeen Angus cattle, and angora goats. He was active in a variety of stockraisers and breeders associations.

Prominent journalist Richard Harding Davis paid the ranch lavish praise in his 1892 tome, *The West from a Car Window.* Giles died here in 1920. Giles' grandson currently lives on and runs Hillingdon, which is several thousand acres reduced in size but still very much a family operation. The old rambling ranch house hasn't changed much since Giles' death; old company portfolios with lovely illustrations of his work still adorn the desk in the front parlor, and blue ribbons from fatstock shows at the turn of the century still hang on the walls.

A little over 6 miles south of the tunnel markers on your right, on the Marquart place, you see a strip of chest-high rock fence about 0.5 mile long, one of the best-preserved stretches of rock fence left in the Hill Country.

The Germans were the only ranchers in the west to build such fences, and the fences can be used to identify areas of German settlement. Ma, Pa, the kids, even Oma and Opa labored months and years to build the fences. They had to do the work themselves; hiring someone else to do it would run $300 to $400 a mile. The construction of rock fences came to an abrupt end, as you might well expect, with the introduction of barbed wire. But many of these centenarians are still functional. What was so slow in going up is now fittingly slow in coming down. Rock fence building is an art. Families sometimes used stone quarried from nearby limestone outcroppings. More often they employed rocks cleared from the fields before the spring plowing. Stones were often laid dry into a trench dug into the ground. This was the fence's foundation.

A good stone fence had a smooth face, which made it hard for animals to climb over, and interlocking stones for strength. Fences with too smooth a face and a rubble fill in between were not nearly as strong. This stretch was obviously built to last.

Seven miles south of the tunnel marker, you see an old tin barn on your right, set back from the road. The front half of it is up on stilts to facilitate loading goods in and out of the F&N boxcars. This now out-of-place building is our only clue that the railroad ran through here.

You cross Block Creek and its tributaries many times during these last few miles. Despite its former preeminence, the old Fredericksburg-to-San Antonio road was neglected until recently by county and state authorities. Homemade warning signs done up in fluorescent red paint warned you of upcoming cattle and low-water crossings. At the water crossings, more of the red paint was daubed on posts, boulders, or whatever else was handy, as further warning to the motorist. Many of these crossings sported homemade flood markers, in contrast to the neatly executed 5-foot graduated flood markers you see on state-maintained roads. But back then, all roads were similarly, crudely marked. Early travel guides told you to "turn left at the red schoolhouse" or "right at the big oak tree with the red ring." Local residents erected signs that warned of various road hazards, identified the road, and told the traveler who lived in which direction. Travel was more an adventure, not just a means of getting from here to there.

When you come to the junction with SH 473, a little over 8 miles from the tunnel marker, continue straight ahead toward Comfort on SH 473.

Now you're smack-dab in the flat, richly green bottomlands of the Guadalupe, and it should be easy to see why the founders of Comfort chose that name, especially when you think back to the arid, hardscrabble hills of the Divide. All of this fertile land was once part of the sprawling Nichols neighborhood.

NICHOLS

About 10 miles from the tunnel marker
The first Anglo settlement here was named Brownsboro after J. S. Brown, who settled at the mouth of Block Creek in 1848 or 1849. Folks began to call it Nichols starting in 1897, the year in which the Nichols Sanitarium for the treatment of pulmonary diseases was created. The Nichols Sanitarium, later the Nichols Ranch, was one of the world's first dude ranches. People from San Antonio and the rest of Texas came up from the Alamo City on the T&NO, then made the switchover and short, two-mile trip up to the Nichols Ranch flag station on the F&N. These visitors might spend the weekend or the entire summer taking the cure or just breathing in the country air here on the banks of the Guadalupe, staying in the big house or in one of the scattered guest cabins.

After traveling a little over a mile on SH 473, you see a stately steel truss bridge to your left, then a road, River Bend Rd., running toward it off SH 473, marked by a three-way intersection sign. It is the first public road left after turning onto SH 473.

GUADALUPE RIVER BRIDGE
About 10.5 miles from the tunnel marker
One of the first things you notice about this big bridge that spans the Guadalupe is that it goes nowhere—there is no road to the bridge, no road from the bridge. It just stands like a giant Colossus of Rhodes, master of the Guadalupe, anchored at either end in uniformly lush green pastures. As such, it looks rather like some eccentric artistic extravagance, serving no purpose other than to decorate the countryside.

This current, purely aesthetic function is a fairly recently acquired role for the turn-of-the-century span. As late as 1953, it was the

Guadalupe crossing of the T&NO line from San Antonio to Kerrville. Just west of the bridge, the F&N tracks met the T&NO rails at Fredericksburg Junction, which no longer exists. Here, a small depot was built which consisted of a small waiting room furnished with wooden benches and a storage room for baggage and mail. The yards of the F&N's southern terminus consisted of a few dozen yards of storage tracks, a water tank, and a turning wye. San Antonio was a mere 2 hours and 50 miles away. If you were lucky, you had covered the 24 haphazard miles from Fredericksburg in about the same time. As the Great Depression tightened its grip on Central Texas and the rest of the country, the F&N's position grew tenuous. When the Southern Pacific refused a chance to buy the F&N for $227,000, it was offered to the citizens of Fredericksburg for $75,000. They refused, declaring that it was impossible to raise even that amount during those hard times, besides balking at the idea of paying for the railroad again. So it remained unsold and limped along. By Pearl Harbor Day, the F&N belonged to one man, Dr. O. H. Judkins of San Antonio, all the other stockholders having bailed out. There was a great demand for scrap metal once the American war machine got rolling, and since the F&N had not been deemed essential to the war effort, Dr. Judkins saw a good chance to rid himself of an albatross. So he applied to the War Production Board and the ICC for permission to abandon the line and sell it for scrap. Permission was duly granted, and bids were invited. A Chicago firm won with the high bid of $77,000. This price included all steel rails, bridges, ties, rights-of-way, buildings, and land—everything but the toot of the locomotive whistle, essentially.

Fredericksburgers experienced a quick change of heart when they learned of the abandonment and sale, unsuccessfully appealing the government's decision, then offering to buy back the line from the salvage firm. The offer was declined. Removal of the rails started immediately, followed by the dismantling of the bridges and trestles. The wooden ties sold for up to a buck apiece. Six carloads of rail went to Australia, but most of the rail was sold to the War Production Board, which used it to build spur lines to all the new army camps. The big timbers went into new bridges across the country, some ending up along the Alcan Highway, which was to be our strategic lifeline to Alaska.

Faced with ever-increasing freight rates, Fredericksburg merchants began to rue the loss of their road. One merchant even went so far as to find out the cost of a replacement line. That figure came to $4,000,000.

But highways and automobiles would have soon done in that line, too, as soon as the travel-restrictive war was over. So the F&N died a rather ignominious though patriotic death, never really having lived up to the expectations of its builders and subsequent owners.

Out of sight, out of mind, goes the shopworn saying; this is exactly what happened to the F&N. It disappeared from the minds of the people it served almost as fast as its rails were ripped up. Its memory has faded just as completely as its physical presence, which is down to a swampy tunnel, some grassy embankments, and a few scattered ties.

Except for the big Guadalupe bridge, not much is left of the old Kerrville branch of the T&NO these days. When the tracks first pushed across the river in 1887, they crossed via a wood piling bridge. This bridge was destroyed by a disastrous flood just after the turn of the century and was replaced by the current one. Funny thing though, of the bridge's three steel truss spans, one bears the date 1904, another reads 1906, and the third is blank. As you follow the road's dip down under the bridge and then its sharp veer to the left over the river, you may wonder why such a high bridge was needed to cross so little a river. If you look into the treetops along the river bank and at the bridge's superstructure, you see why. Most of the graying brush caught up there, some 30 feet above you, was left by the great flood of 1978. Several consecutive days of heavy thunderstorms sent a wall of water crashing down the Guadalupe, engulfing the bridge.

If the river is crossable here (don't attempt to cross if there's more than a foot of water flowing over the bridge), cross on over. You traverse the Guadalupe again about 0.5 mile later. Be alert; the road is paved but only one lane wide. Soon after this second crossing, 0.7 mile later, you pass by the old Brownsboro cemetery on your left, with graves that date from the 1870s to the 1940s. Just after the cemetery, the road dead-ends. Turn left here onto North Riverbend Rd. Turn right on SH Rd. 473 when this road dead-ends in 1.6 miles. After about 0.25 mile on SH Rd. 473, turn right on Waring-Welfare Rd., marked by the "Waring 4" sign.

Note: If the river is too swollen to cross by the old railroad bridge, simply backtrack from the bridge to SH 473, and then turn right on SH 473 toward Sisterdale. After 2.5 miles on SH 473, you come to the Waring-Welfare Rd. Turn right here to get to Waring.

As you drive through this thicketed bottomland, you'll notice another long stretch of aging, knee-high rock fence on your left.

As you prepare to cross the Guadalupe via the low-water bridge, note the 25-foot flood gauge nailed to the stately cypress on the north bank next to the bridge. Most of the time, the Guadalupe flows placidly here. But every decade or so, a flash flood reaches or submerges the top of the gauge. The debris suspended high in the treetops bears testimony to the floods' ravages. Immediately after crossing the cypress-shaded Guadalupe, bear to the right to enter Waring. But if you have the time, you can bear left after crossing the Guadalupe. The road parallels the river for about 1.5 miles, turns right and then left, crossing the river about 2 miles later. At this point, turn around and drive into Waring.

WARING

Kendall County • 73 • About 4 miles from the Waring Rd./RM 473 junction

Waring, like dozens of other Texas towns, was a child of the railroads. And like dozens of other railroad towns, Waring put an older town—Windsor—out of business. Windsor was located on the opposite bank of the Guadalupe from Waring. The area was first settled in 1849, but Windsor didn't get a post office until 1880, although a stage stop was established earlier.

Waring was named for R. P. M. Waring, who donated the right-of-way land for the SA&AP (later known as the T&NO), when the line was being built to Kerrville in 1887. In 1888, the post office was moved across the Guadalupe from Windsor, and the town was properly founded and named Waringford. It retained this name until 1901, when post office authorities shortened it. Today, Waring is a somnolent little river town composed of a couple of dozen homes, a church, a store, and a post office. No matter where you are in Waring, you are always within earshot of the roaring Guadalupe.

The first thing you see as you enter Waring is the steeple of the old whitewashed **Waring Baptist Church,** which sits to your right. It was originally a community church where all denominations worshipped on alternating Sundays. It was then abandoned, except for occasional community functions, until about World War II, when the Baptists took it over; an act that engendered hostility in some quarters. The antagonism has yet to die down. The present wooden-frame sanctuary is the second church building, built around the turn of the century; no one really knows exactly when anymore.

The old **Waring School** sits across from the church on the river bank. The first wing of this wooden schoolhouse was built in 1891; the second in 1903, by public subscription. It is still used for the annual Waring Homecoming and as a polling and meeting place. The old Windsor stage stop is located directly across the river from the school house, up on the hill. All that remains are the rock stables, and they are on private property.

On adjoining corners, at the crossroads with RM 1621, are the **Waring Store** and the old **Waring Post Office.** The post office building began life in 1937 as the local Red and White Grocery Store and Post Office. The grocery closed several years ago along with the post office. Previous to settling down here, the Waring Post Office had changed locations eight times in only 50 years.

Waring still has some nice turn-of-the-century frame and embossed-tin farmhouses. From the Waring Store, head west about a quarter-mile, up the hill, on RM 1621. Turn around, and from atop this hill you can see all of Waring spread out before you.

One of the buildings you see is the old Waring depot, a long yellow-green wooden affair, stting alone in the middle of a grassy field.

WARING DEPOT
One block west of Waring-Welfare Rd. • Not open to the public
A tin roof covers the older wood shingle one; one corner of the tin sheeting is pulled up for you to see. Upon first glance, the abandoned Waring station looks just like dozens of other rural Texas depots. But although these buildings were similar in size and materials used, subtle individuality resulted from variations in detail and patterns of finish. In some stations, the walls were decoratively articulated into panels with a pattern of thin boards. At other stations, ornamental shingle patterns or roof brackets were the distinguishing characteristics. This barn of a depot's most distinguishing characteristic is the mustard color of its simple board-and-batten siding. Even the roof brackets are rudimentary A-line affairs. As you travel through the other little towns in this book, look at the remaining old depot buildings and you'll recognize these small variations. The Shiner and Granger stations are good examples.

The last train passed through Waring 20 years ago, but these days you can scarcely tell that the iron horse ever chugged through. The depot and adjoining grassy right-of-way are your only clues.

The little frame house sitting across the street (to the east) from the depot was originally the hotel. Most of it was torn down years ago, leaving only this several-room section that is now a private residence.

Head back on RM 1621 to the Waring Store and junction, and turn right (south) on narrow little Waring-Welfare Rd. to reach Welfare.

The road to Welfare takes you through rolling, densely wooded ranching country; the trees are so thick that they form a canopy over the road in places. You also cross the old T&NO tracks twice; the silver rails lie embedded in the asphalt and you see the raised roadbed on either side of you.

Welfare sneaks up on you before you know it, 4 miles south out of Waring. There are no highway signs to warn you, only a handful of houses and the slumbering Welfare Store.

WELFARE

Kendall County • 36 • About 4 miles from Waring

Welfare, located in the fertile bottomlands of Big Joshua and Little Joshua Creeks, was first settled by German immigrants in the 1840s, and was known as Boyton or Bon Ton for several decades. The name was changed to Welfare when the railroad came through. But why the name was chosen is harder to pin down. Some say the surrounding rich fields caused people to regard it as a place where one could "fare well." Others say Welfare is a corruption of the German word *Wohlfahrt,* meaning "pleasant trip."

Welfare, after all, had been smack-dab on the main road west from old San Antonio de Bexar for centuries. Only with the comparatively recent construction of US 87 through Comfort has Welfare been bypassed by the mainstream of transcontinental traffic.

Indians traveling the Pinto Trail from the Northern Plains to south and central Texas followed what was later to be the path of the F&N closely, through the pass at Cain City and across the Divide, then the SA&AP's route across the Guadalupe near Waring and over the Spanish Pass through the range of hills south of Welfare, on through Boerne and San Antonio. The Spanish Pass provides a natural passage for travel through the range of high hills located about 6 miles north of Boerne. The pass was used by Spanish missionaries, miners, and soldiers bound for the San Saba de la Cruz Mission (located near present-day Menard), hence the name. Treasure hunters have been combing the Hill Country for the fabled San Saba mines ever since the mission was abandoned in 1758.

American teamsters, soldiers, and settlers continued to use the old Indian trail, and Welfare became a stage stop on the grueling San Antonio-to-San Diego run. The Camp Verde-bound camels also passed through Boyton-Bon Ton on their way west from San Antonio in 1857.

The "SAP," as the SA&AP was sometimes called, also chose this path of least resistance through the pass, and with its arrival in 1887 Boyton got a depot and a new name.

The main highway to Fredericksburg, old Hwy. 28, the Gulf-to-Panhandle highway, ran through Welfare until 1932. Hwy. 28, superseded by US 87, is now just the meandering, barely marked county road on which you have been traveling since the RM 473 turnoff. Welfare, abandoned by the railroad and bypassed by the highway, slumbers.

The 7-Up sign on the Welfare Store porch reads "Welcome to WELFARE, TEXAS," but the store has been closed since the bicentennial year. Mercantile store, post office, cafe, saloon, and home (living quarters are attached out back), the Welfare Store was the heart of the Welfare business district. The saloon had its own private entrance, incidentally. No entrance was allowed from the room that housed the post office—federal law, you know.

The cotton gin is gone, and the little whitewashed frame schoolhouse sits a hundred or so feet east of the road (to your left), even with the "Welfare" highway sign as you continue south out of Welfare. The school started life in 1890, about four miles from here, on Big Joshua Creek. The local men tore it down and rebuilt it here, across the railroad tracks from the store.

Only a brace of houses stand in the immediate vicinity of the store, but folks from several miles around claim Welfare as their home, proudly proclaiming, "We're in Welfare, not on Welfare."

Just after you leave Welfare, continuing south on Welfare Rd., you see the sad old roadbed on your left and then a collection of weather-beaten old homesteads as you continue on toward Boerne.

NICHOLAS ZINK HOMESTEAD
About 5 miles south of Waring; look for historical marker on your left • Private property

Born in Bavaria in 1812, Nicholas Zink came to Texas in 1844 with his wife, Louise. They came as part of the Adelsverein colonization scheme. Zink was a civil engineer and former Bavarian Army officer. From December 1844 to March 1845, he supervised the move of approximately half of the German immigrants from Indianola to New Braunfels. Once they had arrived at the site that would become New Braunfels, Zink supervised the construction of a log palisade, or fort, to protect the immigrants' temporary tent city. This fort was called Zinkenburg. Zink also surveyed the original town site and surrounding farmland.

By 1846, Zink was hauling freight and passengers back and from Houston to New Braunfels. In 1847, he was divorced from Louise for "unhappy differences" and headed for Fredericksburg, but changed his mind and settled on Sister Creek. There he built a large two-story log house, the first building in what would become Sisterdale. He remarried and gained a reputation as a good farmer. But he still wasn't satisfied, so in 1850, he and his new wife, Elisabeth, sold their house and land and moved to Fredericksburg, to build and operate a gristmill on Baron Creek. By 1853, he had moved once again, this time to the Comfort area where he built Perseverance Mill on the Guadalupe River. Its first dam washed away, then drought idled it another year. In 1868, he moved here and built a limestone house, which is the center part of the current two-story ranch house you see from the road.

The 1870 Kendall County census listed Zink as a shinglemaker. By this time he had married again, to an Englishwoman named Agnes who was young enough to be his daughter. When plans were announced to build the SA&AP line to Kerrville, Zink donated land for the railroad right-of-way and helped engineer it. His joy at its successful completion was short-lived, however; he died November 3, 1887, less than a month after the first train steamed into Kerrville. Zink is buried in an unmarked grave on a knoll near this house.

Turn left onto FM 289 (about 1 mile past the Zink homestead), which soon becomes the I-10 frontage road.

PO-PO FAMILY RESTAURANT
US 87/I-10 frontage road, 8 miles north of Boerne and 3 miles from Welfare • 830-537-4194 • Open daily • Lunch and dinner AE, MC, V • Full bar • W

The venerable Po-Po, with its famous, distinctive red neon "EATS" sign out front, started life as a dance hall built in 1929 by local rancher/dairyman Edwin Nelson. He had earlier established a gas station nearby, and this little motorist's oasis midway between Boerne and Comfort, at the junction of old highways 12 and 28, became known as "Nelson City." Nelson City still appears on official

Texas Highway maps, although it has never had a post office or been incorporated.

The Nelson Dance Hall featured a dance every 2 weeks, and the musicians would play from 8 P.M. til 2 A.M. Admission started at 25 cents a head, but as the Depression deepened the price dropped to a dime and finally to the passing of a hat. People just couldn't afford to buy the gas to drive out there, and so the dance hall failed.

The hall was sold in 1932 to Ned Houston, another local and very colorful rancher who exported cattle all over Central and South America. He converted the hall into a restaurant, naming it in all probability for the famous Mexican volcano Popocatepetl, whose nickname is Popo. Houston knew the volcano well, and he had been looking for a short, punchy name.

Houston sold Po-Po in 1938 and it has changed hands several more times since. The plate collection (over 800 plates now), which covers the inside walls, dates to the ownership of Luther and Marie Burgon (1950–81).

Po-Po serves straightforward, simple American food—steaks, barbecue, chops, chicken, seafood. A beer garden and outdoor music stage have been recently added. It's wise to call ahead for reservations on Friday and Saturday nights.

From Po-Po, get on I-10 and head south toward Boerne. After four miles on I-10, take Bus. US 87 into downtown Boerne.

BOERNE

Kendall County Seat • 4,697 • (830) • About 8 miles from Po-Po Restaurant

Townbuilder John James bought the land on which Boerne was built in 1840. Fourteen years later, he and Gustave Theisen laid out a town here and named it for Ludwig Boerne, a radical German political journalist and satirist. Boerne never came to Texas and was dead in Paris by 1837, but his writings maintained a measure of popularity, especially among the German radicals and idealists who immigrated to Texas in the 1840s and founded the communistic society of Bettina.

After the Bettina colony broke up, five of its founders migrated south to a spot near present-day Boerne and established a farm, which they called Tusculum. Like Bettina, Tusculum broke up after a couple of years. But some of the men stayed here individually, as Boerne's earliest settlers. Hundreds of Germans joined them, making

Boerne and Kendall County one of the most thoroughly German regions in Texas. They built a dam across Cibolo Creek and used it to power a gristmill and shingle-making machinery. But these early-comers were continually harassed by raiding, kidnapping Indians.

Even so, Boerne was soon a stage stop on the road west from San Antonio, the Upper Emigrant Road. The SA&AP superseded the bumpy Concord stagecoaches in 1887, and all of a sudden the 31 miles between San Antonio and the romantic hills of Boerne were little more than an hour and 95¢ away.

Boerne quickly grew into a popular tourist resort, famous, as noted in a tourist brochure of that era, for "the purest air God ever made for man or woman, either. The burg is principally noted for the unlimited quantity and excellent quality of its ozone, whatever that is, its surpassing beauty, its beer (imported from San Antonio), its public spirited citizens, pretty girls, good hotels."

The tourists also came here to climb the rugged hills, to drink the cold water bubbling from the iron and sulphur spring four miles out of town, to explore the caves along the Cibolo, or simply to sit around on the hotel porch and breathe the healthy air.

Perhaps while they were here, the visitors also partook of some of the local fruit of the vine. Though the wild grapes and berries gathered around here bore little resemblance to the carefully cultivated grapes of the Rhine and Mosel, the immigrants nonetheless managed to produce a potable wine by adding large amounts of sugar to the juice. The quantities produced were generally quite modest, mostly intended for home consumption, but this was not always the case. Farmers around Boerne produced over 50,000 gallons in one season during the 1870s. A few of the area's old Germans still make mustang grape and dandelion wines. A lot of charcoal burning was also done in and around Boerne, so much so that Boerne was often disparagingly called "Charcoal Capital of the World" by neighboring towns.

Although the SA&AP was a big-time line when compared with the F&N, it received its share of ribbing from its customers. They referred to the SA&AP as the SAP because it "went up in spring and came down in the fall." Of course, a round trip on the SAP didn't take quite that long, though it probably seemed that way sometimes to stranded passengers. The SAP also acted as colonization agent, bringing English settlers to Boerne via the Southern Pacific Colonization Company. (Southern Pacific bought the SAP but kept the old name.)

Boerne has been Kendall County's only county seat. Eighty citizens of Boerne and Sisterdale petitioned the state for the creation of a new county as early as 1859, but Kendall County was not created until 1862, when the Confederate legislature carved it out of Blanco and Kerr counties. Boerne won out over Sisterdale in the subsequent election to determine the county seat. At that time, the county's population was 81 percent German. They were primarily stockraisers, farmers, and cedar choppers. Only recently has this picture begun to change. Just 40 years ago Boerne was described as a "health and recreation resort ringed by wooded hillsides, spreading its winding streets past old stone houses. Narrow windows, outside stairways, steep gables, and prim little front-yard gardens show its Old World influence." With the completion of I-10 through Boerne, the sleepy German town became essentially a San Antonio bedroom town. Some of the old flavor remains. The Boerne Village Band is said to be America's oldest continuously active German music band, going back to the county's founding. It plays regularly at the Abendkonzerte Series at Boerne's Main Square.

A string of Victorian residences lines the Bus. US 87 path toward town, harking back to the days when the SAP ran alongside.

Main at Blanco is the official center of town. Main Plaza is off to your right, the courthouse square to your left.

DIENGER STORE/ANTLERS INN
N. Main and Blanco
The beautifully restored two-story building immediately to your right at this corner was built in 1884 by local merchant Joseph Dienger. Distinguished by its broad two-story wraparound porches, the store was later famous as the Antlers Inn. It typifies the German tradition of fine craftsmanship and construction. The skill of its German masons is evident in the excellent workmanship of the walls. The square wooden porch columns framed with wooden moldings and jigsaw brackets are typically German. The ornate quatrefoil porch decoration constrasts nicely with the roughly polished limestone block walls.

Turn right on Blanco, so as to circle Main Plaza. On down at the end of the block is Ye Kendall Inn.

YE KENDALL INN
128 W. Blanco • 249-2138 • Open 7 days for lunch and dinner
$–$$ • AE, MC, V. • Bar • W with help
The center section of Ye Kendall Inn is the old Reed house, built by Erastus and Sarah Reed, who purchased this land in 1859. The

house and property changed hands several times during the next few years, and after 1869 its fame grew as the King place, under the ownership of Colonel and Senator Henry C. King. By 1878 the Boerne climate had begun to attract health seekers, mostly sufferers from asthma, tuberculosis, and sinusitis, who were willing to make the jolting 31-mile stage ride from San Antonio. To accommodate the growing clientele, subsequent owners C. J. Rountree and W. L. Wadsworth enlarged the building to its present size and renamed it the Boerne Hotel. In 1909 owner Dr. H. D. Barnitz changed the hotel's name to its present appellation.

The original Reed House part of the Inn is constructed of local limestone, with 20" thick walls. The building has a cellar and there is evidence down there of a tunnel, which is rumored to connect the building with another building a block away. Story has it that the tunnel was dug for protection from raiding Indians. The courtyard out back is the old wagon yard, where passengers were loaded and unloaded from passing stagecoaches.

In 1996, several old buildings were moved onto the premises, including a 1920s schoolhouse formerly located on I-10; a carriage house, a 1922 Lutheran church first located in Dobrowolski, Texas; a turn-of-the-century Victorian cottage formerly located on Main St.; a cedar-log cabin from the Fredericksburg area; and an 1820s log cabin moved here from Virginia. Two reproduction storefronts were also constructed.

BOERNE CHAMBER OF COMMERCE
One Main Plaza • 249-8000 • Open Monday through Friday

The Chamber of Commerce is the place to go for tourist information.

Follow San Antonio back to Main. Cross Main on E. San Antonio, past the courthouse and square.

KENDALL COUNTY COURTHOUSE
Main and E. San Antonio

The date on the limestone Kendall County Courthouse reads 1909, but this date is only a half-truth. That was the year the front addition was built. Alfred Giles designed this shyly romantic Italianate addition during his later years, and it contrasts strongly with the severe lines of his 1882 Gillespie County Courthouse. Yet both are distinctively Giles.

The back half was built in 1870, which makes this the second oldest courthouse still in use as such in Texas. The jail next door was built in 1884, and the old sheriff's office is of the same era.

Turn left at the eastern end of the courthouse block onto Saunders. Catercorner to the county jail is the Boerne City Utilities Office.

BOERNE CITY UTILITIES OFFICE
402 E. Blanco

Alfred Giles also designed the two-story limestone building that now houses the City Utilities Office. Built in 1910, it originally housed the Boerne High School. It bears a certain resemblance to the courthouse addition. An older one-story limestone block schoolhouse stands immediately behind it.

HISTORIC HOUSE MUSEUM/KUHLMANN-KING HOUSE
400 E. Blanco, next to City Hall • 249-2807, 249-2469
Museum open Sunday 1–4, Archives open Thursday
9–noon, 1–4 • Adults $1 • W variable

Upon the hill adjacent to the old school is a two-story limestone and cypress home turned museum. Built during the 1880s for local pharmacist and land baron William Kuhlmann, the house was sold in 1908 to Selina King, whose sons operated Boerne's King and King Lumber Company for many years. The Boerne ISD owned the house from 1920–1951, when it was purchased by the city of Boerne.

The **Henry J. Graham Building,** a simple frame turn-of-the-century store, has been moved from its original site in the 100 block of S. Main to its present location next to the museum. It started as a private bank (supposedly Boerne's first bank), then served as real estate office, beauty parlor, barber shop, storage building, and telephone exchange.

Head on back to Main, then turn left on it, toward the city of San Antonio.

Main Street Boerne today bears only passing resemblance to the Main Street of SAP days, but a few nice buildings still line the street.

FABRA SMOKEHOUSE
194 S. Main, behind Benefit Planners Building

Julius Fabra (1827–1910) came to Boerne in 1854, and worked as a freight hauler before opening a meat market here. His son, Ludwig, built the first story of this limestone smokehouse in 1887, and the second story in 1904. Ludwig's son, Henry, operated the market from Ludwig's death in 1929 until his retirement in 1962. The market itself made way for the current building.

BERGMAN LUMBER COMPANY
236 S. Main

The Bergman Lumber building is one of the nicest vintage structures left on Main. Two-story, buff brick with limestone trim, it is topped with a crenellated limestone parapet, which bears the inscription "1902—H. D. Adler –1911." The front porch is supported by svelte cast-iron posts and lacy iron brackets, once all the rage.

THEIS HOUSE
200 block E. Main (Main and Newton) between Bergman
Lumber and Plaza package store • Private residence

Just a few yards south of Bergman Lumber and a few more yards up an alley of a street named Newton is the little Theis house. Obscured from immediate view by a newer building on Main, this is one of Boerne's oldest residences, built in 1858. Originally a dogtrot cabin, its outer walls have been stuccoed and the dogtrot enclosed. But these improvements were made very long ago and the home maintains a certain rustic look.

WENDLER HOUSE
302 E. Main • Currently commercial space

This simple one-story white stuccoed cottage is another of Boerne's oldest residences, built about 1855 by Henry Wendler, a master cabinetmaker from Germany. In 1865 he married a daughter of Albert Luckenbach, namesake of both Luckenbach and Albert communities. They raised seven children in this house.

CIBOLO CREEK

Soon you cross Cibolo Creek. Over the centuries it has been known by a variety of names. Coahuiltecan Indians called it Xoloton, Tonkawas called it Bata Coniquiyoqui. The Spaniards knew it variously as Santa Crecencia, San Ygnacio de Loyola, San Xavier, and finally Cibolo. *Cibolo* is a Spanish-Indian term for "buffalo." The banks of Cibolo Creek are city parkland, from the Main St. bridge east along River Rd./SH 46. It's a nice place to picnic or take a stroll.

ROBERT E. LEE HOUSE
S. Main and Evergreen • Private
Just after you cross the creek, at the corner of Evergreen and S. Main, you see on your left a tiny one-room limestone house. A front porch sign and a small Texas state historical plaque mark the cottage as the occasional quarters of Robert E. Lee, Colonel, Second U.S. Cavalry, back in his Texas frontier days. An interesting barrel-stave cistern surmounting a shingled turret stands a few yards behind the Lee quarters.

PHILLIP MANOR HOUSE
706 S. Main
You can't miss the old Joseph Phillip home, now known as the Phillip House Manor, located on your right a couple of blocks farther south from the Robert E. Lee house. Joseph Phillip built the core of this rambling limestone and mill-sawn lumber complex in 1860. It served as the family home for a few years, but as the years stretched into decades the little house was expanded again and again, serving as inn (during the resort era), athletic and shooting club headquarters, and dance hall. Phillip's complex once included the old two-story Greek Revival Carstangen building, located directly across the street.

RUDOLPH CARSTANGEN HOME
707 S. Main
This two-story, porched Greek Revival building dates to the 1870s when it was home to early settler Rudolph Carstangen.

KRONKOSKY HILL
Kronkosky St., up from S. Main
This is the highest hilltop in Boerne, originally the homestead of Albert Kronkosky. The house was built between 1911 and 1917. It is currently a school and convent for Benedictine sisters. The tower is now the school library and offers a great view. The grounds are open to visitors during daylight hours.

OLD ST. PETER'S CATHOLIC CHURCH
S. Main at Kronkosky
Just south of the old Phillip House and up the hill a bit is the old St. Peter's Catholic Church, now dwarfed by the newer (1923) St. Peter's Church. In 1866, Galveston's Bishop Claude DuBois sent the young French emigrant priest Emil Fleury to Boerne to organize a

congregation to serve the town and surrounding area. This simple, one-story, gabled limestone church was completed in 1867. Fleury left Boerne in 1869, but returned in 1923 to lay the cornerstone for the present St. Peter's. Except for the tin roof, the church retains its original exterior appearance, including the simple wooden steeple. The interior has been remodeled extensively and is of no historic interest. The old church now serves as an educational building.

STENDEBACH HOUSE
103 Kronkosky • Open Mondays only

Behind the Beef and Brew Restaurant at S. Main and Kronkosky is another of Boerne's oldest residences, the Stendebach house. Now housing an antique shop, the Stendebach home is a good example of solid German workmanship, from the second phase of settling down here in the Hill Country, when sturdy rock houses replaced the initial log cabins. Field-dressed limestone blocks, a steeply pitched roof breaking stride over the backside-shed attachment, and casement windows are its distinguishing characteristics.

AREA PARKS

BOERNE CITY PARK
SH 46 East (River Rd.) about 1 mile east of Main • Open daily

Boerne City Park has two areas of interest for the tourist: the Cibolo Wilderness Trail and the Agricultural Heritage Center. The Wilderness Trail, which runs along pretty Cibolo Creek, travels from grassland to creekbed, marshland to woodland, and offers a good cross-section of Hill Country habitats, flora, and fauna. The trail starts in the marshland created by Herff Springs, continues through a patch of native Texas prairie (with lots of wildflowers come spring), along the creek bottom (with tall cypresses and sheer walls), and through the woodlands. The Nature Center building was moved here in 1992 and is over 100 years old. The 6-acre Agricultural Heritage Center features a working blacksmith shop with a steam boiler powering a main drive shaft that drives various pieces of equipment. The Main Display Barn includes old farming and woodworking tools, antique wagons, combine, and other displays. Outdoor equipment exhibits include old tractors, plows, combines and more. The center is open Wednesday and Sunday afternoons or by appointment; call the Chamber of Commerce at 249-8000.

GUADALUPE RIVER STATE PARK
The park is located at the north end of Park Road 31, 13 miles east of Boerne; take SH 46 from Boerne • 830-438-2656
Open daily • Admission • W variable

Guadalupe River State Park (1,938 acres) is located along the boundary of Comal and Kendall Counties. It was acquired by deed from private owners in 1974 and was opened to the public in 1983. Bisected by the clear-flowing waters of the Guadalupe River, the park is notable for its ruggedness and scenic beauty. It has 4 miles of river frontage and is located in the middle of a 9-mile stretch of the Guadalupe River. The Guadalupe River, with banks lined by huge bald cypress trees, is the park's most outstanding natural feature. On its winding path through the park, the river courses over four natural rapids; two steep limestone bluffs are evidence of its awesome erosive power.

Trees in the lower elevations and bottomlands include sycamore, elm, basswood, pecan, walnut, persimmon, willow, and hackberry. In the uplands away from the river, the limestone terrain is typical of the Edwards Plateau and has oak and juniper woodlands, with interspersed grasslands. One area of old-growth ashe juniper woodland provides the proper nesting habitat for the golden-cheeked warbler. Also living in the park are white-tailed deer, coyote, gray fox, skunk, raccoon, opossum, bobcat, and armadillo. Other smaller species abound. In addition to bird-watching and nature study, outdoor activities include canoeing, fishing, swimming, tubing, picnicking, hiking, and camping. There is a 2-hour guided interpretive tour of the adjacent Honey Creek State Natural Area.

The day-use area offers convenient access to the Guadalupe River and has picnic sites and ample parking. Campsites with water and electricity can accommodate recreational vehicles and trailers; another area has campsites with water for tent campers, and a separate area with walk-in tent campsites with water in the area. Special rates are available. Drinking water and sanitary facilities are provided at the picnic and camping areas, and the restrooms at the water or water-and-electricity campsite areas have showers. The park also has a trailer dump station, 3 miles of hiking trails, and a Texas State Park Store with gifts, nature items, and books for children and adults.

Write to 3350 Park Rd. 31, Spring Branch 78070. *Weather:* January average temperature 60 degrees, July average temperature 86 degrees. *First/last freeze:* November 15/March 15. *Busy season:* March through November.

HONEY CREEK STATE NATURAL AREA

Honey Creek State Natural Area (2,293 acres) is located in western Comal County. Chipped stone tools and arrowheads found on the property indicate that Honey Creek was favored by early hunter-gatherers and later Indian tribes who roamed throughout the Edwards Plateau region. Among the German immigrants who accompanied Prince Carl von Solms-Braunfels to Texas were the Doeppenschmidt family from Bavaria. They began to homestead in the Honey Creek area in 1866. Over the years, Doeppenschmidt family members acquired many parcels of land, including what would become Honey Creek Ranch. Adam Doeppenschmidt consolidated the various parcels in 1894 and sold them to Otto Weidner and Fred Rust in 1910. The tracts, which became Honey Creek Ranch, were worked by the Weidners until 1971, at which time they were sold to W. O. Bartle, Jr., of Houston. The area was acquired by deed from the Texas Nature Conservancy in 1985 and by deed from a private individual in 1988 and was opened for limited access in 1985.

Entry into Honey Creek is for guided tours only. The diverse geology, flora, and fauna make Honey Creek a special place. There are 2 miles of trails. A 2-hour, guided interpretive tour emphasizes history, geology, flora, and fauna. Tours are conducted on Saturday mornings, but please call Guadalupe River State Park to confirm. Reservations are not required. Access is through Guadalupe River State Park. There are no facilities at this park except the trails.

The vegetative diversity of the Honey Creek tract is one of its most attractive features. Ashe juniper, live oak, agarita, and Texas persimmon dominate the dry, rocky hills, and a few grasses such as little muhly and curly mesquite have found just enough soil in the cracks to hang on. As the juniper and Baccharis are being removed from the upland flats, the stands of native grasses, like Indiangrass, little bluestem, and switchgrass, are reestablishing themselves as the dominant groundcover. Moving down into the canyon of the creek itself, there is an increase of cedar elm and older junipers; Spanish oak, pecan, walnut, and Mexican buckeye appear rather abruptly. The terrain levels out again in the narrow floodplain and the creek itself. Here, the dominant species are sycamore and bald cypress. Texas palmetto, columbine, and maidenhair fern occur along the rock banks, spatter dock floats on the surface, and a number of emergent plants are plainly visible in the clear, blue-green water. The nine soil types that occur on the property can be distinguished from one another by the dominant vegetation present. The diversity of habitat types have resulted in a varied and abundant fauna. All of the typical Hill Country species, from wild turkeys to fence lizards, ringtails to leopard frogs, plus many types of fish, can be found. Several species of endemics with limited ranges also inhabit the preserve, including Gagle's map turtle, Guadalupe bass, four-lined skink, green kingfisher, Texas salamander, and the Honey Creek Cave salamander. Honey Creek is one of the nesting sites of the threatened golden-cheeked warbler.

Write to the park c/o Guadalupe River State Park, 3350 Park Road 31, Spring Branch 78070.

To resume your path south toward San Antonio, leave Boerne on Main St./Bus. US 87.

One last bit of trivia as we leave Boerne. Perhaps the town's most well-known citizen was one Ad Toepperwein, better known as vaudeville's "Dead-Eye Dick." Ad was so good with a shooting iron that even Buffalo Bill declined a match with him. During a 10-day shooting marathon in San Antonio, Toepperwein fired 72,500 times at 2¼-inch wood blocks tossed into the air. He missed only nine times. The year was 1907, and the record has never been equaled. More on Ol' Dead-Eye in a minute.

When Bus. US 87 merges with I-10, get onto I-10, briefly, toward San Antonio. Take the Scenic Loop/Boerne Stage/Cascade Caverns Rd. exit off I-10. To reach the next station on the SA&AP/ T&NO route— Leon Springs—turn right at the T intersection on the road marked Boerne Stage Rd./Scenic Loop Rd.

But if you like caves, turn left at this intersection, onto Cascade Caverns Rd., in order to reach Boerne's subterranean wonder, Cascade Caverns.

CASCADE CAVERNS
Cascade Caverns Rd., just off I-10 • 755-8080 • April through Labor Day: open daily 9–6; Labor Day through March: open daily 9–5 • Admission

Carlsbad Caverns explorer Frank Nicholson made Cascade Caverns famous with exaggerated descriptions of his Cascade Caverns explorations in 1932. He claimed to have seen blind fish, white bats, beetles, crickets, and milk-colored frogs along the shores of a mile-long underground lake located 500 feet from the mouth of the cave.

Locals had known of the cave's opening for over 60 years, but they believed the cave ended with the body of water. This belief was encouraged by giant formations that hung from the ceiling into the water, giving the appearance of a back wall.

Well anyway, some act of nature caused an opening in the earth below, and all this water disappeared into a still deeper river, and the cave was fully revealed. Originally called Hester's Cave, the hole was first commercially developed in 1933. It remained open until 1941. After a nine-year closure, it reopened in 1950.

Evidence of ancient Indian life has been found in here, and legend has it that an early German settler lived a hermit's life here many years ago. The caverns take their present name from a waterfall that plunges almost 100 feet from a shallow cave containing an underground stream into the main cave. Like most other commercial Texas caves, it is a water-formed cave and considered 95-percent active. The stalactite/stalagmite formations grow at a rate of about an inch every 100 years.

The approximately half-mile tour takes about an hour. Recreational and camping facilities are located on the grounds. For more information write Cascade Caverns, Rt. 4, Box 4110, Boerne 78006.

ANNUAL EVENT

JUNE • Berges Fest • Kendall County Fairgrounds, US 46 Father's Day Weekend
One of the most colorful and diverse German festivals around. There are dances nightly, oompah music, horse races, children's olympics, Mexican dancers, a parade, and arts and crafts.

From Cascade Caverns return to the T intersection and resume your path toward Leon Springs on the Scenic Loop/Boerne Stage Rd.

The road sign does not lie; this is the old stage road, executed now in asphalt instead of rocks and ruts, yet still following the original sinuous toilsome path. For decades traversing a rather lonely course, it can scarcely hold all the traffic generated by recent area residential development. Still, it has a certain charm.

After about 6 miles, Boerne Stage Rd. comes to an intersection with Touton-Beauregard Rd. Turn left here to reach Leon Springs.

LEON SPRINGS

Bexar County • 137 • (830) • About 12 miles from Boerne

Leon Springs' first settler was George von Pleve, a German noble-man and immigrant. Mr. von Pleve established a stage stop here in 1846, and was joined in 1852 by fellow immigrant Max Aue. A veteran of the 1848 Schleswig-Holstein War in northern Germany, Aue came to Texas shortly thereafter. He became a Texas Ranger soon after his arrival. Aue's services were rewarded with a 640-acre grant from the state, the plot being located here at Leon Springs. At the time of his death in 1903, Aue owned more than 20,000 acres. Upon marrying, he forsook the wild life and settled down to open the Leon Springs Supply Company. Soon he was postmaster and the stage line was using his store as a horse-changing station and rest stop. His place got so popular that in 1879 Aue built the Leon Springs Hotel, located next to his store.

This stage route between San Antonio and San Diego was the longest in the country and took nearly a month of day-and-night traveling to traverse. Leon Springs was either the first or last stop out of San Antonio, depending on which way you were headed. When the railroad came through in 1887, the station was named Aue Station in Aue's honor.

Aue's reputation with a gun followed him into civilian life. He was commonly acclaimed as the best hunter in the Hill Country. But even his formidable reputation did not render him immune to brigands. His store was robbed during the 1870s by some young desperadoes. They tied Aue and family up, ate up all the food in the store, and then fled, taking the store's stock of clothing with them as well as Aue's money and horses. As soon as Aue got loose, he headed for Boerne and the sheriff's office. A posse was soon formed. With Aue's ranger experience, the posse soon caught the robbers and shot them down. But the gang actually got the last laugh; just before their leader died, he smiled into the faces of his slayers and murmured, "Tell the old man [Aue] I died in his clothes."

Max passed his talent with a gun down to his sons and his nephew "Dead-Eye Dick" Toepperwein. Good enough to turn Buffalo Bill gunshy, Ad Toepperwein was still never good enough to beat his cousin—Max's boy—Rudolph Aue. Aue refused to shoot professionally because he felt it was just a waste of good ammunition. Toepperwein even acknowledged Rudolph's "deader eye" in a poem, which reads: "I've travelled around the world, but no one could shoot like Rudy could." That, from a man who could shoot your portrait in a matter of seconds into a square of tin.

But Rudy was busy running his business enterprises. Besides inheriting the family hotel and store, Rudolph Aue established five saloons here to service the thirsty troops at nearby Camp Stanley during World War I. It took a refrigerator carload of Pearl beer a day, shipped in from the San Antonio Brewery, to slake their thirst.

Army tents stretched across the countryside during the war, and the troops used the Leon Springs, which outcrop just off the Boerne Stage Rd., as their laundry area. The camp, now known officially as the Leon Springs Military Reservation, has been closed off and on since its creation in 1917. It's currently in active use.

The end of World War I meant the first closing of the Leon Springs camp, and it also signaled the imminent demise of Charcoal City. Charcoal City was the collective name given to the charcoal burners who lined the banks of the Guadalupe River from just north of New Braunfels to just east of Sisterdale. A few of the burners sold or traded their charcoal to local storekeepers, but most of them drove their briquet-laden wagons down to San Antonio. There the burners either sold their charcoal to wholesale dealers or plodded along the city streets, hawking it from their wagons. To say that the charcoal market in San Antonio was variable would be to severely understate the situation. A wagonload might sell for as little as $8 or as much as $24. But as one burner put it, charcoal was always money in the pocket, unlike crops like corn or cotton, which were often beaten down by hail, devoured by grasshoppers, or shriveled by drought.

The round trip from Charcoal City to San Antonio might take two days or a week depending on road conditions (glorified cow paths, remember) and how quickly the load could be sold. If the river was up, burners on the yonder side of the river were in a fix—there were no bridges back then—while burners on the San Antonio banks of the Guadalupe could laugh all the way to market, knowing that their loads would command premium prices.

Most people in San Antonio used charcoal stoves before 1920. One burner said, "Whenever I got to San Antonio with a load of charcoal that I could not sell, I would drive through the red light district, and in no time at all, they would buy every sack of charcoal. I never could figure out just what they did with that coal—and if I couldn't sell it, they were always ready to trade." At Christmas, most burners would throw a few choice cedars on top to sell to the city folk.

All of this is preparatory to telling you that Leon Springs was a favorite camping spot for the burners on their way to San Antonio. The loaded wagons' progress was slow, and very often 10 to 15 of them would end the day at Leon Springs. The water here was good and most of the surrounding land was open country, good grazing for the hungry horses and mules. And so the men would make their camp for the night, telling stories, playing cards, drinking 'shine, fiddling, and fighting into the night. With an early start the next morning, they could be wandering Bexar's streets almost before the dew was dry.

To see what's left of Leon Springs today, cross under I-10 past Rudy's Country Store and turn right onto the Old Fredericksburg Rd., into which Boerne Stage Rd. dead-ends. In a few yards you pass Max Aue's old Leon Springs store and hotel complex on your right.

Continue toward San Antonio on the Old Fredericksburg Rd., past the blacksmith shop, on to the Y intersection with the I-10 frontage road. Turn right on the frontage road, so as to double-back toward Boerne, past the Leon Springs schoolhouse and Max Aue's old store and hotel.

The quaint, cavernous limestone building that houses Romano's Macaroni Grill dates to 1932. It began life as a dance hall and bar, and saw plenty of action during World War II—of the Saturday night cut-and-shoot variety—as the B-29 Club.

Now you're back at Rudy's Country Store, which Rudy Aue, Jr., built in 1926. The present Rudy's claims to have the worst barbecue in Texas; I've had worse, but take them at their word anyway and save your money.

This completes the tour of Leon Springs, the last major stop before San Antonio on the old F&N/T&NO route. From Leon Springs, you can take I-10 into San Antonio. If you wish to return to Fredericksburg, you can retrace the railroad tracks' path or take the following scenic route through scenic, hilly, sparsely settled country.

Return to Boerne on Boerne Stage Rd. or I-10, and take Bus. US 87 into town. Continue on Bus. US 87 past the courthouse square and Market Plaza; 1.2 miles later, turn right on RM 1376. In 11.6 miles you come to an intersection with SH 473 and the hamlet of Sisterdale

(See Hill Country Rivers). Continuing on RM 1376, you again cross the Divide (about 6 miles east of the old railroad tunnel), and in about 17 miles you come to Luckenbach. From Luckenbach, go another 4.5 miles on RM 1376 to its dead end at US 290 at Rocky Hill. Turn left on US 290 to reach Fredericksburg, 5.6 miles to the west.

HERMIT OF THE HILLS/THE HIGHLAND LAKES

Approximately 180 miles

White settlers started coming in numbers to what we now call the Texas Hill Country in the 1840s. The early comers liked what they saw: colorful spring flowers, fields of waist-high native grasses, sparkling rivers, bubbling springs, and live oaks that looked like olive trees from a distance. But this lushness was only skin deep. Only a thin layer of soil overlaid the limestone bedrock. The earliest pioneers' grazing and farming practices quickly destroyed this rich but delicately balanced ecosystem. Without the native grasses' thick root system to hold it together, much of what little topsoil the hills had was washed away by rain into the region's rivers and creeks, or was blown away by the wind. Wildfires, which had previously kept the growth and spread of ashe juniper and other species in check, were not allowed to burn by the settlers. The legendary cattle drives also spread the mesquite tree from South Texas into the Hill Country, via cattle dung. Cows like to eat mesquite beans, and as they walked from one place to another, they deposited the digested remains of what they had eaten miles earlier, including intact mesquite beans. And then there was drought. Drought strikes the Hill Country periodically; some would say mostly. There are some wet years, to be sure, but mostly the Hill Country teeters on the brink of drought. Many early settlers chanced to arrive during one of the Hill Country's rainy seasons. When drought inevitably returned to the Hill Country, they didn't know what to do; all the rivers and streams dried up. Would it ever rain again? There was some doubt and much fear, until someone noticed that the growth rings of Hill Country trees alternated between thin and thick; there would be extended periods, even years, of drought, but the rains would eventually return.

While this promise of future rain gave at least scant hope to the folks who were already living here, it didn't attract very many newcomers to the Hill Country. It took more land out here to sustain a family unit than it did in Texas east of the Balcones Escarpment, where it rained more and the dirt was deeper. Some families prospered but most just managed to hang on, enjoying the good years when they came. Scrimping and saving was a necessary part of life. Spendthrifts perished.

The old pioneer order began to fade in the 1920s as sons and grandsons of the pioneers, no longer willing or able to wrest a living out of this hard ground, began to flee to the cities. Dozens of villages began to fade from the maps. But by the 1960s, a new migration back out to the Hills had begun. These newcomers did not depend on the land for a living, and so the sprawling old pioneer ranches and farms were split up into ranchettes, subdivisions, resorts, planned communities, and such. The mobile homes and California-style ranch houses of retirees and weekenders began to blanket the hills, beginning along the Highland Lakes.

Nothing has done more to change the face of the Texas Hill Country in modern times than the creation of the Highland Lakes chain out of 150 twisting miles of the Colorado River, from San Saba County down to Austin. Previously an isolated and poor region, the Highland Lakes brought flood control, drinking water, electricity, paved roads, and tourists to the scenic but hardscrabble Hill Country. Many of these tourists elected to stay. The bright, sparkling Highland Lakes play such a large recreational role in our lives these days that we tend to forget the first noble purpose of these pools.

The Lower Colorado River Authority was created by the Texas Legislature in 1934 to make the Colorado River more productive for central Texas. Before the LCRA's creation, droughts reduced the river's flow to a trickle, while a heavy rain could trigger horrendous floods that washed property and lives away all the way down to the Gulf of Mexico. Beginning with Adam Johnson in the 1850s, central Texans tried to dam the river, and failed. In 1931, the Insull utility

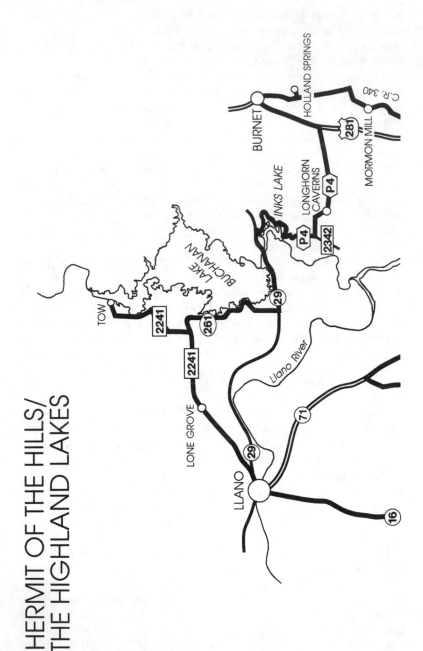

HERMIT OF THE HILLS/
THE HIGHLAND LAKES

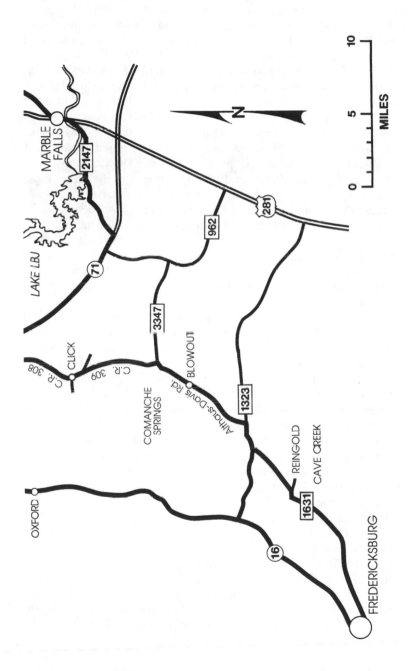

empire began to construct Hamilton Dam (now Buchanan Dam) at the spot Adam Johnson picked out nearly 80 years earlier. The granite bedrock made an ideal foundation. In 1932, Insull declared bankruptcy and the project stalled. The LCRA's first task was to complete construction of the dam, which was finished in 1937.

Besides flood control and water storage, the LCRA's original mission included the generation of electric power. Each dam has its own generating station. Together, the hydroelectric plants provide more than 240 megawatts of capacity to LCRA's electric system. Besides flood control and a dependable supply of water, the Colorado River dams brought electric power to the Hill Country, which transformed the difficult lives that most people led here only 70 years ago.

Without water and the air conditioning that electricity brings, most people would find life in the Hill Country unbearable. But with them, the region's population has exploded, creating power demands far beyond the hydroelectric plants' generating capacity. Once the primary source of power for LCRA's sprawling service area, hydroelectricity today supplies, on the average, less than 7 percent of LCRA's needs. It is used during power emergencies and during power demand "peaks" in extreme weather because it is available at a moment's notice.

Austin, Marble Falls, and dozens of smaller communities depend on the lakes for their water. In the summer, the amount of water used by everyone just about doubles over winter usage levels. A multimillion-dollar-a-year rice farming industry downstream with thousands of acres in production requires summer-long irrigation, using as much water in a single summer as the city of Austin uses in several years. Summertime lake levels are also affected by the customary lack of summer rain, generally 2 inches or less. Evaporation on hot sunny days adds further strain; even if Lakes Buchanan and Travis released no water during the summer, they would lose a foot of water a month due to evaporation alone. Because these demands on water arrive all at once, lake levels at Travis often drop sharply during the summer.

Water quality is an increasingly important mission for the LCRA. Recently, the LCRA created the Colorado River Trail, which follows the Colorado River corridor through 10 Texas counties, from San Saba to the Gulf Coast. The trail incorporates lakes, highways, parks, events, historic places, and other attractions, and is an effort to link cultural, historical, recreational, agricultural, and environmental interests in order to foster awareness and understanding of the importance of clean water and a healthy environment. Throughout the month of April, communities all along the Trail celebrate with a variety of River Fest activities.

Despite all the lake-induced growth, traces of the old, isolated Hill Country still exist, along the seldom-traveled backroads away from the lakes. This trip gives you a taste of both worlds.

FREDERICKSBURG

Gillespie County Seat • 7,745 • (830)

Despite the passing of generations and the encroachment by "outsiders," Fredericksburg, nearly 150 years after its founding, remains Texas' most enduringly German town, and one of the state's quaintest. It is increasingly popular with tourists and expatriate urbanites.

Fredericksburgers tend to be protective of their historic landmarks; the town probably has more historic landmarks per capita than any other Texas municipality, and the number grows steadily. It is just one example of the conservatism that is embedded here as firmly as the granite mountains which overlook the town from the north.

Visitors to Fredericksburg are charmed by the abundance of rock houses and Victorian gingerbread, and by the traces of Old World customs and flavors which still hang on such as the Schuetzenbundes and the annual county Schuetzenfeste, Maennerchor and Damenchor and the annual Saengerfest, the Easter Fires, and the Abendglocken. As recently as 1950, 75% of Fredericksburg's population was of German extraction and German was spoken on the streets as often as English. Today the percentage is down to about 50-50, and only a few of the old folks still speak German amongst themselves on the street, often in hushed tones guaranteed not to attract the tourists' attention.

During World War II, Fredericksburgers just plain quit speaking German—on the streets, in the churches, even at home. Parents quit teaching their children German and never resumed the practice. Churches chose not to resume German-language services after V-E day. Students in the public schools are now taking a renewed interest in learning German, but membership in the singing clubs (German language only) is still declining.

Fredericksburg is a friendlier town than most, but there is a certain resentment that has built up among some of the old-timers. "We're glad they visit; we just wish they wouldn't stay," is an oft-echoed sentiment, even among merchants. Vintage Main Street commercial buildings and residences in the Historical District command six-figure prices, reasonable to someone from Austin or Houston, but bewildering to natives. Dozens of old houses have been turned into B&Bs. The B&B business has gotten so hot in the last few years that old buildings are imported from as far away as Indiana and Pennsylvania and reconstructed on plots of Hill Country pastureland. There is at least one local company that buys, sells, and reconstructs old log cabins and timber frame buildings, plus antique building materials salvaged from razed buildings. Several old Main Street businesses hang on, like **Dooley's 5-10-25¢ Store** (131–133 E. Main), **Crenwelge Motor Sales** (301 E. Main), and **Knopp & Metzger Department Store** (231 W. Main), but most of Main Street's storefronts are given over to antique and specialty shops, which is not to say that all of these newcomers or "auslanders" are ignorant to the customs and traditions of Fredericksburg. "Sometimes the newcomers are more German than we," one native wryly admits.

A small but significant number are artisans and craftspeople who paint, sculpt, carve wood, or make toys, decoys, and gingerbread for Victorian restorations. "Hand-made" is enjoying a renaissance in Fredericksburg.

Fredericksburg is still a small town but definitely growing, from 4,629 inhabitants in 1960 to 7,745 in 1995. Is Fredericksburg in danger of losing its traditional identity?

To get the proper perspective, you have to climb to the top of Cross Mountain. (See also Take a Ride on the Fredericksburg & Northern, Mormon Trails, and Enchanted Rock for more about Fredericksburg.) All of Fredericksburg lays spread out just beneath you, some of it built with limestone from this weathered, scarred hillock. You hear hammers and saws buzzing in nearby subdivisions, and you see two Fredericksburgs—the old standing like Gibraltar in a sea of new. Some of today's old-timers may despair over the current state of affairs, but John Meusebach would probably approve. The very day he sailed for Texas to become the Adelsverein's new Texas commissioner, the Baron Ottfried Hans von Meusebach renounced his title to become John O. Meusebach, Texan. He knew you had to bend a little to fit into the new world.

Begin this trip at the Gillespie County Courthouse, on US 290 in downtown Fredericksburg. Proceed east on US 290 to the intersection with FM 1631, about 8 blocks east of the courthouse. Turn left here and head for Cave Creek.

As you leave town you will notice acres of the trees that produce one of Texas' most famous and tasty products, the Hill Country peach. During a good spring the trees are covered first with a riot of pink blossoms, then with dozens of succulent cling and freestone peaches. Subject as the peaches are to the vicissitudes of spring weather, some years we are blessed with bumper crops, other years the blossoms freeze on the trees and the summer peach crop is barely large enough to feed the growers' families.

Gillespie County peaches are justly favored by connoisseurs. The trees especially favor the area's granite-sand soil and cool winter and spring nights. Approximately 3,000 Gillespie County acres are planted in peaches and nectarines. In a good year the county produces one-fourth to one-third of all peaches consumed in Texas. A good year sees 160,000 bushels harvested. A bad year sees a few hundred bushels.

The earliest peaches begin to ripen in May and by the first of June the peach harvest is in full swing. The roadside stands are open and peaches are being shipped to the big city supermarkets. Some of the orchards allow you to pick your own fruit, which is the most fun because you get to eat while you pick, and nothing beats a ripe peach or nectarine plucked from the tree.

Generally, May peaches are of the cling variety, the early June peaches are semi-freestone, and the late June and July varieties are freestone. Most of the roadside stands and many of the orchards are located along US 290 (see Enchanted Rock—Rocky Hill).

This is a relatively young industry, dating back (in the commercial sense) only about 75 years. Acknowledged as one of the fathers of the peach industry here is B. L. Enderle, a Kerrville boy who moved to Fredericksburg in 1912 to become County Surveyor and schoolteacher at Fredericksburg High. Both his parents were of pioneer German families and were involved in the founding of Comfort and Kerrville. An aunt married Capt. Charles Schreiner. In Kerrville, Enderle's family lived on Earl Garrett Street near the courthouse and next door to "Mother" Butt's grocery store. Mother Butt's husband was a TB victim and he died shortly after the family's arrival in Kerrville to pursue his "cure." The store was established in 1905 and the widow Butt's boys helped out at the store. Her son Howard went on to establish the giant HEB supermarket chain.

In 1921 Enderle and his wife purchased 14½ acres a mile east of Fredericksburg and began to plant peach trees in earnest. He had been growing peaches in his yard since 1915. By 1925 Enderle was producing more peaches than he could sell locally, and had developed a peach sturdy enough to withstand commercial shipment to San Antonio. The delicacy of earlier-era Hill Country peaches had precluded such handling. Other growers were also developing commercially-sized orchards. Because of his boyhood friendship with the Butt family, Enderle obtained the first sales outlet outside the area for Gillespie County peaches in San Antonio's H.E. Butt grocery stores. Soon Austinites were enjoying Gillespie County peaches. But it was not until after World War II that Gillespie County peaches began to muscle in on the state market.

Growing peaches is not easy work—the trees must be severely pruned each year, to say nothing of the work involved in picking and shipping them.

In the last few years, apples also have been grown on a commercial basis. Although the harvests are still pretty small, the apples are worthy enough.

Antedating the peach trees out here was one of Fredericksburg's more memorable failed human blossoms, Peter Berg. Called the Hermit of the Hills, Berg came to Texas in 1857 at the tender age of 20. His wife-to-be had remained in Germany. Berg had planned to earn her passage over here working as a stonemason, then send for his beloved. But when the moment of truth came, Berg's betrothed refused to make the long journey to Texas; she had heard tales of Texas frontier life and opted for the comforts of home.

Heartbroken, Berg retired to a plot of land to which he had no legal claim, located a few miles west of the junction of FM 1631 and FM 2721. Here he built his home, using the natural walls of a ravine and finishing it with stone masonry. The front was two-storied; the back leaned to the hill, where the second floor was ground level. He also built a stone tower, which he used as his observation point for studying the stars and forecasting the weather.

Berg operated a still here for many years, selling his product for 30¢ a gallon. Berg was not a hostile man; he welcomed visitors willing to make the trip out. The owner of the land on which he lived let him stay there unmolested. Berg wanted no pity and accepted no help during most of his life. In his declining years, however, he was granted—and accepted—a small county pension. When he was well into his seventies and declining in health, life became too heavy a burden to bear and Berg ended his life with a single well-placed shot. Hunters found Berg's body atop his smoldering bed; evidently the fire from the gunshot had ignited his straw bed.

Turn left at the FM 1631 and FM 2721 intersection and continue on FM 1631.

CAVE CREEK COMMUNITY

Gillespie County • About 12 miles from Fredericksburg

About 3 miles past the FM 1631 and FM 2721 junction, you encounter a narrow paved road on your right and a sign reading "Cave Creek Rd." Turn right on this little road to reach the old Cave Creek schoolhouse, 0.5 mile down this country lane from FM 1631.

CAVE CREEK SCHOOLHOUSE

This old one-story building is a fine example of vintage Hill Country folk architecture. A frame structure covered with brick-sized patterned-tin siding, the schoolhouse was originally roofed with hand-cut cedar shingles, some of which are still visible under the current corrugated tin roof. The fireplace with its stucco limestone-rubble chimney has been supplanted by a wood-burning stove. It's been years since teacher rang the old bell to call the students to class, but the still-tidy schoolhouse serves as an area polling place on election day.

Return to FM 1631 and continue north. In another mile you come to Cave Creek community's spiritual center, Saint Paul's Lutheran Church.

ST. PAUL'S LUTHERAN CHURCH
About 13 miles from Fredericksburg

St. Paul's Church is the oldest rural Lutheran church in Gillespie County. The sanctuary was built of rough boxing planks, with a 40-foot steeple, in 1884. In 1890 the building was enlarged and a beaded ceiling installed. The building was covered with its present skin of embossed-tin siding in 1928-1929. Its simple soaring style epitomizes the spirit of the hard-working, God-fearing people who settled Cave Creek. The weathervane atop the tinned steeple bespeaks their practicality. Cave Creek community was named for the creek that flows through the neighborhood and eventually enters the Pedernales River near Stonewall.

As you continue north on FM 1631 from St. Paul's Church, it's easy to see why the area was first settled; **Cave and North Grape creeks** water the land well. Some fields are cultivated, others are lush with rich green bermuda, the remainder are just good grazing.

A little less than 4 miles beyond Cave Creek, you see a sign reading "North Grape Creek Rd.," another sign directing you to turn right to reach "Reingold School," and a paved road running off FM 1631 to your right, the first paved right since Cave Creek.

REINGOLD COMMUNITY

Gillespie County • About 17 miles from Fredericksburg

Reingold means "pure gold" in German, and the community was so named because almost all the early-day inhabitants of the neighborhood were from the Gold family. In 1873, for example, 7 out of the 10 children enrolled at the local school were Golds. The Gold family first moved to the area in the 1850s, coming from Germany via New Braunfels. Descendants of Peter and Jakob Gold owned most of the land, and the gin, store, and school in Reingold, also known as Gold community.

The Reingold school still stands, at the end of Reingold School Rd. Unfortunately, public access to it was cut off in 1989, depriving us of the chance to enjoy it and one of the most interesting old houses in the Hill Country.

Continue on FM 1631 to the intersection with FM 1323. Turn right on FM 1323 about 3 miles north of the Reingold turnoff. In less than 2 miles you turn left off FM 1323 onto Althaus-Davis, the first paved road to your left since turning onto FM 1323.

After a few miles on this narrow road, and just west of the "big" branch of **Youngblood Creek,** you pass through a "devil's playground" of great gray granite boulders strewn and stacked helter-skelter over several acres of rolling pastures. You experience a sort of caveman-primeval sensation as you drive amongst these room-sized boulders, reminiscent of the legendary great elephant dying grounds, only these massive chunks double as both corpse and monument. Few spots in the Hill Country evoke such ominous feelings. As one local says, "The world's just plain cock-eyed out here."

As you cross from Gillespie County into Blanco County, after about 4 miles the hard surface peters out and you are soon driving on clean, well-drained and graded granite gravel.

For the next few Blanco County miles you pass through the old Blowout and Comanche Springs communities. Each is more a frame of mind now than a town with an identifiable center. **Comanche Creek** is the stream that flows through Blowout and Comanche Springs. You cross four of its branches in as many miles.

BLOWOUT COMMUNITY

Blanco County • About 25 miles from Fredericksburg

After about a mile and a half on gravel, you pass a set of corrals and a ranch house on your left. This is the Davis Ranch (private property, not open to the public), all that remains of Blowout today. No trace of the post office, or store, or anything else remains.

Perhaps you're wondering where Blowout got its name. Did an oil well blow out here? Or was there a big party or feud here, once upon a time?

Well, after passing the Davis corrals and house on your left, start looking to your right, at the hills. In a half-mile or so, you just might see a big black hole up in the side of one of these hills. It is from this hole that the name Blowout derives.

Story has it that back when Comanches still roamed the area, a band of hunters tracked a bear into a cave. Failing to draw the bear out any other way, they smoked it out, lighting a huge brushfire at the cave's entrance. Sparks from that fire ignited several centuries worth of volatile bat guano. (Like many other Hill Country caves, this cave was a bat roost.) The resulting explosion blew out the mouth of the cave to such a size that it became a landmark to travelers—the Blowout Cave. And Blowout Cave became the namesake for the community which grew up nearby. We do not know what became of the bear or the Indians.

Neighboring Comanche Springs has its heart about 2 miles north of the Davis place, just before the intersection with the road to Click.

COMANCHE SPRINGS

Blanco and Llano counties • About 27 miles from Fredericksburg

As you cross Comanche Creek, you notice on your left a little springhouse built over the creek. This is the **Comanche Spring.** Nearby is an old ranchhouse. Private property! This is Comanche Springs today. Period. It was not always this way.

Twenty-three members of the Anderson, Shelley, and Hardin families came here from Kentucky and Tennessee in the fall of 1854. They found here a broad fair valley where grass waved five feet high, the soil was deep and fertile, and springs watered every draw. It reminded them of home and they decided to stay. Their cattle grew sleek and fat on the tall grasses that have been replaced by the mesquite, scrub cedar, and oaks of today. The school was built the next year, in 1855, from native timber that they hauled to Cypress Mill to be cut, then hauled back. This was the second school in Blanco County.

The land was fertile and well watered, but the surrounding hills were full of Comanches, who raided, burned, and killed at their leisure. When the Civil War came, 9 of the 18 young men here were immediately drafted; the other 9 stayed at home as members of the frontier rangers. This was, after all, the very edge of the frontier, and with so many of the men gone to war, the Indian raids became more daring and frequent. But eventually, even the second 9 were drafted, and life in Comanche Springs was burdensome indeed. Ready-made cloth was unobtainable. Many of the women had to trade for raw cotton, ride 10 or 15 miles over to a neighbor who had a spinning wheel, loom the cotton, spin the thread, and then weave the cloth. When the surviving menfolk marched back home, they came with empty pockets, with no money to rebuild their shattered farms. They had to barter for the goods they needed, tan hides, make furniture, brew moonshine to survive. After four years of cashless living, the men of Comanche Springs planned a desperate adventure: they would pool all the cattle in the region and drive them across the desert to California, where investors made rich from the gold mines were begging for cattle with which to stock their pastures. The drive went well until they crossed the Pecos River into Geronimo's territory. Silas Gipson was killed in the first Indian attack, and though the Comanche Springs men won the battle, they were ready to turn back for home until Tom Shelley talked their spirits back up. They persevered, and eventually did reach California, where their longhorns sold for $40 each, paid in hard gold. Flushed with success, some of the men stayed for years thereafter. Others returned to Comanche Springs two years later, in 1871, with the first hard money the community had seen since the early days of the war.

But the Indian attacks continued through the 1870s and the school had to be abandoned because of them. By 1876, however, the Indians had ceased to be a factor, a post office was established, and both Blowout and Comanche Springs prospered, situated as they were on the Austin-to-Fredericksburg road. Seems hard to imagine now, but this narrow little gravel road, which alternates between a coarse red granite surface and a powdered sugar-like limestone sand surface was *the* road west in its day, the US 290 of its time.

Blowout and Comanche Springs were bypassed over the years, obviously, by the march of modern civilization, and all that remains now of the hamlets are some nice old stone fences, the two old ranches with rail fences and loading pens, and their accompanying weathered outbuildings. Drive slowly to avoid hitting the many roadside cattle and deer. Look closely as you cross **Comanche Creek** and you may see a fat nutria or beaver cutting a path through the water. This is the Hill Country of a past generation, still present.

After a total of 4 miles on gravel road, you come to a three-way intersection. Turn left here onto Blanco Cty. Rd. 309, aka Click Road. (Immediately beyond this point, Althaus-Davis Rd. becomes FM 3347.) You continue on well-drained, smooth granite gravel, easily drivable in all but the very worst of weather. In front of you, on the east side of the road, is Red Mountain, its granite baldness relieved by only occasional stands of cedar and oak. This is about as south and east as the Llano Uplift extends. Depending on the light and time of day, Red Mountain's color ranges from the palest of pinks, to orange, to a rich red. Yet the name fits only this west side of the high hill. The other side is almost completely green, covered with cedars and oaks. Members of the Hardin family have lived and ranched in its shadows for over 100 years. You also get a good view of Packsaddle Mountain, with its loaf-shaped silhouette, off in the north. You cross the path of Comanche Creek several more times as you drive toward Click.

Although you are still in the Comanche Creek neighborhood, you are now in Llano County, and during the Civil War, A. E. Edgeworth operated a saltpeter works here on Comanche Creek. The saltpeter was used to make gunpowder for Confederate troops. The saltpeter was made from bat guano, mined from the caves (like Blowout Cave) that honeycomb the nearby hills.

A little over 5 miles from the intersection of Click Rd. and FM 3347, you cross Sandy Creek, aptly named; a thin silver thread of water courses down the middle of a bed of pink granite sand as wide as the Colorado River. Flakes of gold and silver are occasionally found in the sand, along with fool's gold (iron pyrites) and the occasional arrowhead.

Legend has it that the fabulous lost Los Almagres or Bowie Mine was located atop nearby Packsaddle Mountain, and that several of the ore smelters were located along Sandy Creek.

CLICK COMMUNITY

Llano County • About 2 miles from Sandy Creek

Contrary to what you might first guess, the origin of Click's name is rather unimaginative; the place was named for the family of early settler Malachi Click. Prior to the establishment of the post office in 1880, the settlement was known as Sandy Valley, situated as it was in the fertile bottomlands of Sandy Creek. When George Byfield built his store here, Click was also known as Byfield's Store. In those days Click had a school and Cumberland Presbyterian Church in addition to the post office/store. Now only the stripped-of-paint, shuttered store and an equally weatherbeaten, once elegant clapboard farmhouse remain at the crossroads. A gaunt windmill completes this picture of once prosperous desolation. Members of the Click family still live nearby, on Sandy Creek.

About 6 miles north of Click and after the road has turned to pavement, you cross **Honey Creek,** which, in the words of one old settler, "never ran dry, even during a drought; it flowed with water as fresh and sweet as honey." Honey Creek is now a shadow, on its way to becoming a Hill Country ghost.

When the Click Rd. dead-ends into SH 71, turn right. After about 3 miles, and just after you have passed Packsaddle Mountain, you encounter a historical marker and a road running off to your left, skirting the edge of Packsaddle Mountain.

PACKSADDLE MOUNTAIN
About 10 miles from Click

Though not particularly beautiful or awe-inspiring, there is perhaps no other mountain or hill in all of Texas that has more adventure and romance associated with it than Packsaddle Mountain. Legend and fact have become inextricably intertwined over the centuries.

The legends surrounding Packsaddle Mountain begin with the lost Los Almagres gold and silver mine. According to stories, Don Bernardo de Mirando discovered a rich vein of gold and silver on top of Packsaddle Mountain in 1757. Peons worked the shafts atop old Packsaddle unceasingly until 1775, when the mine workers were attacked by an overwhelmingly large band of Indians. Seeing that they were going to be massacred, the Spaniards filled in the mine shafts so that the Indians could not work them.

Another story has the Indians in possession of the mines, working them for tremendous amounts of wealth. The Spaniards, ever eager to acquire quick wealth, were determined to drive the Indians away from the mountain and gain possession of the fabulous mine. In the course of the battle, the Indians killed all the Spaniards, then filled all the shafts with earth and rock to make the entire mountaintop look the same. They then abandoned the mine, fearing another, more successful attack from a Spanish settlement on the San Saba River. Both stories agree that for years thereafter the top of Packsaddle was covered with human bones, attesting to the fierce struggle.

There is similar ambiguity regarding the origins of Packsaddle's name. Old-timers said it was so named for the depression or gap in the mountain, making it resemble an old-fashioned packsaddle. Others say that the first settlers found an abandoned packsaddle left by some earlier traveler on the mountain and named it accordingly.

Not open to speculation is the story of the last Indian battle fought in Llano County, atop Packsaddle Mountain, in August 1873. A band of 21 Apaches (or Comanches, as some tellers insist) had slipped into Llano County during the summer of 1873 and established a camp atop Packsaddle, from which they proceeded to attack and plunder ranches in the valley below. Their operations had extended from Arizona to Texas.

The Indians' presence was first discovered on the evening of August 9, when cowboys on the nearby Moss Ranch discovered a cow with an arrow protruding from her body. The next morning, eight of the men—W. B., J. R., and L. B. Moss, Eli Lloyd, Archer Martin, Pinckney Ayers, Robert Brown, and L. B. Harrington—mounted up to begin their search for the raiding Indians. Each was armed with a Colt six-shooter and a Sharps repeating carbine, the Uzi of its day. They began to ride a large circle in hopes of picking up the raiding party's trail. After riding about eight miles, the cowboys picked up signs of a fresh trail made by around 20 Indians. Despite being outnumbered, the impetuous cowboys decided to press on and do battle with the raiders. The trail soon led them up Packsaddle Mountain, where they were confident the Indians would be found. About halfway to the top, the eight encountered a lone Indian sentinel. So busy was he adorning his face with war paint and admiring his work in his little hand mirror that he failed to see the cowboys until they were practically upon him. He escaped through the thick brush with a yelp of alarm, and the cowboys followed in hot pursuit. Soon they reached a small plateau, at one end of which was the Indian encampment and at the other end their herd of horses, staked out to graze. The cowboys rushed in quickly between the horses and the camp, so as to cut the Indians off from their mounts, and prepared for battle. The Indians first volley brought down four of the white men, three of them so seriously wounded that they were unable to fight. That left 5 cowboys against 21 Indians. The Texans began their fire just as the Indians made a concerted charge for their mounts. The cowboys' deadly accurate fire drove the Indians back to their original positions. Repeated Indian assaults met similar fates. Finally the Apaches (or Comanches if you prefer) retired to some dense undergrowth behind their encampment. There they were entirely screened from view. Supposing that the Indians had given up the fight, the cowboys laid their arms aside and began to minister to their fallen comrades.

While the cowboys were thus engaged, the Indians sprang from the thicket, ready to charge again. The cowboys, however, went for their guns and the Indians quickly came to a halt, just a few paces from their protective thicket. Their young chief then turned to his band and went on a verbal rampage, trying to persuade his warriors to make another charge. But the braves found the cowboys' Spencer rifles to be too strong a medicine and they refused to advance, whereupon the young chief contemptuously waved them back with his hand and, turning, deliberately advanced upon the Texans. He carried a Winchester rifle and he halted every few paces to fire at the cowboys. In this manner he continued to advance until he was but a few yards from the cowpunchers' position. There he was greeted by a hail of Spencer bullets and he fell dead, pierced by over a half-dozen bullets. As soon as their chief fell, the remaining Indians retreated with some of their dead and wounded, leaving the chief and two others lying dead on the field. The cowboys made no serious attempt to pursue, since half their number lay wounded and in need of medical attention. Besides, the Indians had escaped with nothing but their arms, leaving behind all their horses, blankets and robes, extra weapons, fine tooled saddles, and other equipage. Harrington noted aloud, "Old boy, when you folks kill our people, you always take their scalps," whereupon he stooped down and took the slain chief's scalp, including the ears, and hung it from the horn of his saddle.

Then, spotting another slain foe, he said to himself, "One scalp is lonesome," and he proceeded to get a mate for the chief's scalp.

The wounded Texans were carried down the mountain to the Duncan ranch on Honey Creek, where they all miraculously recovered. More Indian bodies were found in the following weeks, secreted in caverns near the battle site.

In 1924, two Austin men claimed to have found the lost mine atop Packsaddle, and one of the men confidently announced that he expected to find pockets of silver ore yielding $1,000 a ton, and that as soon as he struck that deposit there would be "a great rush to this region." Furthermore, G. W. Burton said, "There is a possibility of this region becoming one of the greatest mining and smelting sections of the world. It has taken years of painstaking work, the cost of many a human life to discover what we believe at last to be the long lost mines of gold and silver of the 17th century Spanish accounts, and if they prove to be, Texas will become the richest mining state in the United States." Their Packsaddle mine ceased operations a couple of years later, the magic vein still undiscovered.

Much of the mountain is 600-million-year-old sandstone in horizontal layers which rests on even older Packsaddle Schist, which is exposed in the bed of Honey Creek at the foot of the mountain, by SH 71. Traces of gold, silver, and other metals are mixed in the sands of Honey Creek. It is a favored launching point for hang gliders.

Continue on SH 71 another 9 miles to the junction with FM 2147. Turn left onto FM 2147. This road offers several good views of Lake LBJ, and then Lake Marble Falls.

LAKE LBJ

Originally named Granite Shoals Lake, this stretch of the Colorado was renamed in 1965 for then-president Lyndon Johnson in gratitude for his efforts on behalf of the LCRA. Construction of **Wirtz Dam,** which forms the lake, began in 1949. It was originally called Granite Shoals Dam and was built mainly to generate electrical power for short periods to meet peak demands. There are 10 floodgates as well. The dam was renamed in 1952 to honor Alvin C. Wirtz, the LCRA's first general counsel and "father."

The lake covers 6,375 acres. Most of the area's power needs are now met by the LCRA's Thomas C. Ferguson Power Plant along Horseshoe Bay, and the lake provides cooling water for the plant. Limestone cliffs give way to granite along the lake's 21.5-mile course. Skiers like the absence of obstructions and the stretches protected from high winds. The many caves and coves make for good fishing. There are many private campgrounds and boat-launch facilities and one LCRA primitive area along the lake.

COTTONWOOD PRIMITIVE AREA
On Lake LBJ, adjacent to the south side of Wirtz Dam, off FM 2147, about 5 miles from the SH 71/FM 2147 intersection
Open daily • Free
Named for an old restaurant and resort area that has since been torn down, this 17-acre tract (part of the LCRA's Primitive Recreation System) offers a boat ramp, parking, observation area, fishing, picnicking, and hiking, but no camping, running water, or restrooms. Day use only. Cottonwood has about 2,100 feet of Lake LBJ shoreline. Granite rock formations protrude throughout. The spring wildflowers are nice out here.

Continue east on FM 2147 toward Marble Falls. Below Alvin Wirtz Dam is Lake Marble Falls.

LAKE MARBLE FALLS
Lake Marble Falls is the smallest of the Highland Lakes, 5.75 miles long and covering about 780 surface acres. The dam was constructed from 1949–1951 for electrical power generation and has 10 floodgates. The dam was originally called Marble Falls; it was renamed in 1962 to honor Max Starcke, LCRA general manager from 1940–1955. Lake Marble Falls is a popular destination for fishers, boaters, skiiers, swimmers, and campers. There are several private campgrounds and boat-launch facilities, as well as a cluster of small city parks in downtown Marble Falls, just upstream from the US 281 bridge.

To reach Marble Falls, turn left at the intersection with US 281 after 7.5 miles on FM 2147. But a trip over to Max Starcke Dam should precede your entry into Marble Falls. To reach the dam, turn right onto US 281, and travel about a mile until you see the highway sign reading "Max Starcke Dam." Turn left here and follow the twisting road about 2 miles across scenic Flatrock Creek, bearing right at each of three forks in the road until you are on a gravel road overlooking the Colorado River, a power substation, and Max Starcke Dam just to your left.

MAX STARCKE DAM OVERLOOK
Off US 281

The falls that gave Marble Falls its name were submerged by the completion of Starcke Dam in 1951. Max Starcke was the LCRA's first general manager. Even though the beautiful falls are gone, the view from up here of the **Colorado River** and its layered, weather-grayed limestone cliffs is nonetheless striking. Once every decade or so, the LCRA lowers Lake Marble Falls for one reason or another, and the first ledges of the stair-stepped Marble Falls are exposed for a few weeks.

Return to US 281, turn right, and drive into Marble Falls.

MARBLE FALLS

Burnet County • 4,266 • (830) • About 17 miles from Packsaddle Mountain

The US 281 bridge across the Colorado River passes over the now submerged Marble Falls. The falls were long prized for both their beauty and their industrial potential, falling 22 feet down a series of slick marble ledges, forming a 3-mile-long lake above. For all its potential, Marble Falls—the city—was a long time in coming to life. A Colonel Charles J. Todd was the first to attempt to "bring in" Marble Falls, buying a tract of land on the east side of the river at the great falls in 1851 for the princely sum of $80.Todd proceeded to lay out a town but failed to attract any buyers. Then, in 1854, young Adam Johnson happened onto the falls and began the project that was to take up the rest of his life, the founding and promotion of a great city and industrial complex here at the Marble Falls. Johnson had recently moved to Hamilton's Valley in Burnet County, which would soon become Burnet, the county seat. He became a surveyor and also worked as a guard/driver for the overland mail along the U.S. government's frontier mail routes. He had been sent down from Ft. Mason (in Mason County) to inspect the falls.

Johnson wrote of his beloved falls: "Simply as the central figure of beautiful scenery, these magnificent falls interest and delight all who visit them; but it is only when their immense power for moving machinery and serving the needs of man is considered that their importance is realized. The practical observer cannot look upon this splendid volume of water, dashing and leaping from ledge to ledge, and hear its ceaseless roar, without being impressed with the thought that nature has fashioned this seeming irregularity and concentrated such titanic power for some grand purpose and that it only waits for man to see the opportunity and turn it to account."

Johnson immediately set out to acquire title to as much of the land around the falls as possible, spending every penny he could get. Imagine his disappointment when he discovered that the titles he held were invalid and he would have to start over again.

About this time the clouds of Civil War loomed on the horizon and when the storm of war came over the land Johnson enlisted in the Confederate Army. He rose to the rank of general under the noted cavalry commander Nathan Bedford Forrest. Johnson was blinded for life during a battle in his home state of Kentucky. After the war he returned to his wife and family in Burnet and resumed his dream of founding his city. He resumed his real estate dealings with a vengeance, acquiring vast acreage in Burnet County and plotting the birth of his city. He and son Robert often traveled by carriage down to the falls, the elder Johnson giving directions through the wilderness maze from memory. Come 1886, Johnson was finally ready, and he spent the next year plotting his town from memory, beginning from a spot on the riverbank near the northwest corner of the present US 281 bridge.

One of the keys to success in Johnson's grandiose plan was railroad service to Marble Falls, and the fate of Marble Falls was inextricably intertwined with that of the new state capital. The Austin and Northwestern railroad had reached Burnet by the spring of 1882, and was projected to run up to Abilene. The old limestone capitol building had burned in November 1881, and state fathers were wrangling over the construction of a new statehouse. Plans had originally called for the building to be built with native limestone from near Austin, but the stone proved to be unfit for exterior use. A fight ensued over what stone to use. Some favored limestone from Indiana, others insisted on native stone. Owners of Granite Mountain just west of Marble Falls (see Mormon Trails trip) offered the state all the granite needed to complete the capitol, free of charge. But Granite Mountain was 16 miles from Burnet and the closest railhead, and the granite could be hauled to Austin no other way.

Enter Johnson. In the summer of 1885, accompanied by son Robert, the general spoke to the assembled legislature and offered seven miles of right-of-way over his land, between Burnet and Granite Mountain, free of charge to the state for the construction of a branch line over which to haul the granite. He assured the state that his fellow landowners would similarly oblige. They did, and the state built the spur using convict labor. So in the end the state got its granite free and Johnson got his railroad for a song, looking like a hero in the process.

With the Granite Mountain spur's completion in the winter of 1885, Johnson could at last see his dream beginning to unfold. Lot sales began in July 1887 at a brisk pace, reported the town's first newspaper, the *Daily Texas Nutshell.*

The thousands of Colorado River Valley acres surrounding Marble Falls were prime cotton acreage, and the next part of Johnson's dream was the construction of a giant cotton mill powered by his beloved falls to process the bumper harvests. To build the factory, he and several other men formed the Texas Mining and Improvement (TM&I) Company and began building a sprawling three-story factory on the north banks of the river next to the falls (northwest corner of the US281 bridge). Johnson sank every penny he had into the project, but TM&I ran out of money just as workers were ready to roof the giant building. Work ground to a halt as Johnson schemed to raise the rest of the money. Finally a rich cousin from Kentucky came through and the shell was completed. But TM&I was out of money again and there wasn't a lick of machinery inside the imposing edifice. Johnson went back east to try and raise money for the machinery but met with failure; the building was not tall enough to accommodate existing cotton mill machinery and then the Colorado went on one of its 40-foot rampages, gutting the building. The eastern capitalists turned Johnson down stone cold. Johnson went home and somehow raised the money to rebuild the factory, taking advantage of massive infusions of free labor courtesy of the local Farmers Alliance, who obviously had a large stake in Johnson's dream. But TM&I continued to suffer from capital problems and eventually went bankrupt. The giant factory building housed a variety of businesses before it went down in a spectacular blaze on a cold night in 1964. Its mill race, however, can be seen whenever the lake level is lowered.

During those early, flush years of expectation, hundreds of folks were drawn here by the brochures touting Marble Falls as "The Manufacturing Center of the Southwest," but many were also drawn here on the promise of a healthy, disease-free life. One land company bragged: "No location in the world surpasses this for benefiting those afflicted with those dreaded diseases so common at this day and time in the crowded cities and harsher climates elsewhere. Here we see daily living evidences of the beneficent results of prolonged residence of those coming here in the last stages of disease, men and women who, as a forlorn hope, have given this place a trial, regained their health, become permanent citizens and reared families of robust boys and girls."

General Adam Johnson's last grandiose plan, which he was promoting in 1922 (the year of his death), was the relocation of the entire Texas prison system to Burnet County. Naturally, the new prison complex was to be located near Marble Falls. "More water flows down the Colorado than any other Texas River," he said. Development of the river could provide cheap electricity for much of the state. Prisoners could build the power plants and the electricity could then be used in the mining of copper, iron, and graphite. A large graphite deposit was located near the proposed prison site, so the prisoners could mine graphite. In addition, Johnson proposed that the convicts quarry granite, gravel, and crushed stone after they were through building the electric plants. The state graciously declined.

The world's biggest graphite mine is located several miles west of Burnet.

ROPER HOUSE
3rd at US 281 • Private offices

A couple of these expectant early-comers were George Roper and his wife Elizabeth. In 1888 they built the Roper Hotel, located at the corner of US 281 and 3rd, two blocks east of Main, and several blocks north of the river. As one of the earliest hotels in the area, Roper Hotel served as a stop for innumerable drummers, or traveling salesmen, and many vacationing Texas politicians, including Governor Stephen Hogg and his family. The Roper changed hands and names several times over the decades, before finally closing and falling into decay. It was completely renovated in 1981. The exterior looks almost exactly as it did in 1888.

A few blocks north of the Roper House on US 281 is the Marble Falls Chamber of Commerce.

MARBLE FALLS CHAMBER OF COMMERCE
US 281 at Broadway • 800-759-8178 • Open daily

This was originally Marble Falls' railroad depot, built in 1893. The iron rails reached from Austin to Granite Mountain by 1885, but they didn't enter Marble Falls until 1889, when the Granite Mountain and Marble Falls Railroad built the necessary four miles of track. With the completion of this line, there commenced a flood of vacationers that continues to this day.

Marble Falls' historic homes district is located behind the Chamber of Commerce in the quadrangle formed by Broadway (north), Ave. E (east), 3rd (south), and Ave. H/US 281 (west). Most notable among the 20-odd old homes is the Otto Ebeling Home, 601 Ave. F at 6th, a frame Victorian house.

From the Chamber of Commerce, cross Ave. H/US 281 on Broadway and turn left on Main. In one block, you come to the O.M. Roberts cottage.

O. M. ROBERTS COTTAGE
7th and Main • Not open to the public
Former Governor (1879–1883) Oran M. Roberts was one of the many Texans lured to Marble Falls in its early years. Preceding many present-day Texas retirees, Roberts retired here in 1893 from his law professorship at the University of Texas and built this whitewashed cottage, which originally stood at 3rd and Main. Mr. and Mrs. H. E. Fabion bought the place in 1903, moved it to its present location, and altered the front porch and roof line, adding Victorian touches such as the tin gingerbread along the roof's peak. A state **historical marker** is posted in the front yard.

Continue south on Main through downtown Marble Falls. A good dozen of the old downtown buildings—limestone, brick, and granite—still stand largely unchanged, notably the City Hall at 2nd and Main.

MICHEL'S DRUG STORE
216 Main • 693-4250 • Open Monday through Saturday • W
The original Michel's Drug Store was built in 1891 and burned down in1927. It was replaced by the present store; the attraction here is the old-fashioned soda fountain, which still serves old-time fountain cokes, floats, sodas, and milkshakes.

Turn right on 2nd to reach the old Marble Falls jail.

OLD MARBLE FALLS JAIL
On 2nd St., one and a half blocks east of US 281 • Not open to the public
One of Marble Falls' oldest still-standing structures, and one that is thankfully no longer used, is the old jail house. Located on 2nd St. in the middle of the block between Main and Ave. J, next door to the GTE offices, the low-slung gray concrete blockhouse served for many years as temporary home for local errants. A two-cell affair, the

jail has a pair of barred slit-hole windows per cell and a cast-iron-strip front door, altogether a most dismal place to spend one's time. The jail is firmly closed to the public, but you can still catch a peek at its gloomy interior through the slit windows.

*From the jail, return to Main and turn right on Main. Go two blocks on Main to S.1st. Turn right on S. 1st and go another block to the intersection with Pecan Valley Rd., which is marked by a stop sign. Turn left here. The road takes you through **Marble Falls City Park**, located on a branch of Lake Marble Falls. Camping is not allowed, but it does have a swimming pool, lighted tennis courts, a free boat ramp, pleasant picnic sites, a playground for the kids, and restrooms.*

After you leave City Park, turn right on S. 4th and go another couple of blocks to reach the home of Brandt Badger, co-founder of Marble Falls.

BRANDT BADGER HOUSE
S. 4th, between M. and N. streets • Private residence

Brandt Badger, Confederate veteran, in the 1880s moved from Gonzales to Burnet where he established a store. Soon after, he sold the store and established a partnership with Adam Johnson to found the town of Marble Falls. He built this two-story house in 1888 of granite from Granite Mountain. In fact the stones were cut from quarry rubble remaining after the shaping of the stone blocks used in the state capitol. Badger lived here until his death in 1920, and the house remained in the family until 1943.

From the Badger House, continue west on S. 4th to its dead end at Ave. S and the Marble Falls Cemetery. Turn right on Ave. S to reach the old Marble Falls Alliance University. Ave. S dead-ends into Broadway; turn left on Broadway, which immediately places you in front of the old University.

MARBLE FALLS ALLIANCE UNIVERSITY
2005 Broadway

Part of Adam Johnson's big plan for Marble Falls included a university. In February 1890 he donated several acres at this site for the school. In August he donated several more lots, the sale of which was to help finance the construction of the school building and accompanying wooden dormitory. In addition, $15,500 was borrowed from TM&I to construct and furnish the buildings. The buildings were finished in 1891, but by the end of that year the university was so deep in debt that in December the property was sold in a sheriff's sale to TM&I for just $605. TM&I owned it until November 1895, when it sold the school property to the Marble Falls Land and Power Company for $100,000. From 1893 to 1907 it was operated as an elementary and secondary school on a tuition basis by the Marble Falls Common School District, which rented the facilities for $100 a year. After voters approved creation of a free public school system in 1907, the Marble Falls Land and Power Company sold the school buildings and property to the school district for about $6,000. The sturdy granite school has served local students ever since, but the dormitory, which stood on the banks of Backbone Creek, has long since disappeared.

From the old University, go to the end of the block, to Ave. U, and turn right. At FM 1431, turn right and proceed to the intersection with US 281. Turn right on US 281 to get to the Bluebonnet Cafe.

THE BLUEBONNET CAFE
211 US 281 S. • 693-2344 • Open Monday through Saturday breakfast, lunch, dinner; Sunday breakfast and lunch • $
No Cr. • W
The Bluebonnet is a 50-year tradition here, although you wouldn't know it once inside. Breakfasts feature great biscuits and homemade doughnuts. Later in the day, fried catfish and homemade pie are popular choices. Chicken-fried steaks, hamburger steaks, fried chicken, burgers and such complete the menu. Overall, the starches are great and the vegetables OK. Best time for vegetables is at lunch. Still, it's worth the tab.

ANNUAL EVENTS

APRIL • Highland Lakes Bluebonnet Trail • Trail winds from Austin through Marble Falls, Burnet, Buchanan Dam, Kingsland, and Llano • First two weekends in April
Features oceans of bluebonnets, historic and scenic sites, local art exhibits and festivals.

MAY • Howdy Fest • 800-759-8178 • Early May
Howdy Fest features street dances, a parade, arts and crafts, sports tournaments, and a carnival.

To continue the trip, go to the intersection of US 281 and FM 1431.
Proceed 2 blocks north on US 281 to the intersection with 12th St.
Just a few feet past 12th St. (which runs at a 90-degree angle), take a
right turn onto Mormon Mills Rd. (aka "Morman Hills" Rd.), which
runs off at a 45-degree angle. To aid you in finding it and making the
correct turn, look for the Comfort Inn on your left, on the west side of
US 281.

If all this sounds complicated, well, it is. But the trip north to
Burnet on the old Mormon Mills Rd. is well worth the extra effort;
it is one of the most scenic backroads in Burnet County and the
Hill Country.

This narrow and winding paved road wanders in and out of Hamilton Creek valley, past the site of the **old Mormon mill and settlement** on **Hamilton Creek** (see Mormon Trails). Watch for wandering cattle and goats on the road. Just south of the Mormon Mills site
you cross Hamilton Creek, and the low-water crossing here usually
has one or two inches of the creek flowing over it. You may very well
have to share the bridge with several of the neighborhoods stolid
Brahma cattle. It's easy to see why the Mormons settled here; the
creek flows wide, cool, clear, and blue, while tall sycamores line the
banks like sentinels.

You need to drive slowly for the next several miles past the old
Mormon Settlement site and **Hamilton Falls** (which you can catch a
glimpse of from the road), for there are some big chuckholes in the
road that you will need to dodge.

About 12 miles north of Marble Falls and 3 miles south of Burnet you
see a rambling white one-story ranch-modern house and assorted
barns off to your left, and a historical marker immediately to your
left on the side of the road.

HOLLAND SPRINGS

Burnet County • About 12 miles from Marble Falls

Located 300 yards to the west on Hamilton Creek are the Holland
Springs, named after Samuel Holland, the first permanent white settler in Burnet County. Indians had visited these cool clear springs for
centuries before Ben McCulloch established a Texas Ranger camp
here in 1847. Samuel Holland, a Mexican War veteran and recent
Georgia emigré, visited the Ranger camp here in 1848 and liked the

lush Hamilton Creek valley so much that he bought 1,280 acres here and settle down. Holland was instrumental in the creation of Burnet County in 1852, and was first county treasurer, a state legislator, and an investor in myriad business projects such as Adam Johnson's Texas Mining and Improvement Company, the Marble Falls Textile Mill, and the Marble Falls Ferry Company. In 1869, Holland bought the Mormon Mills property. The springs are on private property and may only be visited with special permission from the owners.

Several hundred yards past the Holland Springs marker, you come to a "Y" intersection. Take the right fork, which is Cty. Rd. 340, not the left fork (Cty Rd. 340A). To enter Burnet, you pass under two railroad tracks, follow the road's veer 90 degrees to the left, then take the first right, which is S. Pierce. S. Pierce takes you right to the courthouse square in downtown Burnet.

BURNET

Burnet County Seat • 3,569 • (512) • About 15 miles from Marble Falls
The town of Burnet (pronounced Burn-it) got its start in 1849, when the U.S. Army established Fort Croghan, located in what are now the western outskirts of Burnet. The fort was one of a string of eight frontier forts, located about 60 miles apart and stretching from the Rio Grande to the Upper Trinity River, built to protect frontier settlements from Indian depredations. It superseded the old outpost at Holland Springs.

With the protection of Fort Croghan's soldiers the little settlement first known as Hamilton Valley began to grow, attracting such notable early Texans as Noah Smithwick and Peter Carr (from Webberville) and Adam Johnson.

Burnet County's greatest feud took place soon after the county was organized in 1852, as the new county's inhabitants tried to deride where the county seat would be located. The two principal contending sites were the Hamilton Creek location near Fort Croghan and the Oat Meal Creek site (now Oatmeal). The controversy raged back and forth until Peter Carr tipped the balance in favor of Hamilton by donating 160 acres of land for the county seat. County commissioners graciously accepted Carr's offer and Hamilton became the seat of Burnet County. Hamilton/Hamilton Valley became Burnet in 1858, in honor of David Gouverneur Burnet, provisional president of the Republic of Texas.

On December 21, 1861, three days before his death, Peter Carr wrote his will, which gave the city of Burnet 6,359 acres of land and $23,500. His gift was to be used to build a college here. Carr's heirs took the will to court, and in 1868 the Texas Supreme Court ruled in their favor, leaving Burnet County with only two acres for a public school.

Burnet grew as a regional trade center until the Civil War brought unrest to the area. Indian raids, which had subsided in the 1850s, began again in earnest as the county's men were drained off to fill the ranks of the Confederate Army. Bushwhackers terrorized the area, too. Even when the war ended, Burnet and Burnet County remained in a state of unrest.

As Mrs. Nannie Moore Kinser remembered, "Burnet had quite a gang of tough men in the 1870s. . . . They terrified Llano and Burnet Counties. Some were killed, some went to the pen, and some left for parts unknown. I remember [Scott] Coolie well. He was a small man but Dynamite and not afraid of anyone. His hands were smaller than his wrists and they could not handcuff him."

Coolie and his ilk started rounding up cattle after the war without regard to ownership and driving them off to market. A number of men were indicted for this crime, but they were so strong in number that the local judge refused to conduct their trials unless he was protected.

Colonel Samuel Holland, Burnet County's first settler, organized a small police force, and the judge, knowing of what stuff the man was made, said to him: "Holland, I look to you to protect this court, else I can't hold it."

Holland had about 20 determined and well-armed men with which to protect the judge and court. In the courtroom the leader of the opposition party said he would kill the man who swore against him in court. Colonel Holland put a nephew of his behind this man with a five-pound bowie knife and ordered him to cut the renegade's shoulder down if he drew a weapon. But the man did not draw and the trial went on peaceably. It was during this lawless period that arsonists burned down the county courthouse on the windy night of April 10, 1874.

Burnet was not a pretty town in the visual sense in those years either, as one old-timer related: "For many years Burnet remained just a somnolent little town, so much so that a horse-and-buggy drummer, who while spending a night in the one hotel, sat smoking and looking out over the unpaved, mudpuddled, littered square, and quipped, 'When God created the world, he must have raked up the refuse, piled it, and said "Burnet here." ' "

Things picked up in Burnet when the Austin and Northwestern railroad came to town in 1882. The town became the trade center for a large area to the west and north, and thousands of carloads of granite from Granite Mountain passed through Burnet on their way to building the capitol in Austin. With the railroad's arrival and the resulting boost to the local economy, stone and brick buildings began to replace the less permanent wooden ones around the courthouse square, and many still stand today, only slightly altered.

Burnet was named the Bluebonnet Capital of Texas by the 67th Texas Legislature.

BADGER BUILDING/PIONEER MUSEUM
S. Pierce and Jackson • Monday through Friday 9–4:30
Free • W

On the southeast corner of the courthouse square stands the Badger building, a two-story cut-limestone-block edifice completed in 1883. The historical marker on the building reads in part: "This two-story limestone building is representative of other commercial buildings on the courthouse square in the 1880s. Built for local financier Dr. W. H. Westfall and Captain Brandt Badger, who had served in the Civil War from Texas. Badger and son operated a wholesale and retail drugstore on the ground floor. The second floor, divided into five rooms, was used as office space. Badger sold the business in 1885 and later, in conjunction with Adam Johnson, helped establish Marble Falls."

Since that time the Badger building has housed a hardware store, a bank (which closed during the Great Depression), the state Parks Board, the Burnet Rural Telephone Company, the post office, and other businesses before it became a museum and youth and community center in 1966. Westfall, incidentally, was one of the owners of Granite Mountain who donated the free granite for the state capitol's construction. Currently the Badger building houses an ever-expanding collection of Burnet County memorabilia, locally crafted goods, and a small refreshment bar.

WORLD'S SMALLEST CITY PARK
Outside the Badger Building, S. Pierce and Jackson • W

Located outside the Badger Building, this tiny park consists of a small gazebo and a big chunk of granite squeezed onto a several square-foot plot of grass, with a sign identifying the thumbnail plot as the "World's Smallest. "Who would dispute it?

Circumambulating the square, you notice that although many of the structures are essentially vintage, most of the facades have been modernized over the years, detracting somewhat from the desired nineteenth-century effect. The stone building on the corner of Main and Jackson (for many years Dilbeck's Department Store, now an antique mall) is one of the few essentially unaltered structures on the square, as a look at the old pictures of the square displayed inside the Badger building will reveal.

D. L. EMMETT BUILDING
123 E. Jackson • Houses Seidensticker's Men's Store

This two-story limestone building dates to 1883 and features some nice keystone window arch work and a smooth facade, owing to the highly polished, closely fitted stone blocks. Traces of a previous occupant's advertisements still linger across the front of the second story.

BURNET BULLETIN
101 E. Jackson, at Main • Newspaper office

The rougher, quarry-dressed limestone block exterior of this simple, two-story building contrasts with the Emmett Building's smoother skin. This one was built in 1872. The newspaper inside was founded a year later. But the newspaper, Burnet's oldest, didn't move in here until 1979. It was a general store until 1900, then was variously a furniture store/mortuary and a telephone company office. The second story was used as a courtroom during the 1930s when the current courthouse was under construction.

A. I. HABER BUILDING
236 S. Main, at Jackson

Dating to 1883, this two-story rusticated limestone block commercial house was for many years Dilbeck's Department Store. Its facade is essentially unaltered.

OLD MASONIC LODGE
309 S. Main and League • Not open to the public

Located one block south of The Haber Building at the corner of S. Main and League is the old Masonic temple, built in 1854 and the oldest commercial structure in Burnet. Logan Vandeveer, a hero of San Jacinto, came here in 1849 as the beef supplier to Fort Croghan. He became the first postmaster when the Hamilton post office was established in about 1850. After this two-story limestone edifice was completed, Vandeveer ran a store in the bottom story, while the local Masonic Lodge met upstairs. The Valley Lodge No. 175 used the building from 1855 to 1969 and still owns it.

THE GALLOWAY HOUSE
108 E. League, at Pierce • Owned by city
A block east of the Old Masonic Lodge is this rather common-looking two-story frame house with double wrap-around porches. The original part of the house was built in 1856 out of adobe-covered stone by Major Hugh Calvert. It served as an inn for a few years. Enoch Brooks bought it in 1885 and made major changes. W. C. Galloway bought it in 1899 and enlarged it still more. Galloway helped organize the First State Bank of Burnet and served as county tax collector and mayor of Burnet. It now houses the Texas Wild Bunch Museum of Traditional Art.

GEORGE WHITAKER RESIDENCE
802 S. Main • Not open to the public
Several blocks south of the Masonic Lodge, on Main, is the Whitaker house, built in 1870. Whitaker's hand-hewn limestone block house features an inside cistern. With the water supply inside the house, Whitaker and family could withstand Indian attack almost indefinitely, and Indian raids continued well into the 1870s here. A 1939 addition to the house is built of limestone salvaged from the old Burnet County Courthouse, predecessor to the present granite monolith. Whitaker was the first editor of the *Burnet Bulletin*. He spent only one year at the job.

J. G. COOK HOME
200 N. Main • Not open to the public
Heading back north on Main, you see the J. G. Cook home, which was built in 1873 in the early Victorian style and features a staircase and other fittings brought in by ox wagons all the way from New Orleans.

Continue north on Main to Taggard to see other old homes. Return to the square and turn left on Washington (on the north side of the square).

BURNET COUNTY JAIL
Washington and Pierce
Located at the northeast corner of the courthouse square is the county jail, designed by noted architect F. M. Ruffini and built in 1884 of hand-hewn limestone blocks. The roof features elaborate period cast metal work. The jail was used through 1981.

From the jail, proceed north on Pierce one block to SH 29 and turn left to reach old Fort Croghan, a few blocks past the hospital and marked by a highway sign.

FORT CROGHAN
703 Buchanan Dr. (SH 29) • 756-8281 • Call for hours Admission • W

As earlier mentioned, Fort Croghan was built in 1849 as one of a string of frontier forts. The land was first leased from John Hamilton, for whom the town of Burnet was originally named, and then from Peter Carr. The fort was named for George Croghan, illustrious career army officer, but was also known as Fort Hamilton.

As the Texas frontier moved further west, the soldiers stationed in this line of forts also moved westward. Most of the soldiers left Fort Croghan in 1853, and the army officially abandoned the fort in 1855. Fort Croghan did not fall into disuse, however. Locally formed frontier guards used the old fort as a rallying point whenever Indian attacks occurred, and many early county residents lived in the old fort buildings until they could move onto their own land. Most of the buildings disappeared over the years until only the sole stone structure erected by the army, known locally as the "powder house," remained.

In 1957 the Burnet County Historical Society bought 1.6 acres of the fort's original grounds and moved four old stone-and-log buildings from Burnet's past onto the property. Local families donated hundreds of everyday items used by their ancestors, and the resulting conglomeration is now the **Fort Croghan Museum.**

From Fort Croghan, head back toward Burnet and US 281.

BURNET COUNTY BBQ
616 Buchanan/SH 29 W • 756-6468 • Open Wednesday through Monday, lunch and dinner; closed Tuesday • $ • No Cr. • W

Good brisket, also chicken, Elgin sausage, and ribs, cooked with live oak.

At the junction of SH 29 and US 281, turn right on US 281 and go 3 blocks to the corner of S. Water (US 281) and League to reach the first of two houses built by Adam Johnson in Burnet. "Rocky Rest" is set back several hundred feet from Water St., across from the Continental Telephone Co. office.

ROCKY REST
404 S. Water, at League St. • B&B Inn

Adam Johnson built this spacious two-story Greek Revival home on the west bank of Hamilton Creek for his bride, Josephine Eastland, in 1860. They were married on New Years Day 1861. Built of ashlar limestone and hand-hewn logs, the house's thick walls and high, narrow windows gave extra protection in the event of Indian attacks. Johnson organized a local "minuteman" company at nearby Fort Croghan, upon the Army's divestiture of the fort. The house later served as a school, which Johnson helped organize. It is now a bed-and-breakfast.

From Rocky Rest, return to the US 281/SH 29 intersection and turn right on SH 29. Proceed about 1.5 miles east on SH 29 to reach "Airy Mount," Johnson's second home, which will be on your right about 0.75 mile east of town. If you cross the railroad tracks, you've gone too far.

AIRY MOUNT
SH 29 • B&B Inn

The massive limestone barn with attached cistern and nearby house are the principal components of Airy Mount, and have been landmarks to generations of travelers. Long in ruins, both house and barn were restored by Dr. and Mrs. Joe Shepherd, longtime owners of Johnson's Rocky Rest. In attempting to rebuild the Airy Mount house almost from scratch, the only guides they had to rely on were a few fading exterior photographs and the recollections of several Burnet old-timers.

What prompted the Johnsons to leave Rocky Rest for Airy Mount? Story has it that after two of their children died at Rocky Rest, Adam and Josephine said enough is enough and decided to build a new home in a healthier location. Low-lying, creekside locations such as Rocky Rest's were thought to be unhealthy in those days. The most healthy spots were thought to be on high ground, well-drained and exposed to the wind, which Airy Mount certainly is. Johnson was so slight of build that locals say he had to walk around with rocks in his pockets to keep from being blown away, so airy is this hill. Story also has it that the barn was built first and that the Johnsons lived in it for several years as they waited for the new house to be built. One of their children was born in the barn, but when Mrs. Johnson found herself in the family way once again, she categorically refused to bear another child in the barn. Johnson was forced to hurry up construction of the house to the point that he wasn't able to add the originally intended second story. The way the house is constructed hints that Johnson had planned for a second story, thus adding credence to the story.

The main entrance to the house faces toward the railroad tracks and away from the highway, since there was no Highway 29 when the house was finished in 1884.

From Airy Mount, return to Burnet on SH 29.

OTHER AREA ATTRACTIONS

BURNET CHAMBER OF COMMERCE
705 Buchanan Dr. (SH 29 W) • 756-4297, (fax) 756-2548
Located next to Fort Croghan; the place to contact for area tourism information and current hours for area attractions. Write to P.O. Drawer M, Highway 29 West, Burnet 78611.

HAMILTON CREEK PARK
Along Hamilton Creek, south of SH 29 and west of US 281
Open daily • Free • W
A linear park along both sides of Hamilton Creek. There's a walkover bridge, playground for kids, fountains, and a gazebo.

HIGHLAND LAKES CONFEDERATE AIR FORCE MUSEUM
US 281, at the Burnet Airport on the south side of town
756-2226 • Open Saturday and Sunday • Admission
Several World War II and jet-era fighters are permanently based here; see them, plus firearms, photos, and other memorabilia.

THE HILL COUNTRY FLYER
Runs from Cedar Park to Burnet, every Saturday and Sunday, March through December • 512-477-8468 • Reservations recommended • W with assistance
Burnet is the western terminus for this entertaining train, which leaves at 10 a.m. every Saturday and Sunday (during season) from its home station in Cedar Park. Round trip is 33 miles, taking you through Leander across the San Gabriel River, through Liberty Hill and Bertram, and down into the Hamilton Creek valley and Burnet. The spring wildflowers are lovely, as is the fall foliage, and you'll see longhorns and emus along the way, as well as Airy Mount, home

to land tycoon Adam Johnson, the blind man who laid out the town of Marble Falls from memory. You will see big blocks of pink granite lying alongside the tracks periodically; this road was built in 1881 and hauled the capitol's pink granite exterior. These are the pieces that fell off along the way. As the train arrives in Burnet just after 12 noon, passengers are met by a colorful gang of motley ne'er-do-wells bent on plunder, until the good guys come to the rescue, just in the nick of time. The kids love it. You'll have a couple of hours to kill eating lunch, visiting museums, browsing the antique and gift shops, or just walking around. The train leaves Burnet at 3 p.m., arriving at Cedar Park by 5:15. The Twilight Flyer runs on selected Saturday evenings and is a relaxed, romantic, 2-hour version of the same trip, with hors d'oeuvres and beer, wine, or soft drinks.

Number 786, a restored Southern Pacific steam locomotive built in 1916 by the American Locomotive Co., pulls an assortment of cars: 1920s passenger coaches, air-conditioned passenger coaches and streamlined pullmans from the 1950s, a club car, and caboose. Number 786 used to haul freight between Houston and Austin before being retired in 1956. Upon retirement, it ended up on display in a downtown Austin park, where it was a favorite, hands-on, kids' attraction. The City of Austin acquired it in 1986. A few years later, a dedicated group of Austin-area steam train enthusiasts began restoring the engine and acquiring rolling stock. Weekend service was inaugurated in 1992 and the train has been a popular ride ever since.

VANISHING TEXAS RIVER CRUISE

From Burnet, take SH 29 west about 3 miles to FM 2341, then north (right) 13.5 miles to dock • 512-756-6986 • Cruises daily, year round, weather permitting • Reservations required • Fee W call ahead

Cruise Lake Buchanan and the lower end of the upper Colorado River aboard a comfortable air-conditioned river cruiser with open-air observation decks past towering cliffs, wild game, perennial springs, and waterfalls. Bring your camera. Cruises last about 2.5 hours. The lake supports a diverse waterfowl population, including great blue herons, American white pelicans, egrets, osprey, roseate spoonbills, and from November to March, American bald eagles. Spring brings a riot of wildflowers to the lake banks. The 50-foot Fall Creek waterfalls do so year round. White-tail deer, goats, and wild hogs are sometimes at water's edge. Dinner and sunset cruises run on summer weekends. The Osprey offers a fast 4.5-hour trip that includes a visit to Colorado Bend State Park.

BURNET COUNTY PARK (WHITE BLUFF)
On the north side of Lake Buchanan, on FM 2341, about 15 miles west of Burnet • 512-756-4297 • Open daily • Free

This 5-acre park offers a boat ramp, camping, lake access, picnicking, and restrooms.

COLORADO BEND STATE PARK
915-628-3240 • Open daily • Admission • W variable

The park is west of Lampasas, southeast of San Saba. From Burnet, take US 281 to Lampasas, then take FM 580 west 24 miles to Bend and follow the signs 4 miles to the park entrance. From Llano, take SH 19 north to San Saba, take US 190 east about 4 miles to FM 580 and follow the signs 13 miles to Bend; follow the signs 4 miles to the park entrance. The headquarters and main camping are 6 miles past the entrance on the gravel road (unmarked County Road 257). The access road is subject to flooding.

Colorado Bend State Park, a 5,328-acre facility, is located in San Saba and Lampasas Counties above Lake Buchanan. The park, which opened in 1987, used to be the Gorman and Lemons Ranches. Activities include primitive camping, hiking, fishing, swimming, mountain biking, bird and nature watching with a dedicated wildlife viewing area, and guided tours (both walking and crawling) to Gorman Falls and into some of the wild caves.

When Lake Buchanan is near normal levels, the river is navigable from the park's boat ramp all the way to the lake, a distance of approximately 10 miles. This is a trip on slow-moving water through the beautiful canyon lands of the Colorado River. For Texas Conservation Passport holders, observation blinds over a baited site are available for timely and consistent wildlife viewing and photography. Birders can view some of 155 species of birds found in the park including golden-cheeked warblers, black-capped vireos, and bald eagles. Gorman Falls is located on the western bank of the Colorado River approximately 10 miles above Lake Buchanan, and includes a portion of Gorman Creek, which feeds Gorman Falls. Gorman Falls is an impressive, 60-foot-high waterfall. The falls' travertine formations and associated lush vegetation are very scenic. Small travertine dams have formed quiet pools of clear water, which support a variety of aquatic communities. Because of the fragile environment of Gorman Falls, it currently can be visited only through guided tours.

There is a 300-vehicle maximum here and camping reservations are not accepted. Because of various hazards in the caves such as low oxygen levels and poisonous gases, and the fact that the caves are a nonrenewable natural resource, all caves in the park are closed except during guided tours. Reservations are highly recommended for the cave tours.

Public use is primitive at this time, but plans include some development of some area of the park, consistent with the park's natural state. The main camping area has picnic tables, fire rings with cooking grills, potable water, chemical toilets, fish-cleaning table, and a boat ramp. There are also two hike-in camping areas where nothing is provided. In these areas you must carry everything you need and pack out absolutely everything you don't use. Ground fires are also prohibited everywhere in the park except in designated fire rings in the main camping area. There are 11.7 miles of hiking trails and 8 miles of mountain bike trails. Fishing is excellent at certain times.

Write to Box 118, Bend 76824. *Elevation:* 1,025 ft. *Weather:* January average temperature is 46 degrees, July average is 86 degrees. *First/last freeze:* November 20/March 11. *Busy season:* spring white bass run. *Schedule:* Open daily year-round, except for public deer hunts (call for dates). Reservations not accepted. Park fee schedule is different from most other state parks; entrance fee, activity fee. For further information call the park or Park Information at 1-800-792-1112.

From Burnet, go south on US 281 toward Marble Falls. About 5 miles south of Burnet, turn right onto Park Rd. 4 toward Longhorn Caverns and Inks Lake.

Park Rd. 4 is very dramatically hilly on the way to Longhorn Caverns State Park.

LONGHORN CAVERNS
**Park Rd. 4, six miles off US 281 • About 11 miles from Burnet
(512) 756-4680 business office; 756-6976 tour information
Memorial Day to Labor Day: open daily, tours on the half hour
10–5. Labor Day to Memorial Day: open daily, except closed
Monday and Tuesday October through February; tours Monday
through Friday 10, 1, and 3, tours Saturday and Sunday on the
hour 10–5 • Admission, group rates available.**

Geologists say that the Longhorn Caverns were at least a million years in the making, beginning during the Ice Age when the northern part of the U.S. was covered by glaciers. As the glaciers receded, the climate of Texas became drier and the groundwater level began to drop, dissolving the limestone as it fell. Underground rivers flowing through the cave helped to carve out the labyrinthian passageways and huge rooms.

People have made use of the cave since their earliest days on earth; flints and other crude tools have been found over the years in the cave. More recently, stories have it that in 1840 young officer Robert E. Lee captured bands of Indians by driving them into the gaping mouth of the cavern. A secret Confederate powder factory was operated in the cavern's 183-foot main room during the Civil War. Local legend relates that Sam Bass the outlaw hid out in the cave during the1870s. The cavern is said to be the third largest in the world, and became a state park in 1932.

The tour through the cave takes about an hour and a half, and leads you through rooms filled with stalactites and stalagmites, sparkling displays of calcite crystals, unusual flint formations, and the unique Hall of Marble. Rubber-soled shoes are recommended for the tour.

The cave grounds include picnic areas, nature trails, rock formations, and a plethora of wildflowers each spring. Most of the quaint rock buildings dotting the ground were built by WPA workers back in the 1930s.

From Longhorn Caverns, continue west on Park Rd. 4. From this point to the road's dead-end into SH 29, Park Rd. 4 twists and turns back on itself through miles of granite boulders strewn about as casually as toys inside a baby's playpen. About 4 miles past Longhorn Cavern, Park Rd. 4 encounters RM 2342 and takes a hard right. Turn right here and follow Park Rd. 4's path north.

HOOVER VALLEY
Burnet County • About 4 miles from Longhorn Caverns
Very soon after you turn to the north on Park Rd. 4, you see a state **historical marker** on the right side of the road.

Hoover Valley was settled in 1850 by Reverend Isaac Hoover, who established a church here, next to the **Hoover Valley Cemetery.**

The cemetery is located several hundred feet west of the historical marker, on the paved road running to your left off Park Rd. 4, across from the marker.

HOOVER VALLEY CEMETERY
Off Park Rd. 4

Graves here date back to 1850, but the most interesting stone here, with perhaps the most tragic story behind it, marks the final resting place of F. M. and Susan Whitlock and children. The simple, single-scalloped limestone slab reads "Sacred to the memory of F. M. & Susan Whitlock killed by the Indians Dec. 7, 1870." On that fateful day, at the foot of nearby Long Mountain, a band of unknown Indians attacked the Whitlock cabin. Attracted by the smoke, neighbors found the slain Mr. Whitlock lying in the field where he had been surprised. They found the children scattered about the yard, stripped of their clothing. Mrs. Whitlock lay burning in the cabin, which was made of cedar logs. Fire had burned the logs until they had fallen in, and it was not possible to retrieve her body until the next morning, by which time it had been reduced to ashes. The Whitlocks were buried here in the common grave marked by the weathered stone.

Proceeding north from the Hoover Valley marker, you enter Inks Lake State Park.

INKS LAKE STATE PARK
Park Rd. 4, about 8 miles from Longhorn Caverns
512-793-2223 • Open daily • Admission • W variable

Located in the Llano Uplift, Inks Lake State Park is marked by exposed outcroppings of colorful pink gneiss and granite. Many of the outcroppings are covered with colorful lichens—green, yellow, orange, black, gray. Several varieties of oaks and myriad wildflowers thrive on the coarse sandy soil derived from the rock.

There is a great, marked scenic overlook on Park Rd. 4 looking out over the Devil's Waterhole, an arm of Inks Lake. There is a delightful waterfall at the end of the waterhole that flows practically year round. The casually placed giant pink boulders, seemingly tossed about the landscape, probably inspired the waterhole's hellish name, but perhaps the buzzards had something to do with the name too. They hover by the dozens in the late afternoon sky, riding the thermals, plunging and rising hundreds of feet in a matter of seconds as they wheel in lazy, mile-wide circles, sometimes dropping down just low enough for you to catch a glimpse of their red or black wrinkled, featherless heads.

At 4.2 miles in length and covering about 800 surface acres, **Inks Lake** is the second smallest of the Highland Lakes. It was created in

1938 with the completion of Roy Inks Dam (originally called Arnold Dam), named for Llano resident Roy Inks, who was a director on the Lower Colorado River Authority board. The dam was built for hydroelectric generation; it has no floodgates.

The land for Inks Lake State Park (1,201 acres) was acquired by deeds from the Lower Colorado River Authority and private owners in 1940 and was opened to the public in 1950. The land had been used for cattle ranching. Culverts and roads in the park were constructed by the Civilian Conservation Corps from the camp at Longhorn Caverns in the 1930s. Deer, turkey, quail, numerous songbirds, and other species of wildlife abound. Commonly caught fish are bass, crappie, and catfish.

Park activities include camping, backpacking, hiking, golf, lake swimming (unsupervised beach), boating, waterskiing, scuba diving, and fishing. Tours such as nature walks and geology hikes are conducted in the summer (Memorial Day through Labor Day), and by special request through the park office. Facilities include restrooms with showers, picnic sites, screened shelters, campsites with water and electricity, backpack sites (1.5 miles in, ground fires prohibited, no drinking water, primitive toilet on trail), sponsored youth group area (primitive), group picnic pavilion with tables (capacity 25), an amphitheater, lighted fishing piers, boat ramp, playground, 9-hole golf course with golf carts and clubs available to rent, and a Texas State Park Store that rents canoes and paddle boats and sells groceries and gifts.

Write to RR 2, Box 31, Burnet 78611. *Elevation:* 900 ft. *Weather:* July average high temperature 98 degrees; January average low temperature 33 degrees; May, September, and October are wettest months; *First/last freeze:* November 14/March 29. *Busy season:* spring, summer, and fall.

Turn left on SH 29 when Park Rd. 4 comes to an end in a little over 7 miles. In a couple of miles you cross Inks Lake via a graceful Depression-era four-span cantilever bridge. Continue west on SH 29 past Buchanan Dam.

BUCHANAN DAM
About 1 mile from the Bluebonnet Cafe

Lake Buchanan, formed by Buchanan Dam, (pronounced Buck' annon, not Bu' cannon) is the oldest and largest of the Highland Lakes, 32 miles long and 8 miles wide. On windy days whitecaps break over the lake and it looks more like the ocean than an inland lake. At 11,200 feet in length, Buchanan Dam was the largest dam of its type in the world when finished in 1938. Named for congressman James Buchanan, this is still one of the largest multiple-arch dams in the world. The village of Buchanan Dam sprang up after the dam's completion and is a resort, retirement, and fishing community.

An interesting tidbit about Buchanan Dam: In 1854, while surveying the area for public school land, young Adam Johnson came to the Shirley Shoals on the Colorado River and said, "Here we should build a dam." At this same exact spot in 1931, construction of Buchanan Dam commenced.

BUCHANAN DAM MUSEUM
Located inside the LCRA building at dam headquarters, SH 29
Open daily • W
There is a nice view of Lake Buchanan from this building by the dam; the museum has displays on the dam's construction and local history that include a living history video presentation and lots of old photos. There's a Xeriscape garden outside, and the kids can feed the huge school of carp that gathers below the observation deck (when lake levels are normal). Visitors can walk along the top of the dam; it is 2 miles long. Tours of the dam are given on weekends during the summer. Call the Lake Buchanan-Inks Lake Chamber of Commerce for latest schedule. The Lake Buchanan-Inks Lake Chamber of Commerce (512-793-2803) is located at the same site. It is open daily.

The LCRA, Llano County, and Burnet County operate several parks on Lake Buchanan.

BURNET COUNTY PARK AT BUCHANAN DAM
North side of Buchanan Dam, off TX 29, about 10 miles west of Burnet • 512-756-4297 • Open daily • Free
This tiny 5-acre park has a boat ramp, lake access, primitive camping, and picnicking.

Turn right onto SH 261 2 miles past Buchanan Dam and proceed toward Bluffton.

(Option: You can shorten the trip at this point by about 20 miles by continuing west on SH 29 to Llano. About 6 miles west of the SH 261 turnoff, you begin to parallel the picturesque, boulder-strewn Llano River. You catch frequent glimpses of the river for the next 5 miles. The

*City of Austin now owns the old Southern Pacific railroad tracks that
run alongside the highway to Llano; visionaries foresee the day when
commuter and light excursion trains once again run this scenic route.)*

On the way to Bluffton on SH 261, you catch many glimpses of
Lake Buchanan and pass many outcroppings of pink granite. This
is prime resort area, as the numerous fishing camps, motels, and
resorts attest.

BLACK ROCK PARK
**On Lake Buchanan, on TX 261, just off FM 1431, about 15
miles west of Burnet • 473-4083 • Open daily • Fee**
This 10-acre park offers lake access for swimmers, waders, and
anglers (great for stripers), hiking, play area, camp sites with table
and grill, potable water taps, sanitary disposal station, restrooms,
and picnicking.

LLANO COUNTY (BLACK ROCK) PARK
**On Lake Buchanan, next to LCRA's Black Rock Park
915-247-4352 • Open daily • Free**
This 5-acre park has a single-lane public boat ramp for sailboats and
motorboats. There's camping, picnicking, fishing, and swimming.

BARRINGER HILL

Underneath Lake Buchanan
Buried beneath the Waters of Lake Buchanan near the dam is the
legendary Barringer Hill. Only a small mound of rock and dirt 34
feet taller than the surrounding country, Barringer Hill was not even
remotely interesting in appearance to the average viewer, but in the
words of the U.S. Geological Survey, "Few if any deposits in the
world, and certainly no others in America, outside of the localities
where monazite is found, have yielded such quantities of rare earth
metals as that at Barringer Hill."
The mineral wealth contained in Barringer Hill was revealed in
1886 when its owner John Barringer was doing some prospecting. He
accidentally found an outcropping of a heavy greenish black ore,
which he sent to scientists in Philadelphia. As a result, a Dr. Niven
was sent to the hill, where he discovered 47 minerals, 5 of which were
new to science. The ore Barringer had discovered was identified as
gadolinite, which was used in early, pre-incandescent electric light-

bulbs. At that time the only gadolinite known in the world was located in Russia, so in 1889 Niven bought the hill for $5000 in gold for the Piedmont Mining Company.

Piedmont did not commence mining the hill in earnest until 1902. A little gadolinite went a very long way in those days, and only sporadic mining was necessary. Rare earth minerals were quite valuable. Yttrium, of which gadolinite is roughly half composed, cost $144 per ounce in 1887. Shipments were wrapped in tissue paper and sent by express encased in locked iron boxes.

When large-scale mining began in 1902, it lasted only a year. The incandescent lightbulb had been invented, and the need for gadolinite was gone, in the face of a much cheaper wire filament. The Barringer Hill mine closed for good in 1904, and a man nearly lost his life as a result.

Marshall Hanks had been sent down by Westinghouse to supervise mining operations in 1903. Then he received orders to close the mine. The miners were boiling mad at the prospect of unemployment and Hanks had had nothing but trouble with them from the beginning of his stay. The miners had not been told what they had been extracting, and they imagined that they were mining radium. So they struck for hazardous duty pay. Hanks solved that problem, but soon afterward received the closing orders.

It took 13 boxes to hold all the mining equipment that was being shipped back to company headquarters at Pittsburgh, but there were 14 boxes on the railroad station loading dock in Llano. That last box contained Hanks, who rightly surmised that his former employees were out to kill him. Secreted in his box, he could hear the ex-miners rampaging through the streets of Llano in search of him. As they searched, workers loaded the crates onto the train. When the miners could not find Hanks, they began to suspect that he might be in one of the Pittsburgh-bound boxes. They marched to the station and demanded to search the boxes. But the Wells Fargo Express Company did not have a tougher-than-any-desperado reputation for nothing, and the miners didn't get past the angry express agent. Soon after, the train pulled out of Llano, and once it was out of the county the conductor pried open the right box and set Hanks free, alive and well by the skin of his teeth.

No more serious mining was done at Barringer Hill and it was one of the first areas to be covered by Lake Buchanan.

BLUFFTON

Llano County • 75 • About 11 miles from Buchanan Dam

Bluffton is located at the junction of SH 261 and RM 2241, and the community's center is the store at the crossroads and the nearby church. Bluffton has moved around quite a bit since it was first founded in 1852. Along with the Tow Valley community, Bluffton was one of Llano County's first permanent settlements. First located five miles from Tow Valley on the west bank of the Colorado River, it faced a high bluff across the river. Bluffton's first settler was Billy Davis. He was soon joined by Ike Maxwell, who named the village for his hometown of Bluffton, Arkansas. Soon the place had the area's first sawmill, gristmill, and cotton gin, powered by the Colorado River.

Bluffton's first store was opened by one-legged John Pankey, who lost his limb in the Civil War. After he settled in Bluffton, some of the residents chipped in to buy him a wooden leg and to get his store started.

Located on the Austin-to-Mason road, Bluffton was a stage stop and a prosperous town through the 1880s. It had a saloon-hotel and tenpin bowling alley during its heyday. Lots of cotton was grown in the fertile Tow Valley, and Bluffton attracted desperate men, men who made a practice of robbing stages, lone travelers, and gold-laden farmers returning home from market.

One night in 1883, a bunch of cowboys came to old Bluffton to get drunk and ended up burning the whole town down except for the hotel, school, lodge, saloon, and a couple of houses. Undaunted, Bluffton folks rebuilt their town a short distance away. When the route of the Austin-to-Mason road changed, Bluffton began to decline. The remains of old Bluffton were submerged by Lake Buchanan in 1937 and the town moved to its present location.

At the Bluffton Store, located at the junction of SH 261 and RM 2241, turn right on RM 2241 and proceed north to Tow.

Located between old Bluffton and old Tow was one of Llano County's earliest industries, David Cowan's saltworks. David Cowan was a surveyor in Burnet County when he was granted permission by friendly Indians to survey this area. The Indians told him of a salt bank along the west bank of the Colorado. Cowan settled near the salt bank shortly thereafter and started working the bank in 1852. During the Civil War Cowan made salt for the Confederacy, producing 20 to 30 bushels per day. The first Llano district court was held at the saltworks, now submerged under Lake Buchanan.

CEDAR POINT PRIMITIVE AREA
On upper Lake Buchanan, off FM 3014, near Tow Community, about 25 miles from Burnet

Part of the LCRA's Primitive Recreation System. Four hundred acres of undeveloped land for those who like to rough it. There are access roads, parking areas, a single-lane boat ramp, fire rings for campsites, but no tables, running water, or restrooms. There are over 3 miles of shoreline, but no designated swimming areas. Old roads and pathways serve as hiking trails. Lots of nice lake views. Birders and other nature lovers can see blue herons, double-breasted cormorants, roadrunners, and osprey, but the bald eagles that winter on Lake Buchanan rarely come here; you need to go by boat farther up the Colorado River canyon.

TOW

Llano County • 305 • About 5.5 miles from Bluffton

David and Gideon Cowan were Tow's first settlers, in 1852, but the resulting village was named for early resident William Tow. Some of the finest hats made in early Texas came from Tow. Early settler John Morgan first worked at the saltworks, but soon started his own hattery, using the pelts of beavers and other animals he trapped. He charged $8 and $10 for his distinctive, wide-brimmed hats, but in a gesture of patriotism gave them away free to Confederate soldiers.

Tow was also forced to relocate when Lake Buchanan covered its original location. It now centers around the **old white school, church, and fire department** on RM 2241. By the way, you pronounce Tow like *cow,* rather than *tow* as in "tow the car." Locals are very particular about this and it's best to pronounce Tow correctly.

Tow is most famous for its pan barbecue, a barbecuing technique invented here more than 50 years ago and practiced publicly only once a year until 1991 at the annual Memorial Day weekend Tow Fish Fry and Pan Barbecue. To make pan barbecue Tow-style, brisket and/or other favorite meats are cooked over mesquite coals in big pans, rather than resting directly on the grill. The meat still acquires the wonderful mesquite-smoked flavor, but instead of dripping into the fire, the meat juices accumulate in the pan, making a wonderful gravy. This annual event was suspended after 1990 because the volunteer fire department had reached its fund-raising goals. But now that you have the recipe, why not try pan barbecuing for yourself?

From the Tow community grounds, continue north on the road to Tow Village. RM 2241 ceases as a state-maintained road, but a smaller paved road continues north to Fall Creek Vineyards and Tow Village.

FALL CREEK VINEYARDS
Tow Village, 2.2 miles north of the Tow Post Office
512-476-4477 • Open Monday–Friday 11–3, Saturday noon–5, Sunday (March–November only) noon–4 • Free

Vineyards and wineries have sprouted up all over the Hill Country in the last 20 years, beginning with Fall Creek Vineyards in 1975. While in France in the early 1970s, Fall Creek's founder, Ed Auler, noticed that parts of the French wine country were remarkably similar to the soil, terrain, and microclimate of this lakeside ranch.

Being Texas' most geologically and climatically diverse region, the Texas Hill Country possesses countless soil varieties and a hot day/cool night growing season pattern, perfect for growing the finest grapes of a great many varieties.

Fall Creek wines began winning medals in wine competitions in the early 1980s, proving that the Hill Country could grow world-class grapes. Fall Creek wines have been served at the White House; President Bush took some to Beijing to serve at a state barbecue. So many wineries have opened since, that "The Texas Hill Country" has been officially recognized as a wine-producing region.

The entrance to Fall Creek Vineyards is well marked. They have a tasting room where you can sample and buy wine.

ANNUAL EVENT

TEXAS HILL COUNTRY FOOD AND WINE FESTIVAL
Various locations in and around Austin • 512-329-0770
Usually first weekend in April • Admission • W

A celebration of Southwestern cuisine and wines from the Texas Hill Country and beyond. Spotlight on great Austin and Texas restaurants and their food on Friday night, food and wine seminars on Saturday, and a food and wine fair on Sunday. Fall Creek Vineyards' founders helped found this (wine) cellar event. Texas' most celebrated chefs feed you and explain how they do it. Events, locales, and participants vary from year to year, so the festival never gets stale. Fall Creek Vineyards has hosted the Sunday food and wine fair several times.

From Tow, retrace your route back to Bluffton and turn right on RM 2241 toward Llano.

A little less than 3 miles west of the Bluffton store is the Bluffton Cemetery, with a picturesque local-stone fence, entryway, chapel, and well. Buried here are Ike Maxwell and John Barringer, owner of Barringer Hill. This stretch of RM 2241 is part of the Texas Hill Country Trail and is flanked on both sides by bowers of wildflowers each spring.

LONE GROVE

Llano County • 50 • About 5 miles from Bluffton

Lone Grove was established as a post office in 1876 and had one store here on the north side of the Austin-to-Mason road, on the banks of the Little Llano River near Dreary Hollow. The store and post office later moved to the east bank of the Little Llano and were joined by a gin, a sawmill, a couple of saloons, and a gambling house. These houses of ill repute went out of business when the new road bypassed Lone Grove. The old school still serves as a community center.

Just west of Lone Grove, 5 miles northeast of Llano, is the old Heath gold mine located on your right. Gold was discovered accidentally in the early 1890s on land owned by a Mr. Heath. Serious mining commenced in 1896. In 1901, two cars of ore were shipped to a smelter in Pueblo, Colorado, where it assayed at about 1.75 ounces ($35) of gold per ton. Several different optimists sank shafts, dug pits, and cut trenches here, but never found sufficient concentrations of gold to make extraction profitable, not even with cyanide, which is used to leach low-density micro-gold particles from rock formations. Gold mining operations ceased in 1916.

A couple of miles outside of Llano, RM 2241 runs into SH 29. Take SH 29 to enter Llano.

LLANO

Llano County Seat • 3,012 • (915) • About 8 miles from Bluffton

Llano is covered at length in the Mormon Trails trip, so only a few notes of passing interest will be mentioned here.

MALONE MANSION
SH 29 • Not open to the public

A few hundred feet east of the city limits on SH 29, you can see a driveway flanked by twin granite gateposts. The house that stands beyond the gate, atop the hill overlooking the beautiful Llano River valley, is the Malone mansion. Built during the boom days of the late 1880s, when Llano was touted as the Iron City of Texas, this one-and-one-half-story limestone mansion was one of Llano's early-day showcases. Eastern capitalists like F. J. Malone poured into Llano in anticipation of the big iron boom, bringing a new hoity-toity upper-crust social life to this still frontier-raw town. When the boom subsided and the Malones and their ilk were gone, the Malone mansion became a tuberculosis sanatorium for those seeking to regain their health in this "semi-tropical paradise." In 1916, granite magnate Tom Norton bought the house and moved his wife Agnes and five daughters in. Two of the daughters, Cordelia and Catherine, lived in the house until their deaths, two days apart in February 1988, from arsenic poisoning at the hands of a young family friend. He was convicted of their deaths and is now in prison.

Turn left onto SH 16 at the junction of SH 29 and SH 16.

As you pass through town, consider these pieces of Llano trivia:

• After the big iron boom went bust, Llano was widely promoted as a place "unsurpassed in health." An Austin reporter wrote in 1911:

> Llano is great on mines and minerals—the common talk of the day deals in veins and strata of earth and rock; but the mine of vast wealth to the visitor from the hot lands is that stratum of delicious and life-giving ozone to which the face of the earth was projected in those past eons of time. The blessed ozone, nature's own free champagne, with which you may become intoxicated, yet feel better instead of worse the morning after.

> In this ozone-charged air the newcomer recognizes the cause as well as the effect, and the sluggish blood accelerates its pace in a seeming desire to get quickly a full supply of it for fear the supply will run out. The delightful ozone laden air of the Llano region is the constant topic of conversation by visitors and has no relation to 'hot air' talk, which, if stirring, will be found out of town among the prospectors and mining camps.

• One of Texas' foremost sculptors, Frank Teich, spent the last 38 years of his life in Llano. Teich came here from San Antonio after a physical breakdown and a doctor's diagnosis that he would live only six more months. Born and trained in Germany, where he worked under the German sculptor Johannes Schelling, in Texas he superintended the granite cutters for the state capitol and worked on many buildings and monuments throughout Texas and the South, many of them Confederate monuments. He came to Llano in 1901 and opened the Teich Monumental Works, which was a small town in its own right. Teich has been called the father of the granite industry in Texas.

• Llano County has had perhaps more nicknames than any other county in Texas: Rockbound's Paradise (241 different rocks and minerals are found in the county), Deer Capital of Texas, Land of Legend and Lure, Gem of the Hill Country, Iron Capital of Texas, Birmingham of Texas, Granite Capital of Texas, Colorado of Texas, and Livestock Capital of Texas (Llano County brings more hogs to market each year than any other county in Texas). Whew!

OXFORD

Llano County • 33 • About 10 miles from Llano

A little more than 9 miles from the intersection of SH 16 and SH 71 south of Llano, you come to the ghost town of Oxford, marked by a closed red-and-white stucco gas station and store with a tin roof. The cemetery sits in a field directly across the road from the store, and a gravel road runs off to your right by the store, identified by signs directing you to the Ratliff and Inks ranches.

Oxford was once a bustling village, with nearly 300 inhabitants by 1896. Folks had lived here for years scattered along Lost and Hondo creeks. One winter in the 1870s Tom Sims took a load of bacon to Waco to sell. There he met A. J. Johnson, who wanted desperately to come to Llano County. He came in 1880 and laid out the town of Oxford, naming it for his old hometown of Oxford, Mississippi, where he had graduated from Oxford University. Soon Oxford had a gin, a post office, a couple of stores, a drugstore, a doctor, and a blacksmith. The nearby Bedford Academy boasted over 100 pupils. An incident there one night earned Oxford its nickname Cat Town; some young men attending a schoolhouse dance got drunk and threw a cat into a large cauldron of boiling coffee. Oxford was also home to C. T. and John Moss, members of one of Llano County's greatest ranching families.

The cemetery was established in 1881, with the earliest known burial in 1883. Resting here are A. J. Johnson (1832–1912) and James Moss (1843–1924), Confederate veteran and leader of the cowboy band at the nearby Packsaddle Mountain battle in 1873.

From SH 16, turn right on the gravel road by the old Oxford store and proceed a little more than a mile until you come to a collection of old stone buildings dominated by the massive burned-out hulk of a once-proud limestone home.

C. T. MOSS RANCH
One mile west of Oxford • Not open to the public
This is the old C. T. Moss ranch. The big burned-out main house was built in 1888 and burned in 1968, all 10 rooms of it, leaving only the walls. C. T. Moss built the county's first barbed-wire fences, and with his father and brothers owned most of the land and cattle in the southern half of Llano County. Brother Jim led the cowboy band in the battle on Packsaddle Mountain, by the way.

The collection of stone buildings surrounding the big house is one of the most impressive in the Hill Country, and the fancy wrought-iron fence and gate still encircle the crumbling Moss homestead. Jim Moss's frame Victorian house also stands nearby.

Return to SH 16 and continue south toward Fredericksburg.

In another few miles you cross **Sandy Creek** and enter **Legion Valley,** site of one of the worst Indian massacres in the Hill Country. On February 6, 1868, Llano County and Legion Valley were locked in winter's icy grip. Mrs. Boyd Johnson, Mrs. Babe Johnson, Miss Amanda Townsend, and children were spending the day with neighbor Mrs. Mathilda (John) Friend. The menfolk were away that day, believing their families were safe from Indian attack in such intemperate weather.

About three that afternoon, the four children, who were snowballing in the dark, saw a group of horsemen approaching and began to scream. Correctly apprising their identities as Indians, the women rushed the children into the house and bolted the door. Once inside, the women—save Mrs. Friend—went into a state of hysteria greater than the children's. The Indians, hearing the screaming, rightly surmised that there were no men inside and began to batter the doors down. Once they were inside, only Mrs. Friend fought, whereupon she was shot, scalped, and left for dead. The Indians took the other seven hostage and rode off into the sunset.

Mrs. Friend, an arrow sticking from her chest, bound her scalped head and managed to drag herself one and a half miles through the snow to her nearest neighbor. There she begged him to remove the arrow. He failed, and then he and his family fled for the cedar brakes, fearing an attack on their house, too. They left Mrs. Friend alone by the fire with a bucket of water, her wounds undressed, not even her bloody clothes removed.

A posse did not start after the Indians until 36 hours later. The trail they followed was a gruesome one. Five miles from the Friend home, they found one of the babies, its skull bashed in; several hours later another baby, its throat cut ear to ear; next Mrs. Boyd and Mrs. Babe Johnson, ravaged and mutilated, finally Miss Townsend in a similar horrible condition. The Indians' trail had wandered zigzag over to Hell's Half Acre in Gillespie County (see Enchanted Rock—Willow City) back through Blowout community, then up by Kingoland, where they murdered another man before escaping for good.

The two children left alive were restored to their families several years later, and Mrs. Friend miraculously recovered from her wounds and moved to Missouri. The tragedy could have been averted if only the women had been able to maintain a measure of restraint; the Indians attacked only when they realized the men were gone.

In this area you notice an obvious change in the landscape—the gray-and-pink granite and oak trees have given way to white limestone, marl, and juniper trees. This sudden change takes place 14 miles north of Fredericksburg, caused by a large fault that dropped the Cretaceous Trinity limestone into contact with the older pre-Cambrian metamorphic rocks and granite.

OBERHELLMANN VINEYARDS
About 13 miles from Oxford • 830-685-3297 • Open Saturdays, March through mid-December • Free tour • W variable

Located at the base of Bell Mountain, this vineyard began in 1974 on abandoned farmland. Johannesberg Riesling, Gewurztraminer,

Chardonnay, and Pinot Noir are among the grapes grown. After the tour, enjoy complimentary tasting of the wines made here.

From Oberhellmann Vineyards, continue south on SH 16 to Fredericksburg.

MORMON TRAILS

Approximately 190 miles

Texas has been attracting dreamers and schemers for centuries: brigands like Jean LaFitte; treasure hunters like Jim Bowie; empire builders like Philip Nolan, Augustus McGee, Henry Perry, and Dr. James Long; utopians like Nicholas Zink of Sisterdale, Gustav Schleicher of Bettina, and Victor Considerant of La Reunion; religious leaders like Johann Killian and his Wendish Lutheran flock, and Lyman Wight and his Mormon faithful. Few Texans know anything of these men and their dreams, perhaps because most of them failed. Lyman Wight, one of the Latter-Day Saints' original Quorum of Twelve, followed his dream to Texas. This trip traces the wanderings of Wight and his followers through the Hill Country.

Before we start traveling, we need to spend some time looking at the events that led to Wight's migration to Texas. The Latter day Saints movement traces its beginnings back to 1820, when young Joseph Smith received a vision from God. The 15-year-old Smith was attending a Baptist-Methodist revival in his hometown of Palmyra, New York, when a voice from heaven told him not to join any sect, but rather to await a second vision from God. This second vision came in 1823, when a heavenly messenger revealed to Smith the location of some ancient plates buried in a field near Palmyra. These plates supposedly contained the record of ancestry of the American Indians, who were supposed to be the remnants of the ancient House of Israel. Accompanying the plates were two stones, the Urim and the Thummin, which held the key to the plates' translation. Smith was allowed to see the plates during this second vision,

119

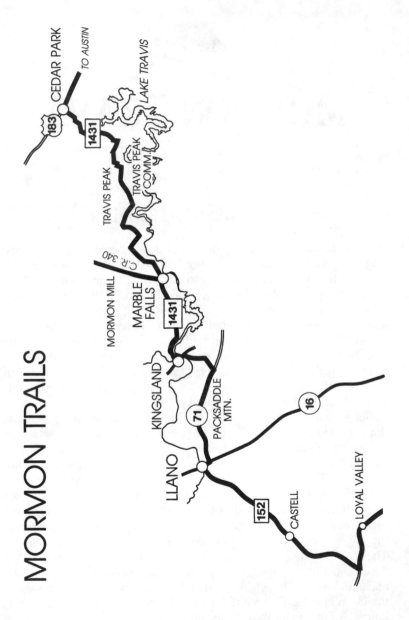

MORMON TRAILS

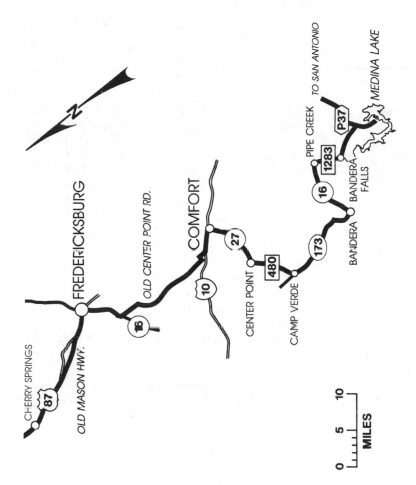

but was not allowed to take possession of them. Four years later the messenger visited Smith again, and this time Smith got to keep the plates. Smith then translated the plates in dictation to several scribes, including his new wife, Emma, and an itinerant schoolteacher, Oliver Cowdery. When completed, the revelations were printed at Palmyra in 1829. This is the Book of Mormon, which Mormons hold in equal esteem with the Bible.

Smith's brand of religion began to attract followers, one of whom was Lyman Wight. Wight was born in Connecticut in 1796. He fought with distinction in the War of 1812. In 1823, Wight married Harriet Benton; they moved in 1826 to Cuyahoga County, Ohio, where Wight joined the Lord's flock under the tutelage of a Baptist-turned-Campbellite preacher named Sidney Rigdon. Rigdon's converts then formed a commune, 12 families strong, which had interests in both farming and mechanics. A year later, the commune members were baptized into the Latter-Day Saints church. Wight became an elder in the Latter-Day Saints church just six days after his baptism.

While in Kirtland, Ohio (their first gathering place), the Mormons adopted the "stewardship plan," a financial plan to which they still adhere, in theory. The stewardship plan is the economic basis for Mormonism. By its terms each man gives all his properties to the church, whereupon he is given stewardship over certain properties, usually the same that he has just given over to God.

Out of these properties he keeps only enough for his "just wants and needs" and turns over the surplus to the church's general fund, which is administered by a bishop. This was a different proposition from the "common stock" proposition of Rigdon's settlement, and the common stock system was the economic set-up employed by Wight in Texas.

Neighbors in Kirtland did not appreciate the presence of the Latter-Day Saints, so it was decided that the main mass of Mormons would move to the western edge of Missouri (which was then the edge of America's western frontier), according to a vision received by Smith. Wight was specifically mentioned in one of Smith's visions as one of those chosen to carry the gospel to Missouri. At the conference of June 3–6, 1831, Joseph Smith laid his hands on Wight and ordained him to the High Priesthood, after the holy order of God, and the spirit fell upon him. But that same month, God, through Smith, also warned Wight: "And let my servant Lyman Wight beware, for Satan desireth to sift him as chaff." As a high priest, Wight would prove to be something of a theological loose cannon. At one church meeting a few years later, John Corrill complained that

Lyman Wight was teaching that "all disease in this church is of the devil, and that medicine administered to the sick is of the devil; for the sick in the church ought to live by faith," a charge that Wight acknowledged to be true. The more practical-minded president told Wight to keep this belief strictly to himself, and affirmed the utility of church-approved roots and herbs as medicine, especially when administered by a church member.

Wight and four other elders came to Independence, the seat of Jackson County, Missouri, in 1831. Smith and other church officials arrived soon after, and announced that this section of Missouri had been revealed as Zion, the promised land of the Mormons. They bought 40 acres of land and laid the cornerstone for a temple that was never constructed. They established a Mormon newspaper, *The Evening and the Morning Star,* in 1832. By 1833, the Mormon population in Jackson County was nearly 1,500, or about one-third of the county's population. The Mormons organized their Missouri Zion as a collective and lived every minute of their lives according to the church's evolving doctrine, which stood in sharp contrast to the individualistic, loosely structured character of most frontier communities. The Mormons' economic success, their ability to control local elections, their clannishness, their church secrets, and their rapid growth in numbers aroused the anger and fear of their mostly Southern, Anglo neighbors, who also objected to the Mormons' abolitionist beliefs and their belief that the American Indians were the lost tribes of Israel.

Tensions between Mormons and gentiles grew. The Mormons saw Jackson County, Missouri, as their final gathering place, the sacred place to which Christ will come for the second resurrection. If this sacred plot were lost to them, the Mormons were to redeem it by force if necessary.

There were minor persecutions and personal conflicts, and then mob violence erupted. The Mormons' printing facilities at Independence were destroyed, and the Mormons as a group were driven from the county in 1833. Lyman Wight claimed that 203 Mormon houses and one mill were burned. He also said: "I saw 190 women and children driven 30 miles across the prairie in the month of November, with 3 decrepit men only in their company. The ground was thinly crusted with sleet and I could easily follow on their trail by the blood that flowed from their lacerated feet on the stubble of the burnt prairie."

The Mormons fled over into neighboring Clay, Ray, and Daviess Counties, but they did not abandon their claim to Zion. They would do whatever it took to get their legally purchased property back.

When a barrage of letters to the governor proved fruitless, the Mormons began to take stronger measures. By May 1834, the Mormons in Clay County had established an armory, where they made weapons like swords, knives, pistols, and repaired rifles and shotguns. Wight, who had held a colonel's commission in the Missouri militia, became the Mormons' chief military commander. General Wight was truly a soldier's general. On June 18, 1834, the Mormon band had to cross a slough that was half a mile wide. The soldiers had to wade through waist-deep mud and water. According to one compatriot, "General Wight, who had traveled from Kirtland [Ohio] without a stocking on his foot, carried Brother Joseph Young on his back." Breakfast that day was watery-thin cornmeal gruel.

On August 16, 1834, Joseph Smith wrote Wight from Kirtland and told him to "enter complaint to the Governor as often as he receives any insult or injury, and in case that they proceed to endeavor to take life, or tear down houses, and if the citizens of Clay County do not befriend us, to gather up the little army and be sent over immediately into Jackson County, and trust in God, and do the best he can in maintaining the ground."

The Clay Countians did not befriend the Mormons, or at least they did not befriend them for long. On June 29, 1836, the gentiles of Clay County called on the Mormons to leave the county. They had first welcomed the Mormons, as refugees, with Christian charity, but the Mormons had worn out their welcome; they were not welcome to live in Clay County, for roughly the same set of reasons given by the Jackson County gentiles. Either the Mormons moved elsewhere (they recommended Wisconsin) or the gentiles would commence a civil war against them. At least partly in response to this threat, the Missouri legislature created Caldwell County on December 29, 1836, as a Mormon refuge. Caldwell County is just north and east of Clay County.

Within a few months of its creation, most of the Mormons moved to Caldwell County, where they founded the towns of Salem and Far West. Far West became the county seat. Far West's square measured 396 feet per side; the four main streets were 100 feet wide. A temple site was selected in 1837 and the population swelled to 4,000. Again, friction developed between the Mormons and their gentile neighbors. Quarrels gave way to shootings, which in turn begat a guerilla war, known as the Mormon War, in 1837.

Meanwhile, Lyman Wight settled in 1837 on a great bend of the Grand River in Daviess County (located above Caldwell County) and established a ferry. In May 1838, Joseph Smith visited Wight's settlement and named it *Adam-ondi-Ahman,* which in the Reformed Egyptian language means "Adam's Consecrated Land." According to church history, this is the valley where three years before his death Adam gathered all the patriarchs—Seth, Enos, Cainan, Mahalaliel, Jared, Enoch, and Methuselah—and gave them his final blessing. As he blessed them, the heavens opened up and the Lord appeared. Here, Smith prophesied, the judgment will sit and the Son of Man will appear and issue a decree that his dominion will be everlasting. At the brow of a hill above the village, Smith discovered a ruined stone altar where he said the patriarchs had worshipped.

Adam-ondi-Ahman grew rapidly. By October 1838, nearly 200 houses had been built, and 40 more Mormon families were living in wagons while waiting for more houses to be built. But the end was near. The Mormons had problems with the gentiles in Daviess County from almost the beginning. Adam-ondi-Ahman was located just four miles north of the county seat of Gallatin. Gallatin was a ragged row of ten houses, three of which were saloons. Almost overnight, the Mormons outnumbered the gentiles in Daviess County and their thriving town quickly left Gallatin in the dust. When a group of unarmed Mormons came to Gallatin to vote on August 6, 1838, they were met by a mob controlled by Col. W. P. Peniston, a member of the county's founding family and candidate for office whom the Mormons opposed. A drunkard picked a quarrel with one of the Mormon leaders, and a fight began. Pistols weren't used, but rocks, clubs, and the occasional butcher knife were pressed into service. Men dropped like flies on all sides. Major Joseph H. McGee saw a Mormon pursued by two Missourians. The Mormon had a butcher knife sticking between his shoulders. As they chased him, another Mormon seized a large club, rushed in between them and their victim, and knocked the gentiles senseless into the dirt. The Mormons retreated, but on October 11, 1838, they attacked Gallatin, and sacked and burned the town's storehouse and tailor shop. Adam-ondi-Ahman came to resemble a fort.

In 1838, Governor Lilburn W. Boggs ordered the state militia to either exterminate the Mormons or drive them from Missouri. When some Mormons moved over into Carroll County (just east of Caldwell County) in the summer of 1838, a civil war with the gentiles flared within weeks of their arrival. The Mormons left Carroll County in September rather than face massacre by their neighbors. On October 30, 1838, 200 Missouri militia attacked a small group of Mormons who had taken refuge at Haun's Mill in Caldwell County.

About 18 Mormons were killed. Rather than allow the Mormons to bury their dead, the militia threw the bodies down a well.

After the Haun's Mill massacre, state militia was dispatched to Far West. The Mormons at Far West surrendered. The leaders were tried by courtmartial and ordered shot, but the sentence wasn't carried out. They were jailed instead. On November 8, 1838, shortly after the Mormons surrendered at Far West, Brigadier General Robert Wilson went to Adam-ondi-Ahman to hold an inquiry into the alleged Mormon transgressions. After a 3-day hearing, every Mormon was acquitted, but Wilson ordered the town to be vacated in 10 days. The Mormons were allowed to spend the winter in Caldwell County, but they had to leave Missouri as soon as it warmed up. The abandoned town quickly fell into ruin, and by 1940, only one crumbling log house—said to be the house of Lyman Wight—remained. Elder Lyman Wight joined his fellow Mormon leaders in jail. On December 1, 1838, Prophet Joseph Smith, his brother Hiram Smith, Lyman Wight, Sidney Rigdon, and two others were placed in the Clay County Jail in Liberty. The town was abuzz with wild rumors of poisoning attempts, gruesome punishments, threats of lynching, and attempted escapes. Joseph Smith had a series of revelations, while the other prisoners denounced any townspeople who came within shouting distance. Rigdon was paroled; the other five Mormon leaders remained in the Liberty jail until April 15, 1839, when they were transferred to Daviess County. While being transferred to another jail in Columbia, Joseph Smith and most of the prisoners escaped; the rest of the Mormons escaped from the Columbia jail and fled to Illinois, where most of their followers had settled after leaving Missouri. The escapes were probably arranged.

The Mormons built a city—Nauvoo—in Illinois and there enjoyed prosperity and peace for a few years, bringing in thousands of converts, the result of the massive proselytizing efforts of the missionary arm of the church, known as the Quorum of Twelve. Wight became a member of the Quorum in 1841. He also became president of the Black River Lumber Company, which the Mormons formed to acquire lumber for the construction of a temple at Nauvoo. By 1843 the Mormons were having trouble with their Nauvoo neighbors, too, and they were looking for a new Zion. The Republic of Texas seemed to offer great possibilities as a place where they could found a nation all their own, so the church began to make plans for a colony in Texas. Wight was at the head of this company. Come 1844, the Texas plan was sidelined for a time while the church organized a harebrained attempt to elect Joseph Smith president of the United States.

Should Smith be defeated, the Texas plan would take effect. The Texas plan provided for the purchase of territory "north of a west line, from the falls of the Colorado River to the Nueces River, thence down same to the Gulf of Mexico and along the Rio Grande and up the same to the United States territory." The Mormons expected to be recognized here as a sovereign nation and to help the struggling Texas republic to defend herself from Mexico.

The Black River Lumber Company was to take possession of the new territory. At the time, the Mormons' desired territory was part of the land in dispute between Mexico and Texas. A Mormon representative went to Texas to negotiate with the government and returned in 1844 with treaty approval by the president's cabinet. Three more men were then appointed commissioners to meet with the Texas congress to ratify the treaty, after which Wight and George Miller were to lead the colony to this territory.

The plan to elect Smith president of the United States came to an abrupt halt in Carthage, Illinois, on June 27, 1844, when Smith was killed by a mob that broke into the jail where he was being held. Confusion followed at Nauvoo, and Brigham Young, president of the Quorum of Twelve, assumed control of the church and declared himself to be the successor to Smith. The Quorum followed his lead, save Wight and two others. Most of the faithful followed Young out to Utah, while other smaller groups went their own way, including Lyman Wight. Wight was not called the Wild Ram of the Mountains for nothing.

When Wight refused the leadership of Brigham Young, he decided to lead the Black River Lumber Company to Texas, following the council's 1844 directive. On March 25, 1845, Wight and 150 followers started down the Mississippi for Texas. They landed near Davenport, Iowa, from which point they prepared for the rest of the trip, which was to be over land. After Indian problems, disease and death, they crossed the Red River into Texas on November 10, 1845, and spent the winter in an abandoned fort in Grayson County. They resumed their journey south on April 24, 1846, arriving at Webberville, east of Austin, on June 6 of that same year (see The Wild West—Webberville).

They didn't stay long. Noah Smithwick, chronicler of early Texas and the Mormons' neighbor at Webberville, wrote: "They were a novelty in the religious world, and curious to know something of their peculiar views, I permitted the elder to preach in my house. Preaching of any kind was so rare that the neighbors all gathered in and listened with respectful attention while the elder expounded the doctrine of the Latter-day Saints, being careful to leave out its more objectionable features. But amongst most people the idea obtained that they were a lawless band and the subject of rising up and driving them from the country was strongly advocated. They were in sufficient numbers to stand off the Indians, and, it being their policy to isolate their communities which relegated them to the outskirts of civilization, I was willing to utilize anything that formed a barrier against the savages. I therefore counseled suspension of hostilities till some overt act called for their expulsion."

Smithwick's advice was not heeded and the Mormons soon moved to a spot on the Colorado River a few miles above Austin by the "Great Falls," near the present location of Tom Miller Dam. Here they settled down to the business of making a living. They took the contract for the first jail in Austin.

Here at the falls of the Colorado the Mormons built the area's first gristmill. Smithwick relates: "Up to this time we were under the necessity of grinding our corn on steel mills run by hand—a tedious and wearying process, so that in building the mill the Mormons became public benefactors and it was a great catastrophe when a rise in the river swept their mill away. They gathered up the machinery, but, discouraged with the prospect, began to look about for a better location."

One report has them moving up the river to Bull Creek, where they established another mill. At any rate, during their stay in Austin they proved to be prodigious workers, building several houses in addition to the jail and several miles of roads to their mills. We know these roads now as Scenic Dr., which runs along the banks of Lake Austin from Enfield Dr. to Pecos St., and Lakewood Dr./Spicewood Springs Rd., which runs along Bull Creek. Most of Lakewood Dr. has now been obliterated by Loop 360. These roads are among the most visually pleasing in Austin.

Hard work notwithstanding, the Mormons managed to debit themselves to the tune of $2,000 to Austin merchants. Before the year 1846 was history, Wight had sent an exploring party west to scout for a new colony location. It reported back a favorable location on the Pedernales "with plenty of good water and timber, abounding with game and honey." Wight had heard of the German settlement at Fredericksburg and hoped that he and his flock might be able to live harmoniously with the mostly abolitionist and Free-Soiler Germans. Adelsverein commissioner John Meusebach welcomed the idea, and so the Mormons prepared to move again, into the valley of the Corderillas or Cordilleras Mountains, as the hills ringing Fredericksburg were variously called. (*Corderilla* means "lambskin dressed with the fleece" in Spanish; *cordillera* means "mountain range.")

By May 1, 1847, a mill site had been selected four miles below Fredericksburg on the Pedernales, and six weeks later the advance guard had a gristmill in operation. Crops were planted, the Austin mill site was sold in August, and the whole colony moved to the new settlement, named Zodiac by Wight.

Soon the Mormons had constructed a sawmill, general store, temple-storehouse, school, blacksmith and wagon shop, cabinet and furniture shops, shingle mill, and houses for the 20-odd Mormon families.

Wight's colony was a godsend to Fredericksburg; the Mormons supplied the Germans with seed, lumber, and shingles from their mill, cornmeal from their gristmill, and furniture from their shops. The Mormons also helped the Germans adjust to the idiosyncrasies of farming on the edge of the Great American Desert. Many of the German immigrants were becoming farmers and herders for the first time, here in America.

On December 13, 1848, two men from Brigham Young's headquarters at Council Bluff, Nebraska, came to Zodiac, their mission being to persuade Wight to journey to Salt Lake City to counsel with his brethren on the Quorum of Twelve. They threatened him with excommunication should he refuse. Wight replied, "Nobody under the light of the heavens except Joseph Smith or John Smith, the president of the Fifty, can call me from Texas to come to Salt Lake City," and said that he had as much authority to call one of the Twelve—or rather Eleven—to Texas, as they had to call him to Utah. The Wild Ram of the Mountains was excommunicated a year later.

Wight apparently tried to get along with neighbors, both red and white. Chief Buffalo Hump and his Comanches visited Zodiac several times during 1849 and 1850 and gave the Mormons the privilege of traveling anywhere through their nation. Wight tried to discuss Mormonism with them, which seemed to please the Comanches greatly.

In 1850, Wight entered secular politics, running for chief justice and judge of probate court of Gillespie County. Wight lost the regular election to Johann Jost Klingelhoefer, but contested the results on the grounds that Klingelhoefer was not a U.S. citizen (he had not yet been naturalized). The contest was decided in Wight's favor, and he took office in September 1850. But since the rest of the county court was comprised of Germans, Wight could not run the county as he pleased. So after attending only five sessions of court, Wight refused to attend any more. He ignored all summons from his fellow commissioners to attend, so the commissioners met, declared the office of chief justice vacant, and called a special election to fill the vacancy. The election was held in August 1851, and Klingelhoefer, by now a U.S. citizen, was elected in Wight's place.

Despite the colony's industriousness, its debts seemed to grow larger and larger, owing to Wight's bad financial management. Come 1851, Wight was anticipating a new move, for a variety of reasons: his inability to get along with the county commissioners; sickness in the colony; no more contract work at Fort Martin Scott, to which they had earlier furnished much lumber and grain; a defect in land title that caused them to lose the land, necessitating repurchase; a flood that swept away their crops and mills; and finally, Wight's seemingly insatiable wanderlust, which prevented him from settling down anywhere for more than a few years at a time.

By February 1851, they were on the move again, this time northeastward. They stopped briefly at the Colorado River near the Marble Falls, and it is at the town of Marble Falls that we take up their wandering path through the Hill Country.

To get to Marble Falls from Austin, take US 183 from I-35 about 16 miles up to Cedar Park, then turn left on FM 1431. Or, take I-35 north to Round Rock, and take the FM 1431 exit. Go west on FM 1431 to Cedar Park, where you cross the Balcones Escarpment and enter the Hill Country. From Cedar Park, FM 1431's path is forever restless.

TRAVIS PEAK COMMUNITY

Travis County • About 13 miles from Cedar Park

Named for the nearby peak, this settlement got its start in 1851 when Herman Hensel built a cabin here. Hensel came to Travis County via Cape Horn and the California gold-mining camps of the great rush of 1849. He bought 80 acres here on Cow Creek and settled down to raising a family. He replaced his cabin in 1878 with a large two-story limestone house that still stands, and also donated land in 1880 for the one-room limestone schoolhouse, which also still stands. These buildings and the cemetery are located just off FM 1431 on Singleton Rd., which runs off to your left down to Lake Travis, just past the Travis Peak community sign. At the end of this road is **Gloster Bend Primitive Area,** the first of several LCRA primitive areas located on Lake Travis, about 3.3 miles off FM 1431.

LCRA PRIMITIVE RECREATION SYSTEM ON LAKE TRAVIS

The Lower Colorado River Authority's Primitive Recreation System on Lake Travis is composed of seven tracts of public land managed by the LCRA. They are open year-round and admission is free, but they *are* primitive (no toilets, no running water, no trash collection facilities). What you pack in, you must pack out. Camping is allowed in designated camping sites, identified by metal fire rings. The only other "improvements" consist of vehicle control barriers, signs, and small parking areas. You can fish at any of the sites. Many varieties of fish, including largemouth bass, sunfish, crappie, striper, and catfish, are in Lake Travis. All anglers must have a Texas fishing license, which can be purchased at area sporting goods stores.

GLOSTER BEND
North side of Lake Travis, on Singleton Rd., off FM 1431
More than a mile of Lake Travis shoreline and a single-lane paved boat ramp distinguish this 600-acre primitive recreation area. The topography is mostly rolling hills with some steep ravines. There are designated access roads and an improved road leading to the boat ramp. There is a paved parking area for vehicles and trailers.

TURKEY BEND (EAST)
North side of Lake Travis; about 3 miles west of Travis Peak Community, Shaw Drive dead-ends into FM 1431 from the south. Turn left on Shaw Dr. and go 1.8 miles to reach the Turkey Bend (East) Primitive Area.
Turkey Bend (East) offers more than two miles of shoreline and one of the prettiest coves on the lake. The property is long and narrow in shape, with varied topography ranging from steep shoreline slopes to gentle flats. The shoreline of the gently sloping southern tip of Turkey Bend fluctuates with lake levels. When Lake Travis is low, more than a quarter-mile of grassy shoreline may be exposed. A looped trail along the upper plateau is for nonmotorized use only. Spectacular views of Lake Travis and the surrounding countryside make it popular with hikers and horseback riders. A trailhead parking area large enough to accommodate horse trailers is provided.

SMITHWICK COMMUNITY

Burnet County • About 11 miles from Travis Peak
Next you encounter Smithwick community, named after the Mormons' Webberville neighbor Noah Smithwick. Smithwick was born in North Carolina on New Year's Day, 1809. He moved to Texas in 1827, working as a blacksmith and smuggling tobacco across the

Mexican border with his old friend Dr. John Webber. After serving in the Republican Army during the Texas war of independence, Smithwick lived first in Bastrop, then in Webberville, where he served as blacksmith, postmaster, and justice of the peace. He moved to Fort Croghan (now Burnet) in 1848, then to the section of the country that now bears his name, located between Doublehorn and Hickory Creeks, in 1855. Doublehorn Creek's name is derived from the interlocked antlers found near the source of the stream by early settlers. Two bucks, presumably having met at the spring to drink, became engaged in an altercation. During the course of their battle they managed to interlock their horns, and unable to extricate themselves, starved to death. Here Smithwick built his first house and a mill on the Colorado.

In 1858, a great grasshopper plague descended upon the countryside, and Smithwick described their onslaught. "They came on the wing and in such numbers that the sun was literally darkened with them. Anyone who has ever looked toward the zenith during a snowstorm will remember that the snowflakes looked like myriads of black specks. That is just the appearance the grasshoppers presented when first discovered. Soon they began to drop, and the ground was alive with them. It was late in the fall and they went into winter quarters, devouring every green thing in sight except the rag-weed, which is intensely bitter, utilizing the denuded branches and weeds for roosting purposes. When the cold came on they were frozen on their perches, and in this state they fell easy victims to the hogs, which devoured millions of them, but there were still enough left to seed the ground for the next season's crop, which they did by boring holes into the earth with their tail-ends. They did not distribute themselves evenly, some farms being almost free of them. On one such place there were only a few dropped down, and the owner thereof, mustering his whole family when the hoppers began to light, gathered tin pans, beating them energetically until the main body of pests passed over. After his neighbors had received the full force of the invasion he was wont to attribute their affliction to shiftlessness. 'If you had just got out and fought them, as I did, you might have saved your crop.' Pretty soon, though, there came on another detachment. When they began to drop our hero got out with his tin pans and brooms and 'beat' and 'shooed' till he was exhausted, but the hoppers kept on dropping, and lost no time in getting to work, cleaning out everything in sight."

With the coming of the Civil War, Smithwick left Texas for California. An avowed unionist, he was threatened by his hot-headed secessionist neighbors, so he sold his farm for $2,000, gave his mill—for which he had been offered $12,000 the year before—to his nephew John Hubbard, and drove a prairie schooner to California. But before leaving Texas, he paid a farewell visit to his old friend and fellow unionist Sam Houston. Smithwick lived out the rest of his 91 years in California. Toward the end of his life, he began to work on his memoirs of life in early Texas. Smithwick didn't let blindness halt his work; he dictated the text to his daughter.

Two more LCRA primitive areas on Lake Travis are located in the Smithwick neighborhood. The first is Shaffer Bend, which is accessed via Burnet County Rd. 343A, about a mile off FM 1431.

SHAFFER BEND
North side of Lake Travis, off FM 1431, about 17 miles west of Lago Vista, near Smithwick community

This 500-acre site exhibits two distinct topographies. The northern portion is very hilly with extensive exposed limestone outcrops and dense stands of cedar. There are several good views of Lake Travis and the surrounding countryside up here, and the area is accessible by gravel road. The southern portion is gently sloping bottomland with large oaks and pecan trees along more than a mile of gently sloping shoreline.

An improved gravel road provides access to the shoreline while avoiding the center of the property, which is habitat for black-capped vireos. Hiking, biking, and horseback riding are allowed in the interior portions of the property. Vehicles with good traction and high ground clearance are recommended.

Another mile west on FM 1431, and you come to the intersection with Burnet County Rd. 343, which runs down to Lake Travis and the Camp Creek Primitive Area.

CAMP CREEK
North side of Lake Travis, on Burnet County Rd. 343, 0.5 mile off FM 1431, near the Smithwick community

Camp Creek features sizable stands of pecan trees and unique creek bottoms. There is excellent diversity of vegetation and wildlife on the 600-acre tract, which has been left largely undisturbed. A hiking trail follows Camp Creek and then climbs to a plateau. The trail provides many scenic opportunities and opportunities for nature study. The shoreline at Camp Creek is shorter and steeper than at many of the other sites in the LCRA's Primitive Recreation System. Burnet County operates and maintains a 5-acre park along Camp Creek's waterfront.

Overnight camping is permitted. The only public boat ramp on the upper north side of Lake Travis is here, along with tables, grills, and trash cans. An improved county road provides access to the park area. There's no running water or restrooms.

Continue on FM 1431 into Marble Falls.

MARBLE FALLS

Burnet County • 4,473 • (830) • About 9 miles from Smithwick

Marble Falls is covered at length in the Hermit of the Hills trip, so only a few pieces of appropriate historical trivia are offered here:

• Some people say that the area around Marble Falls was supposed to have been the first dry land in the world.

• After Colonel Charles J. Todd's ill-fated attempt to establish a town at Marble Falls (although he managed to sell several lots for $200 apiece), a Colonel Dale came down to Burnet County in the summer of 1860 to buy land. Representing a St. Louis manufacturing firm that was looking to build a woolen factory somewhere contiguous to the wool-producing section, Dale was attracted to the Marble Falls of the Colorado for their obvious power-producing capacity. But Colonel Todd held out for too dear a price, and Dale turned to Smithwick at his mill on the Colorado, offering him the aforementioned $12,000 figure. Itching for new worlds to conquer, Smithwick accepted this handsome offer. Dale went back to St. Louis to report to his company, get the cash for the purchase, and obtain the requisite machinery. That winter brought the victory of Lincoln and the first of the ordinances of secession passed by the 13 rebelling states, and the Dale deal fell through.

Wight and the Mormons were also attracted by the Marble Falls; a February 1851 scouting party had chosen a location on the river near the falls. But the colony didn't stay there long, as Wight related in a letter. "We stopped on the Colorado river which we anticipated was a pleasant place to stop till we made choice of a place on which to locate. In an unexpected moment the spring of water failed and weather being extremely dry and hot and not having nother but river water and being exposed to the heat for fear that sickness would again pursue us we made a sudden effort to find good water which we found here in great abundance." "Here" was a spot on Hamilton Creek about 8 miles north of the Marble Falls, to be known thereafter as the Mormon Mills.

At the intersection of FM 1431 with US 281, turn right on US 281 and go 2 blocks to the intersection with 12th St. Just a few feet past 12th St., take a right on Mormon Mills Rd., which runs off to the northeast at a 45-degree angle. To help you find it, look for the Comfort Inn on your left, on the west side of US 281.

MORMON MILLS

Burnet County • About 6 miles from Marble Falls

About 6 miles north of Marble Falls on Mormon Mills Rd., you cross Hamilton Creek, described in the Hermit of the Hills trip. The Mormon cemetery lies up on the west bank of the creek just north of this low-water bridge, hidden from sight on private property. It was here along scenic Hamilton Creek that the Mormons had settled by July 1851. Go another couple of hundred feet and you see a wide blue pond, a historical marker on the left between the road and creek, and a tree-obscured view of the Hamilton Falls, which form the pond.

Smithwick described the falls as follows: "A mountain had been cleft from north to south, to permit the stream to pass through, and then from east to west, the southern portion having been entirely removed so that the almost perpendicular walls between which flowed the creek, turned away at right angles at the mouth of the gorge, where the stream fell over a precipice twenty-eight feet or more in height into a deep pool below: thence rippling away between great banks, shaded by the various trees indigenous to the country."

Today you see a several-tiered limestone cliff, which is the breaking point of a long limestone chute. Several streams of water course over its edge, breaking into smaller rivulets on their stairstep path down to the 2.5-acre pool. The chute's east bluff is conveniently cut away for the roadside viewer; the west bluff continues on for a considerable distance.

You have to settle for a partially obscured glimpse of the falls, for they are on private property very explicitly posted with "no trespassing" signs, but fortunately there is no way for the signs to diminish the melodic tumbling of the waters. It should still be easy to see why the Mormons settled here.

This was the finest land along Hamilton Creek, originally granted to Conrad Rohrer, a German bachelor from Pennsylvania, in compensation for his services in the Texas Revolution. Rohrer, unfortunately, was killed by Indians the same year of grant, 1836, and never cast an eye on the land.

Once settled, the Mormon colony built a new set of mills and shops, but not without problems. They had lost their grain-grinding burrs in the Zodiac floods. Since they had no money to buy new ones, they went out to a nearby quarry and got out blocks of marble, from which they manufactured burrs that sufficed for grinding corn but required frequent dressing.

Smithwick picks up the story: "Old Lyman Wight, the high priest, set about the task of recovering the lost stones. After wrestling alone with the spirits for some little time he arose one morning with joy in his heart, and summoning his people, announced to them that he had a revelation, and bidding them take spades and crowbars and follow him, set out to locate the millstones. Straight ahead he bore as one in a dream, his divining rod in his hand; his awestruck disciples following in silence. Pausing at last in the middle of the sand bar deposited by the flood, he stuck his rod down. " 'Dig right here,' he commanded. His followers, never doubting, set to work, and upon removing a few feet of sand, lo and behold, there were revealed the buried millstones. Wight said he saw them in a vision and his followers believed it."

With the recovered stones in place, the Mormons increased their grinding activities and added a sawmill and turning lathes, with which they manufactured chairs, tables, and all other manner of furniture, supplying the whole countryside. Most of their furniture was made from hackberry wood, which being so white in color required frequent washing to preserve its purity.

Smithwick told another story about this furniture. "One lady in Burnet, to obviate the necessity of such frequent cleaning, concluded to paint her chairs; that was before the days of chemical paint. We bought the pigment and reduced it with linseed oil. This lady, having no oil, and arguing that oil was oil and so was butter, during the summer, mixed her paint with butter and applied the combination to her chairs; the effect can be better imagined than described."

In addition to the furniture business, they operated a farm and the women made willow baskets for sale. But in spite of their industrious habits and frugal living, the Saints fell deeper into debt. In addition, they were plagued by Indian raids. Several times their horses and oxen were stolen and their milk cows were killed. Members of nearby families were slain or kidnapped. Disease also plagued the colony. Wight did his best to stem its tide through the performing of "miracles," but in spite of his best efforts, 23 of the faithful ended up buried along the ridge half a mile downstream from the mill. Smithwick told of one of Wight's healing sessions, as described to him by an eyewitness: "A boy fell from a tree and broke his leg. He was taken to the council chamber and the elder and his council were summoned. They laid their hands upon the broken limb and prayed; the boy then arose and walked. When the narrator had finished . . . I looked him searchingly in the face and said:

"'Did you feel of that leg and satisfy yourself that it was really broken?'

" 'No, I didn't; but "the twelve" did and they said it was broken,' he replied, with an air of wonder that any one should have the audacity to question a verdict rendered by such an authority.

"'I'm glad you didn't,' said I, 'for if you had told me that you yourself felt of that boy's leg and found it broken, I should never believe another word you speak.'

"The poor dupe looked as if thunderstruck. I was not so much surprised at him, but there were some really intelligent men among them, and it was a mystery to me how they could lend themselves to such a course, when there was so little to be gained by it."

By the late fall of 1853 the faithful were on the move again. Wight had never completed his transaction with the land's owner, W. H. Magill, and so the site was sold to Noah Smithwick, who confessed to "having all my life had a penchant for mills." While a youth, Smithwick became fascinated with windmills and whirligigs and constructed a creek-driven circular saw that he used to turn out considerable quantities of cornstalk lumber.

Smithwick described his newly acquired mill, which stood "just at the foot of the falls on the east [bank, the roadside bank you are just a stone's throw from], a three-story frame building, with which it was connected by a gangway. A patriarchal pecan tree lifted its stately head beside the building, caressing it with its slender branches. On the upper side, connected with the falls by a flume, rose the huge overshot wheel, twenty-six feet in diameter, which furnished the power for the mill. The machinery was mostly of the rudest, clumsiest kind, manufactured by the Mormons of such material as was obtainable from natural sources. Great, clumsy, rattling wooden cog wheels and drum and fly-wheels filled up the lower stories, the upper one containing a small corn crackermill and an old up-and-down sash saw, which, after all, had this advantage over the circular saw, that it could handle large timber."

Smithwick and nephew John Hubbard decided to throw out the sawmill, since there was no good milling timber in the vicinity. Then they reorganized the machinery, throwing out all the old wooden cog work and replacing it with cast-iron gearings, a ton's worth. While they were at it, they replaced the overshot wheel with another that was 28 feet in diameter! And as Smithwick related, "We then put in a new set of burrs and added bolting works, the first flouring mill west of Georgetown. This gave a new direction to the farming interest, and soon the rattle of the [wheat] threshing machine was heard in the land, and the reign of the corn-dodger [corn pone] was over in those parts. People came from all points to have their grain ground, and the capacity of the mill being very limited, sometimes when the mill was crowded they had to wait several days for their turn. Those who lived at a distance, many of them thirty or forty miles, struck camp and stayed it out. The Germans came from Fredericksburg. Like other German colonists, they had a hard scramble for the first few years, their crops failing, and for want of a knowledge of the use of firearms they were unable to utilize the game. Many of them gave away their children to keep them from starving."

Farmers waiting for their grain to be milled were not the only visitors to the Mormon Mills while it was under Smithwick's ownership. Political candidates in the election of 1854 managed to penetrate the dense cedar brakes surrounding the mill, as did Gail Borden of condensed milk fame (see Central Texas Stew—Borden), who Smithwick had known in San Felipe de Austin back in the 1820s when Borden was just a blacksmith. Lately, Borden had been to Europe in the interest of condensed milk, and had also taken up the practice of homeopathic medicine and begun prefixing his name with the title "Dr." But Borden's business in Burnet County had to do with gold. He owned land located on Sandy Creek and gold particles had been found in the creek, which had the good "doctor" excited and dreaming of vast wealth. But the gold mines didn't pan out. Ditto for the old Spanish silver mines located nearby (see Hermit of the Hills—Click Community).

While visiting Smithwick, Bordon imparted to him the great secret of his school of medicine as he understood it. Said Borden: "It is no use to be a doctor unless you put on the airs of one. Nine times out of ten sickness is caused by overeating or eating unwholesome food, but a patient gets angry if you tell him so; you must humor him. This I do by taking one grain of calomel [a purgative] and divide it into infinitesimel parts, adding sufficient starch to each part to make one of those little pellets (exhibiting a little vial of tiny white pills), then glaze them over with sugar. In prescribing for a patient I caution him about his diet, warning him that the pills have calomel in them. Well, the result is that he abstains from hurtful articles of food, which is all he needs to do anyway. But I have strong medicine to use in cases of need." Sounds like good advice today.

Smithwick moved in 1855 to the community that now bears his name, after building a rock store here at Mormon Mills. The mill was demolished in 1902; the wooden mill dam that turned the creek toward the flume burned the same year. The last of the old Mormon buildings burned in 1915. In 1935 the landowners sold the stone walls and chimney from Smithwick's store to the Daughters of the Republic of Texas, who used the stones to build a cabin in Houston's Hermann Park.

The placidly flowing creek we see here most of the time turns occasionally into a beast. Hamilton Creek drains quite a scope of country, and when swollen by heavy rains, the runoff becomes congested within the narrow gorge above the falls. The creek then rises rapidly, coming down in a solid wall of water that pours over the falls like a little Niagara. Smithwick related, "I have often seen the creek, which is ordinarily a trivial stream, become a torrent within a few minutes. On one occasion a party of sightseers had a narrow escape. Having wended their way up into the gorge, along the margin of the shallow stream, they were startled by a roar above them, and the guide being acquainted with the vagaries of the stream, ordered them to climb for their lives. Laying hold of the bushes in the face of the steep declivity, they scrambled up out of harm's way and watched the angry flood of waters rush past and leap the falls with a report like thunder, sending up clouds of spray."

But back to the Mormons. A few of them stayed with Smithwick at the mill, the rest moved on. Before we resume our retracing of their wanderings, let us listen to Smithwick's estimation of the Mormons. "I found them just the same as other people in matters of business. While some of them were honest and industrious, others were shiftless and unreliable; and this must ever prove a potent argument against community holdings—the thriftless got just as much as the thrifty. But though the industrious saint was still forced to contribute to the support of his idle brother, he drew the line to exclude the worthless dog that is generally considered an indispensable adjunct to thriftlessness, the canine family being conspicuous by its absence about the domicile of the Mormon. Nor was there anything objectionable in the Mormons as neighbors. If there were any polygamous families, I did not know of them. To still further emphasize the perfect equality of all members of the society, all titles of respect were discarded, men and women being universally called by their first names. And these first names, by the way, were perhaps the most striking peculiarity about the Mormons. The proselytes were permitted to retain their gentile names, but those born in the fold received their names from the Book of Mormon; and have no counterpart elsewhere. There were Abinadi, Maroni, Luami, Lamoni, Romali, Cornoman and many others equally original. The female children, however, were apparently not permitted to participate in this saintly nomenclature. It might be that women cut no figure in the Book of Mormon; at any rate, there was nothing distinctive in the names of girls."

So, the Mormons were on the trail again. For your part, return to Marble Falls and take FM 1431 west to Kingsland.

One last story as you leave Marble Falls. About 4 miles south of Marble Falls, on the old wagon road to Smithwick, is the infamous Dead Man's Hole—a 160-foot-deep cavern into which many a poor unfortunate's body was dumped during the Civil War, victim of the bushwhackers. Bushwhackers were a loose assortment of antisecessionists, army deserters, draft dodgers, and low-lifes who used the war as an excuse to rob and kill anyone who crossed their path. Judge John R. Scott, robbed of $2,000 and thrown dead down the hole, was only one of many bushwhacker victims. In early years the cavern contained some type of deadly gas, which prevented its exploration. A few years after the war, however, an expedition successfully reached the bottom of Dead Man's Hole and brought up two sacks full of bones, of the human variety.

GRANITE MOUNTAIN
FM 1431, about 0.5 mile west of Marble Falls

Just west of Marble Falls you pass the Granite Mountain, home of the state capitol building's granite. Indians swapped the rock to its first white owners for a couple of acres elsewhere. To cut down on building costs, capitol contractors arranged for the use of convict labor at the quarry. Organized labor objected, so the contractors sent to Scotland for stonecutters. Over 15,000 railroad carloads of granite went into the walls and dome of the capitol. Early owner G. W. Lacy once tried to trade this mountain of granite for a good saddle horse. He got no takers. That was B.C. (before the capitol). In 1890 he sold out for $90,000. Granite Mountain has furnished stone for buildings, monuments, the Galveston seawall, and other projects all over the state, the nation, and the world, yet the great dome looks barely disturbed. There are centuries worth of granite left here in the largest quarry of its kind in the United States.

KINGSLAND ARCHEOLOGICAL SITE
Burnet County Rd. 126, off FM 1431 • 915-388-3752
Guided tours on Sunday afternoon and by appointment
This 10-acre wooded site on Lake LBJ is the only public archeological site on the Colorado River and is administered by the Llano Uplift Archeological Society. Humans have inhabited this site for at least 10,000 years. It was discovered in 1988 when vandals were nabbed stealing artifacts, and is now a state archeological landmark. Excavations have since turned up over 100,000 artifacts, including knapped stone tools, grinding stones, and bone fragments. The museum/education center displays prehistoric artifacts, a field-school excavation site is on display, and an outdoor trail goes through nomadic campsites that date back at least 5,000 years. There are restrooms and picnicking facilities.
Write to P.O. Box 302, Kingsland 78639.

KINGSLAND

Llano County • 2,835 • About 13 miles from Marble Falls
Kingsland was first known as Kingsville, and was named for Martin King, who bought this tract of land in 1877. By the 1880s a store had been established here, along with a couple of saloons. In that decade a great business rivalry developed between Kingsville and Buzzard Roost (aka Gainsville), located across the river and several miles northwest. Buzzard Roost had a post office, gin, and store. The rivalry between the towns was resolved in favor of Kingsville when Kingsville merchant J. F. Banks bought the Buzzard Roost gin and store and moved them to Kingsville.
Prosperity really caught up with Kingsville in 1892, when the Burnet-to-Llano branch of the Austin and Northwestern railroad came through town. J. F. Banks built a commodious stone store near the depot that same year. The town's name was changed to Kingsland some time between 1892 and 1901; the post office already had a Kingsville in Kleberg County in South Texas. Kingsland became a hog-and-cattle shipping center with the railroad's arrival. Located at the confluence of the Llano and Colorado Rivers, this area has long been a popular fishing spot. The Austin and Northwestern began run-

ning excursion trains out here soon after the tracks were laid. Governor Hogg was among the avid anglers who made the trip out from Austin. In 1901, the Austin and Northwestern built a resort hotel here: the Antlers Hotel, named for the Antlers Hotel in Colorado Springs, Colorado.

THE ANTLERS HOTEL
Just off FM 1431 • Private residence

Kingsland went into something of an eclipse until Highland Lakes tourists gave it a new shot of life several decades ago. Kingsland now relies on tourists, retirees, and its many second-home-owners for business. But the railroad across the lake with its pink granite pillars still stands.

Situated beside the railroad tracks on the shores of the Colorado River, the Antlers was the area entertainment focal point, where families from across the state came to vacation and local families came to picnic along the river. After a while, ownership of the hotel changed hands. It is now a private residence, and about all that remains of old Kingsland. It is located on your right, just after you cross the railroad tracks on the western edge of Kingsland, a frame two-story affair, with twin front porches running the length of its front.

THE SLAB
At the end of FM 3404, about 1.5 miles west of FM 1431
Open daily • Free • W

FM 3404 crosses the Llano River about 8 miles above its junction with the Colorado and peters into an unimproved county road. At this point, the Llano runs over (and through) granite outcroppings and wide sandy beaches. This is a popular picnicking, swimming, and wading area. There are no restrooms or drinking water.

ANNUAL EVENT

JULY • Aqua-Boom Celebration • 388-6211 (Kingsland/Lake LBJ Chamber of Commerce) • Weekend nearest July 4

The celebration includes ski shows, water parade, boat races, and fireworks.

Turn left on FM 2900 in Kingsland and cross the Llano River branch of the lake. Once across the bridge, take the first right (Cty. Rd. 309), a few feet past Lakewood Forest Subdivision and Comanche Rancheros.

This road west from FM 2900 turns to gravel after a bit but offers a great close-up view of Packsaddle Mountain as you skirt its edges, after about 6 miles on the road. Packsaddle has a plethora of violent and romantic legends and stories surrounding it; these stories are told in the Hermit of the Hills trip.

SILVER PEAK
Cty. Rd. 309, near SH 71 • 915-388-0268 • Open daily, weather permitting, but by reservation only
You can visit old silver and gold mines dating to the 1700s and see the site of the Battle of Packsaddle Mountain between Anglo settlers and Indian warriors in 1873, if you're willing and able to hike a mile or two or three. Hiking ranges from easy to hard. Wear appropriate shoes and bring water. Write to Paydirt Adventures, P.O. Box 1913, Kingsland, TX 78639.

Turn right onto SH 71 and head toward Llano.

Shortly thereafter you cross Honey Creek, on the banks of which the Mormons camped on December 4, 1853, before resuming their journey toward the old German settlement at Castell. The road to Buzzard Roost/Gainsville, about 4 miles north of the Honey Creek Crossing and running east off SH 71, is marked only by a three-way intersection sign. Nothing is left at the old town site.

LLANO

Llano County Seat • 3,012 • (915) • About 21 miles from Kingsland
Llano, which is (and always has been) the seat of government of Llano County, was founded in 1855. Several other settlements, including Castell, Tow, and Bluffton, had already been founded in the area. Among the first settlers of Llano were John Oatman, Sr., and Amariah Wilson. Indians still raided the countryside, and in that first year the Llano pioneers lost their clothes to the raiders.

Llano County was part of the vast Fisher-Miller tract, which was to have been settled by Adelsverein colonists (see Central Texas Stew—Shelby). That tract extended northward into San Saba,

Menard, and other counties. Castell, which was as far north as the first wave of Germans got, was on the southern edge of this tract.

Llano County was created from parts of Bexar and Gillespie counties in 1856 and was named for the river that courses through it from west to east. Llano means "plains" in Spanish; although Llano County is ruggedly hilly, the Llano River rises in the flatland counties of Sutton and Schleicher. One explanation lies in an old (1711) Spanish name for the river, "Rio de las Chanas," or River of the Chanas. The Chanas were a band of Tonkawa Indians that lived in the area. In 1754, the Spanish explorer Pedro de Rabago y Teran identified the river on his map of Texas as the "Sanas" River. "Sano" means "healthy" in Spanish, "sanas" would mean two or more healthy females. Over the years, the local explanation goes, the phonetic similarity between "chanas" and "llano" caused confusion and led to the present name, Llano. As was often the case, the location of the new county seat was hotly contested. Clement Oatman was appointed commissioner of the new county, and as such was charged with holding an election to establish the county seat and to elect the first county officials. The contest narrowed to two sites: the present-day town of Llano built on land donated by John Oatman, Sr., and Amariah Wilson; and a site on Wright Creek north of Llano that was advocated by Uncle Dave Cowan and the Tow Valley/Bluffton crowd, who wouldn't have to cross the Llano River to get to the courthouse. The Llano River was not always easy to cross. Clement Oatman decreed that the county seat election be held under a live oak tree on the south side of the river (near the south end of the SH 16/SH 71 bridge over the river) on June 14, 1856.

On the morning of the election, Oatman sent a boy down to the river to draw a bucket of water so that the thirsty arriving voters could refresh themselves. When Cowan and the Tow Valley-Bluffton crowd arrived, they were thirsty and sampled the bucket of water from the Llano. After tasting it very deliberately, Cowan said, "Boys, boys, it won't do to have our county seat here for this water is unhealthy, there are bugs in it." Whereupon he walked to his horse, rummaged about in his saddlebags, pulled out a quart of moonshine, and poured it into the bucket of water so as to "kill the bugs."

Theatrics notwithstanding, the Wright Creek faction lost the election and the county seat ended up here on the river, which was probably just as well. In 1856 Wright Creek was a bold stream considered to be always able to supply a good-sized town. Now it only flows during the rainy season. Llano finally erected a bridge across the river for the convenience of south-bound travelers (the courthouse is

located on the south side of the river), but it has not even been needed on two recent occasions; the Llano River ran bone-dry in 1952
and 1956.

By 1860 Llano had stores, a hotel, and plenty of saloons, but no
churches. In 1861, Llano County approved the Texas Ordinance of
Secession by 65 percent, one of the largest percentages on the frontier. With the Civil War, Indian attacks increased. Three Confederate
Army companies were raised in the county; so many of the men were
away fighting, leaving many farms as easy targets for the Comanches. A home guard was formed to protect the county, but the Indians
raged through the county until the decisive battle atop Packsaddle
Mountain in 1873.

You would not expect a county known as the "Colorado of Texas"
to be heavily farmed, and Llano County has never had more than 20
percent of its 941-square-mile area in cultivation. Llano County residents have traditionally been stockraisers, and many of the ranchers,
such as the Moss brothers (see Hermit of the Hills—Oxford), drove
thousands of steers north during the great cattle-drive era. Llano was
at the edge of the frontier until 1875.

As was typical with Texas frontier towns and counties, Llano the
city and Llano the county both had their share of banditry and
rustling and feuding. But life here was not as cheap as it was in
neighboring Mason County, home of the infamous "Hoodoo War," a
cattle feud between German-American and Anglo ranchers. Many
early Llano County records were destroyed in the courthouse fire of
1892. But we do know that Llano County ranchers had their share of
cattle rustlers to contend with, and that between 50 and 100 Llano,
Burnet, and San Saba ranchers banded together in a vigilante group
to kill the rustlers and otherwise rid their country of outlaws.

The town of Llano did not have an honest-to-God church building
until 1885. Prior to that year, services were held in private homes or
in the local schoolhouse. Many of the town's young men and boys
enlivened their Sundays by disrupting the worship services of the
faithful. Owing to the disorganized state of organized religion on the
frontier, God's children in Llano were administered to by an ever-
changing assortment of circuit-riding preachers. One Sunday the
Reverend James Moore, a real frontiersman, came to preach. He
entered the schoolroom, which had turned sanctuary for the day, with
his saddlebags in one hand and his long-barreled Winchester rifle in
the other. Drawing his Bible from his saddlebags and setting his rifle
on the table-turned-altar, Moore gazed over the crowd calmly and

announced, "By the grace of God and Winchester there will be no disturbance to the services today."

Llano remained a dusty, rough-edged cow town until 1886, when the Wakefield Iron and Coal Company of Minneapolis came to town in a big way. Prospecting trips had revealed large deposits of magnetic iron ores scattered across the county, the largest concentration of which was located at Smoothingiron Mountain, about 15 miles northwest of Llano as the crow flies. The Wakefield Company and other eastern capitalists who came in on Wakefield's coattails had dreams of making Llano the Birmingham of Texas. Over $300,000 was spent buying up area mineral leases—a considerable amount of money back then, when land sold for mere dollars rather than thousands of dollars an acre.

The many northern and eastern capitalists who came to Llano brought a brand-new snobbish, ostentatious social life with them. The famous Algona hotel was built early in the boom, and it was the hub of the new social lifestyle for Llano and Central Texas. Countless fancy balls, dinners, and parties were held in the grand ballrooms and dining rooms. Of the Algona's 80 rooms, 50 were bedrooms. Built of red brick on the north side of the river, the Algona was named for its builder's hometown of Algona, Iowa. Typical of the vast and rapid changes wrought in Llano by big money, this grand edifice replaced a spread of muddy cattle pens. Most of the stone and brick buildings in downtown Llano were built during this boom era, replacing the more vulnerable wooden structures. The Llano Improvement and Furnace Company was organized to promote the north bank of the Llano River. The company plotted out a large tract of land there with plenty of parks and green space. Lots sold to speculators at highly inflated prices. Some of the streets were given steel-related names: Bessemer, Pittsburg, Sheffield, Birmingham.

The town was full of hope and optimism. Smoothingiron Mountain was celebrated as "bearing the richest grade of magnetic ore to be found in the world." Then, of course, there was Barringer Hill— the greatest field of rare minerals to be found anyplace in the world—located east of Llano.

An iron mine, the Olive Mine, was opened about 10 miles east of town and actually shipped out a few carloads of ore, one to the state prison's foundry at Rusk and the others to Birmingham, Alabama. The mine had a fat-enough payroll during its few years of operation to attract the attention of one bandit, who ambushed the mine's manager as he was driving the payroll wagon from town back out to the mine. The highwayman killed the manager, Captain Thomas Dunn, and made off with the loot.

Llano's once-great granite industry began during the boom, in 1888, when J. K. Finlay polished his first piece of Llano granite. It remained a local commodity until the railroad came in 1892 and loads of granite began to be shipped out across the country.

The railroad was greeted with great excitement as the next step toward making Llano the iron-and-steel capital of the Southwest. The line was a 29-mile-long extension of the Austin and Northwestern railroad from Fairland, which is located between Marble Falls and Burnet. The town was even more excited by the proposed San Antonio and Aransas Pass railroad spur, which was to run from Comfort through Fredericksburg up to Llano. Grading was started from both Llano and Fredericksburg, but the project went bust when Llano citizens couldn't scrape up the money to pay for the first 10 miles of grading and the railroad company couldn't put together enough money to go over or bypass the Great Divide, which is the range of high hills south of Fredericksburg that separate the Pedernales and Guadalupe watersheds.

The iron boom went bust in 1894. You can't make steel without coal, and there was no coal to be found in Llano County or anywhere near it. Carrying it in cost too much. So the big capitalists left town. The Algona closed, the Llano Improvement and Furnace Company went bankrupt, and the Olive Mine shut down. Fires destroyed most of the northside boom buildings, and Llano town, incorporated in 1892, disincorporated in 1895, not to reincorporate for many years. A tornado in 1900 did further damage.

With the steel boom gone bust, the granite industry took up some of the industrial slack. By 1920, Llano had 6 granite quarries and 1 marble works, sending out at least 13 different varieties of granite. 'Twas said of Llano's granite supply that it was "the best and largest deposit of grey granite to be found in the U.S., not excepting the well-known deposits of Massachusetts and Vermont." The granite industry here peaked in 1935, at 10 quarries and 5 finishing plants. But increased rail shipping rates made it cheaper for many customers to use out-of-state granite, so the number of quarries declined, although commercially usable granite remains here in almost limitless quantities.

But even with the capitalists gone, tireless Llanoans continued to push their county as a metallurgical nirvana, where gold, silver, iron ore, serpentine, manganese, graphite, and all manner of rare and precious minerals awaited exploitation, so easily accessible that they would practically jump into their captors' hands.

One of the most energetic proselytizers was N. J. Badu, born in Nancy, France. Badu came to the United States via Mexico, where he had helped build that country's first railroad. In the United States, Badu first went to New Orleans, then to Paris, Texas, where he taught French and married an American, Miss Charlie Neal. A geologist for most of his life, Badu moved to Llano after hearing about its mineral wealth for two years in Paris. The "Prof," as everyone called Badu, managed the Algona Hotel for most of its short life, and later managed Austin's famous Driskill Hotel, while still maintaining a permanent residence in Llano.

In Llano, Badu set up a laboratory, identifying many rare minerals found on prospecting trips. He also operated a manganese mine for several years. Geologists, miners, and capitalists from Washington, New York, and other centers of wealth and power came to visit Badu and to investigate the possibilities of tapping this potential great wealth, but the visits always ended on the same note: a polite no-thank-you, based on the insufficient transportation facilities and power sources to support profitable mining operations. Badu sent mineral samples and displays to expositions and universities all over the country, but died with his dream unfulfilled in 1936. Funeral services were held in the Badu House, and his obituary read in part: "It was more than a citizen that has passed. A landmark had crumbled into dust."

Promoters also touted Llano as a sort of second Eden, to wit: "Lying hidden and protected from the hot, scorching winds of the plains, raised above the malarial infected district of the East, where the nights are too cool for the mosquitos to thrive, where the plagues of Egypt are unknown, where nature has done more to promote the health, wealth, happiness, and prosperity of mankind than any other spot in the great Empire of the Lone Star State, we find Llano.

"The altitude, together with the pure mountain breezes, causes the ruddy glow of health and youth to shine upon the cheeks of him who is so fortunate as to dwell therein. No healthier or prettier spot could be found anywhere.

"The death rate of the county is lower in proportion to the population than any county in the State of Texas. Men of fifty and sixty are sprightly and walk with alacrity and have the same vigor and healthy appearance as the men and women who live at the altitude of Waco, Dallas and in Houston too, at the age of eighteen and twenty-two. So much for the health of the country."

The census bureau has at least partially confirmed these extravagant turn-of-the-century claims, recently rating Llano as the second
healthiest town in the United States.

Llano is still basically a sleepy town except during deer season.
But this may change during the next decade, as Austin's tidal wave
growth laps out west toward Llano.

Turn right on SH 16 from SH 71 to enter Llano.

The historical marker at the SH 71/SH 16 intersection is dedicated
to the local granite industry and reads: "Llano County Granite Quarry
(Original Quarry 6 mi. west). A major source of American building
granite. First stone polished 1888 by J. K. Finlay, using water wheel.
First quarry opened 1890 on David Stewart land. Frank Teich
(1856–1939), famous Texas sculptor, worked here in Llano granite.
Largest stone quarried (40 tons) is base for statue of a Terry's Texas
Ranger, at State Capitol."

*SH 16/SH 71 becomes Ford St. within the city limits. A few blocks
south of the Llano River, you come to the courthouse square and
main business district.*

LLANO COUNTY COURTHOUSE
Ford at Main

A block for the courthouse was laid out and noted on the town plat
soon after the county was organized in 1856, but it was a long time
before a courthouse was actually built. The original building completed in 1885 served Llano well until it was destroyed by fire on January
22, 1892. Built of tan-colored brick with pink granite columns and
trim, it is one of three original Texas courthouses unmarred by subsequent additions or remodeling. It was completed in 1893 at a cost of
$35,000. Under the granite boulders on the west side of the structure
is a time capsule to be opened in 2056, Llano's Bicentennial. Of the
288 county courthouses in Texas, only 66 built prior to 1900 remain.
Llano's is the 39th oldest in Texas. Photos of old Llano are inside. On
the grounds are several statues and monuments.

The Confederate Monument is dedicated to Texans who served in
the Civil War. It was sculptured and erected by James K. Finley &
Sons. The two sons used their father as the model. Governor James
E. Ferguson dedicated the imposing work in 1916.

Dedicated on Veterans Day, November 11, 1987, the Vietnam Monument to veterans of that war was donated by Llano's American Legion Post No. 370 and the Auxiliary.

"Charging Over the Top" is a bronze World War I monument sculptured by Frank Teich, a nationally famous artist who owned the nearby town of Teichville. Governor Dan Moody dedicated the monument in 1928.

Anchoring the corner of Ford St. and Main, at the northeast corner of the courthouse square, is the "Haynie Block."

THE HAYNIE BLOCK
101 W. Main at Ford

This grand (for Llano) two-story commercial building, which fronts on Main St. and stretches north for most of a block on Ford St., was designed by prominent Austin architect A. O. Watson for Elizabeth Haynie of Llano in 1882. The first telephone switchboard in Llano was located here in the 1880s. This building, which has a series of storefronts on Ford St., has housed professionals and merchants as well as a bank for 30 years. During the 1940s, the county hospital occupied the entire second floor.

Despite their appearance, the next three one-story buildings west of the Haynie Block (103–105 W. Main) are believed to be among the oldest on the courthouse square, perhaps dating to the late 1870s. The current brown-brick facades were tacked on to the stone buildings decades later.

ACME DRY GOODS COMPANY
109 W. Main • 247-4457 • Open Monday through Saturday • W

One of downtown Llano's oldest businesses is Acme Dry Goods. The porch awning outside still sports its decorative, pressed tin ceiling; the display window still bears the company name written in the original elegant handpainted script. Walk in and you see modern apparel displayed for sale in a turn-of-the-century setting: shirts and blouses stacked in old wood-and-glass cases; boxes and boxes of shoes stacked on high shelves that are reached via the ceiling ladder that runs on rails the length of the wall-long shelves; the beaded ceiling; a 100-year-old brass cash register; the turn-of-the-century "Pessels Co." safe. The place was the Pessels Company until 1910. This building was constructed of red brick in 1892. The Acme has been in the building since 1923. Acme Dry Goods is one of the three oldest businesses in Llano still operating under the same name.

OLD COMMERCIAL BUILDING
115 W. Main

Directly west of the old Lan-Tex Theater, erected in 1880, this plain, two-story brick commercial building is one of the earliest surviving unaltered structures on the town square. It has been used as a meeting site for the Llano Masonic Lodge, and the back section of the cellar was used as a jail. For a while it housed Pessels mercantile store, then J. Duff Brown's drug store. A furniture store and undertaking business occupied this building until 1894. It has also served as the Martin Telephone Company, a hardware store, confectionery store, millinery shop, grocery store, and as an annex for the Southern Hotel's overflow.

SOUTHERN HOTEL
201 W. Main at Berry • Currently houses Buttery Hardware offices

J. W. Owen built the first two stories of this structure about 1880; the third story was added during the ownership of Colonel W. A. II. Miller, a lawyer who bought the establishment in 1883.

The wide porches were a welcome resting spot for the hotel's many guests. It also served as a stagecoach stop. It was later operated as the Colonial Inn before closing in the 1950s. The old hotel was saved from the wrecking ball by the Buttery Hardware Company, which restored and remodeled the place for use as its offices. Buttery Hardware is one of the three oldest businesses in Llano still operating under the same name.

OLD ICE HOUSE
Berry St., 1 block north of the Southern Hotel, on the bank on the Llano River

In 1904, A. J. Zilker of Austin (for whom the famous Austin park is named) built this ice house and accompanying water-powered mill race to generate electricity for Llano. The smokestack was added later and never used.

THE LLANO NEWS BUILDING
813 Berry, on the west side of the courthouse square

Another plain, brick, essentially unaltered commercial building dating to 1890, this one originally housed the Bon Ton Barber & Bath. It provided the only commercial bath facilities in town.

MASONIC TEMPLE
832 Ford at Sandstone • Cassandra's Antiques

This interesting stone building at the southeast corner of the courthouse square was built in 1907 as the Masonic Temple. The lodge was organized in 1860 and the temple still meets on the second floor. They get up there in an old hand-cranked elevator.

CHARLIE'S STORE
800 block Ford St., on the east side of the courthouse square

Charlie's Store stretches through a series of old storefronts in the 800 block of Ford. This series of buildings dates back to 1880. The large two-story building in mid-block, constructed in 1890, first held a saddle and harness shop, followed by a dry goods store, a saloon, a drugstore, and the Tourist's Hotel. The building at the corner of Ford and Main (built by J. K. Finley) housed a dry goods business until 1908, and was then occupied by Llano National Bank.

To get to the old Llano County Jail, go east on Main Street from the courthouse square.

CORNER DRUG STORE
101 E. Main

Although several architectural changes have been made, this site has operated as the Corner Drug since 1898. It is one of the three oldest businesses in Llano still operating under the same name.

OLD MASONIC LODGE
102 E. Main, just east of the courthouse square

The building was constructed for F. J. Smith and Company as a storage facility in 1883 and is one of the oldest buildings in downtown Llano. Beginning in 1887, the Masons used the second story as their lodge for 21 years.

Turn left on Oatman St. from E. Main St., 1 block after Ford St.

LLANO COUNTY JAIL
Oatman and Haynie • Open on a limited basis

A block east of downtown stands the old Llano County Jail, built in 1895 by the Pauly Jail Building and Manufacturing Company of St. Louis. The gray granite was locally quarried and the red roof of this Romanesque Revival hoosegow earned the jail its nickname, "Old Red

Top." The first floor housed the jailer's office and living quarters. The second floor housed four cells and two drunk tanks. The third and fourth floors housed the gallows, which are still in place.

From the jail, return to Main St. and continue east on Main, past the Fraser House.

FRASER HOUSE
207 E. Main • 247-5183 • B&B Inn
Located in the same block as the "Red Top," the Fraser House was built in 1903 by William Fraser for his new wife Laura. He was one of the master stonecutters brought to Texas from Scotland to complete construction of the state capitol building in Austin. He came to Llano after the granite capitol was finished and he never left. This simply styled two-story granite blockhouse would be perfectly at home on a rugged Scottish moor. The building has been renovated and now houses a bed-and-breakfast.

Return to Oatman St. and continue south on Oatman to Luce St.

HOLTZER HOUSE
107 E. Luce
A few feet west of the Oatman/Luce intersection is the one-story frame house built just before the turn of the century by H. A. Holtzer. Holtzer was a saddlemaker who lived here from 1896 through the 1920s. The gingerbread woodwork and ornate fireplace inside are original to the house.

Continue south on Oatman another 2 blocks to the intersection of Oatman and Brown.

GRACE EPISCOPAL CHURCH
1200 Oatman
Built in 1881 to house the Llano Academy, this simple one-story Gothic building made of locally quarried sandstone was purchased in 1883 by the Episcopal Church's West Texas Missionary District, after the Academy failed. It was the first building in Llano to receive a state historical marker.

Continue south another 2 blocks on Oatman to the corner of Oatman and College. To see the O. Henry School, you will have to walk another half block down Oatman; it becomes a one-way street going north here. Or, you can drive one block west to Ford/SH 16, turn left on Ford and continue 2 blocks, turn left on Lampasas, then left on Oatman, and you can drive right past the school.

O. HENRY JUNIOR HIGH SCHOOL
1400 Oatman, at Ollie

The original section of this two-story school house was completed in 1887 to serve Llano school children south of the river. Built of native sandstone and timber, it was known locally as "the college building" because of its stately style. The northside addition of locally quarried grey granite (with pink granite trim) was completed in 1902. It housed all grades until 1925 when a separate high school building was constructed.

From O. Henry School, return to Ford St. (one block west) and proceed north across the river. Ford St. becomes Bessemer Ave. across the river.

The last block of buildings to your left on Ford just before you cross the river looks almost exactly the way it did 90 years ago, down to the sidewalks out front.

LLANO COUNTY LIBRARY
900 block Ford St., just before you cross the river • 247-5248

The three plain brick one-story buildings that make up the library were built in 1904. They have housed a variety of businesses, including Hargon Furniture, Lange Furniture, Goodman Liquor Company, Southern Mercantile (1908), Pessell's Dry Goods, Hackworth's Variety, C. Bailey's Domino Hall, S. Roundtree's Palace Bar (1916), a Studebaker agency (1920s), as well as pool halls and cafes. Doll collectors will enjoy the collection of dolls from all over the world.

The **Llano River,** which flows so peacefully most of the year, goes into a fit of rage every so often. Perhaps the worst rampage occurred in 1935, when the raging waters swept the highway bridge away.

LLANO COUNTY MUSEUM
310 Bessemer/SH 16 • 247-3026 • June through August: closed Monday, open Tuesday through Sunday 10–noon, 1:30–5:30; September through May, open Friday through Sunday 1:15–5:15 Free • W

Immediately across the bridge and on your right is the Llano County Museum, located in the buff-colored stucco old Bruhl's Drug Store. Here you'll find many items from Llano County's past on display as well as a large collection of photos and clippings. You'll see pictures of the great flood of '35 sweeping the bridge away and of the Lone Star Brewing Company, established here in 1892.

You'll also learn the fate of the magnificent Algona Hotel. Vacant from 1894 to 1898 in the wake of the mineral boom's demise, the Algona was acquired by the Texas Military Institute in 1898. Two years later the Algona was sold to Mr. and Mrs. Ernst Marschall, who reopened it as a hotel. They sold it in 1907. From 1907 to 1910 it was known as the Franklin Hotel, and from 1910 to 1923 it was the Don Carlos Hotel. The block-sized hotel burned on February 11, 1923.

Probably the most interesting and once-controversial article in the museum is the "self-fitting eye-testing machine" that A. J. Bruhl kept in his drugstore. The machine was declared illegal in 1928 by the Texas legislature, and Bruhl was tried and convicted when he refused to retire the machine. The case was appealed and the law was declared unconstitutional. Bruhl reinstalled his machine and it was used until the drugstore closed in 1957.

Another exhibit is devoted to the game of polo and one of polo's greatest players, Cecil Smith of Llano. Indian artifacts from the area, as well as rocks and gems, are also on display.

THE FILLING STATION
502 Bessemer
Built in the early 1920s as a Texaco station, this ex-gas station was famous at the time as the only covered gas station between here and San Antonio.

FINE ARTS GUILD, INC.
503 Bessemer • Open daily • W
The Guild was founded in 1963 to promote the work of Llano artists. Works by members are on exhibit here at the Guild Gallery.

JEANNETTE'S HOMESTYLE BAKERY
501 Bessemer • 247-4564 • Open Tuesday through Saturday • W
This quaint little Mission Revival building was built in 1919 by T. Y. Hill to house the offices of his business, the Cassaday Grey Granite Company. The Cassaday Company was the first to use motor transportation for hauling granite. You can satisfy your sweet

tooth here with a variety of sweet rolls, pastries, cookies, cakes, pies, and breads.

LLANO COUNTY CHAMBER OF COMMERCE
700 Bessemer, 2 blocks south of SH 16/SH 29 intersection
247-5354 • Open Monday through Friday
Hunting lease information, free walking tour maps of Llano, and other local information.

LODGING

BADU HOUSE
601 Bessemer, at Tarrant • B&B Inn • 247-4304
This blocky, two-story Italian Renaissance structure executed in stucco, red brick, and gray granite was built about 1892 as the First National Bank of Llano. Professor Badu bought the place in 1898 at public auction after the bank failed. Located directly across the street from the old Algona Hotel block, the Badu House is the only boom-era building north of the river that survives. The Badu House has been a B&B for nearly 20 years now. Its 6 rooms and 1 suite contain boom-period furniture and fittings.

The pride of the Badu House is the Llanite bar. The bar top is inlaid with polished slabs of the rare (but commercially valueless) rock, the blue quartz crystals glowing in the dark brown feldspar. Professor Badu discovered Llanite, and it is not encountered outside Llano County.

DABBS HOTEL
112 E. Burnet, just off Bessemer on the north bank of the Llano
247-7905
Just a few doors east of the museum, the Dabbs Hotel is the last standing railroad hotel in Llano. It began operation in 1907 and was a home away from home for railroad crewmen, who stayed overnight and returned to Austin the next day. To travel any farther west, you had to go over to the Southern Hotel to catch a stagecoach. Loose, funky, congenial atmosphere. Swimming, fishing, gardens. Huge Southern-style breakfast.

BARBECUE CAPITAL OF TEXAS?
Although towns like Lockhart and Taylor would dispute Llano's claim to this coveted crown, Llano is at least their equal when it

comes to the quality of barbecue served here. There are at least four good places to chow down—three of which are within a rib-bone's throw of each other on SH 29 on the western outskirts of town, on the way to Mason.

BROTHER'S BBQ
405 W. Young/SH 29 • 247-5713 • Open Thursday through Tuesday, lunch and dinner • $ • No Cr. • W

Brother's cooks high-quality beef brisket, chicken, pork ribs, and sausage over mesquite coals and serves it with all the trimmings.

COOPER'S OLD TIME PIT BARBECUE
604 W. Young/SH 29 W • 247-5713 • Open daily • $ No Cr. • W

Brisket, chuck and club steaks, sausage, inch-thick pork chops, pork ribs, lamb, and cabrito are served. Beans and potato salad are also available. Mesquite wood is used exclusively. Pick your meat off the outside pits, then carry it inside to eat. Peel your own onions; white bread, jalapenos, and other condiments can be found on the long picnic tables. Cooper's cooks up more than 1,200 pounds of meat year-round, except during hunting season, when the pounds become tons. Friends whose opinions I respect have come back from Cooper's with less-than-glowing reports, but I have had no such bad luck. If you don't like what you see on the pit, go elsewhere, and remember, the later in the day you come, the less choice you'll have and the greater the chances for dried-out meat. Beer.

INMAN'S KITCHEN
809 W. Young/SH 29 W • 247-5257 • Open Monday through Thursday approximately 7–8, Friday and Saturday approximately 7–9. Closed Sunday, except during deer season when open approximately 7–4. • $ • No Cr. • W

Inman's strongest suit is its locally renowned turkey sausage, smoked turkey, ham, chicken, and jalapeño sausage. The beef brisket is OK, and it's all smoked over live oak coals. Beans, slaw, potato salad, honey-wheat and white bread, fresh apple, peach, pecan, and pumpkin pies (pies available according to the season) are all made on premises. Inman's is open at breakfast time but serves no breakfast food. Very popular during hunting season.

KENNETH LAIRD'S BAR-B-QUE
1404 Ford/SH 71 • 247-5234, 247-5339 • Open Wednesday through Sunday • $ • No Cr. • W

The late Tommy Laird won the 1978 World Barbecue Championship in Taylor and son Kenneth very ably carries the torch now, formerly at Cooper's, and now here at his self-named place. Brisket, sausage, pork chops, chicken, and ribs are slow smoked and served with all the trimmings.

MILLER'S MEATS
Sheffield St., 1 block east of Bessemer • 247-4450

The most interesting feature of this 1892 building is its chunky, granite pillar facade. Several businesses have been operated here over the years. In 1904 the Llano Club, a private club, did a booming business. Prior to World War II it housed the Coca-Cola Bottling Company. Since 1944 the building has housed a meat processing plant.

To continue the trail of the Mormons west, return to the courthouse square and take FM 152 west toward Castell.

ROBINSON PARK
**FM 152, about 2 miles west of the courthouse • 247-4457
Open daily • Free, except for golf course**

Just west of town on the Llano River is this city-owned park. Camping is allowed for no fee, but there is a 14-day limit. A 9-hole golf course, swimming pool, playground, and picnic facilities are here, as well as drinking water and restrooms. Fishing is often good in the river, but the river is too shallow for large boats. The adjacent RV campsites, community center, and rodeo grounds are operated by the Llano County Community Center.

As you leave town, one last bit of Llano trivia. All of us who have ever enjoyed the ease and convenience of an electric typewriter, and more recently the fancy newfangled PCs and word processors, owe some thanks to Llano County native J. Field Smothers, who invented the electric typewriter back in 1912.

THE DUTCH SETTLEMENTS

Leaving Llano on FM 152, you again pick up the wandering Mormons' path west, along the fertile valley of the Llano River, toward the "Dutch settlements" where they were to briefly encamp before turning sharply south toward their eventual home near Bandera. Although you seldom see the river for the next 18 miles, it is always there, just beyond the trees. The Dutch settlements were in fact the Adelsverein's final colonization attempts in Texas. Five projected communities were strung out for several miles along the north bank of the Llano River, which put the Adelsverein just inside the southernmost boundaries of the sprawling Fisher-Miller Grant. This toehold was as far as the Adelsverein would get in its grandiose empire-building scheme.

Despite its dubious claim to the grant land (by 1847 the Fisher-Miller Grant was void) the Adelsverein readied that year to make the final push into the 3-million-plus-acre tract. That land was mostly stone and seldom tillable, and the scanty rainfalls were often months apart. Extremely isolated, it was also a Comanche stronghold. Principal instigators behind the settlements were John Meusebach, Prince Carl of Solms-Braunfels, H. Spies, and Count Carl of Castell.

Schoenburg was the easternmost of these settlements, followed by Meerholz, Leiningen, Bettina, and Castell. The first two were stillborn. Castell, Bettina, and Leiningen made a run at life, but only Castell actually made it, and it is the only one of the Dutch settlements that exists today.

Bettina, the most controversial of these settlements, was composed of recruits from Darmstadt, Germany. Upon his return to Germany from New Braunfels in 1845, Prince Carl hit the university circuit to drum up enthusiasm for the Adelsverein's pretentious colonization project. He told students all over the German states that there was no demand in the old country for all the young professional men the German universities were turning out. They had to find a new and growing country where their services would be in demand. That place was Texas.

The most receptive ears belonged to the members of a fraternity of communistic freethinkers in Darmstadt known as Die Vierziger (the Forty). Prince Carl described Texas to them as "a land of milk and honey, of perennial flowers, of crystal streams, rich and fruitful beyond measures, where roamed myriads of deer and buffalo while the primeval forests abounded in wild fowl of every kind."

After listening to this farfetched spiel, the Forty decided to turn their pipe dreams of a communistic utopia into reality. Early in 1846, they formed the Darmstaedter Kolonie and began to plan apace their colony in Texas, which was to be based on the motto "Friendship, freedom, and equality" and the cardinal principle "Let everyone do as they please." They "had no regular scheme of government," Vierziger member Louis Reinhardt recalled years later. "In fact, being communistic, the association would not brook the tyranny of a ruler. Instead there were guiding spirits by common consent. Being the youngest of the company—I was thirteen—I was, of course, rarely consulted."

The Forty collectively made a contract with the Adelsverein to settle themselves and 200 other families within the boundaries of the Fisher-Miller Grant. In return, they would receive $12,000 or the equivalent in livestock, tools, agricultural implements, wagons, and one year's provisions.

Seven of the Forty came down with cold feet; the other 33 sailed from Hamburg in February 1847. Their occupational makeup was quite diversifed: physicians, architects, lawyers (seven of them), foresters, mechanics, carpenters, engineer, butcher, blacksmith, army artillery officer, shipbuilder, brewer, miller, botanist, hosteler, theologian, musical instrument maker, and agriculturalist. Only the ship's cook spoke English, and few of the 33 had ever actually worked for a living. They were not particularly worried.

The ship landed at Galveston on July 17, 1847, and there they paused long enough to name their colony Bettina, after the forward-thinking, controversial German author Bettina von Arnim, and to resolve that each man would do his share of the work, from tending the fields to building cabins. That done, the men of Bettina sailed again for Indianola—then called Carlshafen—where they disembarked for the long journey inland. Before leaving they received financial assistance from the Adelsverein. The 33 men and their supplies filled up 30 wagons. The cargo included a complete set of mill machinery, barrels of whiskey, and their favorite dogs from back home. "We came prepared to conquer the world," one of them said. The journey to New Braunfels took a leisurely four weeks. They camped out, drank, sang, and frolicked like the schoolboys they had until recently been. "We lived like the Gods of Olympus," one confessed. Their favorite traveling song commenced, "A life we lead, a life full of bliss." Quite a contrast to their countrymen's death-ridden experiences at Carlshafen and New Braunfels only a year earlier. The men of Bettina experienced no Indian hostilities along the way, courtesy of the recently signed Meusebach treaty with the Comanches (see Fort Martin Scott under Zodiac).

Bettina was first laid out under a large oak tree near the confluence of Elm Creek and the Llano River. A cannon was set up and a guard posted. The rest of the men sang and drank until the wee hours of dawn. "Lebe Hoch United States, Lebe Hoch Texas" rang out drunkenly through the night. They started on a huge brush arbor the next day, and followed it with pecan-shingled adobe huts.

Their Indian relations continued to be harmonious. Whenever some raiding rascals stole from the tenderfoot Germans, Chief Santanta tried to bring justice to the thieves if at all possible. When the Germans visited the Indians, the Indians gave them pecans and spread out deerskins for their sitting comfort. They even tried to learn German.

"Heaven on earth" lasted a couple of months. Since everyone could work if and when he pleased, less and less work was done as time progressed. Some spent their time hunting, others chose to while away their days in deep philosophical debate. "Most of the professional men wanted to do the directing and ordering, while the mechanics and laborers were to carry out their plans. Of course, the latter failed to see the justice of their ruling, so no one did anything," one of the 33 later reflected.

By the summer of 1848, members had begun to drift away. Bettina, barely a year old, was a complete bust by the end of 1848. Some of the defectors went to New Braunfels, others to San Antonio, Austin, and Tusculum, which later became Boerne. Several went on to leave prominent marks on Texas history, among them Gustav Schleicher and Dr. Ferdinand Herff. Schleicher served as state legislator and U.S. congressman, and had a West Texas county named for him. Previously a distinguished Hessian Army surgeon, Herff performed a successful cataract operation on an Indian girl out here on the frontier and later became the first doctor in Texas to perform an operation with anesthesia, in 1854. Nothing remains of Bettina today.

Castell, the westernmost of this string of settlements, was named for Count Carl of Castell. Henry Lorenz was the first white man to settle on the north banks of the Llano, but he stayed only a short time, returning to the safety of Fredericksburg. Next came Ludwig Schneider and Henry Vasterling, who settled several miles east of present-day Castell, on the north side of the river. Thus Castell was born. In the coming years Castell moved several times, first across to the south bank of the river, then a mile or so upstream to its present location.

Life here was not easy. For the first couple of years, Castellites depended heavily on supplies and support from the people of Fredericksburg, who had problems enough of their own. A round trip to Fredericksburg—about 50 miles—took four days. Trips to Indianola were also necessary, and they could last from three to four months. Five or six wagons would band together to make the trek. If the wagon train were detained—by bad weather, high rivers, bandits—the folks back home would suffer, sometimes coming close to starving. On one such occasion, two wives whose husbands were away, Mrs. Bader and Mrs. Steele, became so disconsolate that they agreed to divide what little cornmeal they had between them and starve together. To ease the hunger pangs, they gathered tender weeds and cooked them. Once, Mrs. Bader nearly died from eating poisonous weeds.

To survive, many of the German men became wagoneers, supplying the frontier forts. Hunger sharpened their business instincts. They would often spend their limited hard cash to buy whiskey, which they would then trade to the soldiers for corn. Soldiers always had plenty of corn but seldom did they have enough booze. Other times the Germans would comb the stable yards for stray kernels after the soldiers' horses had been fed. When times really got hard, the "Dutchmen" would feed their stock first, then salvage and wash off whatever corn kernels they could find in the barnyard droppings.

Realizing the need for mutual support in these times of adversity, the Castell colony divided its tasks accordingly. One group felled trees, another built the fences, another cooked, and so on. But such careful regimentation of labor failed to surmount all the problems, and by 1850 Castell had only 32 people. Most of the Germans had left, renouncing all claims to their land.

Soon after the string of settlements along the river was established, the Adelsverein collapsed under the weight of its debts, which meant that the Dutch settlements would no longer get even the meager aid that the society had been sending. This was the final straw for most of the settlers. They had lost their taste for life on the Texas frontier. They shared that feeling with the German nobles who had abandoned them. With the annexation of Texas in 1846, most of the Adelsverein's royal patrons lost interest in their scheme to create a model German state in the new world.

Those who chose to hang on here had to work hard and imaginatively. Henry Vasterling established the region's first cheese factory, turning out huge wheels of the stuff and wagoneering it as far away as Austin to sell. Others made and sold bacon in a similar manner. Some even sold their children, or so their Anglo neighbors claimed. These few stalwart survivors were rewarded in a way by the state, which eventually awarded them legal title to the lands settled under terms of the defunct Fisher-Miller Grant. Its beneficence really didn't put the state out much, however; many years later, 320 acres of land out here were sold for a quart of whiskey.

As one wit put it: "In those days a man could obtain title to 640 acres by filing on it and then living on it for 3 years. That's just legal talk for 'The state bets you 640 acres that you'll starve to death before 3 years are up.'"

Almost 9 miles out of Llano, you see a county gravel road, marked by a stop sign, running off FM 152 to your right, across the river. You're entering the Dutch Settlements now. In another 4 miles you come to a 4-way intersection with another gravel road. Turn right onto this gravel road and in a few yards you come to a low-water crossing of the Llano, one of the most pleasantly pastoral river crossings in the Hill Country. Return to FM 152 and continue west from the gravel-road intersection.

You see almost immediately on your left the 1850s two-story fieldstone Oestrich home, one of the finest preserved pieces of early German Texas architecture north of Fredericksburg. It's now a private residence. Then, on your right, you'll notice a section of fieldstone fence as it rises up from Vasterling Creek.

Old Leiningen is across the river from you now. About two miles west of the Lang home, you pass by the E. J. Hoffman Ranch. Look across the river and you will see a stout square fieldstone building with a shiny, hipped tin roof. This was Castell's first permanent Lutheran sanctuary, built in 1893 in the old Leiningen neighborhood, on the edge of Bettina.

Bettina was located at Elm Creek's mouth, just to the west of the old church, which is now used for hay storage and is on private property. A little farther on, you pass on your right the bare shell of the 1850s two-story Peter Lang house, then St. John's Lutheran Church on your left. St. John's is the successor to the old rock church across the river, built in 1925.

It wasn't too many years after Castell's founding that Charley Lehmburg decided that the grass looked greener over on the south bank of the Llano, and so he moved his little empire on over, near where St. John's now stands. Cattleman and drover, Lehmburg also ran the community's store and post office. Theodore Bucholz, newly arrived from Fredericksburg, bought the store in 1881 and moved it to the town's present location.

CASTELL

Llano County • 72 • (915) • About 18 miles from Llano

Residential Castell today is composed of a couple of trailer houses and a dozen turn-of-the-century millsawn-lumber Anglo German farmhouses, quaint but showing their age. The Castell grocery store and the Sunshine Station comprise downtown Castell; its spiritual center is Trinity Methodist Church. Deer and some fishing are Castell's industries today. The Castell Store dates to 1900, give or take a few years, and still has its original beaded ceiling, but not much else of interest. The Sunshine Station dates to 1928, back when FM 152 was SH 29 and the main road through these parts. Owner Emil Holtzer actually set up shop a few years earlier next door, but the first station burned down. The little wooden building across FM 152 from the station was the meat market, and between it and the Castell Store stood one of Castell's cotton gins. Folks around here used to grow a lot of cotton.

TRINITY METHODIST CHURCH
Just off FM 152

The Trinity congregation built a simple shotgun house of worship on these grounds in 1880, enlarging it to its present size and configuration over the next 20 years. The Victorian parsonage dates to 1899; the cedar post-and-tin-roof arbor is at least as old. The old Castell schoolhouse completes the tableau.

A short trek across the windswept, flower-strewn meadow gets you to the burying grounds, where many of the German pioneers lie in eternal sleep. Among all the Vasterlings, Kothes, and Kowierschkes, there is the stone of Christian Oestrich, the first white child born in Llano County (in 1855) and the first man to string "bob wire" north of the Llano. Previous to his use of barbed wire Oestrich had hired Mexicans to build rock fences for him. Oestrich noted that his employees slept on beds of leaves and ate beans flavored with "smoking tobacco." In all probability, the "smoking tobacco" Oestrich referred to was the aromatic herb epazote, which is a common addition to boiled beans in Mexico. When dried, epazote looks very much like home-cured pipe tobacco.

Students of religious history will note the unusually strong presence of Methodism in this overwhelmingly German community. This is largely due to the efforts of one man, the pioneer preacher Charles Grote. Grote rode a regular preaching circuit Fredericksburg north to the Dutch settlements during the 1850s, and often spent the night in a cave near House Mountain, 10 miles south of the river.

The Reverend Grote was not easily deterred from his evangelic mission. To honor one preaching commitment Grote rode the 25 miles from Fredericksburg to Castell through stormy weather in one day, only to be halted by the rain-swollen, impassable Llano River. His flock waited just across the river. They sent three friendly Indians across to help the reverend over. Grote nearly drowned crossing the river, despite his experienced helpmates, but he finally made it across and immediately set about his task of saving souls. Preaching in the shade of a big live oak, Grote chose as the text of his message Jesus' words "Ye must be born again." Before Grote had finished his sermon, his listeners were dropping to their knees and praying for pardon, as impressed by his preaching as by his tenacity. And within this story lies the ultimate reason for Castell's move south across the Llano. During the rainy season the river might be impassable for weeks at a time, no small inconvenience when the nearest civilization lay far south of the river. Every September, the German Methodist congregations of the Llano River Valley (Art, Castell, Hilda, and Mason) gather together to sing the old German hymns of their ancestors, usually on the fourth Sunday.

Speaking of the river, continue on FM 152 west from the church grounds, through the few short yards of commercial Castell. At the intersection, take RM 2768 across the Castell low-water bridge.

As you look out over the **Llano River's** granite-rifted channels and thicketed islands, it seems hard to believe that the Adelsverein officials had assured prospective colonists that steamboats would soon be running up and down the dredged and channeled Llano and Pedernales rivers. No wonder the society failed. So taken in were the German colonists by the Adelsverein's extravagant claims that at first, distant glance they fancied the omnipresent mottes of gnarled live oaks to be olive trees. How disappointed they must have been when they learned otherwise, and when they saw these rivers for the first time.

A historical marker commemorating the Dutch settlements stands just north of the river, where RM 2768 veers off sharply to the right. If you're feeling particularly adventuresome and enjoy good river scenery, you can follow RM 2768's path from the marker, shortly thereafter turning right onto a gravel road just yards north of the river. This road takes you back east, toward Llano, through the Dutch settlements and along the river, which is sometimes only feet away. These miles of river, granite boulders notwithstanding, probably reminded the German emigres of home, and the river and bank look very much the same today. This road makes a number of low-water crossings, so it's not advisable to take it during rainy, flash flood weather. Grazing cattle wander at will along and across the road, so take it easy. Otherwise, the road is smooth but very dusty. If you take this upper-river road, turn right at its dead end some 5 miles later. In a matter of yards you cross the river and come again to FM 152. Turn right on FM 152 to complete the loop back to Castell.

From Castell, continue 9.5 miles west on FM 152 toward its junction with US 87.

You're out of the hills now, and you're entering the comparatively flat, semiarid fringes of the High Plains. You see no cedars here, just scattered mesquites and live oak mottes.

Turn right onto US 87, toward Fredericksburg. Five and a half miles later, turn left on FM 2242, so as to pass through Loyal Valley.

Once known as Cold Spring, this section of the **Cold Spring Creek valley** was settled by unionist Germans, who named their settlement to reflect their political beliefs.

LOYAL VALLEY

Mason County • 50 • About 15 miles from Castell
John Meusebach settled down here in 1869 to raise cattle and fruit. His orchards were locally famous. Fluent in five languages, Meusebach also served as postmaster and justice of the peace.

For many years Loyal Valley had a hotel and the usual secular and spiritual trappings of a Texas village. But when the new highway (now US 87) went through a half-mile west, Loyal Valley withered down to the collection of ranch houses and ruins that you see today.

You shortly rejoin US 87 and begin to enter the hills again. Less than 5 miles later, you come to Cherry Springs. Several hundred yards after you see the "Cherry Springs" highway sign, you see a 4-way intersection sign, followed by a small Lutheran church sign. Turn left here, onto E. Cherry Springs Rd. In the near distance you see the silvery spire and roofs of the Cherry Springs Lutheran Church and the Diedrich Rode homestead.

CHERRY SPRINGS

Gillespie County • 75 • About 5 miles from Loyal Valley

The three-story Rode home is one of the largest Hill Country lime-stone houses still standing, and its tall, shiny tin-hipped roof further heightens its prominence. The energetic evangelic rancher Rode founded the Cherry Springs community in 1853, naming it for the wild cherry trees he found growing along the creek. The settlement was located along the main highway between Fort Mason and Fort Martin Scott.

Rode had been here on the banks of **Marschall Creek** only a few months when the Mormons wandered through, camping first on the banks of Marschall Creek, then on nearby **Squaw Creek.** They must have made a strong impression, for Marschall Creek was commonly known as Mormon Creek for years thereafter.

Rode finished the large house in 1880, and followed it with the other, smaller limestone structures that dot the ranch-house grounds: carriage house, smokehouse, blacksmith shop, and sheep-shearing barn. A lay Lutheran preacher, Rode helped found the church at Castell, and taught catechism classes in his home for years. Along the way he became one of the region's biggest stockraisers and landowners.

Rode's dream was to see a full-fledged Lutheran congregation organized here, and he saw his wish fulfilled with only months to spare. Christ Lutheran Church was organized here in March 1905 and Rode died less than four months later, at the ripe old age of 77.

The present limestone Gothic sanctuary, whose shiny tin steeple can be seen from miles around, was finished in 1907. It is immaculately kept, as is the old Rode ranch just across E. Cherry Springs Rd. from the church. All in all, they form one of the most unique and imposing collections of limestone buildings in the Hill Country. The Kothe family bought the ranch in 1929. It is still a working, 700-acre ranch, but the big house is now a bed-and-breakfast inn as well, with three guest rooms. Guests may take a guided tour of the ranch. For reservations, call Gasthaus Schmidt Reservation Service in Fredericksburg, (830) 997-5612.

Return to US 87 and continue on toward Fredericksburg. You can see the church and ranch house for several miles, over your left shoulder, nestled in the Marschall Creek valley. In 7 miles, you come to an intersection with FM 2323. Slow down here, then slow further at the "Fredericksburg 9" sign. You turn right almost immediately there-

after onto the old Mason highway, which is marked by a T intersection sign but is almost invisible until you come up on it.

Driving this narrow, wandering road, it's hard to imagine that it, not that four-lane Johnny-come-lately dragstrip you just turned off of, was once the main highway north from Fredericksburg.

Soon a creek comes into view—**Barons Creek,** named for Baron John Meusebach—and as you cross it you'll notice on your left an eccentric little house,with tinned first-story walls, a board-and-batten sleeping loft with outside staircase, and a limestone shed attached to the back. The small log cabin that preceded this newer house stands nearby.

A couple of miles later on your left, you see another distinctive little farmhouse, two stories high, one room deep, covered completely by tin with a tin-sheet roof and brick-patterned tin siding. An old telegraph-telephone line runs along the east side of the road, low slung, with many old green and clear-glass insulators nailed to its hand-trimmed poles.

Resume your trek to Fredericksburg by turning right on US 87 when Old Mason Road runs into it a mile or so later.

FREDERICKSBURG

Gillespie County Seat • 7,745 • (830) • About 18 miles from Cherry Springs

Continue into Fredericksburg on US 87, which joins US 290 to become Main St.

Fredericksburg was not built by spendthrifts; the countryside, however pretty, has never allowed for such luxuries. Statistically Fredericksburg averages just under 30″ of rain a year. But statistics don't tell the whole story. Weather in this part of Texas is cyclical. Several wet years are followed by several dry years and so on. Spring and fall are the rainy seasons. Some years it won't rain a drop for months at a time; other years half the annual rain falls on one weekend.

January's average temperature is 46°, but it may be 90° one day and 19° the next. During summer the daily high is seldom below 95°.

Summer is the harshest of seasons here, winter is almost a blessing by comparison. But springtime is joyous. Bluebonnets and peach blossoms are the co-regents of spring in and around Fredericksburg. Bluebonnets favor thin poor soil, which the Hill Country has in abundance, and peach trees thrive on the iron-rich soil of the Pedernales River Valley. Spring also means redbud trees, Indian paintbrushes, phlox, verbena, mountain laurel, yucca, and dozens of other blossoms which splatter and sometimes sweep over the newly green hills and valleys from early March through mid-June.

Fredericksburg's founders arrived here during the height of a banner spring and immediately fell in love with this valley. Miss Margaret Keidel (see Take a Ride on the Fredericksburg & Northern—Keidel Pharmacy and Family Home in Fredericksburg) says that her great-grandfather Wilhelm liked it so much that he abandoned his plans to pursue advanced medical studies at Johns Hopkins to stay here.

Fredericksburg's founders were a diverse lot: doctors, professors, skilled craftsmen, noblemen, artists. Some came searching for political freedom, many more came for the economic opportunities unavailable in the homeland. But to a person, they were romantics, Miss Keidel says. It took a healthy dose of romance to leave home—probably forever—and sail for three months to a country they really knew nothing about, other than what they had read in novels and travel books which often painted a milk-and-honey picture.

As contemporary chronicler Frederick Kapp put it in an 1855 letter to the *New York Tribune,* "The least that even the less sanguine ones expected was to find parrots rocking on the boughs and monkeys playing on the palm-trees."

Romance soon made room for determined resignation. The heat of summer came, as did deadly epidemics and Indian attacks. After the first few wet years, the dry years came. But the German settlers persevered. They had no other choice. The Adelsverein had collapsed, and they had no money to move elsewhere. They learned to save as much as possible during the fat years in anticipation of the lean ones, and they seldom threw anything away.

Their peculiar blend of hard-headed practicality and romanticism was typified in the hotel built by Charles Nimitz, which stands today as the Admiral Nimitz Center at the corner of Main St./US 290 and Washington St.

ADMIRAL NIMITZ STATE HISTORICAL PARK
340 E. Main at Washington • 997-4379 • Open daily, except Christmas Day • Admission • W variable

Charles Nimitz and wife Sophie founded the Nimitz Hotel back in 1852, beginning with four rooms and a huge fireplace in the central hall. Within a few years, it had been enlarged to 30 rooms. The place was always buzzing; after all it was the last real hotel between Fredericksburg and San Diego, California, until the 1870s. And since it happened to be on the road west across the great American desert, everybody stayed there, eager to get their first bath in weeks or to get one last good meal before commencing the weeks-long trek west. Robert E. Lee, General Phil Sheridan, and Elisabet Ney were but a few of the hotel's distinguished guests.

The Nimitz had the frontier's first bathhouse, a cellar brewery, and a great concert-dance hall. Gardens behind the hotel produced most of the dining room fare, even the table wine. Newcomers are invariably impressed by the Nimitz's fanciful, steamboat-like superstructure complete with bridge and crow's nest. Nimitz added it during the 1880s as a nostalgic indulgence. He could well afford it. Despite the horrors of the Civil War, the decline in use of the Military Road, and the closing of the frontier forts, Fredericksburg prospered, slowly but steadily, as a self-contained community. Wagons hauled the region's excess produce down to San Antonio, and hauled back luxury items like the town's first electric light plant (1896) and ice cream-making factory (1907) as well as wrought-iron filigree and white elephants.

Will Porter (O. Henry) visited Fredericksburg at least once during his Austin years (1884-1898), and used it as the setting for his story "A Chaparral Prince." He described it as "a pleasant little Rhine village. . . . They are all German people who live in Fredericksburg. Of evenings they sit at little tables along the sidewalk and drink beer and play pinochle and scat. They are very thrifty people." Nimitz family lore has it that Captain Nimitz regaled the ever-ready-to-listen Porter with a number of stories, one of which eventually grew into "A Chaparral Prince."

Charles' grandson Chester Nimitz spent his early years at the hotel and in Kerrville before entering the Naval Academy and eventually becoming America's highest ranking seaman in World War II.

The old hotel is now headquarters for the Admiral Nimitz Museum and Historical Center, an approximately 7-acre (4.5 for hotel, 3 for the History Walk) day-use museum. Named for Admiral Chester W. Nimitz of World War II fame, the museum was established as a state agency in 1969 by the Texas Legislature, in order to "foster and commemorate the memory of the era of supreme United States Naval Power upon the seas, dedicated to the men and women in the armed forces." In 1981, the 67th Texas Legislature gave control of the Nimitz Museum to the Texas Parks and Wildlife Department and made it responsible for preserving naval documents, relics, and other items of historical interest. It tells the story of Admiral Nimitz within the larger focus of the Pacific War. At Admiral Nimitz's request, it is dedicated to the 2.5 million men and women who served with him in the Pacific. The motto of the museum is "We inspire our youth by honoring our heroes."

Three different museums make up the center. The first is the Pacific War museum in the Nimitz Steamboat Hotel. The second is the Japanese Garden of Peace, which was donated by the people of Japan in honor of Admiral Nimitz. It just happens to be a painstakingly identical replica of the garden of the great Japanese admiral Heihachiro Togo, of whom Nimitz was a self-proclaimed disciple. The third is the History Walk of the Pacific War, a trail that leads the visitor from Pearl Harbor to Tokyo Bay, through a lot full of rusting battlefield paraphernalia—tanks, planes, landing craft, artillery and other weapons, and other equipment used during World War II.

The museum hosts an annual symposium on a Pacific War topic that features prominent historians and veterans of the event or battle under study. Speakers often include foreign veterans from Australia or Japan, as well as Americans. An air show and military field day are held each spring, which feature World War II aircraft, tanks, artillery, and small arms being used just as they were used in the war. Living History exhibits are set up periodically at the museum and at other events across the state.

The museum maintains a series of traveling exhibits available for loan; these include The Yamamoto Mission (the secret mission to shoot down the famous Japanese admiral in 1943); Quiet Shadows: Women in the Pacific War; Cactus Remembered: The Air War for Guadalcanal; Up Periscope!: Submarine Operations in the Pacific War; and Risque Business: Aircraft Nose Art in the Pacific War. Write to P.O. Box 777, Fredericksburg 78624.

Part of the trek around the Center affords a glimpse inside the old bathhouse, with its line of hand-soldered tin bathtubs and center fireplace, where the bathwater was heated.

PIONEER PLACE GARDEN
Behind the Vereinskirche • Free • W

Behind the Vereinskirche is the Pioneer Place Garden, a quiet little green spot whose most obvious feature is the old wooden waterwheel. Said wheel was dedicated by the people of Fredericksburg to Lyman Wight's long vanished Mormon colony at nearby Zodiac, in gratitude for the invaluable help given by the Mormons during the difficult early years here.

As you may have noticed, Main St. in Fredericksburg is one of the broadest streets in any Hill Country town or city. Fredericksburg town fathers laid out Main St. over 100 years ago, making sure that a 16-horse team and wagon could make a clean U-turn in it. One thing you may not have noticed is that, traveling east from the center of town on Main, the first letters of all the cross streets combine to spell "ALL WELCOME." Traveling west from the center of town on Main, the combined first letters of the cross streets read "COME BACK."

From the Nimitz Center, continue east on Main St./US 290. A little more than 4 miles east of the Gillespie County Courthouse in downtown Fredericksburg, US 290 crosses the Pedernales River. Zodiac stood just upstream, in the fields to your left.

ZODIAC

Site on private property; not open to the public
Nothing remains of Zodiac today except a one-acre cemetery plot that lies hidden away, north of the road, on the western banks of the river. Church officials from Salt Lake City visit the plot occasionally to keep it clean, but otherwise Lyman Wight and his followers buried here sleep on undisturbed.

Turn around, recross the river, and head back toward Fredericksburg. Shortly, you see on your right Fort Martin Scott.

FORT MARTIN SCOTT
1606 E. Main, about 2 miles east of downtown Fredericksburg
997-9895 • Open Friday through Sunday • Donation
W with assistance
Texas wasn't even officially a state yet when General Zachary Scott led the Army of Observation into Texas in July 1845. In March 1846, Taylor's army established Fort Brown, the first permanent U.S. military installation in Texas, on the north bank of the Rio Bravo, across from the Mexican city of Matamoros. It was here that the war with Mexico over who owned Texas began.

With the end of the war in 1848, the Army began constructing a line of forts along the Rio Grande from Brownsville to El Paso, and another line of forts along the edge of Texas' rapidly expanding western frontier, from Fort Duncan at Eagle Pass on the Rio Grande, north to Fort Worth. These forts were designed to protect settlers and travelers from attacks by Indians and brigands.

One of these frontier posts was Fort Martin Scott, established in December 1848, two miles east of Fredericksburg on Barons Creek. Folks called the place "the fort at Fredericksburg," or "Camp Houston," until December 1849, when the Army finally got around to officially naming the post, in honor of a U.S. army officer killed in the war with Mexico. Established by Company D of the 1st U.S. infantry, the fort was subsequently garrisoned by companies of the 8th Infantry and the 2nd Dragoons, which were mounted infantry. Mounted infantry was cheaper to fund than cavalry, which was important to the penny-pinching U.S. Congress. At the tail end of 1850, the Army finally decided to build some permanent housing for the troops stationed here. The Army regarded the fort as just a temporary position, so it directed that the buildings be of the most economical character, consistent with the health and comfort of the troops. This meant an assortment of log and adobe buildings for the troops and officers, and a stout stone guardhouse for the prisoners.

The buildings put up by the Army at Fort Martin Scott may have been cheap, but they were well-built, thanks to the meticulous German craftsmen from Fredericksburg who constructed them. Most of the lumber they worked with came from the Mormon sawmills at Zodiac, located east of the fort on the Pedernales River. A government inspector noted in 1853 that "the buildings put up are of a better description than at most of the posts in Texas," where soldiers often lived in tents or stick-and-mud huts of their own construction.

Fort sites were carefully picked. Grassy meadows where the animals could graze, wood for fuel, and building materials such as wood or stone had to be readily available. But the most essential factor in choosing a fort site—for the health and well-being of everyone to be stationed there—was a location near good water—a spring or perennial, clear-running stream. The ideal site also had to have good drainage—standing water was to be avoided like the plague. Malaria, yellow fever, tuberculosis, cholera, dysentery, and breakbone fever were just some of the better-known diseases associated with poor drainage and stagnant water. Scientists didn't know enough yet about the nature of sickness and health to finger mosquitoes and microbes as the culprits; they blamed bad humors, spontaneous generation, or mysterious poisonous mists and vapors that may or may not have been caused by rotting vegetable matter.

Catching and storing rainwater in rain barrels and cisterns was a common way to ensure a supply of clean drinking water in the 1850s, but in the Hill Country, it may not rain a drop for months. Then, the sky will open up for two days straight and dump half the year's rainfall in a torrent that washes away anything and anyone in its path. Fort Martin Scott stood at the eastern edge of what was then called the Great American Desert, which was considered uninhabitable because of the scarity of rain and surface water. Digging a well by hand through the rock was not a practical option. The windmill and mechanical drilling equipment, which would help transform the arid Great American Desert into the irrigated, fertile Great Plains, wouldn't come to the Hill Country and West Texas until the 1880s.

The fort played an important role in the lives of Fredericksburg and Zodiac, but the relationship between the soldiers and the settlers was not always gracious. The soldiers came from many different states and sometimes different countries, so it was inevitable that conflicts would flare up. One incident led to a fire that destroyed the earliest records of Gillespie County, on July, 1, 1850. John Hunter, the county clerk, kept all the county records at his store (located where the **Bank of Fredericksburg** now stands). Like most merchants of his time, Hunter sold whiskey at his store. On the last night of June 1850, a young soldier cursed Hunter when Hunter refused to sell him any more liquor. Angered, Hunter threw the drunken soldier across a table and stabbed the soldier in the chest with a knife, killing him instantly. Naturally, the killing aroused much resentment among the dead man's compatriots, and the next night about 40 of them came to the store looking for revenge. Hunter wasn't there. Forewarned, he was hiding at a friend's place on Live Oak Creek. Since Hunter was not available for slaughter, the soldiers were content to burn down his store. Efforts to rescue the county records from the flaming log structure were thwarted by the vengeful soldiers.

Fredericksburg and Fort Martin Scott were regularly visited by the Penateka Comanches and Lipan Apaches. These visits were usually peaceful. Richard Irving Dodge was stationed at Fort Martin Scott from the spring of 1851 until February 1852. Then a second lieutenant, Dodge oversaw road construction between the fort and San Antonio. He wrote of one visitor: "Years ago, when matches were not so universally used as now, a Lipan Indian was visiting Fort Martin Scott in Texas. One day an officer to whom he was talking took from his pocket a box of what, to the Indian, were merely little sticks, and scratching one on a stone, lit his pipe. The Lipan eagerly inquired into this mystery, and looked on with astonishment while several matches were lighted for his gratification. Going to his camp near by, he soon came back, bringing half a dozen beautifully dressed wildcat skins, which he offered for the wonderful box. The exchange was accepted, and he went off greatly pleased. Some time after he was found sitting by a large stone, on which he was striking match after match, holding each in his fingers until forced to drop it, and then carefully inspecting the scorched fingers, as if to assure himself that it was real fire. This he continued until every match was burned."

By 1853, Fort Martin Scott had been demoted to a forage depot for wagon trains that supplied the new upper frontier posts. The garrison consisted of a sergeant, corporal, and 16 men of the 8th infantry under the command of Lt. Theodore Fink.

A government inspector noted that year, "An Ordnance sgt. is stationed here, but there is little for him to do, the only ordnance at the post being a 12-pounder mountain howitzer, with less than 100 rounds of fixed ammunition and 33 pounds of powder.

"Provisions are obtained from the San Antonio depot. Some 3,000 rations are on hand and they are in good condition. The cost of the rations delivered at the post is 17 and ½ cents. No parts of it could be bought on advantageous terms in the vicinity. On account of the smallness of the command, fresh beef cannot be obtained. It's sold generally at 5 cents per pound."

There was a notable absence of spit and polish at the fort, the inspector noted. "Black belts and white belts are intermixed; some are destitute of parts of their equipment. One was without arms and almost all had a very limited supply of clothing. They had not received much instruction and made but an indifferent appearance on parade."

Soon after this report, the Army closed Fort Martin Scott; in its opinion, the frontier had been tamed. It was certainly swarming with Americans now, at the expense of the Indians. In just three years— between 1847 and 1850—Texas' non-Indian population increased by nearly 50 percent, to over 212,000 persons.

On the other hand, the total Indian population in Texas in 1849 was only about 29,000 souls, and rapidly decreasing. About 20,000 of these were Comanches; the rest were Kiowas, Lipan Apaches, Tonkawas, Wacos, and other smaller groups. Bison and the other game that the hunting tribes of Texas depended on for food, clothing, and shelter had dwindled to the point that the tribes were frequently on the brink of starvation. Disease also hit hard. The Penateka Comanches, whose territory included Fort Martin Scott, were ravaged by epidemics of smallpox, cholera, and venereal diseases in

1848 and 1849. Thousands died, including the great chiefs Old Owl and Santa Anna, who had made peace with Meusebach and the Germans in 1847.

The basic dress of 19th century Lipan and Comanche men was buckskin moccasins, leggins, and breechclout. In cold weather, a buckskin shirt was added, and a buffalo robe or blanket wrapped around the body.

Women—both Lipan and Comanche—dressed in knee-length buckskin skirts, moccasins, leggins, and loose-fitting, poncho-like blouses fashioned from a single deerskin. These were often decorated with fringe, beadwork and tin jingles.

Comanche women were dominated by their men, who refused to do anything beyond eat, fight, and hunt. Lipan women, on the other hand, enjoyed a rough equality with the men. They maintained gardens, and sewed and decorated elaborate outfits. Lipan men, in addition to hunting and fighting, also did drudge work like hauling water and packing meat on the horses. Comanche men would never stoop to such tasks, leaving them to the women.

One notable Comanche woman bucked the tribe's male supremacy. The widow of the great chief Santa Anna formed a semi-autonomous band of seven women, all widows like herself. She owned a large herd of horses and was a successful hunter, having shot with her rifle 15 deer in a morning's hunt.

Comanche warriors painted their bison-hide shields, attached feathers to the rims, and imbued them with much symbolic and magical importance. Though acquainted with firearms, the Lipans and Comanches of the 1850s still preferred the bow and arrow. They used 3- to 4-foot-long bows. The arrows had hardwood shafts and iron points cut from barrel hoops or other metal. Comanches also carried long lances, decorated with feathers and other ornamentation, and tipped with long sharp steel blades as wicked as any Bowie knife. As intimidating as these lances were, they could not hold back all the white people, who outnumbered the indigenous peoples 20 to 1.

Faced with such odds, the tribes could either fight and die, accommodate the whites, which meant settling down and adapting the white lifestyle, or move on, into someone else's territory. In practice, they generally died or moved on.

In 1855, camels came to Texas, the vehicles of an Army experiment to improve trans-continental travel. Fort Martin Scott was first considered, and then dismissed, as home base for the camel corps. Little of the fort remained. Many of its 21 buildings had already been dismantled and recycled into other nearby buildings, like perhaps an adobe wall in Fredericksburg's old Nimitz Hotel, which was a favored hangout for frontier soldiers. The camels, trainers, and troopers finally settled at nearby Camp Verde; you'll read about them elsewhere.

The fort was reoccupied sporadically by the Confederates during the Civil War before being closed for good by the U.S. Cavalry in December 1866. John T. Braeutigam bought the property in 1870. He and his family made the officers' quarters their home. Using materials salvaged from the fort's remaining buildings, Braeutigam built a dance hall and saloon up at the front of the property (alongside present-day US 290) and called it Braeutigam's Garten. It was possibly the county's first such hall; at any rate, the first annual Gillespie County Fair was held on the Garten grounds in 1881. This continued for several years, and then Braeutigam was robbed and murdered at the Garten in 1884. The fair moved elsewhere; the family tried to keep the place going for a while, but it soon closed. The land stayed in the family until 1959, when Raymond Braeutigam sold the property to the city of Fredericksburg. It was closed to the public until 1989, when the old fort grounds were opened as a public park. Of the several buildings on the grounds, only the old guardhouse/stockade is original. The other buildings are reasonably faithful replicas, for example, the adobe, stuccoed officers' quarters, which consist of two rooms, each with a fireplace and a large shaded front porch. Scheduled for reconstruction are the commanding officer's house and a large log barracks. The fort's drill grounds were located across the creek, in what is now a meadow. Tradition says that this is where the county fair's horse races were later run. At any rate, we can be sure that everyone was well lubed. This stretch of Barons Creek is generously littered with the shards of ancient champagne bottles and glasses, long since shattered and worn smooth by 120 years of flowing water.

Fort Martin Scott has its own resident garrison of period reenactors, who do several public reenactments per year, with fascinatingly scrupulous attention to the details of life in that era. Call for current schedule.

From Fort Martin Scott, go back to downtown Fredericksburg to the junction of US 290 and SH 16. Turn left on SH 16 toward Kerrville. About 3.5 miles later, you pass the entrance to Lady Bird Johnson Municipal Park located on Live Oak Creek.

Back in 1851, a bright and confident young German immigrant millwright named Carl Guenther came to Fredericksburg and built a gristmill on Live Oak Creek, taking up where the Mormons left off.

At that time, the nearest mill was a several-day journey away. He built the water wheel and driving gears out of native woods. The millstones were imported from France. But not long after its completion, a flash flood washed the mill away. Although dismayed by the loss, Guenther rebuilt it stronger than before and added a sawmill. By 1859, Live Oak Creek's flow began to diminish and a steam-powered mill opened nearby, so Guenther and family moved to San Antonio where only one water-powered mill served a city of 10,000. Guenther's mill prospered and he became one of the wealthiest men in San Antonio as well as a leader of San Antonio's sizable German population. Guenther died in 1902 at the ripe old age of 76. The company he founded, Pioneer Flour Mills, is the country's oldest continuously owned flour milling business still operated by members of the same family.

Just over 5 miles from the center of Fredericksburg, you see on your right a state sign reading "Picnic Area 1 mi." Go another tenth of a mile and turn left on the little paved road marked by "Old Kerrville Rd." and "Bear Creek" signs. After you cross the Pedernales, bear right at the road's fork (Old Kerrville Rd.). One mile after you leave SH 16, you pass an old limestone home sitting off to your left on a hill overlooking the Pedernales.

PETRI-LUNGKWITZ FARM
Six miles from Fredericksburg • Private residence

This is the old farm of German Texas' first great painters, Richard Petri and Hermann Lungkwitz. The pair had been classmates at the Academy of Fine Arts in Dresden; Hermann also married Richard's sister Elisabeth. The trio immigrated to Texas in 1851, part of the influx of "forty-eighters" seeking the freedom they could not get back home.

After living in New Braunfels, Petri and Lungkwitz bought this plot of land and began life as frontier painters and farmers. Both men painted scenes from everyday life: women milking, Indians, soldiers at Fort Scott, the mills at Comfort, Fredericksburg, Barton Springs.

For his services in the Mexican-American War, Wilhelm Keidel (see Take a Ride on the Fredericksburg & Northern—Keidel Pharmacy and Family Home in Fredericksburg) was awarded a section of land along Bear Creek, adjacent to the Petri/Lungkwitz farm. Family tradition says that Keidel granted them a 50-foot-wide easement across his land so that their cattle could get water at Bear Creek. It was the neighborly thing to do; cooperation was the key to survival. Petri and Lungk-witz needed all the help they could get, for as Miss Margaret Keidel, Wilhelm's granddaughter, observed, "they were patricians who were really out of place living with pigs and cows."

The rigors of farm life proved to be too much for Richard Petri's frail physique. Delirious with fever, he wandered down to the Peder-nales and drowned in December 1857.

Lungkwitz found it impossible to make a living by painting during the Civil War, so he moved to San Antonio and learned photography. He served several years as photographer for the Texas General Land Office, then returned to painting and teaching art. He died in Austin in 1891.

The house that stands here was built by the folks who bought the land from Hermann Lungkwitz and his brother in 1869. The two-story limestone house was built in 1880 right next to the old Petri-Lungkwitz cabin, now vanished.

Continue on the Old Kerrville Rd. south. In about a mile you come to a small paved road running off to your left. It is marked by a "Center Point Rd." sign, a solitary mailbox, and a grove of pecan trees. SH 16 is just ahead across the river. Turn left on Center Point Rd., aka Bear Creek Rd.

About 8 miles out of this road, you begin to follow Bear Creek quite closely for about 2 miles.

Very quickly you are topping the **Divide** between the Pedernales and Guadalupe rivers. You get some great canyon views to the west (your right) and soon you are making a scenic descent toward the Guadalupe valley.

About 5 miles from the Divide, Bear Creek Rd. comes to a T inter-section with RM 1341. Turn left and follow RM 1341 across I-10 and turn left onto the I-10 frontage road. Stay on I-10 about 3 miles, tak-ing the Business 87 exit into Comfort. Turn right on RM 473 in the city, then veer right on SH 27, toward Center Point.

COMFORT

Kendall County • 1,593 • About 25 miles from Fredericksburg

You cross Cypress Creek as you leave town. Back when the Mor-mons camped at this creek while on their way from Cherry Springs to Bandera, only the shingle-makers on down by the Guadalupe lived anywhere nearby.

Take SH 27 to Center Point, turning left onto RM 480.

CENTER POINT

Kerr County • 623 • About 9 miles from Comfort

Local legend has it that the wandering Mormons erected a gristmill on the river here; if they did, they were probably in the employ of somebody else, for the Mormons never stayed put long enough to operate such an enterprise during their long journey from the Mormon Mills to Bandera.

Center Point was also home after the Civil War to "The Fightin' Parson,"Andy Potter. Sent to the rough-and-tumble Kerr County circuit in 1867, Potter chose to hold his first West Texas revival at Center Point. Local believers had been asked to erect an arbor for the occasion. But when Potter arrived he found no arbor, whereupon he told Bandera County Sheriff Buck Hamilton that if he couldn't get the lazy Methodists to build an arbor, he would get Buck and all the sinners to build it. The sinners laid aside their regular work and put up the arbor. Sheriff Buck even kicked in all the beef for the 3-week meeting.

Continue on to Camp Verde on RM 480.

CAMP VERDE

Kerr County • 41 • About 6.5 miles from Center Point

Camp Verde is covered at length in the Hill Country Rivers trip, but while we're still fresh on the subject, here's another Andy Potter story. Upon joining the Confederate Army, Potter was sent with his regiment to Camp Verde to guard prisoners of war.

Potter showed his comrades-in-arms just why he was called The Fightin' Parson early on, when he tamed the regiment's bully. The bully was a muscular giant, dreaded by most of the men in the regiment. Being a bitter enemy of religion, he took great pleasure in hurling insults at the preacher. One morning the bully made a false statement about the parson within hearing range of the latter. Potter walked up to the man and said, "Sir, you are a liar, and if you take *that,* you're a coward." When the bully advanced belligerently, Potter just shoved him back and scoffed, "You won't fight." And the bully didn't; instead he became Potter's friend and was a terror no more. Potter became so popular that the men demanded he be made regimental chaplain, and he was.

At Camp Verde, turn left on SH 173.

SH 173 takes you through the **Bandera Pass** into the valley of the **Medina River** and the town of Bandera. The Mormons no doubt crossed the **Bandera Mountains** via the pass on their way from Center Point to Bandera. This road was part of a winding 100-mile trail from San Antonio to Kerrville traveled by nineteenth-century Texas Rangers in their attempts to guard pioneer settlers from Indian attacks.

BANDERA

Bandera County Seat • 975 • (830) • About 13 miles from Camp Verde

The first settlers here on the Medina River were shingle-makers who set up camp by the river in 1852. In 1853, John James, Charles De Montel, and John Herndon surveyed and laid out the city of Bandera and built a sawmill to make shingles and lumber from the many cypress trees then growing along the river. Shingle-making was not exactly a get-rich-quick proposition; a good shinglemaker could make a thousand shingles a day, and the thousand shingles would sell for about six bucks delivered in San Antonio.

Philip Mazurek, who came to Bandera in 1855 from Poland with his parents when he was 8 months old, became an excellent shingle-maker. Years later he described the shingle-making process: Cypress blocks were sawed into 32-inch lengths (twice the length of a finished shingle). These blocks were hauled up from the river banks, then cut in two and marked off to the proper thickness. Then the blocks were split and rived with a froe knife and wooden mallet. Next they were taken to a shaving horse and trimmed to a feather edge with a drawing knife. The shingles were stacked in huge piles to season. Afterwards they were put up in bundles of a thousand and in due time were hauled to market. Big ox wagons hauled them, 25,000 shingles to the wagon. In San Antonio, the shingles sold for about $4.50 per thousand. Thousands of shingles were produced around Bandera. One cypress could make 30,000 shingles. The road to San Antonio was very bad, especially at a point known as "the slideoff," so-called because in crossing over the steep hill the load would often slide off the back of the wagon. To prevent this a big piece of cypress timber, called the binding pole, had to be placed across the top of the load to keep everything in place, but there was still the danger of the wagon turning over.

People started to join the shingle-makers almost immediately. The Mormons came during the spring of 1854. They camped at first on the north bank of the river, across from the young town. Evidently, they commuted by boat to work across the river at the sawmill each morning. But finally the Mormons bought lots in the little city and built a schoolhouse.

The Mormons passed only the summer of 1854 here at Bandera before moving on. We have no officially recorded reasons as to why they left Bandera, but we can surmise that their proselytizing was a probable cause, considering their hassles at Webberville and the following incident at Gonzales, as recorded in the *San Antonio Texan:* "During the past week a Mormon Missionary has been holding forth in Gonzales. At his last meeting there, he 'pulled off his coat and rolled up his sleeves'—which, alas! caused a stampede of the lady part of his audience. Soon after, he was escorted around the town to the music of tin horns, cow bells, etc., and told to leave ere the dews of night were kissed by early dawn, and he did nothing shorter."

But Bandera suffered only temporarily from the loss of the Mormons. Sixteen Polish families settled here in 1855. Freshly arrived from the motherland, they came first to Panna Maria, then to Castroville, only to find that all the choice acreage had already been taken. Townbuilder Charles DeMontel found them scratching their heads and talked them into moving to his town of Bandera, promising them work at his saw and shingle mill. The Poles started to work almost immediately upon their arrival. The men worked at the mill and cleared land, while the women tilled the soil and dug a millrace for Bandera's first gristmill. The mile-long race diverted water from the Medina River, which powered the mill. The race took the women several months to complete, but they had the satisfaction of seeing families from 75 miles around come to get their grain ground for daily bread. Even the basics of life were hard to come by. To get a milch cow in those early days, two of the Poles walked to Castroville and drove the cow back on foot, a round trip of at least 60 miles.

Indian raids continued until almost 1880, up and down the Medina valley. The Indians were loath to give up this territory, for not only was it a favored hunting spot, it was also the source of their paint supply. The Comanches had discovered in the land around

Bandera deposits of clay that were natural paints. Blue and yellow clays were found a few miles south of town, white and red clays were located northwest of Bandera. Once the Comanches were driven from Bandera County and eventually onto the Oklahoma reservations, they were cut off from their "Valley of Paint."

Follow SH 173's route through town to Main (SH 16). Turn left on Main to the Bandera County Courthouse, located at Main and Pecan.

BANDERA COUNTY COURTHOUSE
Courthouse square, Main St.

Bandera County was organized in 1856, but did not get its first permanent courthouse until this one was built in 1891. A local version of the Second Renaissance Revival style, the shiny tin roof and turret are visible for miles around. It is built from locally quarried limestone, but it did not go up easily. There were factions, well represented in Bandera County Court, that wanted the county seat moved farther west from Bandera City and ostensibly closer to the county's geographical center. At that time Bandera County was slightly larger than it is now and extended about eight miles farther west almost to Leakey. Although the "movers" ultimately failed (unlike those in Blanco County), they managed to delay the courthouse's construction by a year or so.

Several historical markers are in front of the courthouse. One is a great granite boulder with a plaque honoring Amasa Clark, Bandera County's first permanent Anglo settler. Born in 1825, Clark served in the Mexican War, and upon his discharge in 1849 he came to San Antonio. Clark next spent time on the Guadalupe River making cypress shingles. In 1852, Clark first visited the Medina River valley while on a hunting trip with friendly Delaware Indians. At that time there were only three families living on the river where Bandera now stands. They were also shingle-makers and they moved on soon after Clark's visit. Amasa Clark liked the Medina valley so much that he moved here as quickly as possible. Clark worked with the Camp Verde camels for 14 months (1859–60) and sheared some of them to get hair for a mattress and pillows. One of those camel-hair pillows was placed under his head in his casket, and the other was donated to the Frontier Times Museum. Clark established his farm four miles west of Bandera, and worked the place until his death in January 1927 at the ripe age of 101 years and 5 months.

Then there is the "Cowboy Capital of the World" marker, honoring Bandera County's best known champion cowboys starting with the semi-legendary Toots Mansfield, seven-time world champion calf roper.

An (in)famous native son Bandera doesn't talk as much about was Will Carver, who rode with the noted Tom "Black Jack" Ketchum and the Wild Bunch. Ketchurn, who came from Tom Green County, Texas, near the hamlet of Knickerbocker, left Texas for New Mexico about 1890, possibly because of a murder or train robbery. By 1894 his brother Sam and Will Carver had joined him in the Cimarron Mountains of New Mexico, and they commenced a life of robbing post offices and holding upstages, trains, and a railroad station in New Mexico and Arizona. They also spent a lot of time across the border in old Mexico.

Carver also spent some time in El Paso, where he was the final link in an interesting chain of unrelated killings. As you remember, John Wesley Hardin was killed in El Paso in 1895 by the cowardly city constable John Selman. Less than a year later Selman was shot dead by deputy U.S. Marshall George Scarbrough. In 1900 Will Carver shot and killed George Scarbrough. In 1901 Carver's old boss Black Jack Ketchum became the first man to hang for robbing a train.

The historical markers across the street tell of the old Texas Ranger trail and of the last Indian victim in Bandera County.

From the courthouse, proceed east on Pecan as per the signs to the Frontier Times Museum.

FRONTIER TIMES MUSEUM
506 13th at Pecan • 796-3864 • Monday through Saturday 10–4:30, Sunday 1–4:30 • Admission • W

Started by Marvin Hunter in the 1920s, the Frontier Times Museum is an incredible pastiche of relics and artifacts. An eight-inch Brahma fetus mummy, a one-armed man's combination fork and knife, a map of Texas executed in rattlesnake rattles, grisly photos of dead bandits, and a pair of locked deer antlers are just a few of the estimated 30,000 diverse articles on display.

The fireplace in the middle of the room was built from hundreds of fossil snails and the millstone used by Lyman Wight and the Mormons here at the Bandera Mill and then at their camp by Lake Medina. It is the same one lost in the Zodiac flood and later recovered through Wight's "miraculous" vision. The museum is worth the admission. It is owned and maintained by the citizens of Bandera County. Besides the interesting exhibits, the museum sells many interesting and otherwise hard-to-find books and publications about Bandera and Texas history.

As you walk out of the museum, you'll notice that you are on a slight hill. You'd never know it, but this little rise has a lot of local folk history in it. It was first called Poker Hill, back when it was just a dense live oak thicket. 'Tis said that during district court sessions the grand and petit jurors would retire to the thicket and play poker while they deliberated the case at hand. After the thicket was cleared away and the Baptist church was built, the hill became Baptist Ridge, which it stayed until the Methodists and the other denominations started moving up on the hill. They couldn't just call it Baptist Ridge anymore, and Baptist-Methodist-Presbyterian Ridge was too much to say, so the folks just started calling the rise Delightful Hill. Countless other hills out here have similar pasts, though many of the stories have long since faded away, along with their tellers.

From the museum, return to Main and turn left. In 3 blocks you come to Cypress, where SH 16 leaves Main and makes a 90-degree turn to the left.

HUFFMEYER STORE
Main and Cypress

Bandera's oldest Main St. building, Huffmeyer Store was built in 1873 of native limestone and stands at Bandera's historic crossroads. The big fire of 1915 destroyed most of the north side of Main between Cedar and Cypress streets.

Next door is Bandera's chief culinary shrine, the O. S. T. Restaurant.

O. S. T. RESTAURANT
307 Main • 796-3836 • Open daily • Breakfast, lunch, and dinner • MC, V • W with assistance

In business since 1921. Everything on the extensive Tex and Tex-Mex menu is made from scratch. Mexican and American breakfasts are served at any hour, and there is a blueplate special at lunch Mondays through Fridays. Half-orders are okay. Biscuits, onion rings, french fries, chili, beans, soup—all are homemade. Not bad for this day and time. No beer.

And while we're on the subject of food—with absolutely no aspersions being cast on the O. S. T.'s fare—most all of us have a touch of trouble with our stomachs from time to time. An old time Bandera saloonkeeper offered this personally-tested cure to his customers: "When I came here, I had stummick trouble bad. I cured it by eating powdered cedar charcoal mixed with honey. I have passed this information on to many of my friends, and it has helped all of them, that has tried it."

OLD FIRST NATIONAL BANK
309 Main
This two-story limestone building was built in 1875 by W. J. "Short Bill" Davenport, and first operated as a private bank. Note the fading "First National Bank" painted in black and white over the front entrance.

From Main, turn right on Cypress (not left on SH 16). Drive 5 blocks on Cypress to 7th.

FRANZ JURECZKI HOME
7th and Cypress • Private residence
Franz Jureczki built this stucco-over-limestone home in 1876, and it is one of Bandera's oldest residences. Jureczki opened a store in his house and it is said that he sold whiskey for 25¢ a quart, or he would trade a gallon of "the oil of gladness" for a bushel of corn. With a picket fence out front and a woodshed and log barn out back, the Jureczki homestead still looks much as it did at the dawn of this century.

Just across 7th from the Jureczki home is the St. Stanislaus Catholic church and convent-school.

ST. STANISLAUS CATHOLIC CHURCH
7th at Cypress • 796-4712 • Open during daylight hours • Free
When the Polish immigrant families under the leadership of Father Leopold Moczygemba arrived in Bandera in February 1855, they bought the entire block on which the church stands from the James-Montel Company for $1 and organized their congregation, making this the second-oldest Polish Catholic Church in the U.S., after Panna Maria. Soon the congregation built their first church, a 20-foot by 30-foot log building, which no longer stands.

In 1876, construction of the present limestone Gothic vernacular sanctuary began. The steeple was not added until 1906, and in 1912 the baptistry and confessionals were added, bringing the church to its present size. Step inside to admire the high Gothic altar, stained glass windows, and stenciling.

The smaller limestone building on the church grounds was built in 1874 as a convent for the nuns and as a school. It now contains a museum filled with local parish memorabilia dating to the congregation's founding. The museum is open after mass and by appointment.

The one-story limestone building directly across Cypress from the back of the church was built in 1897 as a rectory; previously the priests had lived in a wooden rectory mounted atop the church.

The cemetery contains the graves of most of the Polish immigrants. Stones date to the 1850s, many with Polish inscriptions.

From Cypress, go up 2 blocks to Hackberry. Turn right on Hackberry.

At the corner of 10th and Hackberry (on opposite corners of Hackberry), you'll notice a pair of dressed-limestone block homes, to your left. The first, a one-story house, was built in 1880 for Judge and Mrs. Charles Montague, Jr., who raised 12 children here. The second, a two-story house over in the next block, was built in 1890 by H. H. Carmichel, a Columbia University graduate who came to Texas via Missouri. He married Mary Risinger of Helena, Texas in 1876. (Helena was popularly called "Six-Shooter Junction" and was home of the Helena Duel. In this duel, two adversaries were tied together with a short length of leather strap and then they fought each other with bowie knives until one was dead.) They came to Bandera and established a store in the present Bandera Ranch Store Building.

Proceed another block to 11th and turn right. 11th was Bandera's original main street.

FIRST METHODIST CHURCH
Hackberry at 11th

Andy Potter was the first Methodist minister to preach in Bandera, starting in 1862. He was stationed at Camp Verde at the time. He brought with him from Camp some of his boys who had begged to come along. They even promised, as Potter later remembered, that "if I would select my hymns and loan them my hymnbook, they would practice during the week." The group left Camp Verde at 8 on Sunday morning, neatly dressed. Bandera was 15 miles distant. They ran several horse races down the road along the way. Once in Bandera, Potter "told them they might walk about the town until the hour, but be sure and be there in good time" for preaching. At 11 A.M., Potter walked into the preaching place and found a large congregation waiting. His boys were sitting together on one bench. "I gave out my hymns and started the tune, the soldiers joining in, to the admiration of all. I introduced them to the people of Bandera, who gave them an invitation to dinner. We returned to Camp Verde that afternoon, and the men gave a full detail of our trip."

Potter often got permission to preach out in the country and the young soldiers vied for every opportunity to go with him, so as to enjoy some home cooking and female pulchritude. Potter helped organize the town's first congregation, and assisted in getting the congregation's first sanctuary built in 1867. The present venerable stone building has been enlarged and remodeled since its construction in the last century. Potter continued to visit Bandera and nearby Pipe Creek regularly on his post-war preaching circuit.

Continue on 11th across Cedar.

OLD FIRST STATE BANK
11th at Cedar
This two-story stone building dates to sometime before the Civil War. It housed a school from 1860 through the 1880s. During the '80s it operated as the Bandera Institute, administered by a Professor Ryan, who was thought by some to be the fugitive assassin John Wilkes Booth. Later it served as a bank.

BOYLE STORE
307 11th
Built in 1908, this recently restored one-story frame shotgun building with false facade is a good example of early Texas commercial houses, as is the **old Stevens Store** (now Stein's of Bandera) across the street at 306 11th.

OLD BLACKSMITH SHOP
305 11th
Built sometime during the 1850s, this one-story stuccoed limestone building was used by John James and Charles de Montel while they were platting the town of Bandera. Andy Potter probably preached here, since local Methodists worshipped here before building their first church. It was later a cabinetmaker's shop, blacksmith shop, and doctor's office.

OLDEST STONE BUILDING IN BANDERA
11th at Cypress
Built in 1855 by P. D. Saner, this much-altered, field-dressed limestone building was at various times used as courthouse, school, store, and funeral home.

Turn left on Cypress and go 1 block back to Main. Turn right on Main to reach the Medina River, which is just over a block away.

BANDERA RANCH STORE
Main at Maple, between Cypress and the river
On your left is the sprawling Bandera Ranch Store. The original limestone section was built in 1868 by Henry White, who operated a general store. It has been added on to several times since. The store claims the oldest elevator west of San Antonio.

Turn right on Maple just before you cross the river. This north bank of the river, up to Maple and west for several blocks, is city park land, with picnic tables and grills. You can follow the river on foot, however, for another half-mile or so on the north bank only. Traces of the old Polish mill race can be seen upstream, just past the old low-water bridge at the foot of 1st St. where the river makes a sharp bend.

From Main and Maple and the city park, return to Main and Cypress. Turn right on Cypress/SH 16. One block past Main on SH 16, you see a gas station and convenience store on your right, and a couple of old limestone buildings behind them. They are the old courthouse and jail.

OLD BANDERA COURTHOUSE AND JAIL
12th near Cypress
The courthouse is the simpler of the two buildings. Stonemason Henry White built it from native limestone in 1868 as a store. By 1877 it housed a store on the first floor and the Masonic lodge on the top floor. That year the county bought it to serve as Bandera County's first really substantial courthouse. The county continued to use it even after the current courthouse was occupied in 1891. It currently houses some state bureau offices.

Designed by Alfred Giles, the jail was built of native limestone in 1881. It has ornate window arches and a castellated roof, giving it a very Bastille-like appearance. Such fortress-massive construction was not happenstance. Cowmen began trailing their market-bound herds through Bandera right after the Civil War, and Bandera served as a major supply and rest center right through the big cattle bust of 1893, when practically all trailing ceased.

Bandera welcomed the cowboys' dollars but not their excesses. Any jail built here had to be not only strong enough to corral a dozen drunken cowboys, but also massive enough to resist the assaults frequently launched by their liberation-minded buddies on the outside. This jail was in use as such until after World War II. It is currently undergoing restoration as a museum.

Rowdy cowboys weren't the only disturbers of Bandera's peace; pigs wreaked their own peculiar havoc. Wild hogs were a valuable crop in Bandera County's early days. During the 1890s hog buyers would come through the county and announce the places and times that they would receive hogs. Each hog weighed between 200 and 300 lbs. when sold, and brought 3¢ or 4¢ a lb. on the hoof. This amounted to a considerable piece of coin to most Banderans. Not surprisingly, hog rustling was common, and each term of district court (held twice yearly) at Bandera saw lots of pig theft cases on the docket. Many prominent citizens were among the accused. Most townspeople owned hogs—it's said one man owned 200—and most of the porkers roamed Bandera streets and riverbanks at will, "rooting up gardens, scavenging the premises of townspeople for watermelon rind and eating the offal of the back alleys," as one contemporary put it.

It's also said that on one occasion a Methodist "protracted meeting" was broken up because of the fleas infesting the building to an alarming degree, caused by so many hogs bedding down under the church. Considerable friction was created whenever an election was called to "vote out the hogs," that is, to prohibit them from running loose within the city limits. But since hog owners outnumbered citizens without hogs, the "hog law" propositions were consistently voted down for years.

Banderans have long been connoisseurs of prime horse flesh and the Jan. 21, 1886, edition of the *Bandera Enterprise* went on at length about the previous Saturday's slate of races. Practically the whole town turned out. The principal race of the day matched Brown Jug and Hummingbird. But previous to that contest, doctors Sharpe and Rice ran a 50-yard footrace, with Sharpe representing Hummingbird and Rice filling in for Brown Jug. Sharpe won by 5 feet, and Rice fell flat on his face at the finish line. In the real race, Hummingbird won by 62 feet. Betting was widespread.

100 years later, parimutual betting is again legal, and Bandera Downs was one of the first tracks in the state to open. Bandera may be a horse-race-loving town, but the track couldn't attract enough out-of-town patrons to make a profit, and became one of the first tracks to close.

Bandera was known as a fun-loving town in those days, according to J. Marvin Hunter, who wrote many years ago: "There were all kinds of goodships around Bandera in those good old days. There was good fellowship, comradeship, friendship, social relationship, and sometimes the 'Fighting Parson, old Jack [Andy—ed.] Potter would come around and then they would have worship. When it was announced that Parson Potter or any other minister was in town and was going to preach that night or next day, no matter what was on foot—horse race or dance—everything was called off and everybody went to church. Protracted meetings were often held, always well attended, always earnest and orderly, but it was hard to get up a great revival. Parson Potter said it was no use to tell these people of Paradise, they wanted no place better than Bandera."

SCHMIDTKE-CALLAHAN HOUSE
Cypress/SH 16 at 13th • Houses savings and loan branch

This one-story limestone Greek Revival cottage was built during the 1870s by James Henry White for Charles F. Schmidtke, an early-day merchant, sawmill and gristmill operator. It was later owned by J. C. Callahan, who operated a store next door. His grandson bought the house in 1927, and it stayed in the Callahan family until the 1970s.

OTHER ATTRACTIONS

ARKEY BLUE'S SILVER DOLLAR
308 Main • 796-8826

The name of this club is more in line with the Bandera mentality than the Cabaret. Popular regional country music bands play dancing tunes. Put on yore boots.

BANDERA FORGE
803 Main • 796-7184

A working blacksmith shop that does both traditional and artistic welding. Take the tour, see the demos.

BANDERA VISITORS BUREAU
800-364-3833, fax 830-796-4121

Call for the latest information about rodeos and other local events, river sports, and new B&Bs. Walking and driving tours of Bandera County are available. Write to: P.O. Box 171, Bandera 78003.

THE CABARET
801 Main • 460-3095

Country music is king in Bandera, and it is at the Cabaret too, where you shore won't find Joel Grey or Liza Minelli. Top regional bands and stars play, and have since 1936.

LH7 LONGHORN RANCH TOUR
5 miles from downtown Bandera • 796-4314

This is a working Texas Longhorn ranch, one of the oldest in the state. The Marks family helped save the breed at the beginning of the century. Call for tour.

RODEOS

Open rodeos are generally held twice weekly from Memorial Day weekend through Labor Day weekend, on Tuesday and Saturday nights. On Memorial Day weekend, the Cowboy Capital Rodeo Association sponsors a CCRA Rodeo at Mansfield Park.

SIMS SPUR COMPANY
1108 Main • 796-3716

One of the world's largest spur and bit manufacturers. You can take a tour.

AREA PARKS

BANDERA PARK
On the banks of the Medina River • 796-3765

This 77-acre park offers free, easy access to the Medina River for swimmers and fishers. Picnic areas have grills; bring your own wood or charcoal. Day use only. Several local businesses rent canoes, kayaks, and tubes; some offer shuttle service.

HILL COUNTRY STATE NATURAL AREA

From Bandera, travel south on State Highway 173, go across the Medina River and continue for approximately 0.25 mile to State Highway 1077, turn right and go 8 miles on State Highway 1077 to end of the black top. Continue on the caliche road, crossing 2 cattle guards to the park entrance. 830/796-4413 • Open Thursday through Monday • No overnight camping Monday through Wednesday nights • Admission W variable

The 5,369.8-acre site was acquired by gift and purchase in 1976 and was opened to the public in 1984, primarily for equestrian use. The bulk of the site was a donation from the Merrick Bar-O-Ranch with the stipulation that it "be kept far removed and untouched by modern civilization, where everything is preserved intact, yet put to a useful purpose." The Hill Country State Natural Area features rocky hills, flowing springs, oak groves, grasslands, and canyons. The terrain ranges from flat, broad creek bottoms to steep, rocky canyons up to 1,900 feet in elevation. West Verde Creek has several spring-fed streams, and tanks in the park provide several swimming holes with limited fishing for catfish, perch, and large-mouth bass. Spring water is available for horses, but people should bring their own drinking water.

The park offers a backcountry setting for activities such as primitive camping, backpacking, limited swimming, and fishing in tanks, mountain bicycling, hiking, horseback riding, and equestrian camping. Recreational activity centers around 34 miles of designated, multi-use trails that are open to backpacking, horseback riding, and mountain bicycling. Three miles of trail are reserved strictly for horses and hikers.

The park has Guided Interpretive Horseback Tours, with a two-person maximum. Horses and guide are included in fees for 2-hour and 3-hour tours. (Special Conditions: Advance arrangement/reservation at the park is required. Single rider per horse, 250 lb. weight limit, age minimum 6; liability release required. Tours may be seasonal based on availability of horses and guide.) The adjacent Running "R" Ranch offers horse rentals from 2 hours to all day (830-796-3984).

There is a Texas State Park Store and a composting toilet at the park headquarters. Three walk-in, developed (tent) areas, are located along the creek. Sites have fire rings and picnic tables; there are chemical toilets nearby. West Verde Creek offers swimming and moderate fishing opportunities.

Chapa's Camp is a group camp with a capacity of 20 rigs in a two-acre shaded area with a large barn with a concrete floor and electricity. There is water for horses, fire rings, picnic tables, a chemical toilet, 12 horse stalls and 3 picket lines. Reservations are required. There are six Developed Equestrian Sites, with a capacity of six persons/horses combination, with tables, fire rings, a chemical toilet in the area, corrals, picket lines, and water for horses. These have access to a 34-mile trail system.

A Group Lodge is available to equestrian or nonequestrian use (accommodates 12 persons), and has four bedrooms with bunk beds; one bathroom; a kitchen with a stove and refrigerator; heating and air-conditioning; a separate screened cooking shack with a covered barbecue pit; stalls/corrals for equestrian use; no linens or cooking utensils. Visitors are not required to reserve both Friday and Saturday nights together.

Four Backpack (primitive, designated) Camping Areas have fire rings and are located 1.5 to 3.5 miles from the trail head parking. Call the park for availability.

One Developed Equestrian Area (also used as the day-use parking area, capacity 25 rigs), is located across from the park headquarters in a 6-acre shaded area with 14 (10' x 10') portable stalls, a water trough, a wash area, and fire rings. There is a primitive toilet, a public phone, and a security light. Call the park for availability.

Reservations are recommended for large groups. Fires are permitted in fire rings only, and dead wood can be collected off the ground. But park officials recommend bringing your own wood, because dead wood is scarce. Campers must pack out all trash for disposal, including all hay and animal by-products. Be sure to bring drinking water. Potable water is not available; all water must be treated.

Write to RR 1, Box 601, Bandera 78003. *Elevation:* Up to 1,900 ft. *Weather:* Average January minimum temperature 31 degrees, average July maximum temperature 94 degrees, average annual rainfall 35 in.

LODGING

RIVERFRONT MOTEL
Main at Maple, by the Medina River Bridge • 800-870-5671 • $
The best place to stay in downtown Bandera is on the river. Campers can stay at the private campgrounds on the north side of the bridge; city slickers can bed down at the Riverfront Motel, a collec-

tion of cottages overlooking the river. Reservations are strongly recommended during the summer. AC, TV, 11 cottages.

DUDE RANCHES

Bandera is famous for its dude ranches. Bandera County's dude
ranch industry dates to 1920, when some Houston folk engaged
board for a few weeks in the home of their friends Ebenezer and Kate
Buck, who owned a large ranch on San Julian Creek a few miles
south of Bandera city. The Houstonians returned home and told their
friends about the wonderful time they had. In 1921, several groups
came to stay with the Bucks. The good homecooked food, plus the
Buck's cordial western hospitality became increasingly well-known
in Houston. To accommodate the increasing numbers of guests, the
Bucks had to add on to their already large house. Through the next
two decades the Buck Ranch was so popular that reservations had to
be made months in advance, if they could be obtained at all. With the
Bucks' deaths (within seven months of each other in 1941), the ranch
was sold to W. E. Tedford, who declined to continue taking guests.
But obviously, others took up where the Bucks left off.

DIXIE DUDE RANCH
9 miles out of town (southwest) on FM 1077 • 796-4481 • P.O.
Box 548, Bandera 78003
Bandera's oldest dude ranch, since 1937. But it is also a working
ranch of over 700 acres, home to a herd of registered Texas Longhorns. Guests stay in cabins. There are about 19 rooms. Activities
include horseback riding, swimming, fishing, and hayrides. There is
a playground and live entertainment. Other interesting features are an
old barn and a cemetery with graves that date to the area's post–Civil
War range wars. Full American plan. AE, MC, V, D.

MAYAN RANCH
From the courthouse square on Main St., take Pecan St.
down to 6th, turn right on 6th, and cross the Medina River
796-3312, fax 796-8205 • P.O. Box 577, Bandera 78003
This 324-acre dude ranch offers access to the lovely Medina River,
which is great for swimming, tubing, and fishing. There is also horseback riding, tennis, volleyball, barbecues, hayrides, and cowboy
breakfasts on the trail. The saloon serves mixed drinks. Full American
plan. Cr.

TWIN ELM GUEST RANCH
SH 470, off SH 16 N • 796-3628 • P.O. Box 117, Bandera 78003

In the dude—pardon, guest—ranch business since 1939, Twin Elm has rustic, air-conditioned cabins and activities like swimming, tubing, fishing, horseback riding, campfires, hayrides, and outdoor chuckwagon meals. The Medina River runs through the ranch and there is an outdoor pool as well. The ranch property includes one of the highest of the Bandera Hills, which means lots of nice scenery on your horseback rides. It was previously a stock ranch. Full American plan; some meals are in the dining room, others are outdoors, with real range grub: barbecued beef, biscuits, etc. MC, V, travelers checks, personal checks.

You leave Bandera on SH 16, heading toward San Antonio. The good views start about 4 miles out of town, and bring to mind several of Bandera's many nicknames: Land of Pure Delight, Switzerland of Texas, Cowboy Capital of the World. Do the nicknames fit the terrain? You be the judge.

Turn right on RM 1283 at Pipe Creek.

PIPE CREEK

Bandera County • 66 • About 9 miles from Bandera

Pipe Creek the settlement started about 1872 as a trading post. Pipe Creek the stream takes its name from an incident in which a pioneer returned to the creek to retrieve his pipe in spite of the fact that he and his party were being pursued by hostile Comanches. He made his recovery safely and the creek got itself a name.

Many of Pipe Creek's first settlers were charcoal burners. They hauled it down to San Antonio where it sold for 25¢ to $1 per 40-lb. sack depending on supply. Ladies used it to heat their irons, among other things. Robert Buck, son of an early Pipe Creek settler, described the charcoal making procedure: The cedar trees were cut down and into poles and were hauled to the burning spot. The bark was peeled from the posts and the poles were set up on end, leaning in at the top, like a tepee. At the top a small opening would be left so that smoke could escape while the wood burned slowly. The bark would be piled on the poles, along with dirt, to form a 3- to 4-inch-thick coat over the stacked poles. Another small opening was left at the bottom of this "kiln," so that the burner could light a fire in the center. After the fire was started, the opening was closed, and the cedar poles would slowly smoulder as the fire ate its way through and charred the wood as desired. It took at least four days and sometimes a week to properly char the mass of poles; the slower the fire, the better the coals. Flames were an anathema to charcoal burners—if air got inside the kiln, the fire would break into flames which had to be hurriedly put out with dirt or water, or the cedar would burn too fast and the charcoal would be ruined. When the charcoal was ready and the fire put out, all the charcoal was raked out from the pile of dirt and sacked. It was now ready to be hauled to market, by wagon, 50 sacks to the wagon. The roundtrip to San Antonio and the time spent peddling it took about a week. So for about two weeks work, the burner and his helpers got about $25 or less. But in times of drought and crop failure it was the only income for many families.

Continue on RM 1283 3.5 miles to Bandera Falls, which is a relatively recent residential development. RM 1283 then takes you through rugged, wide-open ranching country. Follow RM 1283's sharp bend left at Bandera Falls, and continue almost 6 miles to the intersection with Park Rd. 37. Turn right onto Park Rd. 37 to reach Medina Lake and the Mormons last stand in early-day Texas.

You experience an abrupt change in terrain after you turn onto Park Rd. 37, which takes a wild and twisting path along the hillsides filled with cedar amd vacation homes that ring Medina Lake.

MEDINA LAKE

Medina and Bandera Counties

Completed in 1912, Medina Lake is the oldest large reservoir project in Texas, unless you count the long-unsuccessful Lake Austin, for which the dam had to be rebuilt two times after its initial failure in 1900. The main dam across the Medina River is 1,580 feet long and 160 feet high, and the lake it created covers over 5,000 acres. The dam was built and is still owned by private interests. During the two years of its construction, 1,350 workers lived in nearby campsite barracks with their families. This camp city had electricity, a hospital, baseball teams, even movies. It also had a steady stream of unsavory visitors—whiskey peddlers, gamblers, and prostitutes—all of whom endeavored to separate the workers from their hard-earned pay, $1.25 for a 10-hour day. At its completion, Medina Dam was the largest dam in Texas, but 70 men, women, and children had died of accidents, sickness, and violence in the process of building it. Medina Lake submerged Mountain Valley, site of the last organized stand of the Lyman Wight colony in Texas.

Continue on Park Rd. 37, following the contours of Medina Lake down to Medina Lake Park where Park Rd. 37 ends and you are treated to a head-on view of jewel-like Medina Lake.

MEDINA LAKE PARK
At the end of Park Rd. 37 • Open daily; day use only
Swimming, picnicking, fishing, and boating (there is a
boat ramp)

Medina Lake Park is about as close as you get to the old Mormon colony of Mountain Valley, which their gentile neighbors called Mormon Camp. The great flood of 1900 destroyed the few buildings that remained, and Lake Medina put the site forever under water. But you can still appreciate the beauty of the Medina valley, and it should be easy to see why Wight settled his colony down here.

In Wight's own words, "We are placed in a valley between several lofty mountains, on a beautiful prairie bottom. The Medina River, a stream a trifle smaller than the Genesee River [in New York state] runs within 30 steps of our doors. Our houses are spaced at a proper distance apart in two straight rows, our gardens lying between, which makes it very pleasant. We have mechancks of almost all descriptions. We make bedsteads and chairs in large quantities, and they sell as well as the finest quality of work brought from the east. We sent off one hundred and thirty chairs and eight or ten bedsteads yesterday and can send as many more in three weeks. We send them sixteen miles and get one dollar apiece for chairs by the thousand. We have a good horse mill to grind for ourselves and neighbors. We have a black smith and white smith. We raise our own cotton and make our own wheels to spin it on; and with all we have a share of farmers . . . our corn is mostly up and growing finely, we have lettice, and in a few days we will have radishes."

The Mormons also had Indian problems. Raiding Comanches hit the colony often, stealing the disciples' horses and mules, firing their crops, and driving off their cattle. Wight wrote pleading letters to Indian agents, the legislature, even the governor, asking for protection. Wight even offered the colony's assistance in civilizing the Indians, teaching the Indians how to use a plow, make wagons and chairs, and handle the blacksmith's furnace and tools. But protection was slow in coming and the raids continued. The Mormons' stock losses mounted, and so did their indebtedness to area merchants.

Wight started dreaming of yet another move, down to Mexico where, in Wight's words, "they have established a pure republic and put down the priests with their craft and made many of them pay one hundred thousand dollars for their lives; they have given free toleration to all sects and denominations and have invited all classes to come, and as the inhabitants are more than three-quarters Indian blood, I shall seek the earliest opportunity of laying the book of Mormon before them, whish treats of many anticuities with which they are perfectly acquainted." (Remember, Smith had been told by God that the Indians were the remnants of the House of Israel.) Wight further hoped that he might find there enough converts to make a republic in Jackson County, Missouri, from which he and the faithful were driven in 1833. But before Wight could turn his Mexican dream into a reality, he received a vision from God in March 1858. Wight claimed God warned him in a vision of a coming war between the North and the South, and further that God told him to move back north. Of course, continued financial reverses and the resultant litigation may have been additional incentive to move, but Wight would never have admitted to any such mundane pressures.

Wight announced the plans to move the following day, but his decision to move all the way back to Missouri met with considerable opposition. Even three of his sons declined to make the move, preferring to stay where they were and face the consequences. Those who chose to follow Wight left shortly thereafter. But only two days into the thousand-mile trek Wight died, eight miles north of San Antonio. Wight's body was taken for burial to Zodiac, where he still rests.

With Wight's death, the expedition fell totally apart. Some drifted back to Mountain Valley and Bandera, while others just dropped off at various points on the route north, such as Burnet and Bell counties. The persistent ones finally ended up in Shelby County, Iowa, in the spring of 1861. Practically all of them affiliated with the Reorganized Church of Jesus Christ of Latter-Day Saints, which established its headquarters in Independence, Missouri, back in the Zion of Joseph Smith.

Of Wight's sons, Levi Lamoni served in the Confederate Army and settled afterward at Medina City, Loami Limhi served the Confederacy and afterward lived in Bandera, Orange Lysander lived in Llano County before moving to Utah, and Lyman Levi lived in Burnet County before settling for good in Missouri.

Thus the Mormon colony of Lyman Wight passed into the history books, like so many other dreams of early settlers who came to Texas with visions of glory.

From Lake Medina, retrace your route on Park Rd. 37 to its junction with RM Rd. 1283. Here you can return to Bandera, or continue on Park Rd. 37 to SH 16, which takes you to San Antonio.

HILL COUNTRY RIVERS

Approximately 280 miles

Limestone and granite are the body of the Hill Country, and the rivers are its lifeblood. Anglo and German pioneers conquered the Hill Country by threading up the valleys of its great rivers—the Colorado, the Llano, the Guadalupe, the Pedernales, the Blanco, the Medina—then fanning out along the lesser tributaries like Cibolo, Little Blanco, Turtle, Cypress, and Verde. They depended on these flowing waters for food, drink, and industrial power. Life was impossible without them.

The Hill Country was not fully populated until the introduction of mechanical drilling rigs and the Halladay windmill during the 1880s. Previously, settlers had to depend on surface water supplies, which meant that the great arid interfluves that comprise most of the Hill Country could not be settled. Now, all you had to do was drill until you hit water, then build a windmill, which could haul water up from previously unreachable depths.

These days, as urban sprawl envelopes the Hill Country, many Central Texans view these streams as little more than seductively beautiful playthings. And they are beautiful, perhaps more beautiful than they were during those pioneer days, when the waters were harnessed to grist-, saw-, and shingle-mills, and served as laundry tubs and garbage dumps.

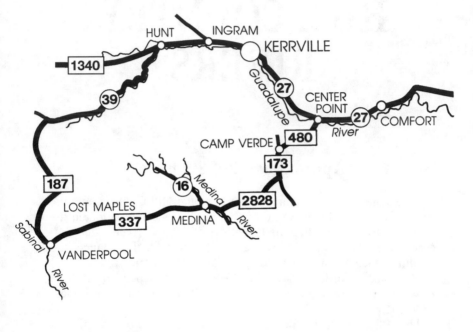

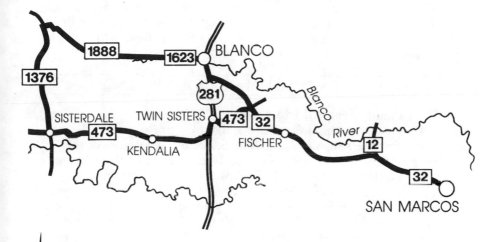

HILL COUNTRY RIVERS

Many of the miles on this trip are river miles, where the water is within view or earshot, and they lead ultimately to one of Central Texas' few remaining natural treasures, the Lost Maples of the Sabinal River Canyon.

The trip begins appropriately in San Marcos, home of the famous San Marcos (Aquarena) Springs, the headwaters of the San Marcos River. Still issuing millions of gallons per day, these springs, along with the Comal Springs in New Braunfels, are the most prolific springs in Central Texas. But that may not be true for long if current groundwater usage rates continue.

SAN MARCOS

Hays County Seat • 31,048 • (512)

Located on the headwaters of the San Marcos River, San Marcos was a favorite Indian campsite long before the appearance of European settlers. It took nearly a hundred years of trying here before a town was finally established. The Spanish made the first attempt in 1755, when they briefly located the San Xavier missions and the presidio of San Francisco Xavier at the giant springs. This settlement lasted about 15 months. In one of their last efforts to colonize Texas, the Spanish established the village of San Marcos de Neve on the San Marcos River at the Old San Antonio Road crossing, a few miles east of present-day San Marcos. Floods, Indian raids, and a filibuster attack caused its abandonment in 1812.

By 1846, San Marcos' first permanent Anglo settlers had arrived. Captain Thomas McGehee and his family set up housekeeping on the banks of the San Marcos near its confluence with the Blanco River. More Anglos began to join them, and in 1851 William Lindsey, Edward Burleson, and Dr. Eli Merriman platted out the townsite of San Marcos as we know it today. But San Marcos had already been the center of Hays County for several years, ever since the day Dr. Caton Erhard opened up his general store here. His original stock consisted of the following items: one barrel of flour, one barrel of whiskey, one sack of coffee, a few pounds of tobacco, a few shingles and nails, and some 10 or 15 pieces of calico at 16 yards to the piece. Eight yards was needed to make a dress in those days and no less than eight yards would Erhard sell. His store served as post office, county clerk's office, and general gathering place as well.

A stage stop on the Austin-to-San Antonio line opened up here the next year—1848—and San Marcos was on its way to becoming a thriving community. The powerful springs at the edge of town (Aquarena Springs) drove gristmills, sawmills, and cotton gins.

San Marcos and Hays County voted in favor of secession, and after the war organized a Ku Klux Klan group to counteract "lawlessness." Meanwhile, cattle and cotton fueled the postwar economy.

Southwest Texas State University was founded in 1899 as San Marcos Normal School, located atop old Chautauqua Hill, where the citizenry had long gathered to listen to the preaching of evangelist extraordinaire the Reverend Sam Jones and to marvel at "sun pictures" (the forerunners of the movie) put on by a Professor Tremaine. University buildings rather than Chatauqua Hill dominate the skyline today.

San Marcos has been the seat of Hays County government ever since the creation of Hays County in 1848, but not without considerable controversy. As the population of western Hays County grew, there became an ever-increasing demand that the county seat be moved nearer to the geographical center of the county. (San Marcos sits in the southern tip.) Inhabitants of the county's western hills had a difficult and long journey over the nonexistent roads down to San Marcos. Farsighted William Cannon had spent a couple of years accumulating thousands of acres in central Hays County, and in 1859 he platted the town of Cannonville and offered it as the site for a county seat. He even went so far as to outline the town's lots with logs and build the county's first courthouse. (After 10 years, Hays County still didn't have a proper courthouse at San Marcos, county officials met in rented buildings.) An election was held in 1860 and Cannonville won over San Marcos by less than 10 votes. A couple of court sessions were held there, but the county records were never moved to Cannonville. Cannon's death and the Civil War hampered relocation efforts, and by war's end county officials had purchased enough land from Comal County to make San Marcos' location a legal one.

In the meantime, Hays County got its first courthouse, courtesy of a defendant in a local murder case who jumped bail after his trial had been transferred to Travis County. The $2,000 sum he forfeited was used to build San Marcos' first courthouse, a 36-by-40-foot two-story pine structure that also served as church, Masonic lodge and school. It burned in 1869.

There's a lot to see in San Marcos these days, and the place to begin is the courthouse square. To get there from I-35, take Loop 82 from either its north or south confluence with I-35. Either way you end up at the courthouse.

HAYS COUNTY COURTHOUSE
Loop 82 at Ranch Rd. 12 • Guadalupe at Hopkins
The locally quarried soft-limestone building that replaced the pine courthouse had to be razed only 10 years later. It in turn was replaced by a harder limestone two-story building designed by noted architect F. M. Ruffini. It was also razed, after burning in 1908. The present courthouse was built in 1909. It is basically of the Greek Revival school, buff brick with a limestone rock foundation. The three-story courthouse is capped with a red tile roof, four corner cupolas, and a large center dome. Massive limestone columns with Corinthian capitols guard the entrances. The roofline's cast-metal cornice and pediments are similarly Corinthian.

The courthouse is the most imposing building on the square. In the last few years, several of the older commercial buildings on the square have had their modern facades stripped away and been returned to more or less their original appearances. However, the square doesn't easily lend itself to leisurely exploration, and there are relatively few quaint or interesting shops. San Marcos is a college town, and preservation and promotion of its historic buildings and past weren't very high on its list of priorities until recently. There are still things to see in town, away from the square.

HAYS COUNTY COURTHOUSE ANNEX
San Antonio at LBJ, on the courthouse square
This building was originally the First National Bank, which was established here in 1879. On May 22, 1933, the bank was robbed by four men with Thompson submachine guns, who got away with $7,040. Hostages were taken, but they were soon released, at the Blanco River bridge five miles north of town. Sometime later, the bank's president saw an account of Machine Gun Kelly's trial and said, "That's the man." When the FBI brought him a photo lineup, he picked Kelly's picture, identifying him as one of the robbers.

OLD CITY HALL AND FIRE STATION
220 N. Guadalupe • Currently houses private offices
Downtown San Marcos has a couple of nice examples of early twentieth-century Spanish Renaissance buildings, one of which is the 1915 City Hall and Fire Station, one-half block north of the courthouse square. Brick, two story, with a red tile roof, it has recently been remodeled into private office space, and the new fire house is just around the corner.

FIRST UNITED METHODIST CHURCH
129 W. Hutchinson
Located 1 block north and west of the courthouse, this 1894 vintage church is a fine example of Gothic Revival church architecture. Its most outstanding features are the identically designed but differently sized belltowers and the curved-at-the-edges, shiny tin roof. The congregation dates to 1847 and included in its membership General Edward Burleson, Republic of Texas vice president under Sam Houston.

BELVIN STREET HISTORIC DISTRICT
San Marcos' finest concentration of vintage homes is in the three blocks of the Belvin St. Historic District.

To get there from the courthouse, take Hopkins (FM 2439) west through the Ranch Rd. 12 intersection. Two blocks past the Ranch Rd. 12 intersection, turn right on Scott. Belvin begins 1 block later, running parallel to Hopkins.

G. T. McGEHEE HOME
727 Belvin • Private residence
Son of original settler Thomas McGehee, George McGehee built this eclectic, rambling house in 1895. A highly pitched shingle roof sprouting gables in several directions, a shingled side turret, and a wraparound porch add distinction to this white frame dwelling.

GEORGE H. TALMADGE HOME
802 Belvin • Private residence
Farmer and carpenter George Talmadge built this Victorian Gothic house of cypress in 1889. Its shuttered windows, porch balustrades, and porch column brackets reflect Talmadge's skill and taste in carpentry.

JOHN F. McGEHEE HOME
832 Belvin • Private residence
John F. McGehee built this house in 1889 from Bastrop pine and cypress siding, along with handmade brick. This home is most notable for its elaborate Eastlake-style gingerbread porch and gable trim.

JOSEPH EARNEST HOME
833 Belvin • Private residence
Merchant and cattleman Joseph Earnest built this frame house in 1892. Constructed according to a stairstep floorplan, each of the three progressively deeper "pens" has its own separate roofline—central French tower overlapped by flanking gables. Other Second Empire details adorn the gables and lintels of this dark-blue-with-white-trim house.

CROOKWOOD
227 N. Mitchell at Belvin • Private residence
This mansion in the Classic Revival style is unique among Belvin St.'s collection of Victorian buildings. Merchant and banker Ike Wood built this imposing residence in 1908. A row of massive Corinthian columns and a hanging second-floor balcony dominate the house's classical facade.

You have now reached the end of the Belvin St. Historic District. There are still more fine old houses to see. Continue past the old Masonic Temple several more blocks, to Bishop. Turn left on Bishop, cross Hopkins/FM 2439, and turn left on San Antonio 1 block later. Proceed up San Antonio back toward downtown San Marcos. San Antonio is also lined with many fine old houses; one is of particular note.

RAGSDALE-JACKMAN HOME
621 San Antonio • Private residence
This simple, white-frame two-story home is one of San Marcos' oldest still-occupied homes. Texas Revolution veteran Peter Ragsdale built it in 1868. Colorful Hays County sheriff Billy Jackman bought it in 1891.

Follow San Antonio's wandering path past the courthouse to its dead end into C. M. Allen Parkway. Turn left onto Allen Parkway. Just after you turn onto Allen Parkway you see on your right the Charles Cock Home.

CHARLES COCK HOME
Allen Parkway and E. Hopkins • 392-1111/3410 • Open all day the first Friday of each month • Open for lunch every Friday Open by appointment to groups • W variable
Built by Charles Cock in 1867, this little cottage is the only stone building of its period left in San Marcos. It was completely restored

and furnished in 1976. Owned by the city, the house is maintained by the Heritage Association of San Marcos, which serves a home-cooked lunch each Friday. Some of the furnishings are from the Cock family, the rest come from all over Central Texas.

AQUARENA SPRINGS
Loop 82 at Aquarena Springs Dr., follow signs around town
245-7575 • Open daily • W variable

Aquarena Springs is San Marcos' bubbliest tourist attraction, built around the prolific (millions of gallons per day!) headsprings of the San Marcos River. They were discovered by a party of Franciscan monks on Saint Mark's Day (April 26) in 1709, hence their original name, the San Marcos Springs. But Spring Lake as we know it is only as old as the town of San Marcos. A dam was built across the San Marcos River a few hundred feet downstream from the head-springs by early settlers who harnessed the power of the springs to power their grist and saw mills. In 1926, A. B. Rogers started a park here, which gradually grew into a full-fledged tourist trap complete with Ralph the diving pig and an underwater submarine theater with mermaids from SWTSU who drank soda water underwater. Well, all good things must come to an end.

Acquired by Southwest Texas State University in 1994, the park is being transformed (as of 1996) from hokey commercial resort to "the natural aquarium of Texas." Ralph and the mermaids are out to pasture. The chief attraction here is again what it originally was—the glassbottom boat tour of Spring Lake, the lake that is fed by the hundreds of springs—large and small—located here on one of the Balcones Fault lines. There is a fee for the cruise; pay it, the ride is worth taking. The rest of the park is free. On the entrance side of Spring Lake, there is an endangered species exhibit and a re-created frontier Texas village that contains both original area buildings and reconstructions. The Merriman cabin, built in 1846 by Dr. Eli Merriman, is San Marcos' oldest standing home. It was originally located near the courthouse square. It served as office, operating room, and home to Eli, Jenette, and their six children. Merriman also served as postmaster and tax collector. He left San Marcos in the 1850s and moved to south Texas. Merriman served as a doctor/officer in the Confederate Army and died in Corpus Christi in 1867 of yellow fever.

The Saloon is a re-creation, but the front bar is from Fredericksburg's famous White Elephant Saloon. Kyle's city jail from 1882–1925 was also moved here. Small and simple, it is of a very rare construction technique. Sawn 2-by-4 boards are laid flat like logs and built like a two-pen log cabin, layer stacked atop layer of boards, reinforced by iron bars and braces. Take the ferry across Spring Lake to see a candle shop, a re-created Kiowa Indian village, the old Burleson home, gristmill, spring house, and Spanish chapel/bell tower. Burleson built this dogtrot log cabin in 1848 of elm and oak logs. In ruins by 1917, it was restored in 1964. The gristmill came from nearby Galle community. The lovely Spanish mission chapel and bell tower was built of stones salvaged from the original mission buildings, built about 1755. The Roaring-20s hotel at the Springs' head was built in 1928 by San Marcos' first tourist-trade entrepreneur, A. B. Rogers. He had started out in the furniture and undertaking business, which was a common combination in those days. Another exhibit details archeological findings, including Clovis points, mastodon bones and teeth, and more recent human detritus. There are several interactive, multimedia kiosks that teach archeological history and early San Marcos history.

SOUTHWEST TEXAS STATE UNIVERSITY
LBJ Dr. and University • 245-2111 • W+ but not all areas
In 1899, the Texas Legislature authorized the establishment of a normal (teacher training) school at San Marcos, to be called the Southwest Texas Normal School. The citizens of San Marcos donated 11 acres of land on Chautauqua Hill, where folks had long gathered to listen to the preaching of evangelist extraordinaire the Reverend Sam Jones and to marvel at "sun pictures" (the forerunners of the movie) put on by a professor Tremaine. The school opened in September 1903 with 303 students. In 1918 it became a full-fledged senior college; in 1969 it became a university. The campus now covers over 360 acres and counts about 20,000 students. Lyndon Johnson received his bachelor's degree and permanent teaching certificate here in 1930. Visitors must obtain a pass at the gate during school hours. The Visitors Center presents a multimedia show about the university and also features some LBJ memorabilia.

WONDER WORLD/WONDER CAVE
Just off FM 2439 about 10 blocks south of the FM 2439/Ranch Rd. 12 intersection; follow signs around town • 392-3760
Open daily, 8–8 summer, 9–5 winter
Wonder Cave is billed as America's only commercial dryformed cave. That means it was formed in a matter of seconds during an earthquake—during the creation of the Balcones Fault, as a matter of fact. It also means that you see none of the spectacular stalactite and stalagmite formations that other Texas caves offer. You do see the

Balcones Fault line running along Wonder Cave's ceiling. Don't go expecting to be visually dazzled; this is more of a thinking man's cave. It used to serve as a distillery and gambling den in the Gay Nineties before the authorities shut down cave discoverer Mark Beavers' illicit operations. Wonder World also features a rather pedestrian antigravity house, an observation tower, and a quaint little wildlife park stocked with llamas, all sorts of exotic deer, and other peaceful animals.

DINING

CAFE ON THE SQUARE & BREW PUB
126 N. LBJ • 353-9289 • Open daily, breakfast, lunch, and dinner • $–$$ • Cr. • W
The cafe started in the 1897 T. A. Talbot building, which still has the original pressed tin ceiling, skylights, and wood floor. Then it moved into the 1896 store building next door and opened a Mexican import shop and brew pub. Same vintage decor, and the owners have a good collection of vintage Texas beer signs and paraphernalia. American and Tex-Mex breakfasts. The lunch and dinner menu is heavy on burgers and sandwiches but also has steaks, fajitas, wild game, and more exotic fare. Try a pint of any of the several house brews, or choose from a fairly extensive selection of domestics and imports. Live music.

FUSCHAK'S PIT BAR-B-Q
920 SH 80, east of I-35 • 353-2712 • Open daily, lunch and dinner • $ • W
Look past the fake log cabin decor and concentrate on the brisket, chicken, and fajita meat. The banana pudding will make puddin' heads happy.

PEPPER'S AT THE FALLS
100 Sessoms Dr. at the dam below Spring Lake • 396-5255 Open daily, lunch and dinner • $–$$ • Cr. • W
Of course you come for the view of the San Marcos River, but the food is okay too. Eclectic menu is informal and has a healthy quotient of appetizers, salads, burgers, and sandwiches. Tex-Mex is prominent throughout, and of course there are steaks, chicken-fried steak, fried and grilled chicken, catfish, and the other usual suspects.

LODGING

CRYSTAL RIVER INN
326 W. Hopkins • 326-3739 • $$

Just 3 blocks from the courthouse square, this B&B is located in a Greek Revival house built about 100 years ago by William D. Wood, who was a newspaper editor, lawyer, legislator, and judge. Guest rooms are named for the various Hill Country rivers.

Close by the Crystal River Inn is the **Cope House** (316 W. Hopkins), built in 1902 for businessman John Matthew Cope. Its two-story wrap-around galleries festooned with gingerbread make it the equal of any of the Belvin St. houses.

ANNUAL EVENTS

MAY • Viva Cinco de Mayo State Menudo Cook-off • Hays County Civic Center, I-35 south • 396-2495 • Weekend nearest May 5 • Free

The menudo cook-off highlights this weekend of beauty pageants, folklorico dances, a parade, and six-kilometer run. Nightly live entertainment, a carnival, and lots of food and beer complement the fiesta.

JUNE • Texas Water Safari • Aquarena Springs, Loop 82 357-6113 • Starts second Sunday in June • Entry fee

Beginning at Aquarena Springs, the race course follows the San Marcos and Guadalupe rivers to San Antonio Bay. The event is considered one of the world's toughest canoe races. It takes contestants eight days to reach the terminus at Seadrift, and they must carry all supplies in their craft. The grueling race draws canoe teams from as far away as Alaska.

SEPTEMBER • Republic of Texas Chilympiad • Hays County Civic Center, exit 201 from I-35 • Third weekend of September

Second only to the chili shootouts at Terlingua is the Annual Republic of Texas Official State Championship Chili Cook-off. The cook-off is accompanied by carnival midway, concerts, arts and crafts shows, and other zany special events. For more information, write the San Marcos Chamber of Commerce, P.O. Box 2310, San Marcos 78666, or call them at 396-2495.

Leave San Marcos on RR 12, heading west. As you leave San Marcos, notice how quickly the landscape changes. About 10 miles out of town, RR 12 suddenly veers north toward Wimberly. You continue straight ahead on what is now RM 32. Less than 5 miles later, you are climbing the Devil's Backbone, a particularly rugged, long hill that helps define the Guadalupe and Blanco rivers' watersheds. The views from the roadside park at the top are worth a pull-over.

FISCHER

Comal County • 20 • About 22.5 miles from San Marcos
See Riding the Fault for more about Fischer.

About 5 miles past Fischer, RM 32 comes to an intersection with SH 473. Turn left on SH 473 toward Twin Sisters. You begin to parallel the delightful Little Blanco River. Quite a collection of vintage stone houses and barns are strung out along this, the old Little Blanco Road. After 5 miles, you come to Twin Sisters.

TWIN SISTERS

Blanco County • 78 • (830) • About 11 miles from Fischer
In 1853, when the first settlers were coming up the Blanco River Valley from New Braunfels and San Marcos, Joel Cherry built a house here on the banks of the Little Blanco River. A number of German settlers soon joined Cherry, and soon a general store and Blanco County's first post office were established. In those days the area was known as Moureau's Valley for Franz Moureau, a New Braunfels lawyer who owned much of the area's land. But since Moureau was an absentee owner who eventually sold off his holdings, the community came to be called Twin Sisters, named for two look-alike peaks in a string of hills to the south.

There are no signs for Twin Sisters on SH 473, but 4.5 miles after you've turned on to SH 473 you'll see a huge limestone barn on your right, the old **Bruemmer Barn,** built by Heinrich Bruemmer, one of Twin Sister's early settlers. Sixty feet long and 25 feet tall, the barn contains its own water system. If ever a Hill Country barn was spectacular, this one is. It's doubtful you'll find one larger. Just a few feet farther on your right are St. Mary's Help of Christians Catholic Church and the Twin Sisters School.

ST. MARY'S HELP OF CHRISTIANS CATHOLIC CHURCH
Church building not open to the public

Unlike their free-thinking, intellectual neighbors in Comfort, the Germans who settled around Twin Sisters were good Catholics. For the first 30 years, they met in local homes or at Twin Sisters Hall. But in 1887, land was donated for a permanent church, and it was built in 1889. The little white frame church is so forthrightly simple in appearance that it tends to stand unnoticed by the speeding traveler—just a big white box with a tin roof and simple little steeple and wooden cross atop. But you can better appreciate its spareness when you realize that the millsawn lumber for the building itself was hauled by wagon over 30 miles of rocky roads and trails. The foundation is of locally quarried limestone. The church is locked up, but you can get a good look inside through the screened windows. Worshipers sit on a dozen rude, homemade, wooden backless benches. The altar is a simple homemade one, with two statues of Jesus and the Virgin Mary, in marked contrast to the opulent interiors of the Catholic Churches you'll see on the Central Texas Stew trip. There is no electricity either. Except for the tin roof, the church looks exactly as it did 100 years ago.

Next to the church is the **Twin Sisters School.** This is Twin Sisters' second school building, built in 1881 by public subscription. The porch was added in 1906. Classes were last held in 1953, but the school still serves as community center and polling place.

In a mile you come to an intersection with US 281. Turn right here for a look at Twin Sisters Hall. In a few hundred feet you will see a sign for Twin Sisters Hall. Turn right, cross the cattle guard, and follow the winding lane to the hall.

TWIN SISTERS HALL
Open the first Saturday night of each month • Admission

The center part of this sprawling hall was built in 1867; the wings were added later, as was the embossed tin siding. It still has its original vaulted, beaded, wooden ceiling, wooden dance floor, and homemade wooden tables and benches, as well as slightly more modern oscillating fans. An advertising board of area business dating from the 1930s still hangs. It is a timeless place; except for the beer prices and cans it could be the 1920s or '30s in here. Come here for a Saturday night dance for the real old-time flavor of Texas—forget the claims of that dancehall-turned-tourist-trap in Gruene—this is the oldest dance hall in Texas.

Across the highway from the Twin Sisters Hall entrance is the old **Twin Sisters cemetery,** where many of the old stones' inscriptions are in German.

From the Hall and Cemetery double back on US 281, and cross the Little Blanco to reach modern-day Twin Sisters, a short string of businesses along the highway.

LITTLE BLANCO INN
US 281 • 833-5637 • Open Wednesday through Monday, lunch and dinner • $ • No Cr. • W

The only place to eat in Twin Sisters is the Little Blanco Inn. Country-style food, including barbecue, catfish, and steak are served. Rolls and bread are also made here. The adjoining gift shop has antiques and homemade quilts for sale.

After nearly 2 miles with US 281, SH 473 turns away again to the west. Follow SH 473 to Kendalia.

KENDALIA

Kendall County • 76 • (830) • About 9 miles from Twin Sisters

Kendalia was named for George Wilkins Kendall, the world's first war reporter. He joined the ill-fated Texan Santa Fe Expedition in 1841 as a reporter, was imprisoned with other expedition members, and lived to write a book about it. In 1846, Kendall joined American forces fighting in Mexico as a foreign correspondent, filing his reports via Pony Express. Kendall was wounded in the knee during the storming of Chapultapec Castle. By 1857 Kendall had bought a ranch here at the place that bears his name and had become one of Central Texas' first sheep ranchers. During the Civil War he produced wool for the Confederate cause, enduring Comanche attacks, roaming outlaws, and natural disasters in the process.

A town had been laid out here by 1883, and contemporary promotional sheets urged readers to "buy a mountain home in the sunny South" in Kendalia, "a great health resort in Kendall County, Tex." Far-seeing promoters had set aside blocks for the Kendalia Steam Mill and Cotton Gin, Mountain College, Vogel Square, and Spring Garden. Five of the original 20 streets exist today.

For the grand tour of Kendalia, continue straight on RM 3351 when SH 473 veers off to the north.

GEORGE ELBEL BUILDING
RM 3351

A few yards down RM 3351 you see on your left the 1911 George Elbel store building. Built of rough-finish limestone blocks, this building's calling card is its cast-iron ground-story facade and imposing pressed-tin false second-story facade. The house next door has some nice gingerbread detailing.

Kendalia Halle, on the other side of the Elbel building, was built some time before 1911, and is still operated as a dance hall. It is available for private parties. Call 830-833-5026.

Just past the Elbel store, you see a sign directing you to turn right to reach the Kendalia Community Church.

KENDALIA COMMUNITY CHURCH
North of RM 3351 • Open to the public and still in use

This simple white-frame church with green trim and louvered window shutters was built about 1887 after Boerne newspaper editor Carl Vogel deeded this lot to a newly formed Methodist congregation.

From the church, continue in the same direction, towards SH 473.

To your left at the stop sign a few yards past the church, the one-story limestone building with the alamo arch is the old Longhorn General Store, built in the 1890s. It is now a private residence. The hotel stood out back of the store; it was torn down years ago.

From the old Longhorn Store go one more block to SH 473, turn left and continue on SH 473 to Sisterdale.

SISTERDALE

Kendall County • 63 • (830) • About 14 miles from Kendalia

Sisterdale is located in the valley of the Sister Creeks, near their confluence with the Guadalupe River. Captain Nicholas Zink, an eccentric Bavarian engineer who had built roads for the Greeks during their war for independence, settled here in 1847. He was soon joined by a group of intellectual refugees from Germany known as "forty-eighters"— forward-thinking men who had seen their dreams evaporate with the failure of the Revolution of 1848. Disillusioned with the world at large, these men had retreated to the hills, having "decided that the quest for Teaming was the only occupation in this world."

Each of these gentlemen farmers had a library and met weekly at the little log schoolhouse to discuss the latest in literature, often in Latin. Indians sometimes came to listen at the door.

In spite of their erudite backgrounds, these men had to hunt and work the fields for their daily bread. This combination of lifestyles presented a bizarrely contrasting sight to contemporary visitors. Frederick Olmstead wrote in *A Journey Through Texas:* "You are welcomed by a figure in blue flannel shirt and pendant beard, quoting Tacitus, having in one hand a long pipe, in the other a butcher's knife; Madonnas upon log walls; coffee in tin cups upon Dresden saucers; barrels for seats, to hear a Beethoven's symphony on the grand piano; 'my wife made these pantaloons, and my stockings grew in the field yonder'; a fowling piece that cost $300, and a saddle that cost $5; a bookcase half-filled with classics, half with sweet potatoes."

Olmstead was referring to the home of Baron Ottomar von Behr, son of the prime minister of Anhalt-Köthen and friend of Bettina von Arnim (see Mormon Trails—The Dutch Settlements) and the scientist Alexander von Humboldt. Von Behr came to Texas in the mid-1840s and wrote a book for German immigrants published in Leipzig in 1847, which served as sort of a bible for many of them. Von Behr was the second settler here and is usually credited with naming the village. A man of many interests, he raised a breed of sheep he had developed by crossing those he had brought from Germany with a hardier Mexican breed, maintained what was probably Texas' first lending library in his house, and served as justice of the peace and postmaster. A meteorologist and naturalist, he made and recorded extensive observations about the area. He made regular trips back to Germany to collect rents on property he owned there, and died there in 1856. His wife remained in Texas to raise their four children; their descendants still live in the area.

Another of the forty-eighters was Dr. Ernst Kapp, a geographer-historian-philosopher turned physician. Imprisoned briefly in Germany in 1849 for a book he had written advocating a more liberal, democratic government, Kapp emigrated to Galveston in December 1849 before settling in Sisterdale. He operated a mineral-water cure sanatorium here, in addition to his farm. In 1853, Kapp was elected President of the Freier Verein, an organization of mostly German intellectual liberals. They held a convention the next year in San Antonio at which they demanded the abolition of slavery. It was the first open convention for abolition held in the South.

Edward Degener was a member of the first, short-lived German National Assembly in 1848. He came to Texas and Sisterdale in

1850, buying the home and farm of the restless Nicholas Zink, who moved on to Fredericksburg that year (see Take a Ride on the Fredericksburg & Northern—Welfare).

The men of Sisterdale joined in with the rest of the region in petitioning for the creation of a new county in 1859. Kendall County was finally organized in 1862, and in the election to determine the location of the county seat, Sisterdale lost to Boerne by less than 10 votes. This loss, plus the forty-eighters' gradual disenchantment with the country life and the Confederacy signaled the end for Sisterdale as a prominent town and major cultural center.

Kapp returned to Germany for a visit in 1865 with the end of the Civil War and never came back, writing books and finally dying in Dusseldorf in 1896. Degener was court-martialed and imprisoned by the Confederate Army during the war for his loyalty to the Union cause. After the war he moved to San Antonio where he got into the wholesale grocery business and politics, serving as Republican Congressman in Washington from 1870–71, and later as San Antonio city councilman.

Other, more practical-minded German immigrants came along to take their places, like Andreas Langbein. Langbein came in 1863 and bought the Kapp place; at one point he owned most of the valley.

SISTERDALE GENERAL STORE
SH 473 • 324-6767 • Tuesday through Sunday 10–7, Closed Monday • No Cr. • W

Inside, up on the wall just inside the front door, is a large framed history of Sisterdale, complete with text and sketches. Several of the old pioneer buildings depicted still stand, but they are located on private property and not accessible or easily visible from the road. You'll also notice a variety of old beer signs and a beautiful hand-carved curly pine bar back, brought to Sisterdale from Fredericksburg in 1919. It used to be across the road in the old dance hall/saloon, but was moved here when this store was built in 1954.

Gus Langbein (Andreas' son) built the dance hall/saloon about 100 years ago, as well as the long, white, one-story house next to it with all the front doors. It served as home, general store, post office, and stage stop, hence all the separate entrances.

As you leave the Sisterdale Store and continue towards Comfort, the small limestone building immediately on your right is the old **Sisterdale school,** built at the tail end of the glory days, when Sisterdale had supposedly the finest primary school in the state.

SISTER CREEK VINEYARDS
RM 1376 • 324-6704 • Open daily (afternoons) • W

The vineyard, located between East and West Sister Creeks, is planted with Chardonnay, Pinot Noir, Cabernet Sauvignon, Cabernet Franc, and Merlot grapes. Sisterdale's old cotton gin houses the winery. Sister Creek's wines have won several silver medals in the annual North American International Wine Competition.

From Sisterdale, continue west on SH 473 to Comfort. Between Sisterdale and Comfort, SH 473 takes you through the fertile Guadalupe River valley.

THE BAT ROOST
SH 473, 11 miles west of the SH 473/RM 1376 intersection at Sisterdale • Private property
Those of us born after World War II tend to take good health and longevity almost for granted, AIDS and cancer notwithstanding. Cholera, diphtheria, yellow fever, polio, rabies, influenza, tuberculosis, and malaria no longer strike terror in our hearts as they did for our parents and grandparents, because of the vaccines and treatments developed to combat these diseases.

Malaria was one of many scourges in early Texas, especially in low-lying areas. After it was discovered that mosquitoes spread the disease, health professionals began searching for ways to control the mosquito population. Since bats are voracious insect eaters, experimental efforts were made between 1907 and 1929 in the U.S. and Italy to promote bat populations in problem areas through the construction of "Hygieostatic Bat Roosts." According to plans drawn up by Dr. Charles A. Campbell, San Antonio's health officer, one of the few roosts in America was built near Comfort in the Guadalupe River bottoms in 1918, on land owned by the family of San Antonio Mayor Albert Steves. Seven roosts were eventually built in Texas, and this site is the only one still in existence. The roost consists of three wooden towers resembling Dutch windmills without blades. Only one tower is visible from the road. The tower is located in a peach orchard just a few feet to your left, directly opposite the intersection with Flat Rock Creek Rd.

COMFORT

Kendall County • 1,593 • (830) • About 13 miles from Sisterdale
The first Anglos to settle the area were shingle-makers who set up camp along Cypress Creek and the Guadalupe River in 1852. A league and labor of land (4,605 acres), which covers the Comfort of

today, was first given by the Republic of Texas to Jose Maria Regalado, who probably never even saw the land. The tract changed hands several times and by 1854 belonged to John F. C. Vles, a New Orleans cotton merchant and real-estate speculator. Theodor Wiedenfeld, his brother-in-law, Heinrich Schladoer, and their families were the first German settlers in the area, having traveled up the Guadalupe from New Braunfels. Not wishing to remain a squatter, Theodor wrote a letter to Vles regarding sale of the land. In response, Vles sent 22-year old Ernst Altgelt, a newly arrived Prussian employee, to check the tract out. It was spring, and Altgelt fell in love with the Comfort valley the first time he laid eyes on it, deciding to build a town here. Vles approved and Altgelt surveyed and laid out a town.

The camp Altgelt set up for his surveying crew on the west bank of Cypress Creek was called Camp Comfort, but no one is quite sure why they chose the name Comfort. Altgelt was so sold on the developmental possibilities that he wrote to his father in Dusseldorf for enough money to buy a thousand-acre tract that adjoined Vles' tract. Vles paid Altgelt off with land, giving Altgelt 2,500 acres to play with. Vles also gave Altgelt power of attorney to sell his land off to settlers.

After 300 lots were laid out, Altgelt declared the town alive and for sale on September 3, 1854. Thirty lots sold immediately, under a grove of oaks (now gone) at the corner of Main and 7th. Eight houses were immediately built.

Soon after the village's founding, Altgelt erected a saw- and gristmill, which came to be called Perseverance Mill. Over sixty families and as many individuals followed Altgelt here in the first year of Comfort's existence. Many of them were highly educated "free thinkers" of the same ilk as their intellectual compatriots at Sisterdale and Bettina. In that way, these settlers were unlike the Catholic and Lutheran farmers, tradesmen, and shopkeepers who left Germany in the 1840s to escape famine and unemployment and settled New Braunfels and Fredericksburg. These later-comers quite openly told people they left Germany to escape not only the political persecution that followed the liberals' failure in the Revolution of 1848, but also religious oppression. From 1854 to 1892, no church was built in Comfort; you could scarcely find a Bible in any of the homes. There were no prayers, and at funerals, sentimental German ballads replaced hymns. Vera Flach wrote in *A Yankee in German America:* "Funerals were always as large as they would be with so many relatives near at hand. The service was conducted by a German lodge and its message was 'Rest in Peace.' The life of the deceased was told and sometimes there was a eulogy read by a man skilled in public speaking. There was no mention of immortality because no one believed in it. We live in our children. That is our only immortality."

So how did Comfort get its name? One story says early settlers wanted to call their settlement "Gemuetlichkeit," a hard-to-spell, pronounce, and translate German word expropriated in the 1960s by the New Braunfels Wurstfest, which handily translates it as "good times." But the word means more, implying a sense of tranquility, serenity, peace, happiness, and comfort.

The erudite backgrounds of many of the Germans here caused another story to be told on them, that "these Freiburg and Heidelberg professors had made a vow to give their descendants a thorough education and therefore to speak only in Latin and German during the intervals of their hard work." At any rate, these hardworking Germans wasted no time in providing themselves with all the comforts of life, including the luxury of wheat flour ground at their own local mill starting in 1860.

Comfort was the county seat of Kerr County for two brief years, from 1860 to 1862. Comfort had wrested away this honor—78 votes to Kerrville's 22 votes—in an 1860 election. Kerrville regained its county seat status with the creation of Kendall County in 1862. Comfort was found to be just inside the new county of Kendall.

Cotton came to Comfort in a big way after the Civil War, for the nearby Guadalupe River bottomland is rich and black. The arrival of the San Antonio and Aransas Pass Railroad in 1887 made Comfort a major cotton shipping center, over more isolated Fredericksburg, which didn't get a railroad until 1913 (see Take A Trip on the Fredericksburg & Northern). Because of its high altitude relative to the Gulf Coast and much of the rest of populated Texas, Comfort was promoted as a cool summer resort; hunters found it to be a "Mecca of the Nimrods." Tuberculars and other respiratory sufferers came for the dry air and mild winters. They liked the clean water and lack of mosquitoes and malaria. By 1910, three hotels were serving hundreds of guests a week. Others stayed at boarding houses or on ranches with guest quarters; many others just pitched tents and lived off the bountiful local provender: fresh milk and butter, fish, fresh meat and game, and lots of fruit and vegetables.

The hospitable climate here was also deemed by E. T. Hall in 1914 "more ideal for ostriches than anywhere else in the country, with the exception of Phoenix, Arizona, where the largest ostrich farm in the world is located." Hall was in charge of Hot Wells Development Company's ostrich farm operation. In 1914, Hot Wells bought one thousand acres along the Guadalupe near Comfort, so that they might raise enough ostriches to supply the contemporary demand for "French plumes" for ladies' hats. You see, ostriches grow 160 of the plumes every nine months, 80 on each wing. All you have to do is pluck them. The ostrich farm never really got off the ground (forgive the pun), because the plumage craze was already at its peak, soon to crash.

Ostrich raising may never have caught on here, but armadillo ranching surely did. For decades, Charles Apelt operated his armadillo farm—the only one in the world—about five miles out of town on SH 27. A basket-weaver, Apelt began trapping armadillos, breeding them, processing them, and turning their shells into baskets, lampshades, and other novelties. A Depression-era pamphlet said of the farm: "Comfort's farm, the only one in the world, has probably done as much as any agency to put this lively 'hill country' town on the map. Not only does the world come to see it whenever it gets a chance, but it buys armadillo baskets in great numbers from the Comfort farm." Notice that back then they put Hill Country in quotations. Anyway, the Comfort Armadillo Farm died along with Charlie Apelt a few years ago.

As pleasant a place as Comfort is to live today, nature still strikes some hard blows. Disastrous floods swept through in 1870, 1900, and 1932. In 1976, a tornado blew through town, most notably razing the old gazebo. August 2, 1978 brought the worst flood yet. Old-timers had long warned of what would happen if the headwaters of Cypress Creek, Verde Creek, and the twin forks of the Guadalupe all received heavy rains simultaneously. On that date it happened, with the greatest concentration between Bandera and Center Point estimated at as much as 43 inches of rain in 48 hours. Cypress Creek exploded into town and ran into the Guadalupe, which had already crested. The flood water ran up to Main Street, and even High Street in one block. The water was up to 12 feet deep in places, and in the park, only the roof of the gazebo could be seen. Three people died and many low-lying homes were destroyed. The July 1987 Guadalupe River flood stranded two summer-camp buses trying to escape and carried ten of the young campers to their deaths as they tried to evacuate the inundated vehicles.

Comfort is full of things to see, reminders of a Teutonic past. There are about 100 pre-1910 buildings within walking distance of the center of town. For a town with so much to see, Comfort remains relatively unspoiled, compared to New Braunfels and the increasingly Disneyland-like Fredericksburg.

Take SH 473 across US 87 to SH 27. Turn right on SH 27, and then after one block turn left onto High Street, the name Comforters gave to their stretch of the Old Spanish Trail, which was, until 1933, the

*main highway through the Hill Country to California, tracing the
same path I-35 follows today. US 87 and SH 27 eclipsed High as the
main drag through town, but it remained Comfort's principal "downtown" street. The street's name refers to its altitude relative to Main
and the streets below, which are closer to Cypress Creek.*

OTTO BRINKMANN HOUSE
701 High • Not open to the public
Otto Brinkmann built this cottage in 1860 and lived here with his
twin brothers until he married in 1867 (hence the house's nickname
"Bachelor Bude"). This house is one of Comfort's best examples of
the "fachwerk" construction technique, that is, half-timbered walls
filled in with native stone—in this case limestone. The cottage was
enlarged in 1879 and restored in 1973.

COMFORT CHAMBER OF COMMERCE
7th at High • Open Friday and Saturday afternoons • W
The Chamber of Commerce is located in the old Comfort State
Bank, a delightful mix of Romanesque Revival and castle Gothic,
built in 1907–08. Richard Doebbler, survivor of the 1862 Nueces
River Massacre, built it of rough-polished limestone blocks with
pink granite pillars. It was Comfort's first formal, chartered bank;
previously local merchants had provided banking services, beginning with August Faltin in 1856. Peter Joseph Ingenhuett began
offering the same services for his customers in 1869. Although this
caused a rift in the community, with inhabitants divided between the
two mercantile families, there was little local interest in organizing a
formal bank until a bank officer from San Antonio came sniffing
around in 1906 to investigate the possibilities of opening a branch
bank here. When they got wind of this, the rival Faltin and Ingenhuett families joined forces with three other Comfort men to organize the Comfort State Bank. The bank stayed in this building until
1960, when it moved to its present location. It was then donated to
the Comfort Independent School District, which in turn made it
available to the Comfort Public Library, now located in the Arno
Schwethelm Building (1916) across the street.
The Chamber of Commerce and the Comfort ISD Board of
Trustees are the closest thing Comfort has to local government;
Comfort is one of the oldest, largest unincorporated towns in Texas
and proud of it. "Live and let live," "We'll take care of our own," and
"The less government the better," are the town's philosophical linch-

pins, and the direct heritage of Comfort's free-thinking founders. A Free Thinkers society is still active. Volunteerism and personal donations built the schools, hospital, theater, and park facilities, and founded and funded the public library, museum, volunteer fire department, and EMS. This "benevolent anarchy," as it has been called, seems to have worked pretty well for nearly 140 years now.

Not too many other towns in Texas have a Bolshevik Hall. Comfort's Bolshevik Hall was a small frame building originally located behind the bank where the old men gathered to play dominoes, skat, pinochle, and other card games and engage in philosophic argument or debate, depending on how many pilsners and lagers were consumed. It has moved several times in recent years and is now located across 7th from its original location.

From the old bank/Chamber of Commerce, go south one block on 7th to Main.

Founder Altgelt had intended that the main business district be located around the two town squares on Main, but early flooding made most businessmen move up to High Street. High, between 6th and 8th Streets, became the main business district, although the Faltins and Brinkmanns remained in business across from each other at 7th and Main.

FALTIN HOMESTEAD
400 block 7th, between High and Main • Not open to the public
On your right in the middle of the block is one of the oldest buildings still in its original location in Comfort. Brothers Theodore and Fritz Goldbeck built it in 1854, and operated Comfort's first general store next door, at the corner where the Faltin Store now stands. Fritz, a member of Altgelt's surveying party, also wrote poetry about early German pioneer life in Texas. Tired of the pioneer life, they sold the cabin and store in 1856 to August and Clara Faltin and moved to San Antonio. Faltin added the fachwerk section and the house has remained in the Faltin family ever since.

FALTIN GENERAL STORE
Main at 7th
Born in Danzig, Prussia (now Gdansk, Poland), in 1831, August Faltin came to Comfort in 1856 and took over operation of the Goldbeck store on the corner, next to the cabin. In 1879 he built this imposing Italianate limestone building, designed by noted San Anto-

nio architect Alfred Giles. It was Giles' first building outside San Antonio. The sheet-metal cornice and heavy consoles were to be repeated two years later in the Giles-designed Gillespie County Courthouse. The store was downstairs, the family lived upstairs, and merchandise was stored in the basement. August retired in 1889 and turned the business over to his sons, who sold it to their brother-in-law, Dan Holekamp, in 1907. He decided to tear down the old Goldbeck store and build the simpler 1907 addition that sits directly on the corner, also designed by Alfred Giles. The second story was used for community meetings.

The Faltin Store started a trend toward limestone construction, as the community recovered economically from the ravages of the Civil War. The limestone was quarried from nearby ranches and hauled in by wagon. Limestone is sedimentary rock, built up layer by layer over the millennia. To split the limestone into manageable blocks, quarriers drilled holes into the rock at regular intervals, pounded round cypress or cedar poles into the holes, then saturated the poles with water. The wood swelled with the water, and their expansion split the limestone along even lines. Holes were also chipped into the sides of the big blocks so the giant tongs used to lift the stone blocks had something to grip on to. This explains the holes and grooves you see in the stones of many of the old stone buildings here and throughout the Hill Country.

They also had to make their own mortar to stick the stones together. Lime, sand, and water made a fine mortar and plaster. To make the lime, they built a kiln by digging an egg-shaped hole in the ground, preferably on a hillside where there would be a good draft for the fire. The hole was then filled with broken limestone rock, but with a hole in the center (like a bundt cake) into which enough burning charcoal was dropped to fill the hole. After burning for three days, the limestone was broken down to a lime component suitable for mortar. More permanent lime kilns were also built into the hillsides, with round stone walls like a well. A good example for public view is on FM 165, 8 miles north of Blanco, at a roadside park in the Peyton Colony area. Peyton Colony was a farming community of Freedmen families that developed after the Civil War, similar to St. John's Colony near Red Rock.

BRINKMANN & SONS STORE
408 7th at Main • Currently houses an antiques cooperative

Otto Brinkmann, whose "Bachelor Bude" you have already seen, built these adjoining store buildings beginning in 1883. The larger section was a general merchandise, hardware, and appliance store. Otto also had a lumberyard. The family lived in the gabled section, before the house next door (facing Main) was built in 1894. Otto's sons joined him in the business as they became of age. Otto's brother Walter, a tinsmith, built the tinwork building next to the corner store in 1894. A furniture store addition came in 1911. Walter lived in the house (1896) next to the tin shop.

From the Faltin General Store, proceed 2 blocks south on 7th (away from downtown) and turn right onto Water. Go 1 block, to the corner of 6th and Water.

COMFORT TURN VEREIN
700 Water, 6th at Water
   This simple one-story white frame shotgun building houses one of the few bowling alleys in Texas where pin boys manually set up the pins after each ball. The Turn Verein was Comfort's first organized social club and dates to 1860. This bowling alley was built in 1901.

From the Turn Verein, return to the Faltin General Store. From the Faltin store, return to High and the Chamber of Commerce.

   The south side of the 800 block of High is cited as one of the most complete 19th-century business districts still standing in Texas. A useful guide for exploring Comfort, including downtown, is *Guide to Historic Comfort,* published by the *Comfort News;* it's free and available at the Chamber of Commerce and other local businesses.

PETER JOSEPH INGENHUETT HOUSE
812 High
   Peter Joseph Ingenhuett came to the Comfort area in the 1850s and tried his hand at farming before moving into town in 1867 to try shopkeeping. He and his family lived in the small fachwerk cottage (built 1863) at the back of this property. A better businessman than farmer, he quickly began to prosper and expand, buying his partner out in 1868 and branching out into a variety of businesses. As his four sons reached maturity, each one took over at least one of his concerns. Ernst took over the hotel; Hubert, the saloon; Paul, the general store and cotton gin; and Herman, the livery stable.
   In 1888, Peter Joseph built the larger, unpretentious, stucco-over-limestone, one-story house that sits out front.

OLD POST OFFICE
814 High

Alfred Giles also designed Comfort's first proper post office, built in 1908; Herman Ingenhuett was postmaster at the time. Giles did not often work in brick; this little building, built of red brick with limestone accents, shows off Giles' ability to work with mixed media, and is in the same simple style as his Center Point School (1911).

INGENHUETT/FAUST HOTEL
818 High • 995-3030 • Open daily • W with help

The original, eight-room wing of this hotel was designed by Alfred Giles for Peter Ingenhuett, who built it in 1880. The hotel's size was doubled by the addition of a back wing in 1894. Out back, wide verandas open onto a courtyard brightened by hanging baskets and flower beds. A charming turn-of-the-century gazebo sits in the middle of the courtyard and provides a nice resting spot. Various members of the Ingenhuett family operated the hotel until about 1903; Louis and Mathilde Faust operated it from 1909–46. It was restored in 1985 and is now home to about a dozen antique dealers. Five rooms/suites are available for overnight (bed-and-breakfast) lodging.

INGENHUETT STORE
830-834 High • 995-2149 • Open Monday through Saturday

Ingenhuett Store can now lay claim to being the oldest general store in continuous existence in Texas, spanning five generations of the same family. The painted sign hanging from the porch still reads "Peter Ingenhuett • Fancy Groceries • Hardware & Implements • Cash Grocery." The store is still, in fact, all of these things. Need service or parts for your 1920 Lavalle cream separator? You'll find both here, along with canned tamales, fresh meat, and overalls. The walls are covered with an amusing 1940s cowboy mural. The oldest, second-story section of the present store building dates to 1880 and was designed by Alfred Giles.

The original store stood where the Ingenhuett/Faust Hotel now stands. Peter Joseph ran his private bank inside the store; the post office was also located here until 1898. He was postmaster nearly 25 years. In addition to this store and the hotel, Peter Ingenhuett also established a livery stable, cotton yard, opera house, and saloon. In 1891, son Paul Ingenhuett assumed operation of the store and expanded the banking business and the marketing of grain and farm implements. He also got into the wool and mohair business in a big way, and added the store's east wing in 1900.

In 1891, Alfred Giles also designed the saloon next door at 828 High (to your right, as you face the store). Church services were held here occasionally before 1900, and the building has also served as dance hall, grocery, meat market, and cabinet shop.

Paul's son, Peter C. Ingenhuett, ran the store from 1921 until 1955, when he was succeeded by his daughter and son-in-law, Gladys and James Krauter, and their son Gregory.

COMFORT HISTORICAL MUSEUM
838 High at 8th • Open second Sunday of month, on special occasions, and by appointment; call Roy Perkins, Jr. at 995-3807 • Donations accepted

This two-story limestone block building was built by Jacob Gass in 1891. During its construction, he walked in from Sisterdale each week, walking back to spend weekends with his family. He lived upstairs and had his blacksmith shop below. Paul Ingenhuett bought it in 1903 for storage for the store next door, then made it available to house the Comfort Museum when the museum was created in the 1930s. The museum consists of natural history artifacts, Indian relics, and historic memorabilia of the early German settlers.

Just around the corner from the museum, to your right down 8th from High, is the Paul Ingenhuett home.

INGENHUETT HOUSE
8th, just south of High, on your right • Private residence

Paul Ingenhuett was born on this block and succeeded his father Peter Joseph in the mercantile business. Young Paul also expanded into farming and stock raising, and helped found the Comfort State Bank. After noted architect Alfred Giles had designed several buildings in Comfort, Ingenhuett commissioned him to design this house in 1897. Of limestone quarried from Ingenhuett's property, the house is simple yet tasteful in its lines. Its only extravagance is the recessed center porch with its Greek pediment and twin supporting pillars. Unaltered, it is currently occupied by the fifth generation of Ingenhuetts.

One of the family reminisced about a hailstorm which struck Comfort about 1928 or 1929. "I was just a little girl then. Hail stones the size of softballs crashed right through the window shutters, screens, and glass. Mother pulled me out of bed just before the hail pounded through, and it was a good thing too, because my bed was left full of broken glass." Her husband remembered that he spent most of the storm under his bed.

Behind the family home, almost hidden from view, stands the old **Ingenhuett Opera House,** built of native limestone about 1890. It is not open to the public, but was Comfort's social center before the Comfort Theatre was built.

Continue east on High. In another few yards you come to the old Meyer Hotel complex on your right, marked by a state historical marker.

THE MEYER BED AND BREAKFAST
845 High • 995-2304
Frederick Meyer came to Comfort in 1862. A wheelwright, he also operated the town's first stagecoach stop and way station (a small log building built in 1857), located here on the banks of Cypress Creek. After purchasing the property, he added a sleeping loft to the cabin, in the style of the Fredericksburg Sunday houses, where passing travelers could spend the night. He built the two-story limestone cottage you see out front here in 1869. The upstairs rooms were rented to stagecoach passengers; he and the family lived downstairs.

In 1872, Meyer built a two-room frame cottage for his wife Ernestine, who was a midwife and needed birthing rooms for her patients who came into town from area farms and ranches. When the railroad came through in 1887, he built the two-story frame hotel with double galleries to accommodate the rail passengers. The Meyers met the passengers at the station and took them by carriage to the hotel. Guests could eat a bountiful 50-cent dinner in the dining room or enjoy a picnic on the grassy banks of Cypress Creek, behind the hotel. Although Frederick Meyer died in 1889, his wife, Ernestine, and then his daughter, Julia Ellenberger, continued to operate the hotel. Julia built the two-story stucco hotel in 1920 to handle the increasing business, and ran the hotel until her death in 1956. It was Comfort's favorite eating place.

The complex changed hands several times before restoration and renovation began in 1973. All 9 units are now air conditioned and have private baths and cable TV, but otherwise retain their original charm. Complimentary country-style breakfast. Call for rates and reservations, or write P.O. Box 514, Comfort, TX 78013.

If you continue east on High, you will cross the Guadalupe at the same point as the pioneers on the Old Spanish Trail, but you'll have to walk the last few hundred feet to the scenic 1920s low-water bridge. Damaged by the 1987 flood, it was closed by the county to car traffic. In the 1930s, SH 27's route through town was modified; the sharp corner at High and 4th was replaced with two blocks of curved road, which accounts for Comfort's apparently somewhat confusing layout. It's actually a very geometric, German town. Turn around and head back up High to 7th. Turn right on 7th.

OLD COMFORT THEATRE
522 7th, at Front

The Spanish Renaissance-styled Comfort Theatre was built in 1930 by public subscription ($50 a share), to fill the local need for a theater and community center. Besides movies and plays, the theater hosted dances, meetings, other civic functions, and served as the high school gymnasium. With the repeal of Prohibition in 1933, beer joints and dance halls popped up all over the countryside and use of the building as a dance hall began to decline. In 1940, a new high school and gym/stage were built, which made community use of the building almost nonexistent. It continued as a movie theater through the 1960s, when new owners began presenting live music and stage plays as well. The building is no longer used as a theater.

Turn right on Front/SH 27 and follow it to its junction with US 87. Continue on SH 27/US 87 toward the Guadalupe River bridge. Just across the bridge you see an old roadhouse named Bruno's Curve.

BRUNO'S TEXAS STAR
On the curve, SH 27/US 87, just past the river bridge
995-9747 • Open daily, 3 P.M. to midnight • No Cr. • W

Stop in at Bruno's for a bit of local color. The original owner moved a chicken coop here and remodeled it in 1938. The place really rocked back in World War II when all the soldiers came up from San Antonio and Leon Springs on the weekends, but somehow it managed to hang on in one piece. The beergarden is nice when the weather is. Live music. Beer, setups, BYOB.

From Bruno's, double back into town. Back across the Comfort side of the bridge, notice the Double D Cafe on your right.

DOUBLE D CAFE
SH 27, west of the bridge • 995-2001 • Open Monday through Saturday, breakfast, lunch, and dinner; Sunday, breakfast and lunch • $ • No Cr. • W

The Double D Cafe serves what most folks call the best hamburgers in Comfort. With a daily ("all-you-can-eat") lunch buffet, this is a place for hearty eaters. Beer only.

Continue through town on SH 27 until you cross High. Turn right on High to visit the only monument to the Union located in the South.

TREUE DER UNION (LOYALTY TO THE UNION)
High, between 3rd and 4th • Open to the public • W

This simple monument, erected in 1865, memorializes the Union sympathizers killed at the Battle of Nueces on August 10, 1862.

Most of the men in Comfort were unionists during the war, and on July 4 of that year, unionists in Kerr, Kendall, and Gillespie counties formed the Union Loyal League. Three companies of men—one from each county—were organized. After learning that the Confederate authorities had declared Gillespie, Kendall, Kerr, Edwards, and Kimble counties to be in open rebellion and thus subject to martial law, the Union Loyal League decided to disband, so as to assure the Confederate government that no rebellion was imminent. All those who did not wish to submit to Rebel rule would meet at Turtle Creek in Kerr County on August 1, 1862, in order to go to Mexico. Sixty-eight men gathered that day, many of them from Comfort. They left the same day for Del Rio and the Rio Grande. Although heavily armed, the unionists were treating their trip as a holiday ride, apparently unworried about Confederate reprisals.

The unionists had gotten to the Nueces River, about 20 miles from Brackettville, on the evening of August 9. There they camped for the night without choosing a defensible position or posting a strong guard. Confederate cavalry, 94 strong, attacked before dawn the next morning. Nineteen of the Germans were killed on the field; nine of them were captured and shot a few hours later. Of the 40 who escaped, 6 were later captured and shot, 20 made it to Mexico, and 11 sneaked back home. The men slain in battle were mutilated and left for the buzzards. Their bones were brought here after the war and buried in a common grave.

Across High from the Treue Der Union monument is the Immanuel Lutheran Church. Behind it is Comfort's first church, the 1892 Deutsche Evangelische Kirche, a simple white frame sanctuary that has been used by all denominations. Before this church was built, services were held in a saloon. The second and third generations of Comfort established the church; Comfort's founders remained free thinkers to the end.

Return to SH 27 and head west for Center Point. As SH 27 makes its bend to the southwest leaving Comfort, you see on your left Comfort Park and on your right the Faltin home.

COMFORT PARK
SH 27 between Main and Broadway

Comfort Park is one of the original blocks laid out as a park by Ernst Altgelt, and a plaque and bust honor him here. After founding Comfort, Altgelt went on to develop San Antonio's prestigious King William Street neighborhood, naming the street and building its first house in 1867. In the center of the park is a gazebo, built in 1904, site of countless summer band concerts, speeches, and celebrations.

Germans tend to be passionate gardeners, and a Farmers Market operates here on Saturdays from May through November, offering a wide variety of locally grown foodstuffs. Comfort also has a number of commercial horticultural and herb businesses, as well as dozens of pretty, carefully tended home flower and vegetable gardens.

Facing the park's north side, at the corner of Main and SH 27, are the **Wilhelm Heuermann homes.** The fachwerk cottage out front was built in 1857; the one-room log cabin in back was built in 1854 or '55.

FALTIN HOUSE
SH 27 at Broadway, across from Comfort Park
Private residence

August Faltin commissioned Albert Beckman to design this grand multigabled two-story limestone residence in 1890. Faltin had come to the Hill Country as a prosperous banker, late of Prussia, and the money he brought with him financed the growth of Comfort and Kerrville. Faltin was especially interested in helping mercantile businesses and industry get started. One of the men he staked was young Charles Schreiner. With Faltin's money, Schreiner established a general store at Kerrville in 1869 and went on to become a millionaire. More on Schreiner later.

Next to the Faltin home, at the corner of Main and 4th, is the home of Ernst Flach, one of Comfort's great entrepreneurs, who built and owned the mill complex one mile upstream on the Guadalupe. It powered a cotton gin, made ice and electricity, cut lumber, and ground grain. The house is an interesting mix of construction styles, showing how additions were attached to houses following original construction. The fachwerk section in the back is the oldest section, post-Civil War. The front part of the house has a limestone center section flanked by wings of whitewashed, millsawn lumber.

CYPRESS CREEK INN
400 block of SH 27 • 995-3977
Open Tuesday through Saturday, lunch and dinner; Sunday,
lunch only • $ • No Cr. • W

The Inn is Comfort's oldest restaurant although it dates only to the mid 1950s. Still it has a loyal clientele of locals and long-time Hill Country travellers. The food is uncomplicated, country-style cooking, though not extraordinary. The pies are homemade, the vegetables frozen. There is a daily lunch special and the Sunday lunch menu includes roast beef, baked ham, barbecued chicken, and steaks.

SHOPPING

MARKETPLATZ ANTIQUE CENTER
7th at Main • 995-2000

Around 15 dealers offer quality antiques in this circa 1883 store building.

ANNUAL EVENT

JULY • Homecoming • Comfort Park • July 4 • $4 per plate

Features a noon barbecue, contests, games, traditional German band music, dancing, and arts and crafts show.

SH 27 west out of Comfort continues to carry you through the flat, rich farmland of the Guadalupe River valley. Although you seldom see it along this 5-mile stretch of road, the river is never more than a few hundred yards away. Turn left off SH 27 onto RM 1350 5.5 miles west of Comfort. RM 1350 takes you into Center Point.

CENTER POINT

Kerr County • 623 • About 9 miles from Comfort

Center Point was originally called Zanzenberg, back when the town was first established on the north bank of the Guadalupe in 1854. Zanzenberg, in the Austrian Tyrol, was the ancestral home of this settlement's first postmaster, Dr. Charles Ganahl. The village was renamed Center Point in 1864 due to its central location between Kerrville, Comfort, Fredericksburg, and Bandera. The post office was moved to the south bank of the river in 1872, where a sizable town grew up. Center Point's growth was spurred on by the local lumber industry, which fed on the many nearby cypress trees, and the arrival of the railroad. It became the railway shipping center for most of Bandera County and once boasted two banks and over a dozen commercial establishments. Development of the Texas highway system diminished Center Point's importance as a trade center and it is now a sleepy little farm and ranching town. Center Point was incorporated in March 1913, but its charter was dissolved that same October, which probably makes Center Point the shortest-lived city in Central Texas.

It is said that there are more Texas Rangers buried at Center Point Cemetery than at any other place in Texas. At least 32 Rangers rest here.

CENTER POINT SCHOOL
219 China/RM 1350, between Ave. A and Ave. C

Indicative of Center Point's former economic prowess is the old Center Point School, still in use and part of a larger, newer Center Point ISD complex. Alfred Giles designed this two-story limestone building, constructed in 1911. Although much simpler in design than earlier Giles buildings, it still bears his distinctive touch. For reference, see his old Post Office (1910) in Comfort, and Kendall County Courthouse addition (1909) and Boerne High School (1910), both located in Boerne.

When RM 1350 dead-ends into RM 480, turn left onto RM 480 toward Camp Verde. RM 480 follows Verde Creek to Camp Verde.

CAMP VERDE

Kerr County • 41 • (830) • About 6.5 miles from Center Point

Camp Verde was one of four camps established in 1856 to accommodate the newly organized U.S. Second Cavalry under the command of Albert Sidney Johnston, and Joseph E. Johnston's First Cavalry. The camp was named after the creek, Verde, where it was located. *Verde* means "green" in Spanish.

Camp had barely been set up here when the camel brigade came marching in. The 33 "ships of the desert" were part of then Secretary of War Jefferson Davis' quest to improve the quality of long distance transportation on the frontier, where water was scarce and forts few and far between.

Major Henry Wayne, who had sailed to Africa in search of the camels, brought them back to Camp Verde complete with native handlers and detailed plans for the construction of an authentic caravanserai.

The camels performed well in several long journeys west except that their feet, accustomed to sandy terrain, were cut and bruised by the rocky terrain. The soldiers used the camels only as pack animals, but the officers' wives occasionally used them as mounts to travel to camp meetings—six women to an animal.

Confederate troops took over Camp Verde with the outbreak of war, and they let many of the animals stray off into the hills. After the war, the federal government lost interest in the great camel experiment and auctioned off the remaining beasts in 1866. Austin lawyer Bethel Coopwood bought several dozen, selling some to circuses and using the others to power an overland freight business between Laredo and Mexico City. Escaped camels roamed the hills around Camp Verde for several decades thereafter, scaring the wits out of travelers and newcomers. Comanche Indians named them "goats of the devil."

The army abandoned the fort in 1869. A 1910 fire destroyed most of what was left of the camp. The adobe officers' barracks were reconstructed to serve as a ranch home.

CAMP VERDE STORE
RM 480 at SH 173 • 634-7722 • Open daily • MC, V

This store first opened in 1853 as Williams Community Store, serving trade around Camp Verde. The store had been opened principally because the army forbade the sale of liquor inside military reservations. Because of the meager population, the store was only open on army paydays. Charles Schreiner and Caspar Real bought the store in 1857, supplementing their store business with army beef and wool contracts. Schreiner moved on to bigger and better things in nearby Kerrville after serving in the war.

But the store at Camp Verde persevered, even after the camp itself was abandoned. A post office was established here in 1858, abandoned in 1892, reestablished in 1898. Today the store contains an inventory of arts and crafts, souvenirs, antiques, and other items designed to appeal to the tourist. Most of the store's fixtures are original, although they are largely obscured by the prodigious inventory.

From the FM 480/SH 173 intersection and the Camp Verde store, proceed south on SH 173 toward Bandera. In 2 miles you cut through the Bandera Pass, the ancient path through the hills that divide the Guadalupe and Medina river watersheds.

BANDERA PASS
SH 173 • About 2 miles from Camp Verde
The history of Bandera Pass is somewhat clouded, but the most plausible story goes something like this: Spanish troops from San Antonio de Bexar met Apache warriors in battle at the pass in 1732. The battle was very bloody, and afterward the Spanish and Apaches held a council and signed a treaty. The Indians would not tread south of the pass, and the Spanish agreed never to set foot north of the pass in Indian hunting grounds. In token of this agreement, a red flag—*bandera* in Spanish—was placed on the highest peak by the pass to remind both sides of their promises.

A second great battle filled the pass in 1842, when 40 Texas Rangers under the command of Captain Jack Hays met a Comanche war party twice their size. The Comanches laid an ambush for the Rangers as the Texans approached the top of the pass from the south. It looked bad for the Texans at first, but Hays rallied his men and drove off the Indians after a desperate hand-to-hand knife battle. The Rangers suffered five dead and six wounded, the Indians a greater, though unspecified, number of casualties. The Comanches slipped away late that night unpursued. Ben McCulloch and Bigfoot Wallace were among the battle's participants. The approximate site of the battle is marked by a state historical marker.

As you descend Bandera Pass, you come to an intersection with RM 2828. Turn right here to reach Medina.

Once you are on RM 2828, you are in the rugged "mountains" of Bandera County, high hills that have earned Bandera County the nickname The Switzerland of Texas.

RM 2828 runs into SH 16 after 9 miles. Turn right onto SH 16 to reach Medina.

MEDINA

Bandera County • 515 • (830) • About 14 miles from Camp Verde
The town of Medina is named for the river on which it is located, which was named, by Spanish explorer Alonso De León, in 1689 for noted Spanish engineer and scholar Pedro Medina. Medina was founded about 1880 as a trading center. The village declined with the development of Texas' high-speed road system, but received a shot

in the arm in recent decades from the vacation trade. Medina is the capital of Texas' fledging apple industry, which explains all the red apples you see hanging or nailed up around here. The harvest begins in late July and continues through September, so be sure to stop by any of the local stands and stores for apples, fresh-pressed cider, and other apple treats. For a good look at the river, turn left on Patterson (before you get to downtown) at the "First Baptist Church 1 Block" sign and go two blocks to the low-water bridge. The small white frame church behind the Baptist Church is the Methodist Church, organized here in 1881.

CIDER MILL & COUNTRY STORE
SH 16, downtown Medina • 589-2588
   Besides cider, you can buy apple jelly, apple jam, apple butter, apple syrup, apple shampoo, apple ice cream, and apple trees.

LOVE CREEK ORCHARDS
589-2588
   Texas' apple industry dates to the early 1980s, when Baxter and Carol Adams began growing dwarf apple trees in the fertile valley of Love Creek, west of Medina. Full-sized apple trees take seven years to produce a crop; dwarf trees yield full-sized apples in less than two years.
   Varieties grown include Red Delicious, Gala, and Crispin. Hill Country apples don't redden as much as their northern relatives, but they are delightfully sweet and crisp, the equal of apples grown anywhere else. Tours of the orchards are given on Saturday mornings from April through October. Harvest starts in late July and runs through August. The Adams family operates the **Cider Mill Store** in downtown Medina.

INTERNATIONAL APPLE FESTIVAL
Late July–early August • 589-2588
   Texas' most unlikely fruit is celebrated with an apple pie contest, crafts, a street dance, family activities, sports tournaments, and the other trappings of small-town Texas festivals.

From SH 16, turn left on RM 337 to reach Vanderpool and the Lost Maples.

RM 337 closely follows the route of the **Medina River** for the next 9 or 10 miles, through and over breathtakingly beautiful but ruggedly desolate hills and valleys. You are forever catching glimpses of the silvery Medina, sometimes beside you, sometimes far below. Best time to drive this road is at sunrise or sunset when the 15 miles of RM 337 are some of the most pleasant you'll find in the entire state.

Turn right on FM 187 when RM 337 dead-ends at Vanderpool.

VANDERPOOL

Bandera County • 20 • About 20 miles from Medina
Vanderpool, named for early settler L. B. Vanderpool, has never been anything more than a wide spot in the road. Today it consists of two churches and some homes. This was one of the last sections of Central Texas to be settled, for the valleys of the Medina and Sabinal rivers were the home of the Comanches. The almost impenetrable hills through which these streams thread made the Indians nearly impossible to root out. Once the Indians were gone, there was little the Anglo settlers could do for a living other than run livestock over this devil's playground.

Take FM 187 the last 5 miles to the Lost Maples through the chute that is the Sabinal River Canyon.

LOST MAPLES STATE NATURAL AREA
FM 187, about 4 miles from Vanderpool • 830-966-3413
Open daily • Admission • W variable
Best known for its stands of Uvalde Bigtooth maples, trees that aren't normally found in this section of the country, hence the name Lost Maples. They're not really lost, they're just a relict population from thousands of years ago when the weather was cooler and the trees more widespread. The microclimate of the Sabinal River valley retains the characteristics of this lost climate, hence the trees line the river for most of its 58-mile length. This 2,200-acre park is the only place along the river where the public can actually get out and commune with the trees. If the weather conditions have been right, the trees go out in a blaze of glory sometime in late October or early November. Conditions vary year to year, so call ahead. Some years, there is no show. In good years, the park is filled to capacity on weekends; weekday visits are more pleasant. Parking capacity is 250

cars and is enforced. The park gets approximately 200,000 visitors a year. Because of the crowds of visitors, the maples are in danger of extinction. Like the cypress trees at Pedernales Falls, the maples' roots don't like compacted soil, and that's what we do when we hike. Each step compacts the soil a bit and makes it less capable of absorbing water. That's why it's important to stay on the designated paths; the trees need their space and loosely packed soil.

Lost Maples is beautiful and interesting any time of the year, though. The park is an outstanding example of Edwards Plateau flora and fauna. It is a combination of steep, rugged limestone canyons, springs, plateau grasslands, wooded slopes, and clear streams. Over 10 miles of trails take you through a variety of habitats and offer glimpses of most of the 350-plus plant species found here. The natural area contains three state champion trees: escarpment chokeberry, Texas ash, and bigtooth maple. The chokeberry and ash have been nominated to the American Forestry Association's Big Tree program for consideration as national champions. The birding is good here. Rare species of birds, such as the green kingfisher, can be seen year-round. The endangered black-capped vireo and golden-cheeked warbler nest and feed in the park in spring and early summer. Wild animals include gray fox, white-tailed deer, armadillo, raccoon, bobcat, rock squirrel, and javelina.

Archaeological evidence shows that this area was used by prehistoric peoples at various times; artifacts have been found that go back 12,000 years. In historic times, which began with Spanish exploration and colonization efforts in the late 17th century, the Apache, Lipan Apache, and Comanche Indians ranged over the land and posed a threat to settlement well into the 19th century.

Visitors can picnic, camp, backpack, sightsee, hike, photograph, watch birds, fish, swim, and study nature. Many natural hazards exist due to the steep/rugged terrain, so do not hike or climb on rocks or hillsides. Facilities provided include restrooms with showers, picnic sites, primitive camping areas, a comfort station, campsites with water and electricity, and a trailer dump station. There is a Texas State Park Store. Accessibility for the disabled: restrooms and picnic tables; can drive approximately 1 mile into park to view foliage.

Write to HCR 1, Box 156, Vanderpool 78885. *Elevation:* Ranges from 1,800 to 2,250 ft. *Weather:* Average rainfall 35.1 in. January average low temperature is 31 degrees; July average high temperature is 94 degrees. *Busy season:* October, November, and spring— March through May.

Continue north on FM 187 from the Lost Maples. Soon you climb out of the river valley and do some ridge-running for the next few miles, through semiarid grazing country. Little more than 100 years ago, this land was commonly referred to as the "rim of the great American Desert." Sinkholes, which are porous basins that feed rainwater into the Edwards Aquifer, are found throughout the Hill Country. You can see a textbook example of a sinkhole at the western edge of FM 187, exactly 8.9 miles north of Lost Maples.

When FM 187 finally dead-ends into SH 39 in the headwaters area of the south fork of the Guadalupe River, turn right onto SH 39.

In the next 20 twisting miles to Hunt, you cross the south fork no less than 14 times as it grows into a full-fledged river. As you draw closer to Hunt, the road is increasingly lined with entrances to resort and summer camps, plush vacation retreats, and little fishing cabins. This stretch of the Guadalupe has been a favorite with vacationers for 50 years.

HUNT

Kerr County • 708 • (830) • About 39 miles from Vanderpool
Within two or three years of Kerrville's founding in 1856, folks began to move up the Guadalupe River valley, first stopping at "the forks," where the north and south branches of the Guadalupe come together. Soon a sawmill, gristmill, and cotton gin were built here. The neighborhood's first post office was located three miles north of present-day Hunt and was called Japonica. Hunt came into existence in 1912, when R. F. Hunt opened a grocery and general merchandise store. The post office was moved from Japonica to Hunt's store that same year, and the settlement took his name. Tourism has been Hunt's major industry since the Great Depression. Perhaps the most illustrious resident was the late flying ace Eddie Rickenbacker, who owned the nearby Bear Creek Ranch. Hunt today is a collection of homes, a dance hall, and a couple of stores and cafes.

CRIDER'S
Downtown Hunt • 238-4874 • Open Saturday nights, May through September
This fair-weather dance hall, located above the Guadalupe River, first opened in 1925. Live bands play C&W dancing music.

STONEHENGE II
On FM 1340, 2 miles west of Hunt • Open daily • W

Stonehenge II is 60 percent as tall and 90 percent as large in circumference as the original. The stones are really made of steel rebar, wire mesh, and cement. You can get out of the car and walk around it. There are also Easter Island-type statues here. If you build it, they will come.

Continue on SH 39 as you leave Hunt to go to Ingram. You cross the south fork of the Guadalupe one last time; the forks are just a few hundred yards north, and it is a united Guadalupe River you cross and follow from here on out.

The historical marker you see a couple of miles east of Hunt marks the former site of pioneer John Sherman's water-powered mill. It was in operation until destroyed by flood in 1932. Ten mills, grinding corn and wheat, cutting lumber, and powering cotton gins, were once located on the Guadalupe between Hunt and Comfort.

INGRAM

Kerr County • 1,493 • (830) • About 6.5 miles from Hunt

Ingram is located on the Old Spanish Trail, on a site originally owned by Abner Morriss. The land was sold to the Reverend J. C. W. Ingram in 1872. He opened up a store, a church and a post office here on the Guadalupe near its confluence with Johnson Creek. A community grew up around the store and church, serving as a commercial center for ranchers, shinglemakers, and cedar choppers. The rough country up Johnson Creek was a favorite outlaw and cattle rustler hangout in olden days. During the Civil War, three German unionists were hung on the banks of Johnson Creek above Ingram and their bodies then thrown into the rocky creekbed 75 feet below. The last recorded Indian massacre in Kerr County took place in 1878 on Johnson Creek, when four children of the James Dowdy family were killed while tending the family's sheep. The town moved slightly north during the 1930s when SH 27 was built, but much of old downtown Ingram still stands.

As you come into Ingram, you first pass the Lake Ingram dam on your right. Just before crossing Johnson Creek, you see the Hill Country Arts Foundation complex on your right.

POINT THEATRE/HILL COUNTRY ARTS FOUNDATION
Entrance is well-marked and complex is just yards from the road • 367-5121

Theatrical productions are staged on summer evenings on the Point Theatre's outdoor stage. Located alongside the scenic, rushing Guadalupe, this used to be a skating rink. Art studios are located inside the Arts Foundation Building, and here art classes are conducted by well-known artists. Concerts and other events are now presented throughout the year. For more information, contact the West Kerr County Chamber of Commerce, P.O. Box 1006, Ingram, TX 78025, 800-257-4322.

After crossing the Johnson Creek bridge, take the first possible right, on a street identified as the Ingram Loop, to see old Ingram.

OLD INGRAM
Old Ingram today is a collection of mostly rock buildings dating to the early 1900s that house a variety of arts, crafts, and antique shops.

Only several hundred feet long, the Ingram Loop rolls you right back onto SH 39. When you come to SH 39, you will see in front of you a multipanel mural on the walls of the T. J. Moore Lumberyard warehouse, depicting various events and eras in Kerr County history. Park the car and take a closer look, as each of the 15 panels is accompanied by written commentary. From the Ingram Loop, turn right onto SH 39, and continue straight on what becomes SH 27 E, into Kerrville.

KERRVILLE

Kerr County Seat • 19,134 • (830) • About 6.5 miles from Ingram

Joshua Brown was the first permanent Anglo settler here. A member of the original Anglo colony at Gonzales, by 1844 Brown had moved west to Curry Creek, where he made shingles. By 1846, the cypress trees around Curry Creek (Kendall County) were about played out and Brown started up the Guadalupe looking for a new source of cypress timber for his shingle-making operation. He ended up at a spring on the Guadalupe, where he made camp and resumed his shingle-making. Indians soon began to attack his camp, so Brown and his coworkers had to move back to Gonzales after just a couple of months here. But in 1848, Brown returned to the camp and started making shingles again. The settlement that grew up around the camp was first called Brownsborough. Brown had acquired legal title to the land by 1856, the year in which Christian Dietert built a lumber and shingle mill on the Guadalupe in what is now downtown Kerrville.

That same year, Kerr County was created from Bexar County, and Brownsborough, consisting of a shingle mill and a couple of log cabins, became Kerrsville, county seat. Kerrsville did not exactly take off like a fast-growing weed. In fact, it lost its county seat status in 1860, when Comfort partisans beat the Kerrsville backers in a special election and the government of Kerr County moved to Comfort. Kerrsville regained its position in 1862, when Kendall County was formed and Comfort was found to be just inside the Kendall County line.

Kerrsville hung on by a thread during the war; Indians and bushwhackers terrorized the whole county. They hid out in the hills north and west of town. During the years before a jailhouse was built, the few offenders who were caught were chained to trees.

The lawlessness continued after war's end; cattle and sheep rustlers ran roughshod over the countryside. Disguised as Indians, the rustlers would steal cattle and horses, commit murder and arson, then head back to the many caves and thick cedar brakes located along the south fork of the Guadalupe.

By 1873, the rustling problem was so out of hand that Kerr County stockraisers organized a vigilante group. One night the anonymous vigilantes stormed the county jail after overpowering the sheriff and deputies and took three prisoners accused of cattle rustling from their cells. One was shot there at the jail. The other two were taken to the outskirts of town and hung from a live-oak tree. Shortly thereafter, Texas Rangers arrested another man as a suspected cattle rustler and again the vigilantes stormed the jail. They took the suspect to Goat Creek four miles west and shot him.

Kerrville (the "s" was dropped from Kerrsville during the Civil War) is named for a man who never lived here, James Kerr. In fact Kerr died six years before "his" county was created. The driving force behind Kerrville's rise to preeminence among Hill Country cities was a man named Charles Schreiner. Schreiner came to Texas from France in 1852. He became a Texas Ranger at the tender age of 16, and by 1857 he had staked his government service claim on Turtle Creek, near Kerrville.

Serving the "Lost Cause" faithfully, Schreiner returned home from the Civil War flat broke. But Comfort merchant and banker August Faltin recognized Schreiner's considerable business acumen and decided to grubstake young Schreiner's first postwar venture. In 1869 Schreiner moved into town and opened up a mercantile company and private bank inside a small lumber store shed. Commonly known as The Captain (by virtue of his Civil War service), Schreiner had a business motto of Live and let live. Well, most of the time. He did not discourage competition; he had confidence in his ability to judge character, and he seldom bet on the wrong horse. He did not hesitate to lend advice to those seemingly on their last knees.

Horace W. Morelock, one-time superintendent of Kerrville schools and later president of Sul Ross University, told the following story. "In the early days, Joseph Pierce owned a ranch near London in Kimble County. But times were hard and he became discouraged. Late one afternoon, he and his wife came to Kerrville with the avowed purpose of transferring their holdings to Captain Schreiner. But the captain had a different idea: 'Go back to the ranch, save every nickle, and the next time you come to Kerrville, do not stop at the St. Charles Hotel; bring your blankets along, and stay in the camp yard.' Within a few years Pierce paid off the debt he owed the captain, sold his ranch at a profit, moved to Crockett County and became a millionaire."

Schreiner soon became a millionaire himself, largely due to innovative thinking and his sense for good deals. Schreiner believed that sheep raising could be highly profitable out here, and so he set out to prove his hunch. By 1900 his Charles Schreiner Company owned 600,000 acres of land, which stretched continuously from Kerrville to Menard, a distance of over 80 miles. He instituted a co-op market and warehouse system for wool growers so that their wool would not be subject to the vagaries of the market. Schreiner made Kerrville the Mohair Center of the World. He was instrumental in bringing the railroad to Kerrville, as well as establishing the Schreiner Institute here. He was also the town's leading banker.

The railroad was an essential part of Schreiner's grand scheme for Kerrville; it was the only form of transportation that was capable of handling the export traffic he had envisioned. But Fredericksburg also coveted the San Antonio and Aransas Pass (SA&AP) rails, and it took every bit of influence Schreiner had to win the rails. They arrived in Kerrville, amidst great rejoicing, in 1887.

The news spread across the rest of Texas that Kerrville was a healthy place to live (a fact still borne out by the census bureau), and soon it was a regular pilgrimage for consumptives seeking a cure. Morelock told of his first trip to Kerrville, via the SA&AP in 1905. "I observed that many passengers were coughing violently and I inquired of the conductor as to its significance. He replied blandly: 'Well, you know the passengers on this train usually go up to Kerrville coughing, and they come back in a coffin.' When I arrived in Kerrville, the first man I met at the station inquired, 'Are you here for your health?' I stammered: 'No, I am here for the other fellow's health.'" In 1921, the U.S. Health Department declared Kerr County to be "the healthiest spot in the nation."

Kerrville's most famous pilgrim in search of a cure was Jimmie Rodgers, the father of modern country music. Born in Meridian, Mississippi, in 1897, Rodgers grew up on the railroad. His father was a railroad gang foreman and Jimmie started work as a water carrier at age 14. He eventually worked up to brakeman. Working on railroads throughout the South, he learned songs from the Negro workers, who also taught him how to play guitar and banjo. He contracted a severe case of tuberculosis in 1924, and was forced to leave railroad work for something less strenuous.

He took up entertaining and in 1927 signed a record contract with the Victor Talking Machine Company. Soon he was a star, recording 111 songs altogether and selling 20 million records before his death. To seek relief from his steadily worsening TB, Rodgers moved to Kerrville in 1929 and built a $25,000 house, calling it "Blue Yodeler's Paradise." He moved into a modest home in San Antonio in 1932, and died on May 26, 1933, in his hotel room in New York City while on a recording trip. He was buried in his hometown of Meridian.

Besides being a major wool and mohair shipping center, Kerrville has also been a major exporter of cedar posts. In fact, the cedar chopper's favorite axe was invented here back in the early 1920s. About that time ranchmen of the cedar section of Texas began to hire cedar choppers to clear out the excessive growth on their land. Most of the choppers were Mexican migrants who complained about the traditional forest axe they were forced to use. They said the forest axe was too heavy, the handle too long, and the blade too short.

Henry Weiss of Kerrville was interested in producing a better axe for cedar cutting than had thus far been on the market. Collaborating with local blacksmith Frank Krueger, Weiss was able to produce a better cedar axe. Using the Weiss-Krueger axe as a model, a company started to make a cedar axe in commercial quantities, but instead of naming the new axe the "Kerrville Axe," the company marketed it as the "Grey Gorge" model. It sold like wildfire, and experienced woodsmen say that this specially designed axe cuts cedar 25 percent more effectively than the old forest axe.

Tourism is now Kerrville's biggest industry. Long recognized by the census bureau as the healthiest place in America to live, Kerrville is now the Hill Country's largest city. This is very much the result of Kerrville's distinct pro-growth mentality. Kerrville boasts the Hill Country's only Hilton Inn, for instance.

Kerrville has elected to pursue the tourist-retiree-weekend home-owner dollar, rather than to run after industry coin, but in the end it doesn't matter. Little of "old Kerrville" remains, and what does remain stands obscured by Kerrville's ebullient ever-expanding present. It is certainly the Hill Country's liveliest city.

BILL'S BARBEQUE
1909 Junction Hwy./SH 27 • 895-5733 • Tuesday through Friday 11–3, Saturday 11–7 • Closed Sunday and Monday $ • No Cr. • W
Bill's cooks up brisket, ribs, sausage, pork loin, turkey, chicken, and on special order, cabrito. The meat is popular with locals, so Bill's usually sells out fast, closing even earlier than their already abbreviated hours. Homemade side dishes and pies, plus cold beer.

Continue east on SH 27, which becomes Main. When you come to the intersection with Sidney Baker (SH 16), turn left onto Baker/SH 16. After a long five blocks, turn right onto RM 1341 (Wheeless) and follow it out of town. After a little more than a mile on RM 1341, you come to a historical marker and a gravel road winding up the steep hill on your right. This is Tivy Mountain, and the marker memorializes Captain Joseph Tivy.

TIVY MOUNTAIN
RM 1341
Joseph Tivy came to Texas in 1837 with his two sisters. After serving as a Texas Ranger, Tivy joined his sisters in California during the great gold rush. The trio returned to Texas in the 1850s, and when Texas went to war Tivy served his time fighting for the Lost Cause, attaining the rank of captain. Tivy and sisters moved to Kerrville about 1870. Soon after arriving, the Tivy siblings made a pact never to marry. Much to the disappointment of his sisters, Tivy broke the vow a few years later, marrying Ella, the widow of his departed best friend. She died shortly after their marriage and her last request was that she be buried atop this high hill of Tivy's. Four days were spent building a road to the summit; it had to be carved out of the mountain. The top of Tivy Mountain is solid rock, and it had to be blasted out to make a vault for the grave. The blasting could be heard for miles around. The casket was taken to the top in a hack pulled by two mules. Mourners had to walk to the top for the services, so rough was the trail. Captain Tivy and his younger sister eventually joined Ella up here. Take the effort to climb up the hill to the gravesite and you'll

see why they wanted to be buried here. An expansive view of Kerrville and the Guadalupe valley unfolds before you.

Tivy served as state legislator, Kerrville's first mayor, and town surveyor. When the railroad came he built the Tivy Hotel nearby. While mayor, he donated land for the city's public school system.

The local high school is named for Tivy. The old Victorian limestone **Tivy High School building** still stands at the corner of Tivy and Barnett streets, beneath Tivy Mountain.

From Tivy Mountain, return to downtown Kerrville by retracing your path on RM 1341 to Sidney Baker/SH 16. (If you wish to see the old Tivy school, leave Tivy Mountain on RM 1341, but when RM 1341's route turns right onto Wheeless a few blocks later, you continue straight ahead on what is now Tivy St. In three blocks you come to the Tivy school. From the Tivy school, return to RM 1341 and proceed to Sidney Baker/SH 16.) Turn left onto Sidney Baker and return to the courthouse and center of town. Proceed one block past Main/SH 27 and turn left onto Water.

Water St. was Kerrville's main business street during the railroad era. Several of the old buildings from that age remain.

PAMPELL'S DRUGSTORE/OPERA HOUSE
701 Water

This Spanish Renaissance two-story brick building replaced an earlier frame structure in the early 1900s. Like that old building, this one had an opera house on the second floor and a pharmacy with soda fountain below. The pharmacy closed in the late 1980s, but reopened in 1989 as a gift store with the old soda fountain still intact, where you can enjoy an old-fashioned soda, malt, ice cream cones, etc.

The building at 709 Water is of two-story cut-limestone block construction, with a nice cast-metal cornice. At the end of this block, anchoring the corner of Earl Garrett and Water, is the Schreiner Store, cornerstone of Charles Schreiner's empire since 1869. For years, it was one of the southwest's largest country stores. Across Water from it was the Schreiner Bank, the town's major financial force until its failure in the mid-1980s.

Turn left on Earl Garrett. This first block of Earl Garrett contains two buildings of note, the Schreiner mansion and the Masonic Hall.

SCHREINER MANSION/THE HILL COUNTRY MUSEUM
216 Earl Garrett • 896-8633 • Closed Tuesday and Sunday, Open all other days 10–12 and 2–4:30 • Admission

Charles Schreiner moved into a small frame house on this lot in 1869. The south portion of this house was built in 1879; Schreiner copied the design of his grandfather's house in Alsace, France.

The house was added to in 1895, and in 1897 was remodeled by Alfred Giles to its present Romanesque Revival appearance. The first house in Kerrville to have electricity and indoor plumbing, it originally had 13 rooms and 2 bathrooms. Schreiner imported masons from Germany to lay the stone walls. Brass light fixtures for the house and the bronze fountain for the formal gardens were imported from France. French immigrant John Michon laid the parquet floor, which uses ten kinds of wood. Upon the Captain's death in 1927, the local Masonic Lodge bought the house to use it as a lodge hall. The Masons sold the house in 1973 to a couple who then sold it to the Hill Country Preservation Society in 1975. The house has been completely restored and contains a collection of Kerr County and Schreiner family memorabilia.

MASONIC HALL
211 Earl Garrett

Designed by Alfred Giles and built in 1890 of rough-finish limestone blocks with a cast-iron cornice and arch, the Masonic Hall followed a common practice of the time, that is, retaining the second floor for lodge use while leasing or selling the ground floor to local merchants. The Masons met here in 1927. The C. C. Butt Grocery Store (predecessor to HEB) occupied the ground floor from 1916 to 1926.

Turn left onto Main/SH 27 from Earl Garrett, then turn left again after one block onto Sidney Baker/SH 16, which takes you across the Guadalupe and out of Kerrville. Turn left on SH 173 at the Kerrville outskirts. Soon you come to the Cowboy Artists of America Museum.

COWBOY ARTISTS OF AMERICA MUSEUM
1550 Bandera Hwy. (SH 173) P.O. Box 1716, Kerrville 78029 • 896-2553 • Open daily • Admission • W with assistance

Although many among us would pony the words "cowboy" and "art" up with other mutually exclusive words like "oil" and "water," the CAA Museum deserves a look-see for the museum building alone.

It was conceived by noted architect O'Neil Ford and was the last non-residential building in which he was personally involved before his death. Heavy timbers and dry-stack limestone retaining walls are part of the entry gardens. There is a heavy Mexican influence throughout. The most impressive feature of the main entrance is the ceiling, composed of 18 boveda brick domes. The construction of boveda domes is almost a lost art, dating back to the Moorish occupation of Spain. Boveda domes use light Mexican brick and are positioned without supporting forms or wires. Only a few artisans from the beautiful colonial Mexican towns of Guanajuato and San Miguel de Allende still construct the domes. The gallery floors are of mesquite. Tree trunks were cut into slices, squared off, glued together, and polished.

The museum galleries house a large collection of paintings and sculpture by the 30 members of the Cowboy Artists of America. It is the only museum devoted to living artists painting and sculpting internationally recognized Western American Realism. The museum offers a variety of changing exhibitions, lectures, historic seminars, artists-in-residence programs, and other cultural and social activities. The museum also includes a library, auditorium, and museum store.

OTHER ATTRACTIONS

KERRVILLE CONVENTION AND VISITORS BUREAU
1700 Sidney Baker • 800-221-7958

BLUE YODELER'S PARADISE
617 W. Main
Jimmie Rodgers' mansion on the hill was finished in May 1929. Mounting medical costs and the price of luxurious living forced Rodgers to sell Blue Yodeler's Paradise and move to San Antonio. In his last two years of life, Rodgers recorded, appeared on radio, and performed in tent shows around Texas, health permitting. Kerrville celebrates his birthday each September with the Jimmie Rodgers Jubilee, a several-day musical tribute featuring dozens of musicians.

JAMES AVERY CRAFTSMAN
FM 783 (Harper Rd.) about 1 mile north of I-10 exit 505
895-1122 • W
The business James Avery started here, in his garage, now has stores all over the southwest and sells nationally by mail. There is a small factory and retail store here. You can see a short video and watch jewelry being made. Write P.O. Box 1367, Kerrville 78029.

Y.O. RANCH
Take I-10 west to SH 41 (exit 490) at Mountain Home, then 18
miles south (left) to ranch entrance sign • 640-3222 • Half-day
tours • Admission • W variable

A working ranch with cattle, sheep, and goats, plus the cowboys
who do all the herding, roping, and all the other daily ranch chores.
Founded by Charles Schreiner in 1880, it is home to over 1,000 longhorns, champion quarterhorses, and free-ranging native wildlife, plus
exotic animals such as axis deer, American elk, antelope, zebras,
giraffes, and ostriches. Several historic buildings have been moved
to the ranch and restored, including an 1850s stagecoach stop, Wells
Fargo office, and pioneer schoolhouse. In addition to the half-day
tours (which include a ranch lunch), you can arrange photo safaris
and year-round hunting. Tours can be customized. There is a summer
camp for boys and girls ages 9 to 15. Lodging is available in the
lodge or in century-old cabins. Also a general store, swimming pool,
and restaurant. Entrance is by reservation only.

LODGING

Y.O. RANCH HOLIDAY INN
2033 Sidney Baker (SH 16) about 2 blocks south of I-10
257-4440 or in Texas 800-531-2800 • $$$–$$$$$ • W+ ten
rooms • No-smoking rooms

The Holiday Inn has 200 rooms and suites including 32 no-smok-
ing rooms. Cable TV. Room phones. Pay transportation to San Anto-
nio airport. Restaurant, two bars, live entertainment weekends. Out-
door heated pool, hot tub, tennis court. Adjoins municipal golf
course. Large lobby with chandeliers made of 350 branding irons and
a bronze of a cowboy on horseback struggling to herd a longhorn.
Custom-made room furnishings. Gift shop.

ANNUAL EVENTS

MAY/JUNE • Kerrville Folk Festival • Quiet Valley Ranch
Take SH 16 (Sidney Baker St.) south 9 miles • 257-3600
About three weeks the end of May, beginning of June
Admission • W variable

More than 100 musicians and groups playing folk, blues, soul, and
a smattering of other styles make this outdoor festival something to
listen to. Many performers are Texas songwriters singing their own

songs. Folk Mass on Sundays. Bring lawn chairs to sit on. Single-day and multi-day tickets are available. Many festival-goers camp out.

MAY/JUNE • Texas State Arts and Crafts Fair • Schreiner College, SH 27E • 896-5711 • Memorial Day weekend and following weekend • Admission • W variable
Not your ordinary arts and crafts fair. The artists and craftsmen are carefully selected for their work, and the number of exhibitors is limited to 200. Demonstrations and free crafts instruction. Also music, entertainment, and children's area. Pay parking, but free shuttle buses run from the Chamber of Commerce office and major motels and hotels.

SEPTEMBER • Kerrville Fly-In • Municipal Airport, SH 27E 896-1155 • Third weekend in September • Admission W variable
As many as 1,500 planes, including many antique, home-built, and experimental, fly in. It's really a convention for members of the Experimental Aircraft Association, but they hold an air show on Saturday that the public can attend.

AREA PARKS

KERRVILLE-SCHREINER STATE PARK
2385 Bandera Highway • 257-5392
Kerrville-Schreiner State Park, 517 acres along the Guadalupe River, was acquired in 1934 by deed from the City of Kerrville. Original park construction was done by the Civilian Conservation Corp (CCC). Activities include boating, fishing, camping, picnicking, unsupervised swimming in the river, bird-watching, hiking, walking, and cycling. The park hosts a bicycle tour each Easter weekend. Facilities include restrooms with showers; picnic sites with and without shade shelters; hike-in primitive campsites (no fire ring; water within one mile); campsites with water nearby; campsites with water, with and without shade shelters; campsites with water and electricity (pull-through); campsites with water, electricity, and sewer (pull-through); screened shelters; an overflow camping area; trailer dump stations; two group picnic areas (large fire pit, drinking water); a group dining hall (with a full kitchen) which can be used as a group shelter area (seven screened shelters and the dining hall can be rented together or separately); recreation hall (day or overnight use, air-

conditioning/heating, tables, chairs, a restroom without showers, and a kitchen); an interpretive center; a Texas State Park Store; an amphitheater on the river banks; a laundry tub available; a concrete boat ramp; 7.7 miles of hiking trails; a lighted fishing pier; a playground; and a convenience store close by.

The park has a typical Hill Country landscape; acres of juniper, live oak, and Spanish oak populate the hills and arroyos. Other plants include redbud, sumac, buckeye, pecan, mesquite, and several varieties of flowers. Bluebonnets usually abound in spring. White-tailed deer are numerous. The park also has squirrels, armadillos, turkeys, jackrabbits, mallard ducks, and several species of birds. Fish in the Guadalupe River for crappie, perch, catfish, and bass.

Write to 2385 Bandera Highway, Kerrville 78028. *Elevation:* 1,645 ft. *Weather:* July average high temperature is 94 degrees, SE breeze; January average low temperature is 34 degrees; low humidity year-round with September the wettest month; *First/last freeze:* November 7/April 5. *Busy season:* March through Thanksgiving.

SOUTH LLANO RIVER STATE PARK
To reach the park, take I-10 from Kerrville to Junction, then go south on US 377 for 5 miles to Park Road 73 • 915-446-3994 Open daily except when wildlife management activities dictate closure of part of the park. The park may be closed during heavy flooding. • Admission • W variable

South Llano River State Park adjoins Walter Buck State Wildlife Management Area, south of Junction in Kimble County. The 2,640-acre site, adjacent to the South Llano River, was donated by Walter Buck to the Texas Parks and Wildlife Department in 1977 and was opened to the public in 1990. The park has two miles of river frontage, a large pecan bottom, and typical Hill Country terrain. The 523-acre, wooded bottomland is home to white-tailed deer and the Rio Grande turkey. The bottomland is one of the most substantial and oldest winter turkey roosts in the central portion of the state. The roosting area is closed to visitors from October through March. Observation blinds allow you to watch the turkeys moving to and from the roost. Other animals include wood duck, white-tailed deer, squirrel, jackrabbit, javelina, fox, beaver, bobcat, cottontail, and armadillo. Exotic species seen here include axis deer, black buck antelope, and fallow deer.

Park activities include camping, picnicking, canoeing, tubing, swimming, fishing, hiking, mountain bike riding, and bird and nature study. Facilities include multi-use campsites with water and electricity with a trailer dump station and restrooms with showers in the area; walk-in campsites with picnic tables, fire rings, and composting toilets in the area; hike-in primitive campsites (1.5 miles) with composting toilets and access to the hike/bike trail (no ground fires allowed, no water in or around the area); a picnic and day-use area near the river with picnic tables, grills, and composting toilets; oxbow lakes; 6.8 miles of trails, which cross into the adjacent wildlife management area; hunting blinds available for wildlife photography; and the Texas State Park Store.

Write to HC 15 Box 224, Junction 76849. *Elevation:* 1,710 ft. *Weather:* July average high temperature is 94 degrees; January's average low is 32 degrees; May, August, and September are wettest months. *First/last freeze:* November 3/April 3; *Busy season:* March through October.

RIVERSIDE NATURE CENTER
150 Lemos St. at the junction of the Guadalupe River and Town Creek • 257-4837 • Open daily
The 3.5-acre center includes a wildflower meadow, butterfly gardens, walking paths, tree trail and native grasses, shrubs, cacti, and trees. The Lawson store, a restored, turn-of-the-century grocery store, serves as office and gift shop.

To continue the trip, leave Kerrville on SH 173 (aka the Bandera Highway). As you leave town, you pass the entrance to Kerrville-Schreiner State Park. Slightly over 2 miles from the park entrance, you come to an intersection with Wharton Rd. Turn left here onto Wharton Rd., which is the original river road to Zanzenburg (Center Point).

Wharton Rd. is named for William Wharton, one of Kerr County's earliest settlers. He bought 640 acres and moved here in 1857 with his wife Thankful and their three sons. They rest now in the family cemetery across the road from the river.

The Wharton crossing of the **Guadalupe River** is one of the finest of the dozens of river crossings you make on this trip. The Guadalupe abruptly narrows from a sluggish, sprawling 50-foot width so that it can squeeze under this low-water bridge, then rush out and into a jagged limestone chute about 12 feet wide and several hundred churning feet long, before it finally spreads out and calms down in the woodlands below.

Once inside Center Point, Wharton Rd. is called River Rd., and you enter town on it through old Zanzenberg. Follow its path to the right, on what is now Park St., crossing the Guadalupe on the old low-water bridge, next to the dam. Just after you cross the river, take the first left onto Skyline Drive, which is marked by a stop sign. Then turn right in another few yards on RM 480/San Antonio St.

Several nice old stone buildings from Center Point's golden days still stand along this downtown stretch of RM 480. About the best is the **old Center Point Bank,** a two-story Romanesque Revival cut-stone building with four front windows. It's located next door to the old Eden Implement Co., a two-story limestone-block building on the corner of Skyline and RM 480, and across the street from the post office.

Turn left on RM 1350 toward Comfort, then right on SH 27 into Comfort.

As you round the bend on SH 27 in Comfort, you pass on your left the old yellow Comfort railroad depot, a simple wooden shed built in 1917, after the original one burned in December 1916. Hotels sent buggies and wagons to pick up their guests and luggage.

Across the highway from the depot is the Frederick Werner home; the fachwerk section of the house visible from the highway was built in the late 1860s, and was later added onto.

The San Antonio and Aransas Pass railroad brought a lot of business to Comfort, but it helped put Peter Ingenhuett out of business. Peter Ingenhuett had a brewery over on Cypress Creek and was said to brew as good a product as San Antonio's famous Menger Hotel brewery. His beer was very popular here until San Antonio's breweries began shipping their ice-cold product up on the SAP (as the railroad was nicknamed). Evidently, Comforters succumbed to the lure of "imported" beer, leaving Ingenhuett and his home brew high and dry.

When it came to beer, the Germans in Comfort were practical minded above all else, even to the point of celebrating the Fourth of July a day early. It seems that one July, Comfort's Goldbeck brothers were responsible for the glorious Fourth being celebrated on the third. Confronted with the delivery of several kegs of Menger Hotel beer a day early, the brothers realized that the beer would spoil if not drunk quickly. Wasting no time, the Goldbecks fired the cannon reserved to call residents together in case of emergency or Indian attack. The town folks, who quickly responded, soon lost their indignation at the ruse and began the annual celebration a day before schedule.

Continue on SH 27 to its junction with US 87, turning left here toward Fredericksburg. In just a few hundred yards on US 87 you turn right on RM 473 and go back toward Sisterdale. At Sisterdale, turn left onto RM 1376 from RM 473.

Sisterdale's decline was hastened by the Civil War. Few of Sisterdale's men sided with the Rebel cause, and many of the men joined the Union Loyal League. Some of these men died in the infamous Battle of the Nueces. One way or another, practically everybody left Sisterdale during the war and practically no one returned.

RM 1376 takes you into the region between the Sister creeks, a broken-up country once favored by outlaws and marauding Indians. It also takes you up and over the High Hills, the Great Divide—the string of hills that separates the Guadalupe and Pedernales watersheds. Few people live in this sparsely watered region.

After 14 wide-open miles on RM 1376, turn right onto RM 1888 to Blanco.

The country continues to be sparsely settled, but the homes along the way are mostly well-aging limestone ones. RM 1888 picks up the **Blanco River** in its infancy and follows its ever-strengthening flow. At first the south banks of the Blanco are high sheer bluffs, then both banks lie low for the rest of the trip to Blanco. *Blanco* means "white" in Spanish, and refers to the river's white limestone bed. There is a legend to the effect that if a person gets a drink of Blanco water, he will never be content at any other place under the sun, but will always have a desire to again quaff the waters of the Blanco River.

When RM 1888 runs into RM 1623, continue straight on what is now RM 1623 into Blanco.

BLANCO

Blanco County • 1,368 • (830) • About 27 miles from Sisterdale
Blanco was first settled when James Callahan and E. C. "Uncle Clem" Hinds moved to the Blanco River valley and built cabins on opposite sides of the river. Callahan had come to Texas from Georgia in 1835 to fight in the Texas Revolution. He fought in the battle of Coleto in 1836 and was taken with James W. Fannin's men to Goliad, where he escaped the massacre because of his skills as a mechanic. When the Mexicans released him, he joined a ranger force. As lieutenant of a Texas Rangers company, he helped expel the

Mexican force that invaded Texas and captured San Antonio in 1842. Callahan had come through the Blanco valley in 1836, and fell so in love with the place that he moved his family out into what was then the wilderness 17 years later. Others followed, so many that real estate entrepreneur John Pitts and Callahan laid out a town on the north side of the river in 1855.

In 1855, Governor Elisha M. Pease ordered three companies of Texas Rangers under Callahan's command to protect the Texas-Mexico border from marauding bands of Lipan Apaches and Kickapoos. On October 1, the rangers arrived at Fort Duncan (present-day Eagle Pass) and crossed the Rio Grande into Mexico, in pursuit of the Indians, and probably in pursuit of runaway slaves as well. At first, Mexican authorities cooperated with the rangers, because the Mexicans suffered even more than the Texans from Indian raids. But then the Mexicans joined with the Indians to drive the Texans back across the Rio Grande. To cover his retreat, Callahan burned the Mexican border town of Piedras Negras on October 6. The commander at Fort Duncan covered the Texans' retreat back across the river. For burning the town, Callahan was dismissed from the service. He returned to his piece of paradise on the Blanco.

But Callahan would enjoy just a few more months of his paradise on earth. He became involved in a dispute with young Calvin Blassengame and Calvin's father, Woodson. Callahan decided to ride over to the Blassengame place with E. C. Hinds and W. S. "Maulheel" Johnson, in order to settle the matter. While talking to Mrs. Blassengame, the three men were fired at by parties concealed in the home. Callahan and Johnson died from the point-blank buckshot; Hinds, though seriously wounded, was able to escape.

Hinds managed to gasp out his story to Callahan's widow, the authorities were notified, and the Blassengame men were arrested without incident. But word of the murders spread like wildfire down the Blanco to San Marcos and then to Seguin. A Texas Ranger captain, Callahan was well known and liked by Central Texans. Nearly a hundred of his friends and admirers saddled up and rode as a group to the Little Blanco River, where the Blassengames were in custody. The posse was determined that justice should be done, so at midnight they overran the guards and shot the men. It had all the makings of a great feud, but fortunately none developed.

Blanco County was created in 1858, and an election that year located the county seat at a spot just across the river from Pittsburg. The court met for the first couple of years under a tree, then in the log schoolhouse. Their approach to law enforcement was equally as casual and as realistic. Take the case of "Dr." McKinney, who settled down four miles above Blanco and started to practice his own brand of medicine, which to his neighbors was quackery. He was also a bigamist, for which illegal practice he was indicted. But when the sheriff and posse rode out to arrest him, McKinney barricaded himself in the house, while his wives sallied forth to meet the posse with a double-barreled shotgun and an axe. The two women looked so determined that the sheriff deemed it prudent to retire from the scene. Shortly thereafter, the good doctor and his entourage left Blanco County for Utah.

Many voters in Blanco County favored secession in 1861, but there was a sizable unionist element in the county, too. While the Rebels were away at war, the unionists managed to divide the county through an election. Western Blanco County then became a part of the new Kendall County. Such division in sentiment made for trouble. Bushwhackers scoured the countryside, molesting anybody they chose, and their Confederate pursuers were very liberal in their definition of "bushwhacker," tormenting and killing German farmers who merely wished to be left out of the conflict. The Comanches were also on the warpath, but the bushwhacker was feared more than the Indian; you knew an Indian was your enemy, but how could you tell whether a strange white man was your friend or foe?

In the fall of 1865, the district court here held its first postwar session. The grand jury went over the various wrongdoings of the past four years, the consequence of which was 73 indictments returned for murder, all of a political nature; that is, involving the killings of bushwhackers and soldiers.

The trouble did not abate. Nearly all the county's men were stock raisers, and they had left most of their stock on the range with little or no care. So after four years of little attention there was a great deal of young stock neither marked nor branded. Some of the returning soldiers argued that this unbranded stock was the natural increase of the stock they had left. This was partly true, and if there had been a fair divide, the harm would have been less, but the man who was most expert with the rope and branding iron got more than his share and the man with a conscience often got none. This led to hard feelings and, even worse, it led greedy men into the habit of branding what they knew was not their own. *Now* they were doing something *very* wrong, but could one expect that after four years of the demoralizing effects of camp life, and the fraud and corruption in many departments in the government, they would not become demoralized and corrupt too? Government corruption had been so bad during the war that one soldier declared that "honest men would steal."

The creation of Kendall County came back to haunt Blanco in 1879. That year the residents of the newly organized Johnson City and the northern part of the county called for an election to relocate the county seat to Johnson City. Blanco residents laughed—until the votes were counted. Johnson City had lost by only seven votes. Blanco won again by a narrow margin in 1886. By this time the county was polarized over the issue. Men were ready to fight at any time over the courthouse location; fistfights and gunfights were not uncommon. Many families even divided over the issue. Johnson City finally wrested away the county seat from Blanco in the third, 1891 election, and within hours all the county records were loaded onto wagons and moved to Johnson City. Ironically, Blanco has remained the larger town.

Cotton came to Blanco in the 1870s, and 1882 was a bumper year for Blanco County and Texas. Blanco farmers grew an astounding number of bales of cotton per acre. It was one of those years that prompted Uncle Clem Hinds to say, "Some years Texas floats in grease."

But then the drought years came. During the dry summer of 1886, a deserted farmhouse near Blanco had the following words chalked onto the board nailed across the door: "250 miles to the nearest post office, 100 miles to wood, 20 miles to water, 6 inches to Hell. God Bless our home! Gone to live with wife's folks." An old farmer remembered, "The corn crop was sorter short that year. We had corn for dinner one day and Paw ate 15 acres of it."

For decades, Blanco was a sleepy little town largely ignored by tourists and travelers. Many of the buildings on the courthouse square stood vacant and forlorn, including the old courthouse. By the 1980s, the courthouse was in danger of being torn down and rebuilt elsewhere. This bleak existence began to change in the 1990s. Thousands of urban refugees from Austin, San Antonio, and elsewhere have been moving into sparsely populated Blanco County. By 1996, a number of restaurants, antique shops, art galleries, B&Bs, a coffee and juice bar, health food store—even a microbrewery—had opened to serve them. Because of the high failure rate of new businesses, this book makes few specific recommendations, but you'll definitely find more things to do and see and eat in Blanco than was the case just a few years ago.

RM 1623 becomes 4th St./Loop 163 in Blanco. When you cross Main St./US 281, you come to the old courthouse and square.

OLD BLANCO COUNTY COURTHOUSE
On the square • Not open to the public
Built in 1885, the old courthouse served its intended function only five years before the county government moved to Johnson City. Designed by noted architect F. M. Ruffini, who crowned its relatively unadorned square limestone body with an elaborate mansard roof, the courthouse was Blanco's pride and joy. Blanco citizens schemed for years after the Johnson City move to reinstate Blanco County government within its walls, but their efforts ultimately failed. In the meantime, the courthouse served as bank, newspaper office, opera house, hospital, school, union hall, and museum. It is currently undergoing restoration but in good condition. You can still see traces of the faded "Bank" signs above the entryways. Few Texas towns can claim a vacant courthouse, and it's a minor miracle that this one has endured for so long a time.

LINDEMAN'S STORE
4th and Main • 833-4350 • Open Monday through Saturday
Located across US 281 from the old courthouse, this old limestone store building dates to at least 1885. Lindeman's is one of that disappearing breed of old-time country stores where you can do your grocery shopping, get fresh meat cut to your specifications at the meat counter, and pick up a new straw hat, jeans, and work gloves. Lindeman's makes its own Deutsche-Tex style smoked ring sausage (pork and turkey), beef jerky, and dried sausage rings, as well as bread, cobblers, cookies, etc. From the parking lot out back, you can see the old Blanco jail, a squat, square, no-nonsense limestone building located on private property a few yards south.

BINDSEIL PARK
On Town Creek, by City Hall, just off the courthouse square
This short little linear park connects you to Blanco State Park. A couple of foot bridges cross the creek.

BLANCO UNITED METHODIST CHURCH
Pecan at 1st, 2 blocks south of the courthouse square
The congregation dates to 1854; the present limestone-block sanctuary dates to 1883, with subsequent additions.

ADRIAN EDWARDS CONN HOME
3rd and Main • Currently houses the Blanco County Title Company

One block south of Lindeman's on Main is the Adrian Edwards Conn home. The little cottage was built before 1873 with 16-inch-thick limestone walls, a rock-walled cellar, and an underground cistern. Remember that Indian raids continued here until at least 1874.

BLANCO BOWLING CLUB CAFE
4th/Loop 163, two blocks east of Main • 833-4416 • Open daily, breakfast, lunch, and dinner • $ • No Cr. • W

The window says "Blanco Valley Cafe," but that name was last correct over 30 years ago; the new owners just haven't gotten around to scraping and repainting the window. The Blanco Bowling Club Cafe is full of anachronisms. Take for instance the made-from-scratch doughnuts and sweet rolls served every morning, and the homemade coconut, lemon, chocolate, apple, and pecan pies, and the hand-breaded chicken-fried steak. Or take the old-fashioned burgers and homemade onion rings and french fries at pre-inflation prices.

BLANCO STATE PARK
The park is 4 blocks south of the town square; take US 281 south, then turn onto Park Road 23 • 833-4333 • Open daily Admission • W variable

Blanco State Park is 104 pleasant acres along the Blanco River. Over 200,000 people visit the park annually. The land was deeded by private owners in 1933; the park was opened in 1934. The area had been used as a campsite by early explorers and settlers. A spring made the location popular when the river was dry. Original park improvements were made by the Civilian Conservation Corps. The park's hilly terrain is dotted with cedar, pecan, and other trees. Animal life includes nutria, mallard duck, raccoon, armadillo, and squirrel. Fish include rainbow trout (in the winter), perch, catfish, and bass.

Park activities include camping, swimming, picnicking, hiking, nature study, boating (electric motors only), fishing, and paddle boat rentals (seasonal). The park's facilities include restrooms with and without showers; campsites with water and electricity; campsites with water, electricity, and sewer; screened shelters; a hiking trail; a short nature study trail; a sanitary dump station; group, day-use facilities; playgrounds; and a Texas State Park Store. Special rates are available.

Write to P.O. Box 493, Blanco 78606. *Elevation:* 1,350 ft. *Weather:* January average low temperature 46.2 degrees; July average high 85.9 degrees; *First/last freeze:* November 6/ March 29.

ANNUAL EVENT

JUNE • Blanco Valley Jamboree • Locations vary • 833-5101
Second weekend in June • Free • W
The event begins with a Friday night dance, unwinds with the chili cook-off on Saturday, and includes a band contest and fiddlers competition sanctioned by the Texas Old Time Fiddlers Association. Other activities include a cow chip (cowboy Frisbee) toss, armadillo races, a jalapeno-eating contest, egg throwing, an armadillo beauty contest, washer pitching, and a Miss Blanco beauty pageant, all climaxed by a street dance.

To leave Blanco and continue the trip, go east from the courthouse square, past the Blanco Bowling Club, on Loop 163 across the Blanco River. When Loop 163 runs into US 281, turn left on US 281. In a half-mile you come to the junction with RM 32. Turn left on RM 32 and head for San Marcos.

As you roll through these arid hills, which are very valuable hills these days nonetheless, consider these remarks by an early settler about the same land: "[We] were dependent in many respects upon each other, but especially for mutual protection and the care of each other's stock, as stock was about all the property we cared for, or counted as property. What did we care for who owned the broad acres while our horses and cattle had the free use of it? A man with large stock did not care for more than land enough on which to build his cabin and pens, with plenty of water convenient. So the men with large tracts of land were to be pitied, for they had their taxes to pay and the land brought no income." So far was this practice carried that the teller claimed to know of a rancher "that claimed to control 10,000 head of cattle on a 160 acre preemption claim, and that not patented; in fact the owner was not willing to pay even the patent fees."
What do you think he would say about the four-digit land prices of today?

Remember that RM 32 becomes Ranch Rd. 12, 10 miles out of San Marcos. And San Marcos is about 35 miles from Blanco.

Since 1990, Hays County has been the fastest growing county in the Austin area. By one estimate, the county's population grew by 18 percent between 1990 and 1995, from 65,000 to 77,000. And as the population rises, the underground watertable drops. Some wells now go down more than 200 feet before they find water.

ENCHANTED ROCK

Approximately 232 miles

Enchanted Rock is the Hill Country's most awe-inspiring natural landmark, a 640-acre bald dome of pink granite rising 325 feet above the bed of Sandy Creek and 1,825 feet above sea level. It is the second largest exposed batholith in the United States, behind Georgia's Stone Mountain, and is one of the oldest geological rock exposures in Texas, formed nearly a billion years ago. Texans have been attracted to it for centuries. The rock's rugged surface conceals entrances to caves and subterranean passages far below. Indians generally feared the mountain, worshipping it from a respectful distance, but on occasion some of them evidently used one cave whose entrance is on top of the rock and whose exit is far below on the back side of the rock.

A correspondent for the *New York Mirror* wrote in 1838 of an "enchanted" or "holy" mountain, which the Comanches regarded with religious veneration and where they frequently assembled to perform "paynim" rites. Modern Texans still flock to Enchanted Rock each year, probably just as awestruck as those Comanches.

Leave Austin on Bee Caves Rd. (FM 2244) west, toward Bee Cave.

The explosive growth that Austin has undergone is typified in Bee Caves Rd. Twenty-five years ago a few scattered houses and the Eanes School stood along the road, and the surrounding hills were mostly green. Now Bee Caves Rd. is lined with dozens of business establishments and the once-verdant hills are brown with rooftops.

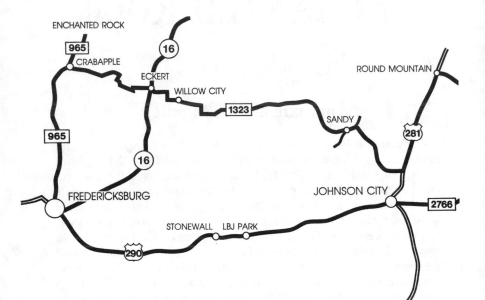

ENCHANTED ROCK

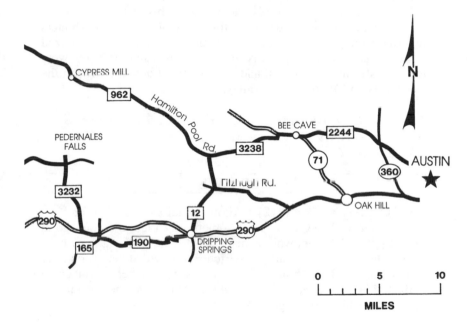

However, this four-lane highway was a winding dirt wagon trail through an isolated cedar choppers' neighborhood called Panther Path back in 1902. That was also the year our own Central Texas version of the Abominable Snowman appeared in Panther Path. Our "Big Foot" first frightened a group of young people who were fishing and hunting several miles above the old McDonald Dam. The eight-foot-tall hairy man-monster flourished a large club and, uttering blood-curdling screams, started to attack. The young people ran for their wagons and managed to make a hairsbreadth escape. The beast followed them for some distance, however, before abandoning the chase and disappearing into a large canyon.

Measurements of Big Foot's tracks showed his feet to be 22 inches long and 7 inches wide, with four toes on each foot. Hunters reported feeling unsafe for quite some time thereafter and organized a well-equipped hunting party to effect his capture. They were unsuccessful in their efforts, and perhaps Big Foot still lurks in the Bee Creek and Barton Creek valley.

Bee Caves Rd. twists and turns, up and down, offering an occasional glimpse of Lake Austin all the way to its junction with SH 71 at the village of Bee Cave.

BEE CAVE

Travis County • 259 • (512) • About 12 miles from Austin
Bee Cave, or Bee Caves as it is sometimes called, was founded in 1870 by Will Johnson, who named the settlement after a large cave of wild bees he found nearby. Dietrich Bohls settled here soon after and you pass a Bohls' homestead on your right just before you come to the SH 71 intersection. Note the old rail fences and the several vintage rock and log buildings tucked away in the trees.

Turn right onto SH 71.

The Trading Post at the intersection was founded at the turn of the century by Will Johnson's son Wiley, back when this intersection was just a crossing of two dirt wagon roads. Continue on SH 71, noting the beautifully preserved zigzag rail fence on your right across from the Trading Post.

BARBARA ELLEN'S
13129 SH 71 W, at RR 620, in Bee Cave • 263-2385
Open daily, lunch and dinner • $–$$ • AE, MC, V • W
Barbara Ellen's serves solid American food, southern style, with healthy portions of vegetables and sinful desserts. Don't miss the bathrooms. Convenient to Lake Travis. Bar.

Continue past the RM 620 turnoff for another couple of hundred yards, then turn left on Hamilton Pool Rd. (RM 3238) as per the sign, which reads "Hamilton Pool Road" and "Boy Scouts of America."

The sharp eye will note a small shed covered with a variety of old advertising signs on your left in the triangle formed by the intersection. Early settler Carl Beck set up shop here at the old Hamilton Pool/Marble Falls Rd. crossroads in 1873. A lot of cotton was grown in the fertile Colorado River valley back then, and Beck soon built a gin, mill, and cigar factory at this crossroads. Beck produced a locally famous stogie using tobaccos imported from New Orleans. He also served as postmaster here for 45 years.

Continue west on Hamilton Pool Rd./RM 3238, past the turnoffs to Fitzhugh and Dripping Springs. At this point the road loses its state-ranch-road status and narrows. Hamilton Pool Rd. also becomes much twistier and slightly rougher at this point.

HAMILTON POOL
Hamilton Pool Rd. • About 14.5 miles from Bee Cave
264-2740
Hamilton Pool is named for a natural pool where a 100-foot waterfall furnishes a constant supply of water. The area was first settled in the 1880s and over the years Hamilton Pool has become a favorite swimming hole. It is now a Travis County park. User capacity is strictly limited to 100 cars, so it's best to call ahead to check.

Shortly past the Hamilton Pool turnoff you will plunge into the Pedernales River valley. The road takes a hairpin course down and across the narrow one-lane low-water bridge, so take it easy and enjoy the scenery.

WESTCAVE PRESERVE
Hamilton Pool Rd. • About 15.5 miles from Bee Cave
825-3442 • Open Saturday and Sunday • Tours 10, noon,
2 and 4 in good weather
As you climb out of the valley you pass the Westcave Preserve. This semitropical 31-acre preserve includes a waterfall and collapsed grotto. The grotto was formed 150,000 or so years ago when falling water washed away enough sand and shale beneath a limestone cliff to make it collapse. The river canyon within the preserve grows a number of unusual plants— for the Hill Country—such as columbine and orchids. The land is operated by the nonprofit Westcave Preserve Corporation. Confirm tours by calling, or write John Ahrns, Westcave Preserve, Star Route 4, Box 30-C, Dripping Springs 78620.

After you cross into Blanco County, Hamilton Pool Rd. resumes its state-maintained status as RM 962.

RM 962 roughly parallels Cypress Creek through fertile bottom-land, pastureland that once grew bales and bales of cotton.

CYPRESS MILL

Blanco County • 56 • About 23 miles from Bee Cave
Not surprisingly, a village grew up along Cypress Creek. William Evans was the first settler here and he built the first waterpowered mill in Blanco County on the swift-flowing Cypress Creek. People came from miles and miles in all directions to have their corn ground and their timber sawed into rough though usable lumber.

Life was good here in those days, for the creek flowed strong and there were many springs in the area. The abundance of cypress trees along the creek—the source of the creek's name is still obvious to the modern traveler—made a bustling business at the mill.

One fly in the ointment was Indians. Blanco County was a favored hunting ground and they resented the white settlers' presence. They made their displeasure known by dozens of raids over the years, the most tragic of which occurred in 1869.

Thomas Felps and his young wife Eliza were ambushed and killed by Comanches on July 21 of that year at a spot along Cypress Creek. They were visiting her father's ranch at the time. Thomas was found unscalped; the superstitious Indians refused to take his redheaded scalp. Eliza was found some distance away savaged and scalped. Her discoverers speculated that the raiders had planned to take her away as a hostage, but Eliza had fought them so stubbornly that they just decided to slay and scalp her and be done with it. The couple left two young children.

The Indian attacks subsided in the 1870s and the locals grew prosperous raising cotton, cattle, and sheep in these fertile bottomlands. But over the years the land and climate changed. The once plentiful springs dried up and Cypress Creek no longer flowed with its former force. Rains no longer fell with the same frequency and the land became barren. The cotton farmers left and the land was given a chance to rest. It is now the almost exclusive domain of cattle and goats.

All that remains now of Cypress Mill is the old schoolhouse which now houses the post office and store.

Continue north on RM 962 through the fertile Cypress Creek valley toward Round Mountain.

ROUND MOUNTAIN

Blanco County • 59 • About 7 miles from Cypress Mill
The Round Mountain community is named for nearby Round Mountain, a small round mountain about 5 miles northeast. Joseph Bird was the first settler here, in 1854. Bird came here to the Cypress Fork of the Pedernales from North Carolina via Arkansas, buying a full league (640 acres) of land, on which he raised cattle. Also a Baptist minister, Bird organized the community's first church. The place was called Birdtown in his honor until the post office was established in 1871, when it took the name of the nearby hill.

OLD ROUND MOUNTAIN SCHOOL AND CHURCH
RM 962 • Not open to the public • Historical marker
Just before you get to Round Mountain and the intersection with US 281 you will see on your left a simple stark white-frame building with an equally utilitarian steeple. A state historical marker stands in front of it. This structure served as community church and school for many years. The school was established in 1871 and had up to 200 students at one time. Before Johnson City was founded in 1878, Round Mountain was the only town in the northern half of Blanco County and was in fact larger than Johnson City when the county seat was moved to the latter town in 1891.

MARTIN COMPLEX
Not open to the public
One of Round Mountain's biggest entrepreneurs in those early years was the widow Martin. She came here from Llano County in 1873 after the death of her husband, John Martin, and with the help of her children built a two-story hotel, livery stable, and general store. The hotel and livery stable still stand a little over 100 yards to the east of the historical marker and are easily visible from both this place and RM 962. The hotel is now a private residence.

Mrs. Martin was appointed postmaster at Round Mountain in 1879 and served in that capacity until 1896, operating the post office out of her store. Round Mountain was on the old stagecoach road west from Austin to Llano at the time and Mrs. Martin did quite a business. She and son David established Blanco County's first telephone company.

When the main road west shifted north, Round Mountain became a predominantly ranching community.

Turn left on US 281 toward Johnson City.

The land here is gently rolling, wide-open, sparsely populated ranch country. As you approach Johnson City and the Pedernales you'll see the wall of hills looming in the distance, the Great Divide that separates the watersheds of the Pedernales River to the north and the Blanco River to the south.

Eight and a half miles south of Round Mountain and just a long mile north of the Pedernales, turn right onto RM 1323.

SANDY

Blanco County • 25 • About 15.5 miles from Round Mountain
The first settlement you come to on RM 1323 is Sandy, named for the deep sandy soil in this section of Blanco County. Never more than a ranching community, Sandy's only identifiable center today is the **Sandy Store and post office.**

Continue on RM 1323 from Sandy towards Willow City.

You are on the Texas Department of Transportation's **Hill Country Trail.** This is typical Hill Country ranching country, and houses are usually tucked away in the rolling hills well away from the road.

One, just inside Gillespie County, stands abandoned beside the road, a vintage limestone dwelling next to an aging windmill. Rectangular, one-story, with cedar doors and window frames and severe, unadorned lines, this house is battered but still strong, waiting for someone to come along and fill it with human warmth.

Cattle fill the pastures prominently, but even more evident are the flocks of sheep and the shaggy, curved-horn, unmistakably Angora goats. **Mt. Hudson** looms large in front of you.

WILLOW CITY

Gillespie County • 75 • About 17 miles from Sandy

Willow City was named by a group of Southern, Scotch/Irish-American families who in the 1870s settled in the valley of a creek bordered by button willows. The first school, a one-room log building with a dirt floor, was built about 1879. It was also used as a church on Sundays; three denominations shared it on a rotating basis. The town soon had a blacksmith, druggist, mill, post office, and store. An early 1880s flood washed much of the town away. Folks rebuilt the town farther away from the creek, in its present location. Cotton became an important crop, and the gristmill became a cotton gin. A two-story, limestone school was built in 1905 and served until 1961. The Willow City Emmanuel Gospel Church meets in a plain white frame church near Hohmann's Store and the Willow City Post Office.

HOHMANN'S GENERAL STORE
RM 1323 • Monday through Thursday 8–5, Friday 8–3, Saturday 8–2:30

Hohmann's is a typical Hill Country store, selling more ranch supplies than groceries; most folks just drive into Fredericksburg to shop at the HEB where food prices are cheaper. The store is usually full, though, mostly populated by good ol' boys in to pick up some feed, salt blocks, bob wire, and the like. There are plenty of stools, chairs, and pop cases to sit around on, and an old Franklin stove sits in the middle of the room to warm things up in the winter. Snake hunting—of the rattlesnake variety—is a favorite topic of conversation. There are a lot of rattlers out there in the rocks, and almost as many different ways of hunting them. Some guys lure them out of their rocky holes by pouring gasoline down the openings while others use a mirror to reflect sunlight into their dens. There's a market for the hides, meat, bones, rattles, and heads these days. Cedar talk also fills the air.

Cedar chopping is a major pastime out here. To kill cedar and keep it killed, you either have to strip off all the needles or cut the tree down at ground level; if even one leaf is left on the tree it will resprout. And they swear that some days the cedar pollen is so dense out here that it looks like thick smoke boiling off the ground. A lot of mesquite is chopped here too, much of which goes to barbecue joints and smokehouses around the area.

Rain (or the lack of it) is also staple talk around here. Most of the talk is in "points"—Hohmann's may have recorded a spotty "10 or 15 points" (.10–.15 inches) while nearby Bell Mountain may have been deluged by "an inch and thirty" (1.3 inches).

But bring up the subject of bluebonnets and you're likely to get some harrumphs and raised eyebrows.

"I wouldn't want to live in a pasture of them. . . . You know what they smell like? I can stand it about five minutes and then I want to mow 'em down. Old so-and-so's house sits in a pasture full of blue-bonnets and he'd just as soon burn them up as smell 'em any longer—but the state law won't let him," is the way one fellow put it. For those of you who don't know, the odor of a bluebonnet changes on a day-by-day basis, starting with a delicate almost indistinguishable scent and ending with a heavy, sickeningly sweet smell like shoe polish.

Backtrack from the store a few hundred feet east on RM 1323 to the 90-degree turn you took to get to the store. Here at this T intersection you see a sign reading "Willow City Loop." Turn left here to drive one of the most wildly beautiful roads in Texas.

If Willow City Loop is impassable due to high water, continue on RM 1323 from Willow City west 2.7 miles to RM 1323's intersection with SH 16 at Eckert. RM 1323 ends here. Turn right on SH 16, then in several feet turn left onto Eckert Rd., marked by "To Crabapple" and "Rabke's" signs.

WILLOW CITY LOOP

You ridge-run the first few miles out of Willow City, then suddenly you dive-bomb down into the brakes of **Coal Creek** where great gray and pink granite boulders lay tossed about the countryside. This is known as **Hell's Half-Acre, the Devil's Kitchen,** or **the Dungeon:** a great troughlike depression where stars fell many centuries ago, leaving many smooth meteoric stones. The brush is almost impenetrable here and was a favorite hiding place for raiding Indians and Civil War bushwhackers. The narrow road twists through the Coal Creek valley, crossing the creek several times, in the shadows of the hundreds-of-feet-high, sheer northern and eastern cliffs of Coal Creek. In the spring this valley is awash in miles and square miles of bluebonnets, which flood the bottomlands and rise high up the inclines of **Cedar Mountain,** where the blooming yuccas stand guard.

Eight miles from Hohmann's Store on the Loop, you'll pass the entrance to Texas' only serpentine quarry, at the foot of Cedar Mountain. Although relatively soft, Texas serpentine takes a beautiful, lustrous polish. It is widely used for terazzo floors, decorative objects and as wainscot in office buildings and hotel lobbies. While there are many deposits, the largest outcropping is here. The Coal Creek serpentine mass is over 3.5 miles long and 1.5 miles at its widest point. It extends over into Blanco County. The importance folks out here attach to rain is best summed up by this sign on the Loop: "K and L Ranch where a good rain and a baby calf are always welcome." Remember, this is all private property—don't trespass. The Willow City Loop has become a very popular springtime weekend "drive," so be prepared for traffic on Saturdays and Sundays during bluebonnet season. Better yet, go on a weekday.

Cattle wander at random along many of this road's 13 miles, so it is imperative to keep your speed down for them, if the valley's wild beauty alone is not enough. In the fall you must also contend with dozens of deer, which cross your path every half-mile or so during the late afternoon. After you've turned west, things calm down a bit and you are out of the Dungeon and into more gently contoured pastureland.

Turn left when you reach SH 16, in about 14 miles. In 3 miles you pass between Mt. Nebo on your right and Bell Mountain on your left. Soon you come to Eckert.

ECKERT

Gillespie County • (830) • About 20 miles from Willow City

Eckert was named for W. R. Eckert, in whose store the post office was established in 1900. Previously the settlement had been known as Nebo, after the mountain. The original Mt. Nebo is the summit of Mt. Pisgah, a mountain ridge in ancient Palestine from which Moses viewed the promised land. Nebo dated to 1875 when eight Anglo families built a log church named Mt. Zion, around which they settled. Not much is left here these days, except for the vacant rock store and a couple of old farmhouses.

*Turn right on Eckert Rd., which is the small road right after the Eck-
ert sign, marked by a sign reading "Rabke's—4 miles" and another
reading "To Crabapple." In 4 miles you cross Riley Creek and come
to Rabke's Table Ready Meats.*

RABKE'S TABLE READY MEATS
**Crabapple Rd., 4 miles from Eckert • 830-685-3266 • No Cr.
W with assistance**

Sandwiched between Crabapple Rd.'s crossings of Riley and
Crabapple creeks is Rabke's, home of some of Texas' best beef jerky
and other smoked meats. Leroy and Geneva Rabke started the business more than 30 years ago. Leroy's ancestors bought this place,
400 acres along Crabapple Creek, in 1880. The barn was built before
1850 and there is another, smaller log-and-rock building from that
era. The Rabkes process deer for hunters and offer a variety of excellent and reasonably priced meats, such as turkey sausage and breast
rolls, whole turkeys, hams, beef brisket, bacon, beef and pork
sausage, turkey jerky, and beef jerky, all slow-smoked over mesquite
and hickory fires.

Only beef round is used for the beef jerky, and you don't know
how tasty jerky can be until you've tried Rabke's rendition. Your
teeth meet a slight resistance as you bite into the very black-peppery
strip of meat, then they slide the rest of the way through, like cutting
through soft butter. The smoky meat almost melts in your mouth; no
fear of breaking a tooth or jaw here, as is the case with many other
jerkies. Rabke's also makes and sells homemade pear relish, bread-
and-butter pickles, and plum, wild grape, and agarita jellies, all made
from fruits and vegetables grown in their garden or picked from the
fields. Write P.O. Box 17, Willow City 78675.

*From Rabke's proceed west to Crabapple community after parallel-
ing scenic Crabapple Creek for several miles. Cattle wander at will
across this pencil-thin road, so take it easy. Less than a mile west of
Rabke's you will come to a T-intersection. Turn right onto "Lower
Crabapple Rd."*

CRABAPPLE COMMUNITY

Gillespie County • About 4 miles from Rabke's

This settlement along fertile **Crabapple Creek** began to grow
almost as soon as Fredericksburg got its feet firmly planted on the

ground. Both New Braunfels and Fredericksburg initially were laid out according to the traditional German farm village plan, where early settlers were granted town lots about one-half acre in size and outlying farms of 10 acres. It was assumed that the immigrants would locate their houses, barns, and other homestead structures on their town lots and then go out to work in their nearby 10-acre fields each day. The farm village plan was a failure in both places from the beginning. Large numbers of cattle and unwise prairie burning quickly exhausted the supply of natural forage nearby, so the settlers began to fan out in search of better grazing lands. The dispersal from town was further aided by cheap land prices. So the Germans fanned out from Fredericksburg, making their homes in the fertile stream valleys scattered throughout the Hill Country and leaving large gaps in the population pattern. The interfluvial lands were not to be settled until the introduction of the windmill in the 1880s.

Heinrich Grobe was one of these expansionists. He moved his family from the New Braunfels area to the Crabapple Creek bottomlands in 1857. Life was good to the Grobes during their first five years at Crabapple. But on the morning of April 4, 1862, Heinrich Grobe went out to work on a rock fence he had been building. His older sons did the morning chores at home and went to help their father. As they approached his place of work, the boys spotted a body in a bush. It was their father, stripped of all raiment save his shoes, 11 arrows buried in his chest. The boys ran home to get mother and together they wrapped father's body in linen and dragged him home on a sled, for the Indians had stolen all their horses. Then a neighbor took poor Mr. Grobe to Fredericksburg for burial. "Widder" Grobe was on her own. She persevered here several more years before moving to the comparative safety of Reingold community, which was more densely populated and less prone to Indian raids. But her neighbors stayed on and Crabapple grew.

CRABAPPLE COMMUNITY BUILDINGS
Feel free to roam the grounds, but all the buildings are locked

Today Crabapple community is one of the nicest collections of essentially unaltered limestone buildings to be found in the Hill Country, kept neat as a pin. The centerpiece of the collection is **St. John's Lutheran Church.** Built in 1897—the date is prominently inscribed in a date stone above the front door—the sanctuary is a cleanly constructed, high-gabled rectangular box. A tin steeple with a weathervane crown St. John's. The Germans who setttled the area were practical above all else; the church steeple is the neighbor-hood's tallest and therefore most visible manmade point, so where else would you put the weathervane?

Scattered across the community center grounds are the limestone schoolhouse, featuring equally simple but pleasing lines, and an unoccupied house of similar design with a shed attached to it, covered with pressed tin in the design of large limestone blocks. In the course of your travels you will be amazed at the diversity in patterned-tin designs that you will see; several different types are found here at Crabapple alone. You'll probably hear wild turkeys in the distance, too.

Continue west on Crabapple Rd. a few hundred yards to the point where the road divides into two forks. Either fork takes you to RM 965, but if you take the low road, you get to cross Crabapple Creek twice. Turn right on RM 965.

WELGEHAUSEN RANCH
Crabapple Rd. at RM 965 • Not open to the public

Just after you cross the creek, you will see on your left another great collection of vintage log and stone buildings. This is the old Welgehausen homestead, now owned by Mr. and Mrs. A. M. Tomforde. The Tomfordes bought this land from Welgehausen family members in 1976. Frederick Welgehausen came here in 1856, back when Crabapple Creek was on the very edge of the western frontier. Welgehausen's first log cabin still stands slightly east of the main residence, restored for use as a guest house.

The main house, a large two-story limestone structure in the center of the group, also began life as a simple one-room log cabin with an outside stairway to the loft. Over the years, as the family grew, rooms were added downstairs, and gradually the little cabin became the core of a larger limestone one-story house. Finally the second story was added, and this expansion is very obvious in the different-sized rocks used. There are many other similarly evolved houses throughout the country, dwellings that had their start nearly a century and a half ago as rude cabins. Sometimes the owners are not even aware of this history until they decide to do some interior work and stumble upon the old log walls, long covered with plaster.

Several other restored log cabins and ranch buildings are scattered across the ranch. Welgehausen family members are buried in the cemetery just north and west of the ranch.

Continue north on RM 965 toward Enchanted Rock. In a scant couple of miles, as you top a hill and turn a corner at its summit, the Enchanted Rock formation unfolds before you.

Awesome is the only adequate word to describe this great bald knob and its smaller companions, which appear every bit as overpowering today as they did 200 and more primitive years ago.

ENCHANTED ROCK
About 18 miles north of Fredericksburg on FM 965, about 7 miles from Crabapple Community • 915-247-3903 Open daily • Admission • W variable
Enchanted Rock is a huge, pink granite boulder that rises 1,825 feet above sea level; it covers about 640 acres. It is the second-largest batholith (underground rock formation uncovered by erosion) in the United States. Enchanted Rock State Natural Area, which contains Enchanted Rock, consists of 1,643.5 acres on Big Sandy Creek north of Fredericksburg on the border between Gillespie and Llano counties. Humans have been coming to marvel at the rock for over 11,000 years.

Legends surround the rock like a fog. Tonkawa Indians believed that ghost fires flickered at the top, and they heard weird creaking and groaning, which geologists now say results from the rock's heating by day and contracting in the cool night. A Spanish conquistador captured by Tonkawas escaped by losing himself in the rock area, giving rise to an Indian legend of a "pale man swallowed by a rock and reborn as one of their own." The Indians believed that he wove enchantments on the area, but the Spaniard explained that the rock wove the spells. "When I was swallowed by the rock, I joined the many spirits who enchant this place." The first well-documented explorations of this area began in 1723 when the Spanish intensified their efforts to colonize Texas. During the mid-1700s, the Spaniards made several trips to the north and northwest of San Antonio, establishing a mission and presidio on the San Saba River and carrying out limited mining on Honey Creek near the Llano River.

Writing in 1834, W. B. Dewees described "a large rock of metal which has for many years been considered a wonder. It is supposed to be platinum. The Indians have held it sacred for centuries, and go there once a year to worship it. They will not permit any white person to approach it. It is almost impossible to make any impression on it with chisel and hammers. When struck it gives forth a ringing sound which can be heard miles around. The party was successful in finding the rock, but were unable to break off any specimens to bring home."

Some legends state that Indians, Comanches in particular, came here once a year from places far away to hold their sacred rites at the summit. But many more stories tell how the Indians held the rock in fearful veneration, refusing to venture much farther up it than the rocky, broken base. They believed it to be haunted, for a variety of reasons. One tale tells of a few brave warriors, the last of a tribe now long extinct, who defended themselves here from the attacks of their hostile brethren for many years, until finally overcome and annihilated in a savage attack. From that time Indians looked upon the rock as the exclusive haunt of the phantom warriors. Others say that a tribal chief sacrificed his daughter on one of the boulders to please the gods. The gods became angry at the sacrifice, struck the chief down, and forced his spirit to walk the rock forever. The depressions you see dotting the rock at its summit are his footprints.

Local historian Julia Estill wrote of Enchanted Rock: "At night spirit fires dance on the summit, and by day millions of isinglass stars glint in the sunlight. During an early morning shower in the hills, when the sun shines out from under the passing cloud, the streams of water coursing down the sides of the boulder resemble sheets of molten silver. Then above the gigantic dome there forms a rainbow path which will lead the seeker directly to a mine of gold, so the old legend goes. In fact the sands of the sluggish stream winding lazily around the base of the rock testify of gold in the vicinity. And the oldest pioneer in the neighborhood will tell you that there is a lost mine somewhere near the rock, the shaft having been sunk by Spaniards in the eighteenth century."

The Indians were further convinced of the rock's spirit infestation by the strange creaking noises you hear on cool nights following hot days. These were powerful spirits and the Comanches would regularly offer human sacrifices in the boulder yards at the base of the rock in order to appease the spirits and win favor for their raids. Once they went clear to San Antonio, to the Mission of San José, to capture their victim. In their attack, they carried off Rosa, the young daughter of the Indian chief Tehuan. Now Rosa had a Spanish boyfriend, the handsome young Spanish soldier Don Hesu Navarro, who had been knocked unconscious by a tomahawk blow during the mission attack. When he awoke, he was distraught to find his beloved gone, on her way to imminent death at the Holy Rock.

Don Hesu rushed to Goliad for aid and with an impetuous band of Spaniards and colonists pursued the raiders to their camp. Don Hesu proposed to attack immediately, but his companions persuaded him to wait until dark so as to play on the Comanches' superstitious beliefs. So that night the rescue party surreptitiously harassed the Indians by stampeding their horses and assaulting their guards. Believing the gods to be incensed with their recent raid, the Comanches found their horses and galloped off with their hostage to the rock, even more determined to appease the spirits with their sacrifice.

Don Hesu and company followed as best they could and reached the rock only to find Rosa already bound to the stake, faggots piled high around her. The rescuers divided into two parties, one group skirting the peak so as to surprise the Indians encamped on the north side of the rock, while Don Hesu and the rest rushed the guards stationed in the sacrificial gulch. Driven to a frenzy by the sight of his beloved about to be immolated, Don Hesu fought like a demon and managed to rescue Rosa and carry her to safety, thus depriving the spirits of the rock of at least one sacrifice.

Enough of legend. Enchanted Rock has been a state park since 1978 and a popular recreational spot for many more decades. Enchanted Rock State Park encompasses 1,643 acres and in addition to Enchanted Rock includes the smaller formations known as **Little Rock, Turkey Peak, Freshman Mountain, Flag Pole,** and **Buzzard's Roost. Sandy and Walnut Springs creeks** flow through it. The "inselberg" (island mountain) we call Enchanted Rock is just one small exposed (albeit the most famous) part of the Enchanted Rock batholith, which covers about 100 square miles. Other angular, blocky outcroppings, which rise as high as 1,800 feet above sea level occur throughout the area.

The batholith is a gigantic mass of molten rock, or magma, that intruded the earth's crust and cooled below the surface millions of years ago. This batholith, as such large igneous rock structures are called, did not initially erupt through the earth's surface but it did create a "bump" about 70 miles across and 1,000 feet high. This molten rock cooled and became the pink and gray granite that we see throughout the uplift. Through millions of years of erosion, this granite bedrock was exposed. The exposed granite then began to erode, and the granite knobs, of which Enchanted Rock is the largest, were formed throughout the uplift. A process called exfoliation, caused by the development of joints or fractures parallel to the rock surface, produced the smooth, rounded onionlike shape of Enchanted Rock. Huge sheets of rock break away (exfoliate) from the main dome along these curved joints, and start inching down towards the base. Its granite is too coarse for commercial quarrying, which has saved it from the fate that has befallen other domes such as Bear Mountain and Granite Mountain.

From a distance, the rock appears barren and devoid of plant life. But once you've started the mile-long climb to the summit, you'll be surprised at the amount of life that Enchanted Rock supports. Gnarled, wind-twisted oaks grow alone and in little island forests. Lichens of varying shades of orange, red, black, yellow, gray, and green mottle the granite; they are the shock troops of the erosion process. Dozens of little seasonal pond, marsh, and prairie ecosystems dot the rock, hosting a variety of grasses, cacti, wildflowers, waterbugs, lizards, and the like. Here's how it works, more or less: Weathering has produced a variety of features, including small circular depressions with raised rims (called rock doughnuts) and shallow depressions up to 50 feet in length (called gnammas or weather pits). Many of these depressions function as temporary rain collectors called vernal pools. As repeated rains dissolve the rock and soil begins to develop, pools that were once devoid of life begin to support algae, quillwort, and fairy shrimp. As more soil accumulates, annual and perennial herbs take over these depressions. Finally, grasses take root and soil islands form, which support larger animal life and trees.

The four major plant communities of Enchanted Rock are open oak woodland, mesquite grassland, floodplain, and granite rock community. Live oak, post oak, and blackjack oak dominate the oak woodland, with black hickory in moister areas. Texas persimmon, agarita, white brush, and prickly pear are common shrubs. Bluestem, three-awn, and grama grass grow in the shade of the oaks; American tripogon is common on gravelly slopes that are seasonally wet. The mesquite grassland, once an area of bluestem grass, is now covered with three-awn, grama, Texas wintergrass, panicum, and sand bur, along with invading mesquite. Elm, pecan, hackberry, black hickory, soapberry, and oak grow in the floodplains. White buckeye, agarita, Texas persimmon, Roosevelt weed, and buttonbush are commonly found shrubs. Grasses and sedges, as well as annual and perennial herbs, form the ground cover. Some of these are water bentgrass, late eupatorium, Indiangrass, bushybeard bluestem, frost weed, and switchgrass. In the spring, bluebonnets, Indian paintbrush, yellow coreopsis, bladderpod, and basin bellflower bloom.

Rock and fox squirrels are common, as are armadillos and rabbits. Lizards and turkey vultures are conspicuous year-round. White-tailed deer are frequently observed. The park's bird life is varied and abundant. Ask and you will receive a bird checklist for the park.

But back to the summit climb. On the east side of the rock, you'll find a seam of quartz uniformly half an inch wide running vertically up to the summit. Also near the summit is a state historical marker commemorating Jack Hays' victory over a band of Comanches in 1841.

Hays was heading up a surveying party in the area that fall. Their work took them to the Indians' sacred rock. Now Hays and company had two strikes against them from the beginning, in the Indians' eyes. They were violating the sanctuary of the sacred rock; and they were surveyors. Indians hated the white surveyors, for they believed the white man's compass was the device that stole their land. Off on his own one day, Hays was surprised by three Comanches. He fled toward a prearranged rendezvous point with his men, pursued by a growing number of Comanches. Hays arrived at the point alone; his men were already fighting for their lives with another band of Indians. He sought refuge atop Enchanted Rock, where, heavily armed and well protected, he managed to repulse his tormentors, killing their war party chief in the process.

From up here you can look to the north and gaze out upon a vast expanse of the Hill Country, which looks almost the same as it did in Hays' day. There are no houses, barns, power lines, or cultivated fields within view, only a narrow dusty jeep trail; you can pretend it is the Pinto Trail used by the Indians in their travels from South and Central Texas to the Northern Plains. The trail roughly followed the more recent route of the San Antonio and Aransas Pass and the Fredericksburg and Northern railroads to Fredericksburg, then farther north, past the rock. The entrance to Enchanted Rock Cave is near the summit, down the north slope a little ways. One of the largest known granite caves, it goes for about 1,000 ft. It developed under talus blocks along a sheeting joint, that is, debris comprised of house-size chunks of exfoliated granite slid down and lodged against a raised joint below and, after centuries of settling, a "cave" evolved. Smaller structures called A-tent caves have also been formed at various places on the Rock by sections of exfoliated sheets.

The various rock formations within the park are a favorite hangout for serious rock climbers and recreational hikers. Visitor activities include primitive backpacking, camping, hiking, technical and rock climbing, picnicking, geological study, bird-watching, and stargazing (minimal light pollution). Do not disturb plant or animal life, geological features, or Indian or historical artifacts. These park resources are protected by law. Bring your own firewood. Rock climbers must check in at headquarters; route maps and climbing rules are available.

Facilities include restrooms with showers; walk-in water sites with tent pads, picnic tables, fire rings, and water and restrooms with showers nearby; hike-in primitive sites, located in three unique areas with composting toilets (backpack camping in designated areas only); picnic sites for day-use with tables and grills; a group picnic area with a pavilion and restrooms; a 4-mile trail winding around the granite formations; a short, steep trail leading up to the top of Enchanted Rock (foot traffic only); an interpretive center; and a Texas State Park Store. No facilities are available for vehicular camping of any type. Park occupancy is now limited so as to minimize park deterioration due to overuse; it would be wise to call ahead for current policy. Parking along FM 965 is now prohibited.

Write to RR 4, Box 170, Fredericksburg 78624. *Elevation:* 1,825 ft. *Weather:* January average minimum temperature 36 degrees; July average maximum temperature 95 degrees; Average annual rainfall 28.7 in. *Busy season:* Year-round, especially during spring, fall, and winter.

From Enchanted Rock park headquarters, head back south to Fredericksburg on FM 965.

As you steal a last look at Enchanted Rock, here are a few final tidbits:

• There was at one time a scheme to create a Texas Rushmore here by carving the faces of famous Texans in the rock.

• The rock was a tourist attraction for Anglo Texans even back in the 1850s, and in 1860 Joe Walker's curiosity cost him his life. He and wife Annie, living in the newly minted town of Llano some 23 miles to the north, had heard of the wondrous knob and were determined to see it. Riding to nearby Legion Valley, where they spent the night with friends, the Walkers started early the next morning to the rock. Within a couple of miles from their destination, they encountered half a dozen horsemen, Indians. The Walkers made a run for it, but the Indians caught up and surrounded the pair, shooting hundreds of arrows at them almost as fast as you can snap your fingers. But the arrows had little effect, for the hard wind blowing that cold Sabbath day made them flutter and fall short of their mark.

But one of the Indians had a gun and shot Mr. Walker, wounding him in the back. Killing one, Walker continued to hold them off with his six-gun for over half an hour until their arrows were exhausted. Then one came walking toward the Walkers with a gun. He stopped at a tree with a waist-high fork in its trunk, placed the rifle in the fork, and took careful aim at the wounded Walker. Mrs. Walker later related: "My poor husband laid his pistol on the ground and put his cold, trembling arms around my shoulders and said, 'Kiss me goodbye dear wife, may God protect you now, for I must go.' I could not cry, nor sob, but kissed him and then took the pistol and put its muzzle to my heart. 'Oh, Annie what are you going to do?' he asked. I told him that I intended to go with him in case he was killed, as he had told me the savages would carry me off if they could kill him, and I did not want to go with his murderers. 'Oh my brave and true little Annie,' exclaimed he, 'Please do not commit such a deed. Oh God stay her hand that she may not take her own life.' During this time, which was only a few seconds, everything else was perfectly quiet. What caused that Indian not to shoot is more than I can tell.

"I had held my breath until I was all in a tremble. As he did not shoot I arose, laid the pistol on the ground, and went toward him. I went within a few yards of the savage, could see his dark clear eyes and into the muzzle of his gun, I then threw up my hands and cried out loud, 'O gracious God of Heaven have mercy and protect a poor helpless woman.' I begged the hostile Indian to please spare my poor husband, that he was already deadly wounded and to please not shoot him in my presence. He took down his gun; stood it against the tree. After pleading until I sank to the ground almost lifeless, my head went up but saying nothing, they all went back to their horses. They layed the dead man across one horse, the others mounted their horse and led our poor bleeding animals away, disappearing over the hill."

Annie returned to her weakening husband, who told her to leave him and try to save herself, that she would find a house about a mile away, and if anyone was home she could get help. Reluctantly agreeing with him, Annie found a thick cluster of bushes by the cliff of a rock where he could hide and be protected from the drizzling rain that had begun to fall. Joe Walker was dead by the time Annie came back to the bloody battleground with help.

Owner Tate Moss opened Enchanted Rock to picnickers and hikers in 1927; it was immediately popular with tourists. On June 22, 1929, Governor Dan Moody was in attendance here to proclaim Enchanted Rock "Texas's most wonderful summer resort." That day, another man drove his new Pontiac automobile to the summit.

Moss's grandson Charles later owned the rock. It was acquired by warranty deed in 1978 by the Nature Conservancy of Texas, Inc., from the Moss family. The state acquired it in 1984, added facilities, and reopened the park in March 1984. Enchanted Rock was designated a National Natural Landmark in 1970 and was placed on the National Register of Historic Places in 1984.

As you continue south on FM 965 toward Fredericksburg, you come to Bear Mountain, located on the east side of FM 965.

BEAR MOUNTAIN
FM 965 • About 14 miles south of Enchanted Rock
Bear Mountain is another of the Llano Uplift's granite hills, and the longtime home of the Bear Mountain Quarry, famous for its red granite. Many buildings in Fredericksburg and the surrounding Hill Country bear special markers proclaiming the source of their stone to be the prize-winning Bear Mountain Quarry. Bear Mountain is not marked as such, but as you pass by you'll recognize it from the tall masts and guy wires on your left, part of the hoisting apparatus for the huge stone blocks, some of which litter the hill's slopes. There's also a roadside park alongside Bear Mountain. Up until 1986, you could park here and hike up Bear Mountain to see one of the area's natural wonders, Balanced Rock, a large granite boulder delicately balanced on three strategic points in a manner seemingly defiant of the basic laws of gravity. That year, vandals blew Balanced Rock off its delicate perch with explosives and sent it tumbling down. Afterwards, the trail was closed off to the public, depriving us of a great panoramic view of the Palo Alto Valley as well.

On the northern outskirts of Fredericksburg, on the west side of FM 965, is Cross Mountain.

CROSS MOUNTAIN
FM 965, just north of Fredericksburg • About 17 miles from Enchanted Rock
Cross Mountain was so named for an aged timber cross found at the summit of this hill in 1847 by John Christian Durst. He raised the old cross up as a sort of sentinel overlooking the young city and a cross has stood up here ever since.

Spanish missionaries traveling from San Antonio to their San Saba Mission probably first raised the crucifix. Cross Mountain lay on the Pinto Trail, and both Indians and the Spanish used the mountain as a point of reference in their journeys. Cross Mountain continued to play an important role in the lives of Fredericksburg citizens over the years. When the settlers began replacing their rude log cabins with more substantial stone ones, they often went to the mountain to quarry the soft limestone found there. Many of the tombstones in Fredericksburg cemeteries came from Cross Mountain limestone.

Cross Mountain is also the home of the annual Easter fires, a tradition here since 1847. In Germany, Easter fires are symbolic of burning the old growth to make way for new life, signaling the dawn of Easter and Christ's resurrection. Here in Fredericksburg, the fires have a different meaning.

Back in 1847, Adelsverein Commissioner John Meusebach negotiated a treaty of peace with the Comanche nation. This treaty allowed the German colonists to live and grow in relative peace and was a great stroke of diplomacy for Meusebach. But the days before the treaty was signed were tense ones. On Easter eve, the hills surrounding Fredericksburg were filled with Comanches awaiting the final negotiations. Their campfires lit up the hills. Frightened by the fires, the children were calmed by resourceful mothers, who told their little ones that the fires were being tended by the Easter Bunny and his helpers, and that they were busy boiling the big cauldrons of dye used to color the traditional Easter eggs. With the successful treaty signing, the Easter fires became a way to celebrate the memory of this landmark event as well as the most sacred of Christian holidays.

You can park at the bottom of the hill and walk up the well-marked trail to the top for a great view of the city and a look at the latest cross now standing guard over Fredericksburg.

Leave Cross Mountain (and Fredericksburg) by continuing south on FM 965 to its junction with US 290, then take US 290 east toward Austin.

ROCKY HILL

Gillespie County • About 5.5 miles from Fredericksburg
Rocky Hill is located roughly where Lyman Wight's colony of Mormons settled in 1847. Wight called his settlement here on the Pedernales "Zodiac." The Mormons were gone by 1853 and the next settlement here was made by German, Danish, and English families. Gillespie County's only cotton plantation employing slave labor operated here through the Civil War. After the war, many of the exslaves remained here on land granted to them. The neighborhood's

name came from the school built in 1885, and the source of the name should be obvious. The old rock school still stands on the north side of US 290 and was in use as such through the early 1970s. It has been remodeled recently.

There are a number of period stone houses along this stretch of US 290 between Fredericksburg and Stonewall. You can usually discern the national origin of the builder by looking at the rooflines of these houses. A shallow-pitched roof with a slight break where the porch joins the house often indicates an Anglo American builder. A steeply pitched and gabled roof is typical of German builders. Deep porches running the length of the house reflect a Deep South influence.

Continue on US 290 east about 4 miles to Blumenthal.

BLUMENTHAL

Gillespie County • About 4 miles from Rocky Hill
Blumenthal is one of Gillespie County's youngest communities, founded about 1900 by two brothers from Grapetown, Max and Eugene Hohenberger. The hamlet received its name either from nearby Blumenthal Creek or from a German town of the same name. Blumenthal means "blooming valley" in German, which it certainly does in the spring. Original buildings here include general store, saloon, house, and cotton gin. In 1996, the hamlet was being renovated as a B&B complex.

Shortly after Blumenthal, you come to the entrances to Grape Creek Vineyard and Becker Vineyards.

GRAPE CREEK VINEYARD
US 290, 10 miles east of Fredericksburg • 800-950-7392
Open daily • Free • W variable
Grapes were first planted in 1986. Cabernet Sauvignon, Chardonnay, Fume Blanc, and Cabernet Blanc grapes are grown. There is a gift shop, tasting room, and B&B. Tours and tastings are given.

BECKER VINEYARDS
Jenschke Lane, off US 290, 10 miles east of Fredericksburg
830-644-2681 • Open daily, closed holidays • W
This vineyard was planted in 1992 (36 acres of vinifera grapes), on the site of an old stand of native mustang grapes, which were used by the neighboring Germans to make wine. The vineyard is surrounded

by fields of wildflowers in the spring, grown by a wildflower seed farm. The native limestone winery stands beside an 1880s log cabin and well. Wines are aged in French oak barrels. The long antique bar came from San Antonio's old Green Tree Saloon. The old mirrored barback was made in St. Louis.

Continue east on US 290 to Stonewall and the intersection with Ranch Rd. 1. Turn left onto Ranch Rd. 1.

STONEWALL

Gillespie County • 245 • (830) • About 5 miles from Blumenthal

This section of the Pedernales was first settled in the 1840s by German immigrants, but the town of Stonewall was not established until 1882, and was named for Civil War Confederate hero Thomas J. "Stonewall" Jackson. Major Israel Nuñez established the area's first store, along with a stage stop and post office in 1870. By 1879, a village by the name of Millville had been established and Nuñez moved his businesses there, renaming the place three years later.

Stonewall may be small, but its size belies its contributions over the years to Texas and the world. When commercial peach growing began in the Hill Country during the 1920s and 1930s, Stonewall farmers adopted the crop with a vengeance, and today Stonewall peaches are recognized as the Hill Country's—and by extension the world's—best. Stonewall celebrates the peach yearly with its Peach Jamboree, held the third Friday and Saturday of each June. Events include a rodeo, dance, parade, and lots of peaches and ice cream.

Emil Sauer was Stonewall's first famous native son. Born here in 1881, Sauer attended the University of Texas and Harvard before joining the consular service in 1911. Serving all over the world, Sauer became consul general in 1923, serving as such in Brazil and Germany. Author of several books on international finance, Sauer retired from the consular service in 1949.

Stonewall is more famous as the birthplace of the only president from Texas, Lyndon B. Johnson. As such, Stonewall was quite a tourist attraction during the presidential years. Things have calmed down here a bit since the president's death in 1973. Most of the souvenir shops have closed down or gone back to selling the merchandise they carried before the Johnson White House era.

Most of the tourist traffic today centers around the **LBJ National Historic Site** and the **LBJ State Historical Park,** established as a cooperative effort by the late President and Mrs. Johnson and federal and state planners. The Texas Parks and Wildlife Department operates the state park located on the south side of the Pedernales River, while the National Park Service operates the LBJ Ranch area directly across the river.

LBJ NATIONAL HISTORIC SITE
Headquarters at the LBJ State Historical Park • 644-2252
Open daily • Summer tours 10–5:30, winter tours 10–4
Free • W

The LBJ National Historic Site was created when President and Mrs. Johnson deeded 200 acres of the LBJ Ranch to the National Park Service. Johnson said he wanted the site to be more than just a memorial to himself or to the abstractions of history. He thought of it as a place where people could enjoy the Hill Country as he had—a place to get away, to relax. And he wanted visitors to be aware of the heritage that had been his—of land-taming pioneers, cattlemen, farmers, overcomers.

Four historically significant sites are located within the LBJ National Historic Site: the LBJ ranch house; the Johnson birthplace; the Junction school; and the Johnson family cemetery. A free bus tour of these sites is available through the visitor center at the LBJ State Historical Park just off Ranch Rd. 1. It lasts a little over an hour.

LBJ RANCH HOUSE
Then Senator Johnson and Lady Bird bought the limestone and frame ranch house from his aunt Frank Johnson Martin in 1951. The original two-story limestone core was built sometime before 1900 by Wilhelm Meier, Sr. The house and acreage surrounding it changed hands several times before Clarence and Frank Johnson Martin— Lyndon's uncle by marriage and aunt by blood—bought the place in 1909, less than a year after Lyndon was born in the little white house just east of the big house. The Martins enlarged the Meier house, adding the frame structure to the limestone house. Johnson visited the Martins often as a youth and was so impressed by the grandeur of their house that he vowed to own it someday. Martin practiced law in Blanco and Gillespie counties and was a district judge for many years. Mrs. Johnson still spends about a third of her time here, and the house is not open to the public.

JOHNSON BIRTHPLACE
Just down river from the big ranch house lies the little white farmhouse in which Lyndon Johnson was born on August 27, 1908. The

current building is actually a faithfully reconstructed replica, for the original was torn down in 1935.

Lyndon's grandparents Sam Ealy Johnson, Sr., and wife Eliza bought the land on which the house stands in 1882, a decade after Sam and his brother Tom had gone bust in the cattle business at Johnson City. Sam built the house in 1889, and in 1907 son Sam Ealy Johnson, Jr., brought his new bride, Rebekah Baines, home to this dogtrot house. He had just finished serving his second term in the Texas House of Representatives and his new wife was the daughter of his predecessor at the statehouse. The family occupied this simple whitewashed one-story L-shaped home through 1913 and the birth of two more children after Lyndon. Today the house is furnished with many articles original to the home or identical to them, such as the telephone and some of the president's childhood toys, including his first teddybear. The place actually has a lived-in look, in spite of the roped-off sections in several of the rooms. The grounds are immaculately kept up with flowers and plants appropriate to that era.

JUNCTION SCHOOL

Further east from the birthplace is Johnson's first school, the Junction school, so named because it sat at a junction of country roads. The simple one-room embossed-tin structure was completed in 1910, although the school itself had operated in a variety of locations since 1881.

Johnson started his education here at the tender age of four. He began to make a practice of hiking over to the school to play with his cousins and the other children during recess. This practice worried his mother no end, since Johnson loved the Pedernales and the path to the school ran along the river; she was forever fearful that he might fall in and drown. So finally she asked the teacher, Miss Kate Deadrich, to please take on one more pupil even though he was a bit young. Miss Kate agreed, and 53 years later they were reunited at the old schoolhouse when Johnson signed the Elementary and Secondary Education Act into law with Miss Kate as his witness.

JOHNSON FAMILY CEMETERY

Lyndon Johnson was buried here under the great live oaks overlooking his beloved Pedernales on January 25, 1973. He rests here with his grandparents Sam Sr. and Eliza Johnson, his parents Sam Jr. and Rebekah, and other members of his family in what is surely one of the most beautiful cemeteries in the Hill Country.

LBJ STATE HISTORICAL PARK
Ranch Rd. 1, about 2 miles east of Stonewall • 830-644-2252
Open daily, except Christmas Day • W variable

The visitor center is the hub of activity for the park. Here you find a room filled with some of the many gifts sent to the president during his administration, ranging from ornate handcrafted jewelry boxes given by heads of state to seed-and-corn kernel portraits sent by admiring Americans. The rest of the center contains exhibits relating to the Hill Country and its people, past and present, memorabilia from Johnson's boyhood, a variety of maps, photographs, and assorted paraphernalia from the presidential years, and finally an auditorium in which a slide show is presented, a show that attempts to explain all the influences on Johnson's character formation, his family, and his life.

Attached to the visitor center is the two-room dogtrot cabin built by German immigrant Johannes Behrens during the 1840s. It is furnished with items typical of the era. Located to the west of the visitor center is the Danz log cabin, one of the oldest in the area. It was discovered when a newer home built around it was being dismantled. Because of its age and historic importance, officials decided that it should be restored and furnished to the period of its use.

To the east of the visitor center is the state park's most interesting feature, the "living" Sauer-Beckmann farmstead. This is an operating historical farm, with all the animals, gardens, buildings, and equipment common to the Texas farm of 1900. Park employees in clothes of the period perform the daily chores and show visitors how life was back then.

Spring at the farm is garden-planting time, fall is butchering and sausage-making time, and Christmastime sees an old-time Christmas tree and tables laden with goodies for the visitors.

Johan Friedrich Sauer bought 188 acres, including the land on which these homes stand, in 1869 from Casper Danz. Born in the duchy of Nassau, Germany, in 1838, Sauer came to Texas with his parents in 1845. Married in 1865, Sauer and his wife moved here after buying the land and proceeded to build a one-room log cabin. As his family grew Sauer added a cellar, a stone shed at the rear of the cabin, and finally two rooms on either side of the original cabin pen. The front room is now the "summer kitchen."

The next home Sauer built is the cut-and-dressed limestone house immediately east of the log cabin. Featured in this house is a functioning turn-of-the-century farm kitchen with a blue enamel wood range. Emil Sauer, the youngest of Johan's 10 children, was born in this house. Another daughter, Augusta Lindig, was the midwife in attendance at the birth of Lyndon Johnson.

The Sauers sold their farm to Herman Beckmann in 1900 and moved to the Doss community in northwestern Gillespie County. Beckmann had bought the farm for his two sons, Emil and Otto. Emil lived in the log cabin and Otto lived in the limestone dwelling. Emil later bought out Otto's interest and married Emma Mayer in 1907. A good cotton crop in 1915 allowed Emil and Emma Beckmann to build a new barn, add a frame room onto the old rock structure, and construct porches connecting to a lovely Victorian house covered with fashionable pressed tin. Milled ornamental columns and gingerbread cornices were used on the large front porch and the small back porch. The L-shaped house is furnished authentically according to the period, down to the period wallpaper. The big house is connected to the smaller stone house by a *Durchgang,* or open hallway. In the Durchgang are a long table and benches, used by the family on summer days and also when feeding the neighbors and hired hands who came to help with the threshing and harvesting.

Behind the big house is the stone smokehouse where the staff hangs the bratwurst, liverwurst, blood sausage, beef and pork sausage, and *Schwademagen* to cure. In front of the house is the stone tankhouse that supports the cypress water tank next to the windmill. Beckmann's big frame barn and battered chicken house stand nearby, still functional. Depending on the day and season in which you visit, you may find the farm staff planting, harvesting, canning, or preserving their garden crop, butchering, or washing the weekly laundry in the big black cast-iron washpot. 'Tis an interesting experience.

In 1966, Edna Beckmann Hightower sold the site to the Texas Parks and Wildlife Department. Archeological surveying and restoration work was undertaken and the farm opened to the public in 1975. Since then, time has stood still and the farm remains forever a small piece of Texas as it was at the beginning of the 20th century. Park visitors can experience the farm at their leisure, and groups can make arrangements for tours.

Tours of the complex, including the Sauer-Beckmann farm with its smokehouse, Victorian-style house, garden, and log house, last approximately an hour; group reservations are accepted. A nature trail wanders through woods and meadows. No entrance fee is required, but donation boxes are available. LBJ Ranch Tram Tours begin at the state park Visitor Center Complex and are operated by the National Park Service. Tours are offered by the National Park

Service and depart from the LBJ State Park Visitor Center. Tours run from 10 a.m. to 4 p.m. daily except Christmas Day. Individuals and families can take the tour on a first-come, first-serve basis. There is a small fee. For group tours, call 830-868-7128.

Facilities include restrooms without showers; picnic sites with and without shelters; a snack bar; a museum; an interpretive center; an auditorium (capacity 234 people); an amphitheater; a swimming pool; playgrounds; a 1.25-mile-long nature trail; historic structures; plus tennis courts and a baseball field, which can be reserved through the park. (Donation boxes are available.) The pool may be rented after-hours by private groups. There is a dining hall (capacity 80) and a group picnic area (capacity 200). A bookstore is operated by Southwest Parks and Monuments Association (SPMA). The Texas State Park Store is in the Visitor Center Complex. The park is famous for its spring-blooming wildflower fields.

Elevation: 1,197 ft. *Weather:* July average high temperature is 95 degrees; January average low is 36 degrees.

Just a few hundred yards east of the LBJ State Historical Park on Ranch Rd. 1 is Trinity Lutheran Church.

TRINITY LUTHERAN CHURCH
Ranch Rd. 1, about 3 miles from downtown Stonewall
Lean, tall stained-glass windows with white frames punctuate the walls and bell tower of this soaring Gothic sanctuary, which are covered with pressed-tin siding in a brick pattern. The church looks blue from all but the shortest of distances, thanks to immaculate care. The congregation organized in 1902. This church building replaced an older, simpler one; its cornerstone was laid in 1904. The Johnsons worshipped here occasionally while staying at the ranch.

LODGING

STONEWALL VALLEY RANCH
North of Stonewall, near the LBJ Ranch
830-644-2380, 512-454-0476
A ranch-style B&B on a scenic, working Texas Longhorn ranch that also has antelope and a herd of bisons. The guest house, which is the original ranch house, sleeps 5 to 6 and has one full bath. You can hike, ride bikes, fish in one of the many stock ponds, or help with ranch chores. Families and children are welcome.

Continue east on Ranch Rd. 1. Just past Trinity Lutheran Church, Ranch Rd. 1 ends. Turn left onto US 290.

HYE

Blanco County • 105 • About 6.5 miles from Stonewall
Hye is the next hamlet east on US 290. Hye was named for Hiram "Hye" Brown, who established the first store here in 1880. The post office was established in 1886.

DEIKE STORE AND HYE POST OFFICE
US 290
Hye's chief attraction is the Deike Store and Hye Post Office. White with green-and-red trim bringing out the highlights of the elaborate Bavarian cast-metal facade, the Hye store was built in 1904. Young Lyndon Johnson mailed his first letter here at the tender age of four, and as you might expect, Johnson's appointee as postmaster general of the United States, Lawrence O'Brien, was sworn into office on these very steps on November 3, 1965.

JOHNSON CITY

Blanco County Seat • 1,032 • (830) • About 10 miles from Hye
Prior to 1850, the land between Austin and Fredericksburg was mostly uninhabited wilderness. The area that was to become Johnson City was first settled in 1856 by James and Martha Provost, back when this was still Hays County. John L. Moss had the first cultivated land here in 1861. Life was hard here in those early years. Indian attacks were frequent. Few Indians lived in Blanco County, but they regarded it as one of their prime hunting grounds, and they looked particularly askance at the white men who came and plowed up their land and drove away the game. During their brief stay here, James and Martha Provost built a log cabin and several modest outbuildings. These structures were to become the core of the Johnson Settlement.

SUGAR PLUM COTTAGE
US 290 at Ave. J • Private residence
On the western edge of Johnson City, on your right a few hundred yards east of the Johnson City historical marker, you see the Sugar Plum cottage, one of Central Texas' most distinctive dwellings. This

frame cottage has been rocked over with a variety of regional rocks and stones. The window casements are concrete, with tiny rocks punctuating the stucco. Ditto for the edging along the porch roof in front. In the center of the porch awning edge, the words "Sugar Plum" are spelled out in the same tiny rock chips. The porch awning is held up by two vastly dissimilar rock posts. The east post is built of little rocks stacked up on top of each other, while the west post is a stack of much larger stones, altogether a very yin-and-yang effect. The west post also has a cactus growing out of one stone. A pair of deer horns are imbedded in the stucco on the east front wall of the house.

LBJ NATIONAL HISTORICAL PARK
Visitor Center is south of US 290 at 10th and G Sts. • 868-7128
Open daily, except Christmas and New Years Day • Free • W
   The Johnson Settlement and Lyndon Johnson's boyhood home are both part of the LBJ National Historical Park. The Johnson Settlement is only accessible via the Visitor Center. You can see the settlement from US 290 as you enter Johnson City from the west. The Visitor Center was formerly LBJ Memorial Hospital. It has two film auditoriums, permanent and temporary exhibit areas, and sales area. Multimedia exhibits (including a 30-minute film) tell the story of Johnson and his presidency in the context of the isolated little Hill Country town that he grew up in. Lady Bird Johnson isn't slighted either. She has her own exhibit and documentary film.

JOHNSON SETTLEMENT
   By 1862 the Provost property had changed hands twice, and the latest owner was an absentee proprietor. His agent was Jesse Thomas Johnson, better known as Tom. Tom Johnson was Lyndon's great uncle.
   Tom Johnson occupied the cabin till 1866, adding an east room and breezeway during that period. The next year, Tom's newly married brother (Lyndon's grandfather), Sam Ealy Johnson, Sr., set up housekeeping in the cabin with wife Eliza.
   In 1868, the two brothers became partners in a cattle-driving business. Due to a cutoff from normal northern markets during the Civil War, the numbers of unattended cattle on the vast open Texas ranges had increased greatly. At war's end, there was great demand for Texas meat from the radically expanding northern markets. There was money to be made in the cattle business, and the Johnson brothers figured on getting their share. A steer worth $6 to $10 on the hoof in Texas might bring $30 to $40 at the railheads in Kansas.

The first year of business was so good that Sam was able to buy the 320 acres and cabin in 1869. Soon after, the Johnsons bought an adjoining 640-acre tract. Located in the valleys of the Blanco and Pedernales rivers, the land was ideal for their operation—plenty of good pasture and water. There was no need for big barns or an elaborate ranch headquarters, just corrals and pens to hold the cattle. The cabin served as headquarters and the pens stretched from the cabin to the Pedernales, virtually covering what was to become Johnson City. Individual owners would deliver their herds to the Johnsons, and the longhorns were held here in the pens until the trail boss and drovers were ready to start for the northern markets. Between 1868 and 1871 the brothers made four great drives north up the Chisholm Trail to Abilene, Kansas, each with herds numbering between 2,500 and 3,000 head. They were the largest trail-driving outfit in Blanco and six surrounding counties.

The Johnson brothers operated on credit. Buying cattle on credit during the spring, they would return home in the autumn with mules to sell and gold to pay for the cattle they had driven north. They had little trouble buying on credit because of the great price differential between range and marketplace.

But in the end, the high market prices led to their demise in the cattle business. The high prices inspired thousands of others to enter the cattle business, which resulted in a flooded market and significantly lower prices paid by buyers. By 1871 the brothers could scarcely sell their beeves for the money they would have to pay upon their return home. After losing their shirts, the brothers dissolved their partnership, sold their holdings to nephew, former ranchhand, and drover James Polk Johnson, and left Blanco County. Sam Johnson moved to Caldwell, then Hays County, before returning to the Pedernales and Stonewall in 1889. With the acquisition of the land and a bride, James Polk made the transition from drover to farmer and rancher. Accordingly, he built a small stone barn northwest of the cabin in which to shelter his horses.

During the years he owned the ranch, James Polk Johnson built a large frame house, which was destroyed in 1918. It was located near the still-standing windmill and water tower erected in 1896. The smokehouse Johnson built still stands next to the water tank.

In 1882 Johnson sold the south portion of the ranch to German immigrant John Bruckner, who built the large, German-style stone barn west of the original cabin.

These buildings today make up the Johnson Settlement, a "living history" project similar to the Sauer-Beckmann farmstead at the LBJ State Historical Park.

LBJ BOYHOOD HOME

In addition to the Johnson Settlement, the LBJ National Historic Site here includes the modest frame home that the Johnson family moved to in 1913. It is a typical middle-class home of its time: six rooms, a screened porch, a front porch swing, and a bit of gingerbread trim on the gables and front porch.

The Johnson home was seldom empty during those years. There were five children to be raised, and State Representative Sam Ealy Johnson, Jr., always seemed to be bringing friends home. The parents conducted regular debates and speaking bees, determined that their children would learn to think on their feet. Mrs. Johnson was one of the few college-educated women in Blanco County and she took her family and civic responsibilities seriously, giving elocution, debate, and declamation lessons on the east front porch and in the parlor of this house. Lyndon Johnson lived here until he started college at Southwest Texas Normal Institute (now Southwest Texas State University) in San Marcos.

The house has been restored to look much as it did during Johnson's boyhood, including many of the original furnishings. It is an excellent restoration with a comfortable lived-in look: toys are scattered on the floor of Lyndon and brother Sam's room, papers and magazines lie casually on the parlor table, the kitchen is full of all the boxes and cans and foodstuffs that you would expect to find. All these little touches make the house like a place where the owners are expected home at any minute, rather than just another sterile museum.

Stop by the visitor center first to sign in and look at the displays there, then await one of the free guided tours of the boyhood home.

From the visitor center, proceed north on Ave. G across US 290 to the courthouse square.

JOHNSON CITY PARK
8th and Ave. G • Free

This is a good place to let the kids run around, but there's no playground equipment—just benches and a gazebo.

BLANCO COUNTY JAIL
7th and G • Not open to the public

Its tall, lean, totally spare appearance perfectly symbolizes the builders' attitudes toward the law and its breakers.

BLANCO COUNTY COURTHOUSE
Courthouse square, 7th and Nugent • One block south of US 290

The present Blanco County Courthouse, a two-story limestone Greek Revival structure, was built in 1916. It replaced Johnson City's first courthouse, built shortly after the county seat was moved here in 1891. The building it replaced still stands across the street at the corner of 7th and Nugent. Construction was supervised by James Waterstone, a Scottish stonemason who came to Texas in 1883 to work on the state capitol.

JOHNSON CITY BANK/OLD COURTHOUSE
7th and Nugent

James Polk Johnson had this two-story limestone building erected in 1885. It served as a store for the first five years, then county courthouse from 1891 to 1916. Since then it has been a store, hotel and restaurant, movie and opera house and community center, and bank.

OLD PEARL HOTEL
7th and Nugent • Currently houses Blanco Title Company

Catercorner to the old courthouse, at the corner of 7th and Nugent, is another one of James Polk Johnson's edifices, the two-story, double-front-porched old Pearl Hotel. Johnson built this hotel in the early 1880s in anticipation of the travelers who would come to Johnson City when it became county seat. The battle over county seat location between Johnson City and Blanco began in 1879 and was not resolved in Johnson City's favor until 1891, six years after James Polk Johnson died. Up until about 15 years ago, it served as city hall.

James Polk Johnson had his finger in a lot of pies. He was Johnson City's namesake and principal promoter. He had the town laid out in 1878 on his land, and it was his intention from the very beginning that his town would become the seat of Blanco County. He didn't wait long to begin his crusade; the first election battle between Blanco and Johnson City came the very next year. Blanco won by a narrow margin, and was to win again two more times before the Johnson City boosters finally won in 1891.

Besides building the Pearl Hotel and the old courthouse, Johnson also built the big cotton gin located on the south side of US 290 just before the US 290/Nugent intersection. In earlier times farmers also brought their corn and wheat here to be ground into flour.

These are just several of the historically significant or interesting structures in Johnson City. For a more complete guide to the city, pick up a copy of *Johnson City Walking Tour* at the LBJ National Historical Park Visitor Center.

OTHER ATTRACTIONS

JOHNSON CITY CHAMBER OF COMMERCE
404 Main/US 290 • 868-7684

The place to come for local information, touristic and otherwise. On the same ground is the Captain Perry Museum, located in an old single-pen log cabin. Cicero R. (Rufe) Perry was born in Alabama in 1822. He came to Texas in 1833 with his parents and became an Indian fighter at the tender age of 14. Perry helped repulse the Adrian Woll invasion of Texas in 1842 and served in the subsequent Somerville Expedition. He joined John C. Hays' Texas Rangers in 1844, fought against Indians in Concho County in 1865, and was commander of Company D, Frontier Battalion, as late as 1874. Perry died in Johnson City in 1898.

THE FEED MILL
U.S. 290, adjacent to the LBJ boyhood home • 868-7299
Open daily

Little Lyndon Johnson and friends used to sneak into this old mill to play; it dates to about 1880. It was renovated and turned into a retail/restaurant complex a couple of years ago. Inside, the old Fairbanks Morse generator that powered the mill and supplied electricity to parts of Johnson City in the pre-REA days has been restored to its original appearance. For the kids, there's a 1934 carousel with lions, tigers, and horses.

ANNUAL EVENTS

LIGHTS SPECTACULAR
Late November through January 1 • Free

The Blanco County Courthouse is wrapped in a hundred thousand tiny lights and brilliantly lighted for the holiday season. There are various special events during the Christmas season, such as concerts and a parade. Contact the Chamber of Commerce for more information.

Leave Johnson City via US 290 east toward Austin. On the east edge of town you come to the junction with US 281. Turn right here, then prepare to turn left in a hundred or so yards onto FM 2766 and head toward the Pedernales Falls State Park.

Two last notes on Johnson City:

• Perhaps more than anything else in his life, Lyndon Johnson wished he had been born in a real log cabin, as had his grandfather. He was enthralled with the pioneer exploits of Sam Sr. and Eliza. If it had not been for Eliza's coolheadedness one day in 1869, Lyndon Johnson might never have been born. Sam was away from the Johnson Settlement Ranch that day and Eliza had been left alone with her baby daughter. Out in the yard with Lyndon's young aunt, she looked up to see a Comanche raiding party approaching the house. Scooping up the baby, she ran for the little cabin without being seen and crawled into a low crawl space beneath the cabin. There the terrified mother and daughter hid from the Indians, not coming forth until hours after the Indians had left.

• Up until Lyndon Johnson, as President of the United States, put Johnson City on the map, Johnson City was proud to call itself the home of the largest Rural Electrification Authority in the world—the Pedernales Electric Cooperative. Congressman Lyndon Johnson was the driving force behind its creation in 1939. Johnson never forgot the folks back home.

About 10 miles east of Johnson City on FM 2766, you encounter the turnoff to the Pedernales Falls State Park. Follow the signs into the park.

PEDERNALES FALLS STATE PARK
FM 2766 • About 10 miles east of Johnson City • 830-868-7304
Open daily • Admission • W variable
Pedernales Falls State Park is a pleasant change from the Hill Country's ubiquitous rock, cedar, and mesquite. This 5,200-acre park stretches along both banks of the Pedernales for 6 miles and along the south bank for an additional 3 miles. Up until 1970, it was a working ranch, the Circle Bar Ranch. That year the state paid nearly a million dollars for the acreage and opened it as a state park in 1971.

Pedernales Falls is the park's main attraction and may be viewed from a scenic overlook at the north end of the park. Here, the emerald-clear river stretches out through a boulder-strewn gorge, tumbles down a pair of stone ledges, and finally spills into a deep, wide, placid pool. In this area, the elevation of the river drops about 50 feet over a distance of 3,000 feet, and the falls are formed by the flow of the water over the tilted, stair-step effect of layered limestone. These river limestones belong to the 300-million-year-old Marble Falls formation and are part of the southwestern flank of the Llano uplift. These layers of limestone were tilted by the uplift, then eroded long before early Cretaceous seas (120 million to 100 million years ago) covered this part of Texas and deposited sands, gravels, more layers of limestone, and marine fossils.

The Pedernales River is the star of the park, but there are other areas of interest. Well-marked trails pass through hills dotted with oak and juniper woodlands; they provide access to more heavily wooded areas of pecan, elm, sycamore, walnut, and hackberry in the major drainages. Ash, buttonbush, and cypress grow on the terrace adjacent to the river. A short nature trail takes you through upland, riverbottom, and canyon habitats. Well over a dozen plant species or groups are identified along the way. The trail takes you to an overlook on the Pedernales that is particularly beautiful at sunrise and sunset, when thick, vaporous clouds float up off the river and bathe the valley in a dreamy haze. Farther on are the Twin Falls of Regal and Bee creeks, where the two creeks meet just prior to entering the Pedernales.

Visitors to the Twin Falls are restricted to an observation deck overlooking the falls. When the park opened, the flat area below the deck was covered with knee-high grass. Excessive visitor foot-traffic in the area caused soil compaction, which killed the grass as well as the bald cypresses that once abundantly grew in the canyon bottom. Soil compaction affects soil structure in such a way as to prevent proper aeration and water percolation. The lower walls of the canyon cut by these creeks are lined with a variety of mosses and ferns.

The Wolf Mountain Trail gives you a good look at some of these canyon habitats, as well as a great view of the Pedernales River valley from atop Wolf Mountain. It is open to hikers and mountain bikers. A primitive camping area is located along the trail, and there are no facilities available. There are also a horseback-riding trail and a rugged, 3.5-mile hiking trail that runs along 60-foot-high rock bluffs and offers panoramic views and access to rock caves.

Wildlife in the park is typical of the Texas Hill Country and includes white-tailed deer, coyotes, rabbits, armadillos, skunks, opossums, and raccoons. Over 150 species of birds have been seen in the park; about one-third of these are permanent residents. Commonly seen birds include hawks, buzzards, herons, quail, doves, owls, roadrunners, and wild turkeys. The endangered golden-cheeked warbler nests in the park.

In 1996, the Hill Country's first public observatory—the Central Texas Observatory—opened in the park with a donated 16-inch Ealing Educator reflecting telescope. Other activities at the park include camping; picnicking; river swimming, tubing, and wading; mountain biking; fishing; bird-watching (checklist available); and horseback riding. River recreation is in a limited area. Facilities include campsites with water and electricity (special rates are available); a sponsored youth group area, which may be used by any youth group with an adult sponsor; hike-in primitive campsites (2-mile minimum; no pets allowed; no groundfires); picnic sites; a trailer dump station; and 19.8 miles of hiking, biking, and equestrian trails. There is a Texas State Park Store. It's wise to make campsite reservations during peak season, March 1 through Thanksgiving.

Write to RR 1, Box 450, Johnson City 78636. *Elevation:* 1,197 ft. *Weather:* July average high temperature is 94 degrees; January average low temperature is 32 degrees; May, August, and September are wettest months. *First/last freeze:* November 3/April 3; Wildlife management activities sometimes dictate closure of all or part of the park.

Leave Pedernales Falls State Park via FM 3232, climbing out of the Pedernales valley toward US 290. You are rewarded with a good 5 miles of panoramic views. At the intersection with US 290, turn left.

You are now in the Henly neighborhood, which is now most notable for New Canaan Farms. Henly was established in the 1880s and named for the owner of the townsite. It had a post office, a justice of the peace, and a couple of businesses in its heyday, but never amounted to much more than a wide spot on the rocky road between Austin and Johnson City.

NEW CANAAN FARMS
US 290, about 1 mile east of the intersection with FM 165
800-727-JAMS • Open daily • W
New Canaan Farms has been making country-style jams, preserves, and sauces since 1979. It is located on the site of the old

Henly Picnic Ground, which served as a gathering place for area families for many years. Lyndon Johnson gave his first political speech here on July 4, 1930, under a massive spreading oak that is actually five large trunks growing from a single root system. You can see the products prepared, see a turn-of-the-century kitchen in action, enjoy fresh-squeezed lemonade and baked goods from the bakery, and browse a gift store filled with antiques, handcrafted items, collectibles, and gourmet foods. Please note: if you go to New Canaan Farms, go back toward Fredericksburg on US 290 to the intersection with FM 165 to continue this trip.

Slightly a mile after you have turned onto US 290 from FM 3232, you come to the junction with FM 165. Turn right on FM 165 toward Blanco, but instead of going to Blanco, turn left on Cty. Rd. 190, less than 100 yards south of US 290.

Onion Creek is one of Central Texas' largest and most scenic creeks, rising in southeastern Blanco County, flowing 22 miles across Hays County, and emptying into the Colorado River in southern Travis County. Cty. Rd. 190 follows Onion Creek for a baker's half-dozen of those 22 miles. The first stream you cross is the **Millseat Branch** of Onion Creek, about a mile past the Cty. Rd. 198 turnoff to **Mt. Sharp** and **Mt. Gainor.**

Louis Capt built a gristmill along this little stream in the 1860s but it was washed away by floods, as were other mills he built both before and after the Millseat Branch one. There was a post office here at the turn of the century, but never an identifiable town.

This narrow lane takes you past rock fences, pecan groves, and the high bluffs of Onion Creek. Several of the ranchers along the way have dammed up the creek, so that it alternates between wide placid pools and a narrow rock-broken path.

Cty. Rd. 190 dead-ends into US 290 in Dripping Springs.

DRIPPING SPRINGS

Hays County • 1,057 • About 16 miles from Pedernales Falls State Park

No one knows for sure who first settled the Dripping Springs area of Hays County, but the first permanent resident was a man named Fawcett who came in about 1849. By the mid-1850s this section was rather thickly settled, as the people were drawn to the plentiful timber, easily obtained water, and fertile soil of the hills and valleys here.

In contrast to the collection of predominantly German communities to the west and south, Dripping Springs' early settlers were almost exclusively of Anglo-southern stock.

At County Rd. 190's dead end into US 290, turn left on US 290, go a couple of hundred feet, then turn right onto Loop 64 to enter downtown Dripping Springs. Just a few hundred feet down Loop 64, you see a white frame-and-limestone house on your left, located on the west bank of Milkhouse Creek. This is the Marshall-Chapman home, bearer of a state historical marker.

MARSHALL-CHAPMAN HOME
Loop 64 • Not open to the public
Burrell Marshall built this residence in 1871 by adding rooms constructed of native limestone to an existing wooden structure.

Postmaster Marshall used his home briefly as the Dripping Springs Post Office till his death in 1872. His widow Martha then married William Thomas Chapman, who became postmaster and later a trustee of the Dripping Springs Academy.

Next to the Marshall-Chapman home on the west bank of Milkhouse Creek is an historical marker explaining the origins of Dripping Springs' name.

DRIPPING SPRINGS MARKER
Loop 64
The marker reads: "Where the Tonkawa once prowled, the cool clear waters of the Edwards Aquifer burst forth along this brook (Milkhouse Branch) and drip musically from the limestone overhang. About 1850, the Moss, Wallace, and Ponds families settled near the Dripping Springs. Mrs. Nannie Moss named the community for the Dripping Springs. Dripping Springs became a stage stop and post office in 1857. The Pedernales Baptist Association operated a boarding school which grew out of an aborted attempt to establish a military academy. During this period (1880s) a town was laid out with names for streets that were bordered by flagstone sidewalks in 1854."

Over the years, several different dripping springs have been offered up as the source for the town's name, but as of 1980 these springs along **Milkhouse Creek** have been declared the official, original dripping springs. Clamber down the shallow creek bank and follow the dripping sounds upstream several yards to the fern-covered overhang where the springs emanate.

Continue on Loop 64 into downtown Dripping Springs. The Dripping Springs business district is a collection of old and not-so-old stone buildings dating from the 1870s up through the 1930s, the most notable of which is the old Dripping Springs Academy, located next to the Dripping Springs post office and bearing a state historical marker.

DRIPPING SPRINGS ACADEMY
Loop 64 downtown • Not open to the public

A rude log school had been erected early on, but the citizens of Dripping Springs yearned for a true institute of higher learning. This dream began to be realized in 1880, when W. M. Jordan moved to Dripping Springs. He was determined to establish a great boarding school in this place of healthful clime and superior moral caliber, despite the area's general poverty and considerable distance from the great centers of population from which the boarding students would have to come.

Despite the odds against his success, Jordan was determined to build his school, and the townspeople pitched in to help. Farmers quarried the limestone from nearby hillsides and carried it to the site. They constructed a lime kiln and burned the lime necessary for mortar. The sand for the mortar came from nearby creekbeds. Cash for the necessary lumber could not be raised readily, but respectable citizens pledged their credit for the amount needed. When the requisite building materials were at hand, the structure was erected by men whose only knowledge of masonry was that learned by the construction of rock fences around their farms. They were supervised by a single mason.

The academy building was completed in time for the 1881 term. Two boarding houses were erected, and when the school opened both were filled with students, while every house in the village and on the adjacent farms with a spare room was filled with boarders. By the second year, the academy's enrollment was around 200.

Operated as a private academy the first year, it was then taken over by the Pedernales Baptist Association. It remained a church school for several years thereafter, eventually becoming part of the country's free school system. Jordan moved on to Kyle in 1883 to found the short-lived Kyle Seminary. The second story was added to the academy in 1920 and it became the home of the local Masonic Lodge in 1952.

From the Dripping Springs Academy, continue east on Loop 64 and turn left on RR 12.

At the edge of town, on your right, is the entrance to Founders Memorial Park. Of principal historical interest at this park is the home of Dr. Joseph M. Pound and his wife Sarah Dunbiben Ward. The first, log portion of this house was built in 1853 using slave labor. Pound served as a private in the Mexican-American War, and was a Confederate Army surgeon in the Civil War. Methodist circuit-riding preachers stopped here and held services. The home was expanded over the years and served as a hospital to Dr. Pound's patients.

From Founders Memorial Park, continue north on RR 12. In about 4.5 miles you come to a 4-way intersection with Fitzhugh Rd. (aka Cty. Rd. 101). Turn right here to reach Fitzhugh.

FITZHUGH

Hays County • About 6.5 miles from Dripping Springs
Fitzhugh was known as Barton Creek until 1898, when an English widow named Mrs. E. A. Brewer established a post office here and named it Fitzhugh for the creek that runs through the community. The old Austin-Llano road used to run through here and the main cattle trail from points west to Austin also ran through Fitzhugh. The post office was discontinued in 1914.

The **Baptist church** that you pass was the first church here. Worshippers first held services under a brush arbor, repairing to the little log schoolhouse when the weather turned nasty. The Methodists organized next, and they alternated services with the Baptists in the schoolhouse. A new sanctuary has been built recently, but the old tin-roofed arbor still sits out back.

Continue east on Cty. Rd. 101 from Fitzhugh. Once in Travis County, the road becomes Fitzhugh Rd. The narrow road twists and turns over numerous seasonal streams and arroyos on its way to US 290. Turn left on US 290 and head for Oak Hill. On your left, you'll see the old San Saba railroad depot, moved here and restored in the late 1980s.

OAK HILL

Travis County • About 11 miles from Fitzhugh

The Oak Hill area was first settled in the 1840s and was being called Live Oak Springs by 1856. The name was changed to Shiloh in 1865 for patriotic reasons. The place was later known as Live Oak and Oatmanville before the present name of Oak Hill was adopted around 1900.

After the capitol building in Austin burned in 1881, plans were drawn up for the new building, and it was decided that native limestone would be used to face the giant structure. That limestone was to come from Oatmanville from the giant limestone hill owned by Tom Oatman.

A railroad spur was built to the quarry site so that the giant limestone slabs could be hauled back to Austin. Sweating convicts in jail-stripe suits cut the stone under the eyes of watchful armed guards. Quarrying here took place from 1882 through 1886. Ten carloads of stone were shipped out of here daily by the 100 stonecutting convicts. But capitol contractors soon found out that the Oatmanville limestone was too soft for exterior use, so they turned to the harder granite from Granite Mountain near Marble Falls. The Oatmanville limestone was used in the basement and inner walls of the capitol building instead. Eight convicts died on top of this hill and are buried nearby, their graves unmarked and lost now. The quarry has been called **Convict Hill** ever since, and it is the hill whose sheer walls line the south side of US 290 (on your right) as you drive through Oak Hill.

Farther east on US 290, on your left and just east of the Williamson Creek bridge, is the two-story limestone Old Rock Store, which bears a state historical marker.

OLD ROCK STORE
6266 US 290

James Patton built the rock store over a period of 19 years, finishing it in 1898. The rock was quarried from his own land here. Patton's father came to Texas in 1836 and fought in the Texas Revolution. Young Patton, born in 1853, joined the Texas Rangers and fought the Comanches before settling down here several miles east of Oatmanville. He later helped consolidate Oatmanville and Oak Hill into one town. Patton established a store here in 1879 in a small frame building and then began work on the rock store. He became postmaster in 1886, serving until the post office closed in 1910. Patton was known affectionately for years as the "Mayor of Oak Hill," although the never-incorporated Oak Hill has never had a mayor.

Oak Hill has experienced explosive growth in the last 20 years as a result of Austin's expansion westward and little remains of the old village.

Continue east on US 290/SH 71 another 6 miles into Austin, and you're done.

RIDING THE FAULT

Approximately 123 miles

The Balcones Escarpment stretches from Del Rio to the Red River in a curved line across Texas. Invisible for most of its length, it rears up prominently from northwest of San Antonio to just beyond Austin, to a height of about 300 feet above the prairie below. Several miles wide, the escarpment—which appears as a range of wooded hills to viewers on the prairie below—separates the Edwards Plateau from the Blackland Prairies and the Coastal Prairies. Its appearance prompted early Spanish explorers to call it *Los Balcones*—"The Balconies."

The Balcones Escarpment, a geologic fault zone consisting of many smaller individual faultings, was formed during a period of geologic turbulence over 70 million years ago, when there was a general downwarping of the earth's crust near the Gulf Coast and a moderate uplift inland. Over the years the older, harder rocks to the west have eroded much less than the younger, softer rocks to the east. The level of topsoil east of the escarpment is much thicker, thus supporting a greater amount of plant life. The fault line breaks across water-bearing formations passing beneath the Edwards Plateau to the prairie. Much of the water is forced to the surface by artesian pressure, resulting in such large and well-known artesian springs as Comal, San Marcos, and Barton springs as well as many smaller springs.

Because of increased consumption of Edwards Aquifer water (principally by the City of San Antonio), the extended drought of the 1980s, and the drought that began in 1995, Comal Springs in New Braunfels is projected to dry up totally by 2010 if current consump-

RIDING THE FAULT

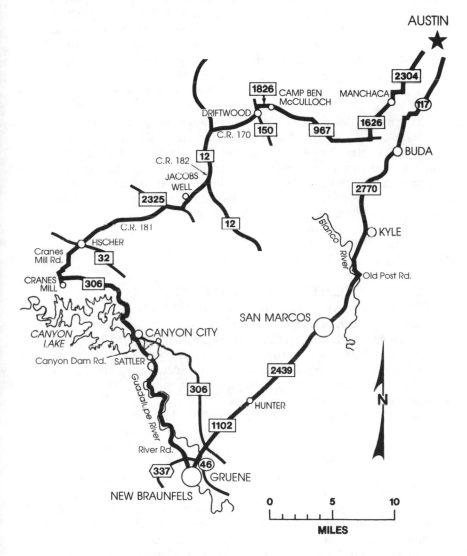

tion rates continue. Flow from the Comal Springs nearly ceased several times during the 1980s, and in 1996 as well. If the springs were to dry up, the blow to tourism in New Braunfels would be devastating, since the Comal River (as we know it) would cease to exist. Next to dry up would be the San Marcos Springs, followed by Austin's Barton Springs. San Antonio's once-famous San Pedro Springs dried up years ago. The water of the San Antonio River along San Antonio's famed River Walk is artificially pumped from the Edwards Aquifer. So enjoy the great springs of the Hill Country while you can, and be sure to conserve water so that future generations enjoy them as well.

This trip carries you down the rocky eastern edge of the Balcones Escarpment to New Braunfels, home of the Comal River, Landa Park, and the Wurstfest. Before the Civil War, New Braunfels and San Antonio were the largest and most prosperous towns along the Escarpment. Austin, the capital city, was much smaller and less civilized.

On the trip back to Austin, you travel along the escarpment's frontier with the flatter, richer Blackland Prairie, along the Old Stagecoach Road that ran from San Antonio to Austin. The trip begins at the National Wildlife Research Center in far southwest Austin, near the intersection of Loop 1 and Slaughter Lane.

NATIONAL WILDFLOWER RESEARCH CENTER
4801 La Crosse Ave. • Far southwest Austin • 292-4200
Tuesday through Sunday • Admission • W

Given our everlasting preoccupation with water (and the lack of it) in the Hill Country, it's appropriate that our trip begins at the National Wildflower Research Center, which is dedicated to natural beauty and water conservation through the propagation of wildflowers and other native plants, shrubs, and trees.

Wildflowers are more than just beautiful: they are also practical problem-solvers in a world which faces increasing shortages in—and quality problems with—soil, water, and air. Fossil fuel and fertilizer prices have skyrocketed, and we have discovered that some of our chemical solutions for problems with soil fertility and with plant or animal pests have had undesirable ecological side effects. With the increased costs have come decreased effectiveness, as some pests have developed resistance to pesticides and herbicides. Add to these problems our declining water supply in Texas and the rest of the western United States, and you can see why planners are telling us that traditional turfgrass and exotic ornamental landscaping will soon go the way of the curly pine.

Alternatively, wildflowers and other native plants and grasses can provide beautiful, low-cost, ecologically balanced landscaping in many instances. Since wildflowers and native plants are used to surviving on their own, annual watering costs can be cut by 50 to 70 percent, and the need for fertilizers, pesticides, and herbicides to protect them is minimal to nonexistent. While turfgrass landscapes need weekly or biweekly mowing, wildflower landscapes do best with minimal maintenance, requiring mowing only after the seed has set. The potential savings in labor, fuel, and equipment maintenance is great. When Mrs. Johnson broke ground for the Center in December 1982, she said that Texas alone—with its one million acres of state rights-of-way—could save $24 million a year if highway mowing could be reduced from four times to one time each year. By expanding its existing wildflower program in 1983, the Texas Highway Department saved 23% of its 1982 mowing costs of highway rights-of-way.

Wildflowers and native plants also provide essential wildlife cover and food, and are useful in stabilizing critically disturbed areas such as construction and mining sites, by preventing wind and water erosion. Many species of wildflowers can thrive in poor soil which can support little else.

Although 25,000 species of wildflowers have been identified in the United State (5,000 grow in Texas), we actually know very little about them beyond theory. Botanists have studied only about 200 species in depth.

The National Wildflower Research Center is a private, nonprofit organization dedicated to the preservation and reestablishment of native plants in their original habitats. Established in 1982, it was seeded by a gift of $125,000 and 60 acres of Colorado River bottom in far east Austin from Lady Bird Johnson. The center educates the public about the ecological and aesthetic importance of native wildflowers and other native plants, trees, and shrubs. Botanists conduct experiments with various species and planting techniques, and do research on the conservation and cultivation of native plants. NWRC acts as a national clearinghouse for information on native plants and habitat. Over 200 fact sheets are available on diverse topics, including how to establish a wildflower garden and propagation and seed collection tips. The center doesn't raise seeds for sale but can direct you to dozens of seed vendors around the country and can advise you on planting times and techniques. Educational programs, materials, and speakers are available for group presentations.

In 1995, after years of planning and fundraising, the NWRC moved from east Austin to its present 42 acres along the Balcones Escarpment. Ground-level attractions include a sprawling, gently rolling wildflower meadow and restored native prairie. There is a half-mile-long nature trail.

The Display Gardens contain over 20 "theme" plots that show some of the different uses of native plants. Three "home comparison gardens" demonstrate different home landscape styles and compare the costs over time of using native versus non-native plants. One is the typical formally designed yard using non-native species such as St. Augustine grass, azaleas, and impatiens. The other two are planted with native species—one duplicating the look of the non-native yard (but using native plants) and the other using native species in a less formal, more natural setting. They provide visual proof of some of the practical, natural approaches that are available for solving environmental problems.

The visitors gallery has exhibits that describe North American prairie, desert, and forest ecosystems; show the medicinal, ceremonial, and agricultural uses of native plants; and tell how to be better stewards of the earth.

Buildings are constructed of native sandstone, limestone, and recycled long-leaf pine and reflect the region's diverse architectural heritage: from the Spanish missions to the sturdy, boxy German farmhouses to western ranch houses. The 43-foot-tall stone observation tower offers great Hill Country views. The Center pumps no water from the Edwards Aquifer; rooftop water runoff captured in specially designed cisterns takes care of the site's irrigation needs. A gift shop offers a wide variety of ecologically correct items. There's also a cafe. You can get married in one of the gardens or celebrate your anniversary in the visitors gallery, hold a conference in the 236-seat auditorium, or stage a fundraiser in the courtyard, but rental policies are EC (environmentally correct), which means no smoking, plasticware, helium balloons, or other environmentally harmful products (including raw rice and confetti).

Short (1 or 2 days) classes like wildflower watercolor painting, papermaking, wildflower photography, dyeing with native plants, and landscaping with native plants are regularly offered. Call for dates and information.

From the National Wildflower Research Center, head north on Loop 1, then east on Slaughter Lane shortly thereafter. In about 3 miles, turn right (south) on Manchaca Rd. (FM 2304).

MANCHACA

Travis County • 4,700 • About 5 miles from the NWRC

Manchaca is now just yards away from the Austin city limits, and a continuous chain of new subdivisions stretches uninterrupted out from Austin to Manchaca and beyond these days. This was not always the case. At the turn of the century, Manchaca was comfortably insulated from Austin by 15-odd miles and several stops on the International and Great Northern (I&GN) railroad, places with names like Vinson, St. Elmo, and Kouns. The capital city, with all of its blandishments and temptations, was a good hour away by train and over three hours distant if you chose to drive the wagon or surrey in over the rattly, dusty Old San Antonio Rd.

Manchaca is larger than you might first suspect, just judging from the highway signs. As old-time Manchacans will tell you, the Manchaca neighborhood stretches for a mile or so north of the present center, east to the Old San Antonio Rd., and south very nearly to Buda, where the Manchaca Springs are located. Manchaca owes its existence to these springs or what is left of them. Local legend tells us that a Colonel Jose Antonio Menchaca discovered the springs and subsequently camped there with his company of soldiers during the days following San Jacinto. Menchaca and company had been charged with protecting early settlers from raiding Indians. Historical research doesn't back up this story, however. Not in question is Menchaca's existence; he came from a well-known Bexar family, fought with the Texans at San Jacinto, and after the war did command a cavalry company charged with protecting the Republic's frontier from Indian depredations. The discrepancy lies in the fact that the springs were called Menchaca well before the evolution, no doubt named for someone else from the Menchaca family. At any rate, the spelling was corrupted slightly to Manchaca over the years, and the pronunciation was corrupted drastically to *Man*-shack. Locally famous, the springs flowed strong, dear, and "99 percent pure," in the words of an early inhabitant. Not surprisingly, they were a regular stop for travelers on the old Austin-to-San Antonio stage line.

With the coming of the I&GN in 1880, the neighborhood's center shifted northward from the springs to its present location. Manchaca is supposedly located on the highest point of land between Longview and Laredo on these old I&GN tracks. Such a location was not happenstance; high ground meant maximum exposure to the cooling winds of summer and greater protection from the various plagues, chills, and fevers that always seemed to prey on bottomlanders.

Location on the railroad was highly prized. The railroad gave life and prosperity to towns like Manchaca and usually meted out death to the towns it bypassed, towns like Mountain City. Manchaca was a magnet to the area farmers, and Texas was overwhelmingly rural then. The daily comings and goings of the "Sunshine Special" were social as well as business events. It is hard to imagine such excitement over a train these days when even supersonic travel is a daily occurrence, but the train was the first and for a time the only means of breaking out of the isolation that was a way of life for rural Texans. The wonderment most of us feel toward commercial space flight or human-powered flight is perhaps comparable to the magic of the train for Texans around the turn of the century. Manchaca's importance as a center of trade and civilization began to fade with the onslaught of the automobile and the great Texas highway system. Nowadays Manchaca is little more than a wide spot in the road. Manchaca's story is not unique. Texas is full of similar hamlets, places with names like Oatmeal, Grapetown, Cain City. Keep this in mind as you roll through these spots; the countryside is full of ghosts.

At FM 2304's demise, turn right on FM 1626. For the next 4.5 miles you teeter on the edge of the Balcones Escarpment. Bear west toward Driftwood on FM 967 at FM 1626's dead end into FM 967.

Hidden away in the thickets is another of these ghosts, Elm Grove, once a bustling village and the location of Hays County's largest public school in 1888.

The pastureland you pass through on FM 967—as the Blackland Prairie gives way to the Hill Country—was the domain of King Cotton 100 years ago. Cotton finally brought the full measure of civilization to this previously sparsely settled area. Cotton was an obsession with Texas farmers from the waning days of Reconstruction till the 1920s when the boll weevil, Johnson grass, urbanization, mechanization, falling prices, and a couple of strategically placed droughts, not to mention cotton's notorious land depletion tendencies, brought cotton farming to its knees. Cotton's disappearance around here was amazingly quick, as was the disappearance of row farming in general. But as crop farming bowed out, sheep and Angora goat raisers from the western edges of the Edwards Plateau moved right in. And now, only 60-odd years later, this pastoral order is giving way to yet another order as the fleeing urbanites move in, seeking their own little patches of rural heaven.

Turn left onto FM 1826 when FM 967 comes to an end after 9.2 miles. Just after you turn onto FM 1826, you come to Camp Ben McCulloch and the Salt Lick.

CAMP BEN MCCULLOCH
FM 1826 • About 12 miles from Manchaca

Camp Ben McCulloch, located on scenic **Onion Creek,** began life as the annual summer meeting ground for the area's Confederate veterans. Their summer-encampment reunions became popular during the Gay Nineties, and since 1904 Hill Country Confederate veterans and their descendants have met here annually for a week of feasting and fun. The veterans named their camp for Confederate General Ben McCulloch. McCulloch died at the Battle of Pea Ridge, Arkansas, in 1862. He had earlier fought Indians on the Texas frontier under the command of Captain Jack Coffee Hays, namesake of Hays County. Many reunion-goers saw their first moving picture, ate their first cotton candy, stole their first adolescent kisses here. The reunion was one of the few breaks in their isolated rural lifestyles until World War II finally opened up their worlds. The reunion still comes off like clockwork each June as the grandchildren and great-grandchildren meet to renew old bonds. Cypress-shaded Onion Creek is very nearly as pleasant a place to take a dip as it was 100 years ago. Incidentally, the great cypresses that once lined Onion Creek and the nearby Blanco River were a prime reason given by President Lamar's 1838 Capitol Commission for locating the new republic's capital at Waterloo. The trees were worth more than the land was back then.

THE SALT LICK
FM 1826, across from Camp Ben McCulloch • 512-255-5638
Open Wednesday through Sunday, lunch and dinner • $
No Cr. • W

The Salt Lick, which dates to 1969, is as much a local institution as Camp Ben McCulloch. Brisket, ribs, and sausage, with traditional side dishes, served family-style in a camp dining hall setting, is what draws eaters here. Co-founder Hisako Robert's Japanese heritage is expressed in the barbecue sauce and the delicious cole slaw, which features toasted sesame seeds. The place can handle groups from 30 to 2,000. It's in a dry precinct, so bring your own beer and wine.

ANNUAL EVENT

JULY • United Confederate Veterans Reunion
Camp Ben McCulloch • Free
The war ended well over a century ago, but descendants of Confederate veterans devote eight days each July to remembering. The camp is named for the prominent Texas general killed in the Battle of Pea Ridge, Arkansas, on March 7, 1862. The United Confederate Veterans Reunion has been held here on Onion Creek annually for some 90 years. Programs dedicated to remembering, fellowship, and dancing are the attractions. A carnival usually operates during the reunion, and there is a barbecue and soft drink concession and a cafe. Everything is free except food, carnival activities, and dances. The general public is welcome.

Continue west on FM 1826 from Camp Ben McCulloch. In just over a mile, turn left onto FM 150.

DRIFTWOOD

Hays County • 21 • About 2 miles from Camp Ben McCulloch
Driftwood. The name seems more appropriate for a Gulf Coast town. But keep in mind that millions of years ago this was the Gulf itself. To fully appreciate the name you will do well to remember the suddenness and severity of the Hill Country flash flood. Most of the year Onion Creek flows placidly along, becoming little more than a string of waterholes during anything approaching a drought. But when the Cen-Tex skies open up and send four or five inches of rain an hour crashing down onto the rocky countryside below, Onion Creek can turn into a rampaging, destructive wall of water. Trees, bridges, stock pens, even houses can be uprooted by the water's force, landing wherever nature and chance deign. Such was the case in 1886, just when local cotton-gin owner and storekeeper Thomas Martin was attempting to get a post office established for the community that had grown up around his business enterprises. What would the name be? The current name—Liberty Hill—was out of the question. There was already a Williamson County post office with the same name. The men of the neighborhood gathered in front of Martin's house, located on the banks of Onion Creek, to come up with a name. Inspired by a pile of drift caught up on a flat in front of Martin's house, one of the men suggested "Driftwood," and the rest is history. Martin thought the name doubly appropriate, since he had used some driftwood to build his store. He died in 1901,

and new postmaster John Puryear moved his store and post office at the corner of FM 150 and County Rd. 170; Onion Creek flooded too often and too severely. The limestone store building that now stands at the crossroads was built in 1915 to replace Puryear's wooden building, which had burned down. Across FM 150 from the store, the simple white frame white church building that houses the "Driftwood Churches" dates to 1884. It was built as a Methodist church. In 1911, the local Southern Baptist church building was destroyed and the Methodist congregation invited the Baptists to share use of their sanctuary (which they have done ever since) according to this formula: members of both faiths worship together each Sunday, but each denomination maintains its identity. The Methodists conduct services on two Sundays per month, the Baptists lead worship the other two Sundays, and they alternate on fifth Sundays. "Union" Sunday school is conducted jointly by teachers of both faiths. Different denominations sharing a church building was a common practice in frontier days, but is very rare today.

Turn right onto Elderhill Rd. (Hays County Rd. 170) next to the Old Driftwood Post Office and Store.

Drivers take heed, for this is quintessential Hill Country road: up, down, twisting and turning back on itself, barely tamed in places. The cattleguards become too numerous to count after a while. Rubberneck at the beautiful countryside, but be prepared to dodge the stray cow or deer that may cross your path. Back in the days when roads were dirt and most folks drove Model T's, **Elder Hill** on this road was the place to see exactly what your flivver could do. You'll know Elder Hill when you dip down it into the Gatlin Creek Valley.

Turn left after 5 miles onto Ranch Rd. 12, where the driving calms down a bit. Stay on Ranch Rd. 12 about 5 miles, taking Hays Cty. Rd. 182 to Wood Creek Resort and Jacob's Well. Cty. Rd. 182 is also marked by a "Veterans Park VFW Post" sign. In about 2 miles, you will come to a yield sign and a junction with Mt. Sharp Rd. Veer left here.

JACOB'S WELL
Off Hays Cty. Rd. 182
Jacob's Well has been luring visitors—sometimes to their deaths—since it was first discovered in the 1840s. A natural well opening out of the bed of **Cypress Creek,** fed by the Edwards Aquifer, it was an important water source for early-day settlers, much like its biblical counterpart. Indeed, its discoverer was supposed to have uttered upon

finding the well, "It is like unto a well in biblical times." The importance of Jacob's Well was underscored by the fact that it served as corner point for four land grants. In more recent times, Jacob's Well has been part of a resort development and a favorite spot for divers, who are drawn to its jewel-like water. No one living knows where the well's narrow passage ultimately leads. Six have died trying to find out. Entrance to the underwater cave has been barred.

As interesting as the well is the man who originally surveyed most of the surrounding miles of countryside, Jacob De Cordova. De Cordova was born in Jamaica in 1808. Merchant, newspaperman, master of five European languages and several Indian dialects, De Cordova moved to Galveston in 1837. He then moved to Houston and served in the Second Legislature as Harris County representative, but decided that politics were not for him, so he packed up and headed for Austin, where he and brother Phineas published a semiweekly paper called the *Texas Herald.* De Cordova was also a land collector, having bought over a million acres in land script by 1859. As "Publicity Agent for an Empire," he traveled Europe and the eastern United States lecturing on Texas and its many virtues. In addition he published a map of Texas and several guidebooks for immigrants. His writings advocating Texas' claims to Rio Grande land at the time of the Compromise of 1850 were said to be vital in securing the $10 million paid to Texas for its claims to the land, territory that was later to make up parts of New Mexico, Colorado, Wyoming, Kansas, and Oklahoma. During the 1860s De Cordova attempted to develop a power project on the Brazos River in Bosque County in order to establish textile mills and other industries. De Cordova's home east of New Braunfels was appropriately known as Wanderer's Retreat.

The well is on private property (Wood Creek Resort), and so to see it you will be technically trespassing. At the nearby **Jacobs Well Cemetery,** the stones date to the 1880s. It is peaceful and nicely shaded by cedars and live oaks.

Turn right on FM 2325 in another 2 miles, then left off FM 2325 after 1.5 miles onto the first paved road—Cty. Rd. 181—to reach Fischer. When the sign says "keep right" do so, for it means business as you twist and turn down to the crossing of the Blanco River.

FISCHER

Comal County • 20 • (830) • About 12 miles from FM 2325/Cty. Rd. 181 intersection
Traces of pre-barbed-wire rock fences herald your arrival at Fischer Store. Mr. and Mrs. Herman Fischer, Sr., set down here in 1852.

Fischer had been a banker in Germany. In 1853, they opened up a "commissary" in one end of their elongated log cabin. In just a few years Fischer had a sizable freight operation going. Huge wagons, the semis of their day, pulled by five and six yoke of oxen—later by horses and mules—hauled goods to and from Johnson City, Blanco, New Braunfels, and smaller points in between. The post office opened in 1876, and a Fischer has always been postmaster.

FISCHER BOWLING HALL
First red frame building on the right as you enter Fischer

Contrary to what you might think, Fischer is alive and kicking every night of the week except Sunday as balls roll and pins fly at the Fischer Bowling Hall. Contact Fischer Store at 935-2351 for bowling hall hours.

FISCHER DANCE HALL
Next door to Fischer Bowling Hall

The bowling hall also closes down on dance nights—usually Saturdays—when the venerable wood floors of the Fischer Dance Hall next door creak beneath the feet of couples two-stepping to the tunes of country bands like the Texas Top Hands. A one-eyed carpenter built the dance hall in 1898. It was used in the filming of Willie Nelson's movie *Honeysuckle Rose*. The Fischer Agricultural Society built and still owns both the dance and bowling halls. First established in the 1880s as a farmers association dedicated to the development and practice of improved farming methods, the Fischer Ag Society is now a recreational organization that anyone may join.

FISCHER STORE AND POST OFFICE
Cty. Rd. 181, Fischer • 935-2351

The present corrugated tin building was built in 1902 along the same simple, elongated lines as the original log structure. It served as a post office through November 1995, when the post office moved into the building next door. The interior has a well-aged and complex, earthy, but pleasant aroma, with traces of dust, leather, wood smoke, old books, and feed. Imagine stopping here in earlier times when the smells of apples, oranges, spices, dried meats, and sausages added to the mix. An old wood-burning stove and woodbox dominate the center of the building. Inside the ancient post office cubicle, you'll see the aged, black-enameled safe still bearing the name "Herman Fischer" in gold gilt letters. A blackboard just inside the south entrance announces all the pertinent weather information and records for the past several decades—a gauge of the quality of life in its most basic sense. Ancient cracker and coffee tins, boxes of locally collected rocks and fossils, barbed wire, and Fischer Store paraphernalia fill the turn-of-the-century shelves and display cases. A national champion tree, the Lindheimer hackberry, grows in the front yard of the farmhouse behind the store. More on Lindheimer later. A little log outbuilding from the days of Fischer Sr. sits in the Y of the road just south of the store.

Veer right at the Y and take Crane's Mill Rd. south at the intersection with FM 32. When you come to a 4-way intersection with a stop sign in about 4 miles, take FM 306 east (left).

CRANE'S MILL

Underneath Canyon Lake

Crane's Mill community now lies at the bottom of Canyon Lake. Crane's Mill once sat smack-dab in the middle of "Charcoal City," which stretched along the Guadalupe River valley from Sisterdale to New Braunfels. Charcoal City owed its beginnings to German settlers like J. B. Crain who fanned out from New Braunfels to tame the Hill Country, starting in the 1850s. Civilization entailed clearing away the thick forests of Mexican juniper (cedar) and oak from their fields and pastures. When the Germans discovered there was a market for charcoal—and Mexican juniper makes superb charcoal—they "burned" (made) charcoal during the time between planting and harvest. Once they were established, the German farmers started hiring drifters to help with the burning. The word went out and by 1880 the rocky hills were filled with burners from as far away as England and Ireland. The charcoal kilns burned the year round and the Guadalupe valley was almost always bathed in a smoky haze, redolent of burning cedar. (See Take a Ride on the Fredericksburg & Northern—Leon Springs, and Mormon Trails—Pipe Creek.) In the days before public utilities, many city dwellers in San Antonio and New Braunfels depended on charcoal-burning stoves for cooking and for warmth, stoves that factories like the one in McDade, Texas, turned out by the boxcar load.

J. B. Crain built a mill here soon after he settled down. The name was anglicized to Crane when a post office was established before the Civil War. The community was also known as Engel's Crossing after the war, in honor of teacher and preacher August Engel, who moved here in 1870. He became postmaster of the reestablished post office in 1872. This crossing of the Guadalupe and its accompanying village are not the only communities killed off by Canyon Lake's creation in 1964. Prosperous farming hamlets like Hidden Valley and Mountain Valley have joined Crane's Mill, engulfed eternally (presumably) in the name of flood control.

CANYON LAKE
964-3341 • Open at all times
The next few miles along Canyon Lake are pleasant ones, particularly at sunset. Completed in 1964, the 8,240-acre lake is accessed by seven Army Corps of Engineers parks. Facilities for boating, fishing, swimming, waterskiing, scuba diving, picnicking, and camping (fee). Commercial facilities around the lake include motels, restaurants, and marinas. For information, write to the Canyon Lake Chamber of Commerce, P.O. Box 1435, Canyon Lake 78130. Recent lake records for fish caught include flathead catfish, 86 lbs.; largemouth bass, 9.94 lbs.; striped bass, 25.5 lbs.; smallmouth bass, 6.13 lbs.

When you reach Canyon City after 9.5 miles on FM 306, take a right on Canyon Dam Rd., just after the "Canyon City" sign.

The awesome earthen walls of **Canyon Dam** loom over you to the west, and a chastened **Guadalupe River** tumbles out of its little window on down toward New Braunfels. You can park on either side of the spillway and walk down the riverbanks for a look at the river.

Canyon Lake is deep, as far as Texas lakes go, and the water released through the dam's bottom gates is from the lowest reaches of the lake, which means that it is very cold—so cold that rainbow and brown trout live year-round in the stretch of river from Canyon Dam to Hueco Springs. They are not native to the river; before the construction of the dam, the habitat of this stretch of the Guadalupe was typical Texas warm-water stream, which is too hot in summer for trout. Now with the lake discharge, summertime temperatures of this stretch of the river seldom exceed 80 degrees, which allows the trout to survive. On the other hand, very few catfish and sunfish now live here; they prefer the warmer water. Trout are stocked in the river every winter by TPWD. Trout fishing is year-round, but is best from November through April. Recent records are rainbow, 7.77 lbs.; brown, 7.12 lbs.

SATTLER

Comal County • 30 • About 15.5 miles from Fischer
Sattler was founded by William Sattler in 1853, as German immigrants spread out across the Guadalupe River valley. Sattler has also been known as Mountain Valley and Walhalla. *Walhalla* is an ancient German pre-Christian word for "heaven." Much of Heaven—Wal-

halla—now lies beneath Canyon Lake. Sattler residents moved uphill when the lake came in.

Continue straight across RM 2673 at Sattler on what becomes River Rd. and go 14 miles, veering left at the intersection with Hueco Springs Rd., about 1.5 miles past the fourth crossing of the Guadalupe River by River Rd. Less than 2 miles after this intersection you come to Loop 337 and the outskirts of New Braunfels.

GUADALUPE RIVER

The emerald waters and powerful rapids of the lower Guadalupe, the sheer cliffs and almost unnatural (for the Hill Country) verdancy of its banks, have been magnetizing visitors and inhabitants since the first day the stream was discovered. Texas Indians, the Wacos and Tonkawas in particular, camped along the length of the river, especially at Waco (Hueco) Springs. Ferdinand Lindheimer recorded a meeting with some Tonkawas in 1846: "There was a Tonkawa Indian Camp on the Guadalupe above New Braunfels which settlers often visited. One day there was a great celebration in the camp. The Tonkawas secretly had killed an Indian and were cooking the flesh. They took great pains to get the idea out of my head that they had killed a man. They said it was the flesh of a Waco Indian whom Americans had killed sometime ago; the flesh was smoked and it stank . . . however the obscene exhibition of parts of the slain Indian's body distinctly showed that it had to do with fresh and not smoked flesh of mankind."

But the Tonkawas were not averse to eating "aged" flesh; they rather prized it. In 1935 Mrs. Augusta Ervendberg Wiegraeffe told a San Antonio reporter: "They [the Indians] always came with a flag of truce to show that they were friendly. The settlers wanted to show a friendly feeling towards the Indians too and decided to give them a big dinner. There was little in the way of food but the women did their best with the material at hand and were justly proud of what was a real feast for those times. The Indians came. They did not make use of knife, fork, and spoon, altogether they were dirty and disgusting and soon had devoured all the food. Leaving the table the Indians went down to the field to a semi-decomposed carcass of a horse and ate the meat."

Problems of a different sort face inhabitants along the river today. The alternately peaceful and wild beauty of the Guadalupe that so entranced Indians and early settlers continues to entrance river visitors today, as is obvious in the nonstop private and commercial development along the river between Sattler and New Braunfels. On summer days you can hardly see the river itself for all the tubes, rafts, canoes, and variously clad bodies inhabiting them, which form a continuous parade down the river. Somehow the Guadalupe manages to maintain a pristine appearance, if you can overlook the beer cans and related flotsam clogging its shoreline at various points. If you are a serious canoer or kayaker and you want to spend your summertime on the river enjoying it, not dodging all the tubers and rafters, hit the water by 7:00 in the morning, no later than 8:00 on weekends especially. It can be a real madhouse out here—on the river, alongside the river, on the narrow winding River Rd. itself.

RIVERBANK OUTFITTERS
River Rd. • Open April through October • 830-625-4928
MC, V
Located between the first and second crossings of the river on the River Rd., Riverbank Outfitters rents canoes, rafts, kayaks, and tubes and offers a shuttle service back to your launch point.

JERRY'S RENTALS
Located above the First Crossing, Hueco Falls • 830-625-2036
Open daily in season
Long-established outfitter offering rafts, tubes, canoes, guided trips, shuttle service, camping, showers, and convenience store.

When the River Rd. intersects with Loop 337/SH 46, turn right. In slightly over a mile you turn left on California Blvd., which is the second paved left after you pass Oakwood Baptist Church and the New Braunfels water tower (on your right, on Loop 337).

NEW BRAUNFELS

Comal County • 30,402 • (830) • About 14 miles from Sattler
New Braunfels owes its name and existence to Prince Carl of Solms-Braunfels, who as commissioner of the Adelsverein desperately searched for a tract of land on which to settle thousands of Texas-bound German immigrants. The Adelsverein purchased land (the Fisher-Miller Grant) on the Llano River but it was too far away to settle immediately, so the colonization had to take place in steps. Prince Carl needed to find some place closer to the coast and civilization to function as a way station. If all this sounds a little half-

baked, it was. (Also see Take a Ride on the Fredericksburg & Northern—Fredericksburg, and Central Texas Stew—Shelby.)

The Adelsverein, or Mainzer Adelsverein, or Verein zum Schutze deutscher Einwanderer in Texas, or Verein, as it was variously known, was a society composed of 10 rich German noblemen who were interested in overseas colonization for economic and philanthropic reasons. Through this "Society for the Protection of German Immigrants in Texas" founded in 1842, these men hoped to make a profit by settling Germans on land they purchased in Texas, assuming that land values would go up as the colony tract was developed. They also counted on heavy trade with their expatriate countrymen. At the same time the noblemen would be providing a safe and prosperous future for folk who otherwise would have faced a bleak future in an overpopulated Germany.

By 1844, the Adelsverein had acquired title to the vast Fisher-Miller tract (located between the Llano and Colorado rivers), or at least thought it had. In reality, all it had was the right to settle the land, ownership of which remained with the Republic of Texas. The land was extremely isolated and inhabited by the unfriendly Comanches. In addition, the soil was generally stony and infertile, the rainfall meager and unreliable. No one from the Adelsverein (other than scouting parties) set foot on the land before 1847, as incredible as it may seem. The two agents sent by the Adelsverein in 1842 to scout for suitable land had not ventured beyond the fertile eastern half of the republic, the characteristics of which they naively attributed to the entire nation in their reports back to Germany.

The Adelsverein's offer to prospective immigrants was very attractive and they had no shortage of applicants. Each single man was to pay $120, and each married man/head of household $240. Each male applicant also agreed to cultivate at least 15 acres for three years and to occupy his house for the same period. In return, the Adelsverein promised the immigrants free transportation to the colony; free land in the colony (160 acres for the single man, 320 acres for the family man); a free log house; provisions and all goods necessary to begin farming, supplied on credit until the second successive crop had been harvested; and numerous public improvements, including roads, mills, cotton gins, schools, hospitals, insane asylums, churches, and even the canalization of rivers. The Adelsverein proposed to do all this with a total capital of roughly $80,000, apparently believing that they would realize great profits by retaining ownership of one half of the colony's land, land that, as has been said, they did not actually own.

Most of the society's funds had already been spent by the time Prince Carl arrived in the summer of 1844. Soon after his arrival in Texas, the prince realized the problems of moving thousands of immigrants from the port of Carlshafen (Indianola) to the Fisher-Miller Grant, a distance of over 200 miles through untamed wilderness. He immediately began a search for land on which to build a way station for the immigrating colonists. After considering a variety of tracts he wrote back to Germany, telling Adelsverein officials that it would only be possible to establish a settlement on the southwestern edge of the grant during the first year. But there were many beautiful places to choose from between the Guadalupe and San Antonio rivers, Carl continued, and his favorite happened to be a four-league tract at the so-called "fountains," located on the Austin-to-San Antonio road. Rich soil, lots of forest timber, water power, and proximity to the major settlements at San Antonio and Seguin were big pluses in its favor. Prince Carl also pointed out that it would be a good headquarters for the colonization projects, owing to its equidistant location from the coast and the upper portion of the Fisher-Miller Grant.

The land of the "fountains" belonged to the heirs of Juan Martin de Veramendi, a governor of Texas while it was under Mexican rule. During the last years of Spanish rule, the tract had belonged to Felipe Enrique Neri, Baron de Bastrop. In San Antonio, Prince Carl was directed to the Veramendi tract by the Swiss Texan Johann Jacob Rahm, who had fought on the frontier with Jack Hays' Texas Rangers. On Rahm's recommendation, Prince Solms purchased 1,265 acres from the Veramendi family on March 15, 1845, for $1,100. These acres lay on the Comal River, the "fountains" in Solms' report.

COMAL RIVER

This 3.25-mile-long stream is the shortest river in the United States, and the springs feeding it were among the four biggest in Texas. Now they are rivaled only by the springs that feed the San Marcos River at San Marcos, commercially known as Aquarena Springs.

Early writer on Texas and geologist Dr. Ferdinand Roemer visited the Comal Springs with Ferdinand Lindheimer and wrote of his impressions: "We had to cross Comal Creek to get there . . . we came to a small, but extremely fertile plain on which dense patches of forests alternated charmingly with small enclosed prairies. A road made by the settlers for hauling the cedar trunks used in building their homes . . . was the only sign of human activity . . . We suddenly heard near us the murmuring of rapidly flowing water, and a few moments later stood at the most beautiful spring I had ever beheld. The natural basin, about forty feet wide, was of incomparable clearness and on its bottom, aquatic plants of an emerald green color formed a carpet. Low shrubs of the palmetto, which I had learned to know at a less attractive place, namely in the dismal swamps of New Orleans, lined the banks. An old live oak, decorated with long festoons of grey Spanish moss, spread its gnarled limbs over the basin. This however is not the only spring of the Comal . . . four or six more springs of even greater volume of even clearness, every one of them could turn a mill at its immediate source, all unite and form the Comal, which, unlike other streams, does not experience a gradual growth, but is born a sizeable stream."

California takes you right into Landa Park across the Comal's headwaters.

LANDA PARK
Landa, near downtown • 625-5818 • Open at all times • Free on weekends from Easter through October, group areas rent for $6 per picnic table • W variable

Although the Comal's springs do not flow quite so forcefully these days, the river is still very nearly as beautiful today as it was in Roemer's time, as a stroll through Landa Park will reveal.

Landa Park is named for early New Braunfels industrialist Joseph Landa. In 1859 he bought the Comal Springs and surrounding land from J. M. Merriweather, who had already built a gristmill, sawmill, and cotton gin, all powered by the Comal's rushing waters. Landa greatly expanded this little industrial complex, adding a grain elevator, electric plant, cotton-oil mill, and ice manufacturing plant. By the 1890s "Landa's Pasture," as the park land was then popularly called, was a favored local picnic and festival ground. In 1897 (so the story goes) Helen Gould, daughter of I&GN railway magnate and robber baron Jay Gould, visited New Braunfels and was so impressed by the beauty of Comal Springs and Landa's Pasture that she suggested the I&GN lay a spur line into the pasture. The railroad needed a recreation ground along the line, and Landa's Pasture was just the ticket. As soon as the Missouri-Kansas-Texas railroad reached New Braunfels, they too laid tracks into the park. In the days before the automobile, special excursion trains ran from as far away as Austin and thousands of happy revelers filled the park on weekends. The Wurstfest complex is located here too.

A miniature train now runs through the 196-acre park. You can take a glass-bottom boat ride on Landa Lake and see the Comal Springs. There are two swimming pools; one is Olympic size, the other is spring fed. You can go tubing down the Comal here or at several other locations along the river.

The tranquil beauty of the Comal River is now overshadowed by the faux-castle towers of the 65-acre Schlitterbahn Waterpark, one of the country's most popular waterparks. The river flows alongside Schlitterbahn, and the river's cool water is circulated through some of the park's rides. Some of the rides take riders into the Comal. In 1991, Schlitterbahn acquired venerable Camp Warnecke and in 1996 opened Blastenhoff and Surfenburg there, with Boogie Bahn surfing and uphill water coasters. You can stay overnight at the Resort at the Bahn (adjacent to the waterpark's main section) or at the Resort at the Rapids (next to Surfenburg). Call 830-625-2351, write to 305 W. Austin, New Braunfels 78130, or check out the web site at http://www.schlitterbahn.com.

Continue through Landa Park on California, past the Wurstfest grounds and the prominent brown-brick municipal power plant. California dead-ends into Landa St. (SH 46). Turn left on Landa, which soon becomes Seguin St. and takes you to New Braunfels' Main Plaza and the Comal County Courthouse.

COMAL COUNTY COURTHOUSE
Seguin at San Antonio

The Victorian Gothic courthouse was built in 1898. The first session of the County Court was held in 1846 in a room in the residence of Conrad Seabaugh, County Clerk, which was located across the Plaza from the current courthouse. The court continued to meet for several years in Seabaugh's room, paying him $2 or $3 per month rent, until the county purchased its own property.

Visitors will find interesting old buildings scattered throughout New Braunfels, but the greatest concentration of vintage commercial buildings is in a two-block stretch of W. San Antonio (from the Main Plaza west to Hill St. and the railroad tracks). Most are two-story brick, really undistinguished, and simply styled, although much of the brickwork is expertly executed. New Braunfels was such a prosperous town during the first quarter of this century that many of the older, Victorian-era commercial buildings were torn down, in favor of the buildings you see today. But a few pre-1900 commercial structures remain.

OLD GUADALUPE HOTEL
471 Main Plaza

New Braunfels' first hotel was the two-story Guadalupe Hotel, built in 1853 by Rudolph Nauendorf. Jacob Schmitz bought the property in 1858, renamed it the Schmitz Hotel, and in 1873 added the third floor and balconies.

HENNE HARDWARE COMPANY
246 W. San Antonio • 625-3318 • Open daily

Henne's cast-metal cornice is about as exuberantly Victorian as the downtown skyline gets. Louis Henne built this store in 1893, and certain newer inventory aside, the store still looks much the same inside as it did back then. An especially nice touch is the pair of "Louis Henne Co." stained-glass transom windows above the front doors. Henne, in business since 1857, claims to be Texas' oldest hardware store.

OLD FIRST NATIONAL BANK BUILDING
278 W. San Antonio • Private offices

The First National Bank opened for business in September 1894. The bank's owners had budgeted $8,000 for its construction; the contractor built it for $13 under that budget. There was one attempted robbery in 1922. One bandit was killed, another wounded, and the third got away. The First National Bank moved over to the main plaza in 1931, and the building housed a variety of businesses before the current owners renovated it in 1982. Years of dull paint were removed, revealing the original bright red brick facade with carved white limestone accents. The original brick bank vault inside now houses the library.

BRAUNTEX THEATRE
290 W. San Antonio • 625-4411

Neon and Art Moderne fans will appreciate the BraunTex's late 1930s sign and stucco-tile exterior.

RAILROAD MUSEUM
102 North Hill

The old 1891 train depot now houses the local Railroad Museum.

NEW BRAUNFELS FIRE MUSEUM
Inside Fire Station No. 1, 100 block S. Hill • Tours given when station is open

New Braunfels' fire department was founded in 1886 and is said to be the fourth-oldest in the state. The museum displays fire-fighting equipment, tools, gear, and pictures that date to the department's founding.

FAUST HOUSE
361 W. San Antonio • Private offices

Just across the railroad tracks is the newly renovated Faust House, built in 1905 by prominent local businessman John Faust, son of one of New Braunfels' first families. Besides its leaded glass doors and stained glass windows selected in Italy, the house was also acclaimed for its modem heating system—a steam boiler in the basement with floor radiators throughout the 4,000-sq.-ft. house. Those original doors and windows as well as the many elaborate light fixtures are still part of the house. Another treat is the inlaid parquet wood floor in the foyer along with the rest of the house's woodwork, which is mostly pine and is now free of its original dark stain. The carriage house out back has also been renovated.

FIRST PROTESTANT CHURCH (CHURCH OF CHRIST)
296 S. Seguin

Two blocks south of the main plaza, this simple Gothic church of ashlar-dressed limestone blocks was built in 1875. A log church was first built on this site in 1846. Its first pastor was the Rev. Louis Cachand-Ervendburg, who was appointed minister to the town's founding settlers by Prince Solms before they left the base camp at Lavaca Bay.

CHAMBER OF COMMERCE
390 S. Seguin • 625-2385, 800-572-2626 • Open daily • W

The Chamber of Commerce has compiled a walking tour of historic New Braunfels. Most of the buildings on the tour are pre-1880, and the tour is worth taking, whether you walk or drive. The New Braunfels *Herald-Zeitung* also publishes a free seasonal visitor's guide, which contains a historic-building tour and a schedule of events. You can pick up a copy at many local businesses and museums, as well as at the chamber. The chamber is located at the Civic Center, two blocks south of the square, at S. Seguin and Garden.

From the main plaza, go south on Seguin (SH 46) to Coll. Turn right onto Coll and go across the railroad tracks to Academy to get to the Sophienburg Museum.

SOPHIENBURG MUSEUM
401 W. Coll at Academy • 629-1572 • Monday through Saturday 10-5, Sunday 1–5 • Admission • W

The Sophienburg Museum is built on the hilltop site of Prince Carl's envisioned Fort Sophia (Sophienburg), which was to have been constructed for the protection of New Braunfels. The prince had a log cottage built here during the spring of 1845 and he lived here for a short time in grand style, raising the Austrian flag (there was no German flag) every morning and receiving guests—red and white—in the full uniform of a Prussian army officer. The cottage, New Braunfels' first seat of government, was destroyed by the great hurricane of 1886, the same storm that wiped out Indianola (Carlshafen), the port of entry that the prince had established for the Adelsverein emigres. Sophia was the name of Prince Carl's fiancee, and the prince returned to Germany in May 1845 to marry her after only a few months in the wilderness. By running home, Prince Carl missed the widespread sickness and pestilence that nearly did the colony in during the first two years following his departure. He left the Adelsverein's accounts hopelessly entangled and the coffers empty.

Because the Adelsverein was already heavily in debt, the 5,000 plus Germans arriving at Carlshafen between the fall of 1845 and April of 1846 found themselves without adequate shelter and supplies. Furthermore, the recently erupted war between the United States and Mexico led to shortages of teamsters who could haul the colonists inland. The army was paying better wages than the Adelsverein. For six months the immigrants had to camp on the cold, rainy, mosquito-infested beaches of Carlshafen, drinking bad water and eating little more than green beef. Small wonder then that hundreds died on the beach, and that in desperation hundreds more attempted to walk the distance to New Braunfels. Some went only as far as Victoria, Goliad, and Gonzales before giving up on their original dreams and settling down to make the best of it in these Coastal Plains towns. Many died along the way, and those who managed to reach New Braunfels brought disease with them. The first batch of colonists, who had come in the spring and summer of 1845 and therefore had missed the initial miseries of their compatriots, were now struck by the newly arrived pestilences. Between 800 and 3,000 died; two or three expired each day in the little town. Prince Solms' successor John O. Meusebach did his best to whip the tottering finances of the colony into shape, but of the 34,000 gulden sent him in 1845, all but a few hundred were spent paying off previous debts. He went everywhere to borrow money—unsuccessfully—hounded at every step by creditors, while society immigrants stacked up steadily at Carlshafen. Disheartened by the incompetency of Adelsverein officials in Germany and the deplorable conditions here in the New World, Meusebach resigned his position in July 1847. The Adelsverein went bankrupt that same year.

Hermann Seele—early New Braunfels farmer, lawyer, teacher, lay minister, mayor, state representative, Confederate major, and newspaper editor—wrote of the suffering he saw here during those miserable months of 1846. "Every campsite between here and the coast and Indianola—and there were many, since the weather and roads, as well as the oxcarts, caused the overland journey to be filled with delays and to last many weeks—was marked with . . . graves, ghastly milestones on the way that the German colonists of West Texas had to traverse . . . I hurried through the forest camp, that upon closer inspection, held only too many sad scenes of sickness and death, in order to return to the ferry. As I passed a large tent, I heard a cry of distress.

"'Isn't there anyone here who will help us?' Looking into the tent, I caught sight of a family of nine persons bedded on the ground, moaning and groaning.

"I asked for pails, with which I brought up fresh water from the river. When I gave it to them, they drank greedily to still their burning thirst, even though the water was neither clear nor cool."

Later that day, upon returning home, Seele fell into a fit of melancholia, to be aroused from it "by the shouts of the children of a man who, with other immigrants, had set up camp on our land. He wanted to see me. He too lay sick of dysentery and dropsy and like others, suffered even more from homesickness. I went with the children to his bedside. With excitement and joy, the man extended his emaciated hand to me. His cheeks were lightly flushed, and his eyes were unnaturally bright. He wanted to let me know that he no longer suffered any pain, that he felt better and would soon be able to return to his beloved homeland with his family. Full of hope and joy, the wife and children listened to the father's words. From the recent, sad experience at the deathbed, I saw his end approaching. I hid my thoughts and spoke a few words of encouragement and sympathy. At home, however, I told my friends, 'We must get up early tomorrow in order to dig another grave.'

"Before sunrise the next morning, the sick man had quietly passed away. We dug his grave in the field and gently laid him to rest. Then we quietly said the Lord's Prayer for the dead man and his family."

The Sophienburg Museum, which chronicles these difficult years and the happier ones that followed, is full of old New Braunfels memorabilia, tidily arranged, and is staffed by enthusiastic docents.

Two blocks west of the Sophienburg Museum is the **von Coll House** (624 W. Coll St.). Jean Jacques von Coll, first lieutenant, retired, of the Duchy of Nassau, was the Fischer-Miller Grant's financial officer and led the first settlers to the Comal Tract in 1845. A year later, Meusebach sent von Coll to Fredericksburg to straighten out the mess caused by the young colony's previous administrator. After returning to New Braunfels he was elected mayor, only to be killed shortly thereafter by an irate colonist who claimed the Colonization Society had shortchanged him.

To get to the Lindheimer Museum, take Seguin (SH 46) south from the main plaza, turn left on Garden, then right on Comal. In case you can't find a copy of the seasonal visitor's guide or the Chamber of Commerce tour map, here's a simplified version of the route that will take you by most of the interesting old homes and buildings. It is about 2 miles long, and can be walked or driven.

From the Lindheimer Museum, proceed up Comal (towards the courthouse) 5 blocks to the old Market Square. Go right at Market Square one block to Market Ave. Turn left on Market, cross San Antonio, and turn left on Mill. Continue on Mill to Academy (4 blocks). Turn left on Academy, go one block, then turn left on San Antonio. After a short block on San Antonio, turn right onto Hill, which runs along the railroad tracks. Turn left onto Coll, cross the tracks, and turn right on Castell, one block later. After 3 blocks on Castell, turn left on Jahn, follow its dogleg across Seguin, and turn left on Comal to complete the tour.

LINDHEIMER MUSEUM
489 Comal • September through May: Saturday and Sunday 2–5; June through August: Monday through Sunday (except Wednesday) 2-5, daily 10-5 during Wurstfest • Admission W with assistance

Smaller and more homey is the Ferdinand Lindheimer home and museum. Born and educated in Germany, Lindheimer left his homeland in 1834 as a result of his revolutionary political beliefs—the advocation of representative government and unification of the separate German states.

Upon his arrival in the United States, Lindheimer wandered through a variety of occupations and latitudes. He volunteered for service in the Texas Republican Army, after being shipwrecked in Mobile, Alabama, but the company of volunteers he joined arrived in Texas a day after the victory at San Jacinto. Prince Carl hired Lindheimer as a guide for the Adelsverein's immigrants. He led the first group of colonists to their raw new settlement at New Braunfels.

For his services Lindheimer was deeded land on the Comal River, where he built a little cabin. Lindheimer collected much of the native Texas flora for Northern botanists, and he used the cabin as a base for his botanical explorations into the Texas wilderness. At one time or another, over 100 species or subspecies of Texas flora have borne his name in their botanical titles.

Lindheimer was one of the few white men the fierce Comanches regarded as a friend. The great Comanche war chief Santanta visited Lindheimer at his home on several occasions.

Lindheimer's intensive botany studies came to an end in 1852 when he became editor of the young city's German-language newspaper. He built this house that year and published the *Neu-Braunfelser Zeitung* for 20 years. Lindheimer had a strong passion for freedom, truth, and right, and his views often brought him threats and abuse, especially during the Civil War. Although antislavery and pro-Union, he urged his readers to be loyal to their new country. To do otherwise would have been insane; unionists elsewhere in the Hill Country were massacred for their beliefs. Lindheimer died here in 1879.

His home, now a museum, has been restored to look much as it did during his lifetime, a typical German fachwerk dwelling. Fachwerk (half-timbering) is an ancient construction technique employing wall frames made of studs and braces, with rocks or brick filling in the spaces between the squared timbers. Lindheimer's home was built from native cedar and limestone. The house is full of fine period furniture, much of it Lindheimer's. Some of the pieces were crafted by master cabinetmaker Johann Jahn. More examples of Jahn's work can be seen at the **Museum of Texas Handmade Furniture.**

To get to Conservation Square and the Museum of Texas Handmade Furniture, take S. Seguin (SH 46) south to its junction with Bus. US 81. Continue on Hwy. 46/81 to the intersection with Loop 337. Turn left onto Loop 337. In just a few yards you will see signs for both Conservation Plaza and the Museum of Texas Handmade Furniture.

Turn right on Church Hill Dr. and follow the signs for a short distance till you reach the Plaza and Museum.

CONSERVATION PLAZA
Church Hill Dr. • 629-2943 • Open Tuesday through Sunday Admission

Created and maintained by the New Braunfels Conservation Society, Conservation Plaza is a collection of six early New Braunfels buildings moved here in recent years. Crown jewel is the Baetge house, built in 1852 by Carl Baetge and originally located on the Demijohn Bend of the Guadalupe River near Sattler. Carl Baetge came to New Braunfels in 1850 with his wife Pauline, whom he met in Russia. A civil engineer, Baetge had been commissioned by the Czar in the early 1840s to build a railroad linking the Winter Palace in St. Petersburg to the Summer Palace in Moscow, a distance of 420 miles. Pauline was a member of the Czarina's Court, and they were married upon completion of the railroad in 1846.

The Baetge House was faced with obliteration with the formation of Canyon Lake, so it was dismantled and later reassembled here. The house is of fachwerk construction, cedar timbers with homemade brick. This was plastered over inside and covered outside with cypress siding. The second story is unfinished inside, the better for the visitor to appreciate the handwork of construction. Some of the furnishings downstairs are original to the house, and many were made by hand in and around New Braunfels. Some of the drawings Baetge made for the Czar's railroad are on display upstairs.

Next to the Baetge House is one of the Hill Country's most interesting log barns, built by an immigrant named Welsch about 1849. Each of the barn's three pens is built in an inverted pyramid fashion; that is, each wall slopes slightly outward (maybe 100°) from ground to roof instead of going straight up at a 90° angle. The best explanation for this sloping was to keep the walls dry from the rain. The barn was originally located on Rock St., which was the old road to San Marcos.

Also present are the **Forke Store,** built about 1865 by Jacob Forke on S. Seguin; the **Haelbig Music Studio,** built about 1850 by New Braunfel's first piano teacher; and the **Star Exchange,** also built about 1850 on S. Seguin. It first housed the Star Exchange and Billiard Room and later the New Braunfels *Zeitung.* Across the street is the 1870 **Church Hill School,** which is built of ashlar-dressed limestone blocks and is still in its original location.

MUSEUM OF TEXAS HANDMADE FURNITURE
1370 Church Hill Dr. • 629-6504 • Memorial Day through Labor Day: open Tuesday through Saturday 10–4, Sunday 1–4, closed Monday; March, April, May, September, October: open Thursday through Monday afternoons; November through February: Saturday and Sunday afternoons • Admission

A few feet up Church Hill from Conservation Plaza, this museum showcases over 75 original pieces of furniture that were made by hand in Texas from the 1830s through the 1860s. They populate the Andreas Breustedt house, built in 1858, which also contains other household artifacts common to the era, in a more-or-less homey atmosphere. Adjacent to the Breustedt house is a log cabin display of more home furnishings and cabinet-making tools used by early Texans.

OTHER MUSEUMS

CHILDREN'S MUSEUM
Inside the New Braunfels Factory Stores mall, 651 I-35 N (Bus.), Ste. 530 • 620-0939 • Open daily • Admission

Hands-on exhibits, puppet palace, other creative areas for kids.

HUMMEL MUSEUM
199 Main Plaza • 800-456-4866

The world's largest collection of original Hummel art; rotating exhibits are assembled from over 350 charcoals, pastels, and oils by Sister Maria Innocentia Hummel, whose work inspired the popular figurines. Her life is chronicled in a video presentation and photos. There are also manufacturing and restoration demonstrations.

SOPHIENBURG ARCHIVES
200 N. Seguin, in the old City Hall building • 629-1900 Open Monday through Friday • Admission

The extensive archives include photos, handwritten original records, newspapers, maps, and oral histories pertaining to New Braunfels and Comal County. The archives are dominated by the leavings of the German immigrants, but they also contain material pertaining to all ethnic groups who have settled in the area since the 1840s.

WAGENFUEHR HOME AND
BUCKHORN BARBERSHOP MUSEUM
521 W. San Antonio • 629-2943 • September through May: Saturday and Sunday afternoons; June through Labor Day: Thursday through Tuesday afternoons; Open daily during Wurstfest • Admission

Among the things on display in this old house and turn-of-the-century barbershop are hundreds of hand-carved circus figurines and pictures made from rocks.

BAKERIES AND RESTAURANTS

EUROPA FINE FOODS
1162 Eikel • 606-1086 • Open Monday through Saturday $ • W

Bavarian-style wurst (as opposed to the Deutsch-Tex sausages that evolved in Texas) are made here at this delicatessen and food import shop. Even the casings come from Germany. No MSG or fillers are used, just pork and beef. Fresh German-style breads and rolls are available daily. Choose from over 30 varieties of sausages, hams, and luncheon meats. The menu features sandwiches, sausages, and complete dinners.

KRAUSE'S CAFE
148 S. Castell • 625-7581 • Monday through Saturday 6:30–8:30, closed Sunday • Breakfast, lunch, and dinner • $ • No Cr. • W

Krause's dispenses simple hearty German American food and cheap cold beer in frosted schooners. The stewed spareribs with dumplings and sauerkraut are particularly seductive. Their sauerbraten, sausage, and barbecue also pass muster with flying colors. Mother always told you to eat a good breakfast and you can get it here— eggs, home fries, homemade sausage, and hot homemade biscuits. The consumer's only bone of contention with Krause's breakfasts has been their sporadic use of margarine and plastic-packaged jellies; their biscuits deserve butter. Fortunately this lapse is only occasional. Good homemade pie is available by the slice or whole pie. A variety of sausages, cured meats, and various condiments are offered as take-out items. In true German tradition, Krause's serves pannas and blood sausage in season, November through March.

LANGSTON HOUSE
190 S. Seguin • 625-1898 • Open Tuesday through Sunday, lunch and dinner • $$-$$$ • Cr.

German food, fresh fish and seafood, and other continental dishes, accompanied by fresh-baked breads and made-on-premises desserts. All in an 1854 mansion furnished with antiques and piano music to boot.

NAEGLIN'S BAKERY
129 S. Seguin • 625-5722 • Monday through Thursday 6:30–6:00, Friday 6:30–6:30, Saturday 6:30–5, closed Sunday • W

Naeglin's peach fried pies, bear claws, and cream puffs are just a few of their tasty offerings. Their loaves of white, whole wheat, French rye, and pumpernickel are cheap and tasty. All their pies are bargains, particularly the great coconut cream pie. Stollen, just like your German grandmother used to make, is a popular Christmas seller. In business since 1868.

WOLFGANG'S KELLER
**In the Prince Solms Inn, 295 E. San Antonio • 625-9169
Open Tuesday through Sunday • $$-$$$ • MC, V**

Named in honor of Wolfgang Mozart and located in the cellar of a historic inn. The continental menu includes German and Italian specialties. Many of the herbs used in the kitchen come from the Inn's garden. A pianist plays in the evening. Exotic after-dinner drinks, like Amaretto Freeze. Bar.

LODGING

If you're looking for more than just run-of-the-mill overnight accommodations, you have two enjoyable choices; both are New Braunfels landmarks and are just two blocks off the main plaza.

THE PRINCE SOLMS INN
295 E. San Antonio • 625-9169

If Victorian is your pleasure, your choice should be the Prince Solms Inn, which was built in 1898 as the Eggering Hotel. The two-story brick Carpenter Gothic structure has been thoroughly restored and decorated in a very busy, very plush late-Victorian manner. Sit awhile in the downstairs parlor with books by Dickens or Doyle and slip back into another era. The Inn has eight rooms and three suites filled with antiques and has a homey atmosphere. Downstairs in the converted cellar is **Wolfgang's Keller,** an intimate restaurant and bar serving classic cuisine at moderate prices. Many of the herbs used are from the Inn's garden. Dinner only Tuesday through Sunday; closed Monday.

Behind the Inn is the Joseph Klein House, built in 1852 on the spot where the hotel now stands. It was moved to the back of the lot in 1898 to make way for the hotel.

THE FAUST HOTEL
240 S. Seguin • 625-7791

If your tastes run more to Art Deco and Greta Garbo, your choice should be Faust. It first opened a couple of days before Black Friday in October 1929 as the "Travelers Hotel." Built by public subscription (like Fredericksburg's railroad) and equipped with all the latest luxuries, it was one of the finest hotels of its size in the state and was a source of civic pride. But despite its instant popularity, the Depression caught up with the Travelers in just a couple of years and its operators went broke. It was saved from closure by Walter Faust Sr., local bank president, whose family originally owned the land where the hotel stands. Faust died shortly thereafter, and in 1936 the Travelers was renamed the Faust to honor him and his family. The hotel gradually slid downhill after World War II, but this trend was reversed starting in the mid-1970s. Under the present ownership, the Faust has been thoroughly refurbished and modernized without sacrificing much of the original beauty.

In contrast to the simple style of the building as a whole are the elaborate Spanish Renaissance details such as the lavish stone carvings above the front entryways and first story windows and the lobby's intricate Spanish tile floor. The Faust has 62 rooms, each with central air and heat and cable TV as counterpoint to the iron beds, candlestick telephones, and flowery carpeting.

The dining room is open for breakfast, lunch, and dinner daily. A small courtyard was enclosed to create the Veranda Bar in 1980.

The Faust family's three-story Victorian mansion, which was displaced by the hotel, now stands half a block south and across the street at the corner of Coll and S. Seguin. It was moved there brick by brick.

ANNUAL EVENT

Ten days in very late October through early November; dates vary slightly year to year • **Wurstfest grounds, adjacent to Landa Park, entrance on Landa St.** • **800-221-4369** **Admission** • **W**

New Braunfels is famous as the home of Wurstfest, a tribute to *Gemuetlichkeit* (good times), beer, and sausage that began in the early 1960s. Live music is played nightly in the cavernous Wursthalle, featuring polka bands (including the much-beloved Myron Floren). The fest's musical lineup also includes choral groups, mariachis, and C&W bands. Beer flows almost as prolifically as the nearby Comal Springs, and sausage is devoured by the mile. Weekend days are the best times for families with small children. The riverwalk area provides a nice break from the madness inside. In any given year, Wurstfest weather can range from beautiful to cold, wet, and nasty; this is the time of year when fall's cool fronts finally begin to roll into Central Texas. It may be 90 degrees one day and 50 degrees the next. A final note of caution: Be careful not to overindulge on the German soda water and then drive; the law will be waiting for you.

As you prepare to leave New Braunfels, here's a last dose of New Braunfels historical trivia that didn't quite fit in anywhere else.

• New Braunfels was founded on Good Friday, March 21, 1845, and named for Prince Carl's hometown of Braunfels, on the Lahn River in Germany.

• The town was founded on its present site on an omen. Prince Solms had been looking at several other sites on the Medina, San Antonio, and several other rivers in Central Texas. The prince wrote: "I myself with a troop of twenty-five men proceeded inland to find a place suitable for a town and to make the necessary preparations and investigations, especially as to whether or not there were hostile Indians in that region. It was on such an excursion that I found snow on my tent one morning, which, though it could be rolled in the hand, by noon had melted. Taking this as a good omen, we established our German colony here to which I gave the name New Braunfels."

• In 1850, New Braunfels was the fourth largest city in Texas, behind San Antonio, Galveston, and Houston.

• During the Civil War, New Braunfels had a saltpeter-extract plant located in what is now Landa Park. It produced 100 pounds of crystal saltpeter daily from bat guano gathered from nearby Cibolo Cave. The saltpeter was used to make gunpowder.

• During the Civil War, the town saw a procession of 20 corn-carrying camels pass through town on their way to San Antonio. The camels had come from Camp Verde, located near the Bandera Pass in Kerr County, remnants of then Secretary of War Jefferson Davis' experiment with camels as an overland transportation system.

• Willie Gebhart, the Father of chili powder in the United States, perfected his creation in New Braunfels. In 1892, Willie opened up a cafe in the back of the Phoenix Saloon. Aiming to please, he soon found out that chili was a popular dish with New Braunfels' Germans. It was a seasonal dish back then, too, since there was only one local ancho pepper harvest per year. Gebhart began to import anchos from Mexico so his customers could enjoy their chili the year round. Sensing the commercial possibilities, he next figured out a way to dry and grind the peppers into a powder, which could then be easily used by the average cook. The year was 1894. Two years later Gebhart was grinding away down in old Santone in his new factory. He could make five cases of powder a week, and he sold it off the back of his wagon. Gebhart also canned the world's first ready-to-eat chili con carne in 1908 and also its first tamales. The Phoenix's old location at 193 W. San Antonio is now occupied by the Jacob Schmidt Company.

• In 1886 New Braunfels was hit by the great hurricane that destroyed Indianola (Carlshafen). Gusts here reached 85 miles per hour and several structures were destroyed. Others suffered major damage.

• In December 1908 Texas Prohibition laws closed New Braunfels saloons on Sundays for the first time ever in the city's existence. No acts of violence were recorded, but the *Dallas Morning News* observed that "'Liberty' was placed in a coffin, given an elaborate funeral, and conducted by a brass band and prominent citizens to her grave on the outskirts of the city."

• During World War I, the nationwide surge of anti-German sentiment led some Texans to demand that New Braunfels' name be changed to a more appropriate, American name. The cooler heads prevailed in the end.

To leave New Braunfels, take E. San Antonio St. from the courthouse square across the Comal River. Turn left on Union, go 6 blocks, then turn right on North and go 3 blocks. Turn left on Central and go one block, and finally right on Gruene. Shortly thereafter Gruene takes a hard left and becomes Guadalupe, then takes another hard right and becomes the Gruene Loop. Follow Gruene Loop across the Guadalupe River crossing to Gruene community. Take the first right across the river to reach downtown Gruene, which is now actually within the New Braunfels city limits.

GRUENE

Comal County • 20 • (830) • About 4 miles from downtown New Braunfels

The Gruene area was first settled in the 1850s by the overflow from New Braunfels and was originally known as Goodwin. Cotton cultivation was introduced to New Braunfels and Comal County in 1852, and it quickly became the county's number one cash crop. The land around Goodwin was prime cotton-growing country. Ernst Gruene and his two sons realized this and moved to Goodwin in 1872. Ernst had come to New Braunfels in 1845. One of Ernst's sons, Henry D. Gruene, became the town's namesake. A hustling entrepreneur, H. D. soon had 20 or 30 families sharecropping on the Gruene family's recently acquired acreage.

By 1878, Gruene had established the town's first mercantile store in the little white-frame building that still stands across Hunter Rd. from the two-story brick H. D. Gruene building. At that time, Hunter Rd. was a stretch on the Old Post Rd., the main road between Austin and San Antonio.

Shortly after the store was established, Henry Gruene built a cotton gin, which was powered by the waters of the Guadalupe River. The wooden structure burned in 1922. Its brick boiler house (the gin was converted to steam power in the early 1900s) now houses the Gristmill Restaurant, located behind the Gruene Hall.

Gruene next opened up a lumberyard, then a dance hall and beer garden in 1882. He also ran the post office and donated land for the local school. A blacksmith shop came along in the 1890s. By this time 8,000 acres around Gruene had been planted in cotton. The town was growing, and so was H. D. Gruene's bank book—so much so that he decided to build his own bank, which he housed in the new (1904) two-story brick building that is still Gruene's most prominent landmark, next to the dunce-cap water tower. The structure also housed his store and post office. Gruene's original bank vault is still inside the bank wing, built of cinder-block-sized bricks and cast-iron doors, with "H. D. Gruene" inscribed in gold gilt thereon.

Gruene the man and Gruene the town prospered until 1920. That year H. D. Gruene passed away. The boll weevil and pink bollworm came along and killed King Cotton, down to the last boll, in 1925. That disaster, combined with drought, falling cotton prices, and the land's decreasing productivity, caused a mass exodus of Gruene's cotton farmers, leaving the place a virtual ghost town until the mid-1970s when a new breed of tourism-oriented entrepreneurs moved in and saved the old town from destruction by developers. Gruene is now on the National Register of Historic Places.

GUADALUPE SMOKED MEAT COMPANY
1299 Gruene Rd. • 629-6121 • Open daily, lunch and dinner $ • AE, MC, V • W

Choose from green hickory-smoked beef brisket, pork ribs, chicken, and Brenham sausage, accompanied by pinto beans, cole slaw, and potato salad. Hamburgers, fries, and dessert are also served. You can eat inside, but on all but the most miserable of days you'll want to dine on the deck outside. The Martinez General Store building that houses the operation was moved here from Martindale. Beer, wine, margaritas.

GRISTMILL RESTAURANT
Behind Gruene Hall • 625-0684 • Memorial Day through Labor Day: open daily; rest of year: closed Monday • $–$$ MC, V, AE

The restaurant operates out of the ruins of the brick cotton gin's boiler room that burned in 1922. Dine on chicken-fried steak, french fries, burgers, grilled chicken, and steak, and drink out of Mason jars while looking out over the scenic Guadalupe River.

GRUENE HALL
606-1281 • Thursday 3 to midnight, Friday and Saturday noon-1, Sunday noon—8:30 • W

Step inside Gruene Hall for a cold beer, and drink in the past. There is no escaping the memory of H. D. Gruene here, for even the front of the bar sports a metal plaque with his name embossed on it. Gruene family photos hang behind the bar. Back in the dance hall, 60-year-old advertising placards for New Braunfels businesses still hang. Some of the businesses they advertise are still hanging on, too. The beer garden is shaded by big cedars, under which picnic tables and old wagon hulks compete for space, and Christmas lights stay up year-round. Gruene Hall's owners advertise it as the oldest dance hall in Texas. The bands playing Gruene Hall are a mix of local country-and-western and regional rock-and-roll favorites.

From Gruene Hall, proceed north on Hunter Rd., past the big brick
H. D. Gruene building, which now houses an antique store open on
weekends.

LODGING

GRUENE MANSION INN
1275 Gruene Rd., New Braunfels, 78130 • 629-2641
Next door to Gruene Hall is the Gruene Mansion Inn, which is not
a mansion but rather the spacious Victorian home that H. D. Gruene
built for his family beginning in the 1870s. Originally one-story stucco-over-brick, Gruene later added the second story, corner gazebo,
and wraparound porches. Guests stay in any of several riverside "cottages" behind the house, which include H. D.'s converted corn crib
and barn. All 17 units are furnished with antiques and handmade
quilts. Some have kitchenettes.

Turn right on FM 1102 to enter Hunter.

HUNTER

Comal County • 30 • About 7 miles from Gruene
Hunter started life as a thousand-acre cotton plantation, operated
by Major A. J. Hunter. The town was laid out and developed with the
coming of the I&GN railroad in 1880. Major Hunter's daughter
Loulie married E. M. House, who was to become one of Texas'—and
the nation's—leading power brokers during the first several decades
of the twentieth century. On his way to the top, House built Hunter
into a major cotton-processing center. With cotton's fall, a new cottage industry grew up. Pablo De La Rosa moved to Hunter in the
1920s and in about 1926 started casting plaster of paris figurines for
sale at the many roadside stands that were springing up along the
ever-improving Texas highways. These figurines became big sellers,
and soon everybody in town had some of De La Rosa's molds and
were making statues of their own. The industry took a nose dive
when the new highway went in about 1933, bypassing Hunter to the
east (the present I-35 route).

From Hunter, turn right on FM 2439 at its junction with FM 1102 to
reach San Marcos. You enter San Marcos on the Old Post Rd. (FM
2439) via Stringtown.

STRINGTOWN

Comal and Hays counties • Just outside San Marcos

Stringtown was settled about 1851 by 16 families who had immigrated as a group from Georgia. The community got its name from the 6-mile string of houses that stretched along the Post Rd. from York Creek on the Hays-Comal county line to near Purgatory Creek southwest of San Marcos. This mass exodus and resettlement was orchestrated by Colonel John D. Pitts, who first bought 1,500 acres here, then persuaded the Georgians to move to the tract with him. Pitts later organized the town of Pittsburg, which later became the present-day town of Blanco.

Situated as it was on *the* road between Austin and San Antonio, Stringtown had its share of famous and infamous visitors. Sam Houston, Governor Oran M. Roberts, General Ed Burleson, University of Texas benefactor George Brackenridge, Bigfoot Wallace, and gambler/gunslinger/Austin city marshall Ben Thompson all left their respective marks here.

Two more young men—well known to all of us—also partook of Stringtown hospitality. Old-timer Sam Kone told this story many years ago: "Two young men appeared at my father's gate one evening and asked politely for shelter for the night. They were gladly welcomed. The strangers took supper, stayed all night, ate breakfast, and upon leaving offered payment. They were met with the command 'Stop again when you are passing this way.' I had the honor of taking care of their very fine horses. A few months later, the pair returned through, but they were riding small mules instead of fine horses. We entertained them as before and later it was found out that we had hosted the James brothers, Jesse and Frank."

As you enter San Marcos, you will notice the many stately, finely crafted old homes, built during the era when this was the main north-south highway and it was considered fashionable to have a house on the main drag.

Once in San Marcos, FM 2439 dead-ends into Ranch Rd. 12. Turn right on Ranch Rd. 12 and follow its path to the courthouse square. At the square, turn left on Lyndon B. Johnson, then right after two blocks onto University.

SAN MARCOS

Hays County • 31,048 • About 8 miles from Hunter

San Marcos is covered at length in the Hill Country Rivers trip, so here's some San Marcos trivia to chew on as you pass through town, beginning with some old legends:

• Once upon a time an Indian maid, the chief's daughter, loved a boy far below her station. One bright spring morning, her lover was slain and laid to rest on the grassy banks of the San Marcos River, with only the blue sky above as a coverlet. That night the moon and stars shone bright and the chieftain's daughter fled in despair to the river bank where he lay. She said a prayer, then threw herself into the river so that she might be reunited with her lover. She was never found; a white water lily bloomed where she dove in.

• A beautiful Spanish maiden and her lover were captured by Indians near San Antonio and carried to their captors' camp near the head of the San Marcos River. Cognizant of the fate awaiting them, the twosome flung themselves as one into the river and sank to their deaths.

• Near San Marcos, there is reputed to be a still-secret spot where Mexican brigands buried their plundered treasure as far back as the beginning of the nineteenth century. The gang was some 800 strong at one time, and their headquarters were located on the high hill later occupied by the Coronal Institute. From that spot they preyed upon donkey trains passing from Natchitoches to Laredo on the Old San Antonio Road. These trains often carried gold and silver from the legendary San Saba and San Gabriel mines. Burying the loot nearby, they sent maps to their accomplices in Mexico showing the treasure's location. The maps, have never surfaced and no clues exist today as to the cache's whereabouts. But justice finally overtook the thieves. When they attacked one of the pack trains at the Blanco River crossing one day, they were repulsed by a large company of armed horsemen who drove them back to their roost and there killed most of the outlaws.

• Dr. Caton Erhard opened San Marcos'—and Hays County's— first store in about 1848 with the following inventory: one barrel of flour, one barrel of whiskey, one sack of coffee, a couple pounds of tobacco, a few shingles and nails, a few bolts of domestic, and a dozen-odd pieces of calico of 16 yards to the piece. Eight yards was required for a dress in those days and Erhard would sell no less than eight yards.

• Shortly thereafter Austin's Colonel John M. Swisher fell in love with the area's beauty while passing through on his way to Mexico and the war with Santa Anna. He returned to open San Marcos' second store, wherein he kept a barrel of whiskey with two faucets, one on the inside and one on the outside. Inside the store, whiskey was a dollar per quart; the same quart drawn from the outdoor spigot went for 50 cents.

• The year 1853 was known as "the year of the grasshopper plague" and a terrible drought prevailed for the next three years. Many cattle died of thirst and starvation, and for the first time stockraisers used prickly pears for cattle feed by burning off the thorns.

• The great hurricane of 1886 destroyed that year's entire cotton crop and not another drop of rain fell until May 1887.

• Gold fever struck San Marcos in 1915 when old-time Arizona miner and San Marcos pioneer Jack Edwards discovered valuable ore in the old Burleson tract on the north edge of town. Assayed samples showed significant amounts of silver per ton with traces of gold. A company was organized, but the operation proved unprofitable.

• Black gold fever struck San Marcos in 1922 when San Marcos pioneer D. D. Compton discovered oil flowing from his 50-year-old water well. Experts estimated that if the well were pumped steadily it would yield five barrels of fine-grade paraffin oil a day. The oil was of such high quality that local motorists used it in their autos straight from Compton's well. With no refinery at hand, Compton had to devise his own method of separating the oil and water. He bailed the oil and water mix from the well with a two-gallon galvanized bucket and poured it into a tub. A hole at the bottom of the tub was left open until all of the water drained off and was then closed to retain the oil.

When University dead-ends into Loop 82, turn left and follow Loop 82 past the Southwest Texas State University campus and Aquarena Springs, then turn left on the Old Post Rd. (Cty. Rd. 140).

The road you have been traveling since you left New Braunfels is the old stagecoach route from Austin to San Antonio. In 1848, Messrs. Turbox and Brown started up a line of four-horse stagecoaches between Austin and San Antonio. Each coach carried a sack of mail along with the passengers and the journey took three days each way. Stage stands were placed at 12-mile intervals, and the horses were changed at each station. A station stood in Stringtown, the next one north stood beside the Blanco River, a ways upstream from the current road's Blanco River crossing.

Bear left at the junction just north of the low-water crossing of the Blanco River. The narrow asphalt strip (you are now on Cty. Rd. 136) hugs the Blanco for a few dozen furlongs. At this point, the Old Post Rd. is Cty. Rd. 136.

NANCE'S MILL

Hays County • About 6 miles from San Marcos
You are passing through the old Nance's Mill neighborhood, which overlapped the southern edges of the Mountain City community and the northern edges of San Marcos. Ezekiel Nance was a prime example of pioneer tenacity and enterprise. Born in Tennessee and orphaned at an early age, Nance began moving west, finally locating on 10,000 acres along the Rio Blanco in 1850. At that time the country was newly and still sparsely settled and the settlers had none of our conveniences, not even a mill to grind their corn crops into meal for cornbread. Nance built the area's first gristmill and cotton gin in 1855, using the tumbling waters of the Blanco as power. People came from miles around. But less than two years later, a rampaging Blanco River swept Nance's little complex downriver. Undaunted, he rebuilt. Over the years he added a cotton mill, a wheat flour mill, a sawmill, and a shingle mill. After the Civil War Nance built a pickled beef factory, taking advantage of the great cattle market glut. But in 1869 the Blanco's waters rolled once more and once again Nance's entire industrial empire went down to the sea. The small gin and gristmill he threw up to handle the 1870 crop were washed away, too. Most men would have given up, but not Nance. He just built another gin and mill. By 1876, Nance had embarked on his most ambitious project, the construction of a big wheat flour roller mill, again on the banks of the fickle Blanco. People came from 40 miles around to have their wheat crops ground. But this enterprise, too, bit the dust, around 1880, victim not of the Blanco River but of Jay Gould and the I&GN railroad. But Nance did not despair; he proceeded to erect newly born Kyle's first cotton gin in 1881. Death took Nance from the people he had labored to serve in 1885.

MOUNTAIN CITY

Hays County • 338 • About 10 miles from San Marcos
The railroad's coming also killed off Mountain City. In its heyday, from 1850 through 1880, Mountain City was a major stop on the Austin-to-San Antonio stage route, a regional supply center, and a

gathering point for many of the great drives of the late 1860s and 1870s. Mountain City's most illustrious citizen was Colonel W. W. Haupt, who came here from Alabama via Bastrop in 1857. A gentleman cotton planter, Haupt was an innovator as well, introducing the Angora goat, Essex hog, and Brahma cow to the area, besides developing the Hauptberry, a cross between the blackberry and dewberry. Mountain City, in its largest sense, stretched from the Kyle bank of the Blanco River up north to Manchaca, a distance of about 10 miles. Haupt's ranch, store, hotel, and post office were the community's center, located across from the present-day Hays High School.

KYLE CABIN
Old Post Rd. • Open the third Saturday in September and on other special occasions

John Claiborne Kyle and his wife, Lucy Bugg, came to Texas from Mississippi in 1844 and built this cabin about 1850. Five of the Kyle boys served in the Confederate Army; one of them was Ferguson Kyle, who founded the nearby town of the same name. John Claiborne Kyle died in 1867. Built of squared-off cedar logs, this large four-pen cabin is the only one of its type left in Texas. Its central chimneys are also rare. The cabin is set back several hundred yards from the road and isn't immediately visible. About 3 miles after turning onto Cty. Rd. 136, start looking for a sign that refers to the cabin, which will be on your left. The cabin is fenced in to protect it from vandals. It is about 0.3 mile south of the Kyle Cemetery, so if you pass the cemetery, you've gone too far.

As you continue up the Old Post Rd. toward the turnoffs to Kyle, you pass the old Kyle Cemetery on your right.

KYLE CEMETERY
Old Post Rd.

The first inhabitant here was an unknown young man whom cow hunters found hanging from an oak tree. Not knowing who he was, why he was hanging there, or who put him there, they buried the poor unfortunate under the oak. He was later joined by such notables as Texas Declaration of Independence signer Colonel John Bunton, W. W. Haupt, Claiborne and Ferguson Kyle, Ezekiel Nance, and Major Edward Burleson.

To get to Kyle, turn right on Center St., at the stop sign, off the Old Post Rd.

KYLE

Hays County • 2,321 • About 11 miles from San Marcos

While Mountain City was dying, Kyle and Buda were springing up to take its place. When railroad magnate Jay Gould came down from New York to check on the progress of his new line, he discovered that there was no town located on the route between Austin and San Marcos. Rather than move the line slightly west to Mountain City, Gould decreed that a new town must be built. Thus was born the town of Kyle, on land belonging to Captain Ferguson Kyle. The town was laid out in 1880 and the first sale of town lots took place that summer under a spreading live oak tree, which still stands, drooping now in its old age. Almost all of the lots sold that first day, but it took a while to get the new town built. Kyle's first railroad station was housed in a tent. N. C. Schlemmer, Kyle's first postmaster, was not overly impressed with his first visit to the young town. Disembarking from the construction train on a dank, foggy November morning, he could not find the town. Spying a figure in the fog, he asked for directions. The man "pointed to the skeleton of a frame building in the distance, on the roof of which some men were working and said that was all there was to it so far, however, that if I wanted a drink I should go a piece farther on, where I would find a tip-top saloon and could get some good stuff . . . It was a wooden shack kept by a very polite and amiable man and seemed to be the center of the town, or practically the town itself, for if there was another habitable structure nearby I couldn't see it."

After a lunch of cheese and crackers and a bottle of Blue Ribbon Beer atop a beer keg, and a short conversation with the Mountain City postmaster, who said he had hoped to become Kyle's first postmaster, Schlemmer decided that since the man seemed to be popular with the locals, he would make everyone happy by resigning his appointment then and there and hopping the first freight train south. But he was back in Kyle as postmaster and merchant by 1885, realizing "that, do what I would, I could not escape Kyle, that the powers that be . . . had decreed and ordered that I must go to that place, nolens volens."

From that rather inauspicious beginning, Kyle grew to be an important trading point and was known as the Prairie City. Kyle had a newspaper, the *Kyle Weekly Nutshell,* by 1881, along with four saloons.

The Kyle Auction Oak is located one block south of Center on Sledge. The Kyle City Hall dates back to the 1890s as does the old rock store facing the city hall to the west and the old Schlemmer Mercantile Company (now Center Grocery), both on Center downtown.

A few interesting tidbits about Kyle:

• The city had a woman mayor—Mary Kyle Hartson—from 1937 to 1946. She headed an all-female city government for four of those years.

• Kyle went through its rough and rowdy period, too. Those four saloons all had a liberal patronage, and these customers drank, gambled, and raced horses. They fought each other with regularity, cutting each other with their bowie knives and shooting each other up with their Winchesters and Colt 45s. A veteran of those early days reminisced, "It was 'dangerous to be safe' then. You'd better attend to your own business and keep out of others' affairs if you wanted to stay healthy."

• In 1882, the great presidential race between Grover Cleveland and Benjamin Harrison was overshadowed—in Kyle at least—by the election battle between Jim Hall and Boliver Greathouse for city constable. The night before the election the local Mexican population was treated to a party at the expense of one of the candidates. They were furnished with eats and drinks, and after a night of dancing those who were not too drunk, or dead from fighting amongst themselves, were shepherded at the crack of dawn to the polling place, handed fifty cents, and told to vote. Some did so two or three times. Several hundred people milled about for three days outside as election judges sweated over the final tabulations. The crowd allowed the judges no sleep during that time. In the end, Jim Hall won.

• Kyle finally began to quiet down in 1898 when the saloons were voted out. With them went most of the bad eggs. Those who remained were too few in number to cause any trouble.

• One of Kyle's old Christmas Eve customs saw half of the town's boys and young men—up to about age 21—lined up along one side of Main St. facing the other half along the other side of the street soon after dark. A furious firecracker and Roman candle war would then ensue. Many a coat and jacket were ruined from powder burns and many an eye was blackened from the fistfights that often followed the pyrotechnical wars.

• The old Ezekiel Nance tradition of fine stone-ground cornmeal and whole wheat flour is being carried on by the Eugene Schnautz family of Kyle. Of superlative quality, their products are available locally and in Austin.

• Noted writer Katherine Anne Porter (famous for the novel *Ship of Fools*) lived in Kyle as a young girl. Her childhood home, a simple one-story frame ranch-style house, still stands at 508 Center St., and a historical marker dedicated to her stands in front of City Hall.

Return to the Old Post Rd. (Cty. Rd. 136) and continue north to Buda. At the intersection with FM 150, the Old Post Rd. becomes FM 2770. Once in Buda, turn left onto Main.

BUDA

Hays County • 1,871 • (512) • About 8 miles from Kyle

The origin of Buda's name poses something of a mystery, although the most common explanation is that Buda is a corruption of the Spanish word *viuda* ("widow") and that the town was so named for the widow or widows who operated a hotel here in the early days. The other popular explanation is that the name Buda derives from Budapest, the capital of Hungary; in olden days, Buda and Pest were separate cities on either side of the Danube River. The Buda area was settled when Phillip Allen moved here in 1846 and began farming what was later to be called Allen's Prairie.

A townsite was laid out in 1880 with the impending arrival of the I&GN and the town was known as Du Pre for the first decade of its life, supposedly as a result of W. W. Haupt's supplications to railroad officials: "Do, pray, give us a depot." At any rate, Du Pre was Buda by 1889.

Buda was once a bustling little town. Captain L. D. Carrington's Carrington Hotel was said to be the most popular eating house on the I&GN line between St. Louis and San Antonio. Two or three trains stopped daily for meals, and the porter's call, "Budy, twenny minutes fo' suppa" was a most welcomed call for I&GN passengers. One day, during a cattlemen's convention in San Antonio, Mrs. Carrington served 1,000 people en route to the convention on several special trains. The old hotel still stands (now a private residence) downtown. Sam Ealy Johnson, Lyndon's daddy, used to drive here from Johnson City in his buggy, park it, and ride the Sunshine Special up to Austin when the state legislature was in session. William Jennings Bryan and Governor Pat Neff came to Buda for a day of feasting and speechmaking in 1924.

In addition to all the standard businesses of a prosperous town of its day, Buda had a cheese factory and chamber of commerce. Buda also got natural gas service before San Marcos and other nearby towns did, because of one man. Will Morgan grew up motherless in Buda, and the women of the town helped Dad Morgan take care of the boys. When Will got rich off oil and gas leases and had a set of plush offices in Houston, he used his influence to get gas lines to Buda in 1931, several years ahead of the other towns in the area.

More recently, Buda was the home of an artisans' colony during the 1970s. Most of the space is currently filled by antique-collectibles shops, the most interesting of which is the 1898 Store.

OLD 1898 STORE
200 Main at Loop 4 • Open Wednesday through Friday afternoons, Saturday and Sunday, 10–6 • No Cr. • W

The first question you ask the first time you walk into the 1898 Store is: How did they get all this stuff in here? Austin geologist Carl Chelf opened the place more than 30 years ago when his collections outgrew his Austin garage. The 1898 Store is as much a museum as a business enterprise; Chelf (now deceased) started collecting at a young age, and most of the wonderful old advertising signs on the walls are not for sale. Ditto for a lot of the store's furniture and fixtures. But there's still lots of merchandise left to choose from: books and magazines, tools, knickknacks, buttons, a dentist's chair, a rock or fossil.

CARRINGTON DRUG STORE
300 Main • Currently houses Memory Lane Antiques

One block north is Buda's most imposing downtown building, this stolid two-story orange brick box built in 1914 by prominent Buda druggist W. D. Carrington. He and his family lived upstairs, a common practice of the times.

OLD BUDA BANK
312 Main (middle of the block) • Currently houses Don's Den

Currently housing an antique-collectibles shop, this low-slung one-story brick building has housed an Indonesian restaurant and a newspaper. It started life, however, as the Farmers National Bank of Buda, and as such was the victim of one of Texas' most unusual bank robberies, back in 1926. Don has an extensive collection of old toys; it's a fun place.

CARRINGTON HOUSE
320 Main • Private residence

At the end of this block is the rambling two-story Carrington House, of travelers' fame.

Now, to the story of that 1926 bank heist. On December 11 of that year, Becky Bradley Rogers, a 22-year-old UT graduate student and part-time stenographer for Attorney General Dan Moody, held up the Farmers National Bank. After an unsuccessful attempt to hold up the Round Rock Farmers Bank the previous day (the same bank Sam Bass had planned to hold up 50 years earlier), Becky walked into the Buda bank that Saturday morning posing as a newspaper reporter working on a story on the local farming economy. At noon, after all the day's customers had left, she pulled a .32 automatic on the cashier. With $1,000 tucked in her purse, she locked the cashier and bookkeeper in the vault and took off for Austin. The shocked employees were out of the vault in 10 minutes and alerted the authorities. Reports had her headed for Fredericksburg, headed up the Old Post Rd. straight for Austin—headed all over Central Texas. In reality she headed for Creedmoor, got stuck in the deep winter mud, got pulled out by an unsuspecting dairy farmer, and then drove leisurely into Austin where she mailed the money and gun to herself at a university post office box and dropped her muddy flivver off for a wash and wax. She was arrested by Austin police when she went to pick up her car. Everyone, the newspapers included, wondered how such a sweet and innocent-looking girl could have pulled off such a daring act. She pulled the job, she said, to finance treatment for her law student fiance's "acute intestinal paralysis," but it turned out she was in debt to the Texas branch of the American Historical Association for $1,500, the result of a membership drive that failed.

Becky went through a series of sensational trials that ended in conviction and a 14-year sentence, reversal of the sentence on appeal, a second trial in La Grange that ended in mistrial, and a second mistrial verdict in a New Braunfels court, whereupon the state threw up its hands in frustration after three years of prosecution and dropped the case. Becky's long-suffering husband (she had been secretly married to him for some time before the robbery) served as counsel for the defense throughout the trial process. Following the dropping of charges in 1929, they dropped out of sight.

In the meantime, the Farmers National Bank had closed up. The bank had gotten its money back, but owner W. D. Carrington had seen enough: "When women start robbing banks I'm selling out." He did so in 1927 to the Austin National Bank. In the meantime, the bank was again robbed by a lone gunman, to the tune of $1,200. Shortly after its acquisition, Austin National Bank closed the Buda bank for good.

Local legend has it that Bonnie and Clyde robbed the bank. The only problem with the story is that Barrow didn't even meet Bonnie until 1930, three years after the bank had closed, and up to 1926, the year of the Buda bank robbery, Clyde's biggest crime had been stealing a rent-a-car to go see his girlfriend.

ANNUAL EVENT

DECEMBER • Buda Fest • Under the oaks in downtown Buda First Sunday in December • Free • W
This Christmas shopping bazaar has arts and crafts, puppeteers, jugglers, musicians, and vendors.

Leave Buda on the first leg of Becky's getaway route. Follow Main/Loop 4 across the railroad tracks, then turn left on the Old San Antonio Rd. (Cty. Rd. 117) just west of I-35 and go 16 miles to Austin.

Incidentally, this road, the I-35 of its time, is believed to be the first paved rural road in Texas. Paving costs were paid by either the U.S. Post Office or Agriculture Department and the project was the first Federal Aid Project in Texas. Paving of this 24-mile strip from the Travis county line through Hays County to the Comal County line was begun in 1915 and finished in 1919. It was also the first paving project of the newly created Texas Highway Department.

ONION CREEK
About 5 miles from Buda
According to legend, somewhere near the Old San Antonio Rd.'s crossing of Onion Creek several miles north of Buda is buried a kettle of Spanish gold and jewels, hidden in a drought crack by a Spanish army pack train under Indian attack. Many have searched, but none have found. This crossing is also known as Sasser Crossing, the place where a frontier bee hunter used to set his saucer of bee bait and lie in wait, hoping to follow the little bait-taker back to its honey tree or cave.

Continue north on the Old San Antonio Rd. past the FM 1626 intersection and across Slaughter Creek to the junction with the I-35 frontage road. Turn right onto the southbound I-35 frontage road, then left a few yards up the hill onto the I-35 overpass, then left again onto the northbound I-35 frontage road. Take the South Congress exit (which comes up shortly), and follow the signs to take S. Congress into Austin.

SOUTH CONGRESS AVENUE (AUSTIN)

Up until the construction of I-35 in the 1950s, S. Congress (US 81) was the main drag out of town. Back then, the Austin city limits didn't extend much farther than St. Edward's University (the campus stretched over 650 acres and contained a large farm in those days), and the stretch of S. Congress/US 81 beyond the city limits was a hotbed of whorehouses and honky-tonks. Hattie Valdes was queen of the Austin madams, running two and three bawdy houses at a time. La Siesta Courts and later the M&M Courts were the best known houses of ill-repute in their day. Many Austin folk objected to the S. Congress strip, but not much was done to shut the houses of ill-repute down because the places had prominent customers and were relatively well-behaved, for whorehouses. It was also suspected that the girls enjoyed more than just a friendly relationship with the forces of law and order. When Sheriff T. O. Lang took office in 1953 he immediately pledged to put the ladies of the night out of business and, true to his word, conducted raid after raid on the houses, but they just kept springing back up. Although the whorehouse era in Austin suffered from the raids in the mid-1950s, it wasn't dealt a final blow until the 1960s when the Tim Overton gang tried to muscle in on Miss Hattie's business.

Tim Overton was a bear of a man. He had played football at the University, climaxing his stint as a Longhorn with a trip to the 1960 Cotton Bowl. Later that year he and brother Charles—who had already done time for burglary—were arrested on forgery charges. Tim soon expanded his repertoire to include bank robbery, whoremongering, and extortion. By 1965 he headed up a gang whose membership ranged from prostitutes to lawyers to two-bit gunmen to fringe members who were prominent Austin citizens. It was at this time that he decided to take over Hattie's, Austin's best established and most reputable whorehouse, then located at the M&M Courts just outside the city limits. Overton went to Hattie and demanded that she install a pair of his girls. She refused, whereupon Tim brashly said, "We're taking over this town anyway, so we'll just take a percentage off the top of what you're taking in." Hattie promptly kicked him out, so Overton went to visit Sheriff Lang. Inside Lang's office, Overton told the sheriff that he was going to take things over, Hattie's included. Lang kicked him out at gunpoint. Undaunted, Overton began assembling a small army of hired guns. Hattie's backers in Austin got wind of Overton's plan and began assembling their own army. The Austin police were powerless since Hattie's was outside the city limits. Hattie's San Antonio gunmen were ready and waiting for the Overton assault, but just as invasion was imminent, the Texas Rangers stepped in, sent everyone home, and closed the place down. This was the last straw for Hattie, and she retired for good after this episode. An Austin era, a seamy one to be sure, had drawn to a close. The M&M Courts were torn down a few years later, and S. Congress these days is noted for its plethora of auto junkyards on the outskirts of town.

What of Tim Overton? He went to prison shortly after the Hattie's fiasco. Released in 1972, he was gunned down in Dallas two months later.

ST. EDWARD'S UNIVERSITY
3001 S. Congress at St. Edward's Dr. • 444-2621 • W

Visible for miles atop South Austin's highest hill is the main building of St. Edward's University. Designed by noted architect Nicholas Clayton, this massive Gothic limestone structure was built 1888-1889 and was gutted by fire in 1903 but was rebuilt. The smaller Victorian Gothic limestone Holy Cross Hall was built after the fire. St. Edward's got its start back in 1872. E. Sorin, founder of Notre Dame University and superior general of the Congregation of the Holy Cross, bought 400 acres here three miles south of the Capitol. Originally envisaged as a boys school, it began with three boys enrolled by 1878. Holy Cross sisters performed the domestic chores, while Holy Cross brothers split the teaching and farming chores. A college charter was obtained in 1885 and enrollment grew rapidly thereafter, despite a tornado in 1922 that leveled practically every building on campus.

Although St. Edwards hasn't fielded an intercollegiate football team since 1939, it became home to the Dallas Cowboy training camp in 1990. The Cowboys play their interteam scrimmages at a local high school stadium.

WILLIAMSON COUNTY

Approximately 165 miles

Set smack-dab in the heart of a state long accustomed to bragging on itself, Williamson County can make, in matters that are quintessentially Texan, a few sizable brags of its own.

Take King Cotton for example—"Gotta pick sum cotton ef it breaks my back"—in a state whose cotton crop has been called the most valuable crop grown in a single political subdivision in the world. Williamson County holds the all-time Texas one-year production record: 168,509 cotton bales produced in 1920, in the days when 70 percent of the Texas population depended on it for a living.

And take the weather—"If you don't like the weather in Texas, just wait a few minutes and it will change." More specifically, consider rain, or the lack of it, which every real Texan feels constrained to discuss at least once a day—Williamson County holds Texas' all-time one-day rainfall record: 23.11 inches at Taylor, September 6 and 7, 1921.

And what about cowboys—"Get along little dogey"—Williamson County was home of Will Pickett, inventor of and arguably the greatest all-time practitioner of the sport of bulldogging, and certainly the world's best cowboy in his day.

Then there were outlaws—"Some rob you with a six gun and some with a fountain pen, but you'll never see an outlaw drive a family from its home." Sam Bass made a patch of Williamson County soil his eternal home under circumstances that made him legendary.

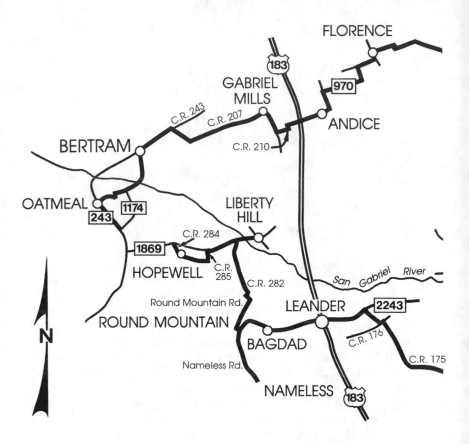

FLORENCE

GABRIEL
MILLS

183

970

ANDICE

C.R. 243

C.R. 207

C.R. 210

BERTRAM

OATMEAL

243

1174

LIBERTY
HILL

C.R. 284

1869

HOPEWELL

C.R.
285

C.R. 282

San Gabriel River

Round Mountain Rd.

LEANDER

2243

ROUND MOUNTAIN

BAGDAD

C.R. 176

C.R. 175

N

Nameless Rd.

NAMELESS

183

WILLIAMSON COUNTY

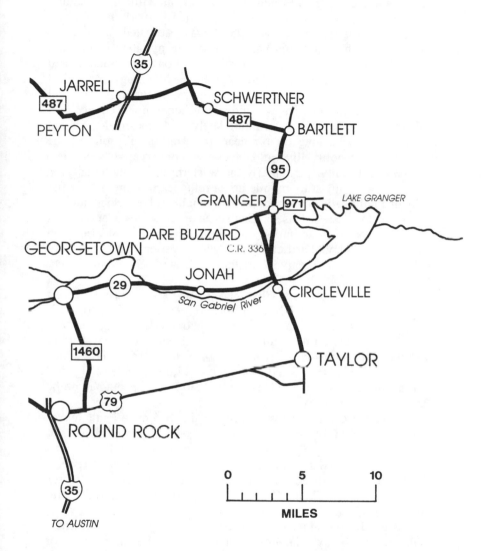

Williamson County's latest brag is that of phenomenal growth; it is one of the fastest-growing counties in the state. In the late 1970s, Austin's explosive growth began to rub off on Williamson County along the I-35 corridor and US 183 North. By 1990, the county's population was 139,551; in 1995 it was estimated at 162,761. Georgetown (the county seat) and the once-sleepy villages of Round Rock, Cedar Park, and Leander now have big-city conveniences and are beginning to experience big-city problems like drugs, gangs, and crime. This growth has created a trichotomy of suburbia vs. small town vs. rural life in what was already a dichotomous county. The suburban lifestyle has been winning lately, with the small-town and rural mindsets hanging on for dear life. Traditionally one of the state's most politically and socially conservative counties, Williamson County (particularly the western half of the county) is filling up with upwardly mobile urban refugees who are mostly fiscally and politically conservative, but often liberal on social and personal-freedom issues. This split between conservatives over the right to choose your own definition of morality has been most evident in Round Rock School District politics, where western moderates have battled eastern conservative Christians in heated school board elections and textbook hearings.

In 1996, Del Webb's Sun City opened. Sun City lies just northwest of Georgetown between RM 2338 and SH 195. This refuge for well-heeled retirees has its admirers and detractors. Regardless, Sun City has certainly altered the landscape. Local businesses have warmly welcomed the infusion of spending money from the enclave's citizens. Population is projected to top out at 17,000 people (and 9,500 houses) by about 2015. Sun City covers 5,300 acres; about half of the land is to be left undeveloped.

Williamson County's posture astride the Balcones Fault makes this trip a delightful mix of rich, rolling, black-earth farmland and rugged Hill Country limestone. There is a reason for the tortured boundary line between Travis and Williamson counties: It reflects the dividing line between the watersheds of the Colorado and Brazos rivers. Williamson County's streams eventually empty into the Brazos, Travis County's into the Colorado.

This trip begins and ends in the heart of downtown Round Rock, Williamson County's largest municipality, at the intersection of Mays, Main, and Round Rock Ave. Mays is also US 81, while Round Rock Ave. doubles as FM 620.

We'll explore Round Rock in depth at the end of this trip. For now, it's time to head up to Georgetown, the county seat.

From downtown Round Rock, proceed north on Mays across Brushy Creek to the intersection with US 79.

HISTORICAL MARKER
Southeast corner of the intersection of Mays and SH 79 • W

The marker commemorates the builders of the Greenwood Masonic Institute and Round Rock Institute. The Greenwood Institute, which was located about a quarter mile west of this marker, is perhaps best remembered as the alma mater of the notorious John Wesley Hardin. Brother Joe Hardin was studying law here in 1870 when his younger brother John, already on the run from the law, decided to join him in his studies. John Wesley camped in the woods near the school, and each afternoon Joe would bring his lessons, which John studied by the light of his campfire. As quick with words as with his gun, John Wesley Hardin purportedly received his diploma in record time.

Turn right on US 79.

About a mile down US 79, on the north side of the highway, you see on your left a spacious **old two-story double-galleried limestone house** with an Indian lookout on top. This is the home Nelson Merrell built for his family in 1870. After this section of Texas had been tamed, Merrell, a noted frontiersman, Indian fighter, and buffalo hunter, settled down to raising cattle and built this spacious home. Why he added the Indian lookout is anybody's guess; by the time he built his house there had been no Indian attacks in the area for over five years and the frontier was being pushed steadily west.

About a half-mile after the Merrell house, turn left on FM 1460 to reach Georgetown.

FM 1460 carries you toward Georgetown through rolling farmland that used to be the exclusive domain of King Cotton but is now dominated by cattle and milo. The hill you top before you drop down into the valley that contains Georgetown is known locally as Rabbit Hill, though nobody around here seems to know why. Tens of thousands of cattle hooves first beat out this particular path into Georgetown during the great cattle drives.

When FM 1460 dead-ends, turn left onto SH 29.

GEORGETOWN

Williamson County Seat • 16,752 • (512) • About 11 miles from Round Rock

The first inhabitants of Georgetown were Tonkawa Indians, who drove buffalo off the high Tonkawa Bluff of the San Gabriel River just east of town and ran footraces around a 500-yard track about four miles northwest of the present courthouse.

White settlers began to drift into the area during the early 1840s, and by 1847 the Brushy post office, at this time a part of sprawling Milam County, was located here. For the settlers living here it was a long trip to Nashville-on-the-Brazos—the seat of government for Milam County—where all legal matters were conducted. So in the early months of 1848, settlers in the western section of Milam County sent a petition to the Texas Legislature asking for the creation of a new county, suggesting San Gabriel and Clear Water as possible names. The legislators promptly acceded to their wishes for a new county but ignored their name suggestions. They chose instead to name the county Williamson, after their esteemed colleague Robert McAlpin "Three-legged Willie" Williamson. Legend has it that when the bill to create the "County of San Gabriel" came before the Texas Senate, Three-legged Willie arose and excitedly protested having any more saints in Texas, whereupon San Gabriel became Williamson. Willie never resided in the county named for him, but traveled through it often.

A popular old-timer's story says that legislators voted to name the county for Williamson after he told the following tale on himself: A few years earlier, Col. Frank W. Johnson had headed a surveying party which had charted a ten-league land grant inside what would become Williamson County. Williamson was part of the surveying party. There were still great herds of buffalo on the scene, and on this particular day Williamson determined to chase down one or more of the massive beasts. Col. Johnson advised against the chase, for the ground was exceedingly wet, uneven, and full of holes. But Williamson was not to be denied, and galloped off astride his horse. They were approaching full speed when his horse suddenly turned a somersault, throwing rider, gun, and crutch off into an inglorious heap. Once the horse was upright, it continued on after the buffalo. Williamson attempted to regain his equilibrium, but each time he stood up his peg-leg and crutch sank deep into the black waxy mud. After "swearing like an army mired in Flanders," he gave up and lay still in the mud until his horse was brought back to him some hours later. Another version of the story says that every time he tried to stand up, a charging buffalo calf would knock him back down. He finally retaliated by shooting the calf from a prone position.

In May of 1848, the men entrusted with the task of locating the new county's seat of government met under a large live oak tree a few blocks south of the two forks of the San Gabriel to deliberate. As the men discussed possible locations, George Washington Glasscock, Sr., member of a land development firm with extensive area holdings, galloped up and made the following offer: if the commissioners would select this site for the county seat and name the town Georgetown in his honor, Glasscock would donate a 173-acre tract of land. "Paying due regard to donations of land" (which was required by law), the commissioners accepted Glasscock's proposition and thereby gained simultaneously a county seat and a new name. One of the commissioners, Washington Anderson, was a cousin by marriage to Glasscock. An Anderson family version of the story has Anderson proposing the land donation and town name to Glasscock, who consented after only a moment's hesitation.

Georgetown residents enjoyed few of life's amenities during the early years. Buffalo, bear, deer, wild turkeys, and Indians wandered at will through the little village. The first time a jail was needed here, a makeshift one was improvised by turning a wagon bed upside down with the prisoner confined underneath while the constable slept on top to prevent his escape.

In the 1850 census (the county's first) Greenlief Fiske was listed as the county's largest taxpayer, paying taxes on $20,000 valuation. Fiske was also Williamson's first county judge. He had come to the area only four years earlier, settling on the South San Gabriel.

While conducting court here in December 1854, Judge Robert Jones Rivers contracted pneumonia. When his condition worsened two days later, the call went out for a minister. Parson Stephen Strickland arrived at the Ake Hotel, where the judge was staying, and informed Rivers that his life was nearing its end. The judge then asked that the curtain over his window be raised. Georgetown, according to an observer, "was then a mere hamlet on a hill, with almost limitless prairies stretching away on every side. There was a thin sheet of sleet on the ground and the brown and sere grass could be seen through it. Altogether it was a desolate and depressing scene." After gazing out the window for some time, Judge Rivers turned toward Parson Strickland and said, "Parson, I have always been a firm believer in the fitness of things and I have never been more forcibly impressed with this doctrine than I am at the present moment. I have been a great traveller in my day and time—have visited Europe, spent some time in the principal colleges, stopped at magnificent hotels, lodged in inns and taverns, and I tell you now, Parson, with all these experiences flashing before me, I know of no place that I can quit with fewer regrets than the new city of Georgetown and particularly this Ake Hotel." It is said that upon uttering these last words, he turned his face to the wall and "was no more." The Ake Hotel was in fact just a log cabin built by John Ake in August 1848, the first house in Georgetown.

After the Civil War, thousands of cattle pounded through downtown Georgetown on their long journey to the northern markets, bringing Georgetown its first real taste of prosperity. Three of the biggest cattle barons in the area were the Snyder brothers—Dudley, Thomas, and John Wesley. The foundation for their fortune was a huge herd of cattle that they collected to drive east to the beleaguered Confederate garrison at Vicksburg. Vicksburg fell before they arrived, however, so the Snyders drifted back to Texas, awaiting orders that never came. At war's end they slipped the herd across the Mexican border, where they sold the beeves for gold. They then returned to Williamson County, bought more cattle, and began driving them north. Innovative in many ways, the Snyders were unusual in that they did not permit their cowboys to drink, play cards, gamble, or swear in their presence.

When Round Rock became a railroad town in 1876, customers and merchants began to desert Georgetown for the tracks 10 miles south. Apprehensive, the remaining Georgetown civic leaders got together, pooled their resources, and built a tap line from Georgetown to Round Rock. The line was built in 1878 and as a result the Georgetown economy rebounded.

Georgetown became famous for its "First Monday" trade-a-thons, which started soon after the Civil War. On the first Monday of each month farmers would bring horses and cattle to the courthouse square to trade. Some visitors considered this event an excuse to go on a drinking spree. Others took it as an excuse to make some ethically questionable trades, and traders would touch up an old graying nag with shoe polish or lamp black to make it look younger. Many a cutting or shooting scrape resulted from these unsavory trades. First Mondays were so popular that horses were hitched in a continuous ring around the courthouse fence and the gravel streets were ankle deep in either dust or mud, depending on the weather.

Considerably more sedate today, the courthouse square is still interesting to see. In fact, it is one of the most complete and best preserved courthouse squares in the state and is a Registered National Historic

District. Georgetown was designated a Texas Main Street City in 1982, and an aggressive plan to completely restore the downtown business district began. By 1986, over $8 million had been invested.

Georgetown calls itself the red poppy capital of Texas. For about a month (usually April) every spring, Georgetown gardens are awash with red poppy flowers. The tradition dates to World War I, when a returning soldier brought home some seeds from Flanders Field for his mother's garden.

Georgetown has three official historic districts. The Downtown Historic District is bounded by Rock St. on the west, Church St. on the east, 7th St. on the north, and 9th St. on the south. It includes the county courthouse and business district. The Belford National Register Historic District includes houses and churches along Austin Ave. and Main St., between University Ave. and 19th St. It was named for Charles Belford, a turn-of-the-century builder who visited his construction sites wearing a suit and derby hat and carrying an umbrella, piece of chalk, and plumb bob. Of the 81 buildings in this 8-block district, 73 are at least 50 years old. The University Avenue/Elm Street National Register Historic District includes homes and churches on University Ave. between Myrtle and Hutto Rd. It has 22 homes of interest, one of which was built for Buffalo Bill Cody's brother. It is notable for its large Victorian houses built in the 1890s on what had formerly been the Thomas Hughes Ranch.

Altogether, Georgetown has over 50 homes that have been deemed historic in one way or another, from grand mansion to shotgun shack; most are over 100 years old. Most of these houses are located immediately east and southeast of the county courthouse in an area that includes the Southwestern University campus and extends below University Avenue to 15th Street.

From SH 29, turn right onto Bus. US 81 (Austin Ave.) to reach the county courthouse.

WILLIAMSON COUNTY COURTHOUSE
Austin at 7th • Open Monday through Friday
The present Greek Revival courthouse was built in 1910 and is the county's fifth. Some of its charm disappeared when its massive marble pediment and roofline balustrade were removed in 1965, but the square's old oaks and pecans still stand guard, offering the weary traveler a bit of shaded rest on those hot Texas summer days. A number of historical monuments and markers dot the grounds.

M. B. LOCKETT BUILDING
119 W. 7th • Currently houses Cafe on the Square
Built in 1896, the old Lockett building anchors this corner of the courthouse square. Built of field-dressed limestone blocks with a red brick facade, it features a pressed-metal cornice and distinctive corner bay window and domed turret.

DAVIDSON GROCERY AND H. C. CRAIG BUILDINGS
115 and 117 W. 7th
Although distinctly separate structures, both turn-of-the-century buildings feature pressed-metal facades in good condition.

GEORGETOWN HISTORY AND VISITOR INFORMATION CENTER
101 W. 7th at Main • 863-5598 • Open daily 9–5, except Sunday 1–5 • W
Eager-to-help volunteers will direct you to a number of free or low-cost pamphlets and books about the area, which are available here.

OLD MASONIC LODGE
701 Main • Currently houses restaurant
The old Masonic Lodge anchors the northeast corner of the square in its own impressive way. The most distinctive feature of this two-story limestone building is its tacked-on cast-metal second-story bay window and onion dome. Shades of Baghdad! The Masons met upstairs and rented out the ground floor to a variety of businesses over the years, until the building was sold in 1982.

DIMMIT BUILDING
719 Main at 8th
Another two-story limestone structure, the 1890s Dimmit building sports a cast-iron facade and full-length cast-metal cornice. The building is still owned by a descendant of the Dimmit family.

P. H. DIMMIT BUILDING
801 Main • Currently serves as an office building
Just across 8th from the old Dimmit building is the P. H. Dimmit building. The P. H. Dimmit Company erected this Richardson Romanesque structure in 1901 as a hotel, but it was never used as such. It later served as store, movie house, drug store, offices, and the like before undergoing renovation in 1960.

LESESNE-STONE BUILDING
102 W. 8th at Main

Built in 1884 and restored 99 years later, this two-story building features some especially nice stone work and a pedimented metal cornice. Stone's Drugstore was the original ground floor occupant and continued there for many years.

FIRE STATION
Main at 9th

A few yards south of the square is the attractively restored two-story limestone building built in 1893 to house Georgetown's volunteer fire department (formed in 1884) and municipal operations. The building was constructed in an L-plan around a metal standpipe which stood 150 ft. tall (15 ft. in diameter) and held the city's water supply. The fire department continues to occupy the building, although most of the city's municipal operations moved into the present city hall in 1971. The perimeter of the standpipe can still be seen in the pavement. The Firefighting Museum displays firefighting memorabilia and equipment from the past.

OLD GRACE EPISCOPAL CHURCH/FOUNDERS PARK
Main at 9th

This whitewashed, wooden-frame, Carpenter Gothic-style church was built in 1881 at the corner of Main and 10th. In 1955, it was moved to University Avenue, across from Southwestern University. By 1989, Grace's congregation had grown to the point that a new sanctuary was built. The Episcopal Diocese of Houston gave the old church building to the City of Georgetown, and in 1992 it was moved to its present site, one block from its original home. The building has been restored and is scheduled to become a tourist and history center that will house the Georgetown Heritage Society's office and history collections. Public restrooms are located behind the church.

Head west down W. 8th, then north on Austin to complete this tour of the courthouse square and surrounding buildings of interest.

STEELE STORE/MAKEMSON HOTEL
800 Austin Ave. at W. 8th • Currently houses a variety of businesses

As early as 1848 a log cabin on this site served as Georgetown's first hotel and stagestop as well as its second post office. Construction of the present sprawling two-story limestone complex commenced about 1870 and continued through about 1911. Previous users of the building included a dry goods store, bank, and hotel/boarding house.

OLD FARMERS STATE BANK
716 Austin

An existing limestone building was remodeled in 1910 to house the Farmers State Bank; the result was a miniature Greek temple, with two massive Ionic columns, sandwiched into this stretch of Victorian buildings. In 1905, Farmers State Bank was one of the first three banks to receive a charter from the state of Texas. The bank moved out in 1962. The county bought the building in 1967. The building is notable for its black-and-white marble wainscoting, 20-foot ceiling with decorative, carved plaster molding, and mosaic tile floor. In 1996, the Williamson County Historical Commission got permission to turn the bank into a county museum.

MILEHAM BUILDING
708–710 Austin

If you like pressed-metal, you'll love the old Mileham building, built in 1898. It sports a two-and-a-half-story pressed-metal facade, which came from the Mesker Brothers Company of St. Louis. The Mesker Brothers sold over 5,000 storefronts nationwide between 1884 and 1907, and furnished decorative metalwork for many other Georgetown buildings.

DAVID LOVE BUILDING
706 Austin Ave. • Currently houses specialty shops

David Love was one of the area's earliest settlers. His name appears on the 1848 petition to form present-day Williamson County. He served as a county commissioner and was an original director of the Georgetown Railroad Company. In 1883 he built this two-story limestone and pressed-metal structure to house his dry goods store.

WILLIAMSON COUNTY JAIL
312 Main, corner of Main and 4th • Three blocks north of the courthouse square

Built in 1889, the still-in-use county jail was patterned after the Bastille, and with good reason. It was built during a time when cattle thieves and desperadoes still roamed the county and prisoners broke the old jail with impunity. Ironically, the first prisoner was one of its builders, who got a little too drunk while celebrating its completion.

From the courthouse square take Main or Austin back down to University Ave./SH 29. Turn left on SH 29 to leave town. SH 29 takes you past several substantial homes and churches, and the campus of Southwestern University, part of the University/Elm St. Historic District.

SOUTHWESTERN UNIVERSITY
University Ave./SH 29 at Maple • 863-6511 • W

Southwestern University traces its beginnings to 1840 and the creation of Rutersville College. The result of a merger of several colleges, Rutersville included, Southwestern opened for business in 1873. Despite its reputation as a respected institution of higher education, Southwestern retained some rough edges during its early days. Many of the male students carried guns, and at one point the school fathers ruled that all student guns must be checked in with the authorities. When one student who felt more comfortable with his gun on was asked to empty his gun, he responded by walking to the nearest window and firing until the chambers were empty. The faculty also maintained a running feud with the town's saloons: the savants accused the saloonkeepers of deliberately enticing the students and getting them drunk as revenge for faculty efforts on behalf of local option laws.

These days, though, the town and university get along fine, and Old Main, one of Georgetown's finest buildings, sits on campus facing SH 29.

One of Southwestern's most distinguished alumni was Jessie Daniel Ames. Born in Palestine, Texas, in 1883, Jessie Daniel moved with her family to Georgetown in 1893. She graduated from Southwestern in 1902 and went with her family to Laredo, where she met Roger Ames, an Army surgeon, whom she married in 1905. When he was assigned to New Orleans during a yellow fever epidemic, Ames sent Jessie home to live with her family, who had moved back to Georgetown and purchased the local telephone company. Roger's work took him all over the world, so they spent little time together; but their troubled union did produce three children between 1907 and 1914, the year Roger died. Widowed at 31, Jessie began to help her mother run the local phone company. Not content to live in the shadows of a male-dominated world, Jessie Daniel Ames soon got into politics, organizing the Georgetown Equal Suffrage League in 1916. She was serving as state treasurer of the Texas Equal Suffrage Association in 1918 when the Texas Legislature passed a bill permitting women to vote in state primaries. The suffragists had only 17 days to register women to vote in the next primary; Ames and her local cohorts registered 3,800 women in Williamson County. One observer commented on the sight of thousands of women pouring into the courthouse to register: "There's never been anything like it since." Mrs. Ames was a founder and first president of the Texas League of Women Voters, and one of the first women delegates to state and national Democratic conventions. During the 1920s, Ames broadened her concerns beyond women's rights to black rights and interracial cooperation.

In 1929, she moved from Georgetown to Atlanta, Ga., to become the national director of women's work for the Commission on Interracial Cooperation. A year later, she founded the Association of Southern Women for the Prevention of Lynching. By 1930, Ames realized that despite its long history in frontier America, lynching was largely a Southern phenomenon, a means of public intimidation designed to keep both blacks and whites in their respective places. She resented the widespread excuse that most lynchings were carried out in the name of chivalry and the protection of white southern womanhood, and she discovered, in fact, that less than one-third of the 204 documented lynching victims between 1922 and 1930 were even accused of crimes against white women. Lurid descriptions of the crimes which the lynch victims were accused of, and equally lurid accounts of the lynchings and mutilations which often followed, served as a sort of "folk pornography" for the Deep South— pornography that was printed in hundreds of southern newspapers. Ames worked tirelessly for state and national antilynching legislation. By the early 1940s Ames felt the movement had been successful enough to allow the Association to be dissolved. In 1944 she resigned from the Commission on Interracial Cooperation and went into retirement.

In 1969 Ames donated her library of more than 1,200 books to Southwestern. She died in 1972 in an Austin nursing home. The spacious two-story frame home in which she and her family lived while in Georgetown still stands a block to the southeast off the courthouse square, at the corner of Farm and 10th streets. It is not open to the public.

Southwestern is also home to the Edward A. Clark Texana Collection, which is housed in the Cody Memorial Library. When Ed Clark (formerly U.S. Ambassador to Australia and Texas Attorney General and Secretary of State) gave his private collection of about 2,400 volumes to Southwestern in 1965, it was described as one of the two greatest Texana collections in private hands. The collection has since grown to more than 10,000 items, including more than 7,000 books, which date from prerepublic days to the present. Parts of the collection may be viewed in the Special Collections Room at the Cody Memorial Library. It's best to call ahead for an appointment, 863-1561.

OLD MAIN
Southwestern University

Southwestern's Old Main, an immense cathedral Gothic limestone structure, was built 1898–1900. The stonecutters employed to build it were the same Scottish artisans imported 10 years earlier to build the new Capitol in Austin.

A couple of trivial tidbits for the ride out of town:

• In 1939 Georgetown came to be known as the Mistletoe or Kissing Capital of the world, when several local men began harvesting mistletoe for Christmas shipping.

• Texaco Oil Company had its beginnings in Georgetown when Judge R. E. Brooks and A. A. Booty organized the Texas Fuel Company. Brooks moved to Beaumont later that year, and in 1902 the Texas Fuel Company became the Texas Company, of which Brooks was treasurer and director.

From Southwestern University, backtrack to the courthouse square.

DINING

CAFE ON THE SQUARE
119 W. 7th, at Austin • 863-0596 • Open daily, lunch and dinner, Sunday brunch • $–$$ • W

Located in the colorful old Lockett Building, this cafe offers a varied menu with daily specials. Lunch menu has lots of sandwiches and salads. Desserts are homemade, except for the Blue Bell ice cream. Inviting atmosphere and decor.

LODGING

THE PAGE HOUSE
1000 Leander Rd., just west of I-35 at exit 260 • 863-8979 Open daily • W

This B&B inn also serves lunch Tuesday through Saturday and dinner on weekends. The house was built in 1903 by J. M. and Olivia

DeCrow Page. Boston-born J. M. Page had been a rancher, postmaster, and businessman in Georgetown since the early 1850s. Olivia died shortly after the house was completed, and the house was sold to her brother Thomas DeCrow. The Polo Barn dates to the ownership of the Horace Weir family. During this period, polo became a popular sport in Texas, and in the 1930s, the Georgetown polo team was based in this big barn. It won several championships during this time. It now has a stage, kitchen, and dance floor and is used for parties, receptions, meetings, and live performances. The Victorian garden is a pleasant place to take tea. Write to 1000 Leander Rd., Georgetown 78628.

OTHER ATTRACTIONS

INNER SPACE CAVERNS
**4200 S. I-35, about 1 mile south of Georgetown at exit 259
863-5545 • Open Memorial Day–Labor Day daily; rest of the
year Wednesday–Sunday. Closed 2 weeks before Christmas
and Christmas Day • Admission • W**
Texas Department of Transportation drillers taking core samples for a proposed overpass discovered these caverns. Waters of the Edwards Aquifer carved them out over a 100-million-year period. Remains of Ice-Age mastodons, wolves, and sabre-toothed tigers have been found inside the cave. Tours last about an hour and leave every half-hour. An inclined railway car takes you down into the caverns, and from there the trip covers less than a mile of relatively easy walking. Be prepared for brief periods of absolute darkness during the sound and light show. Gift shop.

THE CANDLE FACTORY
**4411 S. I-35, about 1 mile south of Georgetown at exit 259
863-6025 • Open daily • W**
More than 300 kinds of candles in 20 colors and fragrances, and a wide selection of candle holders. The candle wax formulas, colors, and fragrances were developed by Dr. Sherman Lesesne, a chemistry professor at Southwestern University who founded the business in 1967. The factory's previous name, Mar-Jon Candles, derived from the first names of his two children, Marcia and John. You can watch the candles being made Monday through Friday.

PALACE THEATRE
812 Austin, just south of the square

Built in 1926, the Palace Theatre is the only Art Deco-style building in Georgetown. It has been undergoing restoration by a community group, and has been featuring classic movies, community theater, and live music.

WINDBERG GALLERY
714-A Austin • 819-9463
Georgetown is home to well-known landscape and still-life artist Dalhart Windberg. Here you'll find original paintings, limited editions on canvas, limited-edition prints, open-edition prints, and plates.

AREA PARKS

SAN GABRIEL PARK
North shore of the San Gabriel River, about 1.5 miles north of downtown, take Austin/US 81 north • 863-9907 • Free
W variable
The North and South forks of the San Gabriel meet in Georgetown, and the town has taken full advantage of its beautiful setting in this 320-acre park. You can swim and fish in the river. There are also a swimming pool, ball fields, and picnic and cookout facilities.

LAKE GEORGETOWN
From Georgetown, take FM 2338 west about 4 miles to Cedar Breaks Rd., then go south (left) to lake headquarters and Cedar Breaks Park • 863-3016 • Open daily • Fee • W variable
Lake Georgetown is formed by an Army Corps of Engineers dam on the North Fork of the San Gabriel River. Overlook is at the dam on the eastern end, off FM 2338. Three parks (Cedar Breaks, Jim Hogg, Russell) have facilities for boating, fishing, swimming, hiking, picnicking, primitive camping, and RV camping. Two hiking trails run along the lake's north and south shores. The northside trail is about 5 miles long; the southside trail is about 11 miles long.

ANNUAL EVENT

LATE MAY–EARLY JUNE • Williamson County Sheriff's Posse Rodeo • 930-3179 • Rodeo Arena in San Gabriel Park
Admission • W
Parade, dance, and several days of rodeo events.

Leave Georgetown on SH 29 east toward Taylor. You are entering the Blackland Prairies of Central Texas, some of the richest farmland found anywhere on earth. Fields of cotton are interspersed with those of milo, corn, and wheat. Except in time of drought, the pastures are usually green and the cattle fat.

Five miles east of Georgetown, you'll see a state historical marker. Near this marker, on the banks of the San Gabriel, the men of the ill-fated **Santa Fe Expedition** camped their first night out.

Aware of the heavy trade at Santa Fe, Texas President Mirabeau Lamar had determined to get a piece of the action. Texas needed trade, and it claimed jurisdiction over the Santa Fe area on the basis of an act of Congress in 1836. So Lamar determined to send an armed expedition north to establish a trade route from Texas to Santa Fe and to establish control of the New Mexico settlements. A call for volunteers was issued, and merchants were promised transportation and protection of their goods. The call was answered by 321 men and $200,000 worth of merchandise. Organized into five companies of infantry and one of artillery, the men loaded up their 21 ox wagons on June 19, 1841, at a spot just east of present-day Round Rock. Their first day's journey along the old Double File Trail took them all of ten miles, to this spot on the San Gabriel River.

The next day, the expedition resumed its journey north. The first few weeks traveling through Central Texas were pleasant ones, filled with hunting and leisurely hours spent fishing. But things changed as they crossed the high arid plains. Losing their way, harassed by Indians, hampered by insufficient provisions and water, the expedition reached Santa Fe only to be met by Mexican troops and convinced by a traitor in their midst to surrender. Exhausted and disheartened, the Texans surrendered without firing a shot. They were then marched to Mexico City and imprisoned; the survivors were released in April of 1842. Although the Santa Fe Expedition was an immediate failure, it stimulated an interest in Texas within both the U.S. and Mexico and formed a basis for Texas' claim to western territory.

After the marker you cross the gravel-bottomed San Gabriel River. There is a low-water bridge just downstream that offers a nice view of the river; it's accessible by turning right on a little loop either just before crossing the river or after crossing. Continue east on SH 29 until you approach the intersection with FM 1660 and Jonah. A few hundred feet before you come to the intersection, a little unsigned paved lane runs off to the right from SH 29 to enter "downtown"

Jonah. This 1-lane path is a patch of old SH 29, from the 1920s. Take the old road, or go to the intersection with FM 1660, turn right, and then turn left a block later. If you cross the San Gabriel River, you've gone too far.

JONAH

Williamson County • 60 • About 8.5 miles from Georgetown

When James Warnock and Joe Mileham built a gristmill on the San Gabriel in 1857, a community gradually developed around it. Mill and community were then called Eureka Mills. About 1880, optimistic Eurekans applied for a post office with the pretty name Water Valley. It didn't float with the Post Office. They applied again with the name Parks, which the Post Office also brushed off.

Community members gathered, for the third time, to pick a name. One of the most exasperated attendees remarked that, as far as picking a name acceptable to the post office was concerned, their hamlet's plight was akin to that of Jonah in the whale. "So why not try Jonah," someone suggested. They did, and postal authorities approved.

Jonah grew up into a prosperous little cotton town with several doctors, drug, grocery, and general merchandise stores. Nearby Willow Hole on the San Gabriel was a popular recreation spot.

But starting in 1921 with the great Williamson County flood, Jonah again entered the whale, so to speak. The demise of tenant farming and King Cotton added to the town's decline. The countryside depopulated. SH 29 bypassed Jonah to the north. A fire several decades ago destroyed most of by-then deserted downtown Jonah.

Three old closed store buildings and the now-closed **Jonah Co-op Gin** are all that remains of downtown Jonah.

Turn left at the T intersection in front of the old cotton gin, following the convoluted path of the old highway. Immediately you cross a little concrete and angle-iron bridge dating from the 1920s, and then you immediately turn right again. In a few hundred feet you rejoin SH 29, heading east toward Circleville. Continue east on SH 29 until it dead-ends into SH 95. Turn right on SH 95.

CIRCLEVILLE

Williamson County • 42 • About 7.5 miles from Jonah

The SH 95 bridge over the San Gabriel started life hundreds of years ago as a favored river crossing of Spanish expeditions. David

McFadin settled nearby in 1846, but the village proper only dates to 1853, when the three Eubank brothers built their separate homes in a semicircle on the south bank of the river, hence the name Circle Ville. The town became an industrial center early on, with gins, tin and pewter shops, and a syrup mill. During the Civil War the Confederacy built a factory to manufacture cotton cards—stiff brushes that made fluffy cotton into firm smooth battings to be spun into cotton or thread, quilted, or made into mattresses. The Union blockade made such industrialization necessary, since Texans could no longer easily trade their raw cotton for finished cloth.

Circleville began to decline with the development of Taylor in the 1880s and today is little more than a string of beer joints along the highway, and stores that serve Lake Granger traffic.

Continue south on SH 95 to Taylor (SH 95 becomes Main St. in Taylor).

TAYLOR

Williamson County • 11,971 • (512) • About 5 miles from Circleville

Taylor owes its existence to the railroad. In 1876, when the International and Great Northern (I&GN) railroad was pushing its way south toward Austin, only a few scattered settlers lived on the prairies near the future site of Taylor. The Palestine-based Texas Land Company bought 500 acres from an I&GN official and proceeded to plat a 60-block townsite. A big lot sale was held in June 1876, even though the tracks of the new rail line were still a month away. But hopes were high for the new town, situated as it was on one of the great feeder branches of the Chisholm Trail and in the middle of one of the state's richest agricultural regions.

Taylor grew rapidly from the start, but life was not easy. Cattle drives passed right up Main St. through the middle of town, and water was available only from springs a couple of miles away. Those who made the trip peddled door to door dispensing the water from wagons. The inadequacy of this system was reflected during the fires of 1878 and 1879: the 1879 fire destroyed 29 buildings, leaving 16 families homeless and 34 businessmen unemployed. The town began to rebuild immediately, however, with brick and stone buildings replacing the earlier wooden ones.

First known as Taylorsville, the town was incorporated in 1882 as Taylor. That same year Taylor drilled a well and built its first water system.

Taylor's economy received a boost when the Missouri-Kansas-Texas railroad came to town in 1882. By 1890, the regional I&GN repair shops were located here and a golden era was dawning. Dr. A. V. Doak established a mule-drawn trolley system to serve the townspeople and also built a pavilion with a seating capacity of 1,000. Dances, plays, concerts, religious revivals, skating parties, even bicycle races and baseball games were held under its broad roof. By 1900 Taylor was the largest inland cotton market in the world. Taylor's principal streets were first paved then, too—not with gold, or even with brick, but with brick-sized wooden blocks. The parquetry has since been covered by asphalt, but if you look carefully around the alley entrances to the 200 and 300 blocks of Main St., you may be able to see a few of these wooden "bricks" peeking out between patches of asphalt.

The level prairie of gummy Bell clay—rich, black, and deep—which surrounds Taylor for miles and miles has long been the best cotton land in the world. Despite cotton's decline, Taylor continued to grow and today is home to some 10,000 people and two dozen industrial firms. Over the years Taylor has also produced several people of note, including Dan Moody, the youngest person ever elected governor of Texas. Moody was elected in 1927 at the age of 34.

Taylor was also the hometown of Elmer "Pet" Brown, the 1914 middleweight wrestling champion of the world. Brown won his title in the Taylor City Hall auditorium, where he defeated Mike Yokel of Salt Lake City.

Will Pickett, "The Dusky Demon," inventor of the art of rodeo bulldogging, could also claim Taylor as his hometown. Pickett worked ranches around Taylor as a young man and it was here that he perfected his bulldogging technique, displaying it for the first time at the Taylor Rodeo. At the turn of the century, the *Houston Post* classed Pickett as one of the "best and toughest of the new breed of folk heroes that dominated the American scene after the Civil War." The story then went on to describe Pickett's unique style, saying he would "leap from his horse onto a galloping steer, grab a horn in each hand and twist until the animal's nose came up. Then, like a bulldog, Pickett would grab the steer's tender upper lip in his teeth, let go of the horns and flap to one side, toppling the steer to the earth. . . . Pickett was as fearless as any cowboy who ever rode the range."

Pickett toured all over the country and the world with wild west shows, thrilling the crowd with his daring skills—most of the time, that is. Some promoters, speculating that Pickett's bulldogging stunt would make a Mexican bullfight look tame by comparison, arranged a bullfight and bulldogging contest at a big arena in Mexico City. A crowd of 25,000 watched Pickett cling to a fierce Mexican bull for 38 minutes before coming out the winner. But instead of applauding his feat, the Mexicans booed Pickett and showered him with bottles and cans. They regarded his art as "beastly primitive." Ironically, at the age of 71, Pickett was trampled to death by a herd of horses, his favorite animals, on a ranch in Oklahoma.

Elmore Torn, tireless promoter of the black-eyed pea and uncle of actor Rip Torn, also hailed from Taylor.

Two phenomena of small-town Texas life in the 1990s are the sale and usage of crack cocaine, and more crime, including murder. In Taylor, for instance, a 6-block area on the south side of town called "the Line" became an open-air drug bazaar. Concerned Taylor citizens founded Turn Around Taylor, a grassroots organization that gained statewide recognition in 1994 when it got the National Guard to bulldoze a number of known crack houses and buildings where drug-trafficking occurred. The demolitions didn't end crime in the area, but did make the drug dealing less open, and they served as an inspiration for other Texas cities and towns concerned about drugs and crime.

To reach the old Moody home, turn right on 9th and proceed 1 block west of Main/SH 95.

MOODY HOME
114 W. 9th at Talbot • 352-7242 • Open Sunday • Free
W variable

Once the residence of Dan Moody, governor of Texas 1927–1931, this two-story frame house (built 1887) with period furnishings is now a museum. Youngest man ever to be elected governor of Texas, Dan Moody was born in this house on June 1, 1893. As Texas' youngest ever attorney general (1925–1927), Moody established himself as a crusader against the Ku Klux Klan and government corruption. As governor Moody continued his program of governmental reform, reorganizing the state prison and highway systems and creating the office of state auditor.

He retired to private law practice at the end of his second term, declining to run for a third term in accordance with contemporary tradition. He emerged from political retirement in 1941 to run for the U.S. Senate, only to finish third against former governors W. Lee O'Daniel and James Allred. It was his only political defeat. He did remain active in party politics. Moody died at Austin in 1966 and was buried in the state cemetery there.

Taylor today has a variety of attractions. Here's how to see them.

From the Moody home, proceed south on Talbot.

ODD FELLOWS LODGE
120 W. 4th at Talbot

Many of Taylor's old brick business buildings still exist essentially unaltered, and this building is one of them. Built as the Odd Fellows Lodge in 1907, the two-story textured brick building features a pair of cast-metal Queen Anne porticos and elaborate diamond-pattern leaded windows, along with a castellated roof-line and Alamo arch, which contains the date of erection—1907—and the inscription "IOOF" and the Odd Fellows' distinctive logo of three interlocked rings.

Proceed 2 more blocks to 2nd.

LOUIE MUELLER'S BARBEQUE
206 W. 2nd • 352-6206 • Open Monday through Friday
8:30–6:30, Saturday 8:30–5:00, closed Sunday • $ • No Cr. • W

When you reach 2nd, turn your head right and you'll catch sight of one of Central Texas' landmark barbecue joints, Louie Mueller's. Master barbecuer Fred Fontaine presides over the pit here and turns out an excellently flavored lean and tender brisket, a good-tasting though slightly greasy sausage, and a good lean flavorful steak. His homemade sauce is heavily laden with onion and is one of the tastiest to be found anywhere. The restaurant serves only barbecue, although it is open during breakfast hours. If you feel like you're inside a gym that just happens to sell barbecue, well, you're right. The Taylor High basketball team played here for years before Mueller took it over. Beer.

THOMPSON BUILDING
201 W. 2nd • Currently houses Taylor Paint and Hardware

Directly across 2nd from Louie Mueller's is the Thompson building. A long, two-story, simply built structure of tan brick, the Thompson Building is lifted from anonymity by its majestic cast-metal cornice, which features six turrets of varying heights, and cast-metal second-story-window architraves painted a bright, contrasting white.

TAYLOR BEDDING COMPANY
601 W. 2nd • 352-6344

Some of the cotton produced in Taylor went to the Taylor Bedding Company, which began business in 1903. Founder D. H. Forwood's dream was to use the area's cotton locally rather than shipping it away, so he started making and selling cotton mattresses. The business grew over the years, and now the makers of the Morning Glory mattress also manufacture furniture, mattress pads, and quilt batting.

Texas' largest bedding manufacturer during the 1930s and 1940s, Taylor Bedding made 90 percent of the U.S. Armed Forces' mattresses during World War II. The plant ran 24 hours a day.

TAYLOR MEAT COMPANY
2211 W. 2nd (US 79, at the Loop • 365-6358 • Open Monday through Saturday • W

Taylor has a healthy Czech population, and Taylor Meat Company makes a wide range of the smoked meats and sausages that the Czech Belt of Central Texas is famous for. Choose from pork and beef/pork links, liver sausage, ring bologna, wieners, head cheese, jerky, beef and cervelat "sticks," country-style bacon, hand-rubbed, hickory-smoked hams, and even chorizo.

TAYLOR NATIONAL BANK
2nd and Main

Located at the northeast corner of 2nd and Main is the old Taylor National Bank building, one of the houses that cotton built. The millions of dollars that cotton injected into the Taylor economy are reflected in the three-story sandstone and brick building's stained glass windows, polished marble columns, and inlaid tile entryway.

The bank building is just one of at least half a dozen notable commercial buildings clustered around this intersection which feature stained glass windows and fine brick and file work, most of which is obscured by years of dirt and drab paint. Downtown Taylor has not yet undergone a wholesale restoration like downtown Georgetown or Fredericksburg, although there are many buildings worth the effort. Most of Taylor's growth effort seems to be focused—regrettably— on strip development along SH 95 on the north side of town.

TAYLOR MOTOR CO.
E. 2nd at Porter

Neon, art moderne, and old car fans . . . don't pass up Taylor Motor Co. Cars aren't the attraction here, but rather the building itself. The white stuccoed wraparound art moderne building is topped by its original revolving, round Buick/Chevrolet neon sign.

TAYLOR CAFE
101 N. Main, under the railroad bridge • 352-8475
Monday through Saturday 7-11, Sunday 11-11 • $ • No Cr. • W

Practically everybody has heard of Louie Mueller's; after all, his barbecue has been featured in *Texas Monthly*. But one place you probably haven't heard of before is the Taylor Cafe, and owner Vencil Mares serves up the best ribs in town here, as well as some tasty lean sausage (from Taylor Meat Company), oak-smoked beef, stew, and plate lunches. Ribs are not served every day, so call ahead. The jukebox here has a good blend of country-and-western, polka, and Mexican selections. Beer.

ANNUAL EVENTS

MARCH • Taylor Rattlesnake Sacking Championship
Murphy Park, on Lake Dr. 3 blocks west of SH 95
Early March • Admission • W variable

Teams race the clock to see who can sack a set number of snakes in the shortest time; one person holds the sack, the other picks up the snakes barehanded. A 60-second penalty is added for each bite. Professional snake handlers perform every hour, and additional prizes are given for the persons bringing in the biggest, longest, and most snakes. Concessions include fried rattlesnake meat, naturally. For more information, call the Taylor Chamber of Commerce at 352-6364, or write them at P.O. Box 231, Taylor 76574.

AUGUST • Taylor International Barbeque Cook-off and Rodeo
Murphy Park, on Lake Dr. 3 blocks west of SH 95
Third weekend in August • Admission • W variable

It's appropriate for a place known as the Barbeque Capital of the World to host the International Championship Barbeque Cook-off. Cooking categories include beef, poultry, sheep, goat, wild game, sausage, seafood, and sauce, in adult and junior categories. A variety of other activities accompanies the cook-off, including a 10,000-meter run and a dance. The rodeo is one of the toughest on the circuit and features a full complement of events. For more information,

call the Taylor Chamber of Commerce at 352-6364, or write them at
P.O. Box 231, Taylor 76574.

*To resume the trip, retrace your route from Taylor back up SH 95 to
Circleville and the San Gabriel River crossing.*

Barely a mile east of the SH 95 bridge across the San Gabriel is
Comanche Peak, a high bluff on the south bank of the river where
Indians were said to run buffalo over the edge, a hunting technique
frowned upon by current-day Parks and Wildlife Department game
wardens.

*Continue north on SH 95 toward Granger. Turn left on Cty. Rd. 336,
about 3 miles north of the San Gabriel River bridge. A highway sign
directing you to Willis Creek Park and a big red prefab building with
a white roof located on your right serve as a tip-off.*

DARE BUZZARD

Williamson County • About 10 miles from Taylor
One of Williamson County's more uniquely named ghost towns,
Dare Buzzard, also known as Dar' Buzzard, lies along Cty. Rd. 336
along **Opossum Creek,** the first little stream you cross once you are
on this road. It was a well-known village by 1856, when the *Georgetown Independent* urged a new mail route between Georgetown and
Cameron via Dare Buzzard and other hamlets. There are a couple of
stories as to how Dare Buzzard received its name. According to one
story, a half-witted boy saw a buzzard flying overhead and pointed
upward saying "Dar' buzzard" ("There's a buzzard"). Others say the
name was for a tavern so rough that even buzzards did not dare stay
there. Take your choice.

Nothing remains of Dare Buzzard today save an old house or two
tucked away and rotting in nearby thickets.

*Less than a mile past old Dare Buzzard, Cty. Rd. 336 dead-ends into
FM 971. Turn right on FM 971 to enter Granger.*

GRANGER

**Williamson County • 1,294 • (512) • About 11 miles from
Taylor**

Folks first came to this area in the 1850s, attracted by cheap and fertile farmland, but it took the Missouri-Kansas-Texas (MKT) railroad to actually see a town organized. When the "Katy" came through in 1882, Captain A. S. Fisher and W. C. Belcher laid out some of their land as a town, along the tracks and "around the station of Granger." By 1884, a number of town lots had been sold here, and the nearby settlements at Macedonia and Dare Buzzard began to shrivel. Although the place was listed on some maps as Pollack, there is no evidence the village was ever called that by its inhabitants. But where the name Granger came from is the subject of minor controversy. Some say the place was named to honor Civil War veteran John R. Granger. Others say it was named for the Grange, a popular nationwide farmers organization of the time.

By the 1880s and especially the 1890s, the rich land had attracted many European immigrants, especially Germans and Czechoslovakians, who became thrifty, industrious farmers. Granger was incorporated by 1891, and had a bank by 1894 and a newspaper by 1897. By 1893 Granger had its second rail line, the 15.5-mile Georgetown and Granger railroad. Promoted by Captain Emzy Taylor of Georgetown, this line was to connect with other lines that crisscrossed the state. Emzy's prominent merchant father Josiah had built the county's first two-story house in Georgetown. Josiah opened a bank in 1882 in Georgetown, helped organize both the Georgetown-Round Rock and the Georgetown-Granger railroad lines, and started the town's water works. Financial problems resulted from expansion attempts, however, and Taylor committed suicide in Georgetown in 1895. The MKT finally bought the line and finished the tracks from Granger to Austin via Georgetown in 1904.

Granger today is a farm town, with a citizenry that is still of predominantly Czech extraction. It has declined from its glory days as a regional trade center, but nearby **Lake Granger** has helped stem the decline. The Blackland Co-op Gin is one of the county's few active cotton gins.

When FM 971 runs into SH 95, turn left, as per the signs. After 2 blocks, 971 veers off to the right. Turn left here onto W. Davilla. West of SH 95, Davilla's asphalt turns to red brick. You don't find too many brick streets left in Texas, and the two western blocks of Davilla are in great shape.

In the 1980s, Granger's old turn-of-the-century railroad depot was removed from its trackside location to the 100 block of W. Davilla, behind a handsome old two-story brick commercial building with bi-chrome brick arches and stained-glass second-story windows. Locals hope to restore the depot and turn it into a museum someday.

Retrace your path east across SH 95 onto E. Davilla. E. Davilla doubles as FM 971 as FM 971 leaves SH 95 and resumes its solo path eastward.

NASINEC
206 E. Davilla • 859-2238 • Thursday through Saturday 9 to noon • W

Granger is the home of *Nasinec,* America's last all-Czech-language newspaper. The paper moved here from Taylor in 1937, and its name roughly translates into English as "Our People." When you enter the *Nasinec* offices, you step into the past. Most of the typesetting is done on pre-World War I black Linotype machines. Tabloid printing is done on a 1940s Kelly B autofeed press, but the full-size printing is done on a massive handfed Babcock Optimus press. *Nasinec* publisher Joe Vrabel can even show you an 1895–1896 Babcock catalogue listing this machine and its specifications. An antique wooden phone booth is also located inside the *Nasinec* offices. Subscriptions to this paper come in from all over the world. The paper folded briefly in the fall of 1981, but resumed publication only two weeks later under longtime typesetter Vrabel's management. "The subscribers wouldn't let us quit," he said. The paper's front window greeting *Vitame Vas*—"We welcome you"—has been unofficially adopted by the town of Granger as its motto.

Photos from the heydays of Granger and *Nasinec* hang on the wall out front. Vrabel also sells poppyseed grinders, poppy seeds, and other imported eastern European spices, as well as a variety of Czech language books and Czech-English dictionaries. If you are a Spades player, Vrabel has the cards for a Czech version of the game called Tarok.

GRANGER CITY HALL
215 E. Davilla

Formerly the Granger bank, the building housing the city hall is two-story brick, with an arched corner entrance and topped by a shiny white corner cupola that is reminiscent of one of the Kremlin's onion-shaped domes.

Davilla used to be lined with substantial and sometimes ornate brick buildings, but as the town declined many of them were vacated and torn down. One such victim was the Granger Opera House, which stood as a local landmark from 1905 until the mid-1970s. It was similar in appearance to the present Granger City Hall.

SAINTS CYRIL AND METHODIUS CATHOLIC CHURCH
W. Davilla at Brazos
Cyril and Methodius are two of the most popular saints in Czech Catholicism. These two brother missionaries came to Bohemia and Moravia from Constantinople spreading the Christian gospel. Many Czechs embraced the faith, and soon young Czech priests conducted services in the native tongue. Cyril and Methodius became known as the Apostles of the Slavonians. After several centuries under the Eastern (Greek Orthodox) branch of Christianity, Bohemia passed to the control of the Western, Roman Catholic branch, through the efforts of German missionaries sent to Bohemia by Rome. Masses were now conducted in Latin rather than in Czech.

This gothic-cathedral-style brick church dates to 1916.

GRANGER BRETHREN CHURCH
W. Broadway at Brazos
Not all the Czechs who settled Texas were Catholic. One block north of—and in stark contrast to—the Catholic Church, stands the Granger Brethren Church. The Brethren are a Protestant denomination that trace their origins to Moravia (in the Czech Republic today) and early Catholic Church reformer Jan Hus, who ultimately burned at the stake in 1415 for his efforts. This simple frame whitewashed church is very much in keeping with its members' beliefs about mankind's relationship with God.

AREA PARKS

LAKE GRANGER
FM 971, about 8 miles east of Granger • 859-2668
Open daily • Free • W variable
This lake was created by damming up the San Gabriel River, for flood control and water conservation purposes. It opened for fishing in 1981, having been well stocked with channel catfish and largemouth bass. There are 36 miles of shoreline. Friendship, Fox, Taylor, and Willis parks provide campsites, hookups (fee charged), picnic

sites, swimming areas, boat ramps, and group shelters. Four wildlife areas also surround the lake.

From Granger, head north on SH 95 to Bartlett.

BARTLETT

Williamson and Bell counties • 1,509 • (512) • About 5.5 miles from Granger

Despite farming's still-prominent contribution to the area economy, Bartlett continues to recede from the prosperity of its heyday. Its many charming, essentially unaltered brick downtown buildings still stand.

Settlers came here in the 1850s, but there was no identifiable town until 1882. John Bartlett, a postwar arrival, caught wind of the MKT's plans to build a railway through the area, and when the Katy surveyors came through laying out the right-of-way, Bartlett and J. E. Pietzsch donated land for the station and platted a townsite. Lot sales began in late 1881 and by the time the MKT rails reached here in the summer of 1882, Bartlett's town was already a bustling village with several business establishments. John Bartlett and A. P. Clark erected the town's first building and engaged in the general mercantile business. Bartlett got its post office that fall, a newspaper in 1886, and a bank, organized by John Bartlett, in 1887. The town was incorporated in 1890.

Agricultural shipments out of Bartlett were so great that the big 1890s fire that destroyed Bartlett's early business district was looked upon as a blessing in disguise, for it brought about the construction of a more substantial brick business district.

The enormous cotton and foodstuff shipments out of Williamson County during these halcyon years led to the construction of the county's last railway, the Bartlett-Florence railway, chartered in 1909. Also known as the Dinky, the Bullfrog Line, and the Four Gospels Line, the railroad was chartered by noncounty residents who believed the tremendous cotton traffic would make the line pay. They also thought they could soon sell the line to one of the county's existing railroads.

Underfinanced, the Dinky ran into trouble from the beginning. The builders got only 11 of the 23 miles of rails laid before money ran out. After refinancing, the rails finally reached the western terminus at Florence in 1912. The Bartlett depot for the Bartlett-Florence was a leased, renovated house.

From SH 95, turn left onto FM 487, Bartlett's chief east-west axis, known in town as Clark St. The two downtown blocks of Clark, between SH 95 and the railroad tracks, are still brick-paved, as is Evie St. for a half-block on either side of Clark.

On March 9, 1936, the Bartlett Electric Co-op became the first electrical co-op in the U.S. to provide electric power to its member customers. The town of Bartlett had enjoyed regular electric service since 1905; but in 1936 most farmers around Bartlett still milked their cows by hand, by the light of a kerosene lamp. They pumped their water, or the Aeromotor windmill did. Wives cooked on wood-burning stoves and scrubbed the laundry on a washboard. There was no radio, and any electrical power a rural family enjoyed came from a noisy, smelly gasoline-engine-driven generator.

President Franklin Roosevelt had signed an Executive Order creating the Rural Electrification Administration in May 1935, so that rural and small-town America might receive dependable, low-cost electrical power. By providing low-cost federal loans for power line construction to the co-ops, the REA eventually brought electric power to 90% of U.S. farmlands and small communities. Inspired by FDR's creation, Bartlett mayor Randy Miller went to Washington to lobby the up-and-coming young Congressman Sam Rayburn to sponsor the legislation to fund the REA.

Later that year, the REA lent $33,000 to Bartlett Community Light and Power, which later became the Bartlett Electric Co-op. The BCL&P built a 59-mile powerline to serve Bartlett-area farmers. Power was supplied by Bartlett's municipal light plant, which had been built in 1934. The first operative section of the line served 110 homes.

Horace Keith, one of the co-op's original employees, recalled that the postholes for those first powerlines were dug by hand, and that it took eight men to set each 35-foot pole into place. They were paid 75¢ an hour. Many of those first poles are still standing in and around Bartlett. Rayburn's REA funding bill finally became law two months after the Bartlett Co-op energized its first line, the first of its kind in the country. Today the Bartlett Co-op serves nearly 5,000 customers with lines that spread over 1,500 miles.

Texas is today the leading electric co-op state by far—87 systems provide service to 1.8 million people using over 250,000 miles of line.

But electrification was not enough to check the steady surge of urbanization, and commercial Bartlett declined. Until recently much of downtown Bartlett stood vacant, its buildings not having met the wholesale demolition which has flattened most of Granger's old business district. Clark's two downtown blocks comprise one of the nicest, intact, late-Victorian, brick, small-town business districts left in central Texas. Like Smithville's business district, none of Bartlett's buildings are individually distinguished, but collectively they make a pleasingly picturesque whole, especially complemented by the brick street.

Bartlett's business district straddles the Bell-Williamson County line. The businesses on the north side of Clark are in Bell County, those on the south side are in Williamson.

A fair number of antique shops line downtown Clark St. now, and thanks to a recent movie filmed here, many of the old buildings have been spruced up. Several of the old buildings' alley walls sport old-style (but not original) painted advertisements for Coca-Cola, Wrigley's Gum, and such.

BARTLETT NATIONAL BANK
Clark and Evie, one block west of SH 95

Essentially a Greek Revival building, the defunct bank's most out-standing features are its carved, wings-outstretched eagles, which line the building's streetside walls, flanked on either side by brickwork Ionic columns. The bank was surely the pride of the town when built.

Continue west on Clark/FM 487. One block west of the railroad tracks, on your left, is the Bartlett Area Museum.

BARTLETT AREA MUSEUM
100 block W. Clark at Emma, across from the police station • W

This red brick building houses the old municipal power plant built in 1934, which supplied power to that historic first REA line. The museum is inside the turbine room, the main exhibit being the power plant itself. Several other display cases hold local memorabilia. The museum is only open on special occasions, but you can get a good look at the old equipment through the plate-glass front door.

Three blocks west of the railroad tracks and one block north of Clark is the old Bartlett School.

BARTLETT PUBLIC SCHOOL
Linderman and Bell • Closed to the public

Built in Bartlett's early twentieth century heyday, this imposing castellated two-story Gothic schoolhouse is another good example of just how prosperous Bartlett was. The three-story hexagonal castellated turret located in the notch of the V-shaped school is the building's focal point. This is appropriate since the main entryway is through the bottom level of the turret. From the school, double back to FM 487.

Pietzch Street runs parallel to Clark, one block south. The five blocks of Pietzch between Emma and Cottrell hold a number of large old turn-of-the-century houses.

Proceeding out of town on FM 487 you pass the squat, Gothic-style Bartlett Methodist Church as well as several good examples of circa 1900 farmhouses. FM 487 follows roughly the route of the Bartlett-Florence railway.

Small as it was, the Dinky still exerted great influence on the lives of the people and towns located along its path. It created new towns like Schwertner and Jarrell; it made a ghost town out of once-prosperous Corn Hill. Schwertner is the first town west of Bartlett on FM 487.

SCHWERTNER

Williamson County • 150 • About 5.5 miles from Bartlett
Schwertner was the Dinky's first depot west of Bartlett, a community settled in 1877 by Bernard Schwertner and his three boys Frank, Edward, and Adolph. These Austrian immigrants farmed and ranched a huge tract of land stretching from Jarrell to Bartlett. The Schwertner family still owns much of this land, as is evidenced by all the ranch signs.

Adolph Schwertner built a gin here in 1903. When he heard of the projected railroad in 1909, Schwertner donated land for a townsite. A depot, general store, dry goods store, hardware store, bank, meat market, blacksmith shop, and post office sprang up in short order. A doctor, saloon, lumberyard, and boarding house were soon added. Schwertner even had its own brass band, as well as a second cotton gin.

Today downtown Schwertner consists of one live tavern and several dead business houses, and the Schwertner State Bank.

ANNUAL EVENT

JUNE • Schwertner Festival • Downtown • Free
First Sunday in June • W
"The little town with a big heart" celebrates life once a year with this big blowout. Athletes can choose between the Farmers Five-

Miler Footrace and the kolache-eating contest. Arts and crafts, pony rides, auctions, games, and a street dance complete the schedule of events, fueled by lots of beer and downhome barbecue with all the trimmings.

A few yards west of "downtown" Schwertner, look to your left (to the south) and you can see a section of the Dinky's roadbed.

About three miles past Schwertner, on FM 487, atop the high ridge to your left overlooking **Donahoe Creek,** you'll see the old **Primrose School,** which once housed 96 pupils. The surrounding neighborhood was known as Lickskillet.

Primrose/Lickskillet was a stone's throw from St. Matthew, the first of the "Four Gospel" flag stations on the Bartlett-Florence rail. These four stations between Bartlett and Florence were listed in official railroad records as Caffrey, John Camp, Atkinson, and Armstrong, but a religious lady gave the stops the names of the four respective New Testament gospels—St. Matthew, St. Mark, St. Luke, and St. John. Each flag station had a roof and benches—no walls—and a picture frame, which contained the station's gospel name and appropriate verses from that gospel, hung from the rafters.

In spite of such divine guidance, the Bartlett-Florence Railway Company was financially plagued. It changed hands a number of times, finally becoming the Bartlett and Western railway. The Bartlett and Western owned two locomotives, ten freight cars, and two passenger cars, but as time passed, the coal-burning locomotives were replaced with gasoline motors. The passenger cars were designed like trolleys and could be caught almost anywhere along the line. Engineers outfitted a Fordson tractor with flanged wheels, allowing this "locomotive" to haul flatcars loaded with as many as 150 quarter-ton bales of cotton at one time. With the acquisition of the mail contract for northern Williamson County, the Bartlett and Western bought several Ford trucks, which were outfitted with railroad wheels and then used to haul the mail up and down the line. Small wonder that many folks along the line called it the Dinky. Its Bullfrog Line appellation was also well deserved; its cars were always jumping the tracks.

Jarrell in four miles, our next big stop on the Dinky line.

JARRELL

Williamson County • 410 • (512) • About 7 miles from Schwertner

Jarrell is Williamson County's youngest town, and it owes its existence to the Bartlett and Western railroad. Jarrell's birth brought the demise of the once thriving village and stage stop of Corn Hill, so named in 1855 because of the fine corn crops the area produced. Corn Hill had a population of 500 and was home to a variety of businesses by 1910. When the Dinky railroad came along, however, instead of coming through Corn Hill, the tracks were laid a little over a mile to the north.

Real estate promoters O. D. Jarrell of Temple and E. C. Haeber of Bartlett purchased land along the railroad's right-of-way, platted a town, and held a sale of lots in December 1909. The new townsite was located at the junction of the old stagecoach road (now I-35) and the new railroad. A saloon and two small stores were built almost immediately, but the nascent town lapsed into a coma when construction of the rails west from Bartlett bogged down.

But by the spring of 1911, the railroad had new owners and new capital, and a second lot sale was held in Jarrell. Residences were built, a bank and churches organized, and the exodus from Corn Hill commenced. A man named Jim Hawkins slowly moved Corn Hill north to the new town, a process that literally took years, although the demise of Corn Hill was further hastened when local farmer S. A. Keeling bought a Case steam engine, which could move buildings in one-third the time required by mule power. By 1916, nearly everyone had left Corn Hill for Jarrell. Today only a building that used to function as a hotel stands at Corn Hill.

Jarrell's population has always been predominantly Czech and German hard-working, conservative farmers and ranchers.

Jarrell happens to be located on the highest point of land along the highway between Oklahoma City and San Antonio, and it seems that just a few feet in elevation can make quite a difference in the weather. Years ago a Georgetown postmaster used to win a regular supply of pocket money off this fact. During the norther season, he would take folks the 13 miles up to Jarrell on the bet that it would have snow and ice, while Georgetown was warm and merely wet. He won so many times that he finally ran out of takers.

These days I-35 is Jarrell's chief industry, as evidenced by the string of roadside gas stations and package stores.

Cross under the interstate on FM 487 and follow its brief coupling with the southbound I-35 frontage road. Continue on 487 as it veers west from the interstate and Jarrell toward Florence.

FM 487 continues to follow the route of the Bartlett and Western in a general way, and occasionally you will catch a glimpse of its roadbed between Jarrell and Florence, where the last three Gospel stops were located. The tracks west of Jarrell were on a difficult grade, so when heavy loads were pulled the crew carried sand along, sprinkling it on the tracks to provide enough traction for the wheels to pull upgrade or to better control them on the downgrade.

After its initial financial problems, the railroad was acquired by career railroad man Thomas Cronin, who hailed from Palestine, Texas. Although Cronin never managed to transform the Dinky into anything more than just what its nickname implied, he at least made it a paying proposition until 1926. In that year Cronin died and Texas experienced a sharp decline in both cotton production and cotton prices. The price the Bartlett and Western received for hauling a bale of cotton fell from $1.59 a bale to 45¢. This was just a harbinger of the hard times to come. Cronin's daughter Marie came back from Paris, to take over the railroad, giving up her career as an internationally known artist to do so. Her French styles and makeup were quite a shock to the stolid inhabitants of Williamson County, but she persevered here for a decade, struggling to keep her father's railroad alive. Finally she bowed to the inevitable and closed the line in 1935. The rails and ties were removed soon thereafter. Some say the rails were sold to Japan, where they were melted down and used against us in World War II; others say that Herman Brown of Brown and Root, Inc. bought them. Neither story has been corroborated. Marie Cronin had planned to return to Paris and her career as an artist, but her eyesight was failing and she elected to remain at the family home in Bartlett, where she died in 1951. You can see an example of her work in the pink granite state capitol building in Austin: a portrait of Johanna Troutman, the "Betsy Ross of Texas."

PEYTON

Williamson County • About 6 miles from Jarrell

Six miles out of Jarrell, FM 487 runs close by Salado Creek, through the ghost town of Peyton. This hamlet was named for early settlers, the W. R. Peyton family. A store and post office were located here on the banks of the creek, and nearby was a half-mile straightaway track where local horse raiser Jay Owens trained his horses and where many an Owens horse raced other local equine speedsters. William Wilson operated the store, and one of his sons, James "Pinky" Wilson, wrote the lyrics to the "Aggie War Hymn" while in the trenches along the Rhine River at Coblenz in 1918. Persistent flooding caused the buildings along the creek to be moved or abandoned; nothing of Peyton is left here today but memories and a nice view of the Salado Creek. *Salado* is Spanish for "salty," which this creek is certainly not. Local plant life suggests that its name was accidentally interchanged with that of the Lampasas River; the Lampasas is salty, but its name means "water plant."

Gold was discovered just a few miles north of here in 1883, samples of which, in some instances, were assayed for as high as $2,500 a ton in gold. It was carried in a formation of decomposed limestone stained with oxide of iron. There was a great flurry of interest, which soon subsided after the field failed to show commercial possibility and evidence of trickery began to surface.

FLORENCE

Williamson County • 921 • About 13 miles from Jarrell
Florence was settled in the late 1840s and early 1850s. It was originally called Brooksville. Some say early settler Enoch D. John named the hamlet after his hometown, Brooksville, Indiana. John built one of the area's first flour mills here. Others say that a man from Bastrop named Brooks set up a store here in 1853 and that the named derived accordingly. Indian attacks were still common in the early 1850s, and preachers usually kept a loaded gun close to the pulpit during Sunday services. When the post office was established in 1857 Brooksville became Florence, named for Brook's daughter Florence or for Florence, Alabama, hometown of the first postmaster, Colonel Fisher, a retired lawyer. Or, there's even the possibility the town was named for the daughter of Colonel King Fisher, the famous Texas pistolero.

Located on a feeder branch of the Chisholm Trail and surrounded by fertile cotton and wheat fields, Florence grew to be a prosperous little town. By the time the Bartlett-Florence Railroad tracks arrived in 1912, Florence already had a bank, creamery, and cheese factory. There was even a college, the Florence College, from 1895 to 1903.

RM 487 becomes Main in Florence.

OLD CITY LIBRARY
Corner of Main and College
Main Street Florence today is a collection of some centenarian limestone buildings and some slightly newer brick ones, many of

which have modernized facades and none of which are particularly distinguished. The most impressive of the lot is the old City Library, a two-story limestone building built as a drugstore in 1906 by J. F. Atkinson, son of Florence's first postmaster. Bigfoot Wallace used to travel down this street as a stagecoach driver on his way to Fort Gates, as Florence was on one of the early roads from Austin to Burnet and points west.

Continue on FM 487 until it dead-ends into SH 195, turn left on SH 195, then right a half-mile later on FM 970, toward Andice. FM 970 stair-steps its way west down to Andice through open high prairie.

ANDICE

Williamson County • 25 • About 7 miles from Florence

Andice was originally called Stapp after Joshua Stapp, who built a log school/church building here in 1857, where Presbyterians, Methodists, and Baptists held joint, or "union" services. The name of the settlement was later changed to Berry Creek. Two of Berry Creek's residents were the Reverend William Isaac Newton and his wife. Their son Audice was born on January 5, 1899, and soon after this blessed event, Reverend Newton applied for a post office, requesting that it be named Audice. Postal authorities misread the name and approved the name Andice that fall, with Newton as postmaster.

All that remains in Andice now are a feed and seed store and an old red brick school, which is now a community center.

When FM 970 reaches US 183, it exchanges its state farm road status for county road status, becoming Cty. Rd. 209. Half a mile later the road forks at an old-time signpost, which lists all the families living on both forks. Arrows next to each name point in the appropriate direction. Take the fork which goes straight ahead, through the fence and across the cattleguard. You are now on Cty. Rd. 210.

This road takes you through rough ranching country, past the highest peak in Williamson County, **Mt. Gabriel** (1,208 feet). Locally known as Pilot's Knob, the peak served as a landmark to traveling Indians and explorers in early Texas. You can best appreciate its size relative to the gently rolling countryside by looking back over your shoulder in another four or five miles. The country here is very rough and sparsely settled, useless for farming and only marginally useful for stock grazing.

When Cty. Rd. 210 dead-ends in the shadow of Mt. Gabriel 1.3 miles later, turn right onto Cty. Rd. 207.

If you were to turn left at Cty. Rd. 210's dead end, you would very shortly enter the **Loafers' Glory** neighborhood. Nothing is there now, but the unusual name derived from the rural Apostolic Church, which was located a mile south of San Gabriel. The name Loafers' Glory was used by people of the vicinity who were not members of the church to describe the peculiar enthusiasm of the members.

Two miles and one 90-degree turn later, you come to a one-story limestone house, with a paved county road running off to the right in front of the house. In your rearview mirror you'll see a "207E" sign marking the road from whence you came.

Turn right on this road by the house in order to reach the ghost town of Gabriel Mills.

GABRIEL MILLS

Williamson County • About 5 miles from Andice

Looking at this rough, thicketed countryside, it's hard to believe that a thriving community existed here as late as the 1920s. The only tip-off is the cemeteries that line the road. The first is the old **Mt. Horeb Church Cemetery,** which is actually a string of family plots stretching along the road for several hundred feet. The road then takes a sharp bend to the right. Shortly thereafter you see on your right another cemetery, the **Gabriel Mills Cemetery.** There is one particularly interesting stone here originally set off from the other, fenced-in markers. This rectangular limestone slab marks the final resting place of one Elizebeth Simpson, whose crudely engraved marker reads: "ELIZEBETH SIMPSON WAS BORNE APRIL The 10 1831X And DIDE SEPTEMBER the 21X 1864 And Remember As YO AR PASING BY YO MUST DY AS WELL AS I." No one knows who Elizebeth Simpson was, but judging from the isolated position of the stone and the crude lettering, Simpson was probably a slave. The stone was moved inside the fence in the late 1980s.

A hundred feet farther, you'll see a gnarled, spreading, centuries-old **live oak tree.** This is a hanging tree; from its branches were hung two horse thieves well over 100 years ago. Just goes to show all hanging trees don't wither up and die.

Continue forward (east) on Cty. Rd. 207 another mile, to the three-way intersection with Cty. Rd. 209 (unmarked). To your left are Gabriel Mill Vineyards. Turn right here, onto Cty. Rd. 209 (you cannot turn left). You are high atop the Shin Oak Ridge now, and the views to the west are great, stretching out some 20 miles. A quaint little Mexican cemetery is on your right in about a mile, and shortly after you come back to the old-time signpost and intersection with Cty. Rd. 210 (the loop you have made is a little more than 7 miles). In case you didn't notice it the first time around, take note of the old "worm" log fence, so named for the zigzag pattern in which it is constructed. From here, continue as before on Cty. Rd. 210 and Cty. Rd. 207 to the one-story limestone house mentioned.

The house was built from rock that previously had been used in the Brizendine Store here at Gabriel Mills.

Gabriel Mills was first settled in 1849 by Englishman Samuel Mather, who built a water-powered gristmill nearby on the North Fork of the San Gabriel River. Mather also did blacksmithing, and one of his early customers was the Comanche chief Yellow Wolf, who brought him some silver ore to be hammered into ornaments. Yellow Wolf offered to lead Mather to the source of the ore "three suns west," but Mather declined.

More settlers joined Mather over the years. A church, school, and Masonic lodge, collectively known as Mt. Horeb, were erected here in the 1850s, although Indians continued to raid the settlement. Stores, a gin, cotton-and-wool-carding machines, and even a telephone exchange were established here in the following years. The town celebrated the erection of a great iron bridge across the North Fork of the San Gabriel River in 1893. But then the Masonic lodge burned down. Nearby Bertram started to grow rapidly and began to lure businesses away. Then the schools were consolidated. People started moving away and Gabriel Mills was literally a ghost town by the Great Depression. The old iron bridge, damaged beyond repair by a flood in 1957, had to be torn down.

Gabriel Mills' famous native son was the noted Indian fighter Andy Mather. The son of Samuel Mather, Andy was born here in 1851 and grew into a strapping six-foot four-inch man. Indian fighter and Texas Ranger, Mather feared no one. Stories of his bravery abound. Mather was the first man to lasso a bear in Texas, killing it with his bowie knife. It was supposedly the biggest bear the state had ever seen. Another time, Mather was engaged in combat with a famous Indian chief. They exhausted their ammunition supply at the same time, whereupon the Indian started to flee the scene. Mather responded by lassoing the Indian around the neck, jerking him from his horse, and dragging him to death. Mather wore his blond hair down to his shoulders, and was never seen without his spurs on. Mather's old friend Buffalo Bill Cody came to visit him once at Georgetown, and the longhaired pair of Wild West legends cut quite a figure together.

Andy Mather died in 1929 and is buried in the Mather family plot in the Mount Horeb Church Cemetery. His stone is easily visible from the road. The Mather plot is the second plot up from the limestone house.

Resume your path west on Cty. Rd. 207.

Soon you will see the **historical marker** that tells the story of this vanished town and cross the North Fork of the San Gabriel. The countryside stretches out a bit now, becoming sparsely treed grazing land. This marker is about 5.5 miles from Andice. When you enter Burnet County, Williamson Cty. Rd. 207 becomes Burnet Cty. Rd. 313.

In about 4 miles this road dead-ends into another road. At this intersection by the Hutto Ranch, turn right onto Burnet Cty. Rd. 312.

Now is as good a time as any to look back at Mt. Gabriel. You'll see why ancient travelers used it as a landmark. You can see the Bertram water tower ahead of you off in the distance.

In a couple of miles Cty. Rd. 312 dead-ends into FM 243. Turn left on FM 243 to reach Bertram.

BERTRAM

Burnet County • 937 • (512) • About 9 miles from Gabriel Mills historical marker
The town we know today as Bertram was a child of the Austin and Northwestern railroad, founded with the arrival of the rails in 1882 and named for the railroad's largest stockholder, Austin businessman Rudolph Bertram. The town of Bertram actually started life 30 years earlier as Cedar Mill. Cedar Mill was located several miles south on a tributary of the South Fork of the San Gabriel. Reflecting a shift northward in the route of the old Austin-to-Burnet road, Cedar Mill moved to a spot on the river that the inhabitants first called Louis-

town (in honor of their first storekeeper), then South Gabriel. The village became prosperous here. When news of the coming railroad drifted into town, progressive South Gabriel residents offered railroad officials $3,000 to route the tracks through their village. But the Austin and Northwestern tracks went through two miles north of South Gabriel instead. Undaunted, the townspeople just picked up and moved to the new town en masse, just as they had earlier moved from Cedar Mill. Brothers Wild and L. R. Gray moved the entire town of South Gabriel—13 houses and two stores—two miles north to the railroad in two days. The Grays used 13 yoke of oxen to accomplish this feat, and the entire town squeezed into one house during the two-day move. Messrs. Lockett and Vaughan continued to run their respective stores here at Bertram.

By June of 1882 the *Austin Statesman* was advertising Saturday excursions on the Austin and Northwestern to Bertram—a four-hour trip—for 75¢ round trip. Bertram went on to become a regional marketing center for farm and ranch products, cedar posts, and pecans. Thousands of carloads of pink granite rumbled through the town during its first decade of life, granite destined for Austin and the state capitol. Today Bertram is best known as home of the Oatmeal Festival.

BERTRAM SCHOOL
FM 243 • Not open to the public
Coming into Bertram on FM 243, you pass the now-vacant two-story red brick Bertram school. Bertram was in the middle of a cotton boom back in 1909, and this rock-solid schoolhouse with its topside belltower reflects this era of prosperity. School sessions were structured around the cotton season then. The school closed in 1970, the result of a merger with the Burnet schools.

At SH 29 in downtown Bertram, turn right and go 1 block to Lampasas St. Then turn right on Lampasas and cross the tracks.

ANTIQUESTONE TILE MANUFACTURING COMPANY
Lampasas, just north of SH 29, and the railroad tracks
Bertram's best brick building is the 1904 structure housing the Antiquestone Tile Manufacturing Company, two-story buff brick with red brick icing and an old-time red tin porch awning.

As you travel the few yards back to SH 29, notice the Reed building across the highway, between Lampasas and Grange.

REED BUILDING
SH 29, between Grange and Lampasas

Built in 1905, the Reed building is Bertram's most imposing business edifice. It is a two-story sandstone structure with a cut limestone-block facade. Inside you'll find high wood-strip ceilings, ceiling fans, a variety of old wood-and-glass cabinets and fixtures, and a nice turned-wood balustrade stairway leading upstairs.

In the alley behind the Reed building you'll note an old tin-sided store whose lettered facade still reads "G. A. Newton Confectionary ICE cold drinks Cigars and Tobacco." It has been closed for years.

JIMMY'S ANTIQUES
SH 29 at Vaughn, next to the Reed Building • 355-2985
Open seven days • W partial

Jimmy's Antiques is located in the first new commercial building erected in Bertram (in 1884), a two-story building with cut limestone block facade and limestone rubble walls. The stone was salvaged from the schoolhouse in the old South Gabriel community. It has housed many different businesses over the years. Jimmy Nuckles' shop is more like a museum than a run-of-the-mill antique shop, although most everything is for sale. Her collection of pre-Columbian pottery, artifacts, arrowheads, and more modern Old West/American Indian memorabilia and jewelry is unequalled in Central Texas, making the place worth a visit even if you don't buy anything. Ask to see the buffalo bone with the embedded arrowhead. Glassware and lots of knickknacks round out an impressive inventory.

From the Reed building, take Lampasas to Vaughn and turn left.

WILKINSON MUSEUM
Vaughn St. between East St. and South Gabriel St. • 355-2682
Open during the Oatmeal Festival and by appointment

The yard is full of wagons, windmills, and farm implements from Bertram's glory days, and the old store and sheds are packed with more old-time area memorabilia. Kids will enjoy Garrett Wilkinson's welded dinosaurs, turkeys, peacocks, and other steel and cast-iron animals.

ANNUAL EVENT

SEPTEMBER • Oatmeal Festival • Downtown Oatmeal
Labor Day weekend • Most events free

Bertram's annual wingding is a bit of insanity known as the Oatmeal Festival. The event used to be held in nearby Oatmeal, naturally, but it got so big that the organizers moved most of the activities to Bertram a couple of years ago. Events include an oatmeal cookoff and eat-off, oatmeal sculpture contest, oatmeal box stacking, oatmeal bowling, the Hours of Oats, and such non-oat events as a footrace, barbecue, parade, and dances.

From the Wilkinson Museum, proceed down Vaughn until it runs into SH 29 east. Continue your eastward path for a few yards on SH 29, then turn right onto FM 1174. You are bound for Oatmeal. About 2 miles after you leave Bertram, you cross the South Fork of the San Gabriel River.

A mile after you cross the river you pass two big red barns on your right, then another red barn and a white board fence. A few hundred feet after you pass these landmarks, you see a paved road that runs into FM 1174 on your right. This is Burnet Cty. Rd. 326. Turn right on this road to reach Oatmeal.

After about 3 miles, this little road, which runs along scenic Oatmeal Creek, dead-ends into FM 243 at the Oatmeal schoolhouse, which is now a community center. The whitewashed frame 1920s vintage schoolhouse is identified by the inscription "Oatmeal" on the windmill vane.

OATMEAL

Burnet County • About 6 miles from Bertram

Oatmeal is the second-oldest settlement in Burnet County. A German family named Hafermehl (locally corrupted to Habermills) came here in 1849 by ox wagon and settled down for a season or two in the lush grasslands adjacent to the headsprings of Oatmeal Creek. *Hafermehl* translates into English as "oatmeal." Some time after they had left, a local resident sent his sons out to look for strayed livestock, giving them instructions to "first look for them around Oatmeal Spring, then go down to the creek." The springs, creek, and community have been known as Oatmeal ever since. The "Oatmeals" were not heard from again until some descendants came back years later and tried to make claim and title to the family's original plot.

The fertile land along Oatmeal Creek attracted many settlers. By 1852 Oatmeal was a bustling village. Burnet County's greatest feud pitted the Oatmeal Creek faction against the Hamilton (Burnet) faction. Hamilton won. But this setback did not mean the end of Oatmeal. A post office was established here in 1853. The next year, John R. Scott arrived from New York via the California gold fields. Here at Oatmeal he planted Burnet County's first orchard and operated the county's first and only cheese factory.

An ardent unionist, Scott was badgered and threatened by his secessionist neighbors once the Civil War started, so much so that he decided to flee to Mexico. He got only as far as the Colorado River between Marble Falls and Smithwick. There he was ambushed and shot by bushwackers who robbed him of the $2,500 he was carrying and threw his body down "Deadman's Hole."

Another prominent area citizen and staunch unionist, John Hubbard, writer Noah Smithwick's son-in-law, was also robbed and murdered by bushwackers. They threw his body into the waterhole beneath the falls of nearby Cow Creek, which have since been known as Hubbard Falls.

After the Civil War a colony of ex-slaves settled in the eastern section of Oatmeal community along Oatmeal Creek. Most of their homes were strung out in a line along Old Oatmeal Rd., so the settlement was called Stringtown; it ceased to exist in the 1920s.

A few years ago the state struck Oatmeal from its highway maps. Thanks to the Oatmeal Festival (see Bertram Annual Events), Oatmeal is back on the map.

From the schoolhouse, start back up Cty. Rd. 326, the road you took to Oatmeal. After 0.2 mile you come to a Y in the road. You came into Oatmeal from Bertram on the fork to the left. Now, take the fork to the right as per the "Oatmeal Church of Christ" sign (Cty. Rd. 327).

In another couple of hundred yards, you come to a brush arbor on your right and the Oatmeal Church of Christ just up the hill on your left.

OATMEAL CHURCH AND ARBOR
On Cty. Rd. 327 • Open only for Sunday services
The brush arbor dates to 1903. Its framework consists of cedar posts and poles and its roof is cedar thatch. There are no walls. An arbor is a roof over one's head and nothing more, the simplest form of mass shelter. Arbors like this were the pioneers' first church buildings. As soon as they were settled in they would build a log church

building, then a frame, stone, or brick permanent sanctuary. The arbor would then be torn down or relegated to use during the hot summer months. Several dozen arbors still exist across rural Central Texas at places like Fitzhugh and High Grove, but they all have solid tin roofs and concrete floors. Here the afternoon sun trickles through the cedar thatch roof like raindrops falling from a tree after a storm, and the floor is packed earth, grassy green from disuse. Worshippers sat on a dozen straight-backed, uncompromisingly hard wooden benches—no chance of falling asleep here during the sermon. A bare light bulb was the only concession to modernity. The Oatmeal Festival's gospel sings have traditionally taken place here at the arbor each Labor Day Sunday.

The church up the hill was built as a combination schoolhouse and church in 1869 for the lordly sum of $65. Except for minor repairs and a board floor, the simple rectangular limestone building looks just like it did in 1869.

From the church and arbor, continue east to the cemetery turnoff. Visit this neatly trimmed plot if you wish, otherwise follow the road's sharp turn to the left. You cross Oatmeal Creek in a few hundred feet. Turn left at the T intersection just beyond the creek crossing. You have just completed the Oatmeal loop and are back on the original road you took to get to Oatmeal. At FM 243 and the Oatmeal school, turn left and proceed south on FM 243. In about 4 miles, you come to the junction with FM 1174.

CEDAR MILL

Burnet County • About 3 miles from Oatmeal
This pretty little valley is the site of old Cedar Mill community, located on the south fork of Oatmeal Creek and on what was once the main road from Austin to Burnet. When the road moved east in the 1860s, the people of Cedar Mill followed it, relocating first on the site known as South Gabriel, then moving to Bertram. Nothing remains of Cedar Mill today except a beautiful view.

Continue on FM 1174 south until you reach the junction with FM 1869. Turn left here onto FM 1869.

(If you went a couple of miles farther on 1174 you would cross a branch of Cow Creek. If you were to walk upstream a ways, which is not advised because this is private property, you would find dinosaur tracks in the rocky creekbed and the names of Captain T. D. Vaughn's Confederate Army company chiseled into the creekbank rocks.)

After about 3 miles on FM 1869, you see the Stocktank General Store on your left and a sign directing you to turn right to reach the Hopewell Cemetery. Despite its appearance, the store dates only to 1987, but its look is 1887: rustic, one story, shotgun layout, with single-stepped facade. The steps are thick cedar logs, the siding is rough-cut, wane-edged board with the bark still on. Fenced in by a worm log fence, the only detail it lacks are the horses tied up to the porch rails.

Turn right here, onto Cty. Rd. 285, as per the "Hopewell Cemetery" sign. In a mile you come to the ghost town of Hopewell, where nothing but a cemetery remains today.

HOPEWELL

Williamson County • About 6.5 miles from Oatmeal

Hopewell was settled in the early 1850s and was first called Burleson's Springs. The name Hopewell was derived from Hope, Arkansas, former home of several early settlers here. Located on one of the early routes of the Austin-to-Burnet road, Hopewell was plagued by Indian raids during the early years. Preachers kept their guns next to their Bibles on the pulpit; the men of the congregation also kept their firearms lapside. Indian attacks in western Williamson County increased during the Civil War because many of the settlers were off fighting and northern traders had furnished the Comanches with the latest in firearms. The most brutal raid occurred here at Hopewell.

The Wofford Johnson family had spent the sweltering day of August 15, 1863, making molasses at the nearby Whitehead place. Returning home that afternoon, Mr. and Mrs. Johnson and their three children were ambushed by the Kiowa-turned-Comanche war chief Big Foot and his band. Wofford and his little girl were killed almost instantly in the dense dogwood thickets along Dog Creek. Mrs. Johnson galloped desperately for home but was shot down a few hundred yards later. The babe in her arms was taken for ransom. The Johnsons' oldest girl managed to escape and ran for help. Local Texas Ranger captain Jeff Maltby organized a posse and set off in pursuit of Big Foot and his band the next morning. The posse found the

Johnson baby alive and unharmed on a cedar bush a few hours into their chase, abandoned by the fleeing Comanches. Maltby's posse got close enough to the Indians to identify Big Foot but were unable to capture the Indians when they leaped off a creek bluff and escaped into the darkness. Maltby spent the next nine years tracking down Big Foot and his lieutenant Jape. He finally confronted them in Runnels County in 1872. Captain Jeff and Big Foot drew simultaneously, but Maltby got his shot off first, breaking Big Foot's neck. In the meantime Jape was fatally wounded by trooper Henry Sackett. Before he died, Jape confessed to the Johnson murders.

The Johnsons were buried in their wagon at the **Hopewell Cemetery,** which is now the only identifiable trace of the Hopewell community. Their common stone reads: "Wofford Johnson Wife and Little Dau MASSACRED BY THE INDIANS AUG 15 1863." They were the last Indian attack victims in Williamson County.

Church services here were first held under an arbor adjacent to the cemetery. After the war a permanent sanctuary was built, followed by a school, gin, store, and Masonic lodge, and a saloon that sold drinks by the dipper. Hopewell had a post office, for less than three months, in 1882. The town started to fade when the Austin-to-Burnet road made one of its many route adjustments. Now only the dead remain.

Continue south on Cty. Rd. 285 from the Hopewell Cemetery. In less than a half-mile, you come to an intersection with Cty. Rd. 286. Bear left here on Cty. Rd. 285. Around the bend and a couple of hundred feet later, Cty. Rd. 284 veers off to the right, but you continue dead ahead on Cty. Rd. 285. Soon you are treated to some nice views of Little Creek, off to your right. Cty. Rd. 285 dead-ends at FM 1869 in another 4 miles. Turn right onto FM Rd. 1869 and go east about 4 miles to reach Liberty Hill.

Williamson County was home to a number of cattle barons during the last half of the nineteenth century. One of the classiest was Dave Harrell, who had a ranch here between Hopewell and Liberty Hill. Harrell was Texas' first shorthorn breeder, and his bull Old Prince was the world champion shorthorn bull at the 1904 St. Louis World's Fair. A huge crowd gathered at the Liberty Hill depot to greet Harrell and the celebrity bull when they returned home.

LIBERTY HILL

Williamson County • 300 • About 7 miles from Hopewell

Captain Cal Putnam was the first settler in these parts. He built a blockhouse near the present-day Liberty Hill in the early 1830s, when his nearest white neighbors were back at Hornsby's Bend. The first settlement was located about three miles west of here on one of the many routes of the Austin-to-Burnet military road. In the 1850s the Reverend W. O. Spencer was the neighborhood's most prominent inhabitant, and when Texas Revolution hero and U.S. Senator Thomas Rusk stopped here one night in 1853, he naturally was invited to stay at the Spencer residence. Rusk was a member of the Senate Post Office Committee and was touring the state looking for new post office sites. As Rusk rose from the breakfast table the next morning to thank his host for his splendid hospitality, he asked Spencer if there were any favor he might do for him. Spencer mentioned that there was not a single post office located on the road between Austin and Burnet, whereupon Rusk sat down and wrote out an order to his post office committee, requesting that a post office be established at this site and that W. O. Spencer be named its postmaster. Then he looked up and asked, "What shall its name be?" Spencer thought for a minute, then said, "These people around here are a peaceful, liberty loving folk. I live upon a hill. I am fond of hills. Let's call it Liberty Hill."

After the Civil War, the village shifted slightly eastward with the stage road, then again to its present site with the coming of the Austin and Northwestern railroad in 1882. The railroad's arrival brought about an explosion in growth here, resulting in the string of brick and limestone business houses that still stands in downtown Liberty Hill.

Liberty Hill was for 25 years home to the Liberty Normal and Business College, which opened in 1885. Many families moved to Liberty Hill to enroll their children in the school, which was touted as the largest and most progressive normal in Texas. "Study is a pleasure and not a burden," its proprietors said. But the school fell on hard times and closed in 1910, and the two-story red brick building was deeded over to the public school system.

In its heyday Liberty Hill had three banks and two gins. It continued to prosper as a local shipping and marketing center until the decline of the railroad and area farming. The town experienced something of a revival in the 1970s when an investor restored many of the old buildings and touted Liberty Hill as a regional arts and crafts center. This boom has gone bust, but Liberty Hill has a magnificently restored downtown just waiting for some enterprising individuals to fill it.

From FM 1869, turn right on Loop 332 and park for a stroll downtown. Loop 332 is Liberty Hill's old main street.

GENERAL STORE
Corner of FM 1869 and Loop 332
This store is your starting point. There used to be old livery stables in back of the store.

OLD MASONIC LODGE
Loop 332
The next block of Loop 332 is a line of well-maintained, though mostly empty, two-story limestone and brick buildings. One of the best is the old Masonic lodge next door to the Liberty Hill Feed and Seed Store; it's identified as such by a state historical marker. John Munro built this two-story limestone structure in 1883, operating a hardware store on the bottom floor. The Masons bought the top floor from him for their meeting hall.

OLD BARNES—McCULLOUGH STORE
Loop 332
Cross the street and begin the short stroll back to FM 1869. You first encounter the old Barnes-McCullough store and lumberyard. Built of multihued brown brick with limestone accents, it is unique in Liberty Hill. The store buildings's facade sports an XXX design executed in black brick. The attached Latinate arched entryway to the lumberyard is similarly executed in brown brick. Barnes and McCullough sold lumber, hardware, and furniture in their time.

STUBBLEFIELD BUILDING
Loop 332, north side
Downtown Liberty Hill's oldest surviving structure, built by S. P. Stubblefield in 1871 of hand-cut limestone. The first floor houses a variety of businesses. The second floor was living space. Stubblefield, a Mexican-American War veteran, died in 1902; his family kept the building until 1907.

From downtown Liberty Hill, proceed east on Loop 332 to Liberty Hill High School and the International Sculpture Park.

SCULPTURE PARK
Liberty Hill High School grounds, Loop 332 at SH 29
Open at all times • W

The late Mel Fowler was the driving force behind the International Sculpture Park, which features 26 works by artists from America and Europe. Fowler lived and worked here for more than 10 years before his untimely death in 1987 while in Italy. Three of the park's works are Fowler's; he loved to work in the Hill Country's native stone.

From downtown Liberty Hill, backtrack on FM 1869 across the San Gabriel River. Less than 0.5 mile later, you see a paved road running off to your left, the first paved left past the river. Turn left onto this road, which is identified by signs as Cty. Rd. 282.

First you overlook the Little Creek valley. When the road forks for the first time, 0.5 mile from FM 1869, bear left.

As you leave Williamson County and the Shinoak Ridge, Cty. Rd. 282 rolls straight on past intersections with Cty. Rds. 284, 283, and 281. It enters Travis County and is now called Round Mountain Rd. A yellow center stripe appears as you approach the Bingham Creek valley, and you are treated to some rugged, expansive Hill Country views. Gradually you dip down to the bottomland and the old Round Mountain community. It has no real organized center anymore. Your tip-off is the Sandy Creek Baptist Church on your right.

ROUND MOUNTAIN

Travis County • 59 • About 9 miles from Liberty Hill
Round Mountain community took its name from a nearby summit; which one is anybody's guess since there is no such peak on any existing map of Travis County. The hamlet centered around a school by the same name, which began life in the 1870s inside a log cabin. A new building was constructed in 1888 on land donated by local pioneer J. R. Faubion, and it remained in use as such until about World War II.

Round Mountain Rd. soon dead-ends into Nameless Rd. An outdoor community bulletin board stands to your right at this intersection. Turn right here to reach the little community of Nameless.

NAMELESS

Travis County • About 3.5 miles from Round Mountain
Three and a half miles after you turn onto Nameless Rd., you reach the town of the same name. "Town" is used euphemistically at best;

there are no highway signs denoting Nameless. What you see is a small road sign reading "Nameless School" on your right and, set back from the road, the small white-frame Nameless schoolhouse, built in 1909. Just a few feet farther on Nameless Rd. you cross Big Sandy Creek, catching it on its brisk-paced meander toward Lake Travis.

Turn around after crossing Big Sandy Creek and head back to Round Mountain.

By now you're probably wondering how on earth this neighborhood came to be called Nameless. The area was first surveyed in 1853 and was well settled by the end of the Civil War. In 1880 the citizens, who had begun to call their settlement Fairview, applied to Washington for a post office. The postal authorities nixed Fairview, along with the next five names offered by the Big Sandy Creek locals. After the sixth rejection, the citizens could stand no more and fired back to the post office bureaucrats: "Let the Post Office be nameless and be damned." Their implied name was accepted, and although the post office here ceased to function in 1890, the place has been known as Nameless ever since. Besides the post office, Nameless had a general store and meat market. The school doubled as a church. Today only the school and cemetery remain. The cemetery is north of the school and not clearly visible from the road.

Back at Round Mountain, do not take Round Mountain Rd. at the T intersection but continue straight on Nameless Rd. past Calkins Country Store. In a few miles, when you enter Williamson County, Nameless Rd. becomes FM 2243. When you have gone 5.3 miles from the Round Mountain/Nameless Rd. intersection, you come to Bagdad.

BAGDAD

Williamson County • About 5 miles from Round Mountain
No sign tells you that you are at Bagdad; you just come to a four-way intersection without even a yield sign to slow you down. The **Bagdad Cemetery** stands windswept to your right, and you can see the **Leander water tower** in the distance.

Charles Babcock arrived here on Christmas Day of 1851. By 1854 he had surveyed a townsite, and soon thereafter businesses began to grow up, for there was money to be made here. Bagdad was located on the Central National road, a military-public thoroughfare northwest out of Austin, halfway between Austin and Burnet's Fort Croghan. It was a popular stage stop and overnight stop. Babcock built an inn here to cater to the traveling trade, and even Robert E. Lee slept here.

The post office came in 1858. Babcock had named his town for the Old World trading city of Bagdad, anticipating a great commercial future for his strategically placed dream. Bagdad had a variety of stores, a boot shop, a marble yard, two schools, a commercial photographer's shop, silver and lead mines, and even telephone service, by 1880. Bagdad eagerly awaited the arrival of the Austin and Northwestern railway and was gravely disappointed when the rails ran through a mile east. So gradually folks just moved over to the new town called Leander. The post office moved in 1882 and by 1900 Bagdad was a ghost town.

Turn right onto Cty. Rd. 278 and go south a few yards to reach the Heinatz store and home.

The only original buildings left in Bagdad today are the old Heinatz home and store. They were built by John Heinatz, who was also Bagdad's first postmaster, in the early 1850s. The home is privately occupied and the old limestone store and post office serves now as a senior citizens center. Remains of the old stage stand were just across the road from the Heinatz buildings.

From the FM 2243/Cty. Rd. 278 intersection proceed east on FM 2243 toward Leander, past the old Bagdad Cemetery. Before you know it, FM 2243 runs into US 183 and you are in the middle of what was Leander's original business district.

LEANDER

Williamson County • 3,634 • About 1 mile from Bagdad

Leander, the successor to nearby Bagdad, owes its existence entirely to the railroad. As the Austin and Northwestern tracks were pushing west toward Burnet, the railroad company sold town lots here on July 17, 1882. The rail magnates named the new town after Leander "Catfish" Brown, a company official. Bagdad's post office moved here that same fall.

For years Leander was a processing and shipping point for local cotton, wool, mohair, cedar, and limestone. It is now on the threshold of becoming another bedroom town for Austin commuters. Not much is left of old Leander these days, just a limestone school building and a few smaller structures. Leander is now mostly new, dating back to the late 1970s.

To follow FM 2243's slightly convoluted path eastward, you turn right onto US 183. In a few hundred feet you turn left on FM 2243 as it leaves US 183 for good. In these few hundred feet you have seen old Leander.

DAVIS CEMETERY/
WEBSTER MASSACRE STATE MARKER
FM 2243 • About 1.5 miles from Leander
A mile and a half east of Leander on FM 2243, you see on your left the pioneer Davis Cemetery. The oldest grave dates to 1839, and tragically, it is a common grave, final resting place for the victims of the Webster massacre.

Their story goes as follows. On June 13, 1839, a group of 17 people—14 men, a woman, a boy, and a girl—left Hornsby's Bend east of Austin. They were heading for a spot on the North Fork of the San Gabriel River in what is now Burnet County where they intended to settle. The group was led by John Webster, who had brought his wife and two children. The rest of their party—13 or so—were to join them at the site several days later. The grant of land was deep in Comanche country.

By August 19 the Webster ox train had come to Pilot's Knob (Mt. Gabriel today), which was only six miles from their land. At Pilot's Knob they spotted Comanche campfires nearby and decided to turn around. While crossing the South Fork of the San Gabriel River (a couple of miles north of here), one of the wagons' axles broke. The train camped here overnight while the axle was repaired. By sunup they had reached Brushy Creek, where the Comanches were lying in wait for them. The settlers voted to fight and formed a wagon circle. It was a brave but hopeless fight, because the Comanches outnumbered them and had the surrounding thick timber for cover. The battle was over in a couple of hours, by 10 o'clock. The Comanches spent the rest of the battle day divvying up the loot; that which they deemed useless they burned or otherwise destroyed. The Comanches had been following the settlers for miles on either side, just waiting for the right spot to attack. They found it here.

All the men were killed; Mrs. Webster and the kids were taken prisoner. The grisly scene was discovered by one of Webster's surveyors, John Harvey, who had been delayed at Hornsby's Bend. By the time he arrived, only skeletons remained. He also found burned wagons. Bullet holes and arrows riddled everything. Only one of the bodies could be properly identified, that of Milton Hicks, whose leg had been broken at the Battle of Anahuac. The bones were put into a common crate and buried. Upon hearing of a Texas-Comanche treaty, Mrs. Webster and daughter managed to escape and fled to San Antonio in 1840. Her son was repatriated six days later according to terms of that Texas-Comanche peace treaty.

The Webster victims rest off in the west corner of the graveyard, partially obscured by a thick clump of cedars. A state granite marker stands on the spot. The next oldest stones dates to 1856, and others display some interesting carvings and verse.

About 1.5 miles farther east on FM 2243, you see a deer crossing sign on your right. A few yards later, turn right onto Cty. Rd. 175, which is marked just after you turn onto it. It's a little over three miles from Leander to Cty. Rd. 175. You're in strictly goat and cattle country now, and you make several low-water crossings.

Next you come to a Y in the road, formed by the junction of Cty. Rd. 177 and Cty. Rd. 175. Veer left, as Cty. Rd. 175 goes eastward. And do not be misled into taking Cty. Rd. 176, which you next encounter to your left almost as soon as you have executed the leftward veer. Continue straight ahead on Cty. Rd. 175, past goat-filled pastures and Aeromotor windmills that still work for a living. You are near Round Rock, and soon the pastures give way to subdivisions.

By this point, the road signs inform you that you are traveling on Sam Bass Rd., the old San Saba Rd. Then all of a sudden little Sam Bass Rd. becomes FM 3406, a four-lane dragstrip built to handle the new commuter traffic. Old Sam Bass Rd. runs brokenly alongside on your right. A half-mile later, turn right off FM 3406 onto Sam Bass Rd., which leaves FM 3406 to enter Round Rock.

ROUND ROCK

Williamson County • 36,924 (unofficial, but probably correct) (512) • About 10 miles from Cty. Rd. 175

Anglo settlers began to inhabit the general Round Rock area during the 1830s. By 1850 an honest-to-God village had grown up here along the banks of Brushy Creek. In fact, the burg was first known as Brushy Creek.

Thomas Oatts opened the first store and post office here in 1852; it was immediately followed by a stage stop and tavern. By 1854 postal authorities had deemed the name Brushy Creek too confusing. Faced with choosing another name, Oatts and friend Jacob Harrell thought a bit, then submitted the name Round Rock, after an enormous anvil-shaped boulder that sat in Brushy Creek by the creek crossing. The two had "spent many happy hours sitting on the rock and fishing."

Other stores, mills, and houses followed. More businesses sprang up after the Civil War, including a cotton gin, newspaper, tombstone carver, and all the other usual businesses of a prosperous village. Round Rock prospered until 1876, when the International and Great Northern railroad came through a mile to the east. Thus Round Rock became "Old" Round Rock, and "New" Round Rock began to build alongside the iron rails. Old and New Round Rocks functioned as separate towns with separate post offices until 1891, when the Old Round Rock post office was abandoned. By this time, Old Round Rock was mostly deserted, and it stayed that way until the 1960s, when many of the remaining structures were restored. Today, the stretch of Chisholm Trail Rd. from Sam Bass Rd. to Brushy Creek is a historic district.

New Round Rock sprouted up as a tent city late in July 1876 on land belonging to Washington Anderson as the rails inched south toward Austin. A year later over a dozen businesses were operating here. Some had moved from Old Round Rock, others had come all the way from Georgetown. That first year a broom factory and lime operation were established here along with a newspaper, the *Round Rock Headlight*. But the new town, despite its prosperity, had no water service for years. Citizens bought their water from wagons that carted the wet stuff in from a spring east of town.

Sam Bass, who is discussed at length below, was not Round Rock's only world famous star. Homegrown boy Vander Clyde Broadway gained fame in Paris during the twenties and thirties as "Barbette," a "dazzling female impersonator aerialist."

As a young boy, Broadway became entranced with the circus, especially the aerialists, and practiced walking on wires, fences, anything he could find in Round Rock. Out of school at 14, he decided that he would become an aerialist. A fan of the Alfaretta Sisters, a family high wire act, he learned that one of the sisters had died and that her survivors were looking for a replacement. With his mother's permission,

Clyde auditioned and got the part. He dressed as a woman because female aerialists were supposed to be more dramatic.

Clyde next decided to go it alone, maintaining the sexual ruse and developing a high wire and trapeze act. He took the act to Europe, where Barbette was an immediate success. Writer Jean Cocteau was entranced by the combination of masculine strength and feminine grace. Barbette played all Europe's major cities, and Cocteau used Barbette in his masterpiece film *The Blood of a Poet*.

But tragedy struck in 1938. A fall and freak illness left Clyde almost totally paralyzed overnight. After a year and a half in hospitals, he came home to Round Rock to recuperate. Defying the doctors who said he would never walk again, Clyde would walk the length of the town every morning, then come home to one of his mother's huge breakfasts. By 1942 he was back in showbiz as aerial director of the Ringling Brothers Circus. At one time or another he worked for almost every major circus in America and is credited with inventing the aerial ballet spectacular that is now a standard in every major American circus.

Round Rock was also home to several cattle barons, including George Washington Cluck and his wife Harriet. When George drove a herd up to Abilene, Kansas, in the spring of 1871, Harriet was right there with him. So were their three children, the oldest of whom was seven. And Harriet was expecting number four in October. But in spite of a flooding Red River, cattle rustlers, and Indians, the Clucks and their herd made it safely to Abilene that fall. The herd was sold, the baby was born, and the next spring the Clucks moved back to Williamson County. They bought a new ranch with their profits, and that ranch eventually became the town of Cedar Park.

In 1970, Round Rock was a sleepy little farm and ranch community with a population of 2,800. By 1980, Round Rock's population was nearly 12,000; it has more than tripled since. Round Rock now does battle with Austin in the courting of business relocations and startups, and sometimes Round Rock wins, as it did when it convinced Dell Computers to move out of Austin in 1993.

Dell Computer Corp.'s announcement in April 1993 that it would build a $25-million, 350-acre facility in Round Rock highlighted the differences between Austin and Round Rock. A Dell memo cited Round Rock's attractive incentives, its fast-track permitting process, inexpensive land, and cooperative attitude as reasons to do business with Round Rock. The same memo criticized Austin city as being inflexible. Round Rock city officials are proud of the city's generous tax abatements, its willingness to hasten the permitting process, and its supply of inexpensive, fully developed industrial sites.

In September 1993, an *Austin American-Statesman* reporter observed that "The 15 miles that separate Round Rock from downtown Austin might as well be 1,000. The two cities are opposites in many ways. The Austin City Council has swung from slow growth to pro-growth and back. The city is characterized as the state's liberal enclave. Round Rock, a former bedroom community that has been pursuing commercial development aggressively, has a conservative, pro-business attitude that never wavers, no matter who sits on the City Council, say city officials. 'There are more Rush Limbaugh fans in Round Rock than in Austin,' said Round Rock City Manager Bob Bennett. 'Round Rock is all the things Austin isn't.' Round Rock's leaders believe these differences are the city's calling card." Round Rock leaders liked this description of themselves so much that they posted the entire story on their World Wide Web page.

After you enter the Round Rock city limits, Sam Bass Rd. takes a hard bend to the left, past Brandt Lane, then Clark St. As soon as you have made this turn, you see on your left the old Round Rock Cemetery.

OLD ROUND ROCK CEMETERY
Clark and Sam Bass • W variable

This graveyard is most famous as the final resting place of the outlaw Sam Bass, but there is much else to look at here.

As you enter this cemetery, you will immediately notice signs of segregation. The large Anglo section is straight ahead, while the Mexican section is to your left. It is a colorful area, contrasting strongly with the somber Anglo spread. Off to the back is the old slave and freedman's section, marked by a sign and historical marker. It dates to about 1851.

Sam Bass and his confederate Seaburn Barnes lie buried along the cemetery's fence line, immediately adjacent to the slave section. Their placement here along the fence, between the Mexican and slave sections, was purposeful. Bass' current gravestone is a new one. The original stone was chipped away by tourists.

The old slave cemetery is full of broken bits and pieces of homemade stones. Only a few have legible inscriptions—crude, loving, and for the most part misspelled. It is the most pleasant section of the cemetery.

From the cemetery, continue on Sam Bass Rd. toward downtown Round Rock. This was the road on which the wounded Bass traveled in his attempt to escape Round Rock and the law back in 1878. Less than a mile later, you come to a four-way intersection with Chisholm Trail Rd. I-35 looms in the background. Turn right here onto the Old Chisholm Trail; this really was part of the historic trail, as you will see.

OLD HOTEL AND TAVERN
Chisholm Trail at Poker Alley

On your right, at the corner of Chisholm Trail and Poker Alley, is an old hotel and tavern, which has been restored.

ST. CHARLES HOTEL AND OLD POST OFFICE
#8 Chisholm Trail at Emmanuel

Next on your right, at the corner of Chisholm Trail and Emmanuel, are the old St. Charles Hotel and the old Round Rock post office. The two-story St. Charles Hotel was built about 1870 and was for many years the home of Dr. William Owen, prominent local physician and businessman. The simple one-story limestone building next to it dates to 1853, and originally housed a mercantile store and post office operated by Thomas Oatts, Round Rock's first postmaster.

INN AT BRUSHY CREEK
I-35 at Taylor exit • 255-2555 • Call for hours • Reservations required • $$–$$$ • AE, DC, MC, V • W

On the east side of Chisholm Trail Rd. is the Inn at Brushy Creek, Round Rock's finest dining establishment. It is housed in an 1850s residence built of locally quarried limestone by a Dr. Cole. The authentic restoration gives dinner here a timeless quality. The food is some of the finest to be found in Central Texas. Most people enter via the I-35 frontage road, which can be reached by doubling back on Chisholm Trail to Sam Bass, turning right there, and then right on the frontage road a few yards before turning into the Inn's drive.

THE CANTINA
Next door to 4 Chisholm Trail

Back at 4 Chisholm Trail, the next building on the right (across Galloping Rd.), is the two-story roofless limestone hulk that was once a boisterous tavern. It stands awaiting restoration.

BRUSHY CREEK/THE ROUND ROCK
Chisholm Trail

In another few yards you cross Brushy Creek. One hundred-plus years ago, herds of dusty market-bound longhorns and innumerable wagons crossed Brushy at this exact same spot. Look to your right as you cross and you can see the wagon ruts worn into the limestone creekbed. Immediately to your left, squatting in the middle of Brushy Creek between stone pillars of the old Georgetown Railroad bridge, is the old Round Rock.

EDWARD QUICK HOME
Chisholm Trail • Private residence

Just after you cross Brushy Creek, you see the old Edward Quick home, set back and well shaded, on your left. It is a private residence.

OLD ROUND ROCK STAGE STOP
901 Round Rock Ave., in the Commons Shopping Center

The old, limestone Round Rock stage stop still stands just south of RM 620, a few feet west of what little remains of the Old Chisholm Trail.

To enter New Round Rock, turn left onto RM 620, which is called Round Rock Ave. inside the city limits. Round Rock Ave. dead-ends at a five-way intersection that includes Main St. and Mays St. You're downtown now, so find a place to park so that you can walk through Round Rock's old downtown, which is a historical district. Many of the older buildings have been restored to their original exterior appearance.

OLD BROOM FACTORY
N. Mays and E. Main • Office building

Round Rock's broom factory produced nationally acclaimed brooms for decades and decades. One of their brooms even won a gold medal for excellence at the 1904 St. Louis World's Fair. From 1887 until 1912, the brooms were manufactured in a building that still stands at the corner of N. Mays and E. Main. This structure, the **Morrow building,** was erected in 1876 of ashlar-cut limestone "bricks," with smooth polished keystone door and window arches. After 1912 the structure housed a general store, furniture store, school, skating rink, and, most recently, an automotive repair shop.

OTTO REINKE BUILDING
102 E. Main
Attached to the Morrow building is its soulmate the Reinke building, built by merchant Otto Reinke in 1879. It, too, is two-story, built of ashlar-surfaced limestone, and has keystone window and door arches, yet the Morrow and Reinke buildings are distinctly different owing to their rooflines. The Morrow building features a fairly simple cast-metal cornice surmounted by a stepped ashlar limestone parapet, while the Reinke building has an arched pediment and graduated pedestals on either side.

ECONOMY DRUG STORE
204 E. Main
The north side of the 200 block of E. Main starts out strongly, with a string of three storefronts united by a common corrugated tin awning and identical, though separate, pressed-metal second-story facades. Unfortunately, the building caught fire in early 1997, and at press time, whether or not it can be restored was unknown.

The old Economy Drugstore has been the most appealing to visitors, even though the building has long since ceased to be a pharmacy. The vintage screen doors, high patterned-tin ceiling, and original wall cabinets and display cases were its most notable features.

PALM HOUSE
212 E. Main • 255-5805 • Monday through Friday 8–5 • Free
Currently houses Chamber of Commerce and a museum
Sandwiched between the Old Economy Pharmacy and old city hall/library is the 1860-vintage Palm home, moved here from a rural location and renovated. T. J. Caldwell built this house, using home-quarried limestone for the walls and home-cut cedar for the rafters, foundation, and floor joists. His slaves did most of the hard work. The house is commonly called the Palm house because Sven and Mary Caldwell Palm bought the place in 1892 from T. J.'s estate. In its new location, the Palm residence houses the Chamber of Commerce and a small museum. Several informative booklets about Round Rock are available here, free or nominally priced. Write Chamber of Commerce, 212 E. Main, Round Rock 78664.

TRINITY LUTHERAN COLLEGE
E. Main at College
Seven blocks east of the Palm house you encounter the old Trinity Lutheran College, which operated here from 1905 to 1929. When the college merged with another to become Texas Lutheran at Seguin, the graceful three-story Spanish Renaissance main building and other school buildings were taken over by the Lutheran Welfare Society. A historical marker tells the school's story.

NELSON-CRIER HOME
400 block of E. Main • Private residence
Heading back downtown, on the south side of E. Main you will encounter the Nelson-Crier home. Andrew Nelson was a prominent early Round Rock merchant, and his survivors built the three-story house over a five-year period, beginning with the year of Nelson's death, 1895. Its current Classical Revival facade dates to 1931. The house and yards take up an entire block.

NELSON BUILDING
E. Main and Lampasas
Back downtown, the John A. Nelson building stands on the corner of E. Main and Lampasas. Nelson built it in 1900 to house his hardware concern. Two-story limestone, with a full-length, top-to-bottom cast-iron and pressed-tin facade, the Nelson building is one of downtown Round Rock's most imposing structures.

SCENE OF THE SAM BASS SHOOTOUT
100 block of E. Main
Now that we're back at the heart of old downtown Round Rock, it's time to address the fate of the outlaw Sam Bass, whose "soft thing turned out rather serious," deadly serious, as we shall see, right here in the 100 block of E. Main, on the afternoon of Friday, July 19, 1878.

Young Bass and his gang had come to Round Rock to rob a bank. Previously they had limited themselves to holding up stagecoaches and trains, but now Bass and the boys were looking to move up in the crime world, but not too fast! They were hoping to cut their teeth on a "soft touch," a fat bank in a podunk town.

Now when you stack Sam Bass up against other outlaws of his time, you see that he cuts a mighty small figure. Born on an Indiana farm in 1851, Sam Bass was orphaned at 13. He came to Denton County, Texas, in 1870, where he found work as a cowboy and team-

WILLIAMSON COUNTY   **419**

ster. But Sam liked racing more than roping, and there was certainly more and easier money in the former. Sam had seen what hard work would get you, and what a good hand of cards or a fast horse would bring. The dime novel glamour of the cowboy life wore off quickly for Sam, and when he acquired a four-legged streak of lightning known as the Denton Mare in 1874, he left the workaday world behind forever. Sam raced her all over Texas, Mexico, and the Indian Territory, winning every bet. But after two years of "swimmin' in grease," Bass could find no more takers, and he sold his fleet mare.

He and friend Joel Collins drove a herd of cattle from San Antonio to Dodge City during the summer of 1876. With the profits from the drive, they decided to set themselves up as gold prospectors in the Black Hills of the Dakotas. They found no gold, and come the spring of 1877, Bass and Collins were broke and hungry. But they weren't about to go back to cowboying; you could blow an entire month's wages—$20 or so—on one wild night in town, then have to work hard for a month so you could blow it all again a couple of fortnights later.

A new friend named Davis convinced them that robbing stages was an easier and quicker way to get gold than digging or roping. So they put together a gang, the Black Hills Bandits, and set to work. Their biggest job was the Union Pacific train robbery at Big Spring Station in September 1877. The take was $60,000, cut six ways. The gang split up after this hit, and Bass hightailed it back to Texas with his 10 grand. Never before and never again would Sam Bass have so much money.

Back in Denton County, Bass called on some friends and put together a gang of his own. The Sam Bass Gang commenced operations in February 1878, robbing stages and trains across north Central Texas and generating big headlines. Often the headlines were bigger than the gang's take. The whole thing mushroomed to the point where the Bass Gang was blamed for every robbery across Texas in the spring of 1878. And there were a lot of stage and train holdups going down back then.

Bass was spending the little money he did get quite freely on fine clothes, saddlery, and the various other, more basic needs of life. Tales of Bass' generosity abound—a double eagle for a homecooked meal or a dozen eggs or a couple of beers—but Bass had barely enough coin to buy a can of beans by the time he reached Round Rock. It was time to do or die—do or starve, actually—for Bass.

Incredibly, Bass had not yet killed a single man. He firmly believed "Discretion is the better part of valor," preferring to run rather than fight. With this attitude, robber Bass provided stark contrast to John Wesley Hardin and Rattlin' Bill Longley, each of whom committed no less a crime than killing dozens of men and a woman or two.

In June, after two stage and four train robberies, Bass decided to move; Denton County was just getting too hot. The gang decided to move south to hit a bank, maybe in Waco, maybe in Belton. They'd figure out exactly where along the way. So off they went, down to Waco, Belton, Georgetown, and finally Round Rock.

Bass' fall at Round Rock was as much the result of politics as hot lead. In 1878, Texas was still mired waist deep in the Reconstruction uproar. Most Texans despised their state government. Bandits and Indians roamed the state at will, and only the carpetbaggers and the bandits had any money. The people demanded that something be done about these brigands, and the government did, too. The buck stopped with the Texas Rangers.

Funded annually by the legislature, the Rangers realized that their jobs, their very existence, depended on bringing law and order—or at least a semblance thereof— to Texas, and bringing it fast. Newspaper editorials were already calling for some other type of peace-keeping force than the Rangers.

Now what the Rangers needed was a scapegoat, one brigand they could rub out quick, so as to appease the wolves. Bass was the perfect candidate. They set the wheels in motion by releasing Jim Murphy from prison. Murphy had been a Bass confederate, and had been jailed for harboring Bass in Denton. Thinking his imprisonment unjustly harsh, Murphy made a deal with the Rangers. In exchange for his freedom, Murphy would play Judas: rejoin the gang and betray them into capture or death.

Bass was just too easygoing and generous to be a good outlaw. He took Murphy back into his confidence, despite the warnings of other more suspicious gang members. It was Murphy who talked Sam out of robbing the bank at Waco and into robbing the Round Rock one. In the meantime Murphy kept in touch with the anxious Rangers by surreptitiously mailed letters. While in Georgetown on July 14, Murphy managed to get word to the Rangers in Austin that Bass was headed for the Round Rock bank, and so the trap was set. That same Sunday evening, the gang rode the 11 miles down to Round Rock, setting up camp near the Old Slave Cemetery on the San Saba Rd. Next morning Bass and Frank Jackson rode into New Round Rock to case the town. Bass came back wanting to rob the bank that evening, but Murphy talked him out of the idea, suggesting they stay four or five days, posing as cattle buyers and thus allowing their horses to rest for the getaway. This would allow the Rangers plenty of time to set their trap. The boys decided to hit the bank on Saturday afternoon, July 20, and then made careful plans. Planning done, they began to count the money they were going to make.

Sam rode into town on Thursday and came back a little disquieted—he had seen some men he thought were Rangers, despite their anonymous cowboy garb. He sent Jackson and Murphy into town the next morning for a second opinion. They found nothing, or at least that's what they told Bass. So Sam quieted his fears and decided that they should ride into town that afternoon to buy some tobacco and a few other odds and ends for their quick flight out of town. While they were there, they could also case the bank one more time and look for Rangers.

Bass, Jackson, and Seab Barnes rode into a seemingly deserted town; the afternoon was a scorcher, and anybody not in the shade was busy looking for some, Rangers included. Murphy had stopped back at the Mays and Black Store in Old Town, on the pretext of looking for Rangers there.

It was about four o'clock when the Bass trio tied their horses up in an elm motte at the corner of Liberty and Lampasas (now a vacant lot). From here, they rounded the corner onto Main St. and walked to Kopperal's Store at 101 E. Main. The bank was next door.

The strolling gang did not go unnoticed. Travis County Deputy Sheriff Maurice Moore had seen them ride in, and had noted their saddlebags and what appeared to be a six-shooter concealed under the coat of one of the men. Bass and company were in turn scrutinizing Moore, who had been standing in front of the livery stable at 110 E. Main across the street from Kopperal's Store.

After the outlaws had disappeared into the store, Moore walked over to Williamson County Deputy Sheriff A. W. Grimes, an ex-Ranger, who was lounging nearby. He told Grimes of his suspicions. The two deputies walked over to the store. Moore hung out near the door, hands in his pockets, whistling. Grimes walked up to the strangers at the counter and asked carelessly of the one man if he didn't have a pistol under his jacket. "Yes," was the reply, and all three immediately drew and pumped Grimes full of lead. Gun still holstered, the words "Don't, boys" still on his lips, Grimes stumbled back a few steps and fell dead by the door. Moore drew as the shooting started, and his fire was immediately answered.

Just the first few shots filled the air with a blinding, acrid black-powder smoke, so the men were firing now at shadows and noises. Bass and company made it out the front door, but Sam's gun hand was shot up and Moore now sported a bullet in his left lung.

By this time, other men had heard the shooting and were running for the store, firing at the fleeing bandits, who were running for their horses. Rangers, deputies, and private citizens were shooting from every direction. The outlaws made it clean through the livery stable and were running down the alley to their horses at the elm motte when the law's shots began to take deadly effect. Sam took a bullet in the back and through the liver and Seab Barnes dropped dead in his tracks from a bullet in the brain, just as they reached the horses. The unscratched Jackson held off the law with one hand while untying Bass' horse and helping him mount with the other. He then mounted his own horse and the two galloped away, Jackson holding up the ashen-faced and bleeding Bass to keep him from falling. They tore out to the north and west, crossing Brushy Creek near the Round Rock and passing Jim Murphy, who was sitting on the front porch of the Mays and Black Store in Old Town. They stopped at the grave-yard camp, then headed north along the road to Georgetown (present-day Cty. Rd. 173).

Disappearing into a live-oak thicket, Bass and Jackson were safe for the time being. Bass declared he could go no farther, so Jackson helped him down and declared that he would stay with Sam—"I can match every one of them Rangers! No Frank, I'm done for," Sam said, and insisted that Frank save his own hide. Reluctantly, Frank obeyed, after first bandaging Sam up and tying his horse nearby, so that Sam might escape if he should feel better that night.

Come morning, the suffering Bass crawled out into a pasture and hailed a passing woodsman, begging the man to take him away into hiding, but the axeman spooked and ran away. Thirsty, Bass staggered to a nearby farmhouse for water, but the woman there ran off without giving him a drink. The bloody Bass finally got some water from a road crew building the new Georgetown tap line from Round Rock to the county seat. Meanwhile, the Rangers had fanned out to find him. When they first saw Bass lying under a live oak tree, less than a third of a mile from where Frank Jackson had left him, the Rangers mistook him for a railroad hand and moved on past. A little later the group's leader inquired of the section workers, who pointed out the dying Bass. Still in the dark as to the wounded man's identity, the Ranger leader approached Bass and asked "Who are you?" Bass raised his left hand as a token of surrender and faintly called, "Don't shoot! I am unarmed and helpless. I'm the man you are looking for. I am Sam Bass."

The Rangers carried him back to New Town, where he was laid on a plain cot in a small plank shed, located roughly in what is now the parking lot between the old Mobil gas station (now an office) and the small frame house on Mays Street, across from the broom factory.

Word was sent to Austin that Bass was in custody, but many there refused to believe the report, thinking it to be an election trick. Bass was questioned repeatedly by the Rangers about his Texas robberies, but he refused to talk names or specific details. Sam clung to life here in the shack through Saturday night and Sunday morning, refusing food, confession, or prayers. Thinking he was getting better, Bass suddenly pronounced "The world is bobbing around," lay back quietly for a moment, twitched his head wordlessly, and died. The day was July 21, 1878, Sam's 27th birthday.

A small group of mixed colors trudged out with Bass' body to the burying grounds early next morning. A few words and a prayer, offered up by a preacher who tagged along at the last minute, was Sam's service, and the black men began to fill the hole with clay. At that moment Frank Jackson galloped up, threw a clod of dirt on the grave in symbolic final tribute to his boss, and sped away.

Sam's demise didn't even make the front page of the local paper but, all the same, legends began to grow about the goodhearted bandit, the Texas Robin Hood, the man betrayed by a man he called friend.

His story was told, suitably embellished, in scores of dime novels, and in a song attributed to old-time cowboy John Denton. Long and sentimental, the ballad was sung by cowboys on the trail as a lullaby to their longhorned charges.

Over the years Bass has become revered as no other outlaw save Jesse James. How did such a feckless bandit become so beloved? After all, no one celebrates Bill Longley or John Wesley Hardin or Black Jack Ketchum Days, or names stores and cafes after them. Yet Round Rock celebrates Sam Bass Days (Frontier Days) every July and has several businesses named after him.

Perhaps his popularity lies in his failure. The average person can relate to Bass on a personal, fellow-mortal level. Bass never made a lot of money robbing, and what he made he gave away. He ran from fights rather than precipitating them. He was betrayed by a friend and died while casing his first bank robbery. In short, he was not a man to be feared, even if he wanted your money. He was just a lazy fellow who was smart enough to see that he could make easy money by waving a gun in the right direction. And once Bass was laid to rest, no one tried to resurrect him, like they did Jesse James, Bill Longley, or Bonnie and Clyde.

"We thought we had a soft thing but it turned out rather . . . serious." The mortally wounded Bass summed up his entire life in that one sentence, on his final trip into Round Rock.

OLD MASONIC LODGE
Northeast corner of Mays and East Bagdad
Not open to the public
A block south of the Mays and Main Street intersection stands the Old Masonic Lodge, built the same year as Sam's demise. The two-story limestone with brick cornice structure looks almost exactly as it did 100 years ago, and not much worse for wear.

LONE STAR BAKERY
106 W. Liberty • 255-3629 • Open daily • W
Another Round Rock institution is the Lone Star Bakery, twice chosen for the best donut in Texas by *Texas Monthly*. The bakery is over 50 years old and on its fifth set of owners, but the donuts are still made from scratch and fried fresh five or six times a day. Lone Star Bakery is located one block north and west of the broom factory.

DINING

COOPER'S PIT BAR-B-QUE
403 N. Mays • 255-5638 • Open Tuesday through Saturday, lunch and dinner • W
If you like Cooper's Old Time Pit Bar-B-Q in Llano, you'll like this place, founded by another member of the family.

POK-E-JO'S SMOKEHOUSE
1202 I-35 North • 388-7578 • Open daily, lunch and dinner
$ • Cr. • W
Mesquite-smoked beef brisket and ribs, pork loin and ribs, mild and hot sausage, ham, chicken, and turkey. Side dishes are made in house and are worthy consorts to the meats. They make a larruping-good cobbler and banana pudding, if you have any room left. Beer.

AREA PARK

OLD SETTLERS PARK AT PALM VALLEY
US 79, 3 miles east of downtown
Palm Valley is named for Mrs. Anders Palm and her six sons, who settled here in 1853 on land that S. M. Swenson, a Swedish immi-

grant, acquired in 1838. Other Swedish immigrants soon joined them here along Brushy Creek. Swenson became a successful businessman just a few years after coming to Texas in 1838. As an immigration agent, he brought several hundred Swedes to Texas, most of whom settled in rural Travis and Williamson counties, in settlements named New Sweden, Manda, Lund, Hutto, and Palm Valley. The Swedes were predominantly Lutheran; Lutheran church services were held in a log cabin as early as 1861, but nearby Palm Valley Lutheran Church was not formally organized until 1870. The present red-brick Gothic Revival church located west of the park was built in 1894.

The two-story Palm house (built about 1904), a barn and other farm outbuildings, and several old log cabins are on the grounds of Old Settlers Village, which adjoins Old Settlers Park at Palm Valley, which is a city park. Old Settlers Village pertains to the Old Settlers Association, a nonprofit organization dedicated to the preservation of cultural diversity in Williamson County. The cabins were donated to the Old Settlers Association in 1936. The little cabin was donated by the Jacob Harrell family. It once served as a one-room schoolhouse (with four students, according to records) and had a little porch out front.

The city park, which covers about 300 acres, has a little lake, hike-and-bike trails, ball fields, and a disc golf course.

ANNUAL EVENTS

APRIL • Old Settlers Week • Old Settlers Village, US 79, 3.3 miles east of I-35 • 255-5805 • Mid-month • W

The foundation of Williamson County is celebrated yearly. After years of July celebrations, in 1997 the event moved to the month of April. There is an old fiddlers' contest and lots of other old-time country and western music.

JULY • Frontier Days • Downtown and other locations 255-5805 • 2 days in mid-July • W

July 19 was the day that Sam Bass was gunned down during an attempted bank robbery, and this is a "celebration" of that event. It includes a reenactment of the fateful robbery, food, games, a parade, and dances.

SHINER-LOCKHART PILGRIMAGE

Approximately 170 miles

Years ago, there was a group of Austin bicycle racers who combined three of their favorite forms of entertainment—bike riding, drinking Shiner beer, and eating barbecue—into a single bike ride. Every other month or so, one of the guys would say, "Want to go to Shiner?" and immediately a spirited consensus sprang up among those present, and they spread the word to everyone else. Those who could make it on the anointed day at the appointed hour pedaled off en masse to our little Lavaca County mecca, the hospitality room at the Spoetzl Brewery, where the venerable Mr. Herbert Siems so ably dispensed the beer and little confidences. We could always count on a host of colorful local characters and employees to enliven our drinking, like Emil Vincik, Cracker Wallace, Joe Green, and Speedy Biel. Emil came for the water, although his girlfriend usually sipped a Shiner. Well into his 80s, the irrepressible Emil never missed a dance, whether it was Friday night at the SPJST Hall or the big Labor Day Shiner Catholic Church Picnic.

Long, lean Joe Green was Shiner's oldest employee and the brewery's unofficial historian; Cracker Wallace is his nephew. Cracker, from our perspective, was one of the brewery's most important employees; he delivered the Shiner beer to Austin twice a week, plus ring sausage from Patek's Market if we asked. Speedy Biel was the brewery's congenial, easy-going sales manager. There was a family

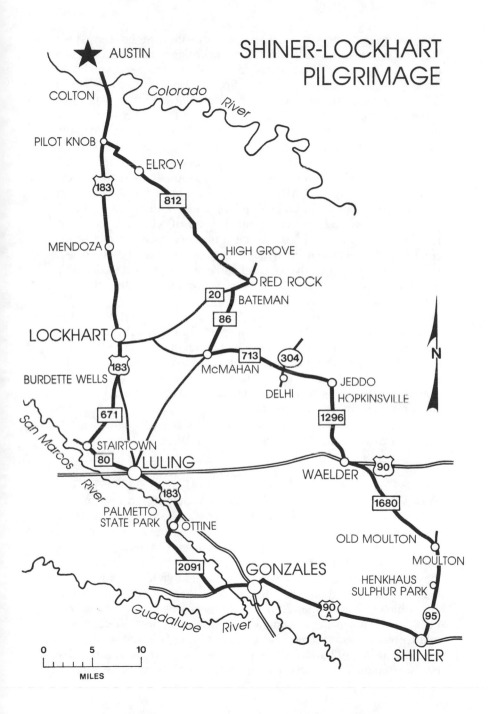

SHINER-LOCKHART PILGRIMAGE

AUSTIN

COLTON

Colorado River

PILOT KNOB

ELROY

183

812

MENDOZA

HIGH GROVE

RED ROCK

20 BATEMAN

86

LOCKHART

183

713 304

McMAHAN

JEDDO

BURDETTE WELLS

DELHI

HOPKINSVILLE

671

1296

San Marcos River

STAIRTOWN

80 LULING

WAELDER 90

183

PALMETTO STATE PARK

OTTINE

1680

OLD MOULTON

MOULTON

2091 GONZALES

HENKHAUS SULPHUR PARK

Guadalupe River

90 A

95

SHINER

N

0 5 10
MILES

atmosphere that one rarely associates with American breweries; we were on a first-name basis with the brewmaster, the kettleman, the bottle shoppers, the administrative staff—in short, everybody. In those pre-microbrewery days, the Spoetzl Brewery was the third smallest brewery in the country, and pulled down just one-third of one percent of Texas' total beer sales. As small a niche as it was at the time, it seemed to satisfy everybody. When our considerable thirsts were slaked, it was time to eat, and where better than Kreuz Market in Lockhart? So we racked up the bikes, and our designated drivers whisked us toward Lockhart. We sometimes detoured for pork ribs at Luling City Market, since there were no ribs at Kreuz and you could not count on getting Kreuz's pork loin past the lunch rush. Once at Kreuz, we wiped out the best of whatever meat was left. The traditionalists among us ate at the benches in the old, unair-conditioned back room next to the pits, where sharp carbon-steel knives with worn-smooth wooden handles were chained to the table tops for your dining pleasure. A sharp, well-pointed knife is the only eating utensil a real man needs.

The little brewery in Shiner isn't so little anymore, but it still begs visiting. Kreuz Market still carves up some of the state's best barbecue, and here you'll find cuts of meat that few other barbecue joints do, like beef clod (shoulder), prime rib, and whole, bone-in pork loin, which is sliced into thick individual chops as ordered. This in addition to the ubiquitous beef brisket and ring sausage. So much for personal raves. Here's how to get there.

From Austin, take US 183 south toward Lockhart.

COLTON

Travis County • 50 • About 7 miles from downtown Austin
Just after you cross **Onion Creek,** south of the US 183/SH 71 intersection, you enter what was once the farming community of Colton. Donald and Jamine McKenzie, two Scottish immigrants with visions of wealth in their heads, established in 1866 a community they called Cotton, an apt name, since the land yielded a bale of cotton to the acre in good years thanks to the soil's wealth of volcanic ash, which had been spewed out millions of years earlier by nearby Pilot Knob. When the community applied for a post office, it was told to pick another name, and Colton it was. The first school was established in 1892 and was named Pine Knob, although this is not pine tree country and there are currently no old pines in the area.

PILOT KNOB COMMUNITY

Travis County • Just south of Colton

Pilot Knob community grew up at about the same time as Colton, as cotton farming enjoyed a strong spurt of growth from the end of the Civil War until the beginning of the First World War. Whole immigrant families, women and little ones included, labored long hours in the fields. But the cotton gins, general stores, and one-room schools are long gone, and the two little settlements are being swallowed up forever by development associated with Austin's new Bergstrom International Airport, which moved out here with the closing of Bergstrom Air Force Base.

PILOT KNOB

One mile west of US 183, just south of the FM 812 junction
Private property

Pilot Knob is the best known of several dozen volcanic craters and mounds that stretch along the Balcones fault zone. The three rounded, knoblike hills that collectively make up Pilot Knob rise up nearly 200 feet higher than the surrounding countryside. Visible for miles around, Pilot Knob has been a guidepost for human travelers for thousands of years. Travelers on the Pinto and Chisholm Trails knew that the Colorado River lay just a few hours north, and that a good place to cross it was a shallow ford about where US 183 crosses the river today.

Pilot Knob was born about 80 million years ago, during the Cretaceous, when Austin and most of the rest of modern-day Texas was covered by a shallow sea that we now call the Gulf of Mexico. Following the creation of the Balcones fault zone from a belt of fractures in the earth's crust, hot molten lava rose from deep inside the earth and pushed up through the seawater. Explosions caused by steam shook the sea's floor, and craters formed around these explosion vents. Ash, debris blown from the volcano, and lava filled the crater, creating a dome that rose above the sea floor. After things cooled off, reef organisms were attracted to the dome's irregular surfaces, and the reefs they formed were not unlike the coral reefs of the South Pacific and the Flower Gardens reef in the Gulf of Mexico, off Galveston. Beach rock formed where the waves lapped at the volcano's peripheries; this beach rock can be seen in nearby McKinney Falls State Park. As we know, the sea eventually receded, leaving Texas behind, and the exposed sea floor began to weather away to its current state. Pilot Knob's volcanic rock has resisted erosion better than the surrounding soft limestone. The hilltops of the knob are the exposed lava core itself, a volcanic rock called nephelinite, which is related to basalt.

Central Texans have long regarded Pilot Knob as a treasure mountain, believing that riches had once been buried here, or more down to earth, that they could find diamonds here. The great diamond mines of South Africa and Arkansas are dug into similar geologic formations. In 1919, professor J. A. Udden announced that the entire dome of the knob was composed of "nephelite basalt," also called "traprock," and that this was the toughest rock to be found in Texas. Promoter Arvid Franke of San Antonio promptly announced his high hopes for turning this noble knob of rock into lowly road-surfacing material. He said that he would build the crusher if the International & Great Northern Railroad would extend their tracks 6.5 miles in his direction. The railroad declined, and so the knobs sit here, covered with scrubby trees and getting a littler smaller each millenia. And with the new airport nearby, Pilot Knob once again marks the crossroads of international commerce. And Travis County's Pilot Knob mustn't be confused with Williamson County's Pilot Knob, which is more commonly known as Mt. Gabriel.

Turn left on FM 812 toward Red Rock. In 5 miles you come to Elroy.

ELROY

Travis County • 125 • About 5 miles from Pilot Knob

It is said that the land on which Elroy is located was once owned by an officer in Santa Anna's army, who traded it for a horse and saddle, presumably to avoid walking home. The area saw its first permanent white settlers around Civil War times. The area was first known as Blocker's Pasture, or Driskill's Pasture, after its owner, Jesse Driskill. (This cattle tycoon's most enduring legacy is the Austin hotel that bears his name.) Driskill eventually sold his pasture to a man named Tolbin, and after that the land began to be subdivided. A. A. Molund was the first to settle here permanently, in 1892.

At this time the neighborhood was also known as Dutch Water Hole. It seems an old Dutch (probably meaning German) sheepherder camped with his flock here regularly on Mayhard-Maha Creek, where it makes its Elroy bend just east of the Elroy Hill and just south of FM 812. The creek was deep enough at the bend to be called a water hole, and one unfortunate day it was also deep enough to drown the old shepherd. The name floated.

Dutch Water Hole had a store and school by 1896, and soon the Water Holers were hankering for a post office. Prominent local healer and shopkeeper Dr. Black spearheaded the hamlet's drive. Dutch Water Hole was not an appropriate name, so Dr. Black circulated through the village soliciting new name suggestions. This is where we lose track of the story for a bit. We know the postal service approved "Elroy," and Elroy it has been ever since, but we do not know how that peculiar moniker was coined. Local historian C. W. Carlson says that Dr. Black asked Thomas Roy Miles, engineer at the local cotton gin, for his suggestion. The two put their heads together and came up with Miles' middle name "Roy." But somewhere, somehow along the way, "El" was tacked on. Was it *el,* the Spanish word for "the"? Was it short for a name like Eldridge or Eleanor? Or was it short for Louis or Louise? No one knows any more. Carlson believes that the store sign may have read "El Roy" at the turn of the century, but he's not sure. Such dual and even triple name combinations were common at the time and resulted in some of Texas' most colorful place names. But an aging Austin newspaper clipping assures us that Elroy resulted from a little switcheroo performed on a local settler's name—Leroy.

Elroy became a predominantly Swedish farming and ranching community and trade center. Its commercial importance began to decline in the 1930s, and the corrugated-tin hulks of the old Elroy general store and gin on your right atop Elroy Hill have long stood vacant.

The land between Elroy and Red Rock on FM 812 is sparsely populated and given over mainly to ranching. As you draw closer to Red Rock, the color of the sandy loam gets progressively redder. About 12 miles from Elroy, watch for the "High Grove" sign, which marks a paved county road. Turn left (north) here and go about 0.5 mile to reach High Grove.

HIGH GROVE

Bastrop County • About 12 miles from Elroy

High Grove is a pleasant place to stop for a bit of rest and reflection. The **old whitewashed building** doubled for years as the "white folks" school and church. The "coloreds" had to go to St. Lytton's school or St. John's school, down the road toward Red Rock and farther south. The **cemetery** at High Grove is kept meticulously clean by an old black gentleman and his wife, and the venerable cedars dotting the yard provide cool aromatic shade. It's easy to lose track of the years out here under the cedars. Most everybody at High Grove moved to Red Rock in the 1890s.

Nearby, back on FM 812 and on your left are an old cabin and log outbuildings used in the filming of Leadbelly *several years ago. Continue eastward on FM 812 toward Red Rock.*

RED ROCK

Bastrop County • 100 • (512) About 16 miles from Elroy
Red Rock was originally known as Hannah—for an early local family of that name—and was originally located several miles west of its present site, about where the cemeteries are now. The **old city cemetery** contains a cast-iron tombstone, something of a rarity. It has a blank square cast for an inscription, but the inscription area is empty, apparently never filled.

The Old Red Rock Cemetery is off FM 812 to your right, down a dirt road (Cty. Rd. 229) about half a mile. The newer cemetery is a mile closer to Red Rock on FM 812, on the left.

As is the case with many small towns, there are several different versions of how Red Rock got its name. One says the name is owed to the red rock used by early settler James Brewer to construct the chimney of his cabin in the 1850s. Another says that it refers to the red rock embedded in the banks of nearby Walnut Creek, where the old Waelder to Austin road used to cross. Early settlers would caravan to Austin once or twice a year to buy supplies, and the "red rock" crossing of Walnut Creek was one of the designated gathering points.

Red Rock was a prosperous community by the 1870s, with both a post office and separate academies for young men and women. Red Rock was also a volatile little town; the Texas Legislature passed a special law forbidding the sale of liquor within a two-mile radius of the schools.

Having been settled by emigres from the Old South, with much of the land farmed plantation-style (i.e., with slave labor) in antebellum days, it is not surprising that Red Rock was a violent place during Reconstruction days. Blacks were flexing their new muscles of freedom, egged on by the carpetbaggers in Austin who made the freedmen many promises they had no intention of keeping. These unwitting ex-slaves were being used to punish southern whites. The postwar years were explosive ones. The Loyalty and Union Leaguers warred with the White Caps and the Ku Kluxers and nobody won, except maybe the carpetbaggers, who took what they could and ran.

Andrew J. "Andy" Potter—the "Fightin' Parson"—was a circuit-riding preacher in those days. Potter was a sort of modern-day St.

Paul, a gambler, saloonkeeper, killer, and blasphemer of the worst sort before finding his God. Potter's rounds took him to Red Rock to preach every so often, in spite of the young hellions' threats to shoot him or run him out of town. Potter always wore a pair of Colt 45s on his hips for just such occasions. While preaching at nearby Lytton Springs one Sunday, Potter was warned not to come to Red Rock on the next Sabbath. Potter replied that he would most certainly be there and that furthermore he expected a fine chicken dinner afterward. When he arrived at the meetinghouse the following Sunday, Potter laid his shootin' irons on the rude pulpit table in front of him and announced, "Now I sent word that I was coming to Red Rock to preach and I'm gonna preach. But I can shoot too. And if anyone wants a fight and starts one, we'll shoot it out." Potter preached his service and got his chicken dinner.

The life of a circuit preacher was not always fried chicken and pound cake for Sunday dinner, as this joke illustrates:

A circuit rider was conducting a prayer meeting out in a recently, thinly settled section where any event beyond the daily routine of staying alive was novelty. Everyone from miles around was present. At the end of his evening's message, the preacher asked of his audience: "Would all Christians please stand up?"

Not a soul moved.

"What! Not a friend of Jesus in the house?" he asked.

At which point one cowboy stood up declaring: "Stranger, I don't know who this Jesus feller is, but I'll stand up for any man that hasn't got any more friends than he has."

Feuds were a way of life in early Red Rock. Folks shot each other in the streets, on the highways, in the fields they worked. At least once, Red Rockers marched over to neighboring Cedar Creek to help their white friends in a big shootout there. Signs posted on the roads leading into Red Rock read: "Negro/Troublemakers don't let the sun set on you in Red Rock." Blacks all over the United States knew about Red Rock's warning signs, and long after the signs were gone, around World War II, blacks were afraid to be found in town after sunset. If they were detained past dark, they asked for a sympathetic white escort out of town. To this day, no blacks live in Red Rock; the closest black community is in St. John's Colony, more than ten miles away.

Like the Knobbs country farther north in Bastrop County (see The Wild West—The Knobbs), it was a rare man in Red Rock who didn't have a killing or two under his belt, well into the twentieth century. And we're talking about pillars of the community too—honorable family men, bank and store owners—not fly-by-night ruffians. Why?

Ask, and you'll get no answer better than "a man has to protect his own." Perhaps it has to do with the isolation of the place, far from the county seat or any other sizable town with law enforcement, in country where the roads were often rendered impassable for weeks at a time by deep red, sticky mud. The railroad was the only dependable way in and out until the 1940s, when the first paved road came through (SH 20). Telephone service didn't come until after World War II. Such isolation attracted and bred an independent lot, which, out of necessity, made its own law. Folks don't kill each other anymore, but nobody's forgotten the past either, and so the feuding hangs on, but in a less bloody manner. Visitors, of course, have nothing to fear; on the contrary, a pleasant conversation is easily commenced.

But Red Rock was a progressive little town, too. Cotton, corn, melons, and other truck crops grew well here, and after the town's move over to the railroad tracks in the 1890s, Red Rock had doctors, hotels, a drugstore, a bank, and all the other customary businesses of a regional trade center. By 1906 Red Rock had its first brick building, a source of pride for the entire town. Red Rock's bank was the largest between Smithville and Lockhart. The Black brothers showed Bastrop County's first talking pictures in the county's first real movie house, built in 1929. Earlier they had shown silent flicks in a makeshift alfresco theater located in the back lot of the lumberyard.

Red Rock was resilient, too. Thirteen businesses burned in 1918 and the town rebuilt. The downtown burned again in 1924 from the **Liberty Garage** (still standing) down to the old depot, and everyone built again. Red Rockers were a proud, stubborn lot— particularly proud of their town baseball team. When asked if the New York Yankees might just possibly be capable of beating the Red Rock nine, the answer was "Not in Red Rock, they couldn't." The Great Depression finally did Red Rock in. Although the discovery of oil during the 1930s brought another spurt of activity to the area, little remains today. The bank used to be on the corner as you entered downtown Red Rock. It collapsed to rubble in the early seventies, and for years thereafter old men sat around cleaning salvageable bricks from the wreckage. Now even the rubble is gone. Only a weedy, uneven lot marks its former location. The Lentz store, Petty's store next door, and the new post office are the sum total of downtown Red Rock today.

RED ROCK GENERAL STORE AND FEED
201 Main, downtown Red Rock • 321-3360 • Open daily
No Cr.
Duncan Lentz ran this store from 1920 until his death in 1990, and could tell many stories of the area, if you knew how to get him

to talk. Dunc is gone now, but his cats are still here. The new owners have cleaned and repaired the building considerably, but held on to Dunc's old Coke cooler and put on display some of the old farm tools they found in the feed store. Ask to see the "Last Supper" mural on the feed store wall, painted in the 1930s by a hobo who got off the train one day, painted this, and then moved on.

From Red Rock, head south on FM 20. In a couple of hundred yards you pass through Bateman.

BATEMAN

Bastrop County • Just outside Red Rock
Bateman, settled in the 1880s, was named for an early resident. The coming of the Missouri-Kansas-Texas railroad in 1887 promised growth and prosperity, but the post office stayed open only from 1900 to 1904 and Red Rock instead became the area's shipping center.

Turn left on FM 86.

Ranching is still the economic mainstay of these thinly settled sandy-loam prairies, along with a little oil activity left over from the salad days of the late 1970s when $40 a barrel prices seduced producers into reviving the original, abandoned Depression-era fields.

TAYLORSVILLE

Caldwell County • About 6 miles from Red Rock
Taylorsville, now more a memory than a village, was named for a local landowner and has no identifiable center.

Turn left on FM 713 at McMahan.

McMAHAN

Caldwell County • 125 • About 10 miles from Red Rock
McMahan lies on Tinney Creek (spelled Tenney on the highway maps), a branch of Plum Creek. The creek was named for Ambrose Tinney, who came here from Germany in 1831 and bought a league of land from the Mexican government for about 9¢ an acre. Other families began to drift in during the 1840s. Sometime during the 1880s, D. W. Ellis established the area's first store, about 0.5 mile

north of present day McMahan at a place called Wildcat. Later a saloon was built on the east bank of Tinney Creek, just east of present day McMahan, near the busy intersection of the Lockhart-to-La Grange and Red Rock-to-Luling roads. The saloon and surrounding neighborhood soon became known as Whizzerville. The story goes that one of the saloon's regular patrons, who seldom stayed sober, got so obnoxiously drunk one day that his neighbors set their dogs on him. The drunkard galloped away on his horse in an effort to rid himself of his tormentors, but the dogs stayed glued to his horse's heels. The horse headed back for the saloon and, without stopping, lumbered through the saloon and out the back door, its half-senseless rider still hanging on. One patron remarked that the rider was sure "in a whiz," whereupon a local answered back, "this is Whizzerville." The name pleased hangers on, and that's what the neighborhood came to be known as.

In 1890 Ed McMahan (no relation to Johnny Carson's second banana) built a store at the crossroads where McMahan now stands. Other businesses followed. A post office was established in 1896, but although locals favored the name Whizzerville, post office authorities rejected it. McMahan, Cole, Blundell, and Jeffrey were among the alternatives suggested, all were last names of prominent early settlers or merchants. Guess who won? R.W. "Bob" McMahan became first postmaster.

Several of the old commercial buildings still stand, including the old post office/general store, a one-story shotgun frame building with three bay windows separated by two sets of front doors. This facade style is not often seen in surviving buildings across the Hill Country. The old "McMahan, Tx." post office sign still hangs from the porch, but the store has been closed since the early 1970s. You cross Tinney Creek just after leaving "downtown" McMahan.

DELHI

Caldwell County • About 8.1 miles from McMahan

Delhi, at the SH 304/FM 713 crossroads, is no longer listed on the maps and not even the old folks know for sure how Delhi got its name. But according to several stories passed down, Delhi got its name from a travelling medicine man named Delhi. He stayed for a couple of months in the area putting on his shows. Since there was little else in the way of fun around here in those days, the young men from surrounding neighborhoods and settlements were always talking about going over to see Delhi, and so the name stuck long after the medicine man packed up his tent and stole away. The name dates at least as far back as 1879. A small church and school turned community center are located a ways south on SH 304.

JEDDO

Bastrop County • 75 • About 5 miles from Delhi
Jeddo is another ghost town. Established in the 1860s, it had a post office from 1874 to 1927. The school is gone; even the two general stores serving ranchers through World War II have disappeared completely.

At Jeddo, FM 713 runs out and you must turn right on FM 1296.

HOPKINSVILLE

Gonzales County • About 2 miles from Jeddo
A couple of miles south of Jeddo is the site of the completely vanished town of Hopkinsville. Founded by D. S. Hopkins in the 1850s, Hopkinsville was a farming community that grew into a cattle town after the Civil War. Herds bound for Kansas via the Chisholm Trail gathered here. When Hopkinsville was bypassed by the railroad, the townspeople moved to Waelder.

WAELDER

Gonzales County • 785 • About 9 miles from Jeddo
Waelder sprang up with the arrival of the Galveston, Harrisburg, and San Antonio (GH&SA) railroad and was named for Jacob Waelder, a German emigre who came from Pennsylvania to San Antonio in 1852. Veteran of the Mexican War of 1848, newspaperman, and lawyer, Waelder served three terms in the Texas Legislature before the Civil War and did a stint in the Confederate Army. Waelder resumed his prominent public stance after the war and labored extensively for the state's railroad interests. Grateful GH&SA officials named the town Waelder in honor of their hardworking company attorney. In 1900 Waelder was Gonzales County's second largest town. Waelder still possesses a number of well-kept Victorian homes, reminders of that era of prosperity.

Turn right on FM 1115 when FM 1296 dead-ends. After 5 blocks on FM 1115, you come to US 90 and the main crossroads of Waelder. There are also some more nice Victorian houses on Ave. D (if you go straight beyond where FM 1296 turns east).

MILLER'S STORE
US 90, one block east of FM 1115

The old R. L. Miller store is identifiable by the historical medallion on the wall. First established in 1866, Miller's was until recently your typical general store, selling everything from horseshoes to sardines to televisions to crockery. A hat and dress shop was located upstairs during Waelder's heyday. In those days Miller gave every newborn boy a pair of pants with an attached card that stated that these pants were to be worn on the boy's first birthday, compliments of Miller's Store. Those were also the days when local boys would wait for the sack of liquor on the Saturday train from Flatonia. Then they would "relax" a bit with their bottles and shoot up whatever came to mind—the sky, the awning, each other, or anyone else foolish enough to come downtown on a Saturday night. You can still see some of the bullet holes in Miller's tin awning.

ANNUAL EVENT

SEPTEMBER • Fiesta Guacamole • Downtown Waelder • Labor Day weekend, Friday through Sunday • Free except dinner • W

Chili cook-offs leave you cold? Then try the Fiesta Guacamole, where you—yes, you—could become the world's champion guacamole masher. Besides Sunday's world championship guacamole mash-off, this Mexican-style celebration includes a carnival and midway, homemade Mexican food, a parade, and lots of hot dance music.

Take US 90 east out of Waelder.

The numerous fading and peeling car lots and business establishments littering the road out of town testify to Waelder's prosperity through the preinterstate era, when US 90 was *the* traveler's route from Houston to San Antonio. The interstate highway system has crippled or killed dozens of towns like Waelder, much as the railroads did towns like Hopkinsville 100 years ago.

At the edge of town, turn right on FM 1680 to Moulton.

As you roll through this gently undulating prairie, you notice that here, too, oil rigs compete with the Hereford, Charolais, and Angus for pasture space.

OLD MOULTON

Lavaca County • About 12 miles from Waelder
Soon you reach the venerable white-frame church that is the surviving total of Old Moulton, the "Queen of the Prairies," so named for its blackland prairie soil that once produced bumper crops. In 1834 the Winters family walked most of the way from Mississippi to East Texas, a two-month trip. In 1852 they settled here on the Lavaca River and named their settlement Moulton after their Mississippi hometown. Or so goes one story. Others say Moulton was named for an early settler. Still others say the name came from a traveler who said the area's live oak mottes reminded him of his hometown of Moulton in Alabama. At any rate, Moulton prospered as a farming community and supply stop on the Chisholm Trail. From 1874 to 1895 it was the home of the Moulton Male and Female Institute, which boasted one of the state's top music departments. The great hurricane of 1886 blew the academy and most of the town down. Locals started to rebuild, but the San Antonio and Aransas Pass (SA&AP) railroad came along the next year two miles east of Old Moulton, on its way from Yoakum to Waco. The exodus to the new townsite laid out alongside the tracks began that same year of 1887. The institute was rebuilt in Old Moulton and hung on there until 1895, when the founder's widow tired of the business and moved to San Antonio.

MOULTON

Lavaca County • 969 • (512) • About 14 miles from Waelder

SAINT JOSEPH'S CATHOLIC CHURCH
Church at Pecan, off FM 1680
Saint Joseph's church and cemetery greets you as you enter Moulton. Built in 1924, the church's interior has recently been restored to its original classic Gothic style with long, narrow nave, side aisles supported by 10 columns, stained glass windows, and chancel.

Soon after you pass Saint Joseph's Catholic Church, you come to an intersection with FM 532. Turn left here to reach downtown Moul-

ton, which runs alongside the railroad tracks. As you approach downtown, you can see that much of old "new" Moulton remains.

Even a fleeting perusal of the two commercial blocks of Main St. reveals that Moulton was once a prosperous, bustling town. All the buildings are built of brick or sandstone, in a rainbow of colors and styles. The collective, mostly continuous rooflines on each block take your eyes on a crazy roller coaster-like ride.

Main St. parallels the tracks but is set back aways up the hill, away from the smoke and dust and general hubbub that used to surround the depot. Between Main St. and the tracks are the rusting cotton gin and sprawling warehouse that were once bursting with bales.

OLD BOEHM STORE
Main at Moore

This sandstone building is one of Moulton's oldest business structures, built in 1906. Ed Boehm started a saloon and general store on this corner in 1887. Boehm was a recently arrived refugee from Moravia via Russia. Russia's governmental restrictions and popular ignorance had disgusted Boehm. A college graduate, he worked for 50 cents a day upon his arrival in the New World, in order to establish a grubstake. Many of his hardworking and hungry Moravian friends joined him here during the next few decades.

The stone used to build the store was quarried a couple of miles west of Moulton at the old Maurin Quarry. New Moulton continued as "Queen of the Prairies" until tenant farmers and the one-crop (cotton) farming system began to fade from the scene. As cotton played out, Moulton became Texas' leading garlic production center for a few years preceding World War II. Frank Wagner, late proprietor of Wagner's General Merchandise, remembered that the whole town reeked of garlic at harvest time as the trackside warehouses were filled with the pungent root. By 1939, Texas was second only to California in garlic production. But the garlic boom faded, as did the smell of garlic, and by the late 1960s it was just a pungent memory.

MOULTON PUBLIC LIBRARY AND MUSEUM
102 Main • Open Monday through Friday

On display are early city and county photos and documents. There are also rotating exhibits.

PAVLA'S TAVERN
114 S. Main • Open daily • 596-4449 • No Cr.

Pavla's Tavern was built in 1922 and has changed little in appearance over the years. You'll enjoy the antique bar and cheap beer.

MAIN BAR
111 N. Main • Open daily • No Cr.
A great vintage place to stop for a cold one. The Main Bar has been here since 1925, as have many of the place's fixtures, both inanimate and human. Beautiful wire-frame bar stools, pressed-tin ceiling, linoleum domino tables, and cheap beer.

Moulton has dozens of late Victorian/pre-World War I homes still standing, mostly along West 1st, West 2nd, and Arnim streets, all of which run parallel to Main.

Up at the corner of North St. and West 2nd, on the north end of Moulton, is the old Sam and Will Moore Institute, now part of the Moulton public school system.

SAM AND WILL MOORE INSTITUTE
North St. at West 2nd
When this two-story brick Greek Revival-style school was built in 1901, it was the pride of the region. Brothers Sam and Will Moore donated the land plus half of the cost of building the school. The rest of the construction money was raised by the rest of the town. Dedication day is celebrated with a parade, concerts, speeches in Czech, German, and English, a big barbecue, and a ball.

KLOESEL'S STEAKHOUSE AND BAR
101 E. Moore • 596-7323 • Open daily, lunch and dinner
$–$$ • W
The Moore Hotel was located here from 1889 to 1940. In 1940 it became Ed's Market and Grocery, and in 1942 it was converted into a restaurant. There is also a full bar and dance floor.

To leave Moulton, return to FM 532 (Moore St.), cross the railroad tracks, and turn right on SH 95 toward Shiner.

PATEK'S MARKET
FM 532 at SH 95 • 596-7116 • Open daily • W
Patek's makes and sells some of the best sausages and smoked meats to be found anywhere: wieners, turkey sausage, pork sausage,

pork and beef sausage, turkey and pork sausage, German sausage, head sausage, liver sausage, bacon, turkey summer sausage, turkey pepper ham, and turkey wieners. Every Saturday they make and sell barbecue brisket, chicken, pork ribs, and pork steaks. The turkey products are made especially for the fat- and cholesterol-conscious who might otherwise abstain.

As you speed away from Moulton, toss your head back at Moulton's water tower, built in 1917 and brought to Moulton in 1935. Moulton has called it the second-tallest water tower in Texas; it's one of the tallest, at any rate.

Moulton's most famous son is musician Adolph Hofner, born here in June 1916. When he was 10, the family moved to San Antonio. Of Czech/German heritage, Hofner first gained fame as leader of a "South Texas" western swing band that rivaled Bob Wills in popularity, at least around San Antonio. He recorded his first songs in 1935. After World War II, he returned to his roots and began playing a unique, delightful blend of Czech and German polkas and waltzes, and western swing music. He's been called the Bing Crosby of Texas swing. Much of his work was recorded by Charlie Fitch's Sarg Records, in Luling. More on Fitch later. Adolph is getting old and only plays a couple of times a year now, so the easiest way to get acquainted with Adolph's music these days is to pick up a copy of an Arhoolie/Folklyric CD titled *Texas-Czech Bohemian & Moravian Bands Historic Recordings 1929–1959*. Among the songs he does is the "Shiner Song," which is a Texanization of the old Czech standard, "Farewell to Prague." The CD also features another band from just down the road in Shiner, the Joe Patek Orchestra.

HENKHAUS

Lavaca County • 60 • About 5 miles from Moulton

Henkhaus, which lies along the old SA&AP line and off the highway to the west a mile or so, is another one of those many faded Texas farm villages. It was named for its founder, a Mr. Henkhaus from Shiner. In its prime, Henkhaus boasted a store, dance and beer hall, cotton gin, and the Evergreen School.

SULPHUR PARK
SH 95 • About 5 miles from Moulton

Sulphur Park, a longtime popular local bathing resort, was founded by Jake Kurc in the 1920s. Its chief attraction was the sulphur-water swimming pool; many people thought the water had special medicinal and therapeutic qualities, much like the warm springs between Gonzales and Luling.

SHINER

Lavaca County • 2,201 • (512) • About 10 miles from Moulton

You are now in sight of mecca—Shiner—which started life as the little hamlet of Half Moon sometime during Civil War days. The name Half Moon came from the peculiar half-moon shape of the stand of timber surrounding the little trading post and community center. Of course in those days most of this area was treeless prairie, waist-high in sage and buffalo grass. Half Moon saw its share of lawlessness and tragedy in those turbulent early days.

In the 1890s a young drifter—barely 19—murdered a local wealthy landowner for his money. A vigilante posse was organized and after 30 hours they tracked the boy into a rough area just east of present-day Shiner, called "The Boundary." The boy and his horse were exhausted, out of water and out of food. When he looked behind him he could see his pursuers and the glint of the setting sun on their gun barrels. The posse drew nearer, and finally at the top of a hill the boy's horse dropped dead. The young killer disentangled himself and stood calmly but defiantly, rifle in hand, facing his pursuers. The posse halted just out of his range to consult among themselves, then started slowly toward the young man, uncertain of what he meant to do. The group halted just within shooting range, and their leader, a brutish man and experienced killer, shouted, "Do you want to give up?"

"No, I don't—shoot if you want to. I want to die like a man and will shoot the first man who comes a foot nearer," was the boy's defiant response, as he braced himself for the inevitable.

The leader stepped forward, rifle cocked, and shouted, "Surrender or I'll shoot the hell out of you." He swung his rifle to shooting position as he spoke, his men and the boy following suit. Their shots rang out as one, and the posse captain fell forward, shot dead through the heart. The vigilantes stood silent for a moment, then started to move, some toward their leader, others toward the boy, who lay "gasping, his chest torn by the rifle fire, trying desperately to raise himself from where he had fallen. His life ebbed away as his life blood poured upon the ground and with it he paid his penalty under the law."

The survivors buried their captain and the boy in a common grave, "a few yards from the creek and near a clump of live oaks" and then galloped away into the night.

Of course, such occurrences were not uncommon here in the "Free State of Lavaca," so named because of Lavaca County's habitual lack of respect for whomever held the reins of government at the time. In 1835 the Lavacans resisted the Mexican government. In 1860 the county voted almost unanimously for secession; four years later it was denouncing Jeff Davis and his war. In the 1880s Lavacans fought barbed wire, railroads, and land monopolists. From 1910 to 1916, the county was a hotbed of socialism, and in 1920 county voters bolted the Democratic Party gubernatorial ticket in favor of impeached governor "Gentleman Jim" Ferguson. Throughout Prohibition, Lavaca County vehemently resisted its enforcement. Lavaca County's Germans and Czechs loved their beer, as evidenced by this chestnut of a joke:

A local option election had been held in a predominantly German Lavaca County precinct, and the election judge was counting out the votes.

"Vet, vet, vet, vet . . ." he droned. Then suddenly frowning, he said, "Dr-r-ry." He continued, "Vet, vet, vet, vet, vet . . ." until his eyebrows bristled and he exclaimed, "The son-of-a-gun—he voted twice!"

But back to Shiner. Henry B. Shiner was born in Victoria in 1848, of Luxembourgian ancestry. He entered the cattle business in the early, open range days and drove herds up the Chisholm Trail. With the widespread distribution of barbed wire, Shiner was one of the first to buy and fence in extensive land holdings, owning some 8,000 acres in Lavaca County by the mid-1880s. It was at this time that Shiner saw the chance to make a bundle off his landholdings by settling the oncoming waves of German and Slavic immigrants there. But he needed the railroads to make his promotion work. He made a deal to split his profits with the SA&AP railway, so when the first SA&AP train chugged through in 1887 Old Half Moon was left high and dry.

Immigrants poured into the nearby new town, known for a time as New Half Moon. The name was soon changed to Shiner and both the town and namesake prospered, in spite of the prairie fires that raged through Shiner during those early years. In 1894 burglars trying to dynamite open the safe in Wangeman's store started a fire that destroyed most of downtown.

The desperadoes escaped with no money and Shiner rebuilt again. In the true stubborn tradition of the Free State of Lavaca, Shiner had two schools in those days, both named the Shiner School. This caused considerable confusion, since the schools were in the same school district. One dated back to the Half Moon days of 1884; the other came with the new town. Neither school would change its name. Shiner No. 1 and Shiner No. 2 was the best compromise they could strike, until the day No. 1 caught fire and Fred Bunjes was the big hero in saving the school. Shiner School No. 1 was officially called the Bunjes School from that day on, but to most of the natives it was still Shiner No. 1.

As you enter Shiner, you see on your left the **Kaspar Wire Works.** Shiner was a cotton town from the word go, but in 1898, farmer August Kaspar began a factory that prospers to this day. In 1895, Kaspar figured out a way to recycle discarded smooth wire into something useful and cheap. With the advent of barbed wire, ranchers began to replace their old smooth-wire fences in favor of the more effective barbed wire. Using a pair of pliers, he handwove the smooth wire into cornshuck baskets and horse muzzles for personal use. When neighbors saw them, they wanted some, and soon Shiner's leading stores were selling his products. By 1905, it was a full-time job, and so Kaspar moved into the town of Shiner. With the decline in demand for baskets and muzzles, the wire works began to make florist easels, coat hangers, gym baskets, shopping baskets, shelving, display racks, and newspaper vending machines and racks. Still family owned and operated, Kaspar Wire Works is the largest producer and renovator of newspaper racks in the world. The product line now includes barber chair stands, fan guards, and computer components.

Shiner is still very much a Czech-German community. You don't hear either language spoken on the streets anymore, but the older generation still speaks it at home. The churches still hold the soul of Shiner and dominate the Shiner skyline, along with the Spoetzl Brewery. Many local youth attend the local Catholic 12-year male and female academies. There are no real mansions in Shiner, but there are few bugtussle shacks either, which befits a town that calls itself the "Cleanest Little City in Texas."

Right across SH 95 from the Kaspar Wire Works is the Spoetzl Brewery.

SPOETZL BREWERY
603 E. Brewery • 594-3383 • W variable

The brewery began business in 1909 as a community-owned concern. In 1914, Kosmos Spoetzl purchased the little brewery. Born in Bavaria in 1874, Spoetzl worked his way through the Augsburg Brewery School and then worked at several breweries in Munich and in Bohemia to gain additional knowledge and experience. Spoetzl spent five years in Cairo, Egypt (where he brewed Pyramid beer), but decided he didn't like the climate, and moved to Canada. On his way to Saskatchewan, he caught pneumonia. At that point, he decided that San Antonio looked better and headed south. That was in 1914. In San Antonio, he read a newspaper ad placed by a little community brewery in Shiner, searching for someone to rent the facility. The local owners were better at drinking beer than brewing it. Spoetzl leapt at the chance and moved to Shiner, where he put all the knowledge and experience at his command into his beer. Soon he bought the brewery outright.

Kosmos Spoetzl had a simple marketing philosophy: A good beer will sell itself. So he set out to brew the very best beer he could. That done, he had to make sure that people drank it. Spoetzl knew that once a man had tasted his Shiner beer, he would buy it. So he bought a Model T, and with a couple of kegs iced down in the back, Spoetzl and his dog bumped across the rolling, fertile prairies that surround Shiner, roping in thirsty farmers and travelers and then plying the adults with ice-cold beer and the kids with silver coins.

Spoetzl produced just one beer, officially called "Old World Bavarian Draft," which was a heavy, dark, all-malt German-style lager that spoke eloquently to his mostly Czech and German audience. The Volstead Act of 1918 put many breweries out of business, but Spoetzl hung on, selling ice, brewing near beer, and storing deer carcasses. But stories abound as to the not-so-near beer that escaped from here. Joe Greene, now deceased, was the brewery's unofficial historian and Methuselah, having first started work here in 1930. He worked over 50 years here; nephew Cracker Wallace is nearing the mark. Average employee tenure here is 25 years; they evidently like what they do for a living.

But back to the near beer; Joe Greene had this to say, for the record: "We just made the beer like we always had, then reboiled it to get the alcohol out and please the Federal men." The reboiling process regularly engulfed the rest of the town with its distinctive sour mash stink. The Spoetzl Brewery trucks starting rolling again the very minute that Prohibition ended in Texas (one minute past midnight on September 15, 1933) to towns like Praha, Muldoon, Dime Box, Nickle Community, and the Sandies. Spoetzl never went much more than 70 miles out of his way in any direction for business.

The end of Prohibition also brought an increase in production, and the brewery now employed between 35 and 40 people during the winter, adding on a few more people during the thirstier summer months. Spoetzl also changed the name (but not the recipe) of his beer to "Texas Special Export," and began bottling it for the first time, in the familiar export bottle (neophytes call it a longneck). Slowly but surely, the brewery grew over the years. The brick Spanish Revival brewhouse and office building were built in 1947. Kosmos died in 1950 and his daughter Cecilie—"Miss Celie"—inherited the brewery and was for a time the only female brewery owner in the country. She didn't exactly rock the boat with radical changes. Shiner did not appear in no-return bottles until 1958, and wasn't canned until 1970, 4 years after Miss Celie sold the brewery to a group of New Braunfels businessmen. But she continued to live across the street from the brewery in a pink brick house that has since been moved elsewhere.

Kosmos' conservative influence was such that after 50 years, the recipe of Texas Special Export remained unchanged. He had been fiercely, colorfully, idiosyncratically protective of his beer. "Water's for washing your feet," he had long ordained, "If you want to drink, drink Shiner beer." Whenever he caught someone salting his beer, he would snatch the salt shaker away and say thunderingly, "If my beer needed salt, I would have put salt in it."

But times and tastes were changing toward lighter beer, and the new owners began experimenting with the recipe, adding corn to the previously all-malt beer, until they came up with Shiner "Premium" beer, a lighter-bodied brew more in line with contemporary tastes. They also upped the brewery's capacity to 72,000 barrels per year.

But despite the change in recipe and brewing capacity, Shiner remained every bit as much a handmade and naturally brewed beer as it was in 1915. It's still brewed with artesian water from the original well drilled for the brewery. Because of the natural brewing process (which takes the better part of a month), it takes up to three times as long to brew a batch of Shiner as some of your bigger sellers. And calorie watchers take note: Because Shiner's brewing process uses less sugar, it has 15 to 20 calories less per beer than most other brands.

Various flavors of Shiner are now brewed (Blonde, Bock, Kosmos Reserve, and Honey-Wheat, as of January 1997), but the brewery's bread-and-butter brand is Shiner Bock. Bock is traditionally an early spring beer, and brewery records indicate that bock was brewed here as early as 1917. But its popularity (and year-round production) is a relatively recent phenomenon that owes to the old Austin hippie scene. Shiner Premium became a popular beer for members of the Austin counterculture during the early 1970s for a variety of reasons (including low price). But when a seasonal shipment of Shiner Bock rode into town in about 1975, it was love at first quaff. By 1978, Spoetzl was brewing Bock the year round, chiefly to slake the Austin market's prodigious thirst. Beer bars in traditional Shiner territory (remember Kosmos's 70-mile radius rule), almost exclusively stocked Shiner Premium; Bock was an Austin thing.

Now the largest regional brewer in the Southwest, Shiner is no longer the only "Little Brewery" in Texas, although it's still far from being a giant. While major brewers can produce up to 3.5 million cases per day, Shiner produced and sold almost 1.8 million cases in 1995 (double its 1993 sales). Shiner is no longer just a central Texas phenomenon; you can buy it in a number of major American cities now. And now there's Kosmos Special Reserve, a pricey boutique beer that attempts to recapture some of the Old-World flavor of Old World Bavarian Draft without its heft. The brewery's one ancient copper brew kettle has been replaced by five new brew kettles; it had worn so thin that you could dent it by leaning on it. The new kettles are made of copper-plated stainless steel. The beer is aged in 300-gallon and 600-gallon glass-lined steel tanks, some of which date to the Kosmos days. Brewery tours are given Monday through Friday at 11 a.m. and 1:30 p.m. The hospitality room is open Monday through Friday after the brewery tour. The gift shop is open Monday through Saturday. Visit the Shiner Web site on the World Wide Web at http://www.shiner.com.

From the Spoetzl Brewery, continue south on SH 95 to downtown Shiner. As you approach the junction with US 90A, you see old downtown Shiner on your right.

As in Moulton, most of Shiner's old business houses line the railroad tracks for several blocks. The elaborate brickwork on these buildings testify to Shiner's turn of the century prosperity.

Turn right on US 90A, cross the tracks, and turn right on 7th St.

PALACE CAFE
103 N. 7th • 594-2711 • Open Monday through Saturday, breakfast and lunch, sometimes later, depending on customer traffic • $ • No Cr. • W partial
Located in the Wm. Green building (1911), the Palace Cafe has a towering mirrored bar back that is worthy of the cafe's name. Daily lunch specials are popular; if they're sold out, content yourself with an old-fashioned hamburger or stew.

SHINER OPERA HOUSE
7th at Ave. D
Back in the Gay Nineties, a town wasn't fully civilized unless it had an opera house. Shiner's opera house was built in 1895 by William Wendtland and Louis Wagner. The opera house was upstairs, with the Opera House Saloon downstairs. The saloon was succeeded by a variety of other businesses over the years, but the opera house has remained in use. A community theater group now performs upstairs several times a year.

Shiner calls itself the "cleanest little city in Texas," and if you drive around a bit through the residential environs you'll probably agree. Many of the immaculate homes date back to the town's founding.

SAINTS CYRIL AND METHODIUS CATHOLIC CHURCH
312 S. Ludmila, just off US 90A and just east of US 90A/SH 95 intersection • Open for services • W
This red brick Romanesque Revival-style church, dedicated in 1921, towers cathedral-like over Shiner. The lovely stained-glass windows were imported from Bavaria. You'll also enjoy the towering altar and statuary. The dome ceiling murals of Jesus alone in prayer are the crowning touch.

PATEK'S GROCERY AND MARKET
US 90A, next to Sts. Cyril and Methodius Catholic Church
594-3171 • W
Patek's makes an interesting variety of link sausages and smoked meats on premises, including green onion pork sausage, low-salt sausage, Polish- and Italian-style sausage, all-pork and all-beef sausage, red hot links, beef wieners and bologna, beef jerky, even chicken sausage and rabbit sausage. Homemade breads and egg noodles are also sold. You can even buy tapes of the Patek Orchestra, one of Texas' most famous Czech bands.

The Patek Orchestra dates to John Patek's arrival in Shiner in 1895. This family orchestra recorded for Decca during the 1930s, then switched to Martin Records in San Antonio. A versatile group, they even played Mexican polkas. The band's demise several years ago was a blow to music lovers; its performance at the annual Shiner Catholic Church picnic was a popular tradition for dancers and listeners alike.

EDB MUSEUM
800 block of US 90A • 594-4343 • W variable

This new and still-developing museum is centered around the 1895 Louis Ehlers cigar factory and the 1853 Green family house. The cigar factory produced several different types of stogies, including the Becky Brown, Katy Lee, and Good Company. Five union men rolled them and were paid a penny for each cigar they rolled. One of Shiner's early, prominent businessmen, William Green, Jr., was born in the rustic dogtrot house, which was originally located in the nearby Winnton community. He ran a post office and general store here for eight years.

EDWIN WOLTERS MEMORIAL MUSEUM
306 S. Ave. I • 594-3362 • Call for hours • Donations accepted

The museum's collections reflect the ethnic diversity of Shiner's history as well as the area's natural history.

SHINER FRIENDLY TAVERN
US 90A • 594-8825 • Tuesday through Friday to midnight, Saturday 10–1, Sunday 2 to midnight • No Cr. • W

Your last-chance stop on the way out of town is the Shiner Friendly Tavern. Tightly cozy and fully deserving of its name, the Friendly Tavern dispenses tap Shiner in an iced mug, and by the bottle, and has a pool table squeezed into one corner for all you pool sharks.

LODGING

THE OLD KASPER HOUSE
219 Ave. C • 594-4336 • $$–$$$$ • Cr.

Bed-and-breakfast inn, in a restored Victorian home. Two blocks east of SH 95, between the Kaspar Wire Works and the SH 95/US 90A intersection. Eight units, private baths, full breakfast.

ANNUAL EVENTS

APRIL • Trade Day • Downtown • 594-3362 • Third Saturday in April • Free • W

Antique show and dealers, arts, crafts, food, livestock, and almost anything else sellable or tradable that's legal can be found here. Dozens upon dozens of dealers set up for business, encouraged by low booth prices; consequently, Shiner Trade Days are better attended and more interesting than those of other towns.

JULY • Half Moon Holidays • Shiner American Legion Hall, 102 S. Ave. G • 594-3362 • Friday and Saturday nearest July 4 Admission to dances • W
Street dancing and beauty pageants happen at night; footraces, tugs-of-war, and outhouse races take up the day.

SEPTEMBER • Shiner Catholic Church Picnic • American Legion Park, 102 S. Ave. G • 594-3836 • Sunday before Labor Day • Admission to dances, dinner
Every rural Catholic church in Texas has some kind of festival or picnic, and this is one of the oldest and biggest. It dates back to 1897. Up to 10,000 locals and visitors attend the affair, dancing to the polka music of such favorites as the Shiner Hobo Band. Dancing—polka and country—runs from noon till midnight, and revelers can take a break at the various games, the bazaar, the auction, or horse-shoe pitching. Be warned—the bidding at the auction gets awfully serious. Dinner is the other big attraction: Shiner Picnic Stew, sausage, fried chicken, and all the trimmings, all at a price you can't resist. Mass is conducted early that day to leave plenty of time for fun. A similar picnic is held on the Sunday of Memorial Day weekend.

OCTOBER • Trade Day • Downtown • 594-3362 • Third Saturday in October • Free • W
Like the April Trade Day.

From Shiner, continue west on US 90A toward Gonzales.

As we leave Shiner, we would do well to remember that times have not always been happy and gay here, but we should also remember that no matter how dark the times may have been, someone has always managed to scratch out some humor in the face of even the worst of tragedies. To wit, in this vicinity just after the Civil War—so the story goes—a man named Martin was passing through, bound for Brownsville from Fayette County with a load of cotton. He had a black man with him to help drive the team of horses. At nightfall, the pair camped on a nearby creek. During the night the hired hand split Martin's head open with an axe as Martin slept. The murderer then skedaddled with Martin's money. The grisly scene was discovered the next morning, a posse organized, and the killer (or a reasonable facsimile thereof) was apprehended and taken back to the scene of the crime. There by the creek the hired hand was dispatched to his fate from the high branch of a stout tree. As was the custom of the time, the corpse was left swinging as a warning to others. Later that day one of the posse members mentioned to another black man that the lynched man had been left wearing a fine felt hat, with a four-bit piece still in his pants pocket. Times being what they were, the freedman headed at dusk for the hanging tree, only to find his victim hanging out of reach. Our ingenious opportunist found a chunk of wood nearby, which when stood upon enabled him to tip-pytoe-reach the dead man's pocket. Feeling the coin deep in the pocket, our protagonist made one final stretch to grasp the coin and in doing so knocked the block of wood over. There he hung by his one hand, which was buried in his dead compatriot's pocket. Try as he might, he could not extricate his hand and so he dangled there for the rest of the night. His cries for help attracted passersby the next morning, who released him. As he fell to the ground and the four-bit piece rolled free, the man vowed never to steal anything again. The tree is said to have withered away and died, as is supposedly tradi-tional with hanging trees.

A little more than 9 miles from downtown Shiner, just before you cross Peach Creek, you'll see a historical marker and a gravel road (County Rd. 361) running to your right, which takes you to the Sam Houston Oak and historic Braches Home, located a few hundred feet north of the highway.

SAM HOUSTON OAK/BRACHES HOME
Tours by appointment only • 830-672-2013 or 830-672-6532
General Sam Houston and his little army rested under the spread-ing branches of this huge, ancient live oak a week after the Alamo fell in March 1836. It was the first rest stop of the Runaway Scrape. The Texians had just burned Gonzales and the flames could be seen from Houston's camp here.

The two-story plantation house you see was built in the 1840s or 1850s. It replaced a log house built in 1831 by Judge Bartlett D. McClure and wife Sarah Ann McClure. Its size and its full, two-story Greek Revival gallery was quite rare for the era and bespoke the Braches' wealth during those hardscrabble times when many Texans were living in cabins or tents. The big house became a stopping place for stage coaches, wagon trains, and mail carriers. After Judge McClure's death in 1842, Sarah Ann married Charles Braches, a rep-resentative in the Republic of Texas congress. Braches had conduct-ed a literary and music school in Mississippi before coming to Texas. Soon after his arrival here, he became an influential citizen and leader. The plantation house became a cultural center for this section of the state.

Drawing closer to Gonzales, about 12 miles out of Shiner, you pass by the turnoff to the old **Maurin Quarry,** which supplied sandstone for buildings in Shiner, Moulton, Gonzales, Flatonia, and surrounding communities. It operated from 1883–1908 and was established by Firmin Maurin from Marseilles, France.

Just after the junction of US 90A with FM 532, take Spur 146 into Gonzales. Spur 146 becomes St. Louis St. within the city limits. St. Louis takes you to the Gonzales County Courthouse.

GONZALES

Gonzales County Seat • 6,519 • (830) • About 18 miles from Shiner
Gonzales is famous as the Lexington of Texas, where on October 2, 1835, defiant Texian irregulars battled Mexican troops sent to take possession of a small brass cannon. The gun had been sent to the settlement four years earlier as protection against Indian attacks. Mexican authorities feared that the increasingly belligerent colonists might use the cannon against them. The Texians buried the cannon in George Davis' peach orchard. But then they disenterred the piece, mounted it on oxcart wheels, and filled its barrel with pieces of chain and scrap iron. On October 2, the Texians crossed the Guadalupe River to confront the Mexican force, which had halted on the west bank of the river. Flying a crude flag with a picture of the cannon and the words "Come and Take It" emblazoned thereon, the Texians attacked, killing one Mexican soldier. Both sides realized that war was now inevitable and retired to their respective home bases. The Texians stepped back to Gonzales and began to prepare for their siege and capture of San Antonio de Bexar.

Gonzales started life in 1825 as capital of Green C. DeWitt's colony of Anglo-American settlers, and was named for Rafael Gonzales, a native of San Fernando de Bexar who was then governor of the state of Coahuila y Texas. Gonzales was abandoned in the summer of 1826 after an Indian attack. On July 4 of that year, most of Gonzales' citizens had gone up to Burnham's Crossing on the Colorado River for a big Independence Day celebration. While they were gone, the Indians attacked. They killed one man who had stayed behind and then plundered and burned the village. Upon returning to their devastated settlement, the survivors promptly fled back to the comparative safety of Burnham's Crossing and other more established settlements. New settlers began rebuilding the town in 1827. In 1832 Gonzales was officially laid out as a town, in the Spanish style, with a central cluster of five public squares in the form of a cross, and an elaborate gridiron of streets and lots that the Anglo-American inhabitants largely ignored.

Gonzales was the only town to answer William B. Travis' pleas for reinforcements at the besieged Alamo; it sent 32 men to martyrdom. On March 11, 1836, Sam Houston arrived to take command of the Texian Army volunteers stationed here. Then, the bad news from the Alamo and Goliad reached Gonzales. So, on March 12, the Texian Army burned Gonzales to the ground and retreated east. This was the beginning of the Runaway Scrape. After the Texian victory at San Jacinto, Gonzalans returned and the town became the county seat of newly formed Gonzales County in 1837.

The noted travel writer Frederick Law Olmstead visited Gonzales in 1856 and described what he found: "Gonzales is a town of perhaps one thousand inhabitants. It is a centre of distribution for hardware and whisky for a rich district, and is probably destined to a steady increase until the soil of the district is exhausted. It has at present nothing to distinguish it from other towns. There is the usual square of dead bare land, surrounded by a collection of stores, shops, drinking and gambling-rooms, a court-house, and a public-house, or two, with the nearly vacant mapped streets behind.

"We could procure no flour, meal, corn, or crackers in town. The price of corn, by the load, was seventy-five cents per bushel; of bacon, twenty-five cents per pound. At a German baker's we found wheat-bread. He informed us that there were about fifty Germans in the town—a few were farmers, most were mechanics."

The nearby rich Guadalupe River bottomland produced a bale of cotton per acre and bumper crops of wild mustang grapes, a local farmer told Olmstead, who wrote, "The mustang grape . . . was not worth much to eat, but made beautiful wine. The Germans made it right fine, he heard. Last year he thought he'd try it himself. He mashed them in a barrel, and let them stand and work for six or eight days, then drained them, and bottled the juice. 'It was splendid; made a splendid drink, sir, splendid; as good as any cider ever you see.' He could get a wagonload in a day if he wanted, and next year he would make a good lot, and squeeze them in his cotton-press."

About 1850, Czech immigrants began settling in Gonzales County, so the town of Gonzales also has a distinctive Czech flavor.

Gonzales was also home to Texas' most notorious pistolero, John Wesley Hardin, during the years following the Civil War. Little Seven-Up, as he was called during his early years, was officially credited with 30 killings, give or take a few. But the late Frank M. Fly, longtime Gonzales County sheriff and justice of the peace, begged to differ with that official figure: "He admitted to 48 and I personally know of several he didn't admit. I don't doubt that Wes Hardin killed any less than 100 men." Regardless of numbers, such renowned shootists as Wild Bill Hickok, Ben Thompson, and Rattlin' Bill Longley avoided any direct confrontation with Hardin's guns.

Wes Hardin was already an experienced killer and wanted man when he settled down in Gonzales County at the behest of his kin here, the Clements family. Hardin had been on his way to old Mexico in order to avoid Governor E. J. Davis' state police, but decided to stay here when cousin Manning Clements assured him he would be safe from arrest here. Besides, the Clementses were in particular need of Hardin's expertise. They and most of the rest of Gonzales and neighboring DeWitt counties were in the middle of the Sutton-Taylor feud, the longest and bloodiest feud in Texas history.

The feud began on Christmas Eve 1868 when deputy sheriff William Sutton shot Buck Taylor and Dick Chisholm to death following an argument over a horse sale. The Taylors and their friends were unreconstructed Rebels and a thorn in the side of the carpet-bagger government in Austin. The Taylors had already whipped Union soldiers sent to tame them and, after the Christmas killing Governor Davis sent a contingent of his state police to try again.

The captain of the carpetbagger force was special officer Jack Helm. Helm and his gunners were known as "regulators," and they joined forces with Sutton and "the law" to bring the "outlaw" Taylor bunch to their knees. In practice there was little difference between the law and the lawless; ambushes and lynchings were the regulators' favored tools.

Helm's past was a shrouded one. Some folks said he was a Confederate veteran and that one day after the war's end he had shot dead a freedman sitting on a fence for doing nothing more than whistling "Yankee Doodle." Helm was dismissed by Davis in the fall of 1870 on misconduct charges; earlier that year he had arrested two of the Taylor clan on trivial charges and then shot them. But Helm remained active in the feud as sheriff of DeWitt County. After Helm's dismissal the regulators became known as the Sutton party.

By the time of Hardin's arrival in 1871, the feud had grown into a little civil war involving hundreds of men. There was no remaining neutral. You picked a side or you left the country. Hardin avoided the fire awhile by heading a Clements herd of longhorns up the Chisholm Trail to Abilene, Kansas, killing six men along the way. While in Abilene he tamed Ben Thompson and Wild Bill Hickok and killed three more slow drawers. He was drawn into the feud on his return to Gonzales County. As Hardin continued to add notches to his gun, Davis became determined that his police would get rid of the gunslinger. Blacks in Austin and Gonzales were of the same persuasion. Fifty of them congregated on the Gonzales courthouse square in the fall of 1871 to ride down south into Clements country, shoot down Wes and his friends, and burn their houses. Word of this posse got to Hardin and the Clements clan. They urged the vigilantes to come on down because "a warm reception" had been arranged. Despite warnings from some of Gonzales' more levelheaded white men, many of the black vigilantes rode down into the area known as the "Sandies." Hardin met them alone, killing three and sending the rest scurrying back to Austin and Gonzales.

It was here that love complicated Wes Hardin's life. Instead of hightailing it down to Mexico, Hardin married Jane Bowen, who had ties to the Taylor party. Wes was determined to settle down in southern Gonzales County. This resolution lasted only a few months. By September 1872 he was in the Gonzales County jail on murder charges. Less than a month later he was out, courtesy of a sharp file and an obliging jailer.

By this time the Sutton-Taylor feud was at its height. Pitkin Taylor, the elderly patriarch of the Taylor clan, had been ambushed and shot in an especially dastardly way. He died a lingering, painful death and the Taylors were out to kill—by any means possible— every Sutton confederate they could find. Hardin traveled to Wilson County to kill Jack Helm. Mission accomplished, Hardin decided to move his family and cattle up to Comanche County. Upon arriving there he killed the deputy sheriff of neighboring Brown County at a horse race in Comanche. All the men in Brown County were soon on his heels and the Hardin bunch was on the run again. Wes got away, but his dear brother Joe and four friends were not so lucky. The posse shot two of them dead and hanged the other three.

Hardin next ran to Florida, killing six more men along the way. He and his family lived in secrecy there for several years before Texas Rangers captured him at Pensacola in 1877. The following year John Wesley Hardin was sentenced to 25 years in the state pen at Huntsville for the killing of deputy Charles Webb in Comanche.

While in the pen Hardin made repeated attempts to escape, studied law and the Bible, and gradually became a model prisoner. He was released in 1894, just a year after his wife's death. Admitted to the bar after his pardon was granted, Hardin settled down in Gonzales with his two children to practice law. He attended the Methodist church regularly, shunned gambling halls, and didn't drink. Only problem was, he couldn't make a living. Folks just wouldn't hire him; his earlier reputation haunted him. Drawn into politics, Hardin campaigned hard for a friend running for county sheriff, vowing to leave the county if the other candidate—who was an old enemy—was elected. Hardin's enemy won and he made good on his promise, moving to El Paso. Again he tried to lead the decent life but his old reputation refused to leave him be. He began to frequent gambling halls and drink. While in one of El Paso's gambling dens, Hardin was shot by city constable John Selman, a low-life creature who deliberately gunned Hardin down from behind on August 19, 1895. Hardin was 42 years old.

Little Seven-Up had killed his first man at age 15, but he was not your typical desperado. Coming from one of Texas' oldest and most respected families, Hardin was believed by many who knew him and his family to be a man more sinned against than sinning. Murderous record aside, Wes Hardin was a handsome, well-mannered man who considered himself a pillar of society. He robbed no banks, he stole no horses in his career. Hardin maintained from the beginning that he never killed anyone who did not deserve it and that he always shot to save his own life.

What of the Sutton-Taylor feud? Suttons continued to kill Taylors; Taylors continued to dispatch Suttons. Even the Texas Rangers failed to break the feud. By 1876, though, the Suttons, many of whom were peace officers, had the upper hand and the feud pretty much came to an end. There were hardly any Taylors left. But the Sutton party boys occupied themselves with other forms of mischief and guns spat lead throughout Gonzales and Dewitt counties into the first decade of the twentieth century.

In spite of the bloodshed, Gonzales County prospered. Cotton was king, and the county also became one of the state's leading poultry and cattle producers. A few million turkeys and chickens saved Gonzales from the full ravages of the Great Depression. In 1936, Gonzales proudly proclaimed itself the first-ranking turkey-producing county in the nation. Gonzales County no longer rules the roost nationally, but still leads Texas in chicken and egg production. And abandoned chicken farms have a new lease on life—as commercial mushroom farms. Mushrooms love to grow in chicken manure.

Life was good to many people in Gonzales, starting in the 1880s. The town is filled with much history and Victorian architecture: public, commercial, and residential.

Downtown Gonzales has a number of interesting buildings and shops, so park somewhere on the courthouse square and perambulate. The greatest concentration of antique and specialty shops is on St. Joseph.

GONZALES COUNTY COURTHOUSE
St. Joseph at St. Louis • 672-2435 • Open Monday through Friday

J. Riely Gordon, responsible for several other grand Texas county courthouses, designed this three-story Romanesque Revival courthouse. It was built in 1895 of red brick from St. Louis, Mo., and is laid out in the form of a Greek cross with a central stairwell inside adorned with ornamental ironwork. Firmin Maurin, owner of the nearby Maurin quarry, supervised construction. The final price: $65,000. The roof was originally slate; it was replaced with red tile in the 1950s. The basement had a dirt floor until 1958, when cement was poured. The Seth Thomas clock was installed in 1896 and cost $900. It ceased to work during the 1920s, and there is a gallows-humor explanation for why. The last man to hang from the Gonzales County jail gallows was Albert Howard in 1921. Toward the end of his stay on earth, Howard became obsessed with the hours he had left, marking their passage by the toll of the courthouse clock. He swore—as many in his position have—his innocence and proclaimed that his innocence would be borne out by the courthouse clock, which would never again keep the correct time. The four faces fell out of sync and remained that way for decades until 1990, when Henry Christian spent his time and $11,000 to repair it.

GONZALES COUNTY JAIL MUSEUM
AND CHAMBER OF COMMERCE
414 St. Lawrence at St. Joseph • 672-6532 • Jail hours: Monday through Saturday 8–5, Sunday 1–5 • Chamber of Commerce hours: Monday through Friday 8–5 • Free • W

The old jail, located on the square, was completed in 1887 and served said purpose for over 80 years. A registered historic landmark, the jail now houses the chamber of commerce and a museum. The cell, dungeon, and jailers quarters remain intact. Six men were hanged from an upstairs gallows, the last in 1921. The original gallows was dismantled in 1953 or 1954, but a replica has been installed in the original location upstairs. It stands amidst the prisoners' cells—not a pleasant sight to wake up to each morning. But such sobering practices were deemed necessary in earlier days. The fortress-like jail was built to hold between 150 and 200 prisoners in case of riot. A well-documented and extensive historical guide and tour of Gonzales is available here free of charge. *Gonzales,* a related, annotated sketchbook of notable local buildings, is also available.

The historical trail is well marked by "Come and Take It" signs. Since the accompanying interpretive guide put out by the Chamber of Commerce is free and so nicely detailed, only a few of its highlights will be touched upon here.

RANDLE-RATHER BUILDING
429 St. George

The Randle-Rather building was built in 1897. This elaborate three-story Roman Revival structure was constructed of locally made natural-clay bricks. Featuring ground-level Roman arcades, second- and third-level balconies with Tuscan columns on either side, topped by a square tower with Roman arched windows, the Randle-Rather building is a study in balance and beauty. A variety of businesses have been housed here. The third floor was devoted to the K. D. (Keep Dry) Club, the region's foremost social club. Their Christmas ball here was the height of the social season; and the women dressed in their finest silks and satins and the gentlemen were attired in "full dress with frocktailed coats."

COWEY'S BAKERY
1619 St. Paul/FM 794 • Open Monday through Saturday
No Cr. • W

Around the corner is Cowey's Bakery, which sells a variety of delectable baked goods displayed in vintage glass-and-wood cases.

ANTON HANZALIK'S BAR
621-B St. Paul, next door to the bakery • Monday through Saturday 7–9 • Beer only • No Cr.

Anton Hanzalik, Jr., has no name for his establishment, Gonzales' vintage bar. The place is identified only by a "Wine and Beer" sign out front. The **City Liquor Store** shares a corner of Hanzalik's establishment. This place has been a bar since 1905; Hanzalik has been proprietor since 1941. Almost nothing has been changed during these 50-plus years. The bar itself is oak, massive, and very Victorian, with enormous pillars and ornate caps. A centrally located wood-burning stove keeps the place warm in winter; the venerable ceiling fans help chase away the summer heat. A sign in the old display case reads "Smoke Mild HWF Cigars Real Value 2 for 15¢." Another sign on the east wall reads "No domino playing after 6 P.M." Hanzalik says he put the sign up during World War II—"Too many fights." He rescinded the 6 P.M. ban after V-J Day in 1945 but never bothered to take down the sign. A tear-away wall calendar on the west wall still reads February 6, 1966. The beer prices harken back to that era, too.

Sheet-iron doors and shutters cover the alleyway orifices of this block's buildings, security measures from another era.

ALCALDE RESTAURANT
614 St. Paul • 672-7071 • Open Monday through Friday, breakfast and lunch • $ • No Cr. • W

A Gonzales institution since 1926, the Alcalde serves homestyle breakfasts, and plate lunches and specials at noon.

Gonzales has many beautiful old homes. On St. Louis St. are the **Old Gonzales College** (820 St. Louis), the **Rather House** (828 St. Louis), and the **Kennard House** (621 St. Louis). Construction on Gonzales College's first building began in 1851, with stone hauled in from nearby Peach Creek. Classes started in 1853. There were separate male and female colleges. School enrollment peaked at 276 students in 1859–60. The college granted a four-year degree. The Civil War disrupted the college's progress and the school continued to decline during Reconstruction. The college property was eventually sold to the city and the buildings became part of the local school system. In 1890, W. M. Atkinson, a graduate of the college, bought this building and remodeled it, using stone from the Maurin Quarry.

The Rather House (828 St. Louis) was built in 1892 for Charles Rather, a prosperous Gonzales County cotton planter and partner of the Randle-Rather Building, on the grounds of the old Gonzales College. The two-story house is built of Louisiana cypress and Bastrop pine. The Rathers moved to Austin in 1910 and the house has gone through a succession of owners. It has recently been restored.

The Kennard House (621 St. Louis) is a good example of the Queen Anne architectural style of the late Victorian period. This frame two-story house was built in 1895 by Mr. and Mrs. James Kennard. The house's original corner tower with third-story open arcade has survived, and the restored house still looks like it did 100 years ago.

The two-story, twin-turret William Buckner Houston home (621 St. George) took three years to build. Mrs. Houston was an artist and painted the parlor ceiling in a manner reminiscent of the Bishop's Palace in Galveston and also painted a mural on the dining room walls. The house has been recently restored and opened as a B&B.

The elaborate red brick Victorian Lewis-Houston Home (619 St. Lawrence) took James Dunn Houston four years to build. He finished it in 1899, then sold it in 1900 to Mr. and Mrs. George N. Dilworth. Their widowed daughter, Margaret Dilworth Lewis, moved into the house with her parents and stayed until her death in 1950. They had plenty of room. The house has 15 main rooms, 5 bathrooms, and an indoor conservatory. Each room has its own fireplace.

OTHER MUSEUMS AND HISTORIC SITES

THE EGGLESTON HOUSE
1300 St. Louis • 672-6532 • Open during "Come and Take It Days" and by appointment
The Eggleston House, built by Horace Eggleston in the 1840s, is Gonzales' oldest standing structure. Built of hand-hewn burr oak logs, it has plank floors whipsawed by Eggleston's slaves. The windows of this dogtrot cabin were originally made of paper liberally coated with bear grease or hog lard, which made the paper more translucent. The cracks in the walls were chinked with moss and clay.

GONZALES MEMORIAL MUSEUM
414 Smith at St. Louis • 672-6350 • Tuesday through Saturday 10–12 and 1–5; Sunday 1–5; closed Monday • Donations accepted
Built in the Texas centennial year (1936), the museum is a good example of the Texas brand of Art Moderne architecture, built from native limestone. The museum honors the "Immortal 32" who answered Travis' pleas for help at the Alamo and the "Old 18" who held off the cannon-demanding Mexican troops at the Battle of Gonzales. The museum also has many items pertinent to the history of Gonzales and Texas, such as the original "Come and Take It" cannon.

Gonzales has many attractive postbellum and Victorian homes. Notable are the multigabled **Bell house** (ca. 1900, 803 St. Lawrence), **J. B. Wells house** (ca. 1885, 829 Mitchell), and the **Fly home** (ca. 1914, 827 St. Joseph). Frank Fly became county sheriff in 1901 after the murder of Sheriff Glover by Gregorio Cortez, the celebrated Tejano outlaw.

CANNON FIGHT BATTLEGROUND
Off SH 97
The cannon fight took place south of town. Several monuments and markers explaining the battle and the events leading up to it are located along US 183 as you head south out of town.

The battle site itself is located 6 miles west of US 183, off SH 97 near Cost. At the large bronze-and-granite monument dedicated to the Texan participants in the battle on SH 97, turn right on Park Rd. 95 and continue to the banks of the Guadalupe River and another monument to those determined men. Then retrace your tracks back to Gonzales and the courthouse.

PIONEER VILLAGE
US 183, as it leaves Gonzales for Luling • 672-2157 • Open Friday through Sunday • Admission

Gonzales' pioneer past is preserved in this collection of 19th-century buildings collected from around the county. The **Greenwood Log Cabin** dates to the 1830s, and was probably built as a slave cabin, then became a sharecropper's house. Instead of clay or mud chinking, chunks of wood were used to fill in the gaps between logs, so that the logs could be removed for better ventilation in summer. The double pen **Knowles-Townsend log house** (1840s) is distinctive for its lack of the almost universal dog run and for its central chimney. The **Samuel Gates House** (1856) was built of elm and oak logs, then covered with expensive, imported cypress boards. The **blacksmith shop** dates to the 1860s, the **Schindler barn** to the 1870s. The **Hamon Church** was built by the people of the nearby Hamon Community in the 1870s. First a Presbyterian church, then Baptist, it is notable for its slanted floor, built so that the worshipers in back could see better. The two-story **Muenzler House** serves as museum for a growing collection of early area artifacts and memorabilia.

The old **Oak Forest schoolhouse** features an old-time doctor's office in one end and a typical school in the other. There is a working blacksmith shop and broom factory. A smokehouse, hog pen, and old-style vegetable and flower garden add to the authenticity.

Started in the late 1980s, the Pioneer Village grows and evolves yearly. In 1994, the **St. Andrews house,** a former slave's quarters, was moved here. Historical reenactments are held here several times during the year.

Adjacent to the Pioneer Village is the site of Fort Waul, a short-lived Confederate fort built early in 1864 to protect Texas from a possible Yankee attack up the "River Route" that led from Victoria on the coast and ran through Gonzales to San Antonio. It was also to be used as a grain depot. It was an earthen fortification measuring 750 feet by 250 feet. The fort was named for Thomas N. Waul, a South Carolina native who came to Texas in 1850. He established a plantation on the Guadalupe River in Gonzales County. In 1862, he organized Waul's Legion at Brenham. This group of approximately 2,000 men served in Mississippi in 1862 and 1863. Much of the Legion was captured at Vicksburg in July 1863. The artillery battery was captured in April 1864 after the Battle of Mansfield. After being paroled, legion members returned to Texas for reorganization and served until the end of the war at Galveston and at other points on the coast.

Waul returned to his plantation after the war, but later moved to Galveston. He died in Greenville in 1903.

LODGING

ST. JAMES INN
723 St. James • 672-7066 • $$ • Cr.

Local cattle baron Walter H. Kokernot had this three-story, four-square-style house built in 1914. It has 30 rooms and 9 fireplaces. It is now a B&B. Each bedroom has its own bathroom and fireplace. A full "gourmet" breakfast is served in the formal dining room. Checks and credit cards accepted. Write to 723 St. James, Gonzales 78629.

AREA PARKS

LAKE WOOD RECREATION AREA
Go 5 miles west from Gonzales on US 90A, and then 5 miles south on FM 2091 • Open daily

The Lake Wood Recreation Area (35 acres) offers access to Lake Wood and the Guadalupe River. The San Marcos River enters the Guadalupe downriver from the park. Gonzales is 10 miles (four leisurely hours) downriver from the park; the river is navigable by canoe the whole way. Lake Wood covers 488 acres. The average depth is 8 feet; in places the river bed is 30 feet deep. For anglers, there are bass, catfish, crappie, rough, and bait fish. There are 16 RV full-hookup sites, as well as tent campsites in a big pecan grove. There are restrooms with hot showers. Picnic facilities include tables, grills, and firepits with water nearby. There is a boat ramp and docks. Skiing is permitted on Lake Wood.

PALMETTO STATE PARK
FM 2091, about 14 miles from Gonzales • 830-672-3266 • Open
daily • Admission • W variable

Palmetto State Park (267 acres), named for the tropical dwarf palmetto (*Sabal minor*) plant found there, hugs a crooked bend of the
San Marcos River and also has a four-acre oxbow lake. The unusually luxuriant vegetation and sulphur springs found here have drawn
naturalists from all over Texas for well over 100 years. The SA&AP
railway ran weekend excursion trains here at the turn of the century,
when the place was known as the Ottine Swamp. Many people
believed the spring waters had medicinal powers. The land was
acquired by deeds from private owners and the City of Gonzales
beginning in 1934 and was opened in 1936. This is an unusual botanical area in which the ranges of eastern and western species merge;
diverse plant and animal life abound. The dwarf palmetto grows in
profusion along with many other plants not seen elsewhere in the
Southwest. Wildlife in the park includes white-tailed deer, raccoons,
armadillos, squirrels, and numerous birds.

The springs are actually now extinct, but two artesian wells supply
the same warm, sulfur-laden water (with its distinctive smell) to different areas of the park. Activities include camping, hiking, fishing,
pedal boating, and swimming.

The San Marcos River runs through the park. You can put in at Luling City Park and travel 14 miles to Palmetto, portaging around one
dam along the way; or put in at Palmetto and take out at Slayden bridge,
7.5 miles downriver. You can make a two-day trip from Luling City
Park to Slayden bridge with an overnight in Palmetto along the way. It
is strongly recommended that boaters wishing to camp overnight at Palmetto call the Central Reservation Center. Take-in and take-out points
are limited; the river is mostly bordered by private land. There are no
rapids, but almost always a steady current. Rentals are available at
Spencer Canoes (512-357-6113) in Martindale. Check river conditions
at the park or Spencer's. You can fish for perch, catfish, and bass.

Facilities include campsites with water and electricity; a campsite
with water, electricity, and sewage; campsites with water; a premium
campsite with water (special rates are available on all campsites); a
group picnic shelter with kitchen; restrooms with showers; a snack
bar within 1 mile; a trailer dump station; picnic tables; an interpretive trail; and over a mile of hiking trails. The Texas State Park Store
rents pedal boats and sells firewood and other sundries.

Write to RR 5 Box 201, Gonzales 78629. *Elevation:* 292 ft.
Weather: Average January maximum temperature 61 degrees, aver-

age minimum 38 degrees; July average maximum temperature 96 degrees, average minimum 73 degrees. *Busy season:* Overnight guests should make reservations two to three weeks ahead of time March through November.

ANNUAL EVENT

OCTOBER • Gonzales Come and Take It Days Celebration
Town square, 414 St. Lawrence • 672-6532 • Weekend nearest
October 2 • Free • W
The activities commemorate the famed battle cry of the opening skirmish of the Texas Revolution, highlighted by a parade, a rodeo, an arts and crafts show, an antique show, a historical pilgrimage, a reenactment of the battle, tours of historical homes and the Pioneer Village, and street dances.

From the Gonzales courthouse square take St. Louis St. west to US 183. Turn right (north) on US 183, continuing until you reach the intersection with US 90A, where you turn left. After about 3.5 miles on US 90A, turn right on FM 2091 to reach Ottine.

OTTINE

Gonzales County • About 13 miles from Gonzales
Ottine owes its existence to Adolph Otto who settled here in 1879. Otto built a cotton gin shortly after his arrival, and a community grew up around it. "Ottine" is a combination of the names of J. A. Otto and his wife Christine. The old store/post office is a piece of classic, turn-of-the-century Texas and is still open to the public.

From Ottine, take either Park Rd. 11 through Palmetto State Park or FM 1586 to US 183, which is about 2 miles from Ottine. Turn left (north) on US 183 to reach Luling.

LULING

Caldwell County • 5,065 • (830) • About 8.5 miles from Ottine
Folks have said—for the better part of the twentieth century—that to get to Luling all you have to do is follow your nose. Oil and gas wells have kept Luling's coffers full, but they have also filled the air with a sulphury reek endured by natives and visitors alike for over 50 years. You are advised of your entry into Luling by a miniature oil

derrick atop a sandstone pedestal bearing the inscription "Luling Oil Since 1922."

Texas knew no Luling before 1874. The place was just a sleepy little farming and plantation neighborhood. Folks got their mail and shopped at old Atlanta or at nearby Josey's Store. Josey was a recently arrived go-getter who had made a deal in the early 1870s with Galveston, Harrisburg, and San Antonio (GH&SA) railway officials to build a station for their new westbound line on his land. The station was to be located smack-dab in front of his store, or so he thought. A town had been laid out and Josey had been selling land to sooners since 1873 in anticipation. But the railroad officials decided to route the tracks a little differently, and when the first train rolled into the station on September 10, 1874, Josey's Store was located on the far outskirts of town. Luling was officially christened that day; it was already a bustling town of 500, thanks mostly to railroad construction crews. For two years Luling served as the terminus of the GH&SA railway and the place roared. Folks called it the wildest town in America. Dogtown, just west of Luling, was known to offer every vice known to man. Luling had no local government in those days, only county and state law haphazardly enforced by a few deputies. Judge Lynch settled more than a few cases. They say Sam Bass, Wes Hardin, the Younger Brothers, King Fisher, Texas Jack, and Austin's onetime marshal Ben Thompson were visitors to Luling during those lawless days. Journalist Alexander Sweet, a visitor to Luling in those early days, recorded the following impressions:

"Walking up the straggling streets, we find the houses in irregular rows, and fronting on the streets at every possible angle of incidence. The houses are mostly of the dry-goods-box style of architecture, the fronts covered with roughly painted signs for the purpose of letting the world know the proprietor's business, and how badly he can spell. Here is a restaurant where the owner advertises 'Squar Meals at Reasonable Figgers, and Bord by the Day or Weak'; next, a Chinese laundry; then a beer saloon; across the street a gun shop; next to it a saloon; then a bakery; a saloon, another saloon with billiards, a lumberyard, a dance-house, a restaurant, a free-and-easy, a saloon, a shooting gallery, a faro-bank, a grocery, a saloon and hotel, a ten-pin alley, a concert hall; and so on to the end of the street. Queer and suggestive signs some of these whiskey dens have,—'The Sunset,' the 'How-Come-You-So,' 'The Panther's Den,' and on one in a north Texas town is inscribed the legend, 'Road-to-Ruin Saloon—Ice-cold Beer 5 cts. a Skooner.'

"While passing the Dew-Drop-Inn Saloon [in Luling] we were startled by several pistol shots being fired in quick succession inside the house, and only a few feet from us. Assuming a safe position behind a convenient cotton bale, we awaited the development of events. A loud-talking crowd was in the saloon. The crash of glass, and the fragments of billiard-cues that came whizzing out the door, indicated that somebody was raising Gehenna inside. As the shooting ceased, the crowd came pouring out, carrying the limp form of a man who was shot in the leg, had a bullet in his left lung, and was bleeding profusely from a knife-cut on the neck. Inquiry elicited the information that he was a cowboy, who, being on a 'high lonesome,' entered the saloon, and incontinently began discharging his six-shooter at the lamps and mirrors behind the bar. This, it seems, is a favorite pastime with the high-spirited cattlekings in their moments of enthusiasm. The Role had been enacted, however, with such frequency, of late, that it had begun to pall on the taste of the spectators. What was at first a tragedy, exciting and dramatic, was now a vapid piece of very weak comedy of questionable taste and doubtful propriety. So thought the barkeeper; and he emphasized his views by placing a few bullets where he thought they would do the most good, and have the most mollifying effect. The wounds were fatal. The playful cowboy died, and, as a bystander remarked, 'never knew what hit him.'

"The barkeeper was never tried. In less than twenty-four hours this 'difficulty' as it was called, passed out of the public mind in the light of a fresh and more interesting incident of a like character, where two men were killed, and one woman dangerously wounded."

As the railroad moved westward toward San Antonio the construction crews and fly-by-nighters moved with it. Luling quieted down and the remaining folks puttied up the bullet holes and started turning the saloons into stores, the shooting galleries into tonsorial parlors, and so on. The town kept growing, even though it wasn't a pretty place. Neighboring townsfolk were wont to say, "Luling has sand, fleas, grass burrs, and so many new people it's hard to tell who is what." Dogtown became Ragtown, Luling's "colored" community.

Luling was officially named for the wife of J. H. Pierce, president of the GH&SA railway, but when the origin of the town's name comes up as a topic of conversation some folks like to speak of the Chinese Ling Lu, who came along with the railroad crews as a laundry man. A generally easygoing man, Ling Lu didn't stand for certain things, such as being called a girl (on account of his pigtail), being asked if he were Mexican or black, or being asked if he used his mouth and teeth to dampen shirts for ironing. Ultimately, Ling Lu—or Lu Ling as he was sometimes called—cut his hair short and adopted the name John Chinaman. He stayed in his town for 10 years without once leaving. In addition to his laundry service, Lu Ling ran a message service and offered the town's first indoor toilets as an adjunct to his laundry shop.

Luling served as a gathering point and supply center for cattle drovers on the Chisholm Trail. It also was the railroad end of a freight road that ran to Chihuahua, Mexico, in those days.

Cotton ruled the local economy until the momentous year 1922. On August 9 of that year Edgar B. Davis' Rafael Rios No. 1 well blew in, opening up an oil field 12 miles long and 2 miles wide. The field was producing 57,000 barrels daily, or 11 million barrels per year, by 1924. Davis had discovered oil where geologists had sworn there was none. For a while it had looked as if the experts were right; the first six wells Davis' United North and South Oil Company drilled were dry. But Davis was a man of faith and a man of mission. Already a self-made millionaire in both the shoe and rubber plantation businesses, Davis came to Luling in 1921 to investigate oil leases purchased from his brother. Deeply religious, Davis believed that God had directed him to come to Luling to deliver the city and Caldwell County from King Cotton's monopolistic grip on the area economy.

Luling roared again during those hectic oil days. A lawman from Luling's Roaring Twenties remembered: "Many a night I put 35–40 men in jail. Weekends you never went to bed; Friday, Saturday, Sunday you might as well stay up all night."

Davis had given away most of his millions before coming to Luling, but when he became rich again he remained true to his generous ways. Early in 1926 Davis sold his field for $12 million. That June he threw the biggest barbecue Luling has ever known. Fifteen thousand people were invited and to feed them Davis purchased 6 tons of beef, 2,000 fryers, 5,000 pounds of lamb, 7,000 cakes, innumerable barrels of ice cream, and truckloads of soda. But Davis had an even bigger problem facing him as he planned his extravaganza. Where would he hold the event? Obviously he couldn't hold it in one of his smelly, dirty oil fields, so he went out and bought 140 acres on both sides of the San Marcos River. One bank was for whites, the other for blacks. Remember, Jim Crow's segregation laws still ruled Texas then. Total bill for the bash: $4 million. Most all his employees were given bonuses between 50 and 100 percent of their total accrued salaries. Davis also gave Luling a golf course and gave Luling's blacks their own athletic clubhouse, among many other gifts. He established the Luling Foundation in 1929, a demonstration farm of over 1,000 acres near Luling, operated for the advancement of all facets of agriculture.

Edgar Davis discovered two more oil fields in Caldwell County and gave most of that money away, too. The Depression broke him and he worked most of the rest of his life to pay off his debts. Davis died in Galveston in 1951 and is buried here, revered as Luling's number one citizen.

Luling was also home for 30 years to another one of Texas' more unique adopted sons. Julius Myer—the last town crier in America to ply his trade—moved here from New York City at age 16 for health reasons. His commercial pronouncements echoed through the streets of Luling until he moved to San Antonio in 1912.

There are almost 200 pumpjacks within the city limits of Luling. Perhaps you noticed, as you drove into Luling on US 90/US 183, the mosquito pumpers strung out every few feet along the railroad tracks, painted up as grasshoppers, mules, crows, melon eaters, and such. The chamber of commerce commissions local artists to create moveable characters. A guide map to these critters is available from the Luling Chamber of Commerce, 308 N. Magnolia, P.O. Box 710, Luling 78648, 875-3214.

Luling's oil may help keep Texas and America moving, but probably more dear to most Texas hearts and palates are Luling's watermelons. One of the state's leading watermelon producers, Luling celebrates its most delicious product each June with the Watermelon Thump.

Davis St., Luling's main business thoroughfare, parallels US 90 along the north side of the railroad tracks. Continue a short distance on US 90, past the intersection where US 183 turns north, and turn right on Ave. N. Cross the tracks and park in one of the shaded parking stalls that are located between Davis and the tracks.

Take a stroll down Davis. Downtown Luling doesn't have the architectural charm of Gonzales, but it has lures of its own.

SARG RECORDS
311 E. Davis • Monday through Saturday 9–6, but not always • W

Located at 311 E. Davis in a nondescript storefront with tattered screen doors and a window bearing a simple neon "Records" sign is Sarg Records, run by Charlie Fitch. In business since 1953, with over 150 singles and 3 albums under his belt, Fitch is one of the few record executives who can say he said no to Willie Nelson. He tells the story, with no remorse, of the day in 1954 when Willie sent him a demo tape in hopes of getting a contract with Sarg. "Nobody—but nobody—would have recorded it, so I just threw the tape in the corner, where it stayed for years. It wasn't recordable, just two times two stuff, you know. Willie was a deejay back then, and the tape he sent me had been recorded over that day's stock market report, so the last song trailed off into the last of that day's stock market quotations. He sent it to me and said, 'If you like it, tell me. If you don't like it, tell me. It won't hurt my feelings.'"

Fitch's 150-odd singles have included records by artists such as Cecil Moore, Homer and Gene and the Westerners, Arnold Parker and the Mustangs, Adolph Hofner and the Pearl Wranglers, the immortal Cajun Link Davis Sr., even San Antonio rock-and-roller Sir Douglas Sahm, back in 1953 when he was just a 12-year-old local prodigy known as "Little Doug." "Real American Joe" and "Rollin', Rollin'" are the record's two songs; it is a collector's item, as is Link Davis Sr.'s 45 rpm single: "Big Houston" backed by "Cockroach." But Fitch's most prolific and interesting artist has been Adolph Hofner (See Moulton). A look at the names of just a few of his recordings with Sarg reveals his musical versatility: Longhorn Stomp, Bandera Waltz, Westphalia Waltz, Shiner Song (Farewell to Prague), El Rancho Grande, Julida Polka, Kansas City, Rockin' and a Boppin', Cotton-eyed Joe, Spanish Two-Step, Dude Ranch Schottische, Krasna Amerika/Beautiful America Waltz, and Steel Guitar Rag. Fitch is also a jukebox distributor, so be sure to check out some of his classic oldies while you're there.

CENTRAL TEXAS OIL PATCH MUSEUM
421 E. Davis • 875-3214 • Open Saturday afternoons
The name says it all; the heady history of the area's oil industry is preserved with examples of equipment, photos, etc. It is housed in the Walker Brothers building, built in 1885 as a mercantile store. Write: P.O. Box 1002, Luling 78648.

CITY MARKET
633 E. Davis, near US 183 • 875-9019 • Monday through Saturday 7–6 • No Cr. • W
If you're hungry, head along Davis to the City Market for Luling's best barbecue. Brisket, pork ribs, and sausage are served up in the little enclosed pit room at the back of the market. The brisket is lean and tender and good—for brisket. The link sausage is also tasty and less greasy than most. Accolades go to the pork ribs—succulent, meaty, with a slightly sweet, smoky flavor. One regular patron from Houston was overheard to say of the ribs: "Sometimes I take $40 worth of ribs home to the kids. They eat on them 'til they're full, run around for a while, then dig in again." 'Nuff said. Your meat is

served on the traditional brown butcher paper with crackers or white bread. You eat in the front room, where beer, pop, potato salad, slaw, and beans are sold. Grab a bottle of their special homemade sauce and dig in. The slightly sweet, tomatoey sauce is not quite hot enough for some tastes but is palatable nonetheless. A little Tabasco would work wonders.

FRANCIS-AINSWORTH HOUSE
214 S. Pecan • 875-9197 • Open Thursday and Saturday afternoons
This 1894 house is operated by the Daughters of the Republic of Texas. It is full of furniture, photos, and early Luling memorabilia. It is available for weddings, meetings, etc.

LULING FOUNDATION FARM
523 S. Mulberry • 875-2438 • Call for a tour
Edgar Davis established this model farm in 1927 to promote alternative agriculture to the farmers of Caldwell, Gonzales, and Guadalupe counties. A free, public institution, it showed the advantages of a diversified livestock operation over the traditional one-crop system. The farm currently measures 1,123 acres; 18 soil types are found. There are six miles of San Marcos River frontage. You can pick your own produce, in season.

BLANCHE PARK
US 183 at Fannin • Open at all times • Free • W
The old log cabin in this little park is notable for its dovetail notch construction, which is a comparative rarity in Texas.

BLUE RIBBON BAKERY
**In Prairie Lea, 7.5 miles west of Luling on SH 80 N
512-488-2222 • Open Friday–Sunday**
This bakery is worth the trip, operated by a state kolache bake-off winner, hence the name. Heavenly kolaches, rolls, pecan cinnamon rolls, cakes, breads, etc.

ANNUAL EVENT

**JUNE • Watermelon Thump • Downtown • 875-3214
Last weekend in June • W variable**
The Watermelon Thump pays tribute to the area's sweetest crop. A parade, Watermelon Queen coronation, dance, food booths, arts-and-

crafts show, fiddling contest, golf tournament, and grand champion watermelon auction are among the activities. The winning melon has fetched over $3,000 in the past.

From the City Market in downtown Luling, go north on US 183 2 blocks and turn left on SH 80, which is also called Austin St. In about 5.5 miles you'll come to Stairtown and an intersection with FM 671. Turn right on FM 671.

STAIRTOWN

Caldwell County • 35 • About 5.5 miles from Luling
The dozens of wells that you see and smell and hear pumping away are working Davis's original golden field. The original Rios No. 1 well is located along FM 671, 0.8 mi. off SH 80. The rotten smell is hydrogen sulfide, which is a by-product of production.

BURDETTE WELLS

Caldwell County • About 10.5 miles from Luling
Mineral and sulphur springs abound in this section of the county, and folks often picnicked at them. One of the most popular springs was Burdette Wells, now known as **Mineral Springs** and located in the Joliet community. The San Antonio and Aransas Pass railroad (locals called it the SAP) stopped here on its daily run between Lockhart and Yoakum. The waters of Burdette Wells were particularly prized and families would often pack a picnic lunch, ride the train down in the morning, and return home on the evening run. A hotel, now long gone, served those who wished to take the waters for an extended period. Not much is left at the Mineral Springs these days save a tranquil, shady cemetery and church. The SAP tracks, which roughly paralleled US 183 and FM 671, were pulled up years ago.

Continue north on FM 671 toward Lockhart, which runs into US 183. Continue north on US 183 to Lockhart.

LOCKHART

Caldwell County Seat • 9,415 • (512) • About 15 miles from Luling
Lockhart was originally known as Plum Creek and had a post office by 1847. Named in 1848 for surveyor and Indian fighter Byrd

Lockhart, on whose land the town was laid out, Lockhart became county seat for the newly organized Caldwell County.

Nearby Plum Creek was the scene of the Battle of Plum Creek, where a volunteer army of Texans including such notables as Mathew "Old Paint" Caldwell, Edward Burleson, and Ben McCulloch decisively defeated a band of marauding Comanches on August 12, 1840. The Comanches had swept down the Guadalupe River valley that summer, pillaging, plundering, and killing. The rampage was their revenge for the Texans' deadly duplicity at the Courthouse Fight in March 1840, where, under pretense of peace talks, Comanches were lured into a San Antonio building and a number of them were slaughtered. After leveling Linnville in Calhoun County, the satiated Comanches began to retreat westward, hotly pursued by the Texans. The warriors suffered heavy casualties on the banks of Plum Creek and were never again to be a serious threat east of the Balcones Escarpment.

Lockhart has had its economic ups and downs over the years, tied as it was for so long to a one-crop—cotton—economy. In the years following the Civil War, Lockhart was a principal staging center for herds starting up the Chisholm Trail. In fact, Lockhart's Colonel Jack Myers really marked out most of what was to become known as the Chisholm Trail when he drove a herd up to Abilene, Kansas, in 1867. A distinguished Civil War veteran (hence his title) and California forty-niner, Myers drove his first herd of cattle up to Salt Lake City. On his way home, he stopped in Kansas at Junction City. There he met Joseph McCoy, a northern entrepreneur who had dreams of shipping thousands of Texas beeves east and north from Kansas via the rapidly expanding railroads. It was a marriage made in heaven; McCoy agreed to build loading pens, a hotel, and all the other facilities the trail drivers would need. He asked only, "If I build these pens, will you bring me 25,000 head of cattle a year?" "We will bring you a million head a year," Myers answered. Myers was true to his word, going home to spread the gospel and gather up a fresh herd. He was the first to reach McCoy's new city. Millions of Texas beeves followed in his wake. Myers died in 1874 and is buried in Lockhart Cemetery.

Lockhart enjoyed a reputation as a tough town, from Reconstruction clear into the twentieth century. As old-timer Geoffrey Wills put it, "They had the White Caps [Ku Kluxers] organization. Everyone packed a six-shooter. We had a high sheriff, but that's the way he run this town. This town was considered a desperado town. It had sporting houses, wide-open gambling places, and all those things. People would never come through this town and they would pass it on account it was so bad. My parents told me it was nothing to wake up Sunday morning and find two or three men dead . . . find them in the alley dead. I was born in 1908 and it was still going on."

In 1950, ex-traildriver Berry Roebuck, then 94 years old, pointed to the courthouse square and told a San Antonio newspaper reporter, "I've seen many a man killed on that square. A good gun used to be the law there."

Merchant Sam Glosserman reminisced several years later, "Everyone came to town on Saturday and what they wanted was a red bottle of soda water or a bottle of beer and Kreuz barbecue. People used to go around and around walking around the square, having the time of their lives, fighting and boozing . . .

"This was really a wild town—one of the wildest in the U.S. This was the wildest town in Texas; I used to stand on Dad's corner and see killings, one after another. I saw police beat people over the head. I remember one guy clubbed a man to death with an axe handle right on that corner!

"I recall one incident. We had a sheriff by the name of John Franks—a tall handsome 6'3" sheriff. He got into some kind of altercation with the city constable John Smith. They had a fight in the courthouse on the steps. Sheriff Franks killed John Smith. It was the talk of the county."

One Pauline Helfin ran a saloon, a rare occupation for a woman during an era when decent women didn't even walk into saloons. One of her regular customers, Morgan White, an honest farmer but a bit of an overindulger, was accused of insulting Pauline. Friends of Morgan sent word to him that Pauline's brother and husband were planning to kill him for his impertinence. Soon after, Morgan came to town, walking down the sidewalk toward the saloon with a musket. "Louis Helfin was shooting from an upstairs window and nailed Morgan through the head on the sidewalk with a Winchester, shot his brains out and men walked on [the brains] out on the sidewalk," Geoffrey Wills related.

Understandably, most Lockhart folks at the turn of the century got skittish when they heard any noise that sounded even remotely like gunfire. So panic gripped downtown Lockhart one hot, dusty late afternoon in July 1902 when local blacksmith Emil Seeliger came bumping and backfiring toward the square in his homemade horseless carriage. This was Seeliger's inaugural run. Folks all over the square ducked for the nearest available cover; they were sure that the feuding was raring up again. Pretty soon the city marshal peeked up and told everyone it was safe to come out; it was just Seeliger and the hossless wagon he's been building on." Seeliger built it out back behind his blacksmith shop, which still stands a few feet north off the courthouse square, at 106-110 N. Main, an orange-with-white-trim brick building (built 1896).

Heads began to pop out to gaze upon Seeliger's wondrously strange contraption. He had spent $125 building his car, $60 of which went to buy its four tubeless motorcycle wheels. Seeliger built the one-cylinder engine himself; it delivered power to the rear wheels via three bicycle-chain drives. The gas tank— Ralph Nader would have had a conniption fit at this—formed the back seat. Seeliger built the unique steering mechanism out of a shotgun barrel and a pair of bicycle handlebars. To steer the car, you just pushed the handlebars in the direction you wished to go. With a body built from trap buggy plans, the "Seeliger Special" topped out at 15 miles per hour, getting 14 miles per gallon. Seeliger had to buy his gasoline at the local drugstore, by the five-gallon can, at 35¢ a gallon. But back to that historic afternoon.

The townsfolk were spellbound, their horses terrified by this belching fire-breathing beast. A light delivery wagon bearing two brand-new sewing machines went bounding down the street pulled by a pair of frightened matched grays. Bam! went the wagon as it hit a dusty pothole and one of the sizable sewing machines bounced off the wagon, wrapping itself around a lightpost. Another few feet, another pothole, and the second heavy machine went flying off as the salesman ran after his wagon, already ruing his losses.

Seeliger even ran his horseless carriage on the railroad tracks. Considering the roads of that era, he doubtless got a smoother ride along the rails. Emil Seeliger's machine eventually ended up on the scrap heap, as he felt it had no historic value.

Seeliger's automobile was not the only harbinger of the new age confronting Lockhart's citizens. The town installed its first water system in 1900, and shortly thereafter county commissioners voted to convert the new courthouse's broom closets into water closets. The county judge said such luxuries were foolish extravagance; there were outhouses behind every saloon in town. But he was voted down and the toilet facilities were installed. Evidently they were an immediate hit; after the first month's water bill the judge ordered all the bathroom doors chained and padlocked, so enraged was he at the size of the bill. It took legal action to get them unlocked.

Today Lockhart is considerably more sedate than in days past, but resurrected old-timers would have no trouble picking their way around the square. The new and modern downtown of 100 years ago is the quaint and historic downtown that visitors find so delightful to stroll today. Lockhart's historic district contains six full blocks and parts of three other blocks. Most of the 84 buildings are commercial.

To get to the historic district, turn off US 183 onto San Antonio and go 2 blocks.

CALDWELL COUNTY COURTHOUSE
Courthouse Square
This immaculate Second Empire courthouse is one of the state's most photographed, and has been in several recent Hollywood movies. It was in built in 1892 of stone from nearby Muldoon with red Pecos sandstone trim for $65,000. The original four-way Seth Thomas clock in the tower was vandalized and replaced by an electric clock in the 1950s. In 1992, a 1916-model Seth Thomas clock, which is very similar to the original, was restored and installed in the clock tower. Restoration of the building is due for completion in 1998.

OLDEST COMMERCIAL BUILDING
118 S. Commerce at Market
The square's oldest building was built in 1873 of locally baked brick. Practically every building on the square is turn-of-the-century and many of them have undergone only minor modification since their erection.

KREUZ MARKET
208 S. Commerce • 398-2361 • Monday through Friday 7–6, Saturday 7–6:30 • $ • No Cr. • W
After rounding the square, head south on Commerce to Kreuz barbecue and meat market for your gastronomic reward. Their beef has already been lovingly described in the introduction to this trip. Their pork is of equally stellar quality. Kreuz doesn't barbecue ribs, they barbecue the entire loin, bone in, and slice off the thick, lean, tender chops to your order. You will even succumb to devouring their thin, crisp, succulent outer layer of fat and gnawing the bones as a final nod to gluttony. Be advised that the chops are a popular item and are usually gone at the end of the lunch rush. Their homemade sausage is good, but a bit greasier than most.

Saturday lunch at Kreuz is a panhumanic experience. Hundreds of folks stream through at noon, lining up dozens deep to buy their meat in the hot smoky pit room. You take your choice of white bread or crackers and the butchers pile it all on brown butcher paper. Some take it home, most eat it here in the dining room. Young and old, black, brown, and white, rich and poor, locals and tourists, Izods and polyesters, farmers, professionals, and bluecollars are all elbow to elbow chowing down at the broad, long picnic-style tables. Accoutrements include fresh and pickled jalapeños, white onions, tomatoes, and avocados. Wash it down with cheap beer or pop. Police your table when done. As you walk out the front door, look down the alley in front of you, and you can see "N. O. Reynolds Saloon" still painted on the alley side of the old brick building which opens onto the courthouse square (108 E. Market). The building and sign both date to 1890.

EMMANUEL EPISCOPAL CHURCH
117 N. Church at Walnut • 398-3342 • Sunday 9–1

A block west of the courthouse square is the Emmanuel Episcopal Church, which has the oldest continually used Protestant church building in Texas. A simple, unpretentious structure, it is easy to miss. Don't make that mistake. The congregation was organized in 1853 and the building was completed in 1856. The sanctuary's two-foot-thick concrete walls are a mixture of sand, gravel, Lockhart caliche, ash, water, and cow manure. The ceiling timbers are hand-hewn cedar. The floor is locally quarried and highly polished limestone slabs. The altar, chancel rails, and window frames are also originals, hand-carved from native walnut. Federal troops used the church as a horse stable during Reconstruction days. A few feet south of the church, at 112 N. Church, is **Holter's Feed Store,** which was built in 1902 as Masur Brothers Hardware. The Masurs' original painted advertisements, as well as a more contemporary "Coca Cola 5¢" ad are still visible on the south side of the building.

FIRST CHRISTIAN CHURCH
W. San Antonio at S. Church, 1 block west of the courthouse square • 398-3129

The First Christian Church in Lockhart was organized in 1852. The present Gothic structure was completed in 1898 at a cost of $28,000, a tribute both to God and the skilled brickmasons who built it. An excellent example of bichromal brickwork, which is now enjoying a revival of sorts in and around Austin, this sanctuary features a combination of flat-sided red brick and textured ivory brick, which looks like limestone from all but inches away. The numerous arches and rounded half-columns and caps are further testament to the bricklayer's skills. All the church's windows are stained glass memorials.

And as long as we're here, let's take a moment to reflect on the strange passing of Texas' most unusual man of God, "Fightin' Parson" Andy Potter (also see Mormon Trails—Camp Verde and Bandera; The Wild West—Bastrop; and Central Texas Stew—Winchester (Buescher State Park). It was in the year of our Lord 1895, on a Sunday evening in a little country church just outside Lockhart, and "as Fighting Parson Potter raised his hands in a closing prayer, the lights of the little church were suddenly blown out by a strong gust of wind, and when the lamps were relighted the audience gasped to see the preacher lying dead in the pulpit. As the lights had gone out, so had gone out the life of Texas' most picturesque preacher. Fighting Parson Potter's wish—that he might die in his pulpit—had been granted."

DR. EUGENE CLARK LIBRARY
217 S. Main, one block south of the courthouse square
398-3223 • Monday through Friday 10–6, Saturday 9 to noon

Also impressive is the Clark Library, Texas' very first city library, built in 1900. A Tulane graduate, Dr. Eugene Clark practiced medicine here from 1883 to 1896. Clark left Lockhart to pursue graduate studies in Europe. He died in his hometown of New Orleans in 1898, leaving $10,000 to the city of Lockhart for the construction of a public library. The library itself cost $6,000 to build. The building is modeled after the Villa Rotunda in Vicenza, Italy. Beautiful stained glass windows are trimmed in walnut and walnut shutters cover the windows. The ceiling is white embossed tin, bearing brass gooseneck light fixtures. Ascend the narrow, winding iron staircase to reach the narrow, horseshoe-shaped second-story gallery, where you can better appreciate the tasteful, very Victorian interior. It is said that President William Howard Taft gave a speech here.

OLD COUNTY JAIL/CALDWELL COUNTY HISTORICAL MUSEUM
315 E. Market St., 1 block east of US 183 and the courthouse square • Open Saturday and Sunday • 398-9643

Located inside the old county jail, the museum features the Mildred Vaughan Memorial Room, Country Store, 1890 kitchen, Pioneer Room, early photographs, and other Texas memorabilia.

This whimsical little brick castle was built after a 1908 election in which the county's voters approved a $25,000 bond sale to finance it. The jailer's quarters were on the first floor. The upper floors have 15 concrete and steel cells. One cell rises from the center of the jail. The gallows were supposedly removed as recently as the 1930s. If you're coming to Lockhart specifically to see the museum, call ahead to verify hours. It's not always open when it's supposed to be.

ANDREW LEE BROCK CABIN
Lions Park, on US 183 across from the HEB supermarket
Open daily
Andrew Lee Brock came to Caldwell County in 1849 and married Rebecca Wayland in 1850. Her daddy gave the newlyweds 200 acres of land on the Clear Fork branch of Plum Creek. That year he built the cabin that is now located in this small city park. He later became a successful businessman and built a grand home that had the county's first bathtub. A number of buildings on the courthouse square were built by Gus Birkner for Andrew Lee Brock. The cabin is furnished for period antiques.

CHISHOLM TRAIL BBQ
1323 S. Colorado (US 183) • 398-6027 • Open daily, breakfast, lunch, and dinner • $ • No Cr. • W
This unpretentious spot is a good BBQ backup when Kreuz Market is closed.

LOCKHART STATE PARK
To reach the park, go 1 mile south of Lockhart on US 183 to FM 20, then southwest on FM 20 for 2 miles to Park Road 10, then 1 mile south on Park Road 10 • 512-398-3479
Open daily • Admission • W variable
Lockhart State Park is on 263.7 acres west of Lockhart. The land was deeded by private owners between 1934 and 1937. The park was constructed by Civilian Conservation Corps (CCC) between 1935 and 1938 and was opened as a state park in 1948.

Activities include picnicking, camping, fishing, hiking, nature study, and a 9-hole golf course. Facilities include restrooms with showers; picnic sites (including a group picnic area); campsites with water and electricity; campsites with water, electricity, and sewer; 1.5 miles of hiking trails; a recreation hall with restrooms (no showers), a patio, a picnic area, playground equipment, and a kitchen with a stove and a refrigerator available, (day-use capacity 75, overnight-use capacity 75); and a swimming pool, with individual and family seasonal passes available. The golf course offers daily, weekend, and holiday rates; annual individual and family passes; and carts for rent; there is a trail fee for private golf carts. The Texas State Park Store is open daily.

Wildlife includes deer, coyote, bobcat, fox, raccoon, opossum, armadillo, nutria, rabbit, squirrel, many varieties of birds, and several types of snakes, including rattlesnake and coral snake. Clear Fork Creek yields bass, catfish, and sunfish.

Write to RR 3, Box 69, Lockhart 78644-9716. *Elevation:* Elevations range from 388 to 705 feet. *Weather:* Average rainfall is 42.2 inches. January minimum low temperature is 44 degrees and July maximum temperature is 93 degrees.

ANNUAL EVENT

MAY • Chisholm Trail Roundup • City park • 398-2818
Third weekend in May • Free
Features a parade, a chili cook-off, dances, food booths, hobby and art shows, and a reenactment of the 1840 Battle of Plum Creek. A shuttle bus from the town square to city park costs $4.

From Lockhart, take US 183 north and continue on toward Austin.

As you leave town, note the rows of old cotton warehouses on your left, reminders of the days when cotton was king in Caldwell County and dozens of gins processed the county's crops. Today Lockhart has only one gin and is more famous for its cottonseed breeding farms, started here in 1882 by A.D. Mebane, than for its cotton. Over the years Mebane puttered and tinkered in his experimental plots, finally developing his world famous Mebane Triumph cottonseed, characterized by great drought resistance and up to 40 percent greater yield than other contemporary seed strains. Mebane's Triumph revolutionized the cotton industry. As you head toward Austin on US 183, you see a few of the roadside fields planted in King Cotton, now a shadow of its once-powerful self.

Many of these fields are now thick with mesquite, as you may have already noticed. Ranchers, farmers, and motorists who suffer flat tires from its sharp thorns may hate it, but to others mesquite has been quite valuable. Indians processed the bean pods into soup, bread, and beer. Cabeza de Vaca was the first European to record the fact that the natives not only ate the pulpy mesquite pods when they ripened, but also made them into a flour. He described the process in a book published in 1540.

A more recent cookbook, *Regional Cooking* (1947), contains the following mesquite-bean cake recipe similar to the old Indian recipe:

> Gather mesquite beans when they are very ripe. Spread them out in the sun until they are dry. Find a stone about a foot long and very narrow. Using that stone as a pestle, grind the beans on another flat stone until you have achieved a flour-like consistency. Sift the flour to get out all the hulls and trash.
>
> Take as much flour as you will need, pour just a little water in it and stir. Then get it out in the sun to dry a little. Then mix in enough water to make a stiff dough. Cut the dough into little cakes and set out in the sun until very dry. They are then ready to be eaten with coffee or milk or stored for future use.

The mesquite served as food of last resort to the traveler and also as a coffee substitute. Mesquite wood has been made into firewood, bows, arrows, fence posts, house lumber, road paving logs, flooring, furniture, even a cannon. A sticky gum exuded from the tree was used for mending pottery cracks and as a hair preparation that would dye hair jet black and kill cooties at the same time. Stephen Austin even advised his colonists to look for the biggest mesquite on their land and drill their water well there. It was erroneously thought that the mesquite pointed the way to sweet, shallow water.

Farming manuals from the 1890s advised also that the mesquite "bean is nutritious, fattening livestock. This tree is taking possession of prairie tracts and gradually rendering the land more valuable. The whole body of wood is also rich in tannin, thus rendering it as a good tanning material. It is said, indeed, to be better than any of the old popular materials, as it better preserves the leather. The bean is very nutritious as feed for horses and cattle. Generations of farm and ranch children have chewed on the sweet beans, especially during Texas' various farm depressions, when mesquite beans were the closest thing to candy they could afford. [The tree] has spread rapidly over the prairies within the past few years and now furnishes firewood in many localities where a few years ago there was not a stick of any kind of fuel to be found."

Ranchers and farmers hate mesquite because it chokes out precious grazing grass; hunters love it because doves love it. Ranchers and farmers hate mesquite because it's nearly impossible to kill off (its long tap root makes it practically drought-proof and impossible to dig out); woodworkers love its handsome pink-to-black burls and shadings. Deer, javelina, rabbits, and birds depend on the tree for food and shelter.

But perhaps mesquite's noblest use is as barbecue wood. It imparts a taste to the meat matched by no other wood. You may confirm this fact by eating any of the smoked meats from Rabke's Table Ready Meats west of Willow City.

Big for a mesquite is about 20 feet tall and perhaps a couple of feet in diameter. Most mesquite trees are little more than big bushes, and this recalls an old Texas joke. It seems a group of horse thieves were nabbed by a posse and "invited" to attend a necktie party. But being civilized men, the posse members allowed the brigands to choose the species of tree from which they wished to swing. Most of the men opted for the more beautiful and romantic oaks, elms, cypresses, and pecans. But one smart thief chose a mesquite. Since the posse were men of honor, they had to give the cagey crook a reprieve when they couldn't find a mesquite tall enough to get his feet off the ground. Which just goes to show that one man's meat is another man's poison.

Since 1980, mesquite has been "discovered" by the world-at-large. Mesquite grilling has recently been the rage in big-city restaurants from coast to coast. Practically every charcoal manufacturer now offers mesquite-tinged briquets for the backyard gourmet. Landscapers now extoll its gnarled lacy-leafed beauty in yards and rock gardens. Researchers at Texas A&I University in Kingsville are attempting to develop a faster-growing, straighter, and thornless mesquite so that the wood can be used commercially for furniture manufacture. They also claim that their research could help provide fuel to the world's impoverished desert regions, where wood is a chief fuel and is increasingly scarce. The tree even has its own fan club, Los Amigos del Mesquite, whose several hundred members devote their resources to educating the public about the mesquite tree.

MENDOZA

Caldwell County • 50 • About 10 miles from Lockhart

The little hamlet of Mendoza near the intersection of US 183 and SH 21 is the home of the Headless Woman of Mendoza, one of Central Texas' better traveled "haints." The story of this unfortunate woman is a variant on the ancient tale of "La Llorona" (the weeping woman). The tale of La Llorona has been told in many forms in many different places. The sad story of the Headless Woman of Mendoza goes something like this.

Once there was a woman who had two children. She didn't love them, and neglected and mistreated them. She was having too much fun dancing and going to parties. First one child, then the other died from her neglect. But she felt no remorse and continued to lead a gay life. On her way home from a party one night, the car in which she was traveling crashed and she was decapitated. When she died she had not confessed her sins or repented of her ill treatment of the children. So now she appears on roadsides all over the area grieving for her children and looking for her head. She is doing penance for her sins. Travelers who stop to pick her up often do not notice anything amiss with the shapely dark figure in the shawl until they look into her eyes and find none.

The Mendoza area was mostly open range land until the 1870s. By 1878 a school had been established to serve the families who had settled down to farm here. It also doubled as church; the school and community around it were known as Rest. A Baptist preacher from Lockhart would ride up to Rest one or two Sunday afternoons a month to conduct services. But during these early days according to the old-timers, who told a story strikingly similar to incidents in Red Rock and Llano, Rest wasn't very peaceful. Not everybody came to church for the preaching. Since this was still largely ranching country, there were a lot of cowboys in the area, and the unwashed among them diverted themselves on preaching days by roping and then pulling the shutters off the church windows during service, or they would sit on the front row jangling their spurs or snoring loudly. Peace finally came to Rest when Mr. Jim Gaddis rode in to preach. He had heard of the cowboys' rowdiness and he wore his six-shooters to church. Like the Rev. Andy Potter, Jim Gaddis laid down one pistol on each side of the Bible on the lectern and announced that everyone would be respectful during church or he would gladly meet the offenders outside afterwards. He got no takers. Sometime during the 1880s, for reasons nobody remembers, Rest's name changed to Mendoza.

From Mendoza, continue on US 183 north about 20 miles to Austin.

Coming back into Austin, just after you pass Pilot Knob (the geographic formation) on your left, you come to the intersection with McKinney Falls Parkway, which leads to McKinney Falls State Park.

McKINNEY FALLS STATE PARK
5808 McKinney Falls Parkway. Take McKinney Falls Parkway from US 183, straight to the park entrance • 243-1643
Open daily • Admission

Located just north of Pilot Knob, McKinney Falls State Park in south Austin is a 640.6-acre park acquired in 1970 from private donation and opened to the public in 1976. The park is named for Thomas F. McKinney, who came to Texas in the early 1820s as one of Stephen F. Austin's first 300 colonists. Sometime between 1850 and 1852, McKinney moved to Travis County and bought this property at the falls on Onion Creek, where he became a prominent breeder of racehorses. McKinney even had his own private track. His large two-story home, stone fences, and the first flour mill in the area were built with slave labor. Preserved in the park are the ruins of McKinney's trainer's cabin and the stabilized ruins of his own homestead. Information on McKinney and the history of the park's land use is interpreted in the Smith Visitor Center.

Within the park, you can also see evidence of the ancient volcanic activity at nearby Pilot Knob. The wide stretch of rock that Onion Creek traverses at the falls is limestone mixed with volcanic rock; elsewhere in the park are outcroppings of basalt and green clay, which was originally volcanic ash.

Camping, hiking, road biking, picnicking, fishing, and wildlife observation are among the park's activities. After being banned for over a decade because of water pollution problems, swimming is now allowed in Onion Creek; call 243-0848 for current creek conditions. Texas Parks and Wildlife Department headquarters adjoin the park.

Park facilities include screened shelters with bunk beds (no mattresses); campsites with water; campsites with water and electricity; walk-in water sites (200 yards in with a picnic table, a fire ring, a grill, and water in area); picnic sites; an interpretive hiking trail approximately 0.75 mile long; 3.7 miles of hike and bike trails; an interpretive center with an exhibit room and audiovisual room; and a group camp which includes the screened shelters located next to the dining hall; the dining hall (capacity 80) may be rented separately for day use. There is also an amphitheater that seats 50 people. There is a Texas State Park Store.

Wildlife that live in the park include white-tailed deer, raccoons, armadillos, squirrels, and numerous birds (checklist available).

Write to 5808 McKinney Falls Parkway, Austin 78744. *Elevation:* 550 feet. *Weather:* July average high temperature 95 degrees, southeast breeze; January average low temperature 37 degrees; moderately humid year round with May the wettest month; first/last freeze: November 28/March 2. *Busy season:* March through November.

As you cross over the **Colorado River** into Austin, one more story of La Llorona is appropriate, for she sometimes appears along the Colorado River on dark nights. One day she took her two children here and drowned them. She never repented, and so she comes back to the river at night, wailing for her children. Some say she has a seductive figure and the face of a horse. Others say she is dressed in black, with long hair, shiny tin-like fingernails, and the face of a skeleton. Still others say she is dressed in white, with the face of a bat. Perhaps you'd like to find out for yourself.

THE WILD WEST

Approximately 160 miles

The Yankees conquered Texas in 1865. The railroads, aided largely by Yankee capital, began their conquest of Texas shortly thereafter.
The six years of Reconstruction following the Civil War whipped
Texas into a feverish turmoil. The railroads were the harbingers of an
industrial revolution that kept Texas in a state of ebullition long after
the despised "bluebellies" and carpetbaggers went home. Violence
was followed by the sudden prosperity the iron rails brought, and for
some years violence and prosperity fed upon each other. Towns lucky
enough to be located along railroad lines were almost guaranteed
immediate prosperity; they were also almost guaranteed a measure of
lawlessness, for much of Texas remained hungry.

This trip takes us through a section of Central Texas that saw both
extraordinary prosperity and extraordinary trouble in the first few
decades following the Great War, courtesy of Reconstruction and the
iron horse.

*Leave Austin via US 290 east. At Manor, take Spur 212 right into
town.*

MANOR

**Travis County • 1,149 • (512) • About 8 miles from Austin
(intersection of US 290 and US 183)**
Manor, like many small Texas towns, has been on the eclipse for
the last couple of generations. But at the turn of the century Manor

was bustling, the second largest city in Travis County. King Cotton and Manor's location on the Houston and Texas Central (H&TC) railroad were the reasons. The surrounding hills with their rich, black, waxy earth produced a half-bale of cotton to the acre, and it took three gins to process the fall crop. H&TC locomotives hauled away 15,000 bales in a good year. Before the advent of World War I, Manor boasted a couple of banks, a newspaper, and electric streetlights, not to mention a mostly brick downtown.

The town dates back to 1850, when James Manor moved here from nearby Webberville. By 1859 the town was one of Travis County's largest and was commonly known as Parson's Seminary after a locally renowned girls school located where Manor Junior High School now stands. Manor was also known as Wheeler's Store before the H&TC came through in 1871. The name Manor was adopted thereafter, in honor of James Manor and family.

Downtown Manor is considerably quieter now than it was during its pre-World War I heyday. Like so many other small Texas towns, Manor began to decline as a commercial center during the 1930s. The **old bank building,** at the corner of Parsons and Lexington/Spur 212/FM 973, is now a hotel. Old downtown Manor consists of a block of brick buildings along the south side of Parsons St. between Lexington and San Marcos Streets. The most impressive of these is the one story red brick **J. F. Nagle building.** One of the **old cotton gins** stands on the south side of the railroad tracks, at the southwest edge of town. Most of Manor's businesses are along US 290, including the Cafe 290.

DINING

CAFE 290
US 290 at Loop 212 • 272-4212 • Open daily, breakfast, lunch and dinner • $–$$ • W
Step into Cafe 290 and it's like stepping into a 1940s cafe. They take great pride in their chicken-fried steak, but you can also get grilled steaks and chicken, fried chicken and catfish, Tex-Mex specialties, burgers, sandwiches, salads, and finger foods. Homemade pies, cobblers, and other goodies for dessert. Breakfasts are Southern country-style and ample. Beer.

Leave Manor by heading east (away from Austin) on Parsons/Spur 212. This is Old Highway 20, the main highway between Austin and Houston during the days of flivvers and bathtub gin. Continue on Old

THE WILD WEST

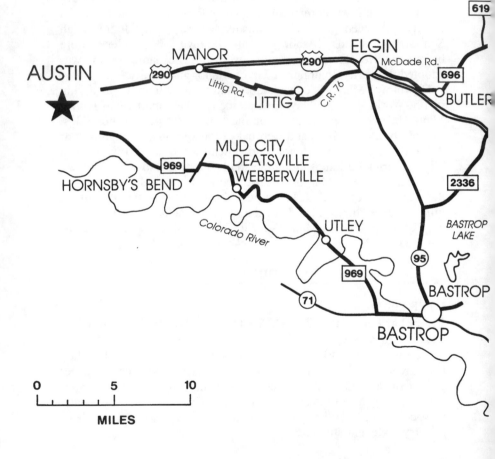

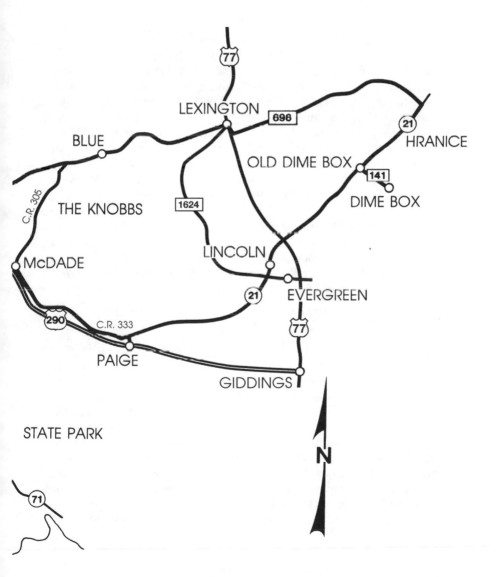

Highway 20 after Spur 212 veers north (to the left). A couple of miles east of Manor, the road comes to a T intersection. Turn right here, onto Littig Rd., which crosses the railroad tracks a few feet later and then makes a hard left to the east. Out here, Old Highway 20 is also called Littig Rd. While cotton is no longer king, it is still grown in many of the fields along this road.

LITTIG

Travis County • 37 • About 8 miles from Manor

Littig is the next sleepy hamlet. This predominantly black community was first called Bittig, in honor of early settler and Manor merchant J. W. Bitting (note the difference in spelling), who donated land for the community school in 1889. The school and later the community became known as Littig.

In those pretypewriter days, when all documents were recorded by hand and the finer points of spelling were oft ignored, place names often evolved in the manner of Littig, as one recorder would misread and misspell the writings of an earlier recorder. None of the locals seem to be able to shed any light on Littig's evolution.

Once in Bastrop County, the old highway is called Cty. Rd. 76. A couple of miles past Littig you come to another T intersection, marked by a yield sign and a Southwest Stallion Station sign. Turn left here onto the old Elgin River Rd., the old settlers' route from Webberville to what we now call Elgin. Soon you enter Elgin.

ELGIN

Bastrop County • 4,535 • (512) • About 6 miles from Littig

Elgin has been known by a variety of names—some very colorful—since the first white settlers moved here in the 1840s. First it was called Young's Settlement, when it was located several miles south of present day Elgin. By 1871, when the newly arrived H&TC established a flag stop here, the place was called Glasscock. Others knew it as Hogeye, named for a popular, bouncy fiddle tune of the day, the only tune a slave belonging to John Litton knew how to fiddle. He might be heard sawing away at this ditty during any spare moment in the day, so travelers and locals alike called the neighborhood Hogeye. Lickskillet was another name given to Elgin in those early, often meager pioneer days when there was only one home in the area and a visiting traveler often had to "lick the skillet" to get his dinner.

The town that was laid out with the coming of the railroad was named to honor H&TC land commissioner Robert Morris Elgin. But some locals tell another story. During Reconstruction days, when law enforcement was nominal and vigilantes battled robbers and murderers for control of dozens of neighborhoods, the H&TC began laying tracks through here on its Houston-to-Austin road. Not too many folks lived in this neck of the woods and some of them did not want a railroad. A Mr. Miles was one of these moss-backs. He headed up the Miles Gang, who announced publicly that they didn't want a railroad and weren't going to have one. The railroad tracks came on through anyway. Once or twice the Miles Gang tore up the tracks; they were promptly repaired. Finally, the first train into the new station was announced. The Miles Gang swore they would "shoot the lights out of it." Of course, they probably had more experience shooting the lights out of their fellow men than out of any train.

This train, like so many H&TC trains over the years, was late in arriving at the Glasscock station. It was already dark when the train passed through Miles' territory, so the engineer had already lit the engine headlight and the conductor had lit the lanterns inside the passenger coach. The Miles Gang was waiting east of town, and when the train roared by they roared too, shooting out all the train's lights. Mission accomplished, the Miles bunch slipped into the thick postoak thickets east of present-day Elgin. The next evening, they were shooting again. It got to the point that whenever the train approached Miles' thickets, the conductor would warn all the passengers to "lay low; we're in for hell agin." Eventually the Miles Gang ceased their nefarious activities but the spot continued to be known up and down the line as "Hell agin," commonly pronounced "Hell'gin." Now, the stationmaster knew that not many town lots were going to sell in a place called "Hell 'gin," but he was also loath to give up a name so rich in connotations. So he struggled with it awhile and further corrupted the corruption to "Elgin."

During those days Bethel Coopwood kept a herd of camels from Camp Verde that he had purchased at an auction for $12 and $14 a head. Elgin began to prosper as an agricultural center and shipping point, particularly after 1886 and the arrival of the Missouri-Kansas-Texas railroad (MKT or Katy), which could haul produce north. Hundreds of carloads of melons were shipped out yearly, as well as thousands of bales of cotton. Brick buildings, a sure sign of prosperity in those times, came early and in great numbers to Elgin. Even the

old cotton gin you pass on the way into town is brick. Little wonder, for Elgin was a center for brick production by the dawn of the twentieth century. Downtown Elgin is still predominantly brick, although the brick streets are now paved over with asphalt.

Once in town, the River Rd. becomes Central Ave.

Downtown Elgin still looks much as it did in 1916 at the apex of its prosperity. Old downtown Elgin is now a certified historical district, from Brenham St. on the south side to 4th St. on the north side; Ave. A to the west and Ave. F to the east. Elgin has one of the best and largest vintage business districts still standing anywhere in Texas, one that straddles both sides of the railroad tracks. There are two blocks worth of brick commercial buildings on the south side of the tracks along and behind Central Ave.; most, unfortunately, are abandoned or barely hanging on.

The first of these historic buildings as you enter town is the old **P. Bassist building** (201 Central Ave. at S. Ave. C), which dates to 1906. The second story of Philip Louis Bassist's red-brick pride and joy served as Elgin's opera house; Lily Langtry is said to have performed here. The ground floor has housed a variety of businesses over the years, including Bassist Produce and the Elgin Post Office.

The east wall of the old (1900) **Schroeder Grocery** at 119 Central Ave. at S. Ave. C still cheerfully urges "Enjoy Bright and Early." Next door (117 Central) is one of **Southside Market's** many past homes; in this instance, for several years. Elgin is famous for its "hot guts" sausage, and Southside Market is the granddaddy of all the local sausage stuffers. William Moon established the Southside Market in 1882 on what is now FM 1704. By 1886, the market had moved to 117 Central. It continued to move around until it settled for a half-century at 109 Central in 1944; Southside Market is now located on US 290, and the south side of Elgin hasn't been the same since.

The humble little depot building on your left next to the tracks is the original (1872) **H&TC freight depot.** For decades, the original board-and-batten walls were covered with asbestos siding. At presstime, restoration of the depot's original appearance was planned.

Elgin has one of the largest collections of painted wall advertisements in Central Texas. Here on the south side of the tracks, you can still read the fading old advertisements painted on several of the commercial buildings, such as the south wall of the two-story former "RIVERs BROS. MERC. Co." building at Austin and S. Main, which sold "Royal Shoes" in the good old days. In the alley behind

Schroeder Grocery, you can see a ca. 1900 Star Tobacco mural painted on the north wall of the building across the alley from Schroeder's. Look through the shop windows at 106 N. Main (the 1901
Dildy/Webster Building) and you'll see two old black-and-white
painted wall advertisements dating to the turn of the century that
were recently uncovered during a building restoration. One ad advertises a grain and feed company; the other touts Owl brand cigars,
complete with a big white owl.

*Central Ave. dead-ends into Main St. Turn left here to see the north
side of the historical district. Main St. is the principal thoroughfare
in downtown Elgin.*

North of the tracks, Main St. is in better shape: many of the old
buildings have been restored, there are new businesses in them, and
a number of longtime local businesses are still active.

UNION DEPOT
15 Depot Ave. at Main
Sandwiched between the railroad tracks and the first block of
business houses on the east side of N. Main is the red brick Union
Depot, built about 1903. It served as the local passenger depot for
both lines for about 65 years. It was undergoing restoration in 1996.

A. CHRISTIAN SALOON
Depot Ave., facing Union Depot
A. S. Christian bought this lot for $300 in 1897 and built a saloon
(one of seven in Elgin at the time), which he named A. Christian
Saloon. According to an old story, the saloon (whose name was
painted in large letters on the side of the building to attract thirsty
passengers from the eight passenger trains that stopped in Elgin
every day) drew the attention of a Bible salesman passing through
town, who detrained and rushed into the saloon to congratulate its
proprietor on his fine establishment. The salesman beat a hasty
retreat when he realized that being Christian had nothing to do with
the den of iniquity he found inside.

ELGIN CHAMBER OF COMMERCE
15 N. Main • 285-4515 • Open Monday through Friday • W
Your best source for visitor information.

CITY CAFE
19 N. Main • 281-FOOD • Open daily, breakfast, lunch and dinner • $–$$ • W

City Cafe is one of the better small-town cafes in Central Texas. The building dates to about 1890 and is said to be the second brick building built downtown. It first housed a general store and drugstore, then a barbershop and bakery; it has housed a cafe since 1910. City Cafe serves the old standards like chicken-fried steak, plus some surprises like a Cajun buffet.

MILLER BROTHERS BUILDING
32 N. Main at E. 1st

The most impressive building on the north side of the tracks is the two-story Miller Brothers Building, built of red brick with tan brick accents. The building dates to about 1890, with a 1911 addition. It was home to Elgin's second bank, the Merchants and Farmers State Bank. The bank's original vault is still inside. It has recently been restored, down to its stained-glass front door and transoms.

NOFSINGER HOUSE
310 N. Main

Dr. I. B. Nofsinger built this Queen Anne-style house out of local brick in 1906. Born in Kentucky in 1864, Nofsinger came to Texas as a young adult and practiced medicine in McDade before moving to Elgin in 1900. His house symbolizes Elgin's turn-of-the-century prosperity. Elgin grew from 832 people in 1890 to 1,709 people in 1910. The house is now Elgin City Hall.

Continue north on Main to Elgin Memorial Park. Along the way you'll see several more substantial old homes from Elgin's golden era.

ELGIN LOG CABIN MUSEUM
Elgin Memorial Park, N. Main at SH 95 • Open by appointment

This little cabin came from the Elm Grove School community in Lee County, about 12 miles from Elgin. It is administered by the New Century Club.

OTHER ATTRACTIONS

ELGIN ANTIQUE MALL
1100 N. US 290 • 285-5655 • Open daily

A number of dealers are located inside, and the inventory constantly changes. Furniture, glassware, and all sorts of specialty collectibles.

DINING

BIGGER'S BARBECUE
US 290 at Loop 109 • 285-3402 • Open daily, breakfast, lunch, and dinner • $ • W
Sausage is the big attraction here, but the beef and ribs pass muster too. Homemade side dishes and pies.

SOUTHSIDE MARKET
1212 US 290 • 285-3407 • Open daily • No Cr. • W
Southside Market makes the sausage that made Elgin sausage famous. Besides the sausage, Southside Market serves up pork and beef steaks, beef and pork ribs, beef brisket, and mutton. The pork steak is plastic-fork tender and peppery—heavenly, in short—and in its own way easily the equal of the pork chops from Kreuz Market in Lockhart or Cooper's in Llano. The side dishes are good too. What's missing is the ambience of the market's old location downtown on Central Ave., on the south side of the tracks. The building that now houses the market used to be a bank, which helps explain the sterile atmosphere.

ANNUAL EVENT

JULY • Western Days • Elgin Memorial Park • 285-4515
Fourth weekend in July
Events include parades, dances, rodeo, fun run, and arts and crafts fair.

To leave Elgin, return to Main St. at the railroad tracks. Go south on Main, past the intersection with Central St., and take the first possible left turn, onto Brenham St., which turns into Cty. Rd. 106, aka the old McDade Rd.

After leaving town, the land to your left (this is the old Miles Gang territory) is East Texas overgrown, while to your right the old H&TC railroad tracks run past new ranch-style houses, old crumbling farmhouses, and gravel pits on the way to Butler.

BUTLER

Bastrop County • About 6 miles from Elgin
Butler is a company town and dates back to the railroad's arrival in 1871. Michael and Patrick Butler came to Austin in the early 1870s and started a brick factory there soon after. The business prospered and Butler bricks were used all over Austin: in the old city hall, the capitol building, and in the streets of downtown Austin. Upon discovery of good clay here on Sandy Creek, the Butlers began moving their operation out here, beginning with a plant built in 1903. Naturally, all of the company's buildings and dwellings are made of brick.

As you enter Butler, you cross some railroad tracks and pass the entrance to the brick works on your left. A few feet later, you come to the intersection with FM 696. At this point, you could continue straight ahead on the old highway to McDade, but instead, turn left on FM 696 and head toward Lexington. On your left, as you cross Sandy Creek, you will see more of the brick works and then the pits where the clay is excavated.

MT. PLEASANT

Bastrop County • About 3 miles from Butler
Texas has had more Mount Pleasants than anyone can keep track of. FM 696's Mount Pleasant, represented these days only by an **old church,** is one of the highest points for miles around, offering lots of shade and cooling breezes.

About 3 miles past the FM 696/FM 619 intersection, you come to an intersection with Lee County Rd. 305, which is also marked by a sign for the Knobbs Springs Baptist Church. Off to your right are the Yegua Knobbs, four hillocks that form the watershed of Yegua Creek, Lee County's major creek. Turn right on Lee Cty. Rd. 305 to reach the Knobbs country.

THE KNOBBS

Lee County • About 11 miles from Butler
You might as well throw your compass away out here for all the good it will do you; the ferruginous sandstone that composes the Knobbs will cause its needle to flutter about wildly, rendering it use-

less. One hundred years ago the Knobbs were not a good place to get lost. Following the war, this area was a favorite hangout for rustlers, murderers, and other ne'er-do-wells, and with good reason. County seat Giddings and the sheriff were a good 20 miles and half a day's ride away, and the thickly wooded hills and valleys made good hideouts. These same hills and valleys made scratching out a living from the soil even more difficult than it already was. Boys from the Yegua Knobbs were known as "notch-cutters," although it is not clear whether the name referred to the notches in their gun handles or the notches in the trees used as trail markers.

Many southern spirits and pockets were empty after the Civil War. For many, rustling and robbing seemed to be the easiest way to make a living, and a well-aimed gun often served as a morale booster as well as a quick and easy method of settling accounts. A human life, even one's own, seemed to have less value after the great conflagration. The words of one Confederate veteran, about to be hung by Lee County vigilantes for rustling, may help us to understand these unsettled times:

> Now gentlemen, as you know, I have just come home from fighting in the war. I found my wife and family almost starved to death and I could not find any of the few head of stock, oxen, cows and canes, steers or hogs that I had to leave behind when I was forced to go to war. I have been gone about four years and, as you know, if I didn't go, I would have been shot. And to fight in a war, as so many others did, that was not any of my business, since I never did believe in slavery and also was too damn poor to own one.
>
> I'm what is called "poor white trash," just cluttering up the countryside.
>
> We came here to try all over again but the slaveholders have the money, the best land and most land, the best and most animals and equipment, besides the cheap slave labor. It has been hard for us to live because no one cares whether we live or die. Mostly they would rather see the latter.
>
> I know the slaves have been mistreated, but on the other hand, being property of the rich people, they were fed and housed and taken care of that way to which we had to fend for ourselves and which was worse than the slaves this way because we had neither the tools or the skills to build a decent home or farm with. Just as they say, "root, hog, or die."
>
> As you know, if the slaveholder had as many as three slaves he did not have to serve in the Confederate Army; but if he did, he was commissioned as an officer and you know how many Privates of us

poor white trash there was. Now the officers stayed behind us, directing us and shooting anyone in the back who faltered or tried to leave. I have had to kill other humans or be killed and I am so damn tired of it all, till I don't give a damn what you do.

Although I would like for you to examine your conscience and if there is a man in this crowd who had not so much as stolen one yearling or hog, then let him whip this worn-out horse out from under me.

The man's words rang true to the posse, so true that by the time he had finished, most of them had gone shamefacedly home. The last man to leave was honorable enough to remove the "convicted" man's noose and untie him. Most vigilante incidents did not end this way, however. Faced with increasing lawlessness and the inability of the law to deal with the problem, certain citizens formed the Knobbs Committee in 1875. This vigilante group worked with similar committees from neighboring settlements like McDade, Lexington, and Giddings. Executions were handled by groups from outside the area where the crimes were committed. Membership in these committees was secret; to be a known member was to court death by those you were after. Members met at night in a variety of wooded locations, using whistles, grunts, and throat clearings for signals. Action came by a simple majority vote. Even prominent citizens were involved, for these were truly desperate times.

Most all the Knobbs men—vigilantes and outlaws—feared for their lives during these years; you might be killed for just being a friend or relative of the wrong man. It was unsafe for the menfolk to leave the house after sunset, so the women answered the door, milked and fed the cattle, and brought in the evening firewood. Some families put up heavy curtains made of dark material to obscure all movements within the house. This practice brought misery on hot summer nights, since the curtains let in none of the cool evening breezes. Some men even wore their wives' nightgowns and caps to further obscure their identities. But occasionally all these precautions were in vain; at least one man was dragged from his home one night and lynched.

In open country, outlaws and vigilantes employed the same methods of waylaying their victims. The favored tactic was for at least two and sometimes up to five men to secret themselves at opportune places along the road on which the victim was to travel. If the first ambush failed, someone on down the line would be successful.

"Convicted" cattle rustlers were sometimes dispatched home and to the promised land—wrapped up in a hide of one of the animals they had stolen. But not all the killings were of the outlaw-vigilante school. On a grudge, George Duncan followed Heywood Beatty up to Parker County, Texas, to kill him. The two had fought as boys at the Knobbs school and Duncan could not let the fight rest. Duncan confronted Beatty after a Sunday baptism and a chase ensued. Beatty had the faster horse and beat Duncan home. Dashing inside, Beatty grabbed his Winchester and stood ready for Duncan beside a window. Duncan rode up gun in hand and was promptly shot dead by Beatty. The feud was done.

The Knobbs are sparsely settled these days and there is little to remind us of those turbulent times, except the old cemetery next to the new church building about 3 miles down this twisting road from FM 696. Turn around and double back to FM 696. Continue east on FM 696. If you want to cut this trip by approximately half, don't double back to FM 696, but continue south on Knobbs Springs Rd. In about 7 miles, you'll reach McDade. Take it easy driving this road. It twists and turns constantly and is booby-trapped with lots of potholes.

BLUE

Lee County • About 11 miles from Butler

Just up FM 696 at Blue, things were much the same. This place was originally known as Blue Branch, named for the waters of **Blue Branch Creek.** By 1879 a half-dozen or so Blue men, including one named Horace Alsup, had been waylaid and killed by unknown assailants. Depending on who you listened to, these unfortunate men had either been brigands or upright men. At any rate, several of them had been found bound in cowhide.

Horace Alsup was assassinated in October 1879. Perhaps a good man at heart, he had nevertheless harbored his son Wade, his son-in-law Young Floyd, and various of their friends whenever the boys got in trouble with the law, which seemed to be pretty often. With the death of the old man, the boys decided it was time to leave the county. But before they left, Alsup, Floyd, and company wanted to have a little fun. So five of them saddled up and headed for a dance in old Blue at fiddlin' Pat Airhart's place. They planned to kill Pat and ride off into the night; not that they had anything against Airhart, they just didn't want to leave the county without a parting shot.

Old "Aunt" Rose Carpenter, years later, spoke of the quintet's atrocious manners that night. "Massa Pat wan' ready f'um to eat yit—hadn' eben ax 'em. Dey cum in and fell in dem cakes and pies and slop coffee all ov' da table. Lor' hit look like a storm been in dere. I wuz dat mad I cudda hit 'em ov' da haid wid a cheer."

The dance was going full blast when suddenly all the windows and doors of Airhart's house were filled with guns. A man outside called out a list of names of the men they wanted: Wade Alsup, Young Floyd, Bake Scott, John Kuykendall, Ab Kaneman, Sol Wheat. Kaneman escaped through a window; Wheat wasn't at the dance. The other four were hustled outside and one of the masked vigilantes told Airhart to keep fiddling and keep the rest of the folks dancing till sunrise. Only then could the dancers stop and go home. As the four started off in the custody of the posse, Kuykendall remarked to one of his comrades, "Another trip to Giddings, boys." His more knowledgeable friend replied, "We will never see Giddings." Truer words were never spoken. The departing dancers found the four next morning, swinging from the stout branch of a tree on Blue Branch, less than a mile from Airhart's place. Apprised of his close call, Airhart traded his fiddle in for a Bible and became a preacher.

Blue once had a chair factory and several stores serving the area farmers. Nowadays it is just a sleepy little ranching community. Prominent Texas potter Ishmael Soto is currently Blue's most illustrious resident. His shop is located a ways up a red gravel road, marked by a simple sign reading "**Soto 4.6 miles.**"

The countryside begins to stretch out a bit as FM 696 approaches Lexington, Lee County's oldest town.

LEXINGTON

Lee County • 991 • (409) • About 9 miles from Blue

San Jacinto veteran James Shaw rode up this way in 1837 looking for a place to settle down. His war service entitled him to a league of land; the new republic had no cash money with which to pay its soldiers. In need to water late one afternoon, Shaw traced a buffalo trail to a clear running spring. A band of Indians was already camped there. Boldly, Shaw decided to ride up to them rather than take flight. They turned out to be friendly Tonkawas, who let Shaw drink his fill and then gave him some of the buffalo meat they were roasting. Shaw named the creek Indian Camp Branch and started staking out his league of land the next day. He built a log cabin with a rock chimney, which also served as post office and schoolhouse, for he was postmaster and teacher between surveying jobs.

Shaw's next encounter with Indians was not as peaceful. Huddling around the campfire one night after the passage of a blue norther, Shaw and the surveying party he headed were attacked by Indians. They sent a shower of arrows into the camp, one of which struck Shaw in the knee. Unable to rise, he was seconds away from being scalped by two knife-wielding Indians when a burly Irishman rushed the pair and knocked them unconscious. He carried Shaw to safety while the other surveyors fought off the marauders.

Other settlers came to live nearby and their community was known as String Prairie, because it strung out for about 10 miles along the narrow band of blackland prairie that runs from Bastrop County through Lee County almost to the Trinity River in East Texas. In 1850 the locals got together and laid out a townsite, naming it Lexington after the embattled Massachusetts village of Revolutionary War fame. When Lee County was created in 1874 Lexington bid to become county seat, but that honor went to Giddings, located on the brand-spanking-new H&TC railroad. Lexington got its railroad in 1890, and with the arrival of the San Antonio and Aransas Pass railroad the whole of Lexington picked up and moved the short distance to its present location. String Prairie was just a memory as folks moved into town. Cotton ruled the Lexington economy during this era, to be supplanted later by ranching and peanuts, and recently by oil. Lexington sits on the oil-rich Austin chalk, as does the rest of Lee County. Lexington may be slightly past its prime but it is still very much alive and proud of its past.

You will see the Lexington city limits sign as you enter town on FM 696. This section of FM 696 is 7th St. within town. Less than a half-mile past the city limits sign, FM 696 meets Loop 123. FM 696 turns right here to join Loop 123 (Rockdale St. within the city limits). Follow Rockdale four blocks (less than a half-mile), turning right on 3rd to reach downtown Lexington and the city square.

LEXINGTON CITY SQUARE
3rd, Laredo, 4th, and Main
The square is located two blocks south of Rockdale, bounded by 3rd, Laredo, 4th, and Main. Most of the town's business establishments still surround the square. Lexington prides itself as a God-fearing town. Not surprisingly, all the town's bars are segregated, side by side, on the far west side of the square. Only one of them is currently open.

The spacious city square today holds the town water tower and not much else. Lexington's founders had envisioned a much grander function for it, intending that the Lee County Courthouse sit here. But, as we know, Giddings won the election.

Lexington may not have the courthouse, but it does have the Lexington Museum. And while the museum isn't nearly as impressive as the Lee County Courthouse, it's at least as interesting.

LEXINGTON MUSEUM
Main at 4th, next to the city square • W variable
Three log buildings make up the Lexington Museum. The Guthrie cabin is the oldest of the lot, built in 1846 by George Washington Guthrie, who fought at San Jacinto and in the Civil War. It was moved here from its original location on the old stage road to Austin. Lawyer Ephraim Roddy built the other cabin in 1850. The Fowler family added onto it in the 1870s. The log farm building was moved here from a site on FM 696. Attached to it are two walls from the old iron calaboose in Giddings, where Rattlin' Bill Longley spent his last days. More on Longley later.

LEXINGTON MERCANTILE COMPANY
South side of the square • 773-2231
This little grocery doesn't make its own sausage, but it does make old-fashioned Texas pies, cookies, and breads. Try the buttermilk pie.

ANNUAL EVENT

MAY • Lexington Homecoming • First weekend in May
Free • W
Barbecue, gospel singing, and a rodeo are just a few of the events in this annual welcome home party for everybody who's ever lived in Lexington, or wanted to.

From the museum, return to Rockdale and turn right. Stay on FM 696 east/Loop 123/Rockdale through the rest of town, until you hit the US 77 intersection. Here FM 696 joins US 77 briefly before resuming its lone path eastward. Following the highway signs, turn left onto US 77, then turn right several hundred feet later, staying on FM 696 as it leaves US 77.

East of Lexington on FM 696, you enter old String Prairie, not leaving it till you turn south onto SH 21. This is one of Texas' oldest

*and most illustrious roads, the Old San Antonio Rd., or El Camino
Real, as documented by the old granite marker in the roadside park
a mile or so south of the junction of FM 696 and SH 21. Actually,
there were at least three documented branches of this road from San
Antonio to Nacogdoches. The branch you are on now—the Old San
Antonio Rd. of 1795—is followed almost exactly by SH 21 to the Brazos River.*

HRANICE

Lee County • About 20 miles from Lexington

You are in the old Hranice community at this point and it was here,
around two centuries ago, that Indians ambushed a Spanish packtrain
carrying a payroll of gold destined for the forts and missions of East
Texas. Surrounded by Indians, with most of their comrades lying
dead at their feet, the surviving soldiers scratched out a hole and
dropped the gold into it. This task accomplished, they attempted to
escape from the ring of Indians. Only one made it back to San Antonio with the bad news.

Treasure hunters have been looking for the $90,000 in gold (pre-
inflationary value) ever since. Some say it lies at the bottom of
Suehs-Gest Lake, others say it rests somewhere on the old Kutej
farm. Still others say a hired hand found the gold, split the loot with
his boss, and then split the scene.

Hranice was first settled by Anglos before the Civil War, but the
1880s saw the beginning of a massive influx of Czech and Moravian
immigrants. Many of them came from a village in Moravia named
Hranice, which means "watershed" or "dividing place."

OLD DIME BOX

Lee County • (409) • About 20 miles from Lexington

Old Dime Box—now a wide spot along SH 21 located just south
of the turnoff to New Dime Box—started life as Brown's Mill, second oldest town in Lee County. Joe Brown built a gristmill, then a
sawmill and cotton gin here before the Civil War. Soon Brown's Mill
had a post office. Once a week the postmaster would ride to Giddings
to pick up the town's mail. Locals would leave their letters in the
mill's mailbox along with a dime for carrying charges. Sometime
around the turn of the century, postal authorities told Brown's Mill to
change its name; mail for Brown's Mill and Brownsville kept getting
mixed up. A town meeting was held and a local wag suggested

"Dime Box," in honor of the old mailing custom. The new name floated, and when the town moved three miles east to the newly laid Southern Pacific tracks in 1913, the name Dime Box went along. So today we have Old Dime Box and New Dime Box. To further confuse matters, Hranice is sometimes referred to as Dime Box. New Dime Box enjoyed a flurry of nationwide fame during World War II when it was chosen for the starting point for the 1944 March of Dimes fundraising drive.

To get to New Dime Box, turn left on FM 141.

NEW DIME BOX

Lee County • 312 • (409) • About 23 miles from Lexington
Oil stirred things up quite a bit in New Dime Box in the late 1970s and early 1980s, but things have declined since and several of the vintage stores and beer joints have closed, though the buildings still stand. For now, Dime Box is comfortably weatherbeaten and slightly frayed at the edges, rather like your favorite pair of comfortable old jeans. The brick buildings facing the railroad tracks were built by Vinc Balcar just after New Dime Box was established. He always closed his store and saloon on the Lord's Day, and children—his own included—were never permitted inside the saloon. One of Balcar's 12 children passed his lunch to him each day at the front door.

WIEDERHOLD MEAT MARKET
FM 141, on the outskirts of town • 884-3535 • Open Monday through Saturday, closed Sunday • W
Wiederhold Meat Market makes an all-pork, old-style Deutsch-Tex ring sausage, perfect for barbecuing.

ANNUAL EVENT

OCTOBER • Dime Box Homecoming • First Saturday in October • Free • W
Homecoming events include a mini-marathon in the morning; barbecue cook-off, games, and crafts booths during the day; and a street dance at night.

Return to SH 21 via FM 141 and continue south toward Lincoln.

LINCOLN

Lee County • 276 • About 12 miles from Dime Box

Lincoln owes its name not to the 16th president but to an old Campbellite circuit-riding preacher by the name of John A. Lincoln. Lincoln was laid out with the arrival of the railroad in 1890. The town rapidly became a regional shipping and supply center with several general stores, saloons, blacksmith shops, and the like.

Turn right from SH 21 at the sign that says Lincoln Community Center and Ball Park.

Not much is left of old downtown Lincoln. The **Lincoln Community Center** grounds and baseball fields are charmingly quaint and from another era, and the barbecue that cooks on the pits at community picnics is first-class. Come spring, the ballfield sports one of the region's best wildflower displays. Electrically colored phlox, from the deepest of blood-red purples to the whitest of pale pinks, dot the diamond in pointillistic fashion, supported by lesser numbers of primroses, morning flowers, winecups, and spiderworts.

Up at the other end of town from the Community Center, old man Wendel's store sits by where the railroad tracks used to run, crumbling slowly, leaning more every year and nearly covered over by vines and other vegetation. The old frame Lincoln post office was torn down in the early 1990s. It sat next to the present post office, built in 1967.

ANNUAL EVENT

AUGUST • Lincoln Community Club Picnic • Usually third Sunday in August • Free • W

Lincoln's population increases several fold once a year for the community picnic, held under the graceful, spreading oaks of the community center grounds. Activities include music, bingo, and various other games, but the stellar attraction is the barbecue—beef, pork, mutton, and Elgin sausage—some of the tastiest you'll find anywhere in Central Texas. It's sold by the pound, starting at 8:30 in the morning, and if you get here much past 1 in the afternoon, you'll have to settle for whatever is left on the pit.

There is another, similar picnic/barbecue held here annually (usually the third Sunday in May) to benefit St. John's Lutheran Church and school of Lincoln.

From Lincoln, continue south on SH 21. Old Evergreen, the town that Lincoln superseded, is just down SH 21 a bit and to your left on FM 1624.

EVERGREEN

Lee County • About 1 mile from Lincoln

Nothing remains but the old Evergreen oak, under whose branches pioneer justice was dispensed and from whose branches errants were hanged. Natives say a small fortune in lead could be mined from the tree, so numerous were the bullets fired into it.

Rattlin' Bill Longley, one of Texas' and the Wild West's most notorious killers, hailed from Evergreen. Son of respected rancher-farmer Campbell Longley, Bill killed his first man at 15. He notched up 31 more victims by his own admission, mostly blacks and Mexicans, and one woman, before his career ended when he was 27. Longley was no robber or rustler; in between murders he was content to work as a cowboy or to hoe his daddy's cotton patch. Bill's problem was that he just plain couldn't abide insults to his own honor, his family's honor, his friends' honor, Texas' honor, womankind's honor, or the white man's honor. Either the offender retracted the insult or he died. It was as simple as that to Bill Longley. He was least tolerant of insults from black men. Longley's first victim was a burly drunken freedman who made the mistake of cursing white men in general and Campbell Longley in particular while galloping up and down the Camino Real, the old royal highway running through Evergreen. Now this was an unwise move, for although Longley was not yet old enough to shave he was already "crack" enough with a gun to gallop his horse past the old Evergreen oak and put six balls into it without missing a shot. The offender swung his rifle up to shooting position after being called down by this young sapling of a boy. His rifle spat out one wild shot before Longley drilled a silver-dollar-size hole in the man's head with one shot from his Dance percussion-fired six-gun. Longley hurriedly buried his first victim in an unmarked grave, his die now cast.

Like Sam Bass, Rattlin' Bill had a weakness for fast horses and racing. He teamed up with friend Johnny McKowen and together they raced their fast ponies at fairs and other gatherings all over the area. One fall day in 1866, they headed up to old Lexington for a day of racing. Blacks outnumbered whites at the races that day, and times being what they were, heated words were exchanged. Longley and McKowen headed back to Evergreen soon after their arrival. Word came back to Longley that afternoon that the blacks were celebrating "that white boy's" flight home. That was enough for Rattlin' Bill; he headed back to Lexington that night. The partying was at a high pitch by then, as were emotions. Longley studied the crowd for a moment, then galloped headlong into it with a Rebel yell, both guns blazing. By the time young Longley had ridden out of the crowd, two men lay dead, six wounded. Bill suffered nary a scratch. From that day on, Longley's name struck terror into the souls of Lee County blacks.

A few weeks later, three blacks rode into Evergreen and stopped at a saloon to drink. As they returned to their horses, one of the men remarked that Evergreen was reported to be dangerous to the well-being of blacks and that he would be glad if someone would undertake to molest him. Longley overheard this, grabbed a couple of friends, and started after the trio. His intention was to disarm the freedmen and allow them to move on. They ignored his command to stop and surrender their arms, however, whereupon the three whites concentrated their fire on the man who had invited trouble at the bar. He fell dead into the dust.

Longley did not always shoot his insulters, to be entirely fair to the man. He once kicked a black porter off a traveling H&TC train because he had kicked Langley's feet into the aisle.

After that last killing on the road to Brenham, Longley had to go on the lam. The law was after him. He headed south to Gonzales County, where the Taylor-Sutton feud was beginning to heat up. Employed as a cowboy, he was riding along one day when a detachment of Yankee cavalry mistook him for Charlie Taylor, who was also on the dodge. Longley lit out and the contingent of "bluebellies" followed. Soon it was a two-man race: Longley versus the detachment commander. Longley had fired five shots at his pursuers, none of which had taken effect. He had dodged over 40 shots. That lone soldier overtook Longley, who had been saving his last shot. As they rode side by side, Longley rammed his pistol into the man's midriff and pulled the trigger, but the hammer had become entangled in the cavalryman's coat lapel. As he pulled the pistol back the hammer was released, the shot fired, and the bullet passed through the soldier's body.

After this affair young Bill headed for Arkansas, where he teamed up with East Texas guerrilla-band captain Cullen Baker, the "Great Granddaddy of Six-Shooterology," the first man to master the quick draw. Baker's band roamed northeastern Texas and southern Arkansas, ambushing Yankee occupation-troop supply trains, firing their supply warehouses, and generally making life deadly miserable for the occupying troops. Remember, Texas and all of the South were under martial law during these years. It was during this period that Bill Longley had his first taste of the hangman's noose. Captured by vigilantes who suspected him of being a cattle rustler (he was in the company of one that night), he and recent acquaintance Tom Johnson were strung up from the same tree. Upon leaving the scene, one of the vigilantes emptied his pistol into the pair. One shot bounced off Longley's money belt, another struck him in the jaw, breaking one of his teeth, the third cut through the two strands of rope from which he hung. Johnson's little 13-year-old brother stumbled onto the necktie party just as the rope 'round Longley's neck broke. The lad cut the ropes from Longley's hands and neck and helped him to a safe place. Tom Johnson was already dead when cut down. Longley got his revenge a bit later on the vigilante who had fired upon him and Johnson as they swung helplessly. He hung the man from the very same tree and emptied his pistol into the fellow.

Longley left Baker after a few more months and took to the road, returning to Evergreen periodically to visit friends and kin. In the meantime he ranged through Llano, Burnet, Gillespie, and the rest of the Hill Country and frontier counties of Texas before heading for the Utah territory. He killed in the Dakotas, Kansas, and Utah. He was thrown in jail several times for his misdeeds but managed to escape every time.

He was finally captured for good in Louisiana in 1877, accused of the murder several years earlier of boyhood friend Will Anderson. Longley believed Anderson had murdered his cousin Caleb "Little Cale" Longley. Most folks around Evergreen believed Little Cale's death was accidental—that as he and Anderson were on their way home from a day of drinking in Giddings, Caleb's horse bolted and he was knocked from his runaway mount by a low-hanging tree limb, whereupon Anderson picked the dead boy up and carried him home. Egged on by Cale's grieving father, Longley went to the field where Anderson was working and shot him with a double-barrelled shotgun. Rattlin' Bill was convicted of this murder and sentenced to death. The 27-year-old died by the hangman's noose in downtown Giddings on October 1, 1878, and was buried just outside the boundaries of the Giddings cemetery, a piece of petrified wood marking his grave. Wild stories of his escape from the noose at Giddings abound.

Some claim that Lee County Sheriff James Madison Brown was paid off to help Longley fake his hanging. They say that a brace kept him from dying when the trap sprang and that his casket was really filled with rocks. From there he disappeared, to Central America or Lousiana depending on who's telling the story. The controversy was

such that just a few years ago an attempt was made to locate Longley's grave and exhume the remains, but after several days of excavation, the grave could not be located and the search was given up.
But given contemporary accounts of his hanging, Longley's escape
seems unlikely. When the trapdoor opened, Bill fell 12 feet until his
feet dragged the ground. The hanging rope had slipped. He writhed
about as the sheriff and aides struggled to take up the rope's slack
and raise him up into the air again to finish the strangulation process.
After about 10 minutes of this, he was pronounced dead by the execution's three doctors, who had been charged with verifying that the
sentence had been successfully carried out. They turned his head 180
degrees in one direction, then 180 degrees in the other direction as
proof. One of his guards that day said that the rope had buried itself
in the side of his neck and had to be cut out.

MANHEIM

Lee County • 40 • (512) • About 6 miles from Lincoln

WACHMANN'S STORE
Hwy. 21, Manheim Community • 253-6630 • Open Monday
through Saturday 8–6 • No Cr.
  Manheim is a little German farming community that never grew
up. Wachmann's store has been Manheim's only business for 50
years. Step inside this sprawling barn of a grocery and feedstore and
admire one of the finest collections of cobwebs and vintage beer
signs in Central Texas. At least half the beers advertised on the walls
aren't made anymore. You can't get a bottle of Shiner Texas Special
Export, but you can get a Shiner Bock Longneck.

*A little over 11 miles down SH 21 from Lincoln are two signed
turnoffs for downtown Paige: Cty. Rds. 173 and 175, which run parallel to each other just a few yards apart along the short distance
into Paige. Once in town, Cty. Rd. 173 is Main St. and Cty. Rd. 175
is Gonzales St.*

PAIGE

Bastrop County • 275 • About 12 miles from Lincoln
  Paige was established as a station on the H&TC railroad in 1871
and was named for H&TC engineer Norman Paige. The new town
was settled for the most part by German immigrants who began to

pour into Texas once again with the end of the Civil War. At the turn of the century, Paige counted a pickle factory as one of its most prominent industries. Old downtown Paige was located along the railroad tracks; new downtown Paige is lined up along busy US 290.

Old Paige is slowly turning into a ghost town; many of the old houses and businesses have been abandoned and enveloped by jungle-like growth. Some of the worst have been torn down in recent years, and the old hotel by the railroad appears to have burned down. The old Sons of Hermann Bar and Hall, with its embossed-tin siding, still hangs on, but management and hours of the bar were up in the air in late 1996.

PAIGE HISTORICAL MUSEUM
South side of US 290 at Main; from old downtown Paige, take Main St. south across US 290 to the grounds of the Paige Community Center and Historical Museum
The Paige Community Center, a large white washed frame hall with a high tin roof that is about 75–80 years old, fronts US 290. Behind is the nascent Paige Historical Museum, which in 1996 consisted of the restored old Paige Depot and a small frame house still undergoing restoration.

From Paige, return to SH 21 on either Cty. Rd. 173 or Cty. Rd. 175. Turn left onto SH 21. As you approach the SH 21/US 290 intersection, you will see a TxDOT sign reading "Austin 42 Giddings 13." Just after this sign, you will turn right onto a little county road marked by the sign "Cty. Rd. 160 Cty. Rd. 333." A few feet later, you will veer left on Cty. Rd. 333, which is Old Highway 20 and the old road to McDade. Don't turn onto Cty. Rd. 160, aka Paint Creek Rd., which runs off to the north. The old highway parallels US 290 and the railroad tracks. The quality of Cty. Rd. 333 is very uneven; stretches of gravel alternate with stretches of relatively smooth asphalt. If the weather is bad, or you're just not adventuresome, you can get to McDade on US 290. Just take SH 21 to the intersection, turn right onto US 290, drive about 10 miles, and turn right into McDade on Loop 223.

As you drive along through this sparsely settled ranching and watermelon country, you can see why early-day train robbers had such an easy time of it. The thickets of brush along the railroad right-of-way obscure the tracks much of the time, even though the tracks are never more than a few yards away from the road. The dense forests on the south side of the road enhanced the bandits' chances for a quick, safe getaway. A rattlesnake farm was once located along this road; the snakes were milked for their venom, which was used in the manufacture of patent medicines.

Once in the town of McDade, Cty. Rd. 333 is called Old 20 S.

McDADE

Bastrop County • 345 • About 10 miles from Paige

McDade was settled in the 1840s by planters from the Old South. The town's namesake, James W. McDade, was one of these men. First known as Tie City because of its status as a regional freight and cotton shipping center, McDade was also home to Bastrop County's oldest industry, a pottery factory using clay from Alum Creek. Mule power turned the mills that ground the clay, and the potters turned out urns, furnaces, milk crocks, mixing bowls, jugs, and flowerpots, all of them fired with a special salt glaze. Some of these pieces can be seen in the little museum located in the Old Rock Saloon at the west end of Old Hwy. 20 S.

The factory's greatest volume of profitable business came from the making of charcoal furnaces. Owner R. L. Williams invented and patented a press for forming the furnaces and practically eliminated his Texas competition. Carloads of these furnaces were shipped out across Texas and the South until the widespread advent of gas and electric service to Texas homes in the 1920s. The product line diversified as charcoal stove sales declined. For instance, art deco lamp bases were produced, but it was to no avail; the pottery closed during the 1930s.

The charcoal furnace is a versatile contrivance. Women cooked and also heated their irons on them. They heated rooms, or at least parts of them. They were used to great advantage when it was preserving time. At the height of summer, preserving sessions usually took place in the back yard, where agarita berries, dew berries, peaches, mulberries, grapes, plums, and figs would bubble away atop charcoal furnaces. Many old-timers maintain that preserves cooked over a charcoal furnace take on an added and desirable flavor from simmering over the charcoal.

The furnace is basically a glorified clay bucket, often bound in heavy tin with a metal loop handle. It has two elevations, with a day grate, which lets air breathe in from below through a ventilation hole. Old charcoal furnaces are collectors items and priced accordingly, especially McDade stoves. But if you just want something to cook your preserves on, a hibachi will do nicely.

But its prosperity and the proximity of the Yegua Knobbs meant trouble for McDade. McDade's citizens suffered from the widespread robbing, rustling, hijacking, and killing that pervaded the area from the days of Reconstruction through the Gay Nineties. As McDade was such a commercial center, much money was spent there. Saloons and gambling places stayed open 24 hours a day. Many tricksters and desperadoes drifted in to take advantage of the free-flowing money and dense woods. Vigilante committees were formed out of desperation; killings and counterkillings went on for years. All this killing came to a head in the Christmas season of 1883.

Remember that four men had been lynched just up the road at Blue several years earlier. Well, things had gotten more tangled and violent from there, until just about everyone had been drawn into the bloodshed.

Bose Herrington, law officer, was murdered in the process of investigating the murder of a Mr. Keuffel and his clerk. This killing was the final straw for the law-abiding citizens of McDade. They decided something had to be done to abate the lawlessness. Their chance came a few days later on Christmas Eve, 1883. That night Heywood Beatty—Yegua Knobbs "notchcutter," rustler, and ne'er-do-well—lay hidden away on the road from McDade to the Knobbs, waiting for a friend. Together, they were scheduled to murder another man.

Beatty waited all night. His friend never showed, so at daybreak Beatty began to ride toward McDade, wondering what had become of his pal. He got his answer about a mile from town when he looked up and saw Henry Pfeiffer, Wright McLemore, and Thad McLemore hanging from a blackjack tree. They had been drinking in the Old Rock Saloon that Christmas Eve when 40 or 50 masked men surrounded the saloon and called out their names, plus the name of another man who got away by hiding behind some boxes in the back. The three answerees were swiftly dispatched to their fates. The fourth left the county as fast as he could.

Heywood Beatty rode into town with blood in his eyes. He had an idea of who might have been in that lynching party and he was determined to make amends for his late friends. He met up with his brothers Jack and Az and friends Charlie Goodman, Burt Hasley, and Bob Stevens.

Heywood Beatty had recently been implicated in the murder of Bose Heffington. Az and Jack Beatty walked over to George Milton's store, where Jack walked inside and confronted Milton with the rumors linking brother Heywood to the Heffington slaying. In the meantime Az attacked Thomas Bishop, who was sitting on the Milton Store gallery (porch). The two rolled into the street before Bishop managed to jam his pistol into Az Beatty's gut and shoot him dead. At this, Jack came at Bishop through the front door with a knife, Milton following. From down the street Heywood Beatty fired upon Bishop. Bishop returned the fire, badly wounding Heywood. Milton began firing as he reached the front of his store, killing Jack Beatty. At this moment Bishop's cousin Willie Griffith came running up to assist; he was shot in the head for his efforts. Heywood's friends Stevens, Goodman, and Hasley were involved by now and over 100 shots were fired before the fight ended. As the smoke began to clear, two Beattys were dead, one was fleeing badly wounded for the safety of the Knobbs, Griffith lay dying, and Stevens, Goodman, and Hasley lay wounded. Milton and Bishop were unhurt. Public sentiment was on the side of Milton and Bishop and they were not punished for the shootings. Governor Ireland dispatched the Brenham Grays, in full uniform with ammunition and equipment, to McDade on Christmas Day to prevent further bloodshed. Many folks say the bodies of the five outlaws lay stretched out on the McDade station platform that Christmas Day, a gruesome sight for those on the Houston-to-Austin train.

Most of the bad boys left the country after this blowout, but the violence did not finally die out till the mid-1890s.

OLD ROCK SALOON
Old 20 S. at Waco • No set hours; open during Watermelon Festival and by appointment

The Old Rock Saloon, which was later covered with stucco, now serves as the local museum. It is the westernmost building in one-block-long downtown McDade. McDade's hotel stood directly across from the Old Rock Saloon by the tracks. The hanging tree stood across from the McDade General Store. McDade is considerably tamer now, over 100 years after the troubled times. Locals brag on the size of their watermelons; according to them, Luling's melons are marble-sized in comparison. The train station has been moved from across the tracks from its original site and is now the **McDade General Store,** which sells local melons at bargain prices during season. In the string of store buildings between the McDade store and the saloon, Dungan's Drug Store closed about 1993, and the wonderful old Underwood Pharmacy signage ("J. B. Underwood Prop., Dr. E. S. Mullen Prescriptions Patent Medicines Stationery

Candies") has been painted over. About the only good news is that the old **McDade Guaranty State Bank** building, a simple square one-story red brick affair, has been undergoing restoration. It is located on Bastrop St., behind the post office. The bank building dates to about 1910; the bank itself closed during the Depression.

ANNUAL EVENT

JULY • Watermelon Festival • Downtown McDade • Second Saturday in July • W
The festival includes a parade, dance, an auction of the area's largest watermelons, and free watermelon for all.

To leave McDade, take Old 20 S. east to Loop 223. Turn right on Loop 223, which takes you to US 290. Along the way is the McDade Cemetery, where some of the feud participants are buried. Cross US 290 here, and continue south toward Bastrop on what becomes FM 2336.

CAMP SWIFT
About 7.5 miles from McDade
FM 2336 skirts the eastern edge of Camp Swift, built at the beginning of World War II as an infantry training center. It now serves as a National Guard reservation. You may see dozens of camouflaged choppers hunkered down amid the mesquites and oaks.

When FM 2336 runs into SH 95, turn left on SH 95 to reach Bastrop. About 7 miles later, turn right on Loop 150, which takes you to downtown Bastrop.

BASTROP

Bastrop County • 4,389 • (512) • About 9 miles from Camp Swift
The town we now call Bastrop started as a Spanish fort, established in 1805 to protect commerce on the Old San Antonio Rd., which crossed the Colorado River here. It was to have been the nucleus of a colony established by Felipe Enrique Neff, Baron de Bastrop, but it was abandoned shortly after its settlement in 1823 because of Indian attacks. Stephen F. Austin next attempted to settle the area, starting in 1829. The Anglos first called their settlement Bastrop in honor of the man who did so much to facilitate Moses and

Stephen Austin's dealings with the Mexican government regarding their colonization projects.

Phillip Hendrick Nering Boegel left Holland in 1793, ostensibly because of the French invasion of Holland. Actually Boegel was a fugitive from the law, accused of embezzling funds while collector general of taxes for the province of Friesland. Arriving in Spanish Louisiana, he latinized the spelling of his name, adopted the title Baron de Bastrop, and started establishing colonies. With the Louisiana Purchase he headed first to Nacogdoches, then to Bexar (San Antonio), where he continued his colonizing business and ran a freight business, too. Eventually he became second alcalde (vice mayor) of the *ayuntamiento de Bexar* (Bexar County, then encompassing all of Central Texas). Bastrop served as Bexar's representative in the Congress of Coahuila y Texas from 1824 till his death in 1827. He died a pauper and friends bore his burial expenses.

Austin's colonists began pouring into Bastrop in 1829 and the town served as a jumping-off point for many western-bound Texans, including Noah Smithwick, William "Uncle Billy" Barton (of Austin's Barton Springs fame), and Reuben Hornsby.

The Mexican government changed the town of Bastrop's name to Mina in 1834 to honor the patriot Francisco Javier Mina. This name change did not set well at all with the Texans. Santa Anna burned the town in 1836; in 1837 the Republic of Texas changed the town's name back to Bastrop and made it seat of Bastrop County, one of Texas' original 23 counties. Originally Bastrop County encompassed all or parts of 15 present-day counties.

Bastrop prospered after the Texas War for Independence, boasting a newspaper, library, and several schools by the 1850s. The newspaper—the *Bastrop Advertiser*—is the oldest still-publishing weekly in Texas, dating back to March 1, 1853. Bastrop's economy was supported by cotton, naturally, but also by coal mining, brickmaking, and lumbering in the Lost Pines. Bastrop pine was used in the construction of Austin's first capitol building and in many other Austin and Central Texas buildings. Steamboats plied the Colorado River in those days, carrying cotton and lumber down to the coast and bringing back all manner of highly demanded consumer goods.

In those antebellum days one of Bastrop's most visible visitors was Andy Potter, who was later to become the "Fightin' Parson." Potter was a heathen back then, though, and was invited to visit the mayor's office almost every time he hit Bastrop, for he was forever being charged with violating some law, particularly the one forbidding fighting. Mayor/Judge O'Connor, being a hot-tempered Irishman himself, generally let Potter off with a moderate fine. This happened so many times that Potter was going broke and the town coffers were becoming full of his fines. Therefore, Potter devised a plan to soak the town of Bastrop and get his money back.

Potter's plan involved a concert, and the only townsperson let in on the secret was the printer. Potter had printed and distributed the following playbill: "Signor Blitz, from the London and New York theatres, informs the citizens of this place that he will give one of his celebrated entertainments at the courthouse, at early candle-lighting Saturday night—the extraordinary vocal powers of Signor Blitz have been the theme of universal commendation throughout the North and in Havana, as well as in Europe, where his concerts have been honored with the presence of royalty. Admittance fees: For grown persons, $1; for man and wife $1.50; for children and servants, half price; Front seats reserved for ladies."

The house was packed for Signor Blitz's show. Potter blacked his face and, arming himself with a bowie knife and pistol, walked out on stage and announced that Signor Blitz had failed to arrive, but that he would substitute for the great Signor. Potter then burst forth into a black minstrel song. A prominent doctor approached the stage with pistol in hand and demanded to know who the singer was. Potter pulled his own pistol and waved the doctor back to his seat. Then he told them who he was. The crowd roared, laughed, and stomped as if to tear down the house, then carried Potter up on their shoulders to a barroom and made him sing till one in the morning. Potter was the only man in Bastrop who could have pulled such a trick; anyone else would have been arrested or abused within an inch of his hoaxing life.

By the start of the Civil War, Bastrop's business district was one of the state's biggest, consisting of two blocks of two-story wooden buildings on the banks of the Colorado River, along the same stretch of Main that comprises downtown today. At the time, it was one of the most imposing business districts anywhere in the state. The great fire of 1862 burned almost all of downtown down. The 1852 Union Hall (813 Main) is the only antebellum business building standing today.

Bastrop County's plantation economy was in shambles by war's end, and the town struggled to rebuild. Hopes were buoyed by the prospect of the new Houston-to-Austin railroad coming through town, but those hopes were washed away by the great Colorado River flood of 1869. Fearful of future floods, the Houston and Texas Central railroad chose a more upland route through northern Bastrop County, which spawned the towns of Elgin, McDade, and Paige in 1871. Goods had to be hauled to and from the station at McDade, 15 miles to the north. This limited Bastrop's growth. But 1887 would bring great changes: The MKT railroad had come to town. Bastrop quickly blossomed as a commercial center, as a look at the old downtown district indicates. Most of the buildings were built after 1887. The same may be said of old Bastrop's residential district. A few homes date to the 1830s, but most houses (and certainly the fanciest ones) postdate the railroad's arrival.

Bastrop's most famous son (or daughter) was Joseph Draper Sayers, born in 1841 in Mississippi. In 1851, he came to Bastrop with his father. He attended the Bastrop Military Academy from 1852 to 1860. He served in the Confederate Army during the Civil War, after which he returned to Bastrop and began to study the law. He was elected to the Texas Legislature and was then elected lieutenant governor. Next, Sayers was elected to the U.S. Congress. He resigned from Congress to run for governor in 1898. He won, and was reelected in 1900. His administration is remembered chiefly for the disasters that occurred during that time, such as the burning of the state penitentiary in Huntsville, the great Brazos River flood of 1899, and the great Galveston hurricane and flood of 1900. In retirement, he served as a regent of the University of Texas and on various state regulatory boards. Sayers died in 1929.

Through the years, Bastrop has been able to retain much of its old-time flavor. Unfortunately, Texas' oldest pharmacy—Erhard and Son—started in 1847, burned down in 1980. But much of Bastrop remains almost as it was 100 years ago. Over 130 homes and buildings are listed in the National Register of Historic Places.

Long a slumbering little town, Bastrop awakened in the 1980s as Austin-related growth began to spill over into Bastrop County. In 1985, the City of Austin and Bastrop County went toe to toe in court as Austin tried to extend its territorial jurisdiction into Bastrop County, ostensibly to control the quality of development. Ever suspicious of the big city's motives and bitter over Austin's pollution of the Colorado River, Bastrop County met Austin at the county line, filing suit against Austin for routinely releasing poorly treated or untreated sewage effluent into the Colorado, which Bastrop was the first to receive. The river at Bastrop was so brown and uninviting that even the cows wouldn't go near it, much less anglers or swimmers. In response to the Bastrop suits, a moratorium was imposed on any more hookups for sewage service in parts of Austin that were overloading the sewage treatment system. The situation began to improve in 1986, when the City of Austin upgraded and expanded its sewage treatment facilities. The quality of Austin's release is now so high that the stretch of the Colorado from Austin to La Grange is rated exceptional in terms of being a quality habitat for aquatic life, which means that it is also now safe again for boating, fishing, and swimming.

But while they were able to keep Austin government out of Bastrop, they weren't able to keep Austinites from moving to Bastrop. The most famous of these was Dr. Gerald Wagner, who was the catalyst behind the renovation of much of Bastrop's venerable business district in the 1980s. Wagner discovered Bastrop in 1982, at a time when an ambitious development project of his in Austin was going sour. He had been looking for alternative sites, and two of Bastrop's stately homes happened to be for sale. Wagner snapped them up and didn't stop buying until he owned several dozen buildings downtown and elsewhere in Bastrop, many of them located in his Crocheron Compound, aka the Wilson Street project. A dozen old cabins, barns, and other buildings were moved in here from their original sites in Bastrop and nearby counties, placed in a plantation-like arrangement, and meticulously restored.

BASTROP COUNTY COURTHOUSE
Courthouse square, Pine at Water • 321-2579
Monday through Friday • W
J. W. Preston designed this three-story brick courthouse. It was built in 1883 and contains 1,383,512 bricks. During a subsequent post-World War I remodeling, the exterior brick walls were covered over with stucco, the clock tower was reduced in size, and some of the Victorian ornamentation was removed, which gave the courthouse its current Mission Revival appearance.

OLD BASTROP COUNTY JAIL
Courthouse square • 321-2419
Built in 1891–92 in the Second Empire style, this building looks more like an old city hall or bank than a jail. The jail moved out in 1974. A recent refurbishment converted much of the old jail space into county offices and a jury room, but a few of the original cells remain on display. The intricate lever-action cell-locking mechanism ("1874, Pauly Jail Bld'g & Lever; Lock Patd. Sept. 15 1874 St. Louis Mo.") still works, and the thick metal stripping used in lieu of bars reminds you of being imprisoned inside a woven basket. The cells are low-slung and cramped. They must have been hellishly uncomfortable on one of our sultry Central Texas summer days.

From the jail, walk on over to Main and the Bastrop County Historical Museum.

BASTROP COUNTY HISTORICAL MUSEUM
702 Main • 321-6177 • Open Monday through Friday afternoons • Admission • W

The museum is located in the **Cornelson-Fehr house,** built in 1850 and enlarged in 1854. It sits on the site of the old Spanish fort Puesta del Colorado. The museum has rare manuscripts and miscellaneous pioneer and Indian artifacts. Notable among the contents are some silver spoons supposedly fashioned from coins taken from Santa Anna after his capture at San Jacinto. Recently added exhibits examine the lives of African Texans in Bastrop County and the Tonkawa tribe in Bastrop County.

From the museum, stroll up Main to old downtown Bastrop.

ELZNER COTTAGE
802 Main • Private residence

A few feet north of the museum is the gingerbreaded P. O. Elzner cottage, built about 1876 with Bastrop pine. It stayed in the Elzner family until 1968. More on Elzner in a moment.

PROKOP BUILDING
913 Main • 321-5765 • W

Inside the brick 1887 Prokop building, potter Marie Blazek keeps Bastrop County's oldest industry alive, creating stoneware and porcelain mugs, steins, casseroles, tortilla warmers, shaving mugs, pitchers, and more.

BASTROP BBQ AND MEAT MARKET
919 Main • 321-7719 • Open Monday through Saturday, breakfast, lunch, and dinner • $ • W

The roofline is all that remains of the 1890 Louis Eilers building, which was destroyed by fire in 1980. Breakfast is served until 11 a.m. Later on, choose from brisket, steaks, chicken, and babyback pork ribs and the standard side dishes.

THE OLD BRIDGE

The 1923 Parker-style, arched steel truss highway bridge over the Colorado River at Chestnut Street was recently retired from four-wheel service and has been integrated into the city parks system as a walkway. This type of bridge was commonly built in the 1920s and 1930s to cross long expanses. It has been added to the National Register of Historic Places, along with another Parker-style bridge (on SH 16) that crosses the Llano River in Llano (See Mormon Trails).

LOCK DRUG STORE
1003 Main • 321-2422 • Open Monday through Saturday • W

A favored local hangout since 1905 when it was built by W. J. Miley, Lock Drug's soda fountain serves juices, coffee, ice cream cones, sodas, and banana splits from one of the few old-time soda fountains still in use in Central Texas. Sit at the bar and admire the marble fountain and stained glass cabinets. If there's no room at the fountain (which is often the case), sit at one of the round tables in one of the old curved-wire chairs. Notice the pressed tin ceiling and the old pharmacy drawers lining the walls. The **W. J. Miley house,** built in 1860, is located at 509 Spring. Before the drugstore was built, Dr. David Sayers, father of turn-of-the-century Texas governor Joseph D. Sayers, practiced medicine here.

ELZNER'S CORNER
Main at Spring

The corner of Spring and Main has been known as Elzner's Corner since the 1890s. For years P. O. Elzner was Bastrop County's best-known merchant; and at its zenith, his little empire stretched east to the Opera House and south half a block to the liquor store. "Elzner's got 'em" was a commonly heard phrase around these parts, as evidenced by this story told a few decades back in the *Bastrop Advertiser,* which is the oldest weekly newspaper in Texas:

If a stranger came to town and didn't know his way around, he soon found out where to go.

Where can I buy a pair of good boots?" the outlander would ask.

The local citizen would point to the corner of the block. "Elzner's got 'em."

"And I have to get a load of groceries."

"Elzner's got 'em."

"Yes, but I haven't got a wagon yet."

"Buy one at Elzner's."

Elzner sold nearly everything: dry goods, groceries, hardware, furniture, farm machinery, liquor. Bruno Elzner later took over the corner and you see signs from his era painted on the backs and sides of the Elzner Corner buildings.

BASTROP CHAMBER OF COMMERCE VISITOR INFORMATION CENTER

Main at Spring • Open daily during tourism season • W

Across Spring from Elzner's corner is the Visitor Information Center, housed in a whimsical little Victorian-styled kiosk. It stocks a variety of free, informative local pamphlets, including "Discover Bastrop's Historic Places: A Guide to Structures Included on the National Register of Historic Places."

When in Bastrop, tune your car radio to AM 530 for the latest information on local attractions and events.

BASTROP OPERA HOUSE

711 Spring • 321-6382

P. O. Elzner and D. S. Green built the Opera House in 1889. It is two story, stucco over brick. Elzner became sole owner in 1901. But he went bankrupt soon after, and the opera house got new owners. It was converted into a movie theater some time after 1910. For years the pride of Bastrop, the Opera House eventually lost its luster, and by 1978 was threatened with demolition. But a group of concerned citizens decided it should be restored instead and launched a campaign that year to restore the house to its former glory. Plays and musicals are staged throughout the year. Dinner/show packages are available

CALVARY EPISCOPAL CHURCH

603 Spring, one block west of Main

Calvary's cornerstone was laid in 1881. The bricks were locally made. Its simple Gothic exterior hasn't been altered since its construction, and the interior has been only slightly altered. The church was also the first building in Bastrop to get a Texas Historic Medallion. The interior is similarly dark, massive, and Gothic, with hand-carved pews, altar, vaulted ceiling, and exposed wood beams. The stained glass windows are especially beautiful.

The streets with the greatest number of vintage commercial buildings and/or homes are Main, Church, and Pecan Streets. Church runs parallel to Main one block west. Pecan runs parallel to Main two blocks east.

The **Jenkins House** (1710 Main) began as a log home in 1832 and was expanded over the years. The ornate porch was added at the height of the Victorian era. The **Greenleif Fisk House** (1005 Hill) is a frame house with a heavy skeleton of hand-hewn logs, a building method that goes back to medieval England. German immigrants settled here in number as well and built houses similar to those in the fatherland, but the last of these was razed in the 1970s. Most of Bastrop's old homes are in the Greek Revival style and the later, more exuberant Victorian styles. One of the best examples of Bastrop's Victorian-era houses is the flamboyantly gingerbreaded **Orgain House** (1508 Church), built about 1881. At 1703 Wilson Street is the home of Texas governor **Joe Sayers,** which was built in 1868. But the best known of Bastrop's stately old homes is the **Wilbarger House** on Main St., 4 blocks north of downtown.

WILBARGER HOUSE
1403 Main • Private residence
This stately Greek Revival house was built sometime between 1842 and 1847. In 1850 James Wilbarger bought it. James was the son of Josiah Wilbarger, whom you will encounter later on this trip. Josiah came to Texas late in 1827 from Missouri with his bride Margaret. After a year at Matagorda, Wilbarger moved to what would soon become La Grange, in Austin's Colony. A year or so later he moved farther west, into Bastrop County, where he established a plantation and sawmill on the Colorado River about ten miles upstream from Bastrop. Son James built upon his father's enterprises after blazing a trail which would later be called Wilbarger's Trace, which led from the plantation to Columbus and eventually Galveston. Along this "road" James drove ox wagon trains loaded with cotton, hides, and lumber. He returned with sugar, flour, yard goods, and supplies for the store he operated at Wilbarger's Bend in the Colorado River. The Wilbargers were lavish entertainers, and Governor Sam Houston and future Governor Joe Sayers were among their guests. The house remained in the Wilbarger family for four generations, until the late 1970s.

LCRA RIVERSIDE CONFERENCE CENTER
1500 Wilson
The Crocheron Compound was recently acquired by the Lower Colorado River Authority and serves as a conference center, complete with dormitories and a dining room. The only vintage building original to the site is the **Crocheron-McDowall home,** built in 1857. This two-story Greek Revival home is furnished with period antiques and is available for small meetings.

LODGING

PFEIFFER HOUSE
1802 Main, 78602 • 321-2100 • $$ • No Cr.
The Pfeiffer House is a Carpenter Gothic home built in 1901 by local builder J. R. Pfeiffer for his wife Freda. The house has been lovingly restored and furnished with period antiques. The house contains three guest rooms; there is a shared bath. No children or pets. It's best to call ahead or write for reservations, especially during the spring, summer, and early fall months. Full breakfast.

PARKS

LAKE BASTROP
Take TX 95 north about 3 miles to FM 1441, then east to North Shore Recreation Area • 321-3307 • Open daily • Admission
W variable
This 906-acre lake offers recreational facilities in two parks for boating, fishing, swimming, waterskiing, picnicking, and camping. A 12-lb. Florida largemouth bass and 56-lb. catfish have been pulled from the lake; species include black striped bass, Florida largemouth, crappie, channel, yellow, blue, and flathead catfish, and perch. Best bass fishing is December through March. An observation-picnic area adjacent to the power plant is open, free of charge, from 8 a.m. to sundown daily from March to mid-September. To reach it, take the Plant Access Rd., off TX 21.

BASTROP STATE PARK
One mile east of town on SH 21; take Chestnut St. (Loop 150) from downtown • 321-2101 • Open daily • Admission
W variable
This park is one of the most beautiful in Texas. Many visitors return to the park year after year.

The loblolly pine woodland is isolated from the main body of East Texas pines by approximately 100 miles of rolling post oak woodlands. This pine-oak woodland covers approximately 70 square miles and is part of the most westerly stand of loblolly pines in the state. The most commonly accepted hypothesis for their existence is that they were once part of a vast prehistoric pine forest that covered most of Texas. This forest was the result of extensive rainfall caused by glacier activity that extended as far south as Kansas. As the glaciers subsided and the land dried out, most of the pines west of the East

Texas pine belt died out. But this 70-square-mile stand of loblolly pines remained due to generous rainfall, acidic soil, and good drainage. White-tail deer, rabbits, squirrels, opossums, and armadillos scurry through the woods. A checklist of the bird life in Bastrop and Buescher State Parks is available at the park headquarters.

Bastrop State Park comprises 3,503 acres (land acreage, 3,493; water acreage, 10). The park was acquired by deeds from the city of Bastrop and private owners from 1933 to 1935; the park opened in 1937. Additional acreage was acquired in 1979. The Civilian Conservation Corps built the original park facilities. Park activities include backpacking, camping, picnicking, fishing, swimming, golf, bicycling, wildlife viewing, hiking, and special tours. There is an interpretive tour in summer months. The Houston toad is an endangered species resident in the park; call for information on guided toad tours.

Facilities include restrooms with showers; picnic sites; backpack areas along an 8.5-mile hiking trail; 3.5 additional miles of hiking trails; campsites with water; campsites with water and electricity; cabins; lodges; group barracks; a dining hall (accommodates 90); a swimming pool; an outdoor sports area; a trail area; a day-use dining hall (refectory) with a kitchen area, tables and chairs for 90, a patio area, air-conditioning, and two fireplaces; and a sponsored youth group area. Special rates are available. A golf course is operated by the Lost Pines Golf Association. The course has Bermuda grass greens, is playable year-round, and has electric and pull carts available for rent. For detailed information, call 512-321-2327.

Rustic cabins, which accommodate two to six people, overlook a small lake. Each cabin has air-conditioning, a microwave, and kitchen facilities (linens and towels are furnished, but no utensils, dishes, or silverware). Any cabin or lodge reservation for either Friday or Saturday must include both nights; hotel/motel tax is added to cabin rates. The park has a large 60-ft. by 100-ft. freshwater swimming pool (open from the fourth Friday in May through Labor Day; equipped with two children's wading pools). Lifeguards are provided during pool hours. There is a Texas State Park Store.

Write to P.O. Box 518, Bastrop 78602-0518. *Elevation:* 374 to 600 ft. *Weather:* Average rainfall: 36.5 in., January minimum temperature 38 degrees, July maximum temperature 96 degrees.

A marker at the entrance of Bastrop State Park just off US 95 commemorates early settler James Goacher, who first settled in southern Lee County in 1828. He was commissioned by Stephen F. Austin to blaze a road linking Austin's lower colony at San Felipe to the upper colony at Bastrop. In return, Goacher received a league and a labor of land. Goacher chose as his smaller plot of land a worthless-for-farming section on Rabbs Creek. Why did he choose such an apparently worthless piece of land? Legend has it that Goacher had stumbled onto a lead mine on the tract in the process of laying out the "trace" (road) that bore his name. Frank Dobie wrote of the lost lead mine of James Goacher in *Coronado's Children:*

> When settlers came to Goacher's home to buy lead, so legend remembers, he would, if he did not have a sufficient supply on hand, insist on their staying at the house while he went for some. He always reappeared from a different quarter from that in which he had gone out. Sometimes he would be gone for hours, again, only for a short time. He guarded the secret of his lead ore as jealously as though it had been a trove of precious gems. Only three souls shared with him knowledge of the whereabouts of the mine; they were his two sons and a son-in-law named Crawford. One day about two years after they had settled on Rabbs Creek (1837) all four of the men met death while rushing to the house, unarmed, to repel a horde of savages. These savages, so it is claimed, knew the whereabouts of the lead, knew the fatal worth of lead bullets, and in annihilating the Goacher men and carrying off the women and children they did not kill, were but following a plan to render the colonists less formidable.
>
> Perhaps, after the massacre, they covered up all traces of the lead mine; so remote was the Goacher homestead that other settlers knew nothing of the havoc until several days later.

The mine has never been found, although several locals over the years have found large chunks of lead in and around the Rabbs Creek/Goacher area.

Head west toward Austin from Bastrop on SH 71. Two miles later, turn right onto FM 969, once the road of westward-pushing Austin colony pioneers.

Bastrop was just this side of a pipe dream in Stephen F. Austin's mind when land-hungry colonists began inching their way west toward what would become the capital city. By 1828 Lehman Barker, his son-in-law Josiah Wilbarger, and their families had built a little stockade 10 or so miles up the Colorado River from Bastrop on the bend of the river that still bears Wilbarger's name. These little family fortresses were a necessity, for Indian raids continued through the 1850s in these parts. The first settlement west of Bastrop on what we now call FM 969 was Utley.

UTLEY

Bastrop County • 30 • About 9.5 miles from Bastrop
Utley started as a trading post run by James Wilbarger, son of Josiah. Utley today is actually up the road a bit from the time-honored crossing of the Colorado where the hamlet first started. A smattering of houses is located at the original townsite, at the top of the hill. The rich bottomland this road traverses was highly prized by early settlers. Take a drive out here during the spring and you will see why. The soil that produced bountiful crops of cotton and corn now produces bowers of flowers, starting with bluebonnets, paintbrushes, and primroses. Prickly poppies, phlox, verbena, gay feathers, winecups, ragworts, and lazy daisies pop out to reinforce the early bloomers, and about the time the first wave begins to fade along come the gaillardias, horsemint, day flowers, wild petunias, trompillos, and the rest of the hot weather flowers. Such a thorough mix of species comes only with age, and the roadside from Bastrop to Austin is a riot of color from early March through June.

Wells Prairie was the next settlement west on FM 969, generally in the area of Cedar Valley and the FM 1704 turnoff, about two miles from Utley. Martin Wells settled here in 1831. The next road to your right is the Old Upper Elgin River Rd. You continue west on FM 969.

Close by the Upper Elgin River Rd. turnoff on your left are the **Robert Coleman historical markers.** Colonel Robert M. Coleman and his family settled here in the early 1830s. Coleman was clearly a man going places in early Texas. He was the first *presidente* of the municipality of Mina in 1834. In the summer of 1835 Coleman commanded one of four volunteer companies organized to fight the Tawakoni Indians. Later that year he commanded the Mina Volunteers, who played a supporting role in the Texas siege of Bexar (San Antonio). Coleman was a signer of the Declaration of Independence at Washington-on-the Brazos and served as aide-de-camp to General Sam Houston at San Jacinto. Following his army discharge, Coleman commanded a company of Texas Rangers at the fort bearing his name, located in what is now east Austin. But then Coleman's luck began to run out, and not without irony. He was not too popular, it seems, with many of the men under his command. He was relieved from his Ranger command after the death of one of his men; he had encountered the subordinate in a deadly drunk state and had the man bound to a tree, supposedly till he sobered up. The man did not sober up— he was strangled to death by his bindings. Coleman had to go down to Velasco to await the decision on his case. While at Velasco he died, drowned while bathing in the Brazos River in the year 1837. This bad luck dogged his family. His wife and oldest son were killed by marauding Indians here in 1839. A younger son was taken prisoner.

Just inside the Travis County line, about two miles from the Coleman Markers, is the entry to pecan-shaded Webberville County Park on the Colorado River. It has a boat ramp, a fishing dock, softball fields, basketball courts, a hike and bike trail, and picnic facilities.

At the Blake-Manor Rd. turnoff, you enter Webberville, one of Travis County's earliest and wildest settlements. Stay on FM 969 through town.

WEBBERVILLE

Travis County • 50 • About 8 miles from Utley
"Dr." John F. Webber, Vermont native and War of 1812 veteran, settled and built a stockade here before the Texas Revolution. Webber was—to say the least—an interesting character. His doctor title dated back to the 1820s, when on a tobacco-smuggling expedition to Mexico he acted as a doctor for the duration of his stay, in order to divert suspicion from his real activities. It took time to disperse the tobacco, since it had to be sold in small lots so as not to arouse suspicion. American doctors were held in high esteem by the Mexicans, so Webber's services were in great demand. He achieved great fame as a healer during his lengthy stay, despite his inexperience. Webber managed to avoid service in the Revolutionary Army, and what is more he took a slave, Silvia Hector, for his wife. Even so, most of his early neighbors took a "Live and let live" attitude; everyone was busy enough as it was already, fighting off the Indians and trying to scratch out a living. What your neighbor did was pretty much his own business as long as it did not directly impinge on your own existence. This easygoing attitude no doubt contributed to the growth of Webber's Prairie. By 1840 James Manor and Frank Nash had opened up a store and saloon here and Webberville became known as Hell's Half-Acre, or Half-Acre for short. Hard liquor flowed at several saloons and there was little interference from the organized constab-

ulary. A man might just ride through the saloon's front door and out the back if he had a mind to, and if he was man enough to deal with any objections to such a move. Anyone looking for a lively time came to Webberville. Lyman Wight and his bank of Mormons lived here for a while before moving to Austin, spurred on by threats of tar and feathers, and rails and ropes.

Many of the newcomers after 1840 were from the Deep South and did not approve of Webber's unorthodox marriage. He and "Puss," as Silvia was familiarly known, had eight children. Aunt Puss was known as the settlement's most compassionate woman, taking in anyone who came to her door no matter how much of a social pariah the unfortunate wretch might be. But such merciful ways were lost on these new, prejudiced neighbors. The Webbers were increasingly ostracized and Dr. Webber lived in fear of "black-birders," those men who made a living by kidnapping free people of color and selling them into slavery. Wilting in the face of his neighbors' threats, Webber finally sold out his holdings and moved the family down to South Texas, near Donna, in 1851. A Colonel John Banks bought the Webber tract, established a plantation, and laid out a townsite. After the Civil War Webberville was elated at the prospect of a Houston-to-Austin railroad. But elation turned to consternation when the original route through Webberville was moved upland to the present Giddings-Elgin-Manor route. The Webberville route was too easily flooded by the Colorado River. Bypassed, Webberville started its gradual slide downward.

The county park on the river makes a pleasant stop. To get there, turn left (south) off FM 969, proceed several hundred feet, and follow the sign. When you leave the park, backtrack to FM 969 and head for Deatsville.

DEATSVILLE

Travis County • About 2 miles from Webberville
Farther toward Austin on FM 969 is a collection of houses known as Deatsville, which was the far western edge of old Webberville. This was the home of Peter Carr, Travis County's first mailman. Carr made the once-a-week trip from Austin to La Grande on horseback, carrying his fiddle. Carr would stop often along the way to entertain his friends with a tune or two. In those days the receiver rather than the sender paid the letter's postage, and Carr's habit of letting his friends root through the bag and take their letters without charge

greatly annoyed postal authorities. He was also one of Texas earliest cattlemen, raising cattle at Deatsville and branding them with his registered brand KER.

Many wild cattle were found in the thickets here along the Colorado River. Noah Smithwick, who lived for a time at Webberville, wrote of them as "handsome brutes, coal black and clean limbed, their white horns glistening as if polished."

Continue on FM 969.

MUD CITY

Travis County • About 6 miles from Webberville
You see no highway sign for Mud City anymore. Mud City was once a proud little community with a sense of humor. A few houses and an abandoned cotton gin and store still stand today. Mud City— or just plain Mud for short—grew up in the 1880s as a spillover from Hornsby's Bend. Old-timers say a constantly overflowing creek nearby was responsible for the name. It made a perpetual bog out of this stretch of the Austin-to-Bastrop road and travelers were constantly cursing the mud. Locals liked the name others used in anger, so Mud it was. Mud City even had a baseball team for a while, named the Daubers.

Continue on FM 969.

HORNSBY'S BEND

Travis County • 20 • About 8 miles from Webberville
Hornsby's Bend is Travis County's oldest settlement. Travis County's original surveyor, Reuben Hornsby, settled here with his family in 1832, when this was the very edge of the frontier. Life was not easy here, for the Indians attacked often and civilization—at Bastrop—was a couple of days away. When the menfolk were away, Reuben's wife Sally had to fend off the Indians by herself. She accomplished this one time by dressing the women in men's clothes and parading them around with broomsticks on their shoulders. The ruse worked; the Indians left. Other times they were not as lucky. Violent deaths were a sad but unavoidable part of life. John Williams and Howell Haggett were killed while hoeing corn in Hornsby's field in 1836. Daniel Hornsby and William Atkinson were killed by Indians while fishing in the Colorado in 1845.

The best Indian story of all involves Josiah Wilbarger, who, you will remember, settled back toward Bastrop on the Colorado. In 1830 he, Reuben Hornsby, John Webber, Martin Wells, William Barton, and Jesse Tannehill had surveyed the north bank of the Colorado between Bastrop and Austin and then selected their head-right claims. In 1833 Wilbarger came up to Hornsby's Bend, where he was joined by William Strother, James Standifer, Thomas Christian, and John Haynie. Together they rode off for a look at the land northwest of Hornsby's grant, in the Pecan Springs area of Austin. The party had found Indian tracks but failed to find the Indians themselves, so they gave up the search and stopped for a bit of lunch before heading back for Hornsby's. Wilbarger, Christian, and Strother unsaddled and hobbled their horses, but Standifer and Haynie left their mounts saddled and staked. As they ate, a band of Indians attacked. Haynie and Standifer leapt for their horses and escaped, leaving the others to fend off the Indians as best they could. Strother and Christian were killed. Wilbarger took arrows in both legs and a rifle ball in his scalp. But Wilbarger was not dead—he was in fact conscious and paralyzed by the rifle ball. He could feel no pain as the Indians ripped off his scalp, he could only hear the sound of it, a sound like thunder. He had been stripped naked except for one sock. Wilbarger was soon able to move again and he crawled a few hundred yards toward Hornsby's before he was forced to stop, exhausted. He lay down under an oak tree and fell asleep at nightfall.

During his fitful sleep his sister Margaret—who had died the day before in Missouri, although Wilbarger had no way of knowing this—came to him in a dream and told him not to despair, help would come. She then disappeared in Hornsby's direction. In the meantime Standifer and Haynie had reached the Hornsby cabin and reported the deaths of Strother, Christian, and Wilbarger.

That night Sally Hornsby dreamed twice that Wilbarger was not dead but badly wounded and lying under a tree. The next morning she insisted that the men go rescue Wilbarger. They were reticent to sally forth, but Hornsby prevailed. A search party went out and advance scout Joe Rogers sighted Wilbarger first, sitting under the oak tree. He was so sunburned that Rogers first mistook him for an Indian and started to shoot, but the wounded man managed to shout out, "Don't shoot. It's Wilbarger." He was carried back to Hornsby's Bend, where he was nursed back to health. Wilbarger lived 13 years after the scalping, but his scalp wound never healed completely and he wore a cap of black silk over the wound for the rest of his life. His death was reportedly hastened as the result of bumping his wounded

head on the doorway of his home. Wilbarger died at his home on the
Colorado and is now buried in the state cemetery in Austin.

Tucked away in a grove of trees to your right as FM 969 approach-
es the FM 973 intersection are a couple of homes dating back to the
one-time prosperous cotton economy of Hornsby's Bend. You won't
find a cotton boll for miles around today. Cattle, milo, and some
truck farming sustain the hangers-on these days.
At the intersection of FM 969 and FM 973 is a historical marker
that tells the Hornsby saga. Most of the Hornsby family, including
the Indians' victims and baseball great Rogers Hornsby, are at rest
in the nearby Hornsby Cemetery. Farther on, Wilbarger's discoverer
Joe Rogers is buried on the hill bearing his name. Rogers was him-
self the victim of an Indian ambush in 1837.

Two miles east of the Wilbarger marker, you pass by the Travis
State School (on your left) and descend down Rogers Hill. Austin
lies spread out before you and Joe Rogers lies forever at rest in a
thicket a few hundred feet north of FM 969, across from the school.
Old old-timers will remember Rogers Hill by another name—Hungry Hill. An anonymous *Austin Statesman* reporter went searching
for Hungry Hill in 1935 and reported:

> A negro settlement, Hungry Hill was so named because its soil
> was thin and unproductive. The stranger pulling up the hill in sec-
> ond gear and stopping to inquire directions gets an almost inevitable
> reply, "Yas suh, this is Hungry Hill and I'se the hungry man." All of
> which leads to the passage of a quarter from one palm to the other
> and silent gratitude that no hungrier hill lies beyond.

After 6 miles you are back in Austin. It is unlikely that any of these
pioneers—even in their wildest dreams—would have foreseen the
Austin of today.

CENTRAL TEXAS STEW

Approximately 165 miles

Of all the European peoples who migrated to Texas between 1836 and World War I, the Germans came in the greatest numbers. Germans began the European exodus to Texas in the 1830s and 1840s. Thousands of their Slavic neighbors from Central Europe—Bohemians, Moravians, Silesians, and Wends—soon followed. All were seeking better lives, religious freedom, and liberation from the political domination of their German or Austrian rulers. The Civil War interrupted the flood of immigrants only temporarily. The flow began again in 1866 and continued until World War I. Germans of every religious faith, social class, and job category settled in Texas, but the Slavs were almost exclusively farmers and mostly Catholic. Czechs generally settled on farms in the country, rather than in towns, where many Germans settled.

Most Czech (Bohemian and Moravian) immigrants to Texas were *chalupnici,* or "cottagers" (families owning fewer than 20 acres). To people who lived 10 or more to a one- or two-room cottage, whose farm was so small and narrow that you could clear it in a flying leap, the lure of 100 acres in Texas proved irresistible, and some 40,000 Czechs came to Texas between about 1851 and 1939. They methodically sought out the best farmland they could find, so that by 1900, a "Czech Belt" stretched across Texas' fertile Blackland Prairies, from the town of West southward 200 miles to Victoria.

This trip takes you through an area of Central Texas in which many Germans and Czechs settled. Much of the territory was originally settled by Anglo, Southern immigrants who came here as members of Austin's colonies. A decidedly German flavor still pervades towns and villages like Round Top and Winedale. The Czech presence is strong in Fayetteville and Praha. They comingle in La Grange and Schulenburg. Several area Lutheran churches still hold German-language services on a regular basis, and polka music is a staple sound on a number of area radio stations. One of the best-known polka music shows is hosted by Lee Roy Matocha, the "Fayetteville Flash" and his orchestra. Sometimes Lee Roy speaks English, but most of the time it's Czech, which is still fun to listen to, even if the only Czech you speak is pilsner. The Lee Roy Matocha Orchestra plays several times a month around greater Central Texas, at church and Czech heritage festivals, weddings, and SPJST halls, often alternating with other popular Tex-Czech groups such as the Red Ravens, Djuka Brothers, Kovanda's Czech Band, and the Columbus Travelers. Faith, family, the farm, and fraternal orders such as the SPJST have helped preserve the Czech identity. SPJST stands for *Slovanska podporujici jednota statu texasu,* which translates as The Slavonic Benevolent Order of the State of Texas. It was founded at La Grange in July 1897 by a group of Czech immigrants who felt that the similar national order, CSPS (Czech-Slovakian Fraternal Union), to which they belonged did not meet their needs. The nonpolitical, nonreligious SPJST provided Czechs with social affairs at which they could meet fellow Czechs, and also be assured of help in case of sickness or need of a decent burial. More than 140 lodges are now scattered across the state, and the SPJST maintains a Czech heritage museum at its Temple headquarters. Another organization, the Czech Catholic Union of Texas (*Katolicka jednota texaska*), or KJT, was founded in Hostyn (south of La Grange) in 1889 and claims about 100 lodges. The Texas Germans, for their part, have the Sons of Hermann lodges.

For my money, the best sausage and smoked meats in Texas come from this region, and you'll find other locally grown or homemade products for sale at various businesses or from the farmer or butcher himself: honey, molasses, bread, kolaches, noodles, sauerkraut, flour, pickles, eggs, butter. The title of this chapter reflects the region's ethnic diversity and the tasty stews served at area restaurants and festivals.

Regrettably, this distinctive flavor fades a little more every year as the old-timers pass on and new folks move in. We begin in Smithville.

CENTRAL TEXAS STEW

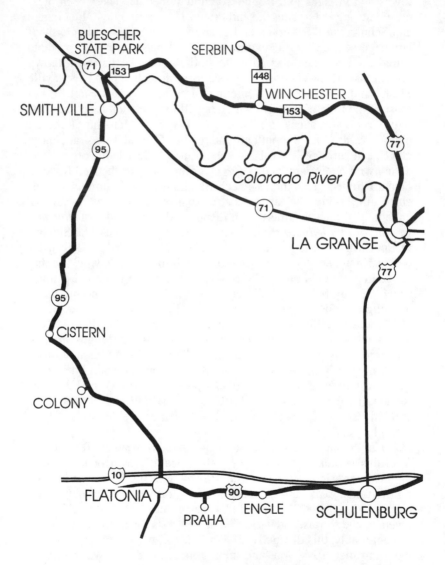

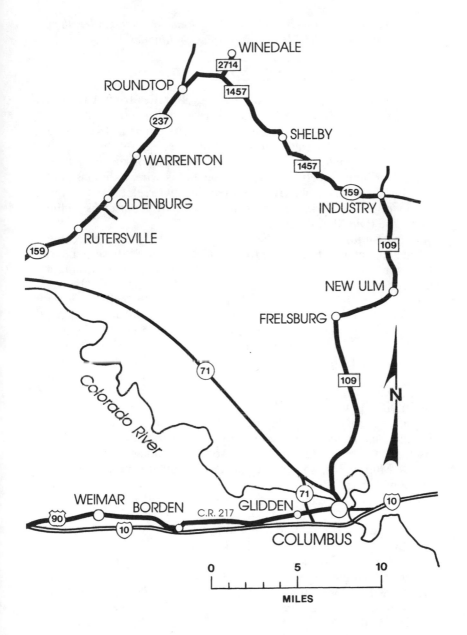

To reach Smithville from Austin, take SH 71 east about 40 miles, then take Loop 230 (old SH 71) into downtown Smithville.

SMITHVILLE

Bastrop County • 3,444 • (512) • About 40 miles from Austin

Records show that in early years Mexican miners probed the area searching for silver. A Dr. Thomas Gazely settled here in 1827, lured by silvery tales of wealth. He placed his headright—which was a patent to a league of land—on an expanse located on the creek now named for him, **Gazely Creek.** He brought his wife, four sons, and the area's first slaves shortly thereafter. Gazely Creek flows through southwestern Smithville, entering the Colorado River just west of the Loop 230 (Old SH 71) bridge.

Frank Smith, for whom the town was eventually named, came to this area at about the same time as Gazely. The little settlement that would eventually grow to become Smithville began around a trading post and ferry across the Colorado, located in the far northeastern tip of present-day Smithville. These facilities were operated by one Frederick W. Grasmeyer. Steamboats plied the Colorado from the coast up to Bastrop from 1845 until the end of the Civil War, and the little village at Grasmeyer's Crossing grew steadily. This village had several dry goods stores, a Masonic Lodge, and a post office by the centennial year of 1876. That same year, Murray Burleson bought most of the land on which Smithville now stands.

But Smithville didn't really take off until the arrival of the Taylor, Bastrop, and Houston railroad in 1887. At this time the town picked itself up and relocated a mile or so southwest along the newly laid tracks. Murray Burleson donated the land for the first railroad station and a movement was afoot to rename the town Burlesonville in his honor. Legend has it that the name dispute was settled by a coin toss; Burleson lost. The still-publishing *Smithville Times* was born in 1893. Town incorporation came in 1895, as did the Bank of Smithville, now the First State Bank. Smithville became a division point on the Missouri-Kansas-Texas (MKT) railway and as such was the home of a great regional railroad shop complex for many years. But the MKT closed its shops in 1957, and Smithville struggled for years to recover. The First Bank of Smithville, however, has managed to hold on through the fall of King Cotton, the Great Depression, and the railroad's pullout.

Main Street, Smithville's traditional business artery, begins at the railroad tracks, goes north across Loop 230, and peters out a block later. Main Street is a quaint three-block stretch of late Victorian commercial buildings. Over 30 of these were built between the years 1895 and 1910, Smithville's golden era. A number of them still look pretty much like they did when first built. Many have been recently restored or are undergoing restoration. The city has purchased and installed old-fashioned street lamps. While none of the buildings are individually impressive, together they make for one of the most complete late Victorian commercial districts in this region of Texas. The Smithville Commercial Historic District was established in 1982 to aid in its preservation.

The **Old Masonic Lodge** (301 Main at Loop 230), a three-story red brick building built in 1902, towers over the rest of Smithville. Its south side bears fading painted advertising that dates back to well before World War II. Across the street, the old **Rabb-McCollum Building** (302 Main) is Smithville's most ornate commercial building. Built in 1907, this red brick building has buff brick trim and a simple but imposingly large cast-metal pediment.

CHARLIE'S BAR B QUE
110 Main • 237-4242 • Open Monday through Saturday
$ • No Cr.
This simple one-story brick place was built in 1905 as a meat market. Charlie's just sells barbecue now. One of the brick pits out back dates back to 1905. The all-beef and pork/beef sausage are made in the back room. Charlie's also smokes chicken, brisket, pork ribs, and mutton in an oak-fired brick pit. There is also made-on-premises cole slaw, potato salad, and beans. Charlie says Willie Nelson has eaten here; if it's good enough for Willie, it's good enough for us.

SMITHVILLE RAILROAD MUSEUM AND PARK/
SMITHVILLE CHAMBER OF COMMERCE
First Street, at the foot of Main Street, by the railroad tracks
237-2313 • Park open daily
Smithville would be nowhere without the railroad, so the town pays homage to the iron horse with this little, though growing, museum. Kids love going through the old cabooses and motor car outside. The museum inside is an authentic reproduction of an 1895-era station built with recycled vintage materials. It is full of early railroad artifacts, photos, logs, schedules, and such. The Chamber of Commerce building is also located inside the museum building. Just south

of the museum and park, where the MKT roundhouse was located, the Lower Colorado River Authority maintains its Smithville Railcar Facility, where the LCRA's fleet of 1,000-plus railcars are maintained. The cars annually haul millions of tons of coal from Wyoming to LCRA's Fayette Power Plant near La Grange.

Smithville has around 30 Victorian-era homes scattered about the residential district between Loop 230, the Colorado River, and Garwood Street to the east. To start your exploration, drive north on Main from downtown to its dead end at the river and then branch out from there. In 1995, the Smithville Residential Historic District was created. It includes the area of town from 1st St. to the Colorado River, an area of about 50 city blocks.

SMITHVILLE HERITAGE SOCIETY HOUSE AND MUSEUM
602 Main • 237-2313 (Chamber of Commerce) • Open Tuesdays, during citywide events, and by appointment • Donations

This two-story frame house was built in 1908 by an MKT employee. Another metal building out back holds additional items of local history.

Other houses of note are the **Burleson house,** (207 E. 8th), a 2½-story Queen Anne style house built about 1899 for Murray Burleson; and the 1915 Classical Revival **Chapman-Trousdale house** (201 E. 8th).

RIVERBEND PARK
Off SH 71 • 237-3282

Located on the Colorado River, the park offers boating, a fishing pier, camping (including full RV hookups), and picnicking. There are barbecue pits. Lots of spreading oak trees provide welcome shade in the summer. Many local celebrations are held here.

ZIMMERHANZEL'S BAR B QUE
Loop 230, just east of the Colorado River bridge, on the west edge of town • 237-4244 • Open Monday through Saturday 10–5 • $ • No Cr. • W

Zimmerhanzel's bright red corrugated metal building belies the barbecue inside. We've had some of the best ever brisket here, very lean and flavorful. We can't guarantee you such perfection with each brisket—it's not that good a cut of beef—but they do trim it leaner than most places at Zimmerhanzel's. They make their own lean all-beef sausage. Chicken and lean meaty pork ribs all cooked over oak make up the meat menu. Homemade slaw, macaroni salad, potato salad (with boiled egg), and pinto beans are worthy accompaniments. No beer.

The best place in Smithville to stop for a cold one and for some local color is Huebel's, located at the corner of W. 2nd and Cleveland. Take Cleveland off Loop 230 and go one block south.

HUEBEL'S
W. 2nd and Cleveland • 237-2221 • Open daily • W
Huebel's is housed in a Depression-era gas station and garage. The main repair room has been cleaned out in favor of an assortment of tables and chairs for patrons. The northeast side has a little bar, stools, and an enclosed grocery area.

A jukebox with a good mix of country-and-western and polka blasts out from over by the door. The place really starts to hop in the afternoon when the domino games get going. The patrons are a good combination of old and young.

ANNUAL EVENT

APRIL • Smithville Jamboree • Crockett Riverbend Park 237-2313 • First weekend after Easter • Admission • W
A community festival complete with a carnival, a youth parade, a livestock show, a pet show, horseshoe pitching, volleyball, softball, fireworks—you name it and it's probably here.

From Huebel's in Smithville, take Loop 230 back toward Austin a few hundred yards until you come to the intersection with SH 95. Travel south a little over 14 miles on SH 95 to Cistern.

CISTERN

Fayette County • 75 • About 14 miles from Smithville
Cistern was settled in the early 1850s. The community was known by a variety of names during the early years, but when locals applied for a post office they had to come up with one permanent name. At first they submitted Whiteside Prairie, after an early pioneer family.

The post office nixed this name, as well as the next two proposed, Cockrill's Hill and Milton. In desperation, the locals submitted a name descriptive of the community's most distinctive feature: the cisterns dotting each yard. Local well water contained so much iron and sulfur that it was undrinkable and each family had to build a cistern to catch their drinking water as it fell from the heavens. The post office authorities liked the name.

Cistern made history in 1886 when a hailstorm ruined all the area crops, demolished every roof in the community, and killed every animal caught outside during the storm.

"Downtown" Cistern today consists of the V&V Sausage Company and the Cistern Country Store, located across from each other on SH 95.

From the V&V Sausage Company and downtown Cistern, follow SH 95 and the signs a mile south to Gladys' Cookie Shop, home of what is arguably the best fruitcake you'll ever taste.

GLADYS' COOKIE SHOP
Just outside Cistern • 865-3682 • Monday through Saturday No set hours • W

Gladys Farek mixes her fruitcake batter in a cement mixer, and she can make up to 1,000 pounds of fruitcake a day. Each cake is 50 percent pecans, with candied fruit and just enough flour, egg, and molasses batter to hold all this together—no citron, raisins, or spices added. Gladys also bakes bread, poppyseed kolache rings, iced raisin bread, cinnamon nut rolls, and giant five-inch cookies—oatmeal, chocolate chip, sugar, and molasses. Don't leave without some of her homemade noodles—a tad expensive but worth the tariff.

The Fareks have no set hours; if you're around at a decent daylight hour Monday through Saturday, just pull in off the highway. If anyone's home, they'll soon be out to show you around.

ANNUAL EVENT

JULY • Cistern Catholic Church Picnic • First Sunday in July Adults $4, under 12, $2

Food is the big reason to show up in Cistern this particular Sunday noon. Sausage, stew, and all the homemade trimmings round out the menu.

COLONY

Fayette County • About 5 miles from Cistern
The Colony community was established in the 1870s by former residents of Mississippi. Three churches, several stores, and a post office once served the community. John and Margaret Young donated land in 1876 for a Methodist church and cemetery, which became the community's primary burying ground. Earliest known grave is of Methodist minister Samul J. Brown, who died in 1879. The cemetery, which is located just west of SH 95 on Colony Cemetery Rd., is about all that is left of the Colony.

From Colony, continue south on SH 95 into Flatonia.

FLATONIA

Fayette County • 1,373 • (512) • About 12 miles from Cistern
The present town of Flatonia has had two predecessors: Oso, which you pass through coming into Flatonia from the north, and Old Flatonia, aka Flatonia Junction, located a mile or so south.

Oso was a bustling little farm settlement with three stores, a mill, a gin, a tannery, and a blacksmith shop before the Galveston, Harrisburg and San Antonio (GH&SA) railroad was built to Flatonia. With the railroad's arrival, Oso moved to the new townsite lock, stock, and barrel.

Ditto for Old Flatonia. In the early days of Anglo Texas, Flatonia junction was a stopping point on the old wagon road between La Grange and Gonzales. The village was named for F. W. Flato, who came to Texas in the 1840s as a ship captain. In that capacity, he carried over hundreds of Texas-bound Adelsverein immigrants. Eventually he settled down at this wagon road junction and opened up a store.

In the early 1870s Flato caught wind of plans by the GH&SA railroad company (later the Southern Pacific railroad) to extend their line from Alleyton to San Antonio. In 1873 Flato, John Lattimore, and John Kline bought the present Flatonia townsite from the Faires brothers and offered GH&SA president T. W. Pierce one-half interest in the new town if Pierce would route his new line through the town. It was an offer Pierce couldn't refuse. When the railroad came in 1874, the whole population of Old Flatonia loaded their houses and goods on wagons and moved en masse to the new townsite.

Incorporated in 1875, Flatonia immediately boomed. For the first several years after the railroad's arrival, Flatonia served as its western terminus. During that time Flatonia was a crossroads market for cattle and produce. The town was full of cowboys and gandy dancers whose idea of a good time was drinking, gambling, whoring, and shooting up the town whenever the urge struck them, much to the consternation of the law-abiding Flatonians.

Things eventually calmed down as the railroad progressed westward to San Antonio. But Flatonia continued to prosper. Flatonians were overjoyed in 1880 when the San Antonio and Aransas Pass railway announced its plans to build a new line from Waco to the Gulf Coast, smack-dab through Flatonia. The town envisioned itself as the future rail center of Texas.

In 1880, Flatonia was a booming town with 2,000 inhabitants. Two Vienna-trained pharmacists—Pellar and Webb—opened up a drugstore. Fur-buying was a brisk industry, and tens of thousands of pounds of cotton were ginned and shipped out. Many substantial brick and limestone buildings were erected. Colonel Pocahontas Edmondson founded the *Flatonia Argus* on January 1, 1875. It is still published weekly, Fayette County's oldest paper and Flatonia's oldest continuous business. Flatonia had several mercantile stores, a furniture store, a community dance hall, and an opera house. Many of the commercial buildings from Flatonia's golden era still stand, but at least 40 percent of them are deserted today.

The SA&AP came through in 1888, but its arrival had just the opposite effect from the anticipated one. Instead of unparalleled growth, business fell off in the town. The farmers and ranchers who used to come in from miles around to trade in Flatonia started going instead to the new towns that sprang up along the railroad. In just a few years the population dropped to 800. Flatonia has not yet recovered; in 1970 it had slightly over 1,100 citizens.

But Flatonia is not dead by any means. "The Twinkle in the Lone Star," as the town calls itself, is home to several industries, the most interesting of which is the mining of fuller's earth. The countryside around Flatonia is full of fuller's earth, and the material plays several very important roles in our lives—roles that not many of us are aware of. Fuller's earth serves the oil drilling industry as a well filler and sealer. A coarser, granular grade of fuller's earth serves the average American as an oil absorbent for garage floors and as kitty litter.

Downtown Flatonia has two main streets: North Main, which is US 90; and South Main, which parallels US 90 on the south side of the railroad tracks. SH 95 becomes Penn St. within Flatonia. Many of Flatonia's oldest buildings are located on North Main, South Main, and Penn.

ARNIM AND LANE MERCANTILE
102 W. North Main at Penn • 865-3552 • Monday through Friday 9–3 • W

The 1886 Arnim and Lane Mercantile building is one of Flatonia's most attractive and enduring commercial buildings. Essentially unaltered over the years, it is a great example, inside and out, of brick commercial architecture from that era. One of hundreds of brick commercial buildings with classical overtones erected in Central Texas, the Arnim and Lane building is striking in appearance despite its simple lines. Clever use of pilasters (rectangular piers projecting from a wall, made to resemble a column) and relief of the arches enriches an otherwise austerely flat facade; sunlight catches these details, producing shadow patterns that contrast nicely with the buff-colored flat surface. It is topped with a cast-iron pediment that bears the name and date. Genie-bottle finials stand guard at either corner.

E. A. Arnim and Jonathon Lane founded the store in 1878; E. A.'s son, Douglas, is the current owner. It is one of the oldest stores in the state, and as much a museum as a store, although much of the merchandise is for sale. You won't find a computer, electronic cash register, or even a water fountain here. You want a drink of water? Arnim has a tin water can with spigot. Most all the fixtures are a century old, including the cast-iron rope dispensers. The wraparound interior balcony was added in the early 1920s. Arnim hasn't ordered any new merchandise since the 1960s, and much of it dates to the 1920s, '30s, and '40s. The store isn't open to make Arnim money; it's more like a public service gesture on his part. The store is truly a step back in time and worth a special weekday trip out to see.

E. A. ARNIM ARCHIVES AND MUSEUM
101 N. Main at Penn, across from Arnim and Lane Mercantile 865-3720, 865-3368, 865-3643 • Open Sunday 9–3 • Donations W partial

This museum is based upon the extensive collections of Douglas Arnim's brother, the late E. A. Arnim, Jr., known as "Uncle Sam." E. A. Arnim, Sr. had wanted to name him Ulysses Samuel Arnim, so that his initials would be U.S.A. Mrs. Arnim vetoed that, but people began calling him Uncle Sam anyway. He grew up to be a lawyer and Fayette County judge, but his great passion was scouring the countryside collecting things, with the idea of establishing a museum in Flatonia. Out back of the museum is a nineteenth-century livery stable crammed with his accumulation of early farm machinery, tools, and household items.

Continue on Penn across US 90 to South Main. Turn left on South Main (E. South Main). This 100 block of E. South Main has several interesting buildings.

OLD POST OFFICE
116 E. South Main • Currently houses a shoe repair shop

Flatonia's old post office is also of the commercial-classical school, but not nearly so striking in its simplicity, due in part to the use of dark-red brick. But it has its charm—note the complete absence of pressed-metal gaiety in the roofline: it's all brick, except for the coffeepot center finial and flanking volute.

FOSTER BUILDING
120–122 E. South Main • Currently houses City Market

Down at the east end of the block is the 1886 Foster building, yet another example of this commercial-classical style, a fortress-like building with Gothic overtones. But the Foster building is most notable for the fading old signs painted on its western wall: "Piedmont The Cigarette of Quality 10 for 5¢" and "Meet Me at the Happy Hour Theatre Tonight." Once a favorite advertising medium, the walls of buildings stand increasingly pristine these days (except for the work of vandals), and the signs that remain fade a little more each year.

CITY MARKET
865-3384 • Open Monday through Saturday • $ • No cr. • W

At press time, the City Market had forsaken the grocery business and become a restaurant with a good, down-home lunch buffet, with barbecue served on Saturdays.

OLD HOSPITAL AND OPERA HOUSE
109 W. South Main

A block west of the City Market is the Old Flatonia Hospital and Opera House. Dr. George Washington Allen founded Flatonia's first hospital in 1896, and built this brick, Romanesque Revival building in 1897 to house it. In 1910, the Opera House was established upstairs. The building was sold in 1914 and has housed a variety of businesses since.

Turn around at the end of the block and return to Penn. Turn left onto the 200 block of S. Penn.

MILLER BUILDING
214 S. Penn
The *Flatonia Argus,* Flatonia's oldest ongoing business, is published inside this little 1886 brick building. The *Argus* is now printed on computerized presses, but the old ones are still inside, gathering dust.

FRIENDLY TAVERN
216 S. Penn • Open daily • No Cr. • W
The Friendly Tavern is short on decor (except for the domino tables) but long on local color. The hours are casual; it opens around noon and closes when everyone leaves, no later than midnight. Cheap cold beer (tap or bottle) and casual service.

Flatonia's old home district is located behind S. Main; the greatest concentration of Victorian and pre-World War I homes are on S. Penn, S. Market, and S. Converse. S. Market and S. Converse run parallel to S. Penn.

To leave Flatonia, go north on S. Penn to SH 90 and turn right (east) on US 90. To get to Grumpy's, turn right on La Grange St. (FM 609) three blocks later and follow it to the intersection with I-10, less than a mile later.

GRUMPY'S RESTAURANT
FM 609 at I-10 • 865-3374 • Open daily • Breakfast, lunch, and dinner • $ • MC, V • W
Flatonia is not exactly long on eating places; Grumpy's is one of the few good places in town to get a sit-down meal. Located on I-10, it is a truckstop cafe with the usual truckstop decor and menu. They do have pretty good homemade pie.

Just reverse your route to get back on US 90 when you leave Grumpy's.

ANNUAL EVENT

OCTOBER • Czhilispiel • Downtown • 865-3920
Last weekend in October • Most events free • W variable
Flatonia's big annual blowout is the Czhilispiel, a 3-day *Czhili* cookoff-cum-everything-else affair. A Biergarten, a carnival midway, and street and folk dances are just a few of the Czhilispiel's draws.

Leave Flatonia on US 90, heading east toward Schulenburg.

As you drive through these gently rolling hills, now rather thickly covered with trees, reflect on this fact: When the railroad came through this then-sparsely populated territory, scarcely a tree grew as far as the eye could see, just a sea of chest-high wind-waving grass.

Not quite 3 miles out of Flatonia, you come to the FM 1295 intersection, and if you look right down that road, you'll see the tall Gothic steeple of St. Mary's Catholic Church in Praha (one of Fayette County's four "painted" Catholic Churches), about a mile south of you. Go south on FM 1295 to reach Praha.

PRAHA

Fayette County • 25 • About 3 miles from Flatonia
Anglo Texans like James Duff and the Criswell brothers—William and Leroy—first settled this area. These Texas Revolution vets called the place Mulberry. With the arrival of an outlaw gang who made this pretty little valley their new base of operations, the place was more popularly known as Hottentot. Czech immigrants began to move here in 1858 and they renamed the hamlet Praha after their capital and cultural center in the homeland. It was also called Maticka Praha (Mother Prague) because it was the mother parish for surrounding towns. The soaring, circa 1890 **Saint Mary's sanctuary** on FM 1295 is commonly regarded today as the mother church for Texas Czechs. It cost $12,000 to build. The church is spare, void of gargoyles and other gewgaws, but a Gothic masterpiece nonetheless. Religious paintings dating from 1895 adorn the interior walls and ceilings. Over the altar, there are two small paintings. One depicts the great cathedral at Prague; the other is of a well-known convent outside Prague. Back then, Praha also boasted America's first Czech parochial school. Close to 700 people lived around here then. But the town slowly declined, and the school closed in 1973.
Praha today consists of little more than St. Mary's Church, a repair garage, and a couple of houses; but Praha is more than just a tiny town, it is a community whose citizens live all over Texas. These Czechs and their friends—over five thousand of them—squeeze into Praha every year to celebrate Czech homecoming at the Praha Homecoming or "Praha Pout."

ANNUAL EVENTS

AUGUST • Praha Homecoming • St. Mary's Catholic Church, FM 1295 • 865-3560 • August 15 • Meal and dance tickets • W

A celebration of mass opens the day's festivities, which continue with eating, dancing, drinking, and reminiscing. Everyone—but everyone—comes out for the celebration.

In the afternoon, the Columbus Travellers perform for your dancing and listening pleasure. Despite their pedestrian name, the Travellers are one of only two traditional Czech brass bands still active in Texas (Kovanda's Czech Band of Fayetteville is the other one). None of the band members are from Columbus, incidentally; they all hail from different towns, so they do a lot of traveling every time they rehearse and play.

NOVEMBER • Veterans Day Memorial Ceremonies St. Mary's Catholic Church, FM 1295 • 865-3560 November 11 • Free • W

The Czechs of Praha are proudly patriotic, and their annual Veterans Day ceremonies are among the largest and most impressive in the country. Thousands of visitors come to praise and remember our soldiers. Ceremonies usually include a 21-gun salute, silver taps with echo, a missing man formation flown by the U.S. or Confederate Air Force, bands, speakers, an air show, a dinner, and, of course, beer.

JERRY SIMEK PLACE US 90, 2.9 miles east of the Praha turnoff and 1 mile west of Engle on the north side of the road • 409-561-8485 Open daily • W

This small whitewashed wooden box of a place along the highway is easy to dismiss as uninteresting or—at 60 miles per hour—just plain easy to miss. Period. But do yourself the favor of stopping, anyway. The inside of Simek's place isn't much more impressive, frankly, but that's not the reason for stopping. The Shiner beer here is cold and cheaper than at most places. The Simeks will also sell you homemade egg noodles, locally grown peanuts and peppers, mustang grape jelly, sauerkraut, locally canned pickles, and pickled okra. Now aren't you glad you stopped?

ENGLE

Fayette County • 106 • About 4 miles from Flatonia, excluding Praha side trip
The next little burg down US 90 is Engle, which grew up along the GH&SA railroad in the 1880s. The place was named after railroad engineer J. E. Engle. Precious little is left here these days.

CHUDEJ'S SALOON
US 90 at FM 2238 • Open Wednesday through Monday • No Cr.
It's easy to miss this local landmark; the sign has faded over the years, and the owners aren't too worried about attracting new customers. J. C. Bucek began selling beer in this little wooden one-story shotgun storefront in 1890; the Chudej (pronounced Khoo-day) brothers bought it from him in 1948, and have done little to disturb the furnishings and decor since, including leaving the outhouses out back. Have a cold Shiner beer and relax; there's usually a game of dominoes going on, or conversation amongst the local Bohemian patrons. Just don't tell them I sent you!

Five miles east of Engle, turn left on FM 2672 to reach the old High Hill community, approximately 4 miles north of US 90.

HIGH HILL

Fayette County • 116 • About 9 miles from Engle
High Hill was established about 1848 by German immigrants, and was previously known as Oldenburg, Wursten, and Blum Hill. The Germans were supplanted by a wave of Czech immigrants starting in 1860. High Hill was the only town in south Fayette County until after the Civil War. With two private schools drawing students from all over the state, High Hill was a center of culture for the region. The local choir and orchestra were in great demand at Saenger Fests throughout Texas. High Hill had several stores and blacksmith shops, a hotel, and a brewery among its business establishments.

Things were looking up in High Hill when Colonel T. W. Pierce and James Converse came wandering through the area in 1873 looking for a route to San Antonio for their GH&SA rails. Naturally they were interested in establishing a station in High Hill, already a prominent stagecoach stop on the first overland mail route between Washington, D.C. and San Francisco. But Pierce and Converse were rebuffed in their search for a right-of-way through High Hill.

"Railroads are just a fad," High Hillers told them. "Go back home; we don't want to ruin our country with a railroad. We can go off and leave our houses unlocked. We won't be able to do that if your railroad comes through," they jeered. So the GH&SA line went through two miles south of High Hill. Pierce chose a spot for the terminal near the home of local farmer Louis Schulenburg. The first train arrived here on December 8, 1873. The new town was built on land owned by Schulenburg, Franz Stanzel, and Christian Baumgarten. In just a few years High Hill was a ghost town; everyone had moved to Schulenburg and the railroad, rolling their houses and businesses over on logs.

Ghost town or not, there were still enough people in the neighborhood to build **St. Mary's Catholic Church,** a red brick Gothic Revival sanctuary built in 1906. Another of the "painted" churches of Fayette County, it is actually the third church to be built by High Hill Catholics, and is partially built with material from the smaller sanctuary it replaced. Its interior shows some of the most elaborate and sophisticated decorative painting to be found in Texas churches. All the ceiling, walls, and columns are painted. The nave is separated from the two side aisles by octagonal wooden columns painted to look like marble. The ceilings and walls are painted with Greek and religious motifs. San Antonio artists Ferdinand Stockert and Hermann Kern did the work in 1912, combining freehand painting with stenciling. The High Hill cemetery (one mile south) has many old stones with Czech and German inscriptions.

A few dozen yards north and west of the church, off County Rd. 440, stands **Texas' first cottonseed oil mill,** a barnlike structure of stucco over brick built in 1866 by Frederick Hillje. Hillje first used a modified sugar beet crusher imported from Germany. Later, he installed regular cottonseed milling machinery. But the mill failed after just a few years, for cottonseed oil was then an almost unknown commodity.

From High Hill, return to US 90 on FM 2672, and continue east on US 90 into Schulenburg.

SCHULENBURG

Fayette County • 2,736 • (409) • About 13 miles from Flatonia, excluding Praha side trip
Schulenburg was a child of the GH&SA railway. As was often the case all over Texas, the railroad spawned one town and killed off another; Schulenburg's birth was accompanied by the death of High Hill. Schulenburg was part of a 4,428-acre tract of land granted to Kesiah Crier by the Mexican government in 1831, which ran along

the West Navidad River. After 1845, the Crier family began to sell off pieces of the league, which brought more population to the southern half of Fayette County. In 1873, the railroad bought Louis Schulenburg's 450-acre farm, along with several other local tracts. Since the railroad's depot was to be located on Schulenburg's land, Christian Baumgarten suggested that the new town should be named after him. On New Year's Eve 1873, the first train chugged into Schulenburg, which in German means "city of schools." The town may have been named for Louis Schulenburg, but Schulenburg's most prominent early resident was Christian Baumgarten, whom the town reveres as the "Father of Schulenburg." The first business in Schulenburg was the Baumgarten Lumber Company, located at the railroad tracks on N. Main at Wolters. Baumgarten built Schulenburg's first frame, stone, and brick buildings, respectively, and also established a lumber company, furniture and hardware stores, a cotton gin, a mill, and a sash and door factory, and initiated the first commercial manufacturing of curly pine furniture in Texas. The working of curly pine is now an extinct art, but a prime example of the wood's beauty can be found at the Sisterdale general store in Sisterdale (see Hill Country Rivers).

But Baumgarten is most famous for his work with cottonseed oil. Baumgarten and his son Gus built a cottonseed oil mill here in 1883. Gus took up where his father left off, building oil mills in Hempstead, Rockdale, Caldwell, Taylor, Kyle, Luling, and Hallettsville. Gus Baumgarten worked tirelessly promoting cottonseed oil as a cooking fat. The result was a revolution in American cooking; housewives began to use vegetable fats in their kitchens rather than the traditional butter and animal fats, a trend that has continued right into the 1990s.

Baumgarten the younger also developed a starch-free flour from cottonseed meal, which is useful for diabetics. His Baumgarten Process Allison Flour has five times the nutritive value of wheat flour. It was while government chemists were in Schulenburg studying the Baumgarten flour-making process in 1917 that Gus Baumgarten effected another revolutionary change in the American kitchen. At that time, Baumgarten had been fiddling around with a thermometer in his home oven. He invented controlled-heat baking in the process. Herbert Hoover, who had sent the government chemists down to the Schulenburg mill, heard of Baumgarten's experiments and wrote asking if he would please instruct by mail 2,385 home economists, who would then demonstrate this new baking method all over the country. The end result was a thermostat on almost every oven subsequently produced in America. These days it's hard to imagine an oven without one.

The elder Baumgarten, Christian, was obviously a smart cookie. Born in Prussia in 1836, he was a carpenter by age 14 and an orphan by 18. Thereupon he set sail for America, landing at Galveston where he worked till he had saved enough money to move inland. Baumgarten came to Fayette County in 1857, buying land in this area shortly thereafter for $10 an acre. Its value mushroomed when Schulenburg was born.

Baumgarten built the Immigration House in 1875 for Franz Russek. Russek, who was immigration agent for the railroad, helped bring hundreds of newly immigrated German and Czech families to the area. Most of the Czechs were farmers, and Schulenburg served as a trading center for them. They and other local farmers raised many bumper crops of cotton from the rich soil. Schulenburg had one of the area's biggest cotton presses. From here, the bales went by train to the great ports of Houston and Galveston.

In 1875, Schulenburg incorporated. During its time as the railroad's western terminus, Schulenburg attracted its share of opportunistic scalawags and was a rowdy town until the law-abiding citizens hired a man named Jamison to bring law and order to town. He "had to shoot and stab some of the bad men," but he succeeded, and Schulenburg has led a peaceful existence for the most part since.

In his 1883 bestseller *On a Mexican Mustang Through Texas,* humorist Alex Sweet depicted the young town of Schulenburg:

> Schulenberg [sic] is a small town on the railroad. Almost all the inhabitants are Germans—thrifty, hard-working people, who attend to their own business with more enthusiasm than the native American can ever be accused of doing.
>
> They have a mayor and a board of aldermen in Schulenberg, and city ordinances are made by the aldermen. Those that are not vetoed by the mayor are broken by vagrant hogs, stray cows, and inebriated cowboys. There is a newspaper published in Schulenberg. Its columns are devoted to the mayor's proclamations, the railroad time-table, patent-medicine advertisements, and reports of aldermanic discussions on municipal affairs. The absorbing topic at Schulenberg, when we were there, was, "Shall we continue to employ our present efficient police-force?"
>
> The "efficient police-force" consisted of a large man, whose clothes had apparently been made for a smaller policeman. He was armed with a very large revolver. His trousers did not quite reach his ankles; they had evidently been pulled before they were ripe.

Schulenburg has always been an industrious little town. Texas' first evaporated milk plant (begun in 1929), the Oak Ridge Smokehouse, poultry and egg processing plants, and the Victor Stanzel Company (maker of model airplane kits) have been just a few of Schulenburg's industries over the years. The Texas Jersey Cheese Company opened here in 1996, making a variety of cheeses from local milk.

Schulenburg is also famous as the home of the jumbo hamburger. They were 10¢ a shot when longtime local restaurateur Frank Tilicek invented them during the Depression as a way to get travelers to stop at his place. **Frank's Restaurant,** a Schulenburg institution for over 50 years, is still open and still serving jumbo burgers.

To get to Frank's Restaurant, take Kessler/US 77 north from US 90. Turn left on Kessler and travel about a mile to the intersection with I-10.

FRANK'S RESTAURANT
I-10 and US 77 • 743-3555 • Open daily • Breakfast, lunch, and dinner • $ • MC, V • W

Frank and Rozine Tilicek founded this place way back when US 90 was the main drag through town. They were right there, ready to cater to the hungry traveler.

When I-10 lifted the traffic burden from US 90, the Tiliceks moved with the traffic. The building may be new and devoid of the old roadhouse charm of earlier Frank's establishments, but the food is the same: steaks, chicken, Mexican food, homemade bread and pies, and, of course, those venerable jumbo hamburgers. They also serve a good weekday blue plate lunch.

CITY MARKET
Kessler/US 77 at College St., between Frank's Restaurant and Summit/US 90 • 743-3440 • Open Monday through Saturday 7:30–5:30 • W

The City Market is one of Central Texas' best meat markets, offering their own smoked pork loin, jerky, bacon, sausage, wieners, and barbecue as well as fresh meats. You can sit down and eat it here, or take it with you.

KOUNTRY BAKERY
Kessler/US 77 at College St., across from City Market
743-4342 • Open Monday, Tuesday, Thursday, and Friday
5:30–5; Saturday 5:30–2; closed Sunday and Wednesday • W

Good kolaches (I'm partial to the cream cheese and the poppy-seed; there is also a variety of fruit fillings), pigs in a blanket, bread, pies, cookies, and apple strudel. Old-fashioned hamburgers and sandwiches are also served. Kolaches freeze well, so you can take a dozen home with you.

The best of Schulenburg's old commercial buildings are located on N. Main, two blocks south of Summit/US 90. To get to N. Main from Summit/US 90, go south on Kessler/US 77. After one block, the road bifurcates: US 77 continues straight, passing under N. Main, the railroad tracks, and S. Main, while Kessler veers to the right, dead-ending one block later at N. Main. You follow Kessler's veer, then turn right on N. Main.

N. Main truly lived up to its name in the days when the GH&SA railroad was the only highway through town. Compared to the rather subdued styles of Flatonia's downtown buildings, Main Street Schulenburg is a riot of elaborate brick arches, turrets, gingerbread, and frosting. Schulenburg was a prosperous town almost immediately, and substantial business buildings and homes began to be erected almost as soon as the town was created. Several of the buildings on the east end of N. Main date to the 1870s. In 1893, the "Great Fire" of Schulenburg destroyed a half-block of buildings that had been built in 1874, specifically buildings from the west half of North Main, along Upton Ave., to the west portion of Anderson.

SCHAEFER BUILDING
N. Main at Kessler

Sigmund T. Schaefer built this brick building with fanciful, pinnacled roofline in 1896 to house his hardware and building supply store. He was also an undertaker; this was a common business combination in those days. The Palace was located in the eastern corner; "Palace Saloon" is still painted over the building's back entrance, which you see just before you turn onto N. Main. The *Schulenburg Sticker* newspaper (established 1894) is now located here.

The 500 block is notable for the 1894 building that now houses the **Upstairs at the Downstairs** club (525 N. Main, 743-4040, beer, pool, darts, dance floor). The brickwork on this two-story building is a decorative exercise in geometry and repetition that creates buff brick icing on a red brick cake. The red brick **Englemann Brothers building** (531 N. Main) is downtown's tallest. In the 600 block, an otherwise plain commercial building (607–609 N. Main) is saved from anonymity by the fanciful tower and pinnacles up top.

SCHULENBURG HISTORICAL MUSEUM
631 N. Main • 743-4514 (Tourist Information Center)
Open Sunday afternoons • Donations • W
Located in the 1886 C. Bohms building, the museum depicts life in Schulenburg's early days. There's a lot to see.

BAUMGARTEN COTTON GIN
700 block of N. Main
This compact, square brick building on your right was built in the mid-1870s. The bricks were made at Baumgarten's nearby brick kiln. It originally housed his mule-powered cotton gin. Such a gin might take up to three hours to compress one bale of cotton. Located at this site, at one time or another, have been a mattress factory, a wire basket works, and Gus Russek's Enterprise Bottling Works.

Continue on N. Main to West Ave. and turn right on West. One block north, at the corner of West and Anderson, is one of Schulenburg's most elaborate residences.

GUS CRANZ HOUSE
701 West at Anderson • Private residence
Whoever coined the term *gingerbread* for elaborate building ornamentation could have been looking at this house styled after an Austrian villa. The full-length front porch and twin staircases leading up to it are lined by balustrades comprised of dozens of balled balusters. The porch is curved to create twin porticoes and its roofline is trimmed with an overhang of dozens more balled balusters. The gable windows are leaded glass; the foundation is covered with panels of whitewashed wood-strip fretwork. Dating to 1874, the house was meticulously built, down to its mitred and doweled joints.

Builder Gus Cranz later acquired a son-in-law of some note, Hugh Roy Cullen, who became a leading Texas oil man.

BAUMGARTEN HOME
607 West
This home encases the original cedar log cabin built by John Christian Baumgarten in 1850, which was the first home built in what is now Schulenburg. The home was enlarged over the years as

the family grew. The oak tree in the yard is estimated to be over 400 years old.

MYRNA LOY APARTMENTS
601 West at Summit • Private residence
Located one block north of the gingerbread house is an anonymous two-story green-asbestos-sided building, distinguished only by the Art Deco black-glass sign mounted over the front entrance bearing the white Deco-lettered inscription "Myrna Loy Apts." There is not a more tastefully executed sign in Central Texas, nor a more uniquely named apartment complex.

Continue north, across US 90, on West Ave. to see two more of Schulenburg's old Victorian-style homes.

The **Gus Russek home** (409 West) is an elaborate two-story showplace built in 1909 by this business magnate of early-day Schulenburg who also served in the Texas Senate for 10 years. At the far north end of West Ave. (just after it becomes Cty. Rd. 415), on your left, is the two-story **Ignac Russek home,** built in 1893.

LODGING

VON MINDEN HOTEL
607 Lyons (US 90 at Lyons) • 743-3493 • $
Built in 1927, this building contains both a 40-room hotel that still has much of its original furnishings and a movie theatre that still shows first-run movies. The Cozy Theatre opened in November 1927; the hotel in May 1928. The hotel has a restaurant that serves pizza and American homestyle cooking.

OTHER ATTRACTIONS

SAINT ISIDORE SCULPTURE
1010 Lyons Ave., southeast of St. Rose Catholic Church
The importance of agriculture and God in the lives of Schulenburgers is expressed by this sculpture, which memorializes Saint Isidore, patron saint of farmers. The sculpture was created by local artist Gene Mikulik and was dedicated in 1982. The parish celebrates the feast day of Saint Isidore every year on May 15.

GALIPP'S SUPER MARKET
236 College, just off US 77, across from Kountry Bakery
743-4866

Other than supercheap prices for Shiner beer, Galipp's is noteworthy to the traveler only because of its Saturday barbecue and fixings. In the grand old tradition, Galipp's meat market slow-smokes all the week's unsold meat to fingerlicking perfection and serves it with homemade bread, pinto beans, and potato salad. Besides brisket, you'll find steaks, roasts, chops, and goodness knows what else.

SCHULENBURG TOURIST INFORMATION CENTER
101-B Kessler (US 77) • 743-4514 • Open Monday through Friday

Even when the center is closed, you can pick up an informative area guide from the rack of brochures outside, by the front door. The Schaefer Observatory next door was built by local astronomer Rip Schaefer. A number of his photos and observations are on file at UT's McDonald Observatory, including the phases of a 1940 solar eclipse. It is no longer in use.

WOLTERS PARK
West Ave., 4 blocks south of US 90, follow signs
Open daily • Free

Schulenburg's city park is named after R. A. Wolters, who donated the land for a park in 1936. The first building moved here was the Turner Hall, built in 1886 and originally located at Summit and Upton streets. It was put on logs 10 inches in diameter and rolled across town to the park. Turner Hall is now the American Legion Hall. In 1941, a log cabin built by Jacob Wolters at Industry in 1835 was moved here. The spacious tree shaded grounds are perfect for picnicking.

ANNUAL EVENT

ST. JOHN'S PARISH PICNIC
St. John's Catholic Church grounds, 6 miles southwest of
Schulenburg on FM 957 • Every July 4th • W

St. John's Parish is over 100 years old; parishioners and guests have been celebrating on July 4th for almost as long. The day starts with 9:30 mass, a flag-raising ceremony, and then the fun and feasting begin. Dinner is stew, fried chicken, and all the trimmings. Popular Czech-Tex groups like the Dujka Brothers, the Red Ravens, and the Jolly Texans play all afternoon for your dancing and listening pleasure. There are lots of games for kids, a cakewalk, auction, lots of cold German soda water, and more.

Leave Schulenburg on US 90 and head east toward Weimar. Five miles east of Schulenburg, turn left on FM 1383 to reach the picturesque hamlets of Dubina and Ammansville. In 2.5 miles, you come to Dubina. Turn left on Fayette Cty. Rd. 480.

DUBINA

Fayette County • About 7.5 miles from Schulenburg
"Dub" is the Czech word for oak; later the "ina" was added, although no one remembers why any more. The area was first settled in late 1856 by seven Bohemian emigrant families who spent their first night here huddled under a large oak tree, seeking shelter from a brutal sleet storm. The community that grew up here was also known as Navidad, Bohemia Navidad, and East Navidad, owing to its location near the Navidad River and its overwhelmingly Bohemian population. The community prospered, servicing about 600 families by the turn of the century, with cotton gin, grist mill, general store, school, post office, and even a zoo.

Only 200 people live in the area today, and the only active institution is Saints Cyril and Methodius Catholic Church.

STS. CYRIL AND METHODIUS CHURCH
Open daily • Donations accepted • W with help
The current white frame sanctuary was built in 1912; it replaced the 1877 church, which was destroyed by the great hurricane of 1909. Before that, the faithful worshipped in a log cabin. The church is most notable for its stencilled and painted interior walls and vaulted ceiling, stained-glass windows, and Gothic altar. The church is open for viewing daily from 9–5.

Besides the church and some aging local farm houses, all that remains of Dubina today are the old saloon/post office/store (long closed), and the local **K.J.T. Lodge, No. 6.** K.J.T. stands for "Katolik Jednota Texaska," or Catholic Union of Texas, similar to the S.P.J.S.T. The signs on the white-washed outhouses behind the hall still say "Muzke" (men) and "Zenske" (women). The adjacent cemetery has many tombstones inscribed in Czech. The Czech legend at the cemetery entrance translates roughly as: "Here lies a large number of us who were sent to God. If you don't want to pray for us, then leave us alone."

If you continue on Cty. Rd. 480 for another 0.75 mile, you will cross a quaint one-lane bridge, then another one that dates to 1885, built by the King Iron Bridge Co. of Cleveland, Ohio. This truss "pianowire" bridge is one of the few of its type still in use in Central Texas. From the bridge, return to the church.

The parish hall next to the church is site of the parish's annual picnic and Feast Day, held the first Sunday in July. It's similar to the Shiner Catholic Church Picnic (see Shiner-Lockhart Pilgrimage— Shiner, Annual Events). Mass is still celebrated regularly, and on Christmas Eve, the carols are still sung in Czech, German, and English.

From Dubina, continue north on FM 1383 5 more miles to Ammansville.

AMMANSVILLE

Fayette County • About 5 miles from Dubina
Ammansville was named for its first settler, J. Amman, and began to jell as a town with the establishment of its first public school in 1876. St. John the Baptist Catholic Church and a German private school were established in 1890.

ST. JOHN THE BAPTIST CHURCH
Open daily • Donations accepted • W
The first church building was destroyed by the 1900 hurricane that ravaged Galveston. The church was destroyed a second time by fire, and was replaced by the present wooden sanctuary in 1919. The interior is outstanding, with its Gothic altars and intricately stenciled walls and vaulted ceilings. St. John's is the fourth of the Schulenburg area's "Painted Churches," along with those previously described at Dubina, High Hill, and Praha, all true Texas treasures. The church is open for viewing daily from 9 to 5.

In its pre-World War I heyday, Ammansville boasted two cotton gins, a bank, general stores, a courthouse, and a jail. Several of the old commercial storefronts still stand, but the only one still open for business (at this time) is **Tofel's Place** (open daily, except Sunday), where you can still get a cold Shiner Beer, kibbutz a domino game, or horn in on the local conversation. The local **K.J.T. hall,** or "beseda," (Czech for "get-together") has served over the years as church, school, and library, and is still used for local weddings, reunions, meetings, and the **St. John's Parish annual picnic and Feast Day,** held each Father's Day in June. This picnic, or any of the German/Czech Belts' parish picnics, is a lot of fun, with plenty of Czech-Tex food, polka dancing, and such.

From Ammansville, return to US 90 and continue east towards Weimar.

WEIMAR

Colorado County • 2,162 • (409) • About 8 miles from Schulenburg

Weimar is a German and Czech community located in the rolling hills of Colorado County. Weimar started out as the Jackson's Ranch Settlement, named after the man who owned much of the local land. When the GH&SA railroad came through in 1873, the name was altered slightly to Jackson's Station.

There are two stories as to how Jackson's Station became Weimar. The first story tells of an 1882 meeting of the local German club Verein Frohsinn, whose members gathered together for the purpose of renaming the town. All suggestions were written on slips of paper and dropped in a hat, and then the winning name, Weimar, submitted by a Bohemian clerk, was drawn.

Story number two has a GH&SA engineer rolling into town one day and telling the folks of Jackson's Station they should rename their town Weimar. It seems the engineer had a son enrolled at a school in Weimar, Germany. In letters home, the son had described the countryside around Weimar in detail and the engineer thought his son's description of the German town's terrain fit Jackson's Station to a tee. The German and Czech settlers agreed and renamed their town accordingly.

On November 16, 1880, the Colorado River at Weimar was so thick with ice that a wagon with a double team of horses could cross safely. An enterprising Weimar photographer was sharp enough to record this once-in-a-century occurrence for posterity. During the same blue norther the snow stood four and five inches thick on level ground. Cattle edged up against the recently introduced barbed wire fences and froze to death by the hundreds.

Weimar has always been a God-fearing little town, but it has known its moments of violent passion and cold-blooded murder. On January 10, 1895, two prominent Weimar physicians, Drs. J. E. Grace and Eugene Pottost, met on one of the town's principal streets, whipped out their revolvers, and settled their differences with a burst of gunfire. Grace was killed, struck by two bullets. Pottost was hit three times but survived. A contemporary newspaper account further describes the Grace-Pottost confrontation: "The affair was caused by a little difficulty between the two men about a small matter about two weeks ago, in which a blow or two was passed. It seems they met this evening for the first time since. Insults were passed and soon the shooting began. The affair is much regretted and has caused great excitement."

But Weimar settled down and became a livestock and poultry processing center, and for years even had a pickle factory. Weimar's most prominent edifice is the soaring St. Michael's Catholic Church, whose steeple you saw coming into town. To get there from US 90, turn left on Center St.

ST. MICHAEL'S CATHOLIC CHURCH
410 N. Center, four blocks north of US 90 • 725-6714
W with assistance
The imposing, Gothic St. Michael's was completed in 1913. Brick from Elgin was used in its construction. Inside, the high vaulted ceiling and elaborately carved altar and statuary tend to leave the viewer breathless, then contemplative.

From St. Michael's, double back on Center toward US 90, but turn left on Post Office St. Post Office runs north of and parallel to Main St./US 90.

Weimar is short on restaurants these days, but tasty treats can be found at two other places in town.

SUSIE'S BAKERY
124 E. Post Office • Monday through Saturday 7–5:30
No Cr. • W
Located on Post Office St. (the post office, incidentally, is now located on Main), is Susie's Bakery, purveyor of cheap and tasty kolaches in various guises (try the poppyseed and cheese ones), white and whole wheat bread, filled doughnuts, sweet rolls, cookies, and pigs in blankets, all baked on the premises.

KASPER MEAT MARKET
119 E. Post Office • 725-8227 • Open Monday through Saturday
No Cr. • W
Across Post Office from Susie's Bakery is the Kasper Meat Market, a real old-time meat market, the kind that is rapidly van-

ishing from the Texas scene. The place has been run by the Kasper family for several generations, long enough for them to perfect their art; over a ton of sausage is sold every Saturday. They put out hogshead sausage, beef-and-pork sausage, pork sausage, and smoked hams year-round and smoked turkey in season. The Kaspers also smoke some pretty good beef jerky. Patrons sit on old handmade cedar furniture while they wait for their orders to be filled. As said earlier, this is a real old-time meat market, where they do all the cutting in the front room, just across the counter from you. So, don't be surprised if you walk in on a mass cow-head-splitting session; brains seem to be a popular item with the locals. Definitely a million miles away from your supermarket meat counter.

Just south of the railroad tracks, the 100 block of E. Jackson sports several old commercial buildings. The **old train station** now houses the public library. It's just across the street, on the north side of E. Jackson, and faces the opera house.

WEIMAR HERITAGE SOCIETY MUSEUM
125 E. Main (US 90) • Open Wednesday and Sunday afternoons • W
Exhibits trace the city from its beginnings. There are a turn-of-the-century doctor's office, farm implements, photos, and more. One room is dedicated to World War I, World War II, Korean conflict, and Vietnam war veterans.

Leave Weimar on US 90, heading east toward Columbus.

BORDEN

Colorado County • (409) • About 5 miles from Weimar
Borden is the next wide spot on US 90, named for and found-ed by Gail Borden. Jack-of-all-trades and inventor, Borden arrived at Galveston Island on Christmas Eve, 1829. He spent time ranching, surveying for Austin's colony, and publishing a newspaper before becoming first collector of the port of Galveston. He next served as land agent, Sunday School teacher, and Galveston city alderman.

Borden started inventing in the 1840s, creating among other things a "terraqueous machine," a sort of prairie schooner that could travel on land or water. By 1849 Borden had perfected his "meat biscuit," a dehydrated meat patty compounded with flour. He spent the next few years traveling all over the world trying to sell it, mostly to the war ministries of various countries, as the ideal traveling ration for armies on the move. The only problem was it tasted awful, and it didn't keep well in damp coastal climates. In his effort to market the meat biscuit, Borden moved to New York in 1851. By 1853 he had invented a process for condensing milk. After two failed attempts at establishing a condensing factory, Borden managed to open one and keep it running in Connecticut in 1858. The Civil War and the resulting upsurge in demand for condensed milk made Borden a wealthy man. Along the way he also invented processes for condensing fruit juices, coffee, and extracts of beef.

At war's end Borden returned to Texas, where he erected a beef packing plant at the village that was to bear his name. By 1871 he had accumulated 1,600 acres here, where he built houses for himself, his sons, and his brother. His beautiful house featured all the delights and comforts of its age, including the luxury of running water. The house was surrounded by acres of orchards and by flower and vegetable gardens, in accordance with his motto: "Beautiful surroundings for home and work." In 1872 Borden built a milk processing plant at Bordenville, as the place was then known.

About the same time, the GH&SA railroad came rolling through on its way to San Antonio. One of the GH&SA locomotives bore the name Gail Borden, a great advertising coup for him. Merchants up and down the line began stocking his canned meat in addition to his milk.

Borden spent much of his profits building churches and schools for both black and white Texans, and partially supporting many poorly paid teachers and ministers. He died in 1874, and the plants shut down soon thereafter. His magnificent home burned to the ground in 1885. As time marched on the old factory buildings were torn down, some of the materials being used to build the bustling town of Weimar. Borden was buried in New York City's Woodlawn Cemetery.

Borden's identifiable center these days consists of one business establishment, the **Borden Store.**

Turn left at the Borden Store onto Cty. Rd. 217, which offers you a glimpse of the rolling Colorado County ranch country. Resume your course east on US 90 when Cty. Rd. 217 rejoins it.

GLIDDEN

Colorado County • 255 • About 8 miles from Borden
Glidden, which is now a suburb of Columbus, was founded in 1887 and named for railroad engineer F. J. Glidden.

COLUMBUS

Colorado County • 3,605 • (409) • About 10 miles from Borden

Columbus started life as an Indian village located on the banks of the Colorado River, identified on old Spanish maps as Montezuma. Montezuma happened to be located in the western corner of the 200,000-acre area of Texas along the Brazos and Colorado rivers granted to Moses and Stephen F. Austin for the purpose of settling American immigrant families. The first white settlers in the Montezuma area were Robert and Joseph Kuykendall and Daniel Gilleland, who arrived about Christmas of 1821. In August 1823 Stephen F. Austin and the Baron de Bastrop, Felipe Enrique Neri, surveyed 170 acres here on the Colorado River. This plot, the present site of Columbus, was to be capital and headquarters for the Austin colony. But Austin relocated his capital to a similar spot on the Brazos River, due to the frequency of Indian attacks here and the fact that most of the settlers had already located along the Brazos.

But the settlers here stayed on. That same year, 1823, W. B. DeWees, commonly regarded as the founder of Columbus, married the daughter of Leander Beason and built a home here. Others joined the Gillelands, Kuykendalls, and DeWeeses, and the little settlement was first known as Beason's Ferry.

Austin's contract with the Mexican government called for the family to be the basic unit of settlement. Each family that farmed and raised stock for a living was to receive a minimum land grant of one square league (4,428 acres). Because of the vagueness of the Mexican grant to Austin, the money paid by the settlers for their land ranged from nothing to about 3¢ per acre.

In order to gain legal title to the land, settlers had to satisfy a number of requirements, including such quaint practices as walking the land's perimeters while shouting out the transfer of title from the Mexican government to the settler, pulling up herbs, throwing stones, and setting out stakes. They also had to cultivate the land and build a residence within two years of the grant.

Austin had his hands full trying to collect surveying fees from his colonists, creating and maintaining conditions in the colony conducive to its prosperous development, and dealing with the ever-changing Mexican government. In trying to walk the tightrope between the desires of the Mexican government and those of his colonists, Austin traveled thousands of harsh, strength-sapping miles through the Texas wilderness and spent over two years in a Mexico City prison. Meanwhile, relations between the Mexican government and the Anglo Texans deteriorated.

By 1835 the village of Columbus had been laid out and named, and Texas was on the brink of rebellion. The village sent a contingent of men to Gonzales that fall, where they took part in the Battle of Gonzales. The war came to Columbus the next spring, as the Republican Army under the command of Sam Houston retreated from Gonzales. The Mexican Army was in hot pursuit. By March 6, 1836, Houston's troops were camped on the east bank of the Colorado near Columbus. Here Houston tried to train his raw troops in the fine art of organized warfare. By March 24, the Mexican Army was camped on the west bank of the Colorado, reinforced by the arrival of Santa Anna.

Most of the Texans wanted to do battle then and there, but Houston counseled caution, saying he wanted to wait for the proper time and place, and this was neither. So the Republican Army burned every building in Columbus to the ground and hightailed it east, where they finally confronted and whipped Santa Anna at San Jacinto on April 21, 1836.

With the cessation of hostilities, the Anglo Texans began to drift back to the homes and settlements they had abandoned in the face of the Mexican Army's rampage. Their hasty and ungainly retreat is known today as the Runaway Scrape.

Colorado County was organized in the spring of 1837 and the first court session was held under a giant live oak, since all the town buildings had been burned during the Runaway Scrape, and the new courthouse had literally slipped through the fingers of its builders. Preparations had been made for the construction of a county courthouse here. Lumber had been cut upriver at Bastrop and then floated to Columbus, but the obstruction built across the river to catch the lumber failed to hold and the timber continued merrily on to the Gulf. The court was presided over by Judge Robert McAlphin Williamson, more colorfully known as "Three-Legged Willie," by virtue of the wooden leg he had attached to the knee of his withered left leg. The lower, natural half of that leg he left protruding rearward, and he had all his pants tailored accordingly.

Justice in those days was of a no-nonsense nature. In May 1838, one Wilson H. Bibbs was charged with grand larceny (probably cattle theft). Pleading guilty as charged, Bibbs threw himself on the mercy of the court. The court's mercy consisted of the following sentence: "That Wilson H. Bibbs should receive on this day 39 lashes on his bare back and be branded on the right hand with the letter T." The T presumably stood for "thief." He was also to be held in "outside" until a $500 fine was paid, but this portion of the sentence was later remitted when it was shown that the sum of $500 was not to be found anywhere west of the Colorado River. Bibbs was then released "from outside," where he had presumably been chained to a tree, there being no jail built as yet.

Columbus eventually got its courthouse and jail built and proceeded to grow into a prosperous little city. One of the town's more memorable settlers during this era was Colonel Robert Robson, who hailed from Dumfries, Scotland. Once in Columbus, Robson erected a castle of homemade lime and gravel on the south side of the Colorado, on the site where Austin had planned to establish his colonial headquarters. Robson's three-story fortress was surrounded by a moat, and entrance was gained via a drawbridge. Most of the rooms were 20 feet by 20 feet, with a grand ballroom three times the length of the other rooms. The castle was also the first building in Texas to have running water and a roof garden. Colonel Robson also introduced the Mexican huisache tree to Texas. The Robson house was undermined by a severe river flood in 1869 and torn down in 1883 to make way for a beef processing plant.

Steamboats plied the river from the Gulf up to Columbus through the Civil War, so Columbus served as a shipping point for inland farm products and as a supply center for wagon trains headed west.

Cotton was a mainstay of the Colorado County economy from the beginning, and much of the cotton was grown on plantations, using slave labor. One of the slaveowners' most persistent fears was the possibility of slave insurrection. They attempted to prevent such uprisings by a variety of practices, such as denying their chattel any formal education or the right to congregate except in small, supervised groups. But plots were concocted among the slaves despite their masters' efforts.

According to contemporary newspaper accounts, Colorado County was very nearly laid to waste in the late summer of 1856. The reports say that the white slaveowners of the county uncovered a plot for mass rebellion just days before it was to occur. Supposedly, over 200 blacks were in on the plot, along with "every Mexican in the county." Possessing large numbers of guns and homemade knives, the rebels were to have indiscriminately murdered all the county's white inhabitants—men, women, and children. No mention was made of just what the blacks and Mexicans were to do once this wholesale butchery had been accomplished. At any rate, the "diabolical" plan was unearthed just in the nick of time. The three slave ringleaders were hanged, two more were whipped to death, and all Mexicans were ordered to leave the county within five days, never to return upon pain of death. And life in Colorado County settled back down to the norm.

Five years later, Columbus and Colorado County voted overwhelmingly for secession and sent hundreds of able-bodied men into the fray. The very old and very young men stayed at home serving in the Home Guard, or "Heel Flies."

The Reconstruction years in Colorado County were restless, sometimes violent ones. At war's end, the newly freed slaves came to the courthouse square in great jubilant crowds singing, "Lincoln rode de big black horse, Davis rode de mule, Lincoln wuz de nobleman and Davis wuz de fool." Naturally, the recently subdued white Rebels didn't take to this behavior too well, and the Yankee occupation troops, to rub it in further, put the freedmen in uniform and commissioned them to keep the peace in Colorado County. A chapter of the Klan was formed and these unreconstructed Rebels would ride into town, fire a couple dozen shots, then dash back into the wooded night. The bluebellies would then halfheartedly pursue the raiders a mile or two before turning back. Federal authorities and county officers often clashed.

Despite the unrest of Reconstruction, there were fortunes to be made now that the war was over, mostly in cattle and cotton. In 1869, the railroad finally came to Columbus. The Buffalo Bayou, Brazos, and Colorado Railway had reached Alleyton (three miles east of Columbus) by 1860, but the Colorado River still stood in the way. After the war, the Buffalo Bayou, Brazos, and Colorado Railway reorganized as the Galveston, Harrisburg, and San Antonio Railway and finally made the big leap over the Colorado and into Columbus. The railroad made it much cheaper to ship out Colorado County cotton and bring in all sorts of consumer goods. But instead of riding the rails to market, Colorado County cattle were trailed north. At least one man, Robert Earl "Bob" Stafford, made a million dollars from Texas Longhorns, which were almost as numerous as grasshoppers in the region after the war. But prosperity did not bring peace to Colorado County. During the pre-barbed-wire days of free range and wild cattle (about 1875), a feud developed between the Townsend family—longtime pillars of Colorado County—and the Staffords, relative Johnny-come-latelies who had wasted little time in getting wealthy. No one knows exactly how the feud got started, but once it got going, it was a hot one. Things came to a head when J. L. "Light" Townsend was elected county sheriff. The Stafford faction tried to unseat him at succeeding elections, but failed.

The Townsend clan (Asa and Rebecca Harper Townsend and their nine children) had come to Columbus in 1838. Asa was involved in Texas politics by 1845, when he served on a committee involved with the annexation of the Republic of Texas to the United States. He was also director of the Colorado [River] Navigation Association and an active Mason.

Robert Stafford, born in Georgia in 1834, came to Texas in 1856 and settled in Colorado County, where he farmed and raised livestock on a small scale, using the I.C.U. brand. The oldest child in his family, he was soon joined by several siblings, including his brother John, who was 20 years younger than Bob. Stafford joined Hood's Texas Brigade in 1861, served honorably, and came home from the Civil War penniless but full of hope and determination. In 1869, he successfully drove a herd of cattle to Kansas. Emboldened by his success, he enlarged his business by buying up all the brands in his section of the county that were for sale. In 1872, he contracted to deliver beef to Havana, Cuba. He also sold cattle that went to pacified Indians out west. His fortune increased rapidly, to the point that he organized his own bank in 1882 of which he was president and sole owner. The following year, Stafford realized that he and his fellow stockmen could make more money off their beeves by shipping dressed, chilled beef to distant markets than by driving live cows up the long and arduous Chisholm Trail. He organized the Columbus, Texas Meat and Ice Co. and became its president. The Columbus, Texas Meat and Ice Co. built a $250,000 three-story plant on the site of the old Robson Castle in 1884. At the time, it was one of only three packing houses in Texas. The plant could process either 125 or 250 head of cattle per day, depending on who you believe, and could make 40 tons of ice daily. The company filled an order for an English syndicate and also shipped dressed carcasses to Chicago, New Orleans, Galveston, and other points via the new refrigerated rail cars that were the wonder of the age. The plant closed in 1891 and was later torn down.

In 1889, a group of progress-minded Colorado County citizens decided that the little 1855 courthouse no longer befitted a town of Columbus's stature and they persuaded county commissioners to build a new one. Despite considerable opposition from county citizens who lived outside Columbus, the commissioners went ahead with their plans. But the project was plagued by delays. Citizens demanded that the brick be manufactured in Colorado County, so the schedule was relaxed. By April 1890, the foundation had finally been poured. The county decided to incorporate the laying of the new courthouse's cornerstone into the county's traditional July 4th celebration. But that date couldn't be met, so it was delayed until July 7, 1890. At 11 that morning, about 3,000 folks from around the county began gathering on the north side of Columbus for a barbecue. About 5 that afternoon, they assembled in parade formation and marched down Milam Street to the courthouse square. The Masons of Caledonia Lodge #68 conducted the cornerstone laying and ceremony, and then the group paraded back to the barbecue grounds. At this point, the crowd began to disperse. Many went off to prepare for the big dance to be held that night at the Opera House. But about an hour before the dance was scheduled to start, Opera House owner Bob Stafford got into an argument with city marshal Larkin Hope, who was Sheriff Townsend's son-in-law. What transpired between them depends on whose side you're on, and some folks in Columbus still take sides over 100 years later. At any rate, the argument ended when Larkin Hope and his brother Marion shot and killed Bob Stafford and his brother John.

There was considerable outrage over the killings, and many called for Townsend's removal, but this was not effected until his death several years later. But the feud did not cease then; it expanded and drew in new participants. By 1899, there had been so much bloodshed here that the place was called "Hell's Half-Acre" and many travelers skirted the town altogether for years thereafter. By 1906, things were so bad that the citizens of Columbus voted to abolish their town charter (Columbus had incorporated in 1866), and a Texas Ranger was permanently stationed here to keep the peace. With that, the feud was pretty much over, at least the shooting part. Eight men had died in the process.

But this period of trial and tribulation was not without its humorous incidents. At the north end of Columbus, the Colorado River makes a big loop north, returning to the south end of Columbus some six miles later. One day a man robbed a store in town and escaped down to the river, where he commandeered a boat and made clean his getaway. After miles of rowing he came to a town, which he supposed to be Wharton, whereupon he got out of the boat with his loot and proceeded to walk downtown to peddle his heisted goods to the unsuspecting citizens. Almost as soon as he had set up shop on a street corner, he was accosted by the sheriff of Columbus. The hapless criminal had rowed down-river right back to the scene of his crime.

More recently, the gravel and oil industries have supplanted Colorado County's traditional sources of agricultural income.

Today Columbus is considerably more peaceful but a person brought up in those wild and woolly days would not have too much trouble finding his or her way around, so much remains of old Columbus—enough, in fact, to merit a small book all its own.

From the western outskirts of Columbus, continue east on US 90 past the old city cemetery where most of the county's illustrious early settlers now rest. Among them are W. B. Dewees, Dr. John G. Logue (founder of Texas' first drug store), and Dilue Rose Harris (famous for her reminiscences of early life in Texas). US 90 becomes Walnut once you are in Columbus. The courthouse square is located 6 blocks west of the US 90/SH 71 intersection at Walnut and Milam.

COLORADO COUNTY COURTHOUSE

Walnut and Milam • 732-2604 • Monday through Friday • W

Built of locally made brick with Belton limestone trim in the Second Empire style, this is the courthouse whose cornerstone played a catalyst role on the bloody day of July 7, 1890. In November 1890, the commissioners voted to install a clock in the tower. Even this caused controversy. The city of Columbus provided about 25 percent of the purchase price and an employee to maintain it, but many rural Colorado Countians were against the "Columbus town clock," saying among other things that the county paid too much for it. The courthouse was finally completed in February 1891, and a grand ball on February 24 inaugurated it. The neoclassical copper dome that now tops the courthouse replaced the original bell tower, which was knocked to the ground by the hurricane of 1909. The clock was never replaced, and so the clockwinder lost his $15-a-month job.

Step inside for a look at the District Courtroom, most notable for its Tiffany-style stained-glass dome and matching lampshade. The courtroom looks just as it did when first built, down to the hardbacked wooden spectator benches, pine wainscoting, and wreathed ceiling. Stained-glass enthusiasts come from all over the country to see the dome.

OLD WATER TOWER

Courthouse square, Spring and Milam • Open the first and third Thursdays and third Saturday of month, during Magnolia Days (third weekend in May), and by appointment • Admission Currently houses museum • W variable

Located on the southwest corner of the courthouse square is the old water tower. The tower was built in 1883 using 400,000 bricks. A wooden water tank up top and a horse-drawn firewagon beneath comprised Columbus' first fire department. The tower served in that capacity until 1912. The town tried to demolish it a few years later, but the 32-inch-thick walls proved indestructible. In 1926 it became the local **Daughters of the Confederacy museum.**

STAFFORD OPERA HOUSE AND COLUMBUS CHAMBER OF COMMERCE
425 Spring at Milam • 732-5881 • Monday through Friday • W

Located across from the courthouse and next to the Bob Stafford house is the Stafford Opera House, built by Bob Stafford in 1886 for the princely sum of $50,000. Stafford acquired the property after fire destroyed Bond's Hotel, which had previously occupied this corner. He planned to build two commercial buildings, but was asked by local citizens to build something large enough to host theatrical productions and other social events. Stafford acceded to their wishes, and prominent Galveston architect Nicholas J. Clayton designed the opera house in the French Second Empire style. The bricks were made south of town. Bob's Stafford Bank (capitalized at $50,000) and the Senftenberg Mercantile Co. occupied the first floor, with the elaborate Opera House upstairs. It was lit by bottled-gas-burning chandeliers. The curtain, wings, and additional stage equipment cost Stafford an additional $10,000. One thousand people filled the hall on opening night; special trains were run to bring in folk from surrounding counties. It is said that Stafford could watch the shows from his bedroom next door. The marble cornerstone of "R. E. Stafford's Building," depicting a steer roped by the horns, the rope being held by a single right hand, is one of the more unusual cornerstones you'll ever see. After Stafford's death, the bank, store, and opera house continued to operate in the same manner until the building was sold in 1916. The last show upstairs was held in 1916. The first floor housed the local Ford dealership from 1918 to 1974. The upstairs was used as a boxing arena, for basketball games, and as a roller-skating rink. The stage was torn out in World War II and the area converted into eight apartments in response to the wartime housing shortage. Finally it became a tire-storage area.

Preservation-minded citizens purchased the building in 1972 for $30,000 and began restoring it in 1975; $1.3 million later, the Opera House is once more a community and cultural center. Plays and other live entertainment are presented on a regular basis. The Chamber of Commerce offices are located downstairs. Here you can obtain information about Opera House events and tours, as well as a variety of informative local literature including self-guided tours of historic Columbus. Guided tours of historic Columbus are given on the first and third Thursdays and third Saturday of each month. There are over 70 historical markers scattered about town.

R. E. "BOB" STAFFORD HOUSE
400 block of Spring, next to the opera house • Private residence
Stafford built his residence next door to his bank and opera house. This two-story, cypress-and-pine frame house with a cupola on top is a good example of the Carpenter Gothic style, with ornate, jigsaw-cut porch-column brackets, fascia, and balustrades. At the time of his murder, Bob Stafford's range extended from Colorado County to the Gulf of Mexico, and his herd numbered somewhere between 50,000 and 75,000 head. He had a horse ranch in Presidio County and about 90,000 acres of various properties in other counties and in the San Antonio area.

COURTHOUSE OAK
Walnut at Travis
The last few years have not been kind to this once majestic historic live oak. It is now just a stump with some sawed-off branches, reminding the viewer of a human heart.

From the Stafford Opera House, head north on Milam.

EHRENWERTH-RAMSEY-UNTERMEYER BUILDING
1120 Milam
Built in 1875 with bricks from a local kiln and one of Columbus's oldest commercial buildings, this is about the most elaborate business structure downtown. Ehrenwerth built it to house his mercantile store, but it housed L. G. Smith's Red Elk Saloon and Gambling Hall during the 1880s. The Untermeyer Hardware Store was here for nearly 70 years, beginning in 1925. The building was recently restored and renovated as a community hall.

BRUNSON BUILDING
1014 Milam • Currently houses the Live Oak Arts Center
Charles Brunson built the building which bears his name in 1891. A native of Westphalia, Germany, Brunson came to the U.S. in 1845 at age 15. After driving stagecoaches and mule teams for years, he settled in Columbus in 1866 and went into the saloon business, at which he prospered. In the early days, the second story of his saloon served as an opera house/theater. In 1896 he built the structure at **1010 Milam,** which was later known as the **Waldvogel building.** The Brunson building was used as a saloon until Prohibition, and has since housed a variety of businesses. Except for the lowering of the

canopy and some changes in the windows, it has maintained its original style, down to the cast-iron porch columns and step-up out front.

PRESTON KYLE SHATTO WILDLIFE MUSEUM
1002 Milam • 732-2664 • Open first and third Thursdays, third Saturday each month
Wildlife from around the world are on display; the collection was gathered over the years by two local families. There are more than 65 species from North America, Africa, Australia, and New Zealand, ranging from bull elk to elephant, rhinoceros, lion, leopard, and cape buffalo.

HANCOCK-HELLER HOME
934 Milam • Private residence
One of Columbus' more unique homes is the Hancock-Heller home. It was built in 1865 by county tax collector John Hancock as a simple one-story dogtrot house with cypress walls and cedar floors. The house received its current, radical face-lift in 1884, when another owner added the gable with its sinfully rich scrollwork bargeboards, the equally elaborate porch fascia, the lacy porch-column brackets, and the ball-and-spindle porch balustrade. Seldom do you see so much gingerbread on a small one-story house. You gain weight just looking at it.

SIMPSON-YOUENS-HOPKINS HOUSE
617 Milam • Private residence
Joseph Hopkins had this cottage built sometime after the Civil War. James Simpson, the county's first banker, bought it in 1875. It has a local-brick foundation, and is constructed of pine and cypress. Cypress is a very durable wood, especially impervious to moisture, and you'll find that cypress and cedar were used extensively in many of the old homes still standing today.

Double back to Walnut, then turn right on Walnut to reach the next two attractions.

ILSE-RAU HOME/RAUMONDA
1100 Bowie at Walnut • B&B Inn; also open for tours the first and third Thursday of each month and during Magnolia Homes Tour the third weekend in May • Admission • W variable

Another of Columbus' showcase homes is the graceful Ilse-Rau home, built by farmer-rancher-saloonkeeper Henry Ilse in 1887. Constructed in a symmetric Carpenter Gothic style, the two-story home is cypress with wood floors, and a roof of stamped-metal rectangles. The porch balustrades are of an elaborate interlocking circle design.

SENFTENBERG-BRANDON HOUSE MUSEUM
616 Walnut (US 90), between Bowie and Live Oak
This house started as a simple one-story, four-room Greek Revival cottage with four fireplaces and a basement made of handmade brick. It was remodeled by the Senftenberg family in the 1880s to its present two-story ornate Victorian appearance. Kenneth Brandon bought the house in 1900 and added the northeast wing. The basement is made of locally made brick. The house was acquired by the Magnolia Homes Tour, Inc., in 1968 and is a museum that depicts life in Columbus in the late nineteenth century and includes many antique items donated by local families, including crazy quilts from the Bob Stafford family.

Now take Live Oak back to Spring, where you turn left, past the Townsend-West-Stiles home.

TOWNSEND-WEST-STILES HOME
634 Spring • 732-2726 • B&B Inn (see Lodging)
This Eastlake-style house was built in 1890 for Marcus and Annie Burford Townsend on the site of the old Southern Pacific Railway Hospital, which burned down in 1886. Marcus was one of the principals in the Stafford-Townsend feud; he served as state representative from 1883–85, and state senator from 1889–93. Townsend's main legislative accomplishments amounted to sponsoring the bill for the state to buy the Alamo and another bill to name a county after his law partner, Robert Foard. Built in the shape of a cross, it features ornate lacy gingerbread trim along the roofline and gables, ball-and-spindle porch balustrade, intricately carved doors and woodwork and stained-glass windows. The house also features 10-foot-tall windows that go to the floor; some say Townsend had the windows installed that way so that he could easily watch for potential assailants. Thurman West bought the place from Townsend in 1906, and the West family occupied the house until 1989.

Head back toward the courthouse square. At Bowie, turn right to reach the Alley Log Cabin, Dilue Rose Harris House, and Mary Elizabeth Hopkins Santa Claus Museum.

ALLEY LOG CABIN
200 block Bowie • Open Thursday through Saturday and during Magnolia Homes Tour the third weekend in May

In 1822, 18-year-old Abraham Alley and three brothers came to Texas from Missouri to join their older brother, Rawson, who had settled in Colorado County the year before as a member of Austin's "Old Three Hundred." A farmer, Abraham also participated in several campaigns against the Waco, Tawakoni, and Comanche Indians as far away as San Saba during the 1820s. Alley built this cabin from oak logs in late 1836 to replace the cabin burned during the Runaway Scrape; he and wife Nancy raised five children in it. The cabin was moved here from its original site at Alleyton in 1976. It is furnished with period antiques. Alleyton was named for the Alley brothers, all of whom settled near each other about three miles east of Columbus. Brother William donated land for the townsite in 1859. In 1860, Alleyton became the terminus of the Buffalo Bayou, Brazos, and Colorado and was briefly the biggest town in the county.

DILUE ROSE HARRIS HOUSE MUSEUM
602 Washington • Open first and third Thursdays, third Saturday each month • Admission

Dilue Rose Harris came to Texas as a young girl in 1833. She married Ira Harris in 1839 at the tender age of 13 and they moved to Columbus in 1845. Ira served as county sheriff and city marshal. They built this house in 1858. It has masonry walls of gravel and lime, plastered over and scored to resemble stone blocks, and is decidedly uncharacteristic of the era. Ira died in 1869, leaving her and nine children behind. Intimately acquainted with the leaders of the Texas Revolution and the Republic, she wrote extensively of her early life in Texas. Her reminiscences have been heavily relied on by historians since. The house is filled with personal effects and period furnishings. She died in nearby Eagle Lake in 1914.

MARY ELIZABETH HOPKINS SANTA CLAUS MUSEUM
604 Washington • 732-5135 • Open Thursday through Saturday Admission

Over 2,000 Santas are here on display. There are Santa music boxes, banks, creamers, pitchers, salt and pepper shakers, cookie jars, and homemade Santas. The collection memorializes Mary Elizabeth Hopkins, who got her first Santa in 1913. After her death in 1990, her husband donated the collection to the Magnolia Homes Tour, Inc., which led to creation of the museum. Call for group tours.

NESBITT MEMORIAL LIBRARY
529 Washington • 732-3392
This public library is enhanced by a collection of old dolls and kids' toys donated by Miss Lee Nesbitt. The library is also notable for its Texas history and genealogy archives.

OTHER ATTRACTIONS

KEITH-TRAYLOR HOUSE MUSEUM
806 Live Oak
This gingerbread-festooned cottage was built around 1871 by John Keith, a Civil War veteran who moved here in 1870 and became a lumber dealer. Charles and Lura Traylor bought it in 1875. In 1896, one of the Traylor daughters married a son of the Keith family in the same room of the house that both were born in.

TAIT TOWN HOUSE
526 Wallace
Born in Georgia, Dr. Charles Tait (1815–1878) came to Texas from Alabama in 1844. A former U.S. Navy surgeon who also had a civil engineering degree, Tait surveyed land for a railroad company and was paid with a 6,000-acre tract of land south of Columbus. He used the land to establish a plantation he called Sylvania that was headquartered about 10 miles south of Columbus. The plantation grew corn, cotton, and cane, and produced lime. Slaves hewed the logs and fired brick in the plantation's kiln that they used to build the plantation house in 1847. Tait found the time to fight in the Mexican War of 1846–48, serving as surgeon with Jack Hay's Texas Mounted Cavalry. In 1848, he married Louisa Williams of Bastrop. He was elected to the state legislature in 1853 and 1855. But by 1856, Tait had decided to move his family into town; he felt that the damp river-bottom climate was dangerous to their health, and he wanted his children to attend a good school. So construction began in 1856 on a town house located on a 640-acre tract on the edge of Columbus.

Bricks for the two-story Greek Revival house were made at the plantation. Stone quarried there formed the foundation. The lumber came from trees cut at Sylvania; they were cut into lumber by a saw powered by the engine of a small steamboat that had gotten stuck in the silt-laden Colorado River near the plantation. The *Moccasin Belle* had carried Tait's cotton to Galveston. Tait bought the marooned boat and salvaged what he could. The pine flooring and window frames came by boat from Bastrop. The family moved into the house in 1859, but it wasn't finished until Dr. Tait returned from service with the Confederate Army. From the high "widow's walk," Tait could see all the way to his plantation. Dr. Tait died in 1878, but members of the family have continued to live in the house ever since. The anchor from the *Moccasin Belle* still sits in the front yard.

MONTGOMERY HOUSE
1419 Milam
This L-shaped cottage was built in 1867 by land agent A. J. Gallilee. It has a handmade brick foundation, native oak sills, and pine flooring. The siding, doors, and window shutters are cypress. J. T. and Fanny Montgomery bought it in 1876.

SECOND-LARGEST LIVE OAK
1218 Walnut
This venerable, low-spreading tree is recognized as the second-largest recorded live oak in Texas by the Texas Forest Service. It is also recorded in their Registry of Champion Big Trees in Texas. It tops out at 75 feet and has a trunk circumference of 310 inches.

DINING

About the best place to eat in Columbus is Schobel's. To get there, take Milam south, away from the courthouse and Walnut/US 90.

SCHOBEL'S RESTAURANT
2020 Milam at SH 71, just north of I-10 • 732-2385
Open daily, breakfast, lunch, and dinner • $ • DC, MC, V • W
Located in a modern prefab building, which fortunately does not reflect upon the downhome food, Schobel's has a basic Texas rural cafe menu: steaks, seafood, fried chicken, and Mexican food. They do serve homemade bread and pie. Beer, wine, and mixed drinks.

HACKEMACK'S HOFBRAUHAUS RESTAURANT
Take SH 71 north to FM 109, then north (right) 10 miles to the restaurant • 732-6321 • Dinner Thursday through Saturday; open Sundays during the summer • $-$$ • MC, V • W

German and American food are served. German dishes include wienerschnitzel (Texas style), beef rouladen, sauerbraten, jagerschnitzel, and the Neu Ulm Bauernschmaus (for the very hungry) with knackwurst, bratwurst, Texas wurst, jagerschnitzel, kraut, potatoes, rye bread, and salad.

LODGING

The Columbus area has a number of B&Bs. Call the B&B Registry at 732-5135 for current establishments and reservations.

GANT HOUSE
926 Bowie • 732-2190 • $$$

German cottage built in 1860 with original wall stenciling and decorative painting. It's been featured in *Country Living,* and the stenciling in one room was copied for the Texas Room in the DAR Museum in Washington, D.C. Two bedrooms with shared bath. No children under 12. No pets. Cable TV. Continental breakfast. Kitchen privileges. Furnished with antiques.

MAGNOLIA OAKS
634 Spring • 732-2726 • $$$-$$$$

This old mansion has six units with private baths. It is shaded by massive trees and is beautifully decorated. Smoking allowed on porches. No credit cards; checks OK.

RAUMONDA
1100 Bowie • 732-2190 • $$$

Three bedrooms, one with private bath. No children under 12. No pets. Cable TV. Enhanced continental breakfast. Juices, other soft drinks, ice in the evening. Furnished with antiques. Outdoor pool.

THE VICTORIAN
1336 Milam • 732-2125 • $$$

This two-story 1883 house with double porches has three units that sleep a total of seven people. Complimentary juices, soft drinks, and wine are available throughout the day. Enjoy a complimentary tour of Columbus. No credit cards; checks OK.

AREA PARKS

BEASON'S PARK
US 90 at Colorado River bridge, east of town • W
This new park has primitive camping and picnic areas, playing fields, swimming in the river, canoeing, and fishing for catfish, perch, gasper goo, and bass.

ATTWATER PRAIRIE CHICKEN
NATIONAL WILDLIFE REFUGE
Take SH 71 south to US 90A, then east to FM 3013 at Eagle Lake, then east (left) about 7 miles to refuge • 234-3021
Open daily dawn to dusk • Free • W variable
During mating season, male prairie chickens make a mating call that sounds like someone blowing across the mouth of a bottle. You can watch this endangered species' mating dance and hear the male's "booming" mating call from late February to early May in this 8,000-acre U.S. Fish and Wildlife Service refuge. Write P.O. Box 518, Eagle Lake 77343.

ANNUAL EVENT

MAY • Springtime Festival • 732-5135 • Third weekend in May
Admission to some events • W
Street dances and live music, antique cars, arts and crafts show, live entertainment at the Stafford Opera House, beer garden, and the famous Magnolia Homes Tour. Each year, several of Columbus's historic old homes and buildings are on public display. Many are private homes that folks would otherwise never get a chance to see.

To leave Columbus, proceed west on Walnut/US 90 from the courthouse square, then turn right on SH 71 toward La Grange.

As you cross the **Colorado River,** you pass by the site of the fabulous Robson castle, located on your right on the south bank of the river. Nothing remains of the castle.

A little more than a half-mile from the river bridge, turn right on FM 109 to Frelsburg.

ZIMMERSCHEIDT SCHOOL
Zimmerscheidt Community • About 8 miles from SH 71 and 3 miles south of Frelsburg.

At a four-way intersection with unpaved Zimmerscheidt Rd., you'll see on your left a small one-story red frame building, the old Zimmerscheidt School, one of the few one-room schools left standing in Central Texas. In 1855 Frederick Zimmerscheidt donated an acre of land so that a school might be established to educate local children. That school served the community which took on Zimmerscheidt's name from the time of its establishment in 1857 till its consolidation with the Columbus Independent School District in 1948. The building then served as community center until 1962.

FRELSBURG

Colorado County • 75 • About 12 miles from Columbus

Frelsburg was named for John and William Frels, pre-Adelsverein German immigrants who settled here in the early 1830s. There's not much to see or do in Frelsburg these days, but if things had worked out a little differently, Frelsburg might be a bustling college town today. Frelsburg, you see, was to be the home of Hermann's University, an institute of higher learning that would offer German instruction in liberal arts, theology, medicine, and the law. The Republic of Texas Congress chartered the university in 1844 and donated a league of land. The school was to be financed by sales of stock shares, at $50 a pop. But evidently Texans deemed the price too steep, and at any rate the Civil War came along and disrupted plans. Hermann's University was reincorporated in 1870, with $25 shares, a league of land donated by the state in Gillespie County, and an actual building site located at Frelsburg. A two-story building was erected here, but classes were never held. The act of incorporation was repealed in 1871, and the Frelsburg public school inherited the building.

SAINTS PETER AND PAUL CATHOLIC CHURCH
East side of FM 109, 1 mile south of the intersection with FM 1291

Established in 1847 by German Catholics, it is one of the state's oldest Catholic parishes. The current sanctuary was built in 1912 and features ornate statuary.

TRINITY LUTHERAN CHURCH
FM 1291, just off FM 109, several hundred feet west of Frelsburg store

In 1855, William Frels donated land for a cemetery and church. A Lutheran congregation was formed as well as a day school. English-language services were not conducted here until 1932, so over-whelmingly German was the membership.

The present white-frame sanctuary (built in 1927) reflects the basic philosophy of its congregation. The structure is severely straightforward, of minimal physical ornamentation save the gables projecting from the tinned steeple. The steeple is covered with embossed tin, the pattern of which looks like nothing so much as the Pentecostal water-droplet symbol. It is capped by a crucifix resting atop a ball (the earth). Even the stained glass windows are mostly black and white and a somber, severe green. Porch railings are no-nonsense plumbing pipe. The inscription "Evan. Luth. Trinity Congregation Frelsburg" is executed in stained glass over the front entrance.

At Frelsburg, follow FM 109's path east, then north into New Ulm.

Just east of Frelsburg is a handsome, fragrant stand of pines and cedars.

NEW ULM

Austin County • 650 • (409) • About 4 miles from Frelsburg

New Ulm was originally known as Duff's Settlement after James Duff, to whom this land was granted in 1841. After 1845 the area's population became increasingly German, many of them coming here from the previously established communities of Nassau, Shelby, and Industry. They renamed the community after the city of Ulm in Wuerttemberg, Germany. New Ulm has been, and continues to be, a prosperous farming community, with its very own bank. And by virtue of its pioneer architecture, New Ulm is one of Central Texas' most unique communities.

As Texas towns developed during the last half of the nineteenth century, they went through several transformations. Almost always, the first permanent commercial buildings to be erected were small, one-story, wood-framed shotgun affairs. The omnipresent gabled roof was always hidden by a false front. The front entrance was always symmetrically arranged, with centered double doors flanked by single windows or display bays. You've seen these buildings in countless Hollywood westerns, but you hardly ever see them in real life anymore.

Almost universally, time has been harsh to these structures. Those that remain are found only in isolated communities and are usually abandoned and decaying. But in New Ulm, these frontier relics are alive and well. One of Central Texas' most timeless communities, New Ulm is full of turn-of-the-century commercial buildings and farmhouses.

As small as the town is, it's hard to get lost, and it's pretty easy to find places despite the less-than-comprehensive street signing.

Every north-south street that concerns us is marked along FM 1094 (Bastrop, New Ulm's principal east-west artery). In order, from west to east and starting with FM 109 (the principal north-south artery), they are FM 109, Elm, Pecan, Walnut, and Main. Cross streets (running east to west) as you come into New Ulm from Frelsburg are Front, Taylor, and Bastrop (FM 1094).

All of the buildings of interest are within the confines of this 12-block area. The buildings seemingly dot the blocks at random, punctuating the gridded grasslands rather than obliterating them, just as they have done for the last century. In this rare collection, one home stands out from the rest as an exercise in fanciful deception.

FINK HOUSE
Walnut and Bastrop/FM 1094 • Private residence
Built in 1893 for the Fink family, who moved here from Bastrop, this interesting house has a facade in the shingle style of architecture. True shingle-style houses have floor plans that feature irregular rooms freely grouped around a large hall. The rooms open up to each other in a continuous flow of space, and the theme of spatial flow and unity continues outside, with wide porches encircling most of the house. Broad horizontal lines on the exterior emphasize the theme of interior flow by the use of huge, massive roofs, horizontal bands of windows, and the fusion of roof shingles and shingles as wall surface, creating a house with sprawling, lazy lines.

The Fink House features a broad, massive roof that unites with a portholed, shingled front porch, but the floor plan is traditionally symmetrical. Altogether, the house is a unique exercise in Swiss-flavored geometric gingerbread and shingle styling.

Most of commercial New Ulm is vacant (though recently renovated), but a few businesses hang on in the old storefronts. Good examples of the frontier shotgun buildings are located along the first 2 blocks of Taylor east of FM 109, both sides of Pecan in the first block between Front and Taylor (2 blocks east of FM 109), and the fourth block of Front (4 blocks east of FM 109). These locations include both free-standing structures and strings of three or more contiguous buildings. The old creamery complex stands at the corner of Taylor and Main, 4 blocks east of FM 109 and 1 block south of Bastrop/FM 1094.

VOSKAMP MARKET
Pecan and Front • 992-3388 • Monday through Saturday 8–6 • W

Although the Voskamps have run this market for only the last 20 years, the Voskamp name is well-known to area carnivores. Several previous generations tended to the butchering needs of folks in Austin and Fayette Counties. These Voskamps stay busy baking their own cookies, cakes, bread, and pies. Their profit is your gain as well, for these reasonably priced comestibles are made with family care.

Another block and a half east on Front (facing the railroad tracks) is another series of commercial buildings.

This was once a row of six or eight separate though contiguously porched business establishments dating to 1894, one of which happened to be the local undertaker's. Although all the buildings were pretty much the same in size and shape, distinct identities were achieved via variations in the contiguous false fronts—a step here, a pediment there. Only about half the row stands today—several of the buildings were torn down to make room for a beer garden. The remaining structures, including the old funeral parlor, have been left largely intact.

To reach Fireman's Park, follow the signs from FM 109.

FIREMAN'S PARK
One mile west of town on Taylor • Open during daylight hours Free • W

This park/baseball diamond/picnic area is quiet, secluded, shaded, and big enough to let the kids run around in. Community baseball league games every Sunday afternoon in the summer.

Retrace your route back to town from the park. Continue north on FM 109 from New Ulm to Industry.

As you leave New Ulm, you will notice more of New Ulm's old homes and the **Lutheran church** atop the gently rising hill to your left.

INDUSTRY

Austin County • 475 • About 6 miles from New Ulm
Industry can properly be regarded as the first German settlement in Texas, and the beginning of the great German migrations to Texas can properly be dated to the 1831 arrival of Friedrich Ernst and Charles Fordtran. Ernst, a former postal clerk, and Fordtran, a tanner from Westphalia, met in New York and joined forces to find a new home. Their search led them to Texas, where Ernst, as a married man with a family, was eligible for a full league of land in Austin's colony. The single Fordtran was eligible for only one-quarter league. The two settled as neighbors here in the Mill Creek valley, in the northwest corner of present-day Austin County. Ernst, the "Father of German Immigration in Texas," was ill-prepared for his new pioneer lifestyle. He did not know how to build a cabin, hated guns, and had brought none of the equipment necessary for clothing his family out here on the fringe of civilization. Still, he had a boundless love for his new homeland with its rich soil, mild climate, political freedom, and unlimited opportunities. He poured out all these feelings in an eloquent letter to a friend back home in Oldenburg. The friend passed Ernst's letter to a friend, who copied the letter and passed it on to others, who did the same. Ernst's enthusiasm spread to the letter's many readers, and the stream of German migration to Texas commenced.

Meanwhile, Ernst and Fordtran were adapting to life out here on the frontier and beginning to prosper. Ernst laid out a townsite on his land in 1838. He had invited all German immigrants who so desired to stop at his estate until they had selected land of their own. A number of them chose to settle down here. Some of these visitors suggested that Ernst make cigars from the tobacco grown in his garden, and the cigar-making industry that developed gave the town its name. The industrious Germans would spend their lunch breaks from the fields rolling cigars; their Anglo American neighbors were so impressed with the Germans' industriousness that they referred to the village accordingly.

Industry also prospered as a farm community, with its own gin and sawmill, well into the twentieth century. Today Industry is a quiet collection of farmhouses, ranch and feed stores, a gas station and convenience store or two.

To get to the heart of old downtown Industry, turn right off FM 109 onto Main, the first street after the FM 109/SH 159 intersection, by the post office.

WEIGE BUILDING
Main St., 1 block north of SH 159

The Weige building, on your left, was built in 1888. The Weige Store closed in 1973. A third of the building was detached and moved a short distance away, where it became Assman's Cafe. Before it was detached, it had housed the Industry Bottling Works (1903–1928), which bottled soft drinks. It also contained a saloon then. The bar was still in use when Assman's Cafe burned down several years ago. It was not the first time that fire ravaged downtown Industry. In 1917 the other side of Main St. burned down. The only survivor was the small old wooden store across the street from Weige's Store.

*Continue east on Main to the modern Immaculate Conception Catholic Church to see the "East End" of old Industry. Of the various old houses strung out along this section of Main, the most interesting is the **Schramm House,** which is also the last house, as the town plays out, located at the corner of Main and the first cross street running to your right, just before you reach the cotton gin, and then Immaculate Conception Church.*

SCHRAMM HOUSE
Private Residence

This large two-story white frame house with the massive pillared plantation-style front porch, was built by German businessman C. C. Koch in the 1860s. After his death in 1891, his widow converted the house into a hotel. It reverted to a family residence in 1908. A detached building behind the house (you can see it as you double back into town) is supposedly a pre-Civil War kitchen, back when kitchens were separated from the rest of the house because of possible fire hazard.

From Immaculate Conception Church, backtrack on Main, past the Weige Building, to the intersection with FM 109. The little white frame shotgun building you see on your right, across from Firemen's Park and just before you pass Bermuda Street, is the old saddle shop of Ferdinand Ernst, grandson of Friedrich Ernst. Later it was a weekend meat market.

Continue west on Main to see the "West End" of old Industry. Follow the sign, to your right, to **Industry Methodist Church.**

The simple whitewashed wooden sanctuary behind the newer church was built in 1867. Men from the congregation did most of the construction work, since hard money to pay professional carpenters was almost nonexistent after the Civil War. The adjacent **Pilgrims' Rest Cemetery** offers one of the best panoramic views of the bucolic countryside in Austin County. Friedrich Ernst's widow and children are buried here. Farther west on Main, after you cross FM 159, is the 1899 **Lindemann Home** and store, and a historical marker describing the family's prominent role in Industry's business life. The old, rusting, corrugated metal shed next to Zaskoda Funeral Chapel was Industry's last blacksmith shop. It closed in 1972.

INDUSTRY POST OFFICE
Friedrich Ernst Park, just off FM 109, about 0.5 mile north of FM 109/FM 159 intersection; turn left at "Historic Site" sign Always open • No admission • W

As best as anyone can tell, this small, one-room rock building was built from locally quarried stone in 1838 as a store for Friedrich Ernst and his son-in-law, John Sieper. It was also the area post office, supposedly the first post office in Texas west of Galveston. The adjoining park is a good picnic spot.

From Ernst Park, return to the FM 109/FM 159 intersection. Head west on FM 159 (toward Fayetteville and La Grange).

In 2.5 miles, turn right onto FM 1457 toward Shelby.

ECKERMANN'S MEAT MARKET
FM 1457, about 4.5 miles from Industry • 836-8858 • Open Monday–Friday 8–12, 1–5; Saturday 8–3 • W

It seems like every neighborhood big enough to have a name in this part of Texas has a meat market or a local sausagemaker, and Shelby is no exception. Eckermann's makes two kinds of pork/beef sausage (one with garlic, one without), liver sausage, bacon, and ham, all locally popular. If you want to cook your sausage the way the natives do, try this recipe, given me by Shelby's master sausage chef, who has been doing it for over 30 years at Shelby's annual wingding.

Place sausage links in large pot with enough water to cover. To the water, add a couple of bay leaves, garlic, the juice of a couple of fresh lemons, and a couple of tablespoons of pickling spice tied up in cheesecloth. Simmer slowly for an hour and a half. Do not bring to a hard boil or you'll split the sausage casings. It's important that the casing not burst, he emphasized. This recipe is good for about 5 lbs. of sausage. Adjust accordingly for larger or smaller portions.

SHELBY

Austin County • 175 • (409) • About 6.5 miles from Industry

Shelby owes its name to David Shelby, who settled here in 1822 as one of Stephen F. Austin's "Old Three Hundred." (The Old Three Hundred were the settlers who filled Austin's quota of 300 families to settle his first land grant.) But the village did not really come into existence until Otto von Roeder built a gristmill, which acted as a magnet to prospective settlers. The village took on a decidedly German flavor after 1845, being known for a time as Rödersmühle. David Shelby became the village's first postmaster in 1846. The Germans' desire for a cultured life led to the founding of an agricultural society, singing society, school, and band by the start of the Civil War. Shelby had 200 residents and a dozen businesses by 1900. By 1940, the number of commercial establishments was down to seven. Today there are two, as the farm life has given way to the city.

The cemetery is nice, with its collection of graceful cedars and German tombstones, and there are a couple of aging gabled Victorian farmhouses, but not much else here.

The rustic log chapel was built in 1988, but gives you an idea of how the early churches looked. Just a few yards down FM 389 (to your left), you'll see the whitewashed **Harmonie Hall.** The Harmonie (singing) Society was established here in 1875, and began work on this hall soon after. Every German community of any size had a Harmonie Society or something like it, and they all built sprawling wooden pavilions like this in which to hold their functions. This hall is still used; its events include a spring antique show that draws dealers from all over the state.

About 3 miles west of Shelby on FM 1457, you see a historical marker, which tells the story of the Nassau Farm and the early days of the Adelsverein.

NASSAU FARM HISTORICAL MARKER
FM 1457 • About 3 miles from Shelby

Books and novels about Texas had captured the fancy of Germans by 1842, among them 14 noblemen who met to form an informal society "for the purpose of purchasing landed property in the Republic of Texas." The very same day they met to organize—April 20, 1842—the nobles decided to send two of their group as delegates to Texas to investigate firsthand the land, the people, and the climate, and to report back to the society on their findings. Counts Boos-Waldeck and Victor Leiningen left for Texas in May.

In February 1842, Sam Houston, the President of the Republic of Texas, had been authorized by the Congress to grant, under certain conditions, entire tracts of land to contractors who would colonize the land as stipulated by law. Count Leiningen negotiated with President Houston, but being inexperienced in legal matters and lacking in counsel, he made demands that could not be granted without nullifying the legality of the contract, changes that even the president could not make.

The Congress did not see fit to alter its colonization law to fit Leiningen's desires. Leiningen was intransigent, so no agreement was reached. But when he returned to Germany in 1843, Leiningen submitted a *favorable* report for a large-scale colonization project.

Meanwhile, Count Boos-Waldeck had acquired a beautiful league of land in Fayette County with rich soil, good water, and heavy forests. The 4,428 acres had cost a little over $3,000; the big house, outbuildings, slaves, and equipment were to cost another $18,000. The Nassau Farm was the showplace of the region. Boos-Waldeck returned to Germany in January 1844 opposing large-scale colonization because of insufficient funds. His advice went unheeded.

Count Castell, one of the society's leaders, had grandiose plans for an enterprise like the British East India Company. By July 1843 a joint stock company had been formed "for the purchase and colonization of land-grants in the Republic of Texas."

That summer society members had been approached by one Alexander Bourgeois d'Orvanne, a French flimflam man who, with his wealth of Texas knowledge, soon gained the confidence of the society's directors. The commoner Bourgeois had added the title "d'Orvanne" to his name in order to facilitate his approach to the

Society of German noblemen. By mid-September 1843, he had conned the society into the tentative purchase of his colonization rights in Texas, although the rights were to expire only three months later. His contract with the Republic had called for the arrival of 400 families in Texas within an 18-month period, but it expired in December 1843 without his having settled a single colonist. At that time "d'Orvanne" had not yet moved the slow-acting German nobles to final purchase of his contract, either.

By the time the nobles finally ratified the purchase agreement in April 1844, d'Orvanne no longer had any colonization rights to sell. But the nobles knew nothing of this; in the six months spent mulling over the purchase they had apparently failed to inform themselves fully of the contract's ramifications. Any hope of negotiating an extension on the contract was lost by February 1, 1844, for the Texas Congress had passed a law nullifying all unfulfilled contracts and prohibiting any extensions favorable to the contractors. If Castell and Leiningen, the society's major leaders, knew anything of this law, they probably expected the society's good reputation to ensure renewal of the d'Orvanne contract.

By the time the society was officially chartered as the Adelsverein on May 3, 1844, d'Orvanne was colonial director for the organization, at the disposal of the commissioner general, Prince Carl of Solms-Braunfels. Both men left for Texas later that month.

Once in Texas, d'Orvanne pleaded with President Houston for a contract extension but in vain. It didn't take Prince Carl long to catch on to the true state of affairs, and he wrote back to Germany telling of the difficult situation he was in: the arrival of immigrants was expected soon and there was no land on which to settle them.

By this time the society had been approached by another con artist, Henry Fisher, who talked the nobles into buying *his* colonization contract, the infamous Fisher-Miller contract, for $9,000. Again, the society had neglected to find out what it was getting itself into. Meanwhile, d'Orvanne was canned unceremoniously in August 1844.

Under terms of the Fisher-Miller contract, the society was bound by law to settle 6,000 immigrants on land that was 300 miles from the coast, 150 miles from the closest settlement, completely unexplored, and in the hands of hostile Indians. The Adelsverein believed it held title to the land; all it really held was the right to settle the land. It was responsible for surveying the land and dealing with the Indians. The nobles did not know it at the time, but they had acquired an albatross, and Messrs. Fisher and Miller had extricated themselves from an impossible-to-fulfill contract, with $9,000 to boot.

Nassau Farm remained in the hands of the Adelsverein and would have made an ideal mid-journey way station for the German immigrants bound for the interior of Texas, but Prince Carl rejected this idea. He feared that the plantation's close proximity to non-German settlements would cause the immigrants to lose their native culture. For the first way station north, he chose instead the tract of land we now call New Braunfels. Prince Carl did, however, use the Nassau Farm as a place for personal rest and recreation, especially horse racing. The big house, two stories of solid oak, had two glass windows from the beginning, and glass was a true frontier luxury. Prince Carl's successor as commissioner general, John Meusebach, also used the farm as a vacation spot. When the Adelsverein went bankrupt in 1848, the Nassau Farm was sold to Otto von Roeder, who sold some of the land and eventually lost the rest in a lawsuit. Thereafter, the farm was gradually broken down into smaller plots. All that remains today are the old cemetery and two large, weathered barns which stand atop the high hill to the south of the historical marker. They are easily visible from the road, but are on private property.

Turn right on FM 2714 to reach Winedale.

WINEDALE

Fayette County • (409) • About 7 miles from Shelby

Although the Nassau Farm was never used by the Adelsverein for colonization, it nonetheless acted as a magnet to many German immigrants, who settled in the fertile rolling countryside surrounding the plantation. Winedale was founded by one of those German settlers, Charles Windewehen, about 1870. The village's original name of Truebsal—"trouble" in English—was changed to Winedale because of the wine industry that resulted from abundant crops of grapes.

WINEDALE HISTORICAL CENTER
FM 2714 • 278-3530 • Weekday tours by appointment year-round • Weekend tours May through October: Saturday 10–6, Sunday 12–6; November through April: Saturday 9–5, Sunday 12–5 • Admission • W variable

Today Winedale is best known as home of the Winedale Historical Center and the annual summer Shakespeare workshops taught by UT professor James Ayres. The historical center is a collection of restored farm buildings and their furnishings, donated by the late philanthropist Miss Ima Hogg to the University of Texas in 1965. The centerpiece is the **Lewis House.** It was originally built by William Townsend about 1834 as a one-room cabin with a sleeping loft, using locally cut cedar timber. Sam Lewis acquired the property in 1848 and enlarged the cabin to its present state sometime during the 1850s. With two stories, eight rooms, a galleried porch across the front, and a dogtrot through the center, the building reflects both Anglo American and German influences. The room arrangement, with a wide central hall and double gallery, is typically southern, while the steeply pitched roof, small windows, and other structural details reflect the work of German craftsmen.

The Lewis House's most outstanding feature is the decorative painting found inside, executed by the locally renowned Rudolph Melchior. A successful artist in Germany, Melchior immigrated to Texas in 1853. Two of the rooms contain his stenciled borders and freehand overmantle paintings. One of the rooms also contains a ceiling painting full of neoclassic details—medallions containing symbols of the four seasons and in the center a green parrot.

The Lewis place became a stage stop and popular overnight stop for travelers when the public road from Brenham to La Grange was relocated to run past the Lewis farm in 1859. Joseph Wagner bought the house and surrounding farmland in 1882.

Miss Ima acquired the property in 1963 and supervised the painstaking restoration of the Lewis home and two handsome barns. The larger barn was converted into the present theater. Several more buildings were added after 1965.

Behind the Lewis House are a log kitchen and smoke house moved to Winedale during restoration and placed on the sites of similar structures which were torn down in the 1920s. A nineteenth century vegetable and flower garden faces the buildings. The theatre barn was built in 1894 from cedar beams salvaged from an animal-powered cotton gin dating to the 1850s. It served as Wagner's hay barn. The other barn was for the animals. **Hazel's Lone Oak Cottage** is a typical Texas dogtrot home, built about 1855 by German immigrant Franz Gaentschke on Jack's Creek, about two miles south of Winedale. It was moved here in 1965, the gift of Miss Ima's friend, Mrs. Hazel Ledbetter.

The **McGregor-Grimm House** is a two-story Greek Revival farmhouse built in 1861 by Washington County planter and land speculator Dr. Gregor McGregor for his bride, Anna Portia Fordtran. It was moved here in 1967 from the Wesley community, 15 miles to the east, and has been furnished to reflect the lifestyle of a wealthy Anglo-German family of the Anglo-German family of the 1860s. The rooms contain several more examples of decorative wall stencilling and painting believed to have been done by Rudolph Melchior.

The **Lauderdale house,** an 1858 Greek Revival farmhouse, was brought from Somerville to serve as a dormitory and conference center. It burned to the ground in the fall of 1981; only the twin brick chimneys are left standing.

Picnic tables are located behind the theatre barn in the shade of four large post-oak trees where black tenant farmers had an outdoor dancing platform at the turn of the century. A self-guiding nature trail along which native Texas trees and plants are identified begins here. It takes about an hour to walk.

Visitors should first report to the office across the road, where a library and gift shop are also located.

Call for tour information or appointments or write Winedale Historical Center, P.O. Box 11, Round Top 78954.

ANNUAL EVENTS

MARCH • Spring Festival and Texas Craft Exhibition Winedale Historical Center (see above) • 278-3530 Third or fourth weekend in March • W variable

Features traditional German/Texas crafts and the best in contemporary crafts (juried show, by invitation). Watch demonstrations of blacksmithing, soapmaking, quilting, gooseplucking, and more. Live folk music, food served on grounds. A traditional German play opens the festival on Friday night.

APRIL or MAY • Eeyore's Birthday • Winedale Historical Center (see above) • 278-3530 • End of April or beginning of May • Free

University of Texas students began the tradition of celebrating the rites of spring in a city park with a party marking the birthday of lonesome Eeyore from *Winnie the Pooh.* Later part of the fun moved to Winedale. Much the milder of the two parties, the Winedale celebration features maypoles, games, and a costume contest.

JULY AND AUGUST • Shakespeare at Winedale • Winedale Historical Center (see above) • 278-3530 • Weekends in late July and August • Write or call Winedale Historical Center for reservations • W

Each summer, a special group of UT-Austin students comes to live Shakespeare out here at Winedale. And at the end of the session, the troupe presents several selections from the master's catalogue, a different program each weekend.

OCTOBER • German Oktoberfest • Winedale Historical Center (see above) • 278-3530 • Early October • Admissiom • W variable
Highlights of the festival include demonstrations of crafts and pioneer skills, tours of restored buildings, and food and music on the grounds.

DECEMBER • Christmas Open House • Winedale Historical Center • Last Sunday before Christmas • Free • W variable
In the beautiful old Lewis house, there's a special cedar tree, live ethnic music, and refreshments to create the spirit of an old-fashioned Christmas. Other center buildings are open.

From Winedale, return to FM 1457, turn right and head for Round Top.

Tidy old German farmhouses dot the gently rolling hills along the way. Just before you enter Round Top, you pass the collection of neatly kept, whitewashed buildings that comprise the Round Top Rifle Association, which has been in existence since 1873.

ROUND TOP

Fayette County • 87 • (409) • About 4 miles from Winedale
Round Top occupies a unique spot in Texas. For many years the state's smallest incorporated city, Round Top has managed to maintain a certain rural German antiquity while resisting both the charm-sapping growth that has plagued Fredericksburg and New Braunfels and the decline that has killed many other German hamlets.

The Townsends were the first white settlers here, and the locality was known as Townsend for several years due to the presence of five families by that name. But the post office created here during the Republic days was known as the Jones post office, after postmaster John Jones, brother of the Republic's postmaster general.

With the coming of the stagecoach, which ran from Goliad to Washington-on-the-Brazos, the area became known as Round Top after the distinctive house with the round top built by German immigrant Alwin Soergel in 1847.

Originally settled by Southern Anglos, many of whom fought in the Texas Revolution, Round Top was heavily German by the Civil War. It was then a prosperous village of 300, including doctors, lawyers, teachers, carpenters, blacksmiths, painters, two ministers, a saddlemaker, a cabinetmaker, a bookbinder, and a cobbler. The town even had a brewery and a cigar factory.

The Round Top Academy operated on the Ledbetter Plantation, located 2 miles northeast, from 1854 until 1867. The curriculum included the three Rs, plus advanced studies in philosophy, chemistry, algebra, Latin, German, Spanish, and French.

Round Top's Lutheran church was organized in January 1861. During the Civil War the town served as Confederate Army recruiting station for northern Fayette County. Round Top contributed two companies—the Round Top Mounted Infantry and the Round Top Guerrillas—to the Confederate war effort. Federal troops were stationed here at war's end. Local citizens organized a community militia to combat postwar lawlessness and applied for a town charter in 1870, which was not approved until 1877.

Round Top continued on as a sleepy little farm town until the 1960s, when Houstonians discovered its charms and began buying up the many old buildings here and restoring them. For a small city, Round Top has an awful lot to see.

FM 1457 dead-ends into FM 237 at the Round Top town square.

ROUND TOP VISITORS CENTER
South side, town square • Open daily

The Visitors Center is built on the ruins of Round Top's first brewery, built in the 1860s. The only original part of the building is the basement, which was carved out of the native sandstone bedrock. Faith P. Bybee, who established the Texas Pioneer Arts Foundation and Henkel Square, bought the property in the 1970s and had a facsimile of the brewery built upon the original foundation. It became the local visitors center in 1995. Inside are information and displays about area history and attractions.

HENKEL SQUARE
FM 1457 • 249-3308 • Open daily noon to 5 • Admission

Henkel Square is a collection of local and imported early Texas structures administered by the Texas Pioneer Arts Foundation. Most of the buildings have been restored both inside and out and are furnished with period pieces. Among the highlights here are the stenciled walls in the **Schumann and Henkel homes,** the bluing walls inside the old Muckleberry log cabin (imported from Frelsburg), and the German-language sign inside the **Haw Creek schoolhouse and church,** which translated into English reads: "I call the living to church and the dead to the grave." "Squire" Henkel laid out the town of Round Top, and his old home is the centerpiece of the collection. For more information about Henkel Square, write P.O. Box 82, Round Top 78954.

BETHLEHEM LUTHERAN CHURCH
Southwest of the town square, 1 block west of FM 237
249-3686 • Open at all times • W variable

Follow the signs and white steeple to the Bethlehem Lutheran Church, built in 1866 of stuccoed native stone. Johann Traugott Wantke built for the church a native-cedar pipe organ, which is still played the fourth Sunday of each month. The church interior features native cedar floors and doors and traditional German Lutheran fittings.

Only three Wantke cedar pipe organs are known to exist, and this one took over two years to build. Wantke built it on the premises. He had no tuning fork, and local legend has it that to tune the organ Wantke would play a note on his piano at home, then scurry down to the church with the note fresh in his mind to tune the corresponding pipe on the organ. Wantke's distinctive one-story stone home still stands just a block north of the church, a block west of FM 237. The old cigar factory stands just a few yards south and east of Wantke's house, a small brown-painted frame building whose back overlooks FM 237. It is inside a white picket fence, in a compound with several other old frame buildings. It still contains the original cigar-making equipment.

ROUND TOP HISTORICAL SOCIETY MUSEUM
SH 237, just off the town square

Opened in 1995, the museum is filled with items of local historical significance.

INTERNATIONAL FESTIVAL-INSTITUTE AT ROUND TOP
SH 237, 0.5 mile north of the town square • 249-2139
Admission • W

The International Festival-Institute at Round Top was founded by American concert pianist James Dick in 1971. The project, which began in a small converted school building on a 6-acre campus, has experienced phenomenal growth under his guidance. Today, the 130-acre campus is dotted with several beautifully restored mansions, gardens and fountains, and the massive, 1,000-seat Festival Concert Hall.

The Institute offers advanced young musicians an intensive summer program that includes individual lessons, master classes, and public performances of chamber, vocal, and orchestral works, as well as seminars on theory, advanced musicology, and music criticism. The faculty includes distinguished musicians and teachers from the

U.S. and abroad. The student body is similarly international. Annual auditions are held in New York, Los Angeles, France, and England. Each student chosen receives a major scholarship.

The Institute has two performance seasons. The first season begins in May, with a Festival of Early Music, followed by the 6-week Summer Institute for Advanced Study and Performance in June and July. During June and July, concerts are presented by festival participants, faculty members, and the Texas Festival Orchestra.

The second, August-to-April benefit season features outstanding faculty members and visiting artists who perform solo and chamber music each month. Proceeds go to the scholarship fund. After the Saturday afternoon concerts, you may wish to stay for dinner and a classic film at the **Menke House.** Rooms in the historic Menke House and attractive studio residences are available as overnight accommodations following the Saturday afternoon concerts. Each room has a private bath and entrance. Breakfast is served Sunday morning in the Menke House dining room. Reservations are necessary.

The Museum Forum is an annual forum on the decorative arts held each September, with speakers drawn from across the country. An outreach program presents an annual series of free concerts for area schoolchildren. A Christmas open house and concert are held in mid-December.

The one-story frame **Clayton House** was built in 1885 near La Grange and was moved here in 1976, where it underwent restoration and enlargement. The C. A. Menke House was built in 1902 at Hempstead and moved here a few years after the Clayton House. The restored house is a tribute to Dick's other passion, the preservation of fine carpentry and woodworking skills. He keeps his in-house crew of local carpenters and craftsman busy these days on the interior of the great concert hall, which features an intricate inlaid, patterned wood ceiling. The latest addition to the Festival-Institute campus is the old **La Grange Methodist Church,** a simple but pleasing wooden Carpenter Gothic building.

Tours of the facility (there is a fee) may be arranged by appointment for any number of people. Write to P.O. Box 89, Round Top 78954, or visit the Web site at http.//www.fais.net/~festinst.

SHOPPING

ROUND TOP GENERAL STORE
SH 237, on the west side of town square • 249-3600
On the square since 1848, the general store now features antiques, gifts, and fudge made on the premises.

WAGNER'S WOODCRAFT
1.5 miles north of town on FM 1457 • 249-5364

Swings, outdoor furniture, and gifts made out of native aromatic cedar feature traditional German craftsmanship by members of a pioneer Round Top family.

DINING

KLUMP'S RESTAURANT
SH 237, on the town square • 249-5696 • Open Tuesday through Sunday breakfast and lunch; Wednesday through Saturday dinner • $ • W

Located in what used to be a tinsmith's shop, Klump's has regular Texas breakfasts, lunch specials, burgers, steaks, catfish, fried chicken, and good Saturday noon barbecue. Good local atmosphere. Beer.

ROYERS' ROUND TOP CAFE
Town square • Open Thursday through Sunday, lunch and dinner • $–$$ • Beer and wine • W

The *Houston Chronicle* has called it the best country cafe in Texas, and the food is good. It's a mix of country and city cooking. Local ingredients are used and the cafe makes its own breads, rolls, pies, and such. Old country standards such as fried steak and grilled porkchops and quail are joined by city favorites like grilled salmon and fresh pastas. Various sandwiches (including a great hamburger), plus soups and salads, round out the menu.

LODGING

GASTE HAUS ROUND TOP
Various locations in Round Top • 249-3308, 259-5781 • $$–$$$ No Cr., checks OK

Operated by the Texas Pioneer Arts Foundation, lodging is offered in three restored area homes. Two are "downtown," the third is slightly out of town. Write to P.O. Box 82, Round Top 78954.

HEART OF MY HEART RANCH
Florida Chapel Rd., off SH 237 • 800-327-1242

All guest rooms in this comfortable Victorian-style home have private baths, and those on the ground floor have separate entrances. Or you can stay in an 1839 log cabin with stone fireplace and complete kitchen. There is a pond you can fish or float in, or you can walk through the woods down to Cummins Creek. In the morning, there's a hearty country breakfast that features locally grown or produced foods. Write to P.O. Box 106, Round Top 78954.

ROUND TOP INN
SH 237, 3 blocks south of the town square • 249-5294
The Inn is a collection of old pioneer buildings (1840–1879) spread out over a city block that have been restored and refurbished with modern conveniences. Seven guest rooms with private baths. Write to P.O. Box 212, Round Top 78954.

ANNUAL EVENTS

JUNE AND JULY • Summer concert series at the International Festival-Institute at Round Top • SH 237, 0.5 mile north of the town square • 249-2139 • Admission • W
During June and July, the Institute hosts the 6-week Summer Institute for Advanced Study and Performance; weekend Festival-Institute Concerts are presented by participants, faculty members, and the Texas Festival Orchestra.

JULY • Fourth of July Celebration • Round Top Rifle Association Hall • July 4 • W
Round Top's celebration of our national day of independence dates back to 1826 and is believed to be the oldest Fourth of July fest west of the Mississippi. These celebrations have been widely publicized since 1851. In 1876, for example, the featured speaker was local Texas Revolution veteran Joel Robison, who transported the captured Santa Anna to General Sam Houston. For his services, Robison received Santa Anna's gold brocaded vest. It became customary for the young men of Fayette County to borrow this vest for their wedding day. But back to the Fourth of July.

These days, the glorious Fourth is marked by a trail ride from Carmine to Round Top, speeches at the town square, and a parade out to the Rifle Association Hall, the start of which is signaled by a shot from the town's Civil War cannon. Barbecue is served at the hall, and the Round Top Brass Band and a variety of polka and country-and-western bands play throughout the day and well into the night.

AUGUST–APRIL • Benefit concert series at the International Festival-Institute at Round Top • SH 237, 0.5 mile north of the town square • 249-2139 • Admission • W

The August-to-April benefit season features outstanding faculty members and visiting artists who perform solo and chamber music each month. Proceeds go to the scholarship fund. After the Saturday afternoon concerts, you may wish to stay for dinner and a classic film at the Menke House. Rooms in the historic Menke House and attractive studio residences are available as overnight accommodations following the Saturday afternoon concerts. Each room has a private bath and entrance. Breakfast is served Sunday morning in the Menke House dining room. Reservations are necessary.

DECEMBER • Round Top Christmas • Downtown • Usually first weekend • 249-4042 • Free • W

Sponsored by the local Do Your Duty Club, the celebration includes Christmas carols, tree lighting, Santa's arrival, open house at local shops, and the Second Shepherds' Play, a medieval English morality play about the birth of Christ. The famous Winedale stew is served before the play.

Leave Round Top via SH 237 south, toward La Grange.

Vintage German farmhouses continue to line the road south of Round Top to Warrenton.

ST. MARTIN'S CHAPEL
SH 237, about 4.5 miles from Round Top on the west side of the road

St. Martin's Chapel is called the world's smallest Catholic church. The history of St. Martin's goes back to 1886, when it served 100 families. It was a mission of the Fayetteville parish then, as it is now. In 1915 the parish built a schoolhouse in Fayetteville. Since many Warrenton families were moving to Fayetteville, the Warrenton church was torn down so its lumber could be used to build the new school. Just enough wood was retained to build this tiny 12-pew chapel. Mass is celebrated here once a year, on All Saints Day. The bell in the steeple still works.

WARRENTON

Fayette County • 50 • (409) • About 5 miles from Round Top

Warrenton was founded by William Neese, a German immigrant who bought land here in 1854 from Conrad Tiemann. The land had been owned originally by John G. Robison, who was killed by Indians one mile east of here in 1837. His son was Joel Robison, captor of Santa Anna.

Neese married Tiemann's daughter Wilhelmine on New Years Day 1855. He had just built Neese's Store a few months earlier, and so became the settlement's first merchant and postmaster. It was first named for his store, but finally was permanently named for his friend and neighbor Warren Ligon, who had bought 500 acres here in 1852. Ligon wanted to call the settlement Neeseville; Neese favored Warrenton.

Neese also built a cotton gin. He bought local cotton, ginned it, and hauled it to Galveston for sale. In 1868, he started building the two-story sandstone house which stands across the road and a few yards north from the current Warrenton Store. He meant for it to be the finest home between Brenham and La Grange. The Neese family was still living in a double pen log cabin at the time. The sandstone came from a quarry five miles east, toward Willow Springs. The double column two-story portico with iron bannister came from New Orleans.

He didn't enjoy his new house for long. On the evening of 3 October 1872, Neese returned from visiting his brother-in-law and noticed a light on in his store, which stood opposite his house just a few feet south of the current Warrenton Store. He went to investigate, opened the door, and was gunned down by the robber—a freedman. The murderer escaped to La Grange on horseback, but was caught and later convicted of first degree murder. Curiously, he was not hanged—which was the common practice of the time—but was sent instead to the penitentiary at Huntsville. Neese was buried at the Drawe Cemetery two miles east of Warrenton.

The open area directly across the road from the Warrenton Store was originally laid out as the town square. Today it is just a pleasant field, well-shaded by live oaks and surrounded by a half-dozen or so old farmhouses, several of which now house antique shops.

Most of Warrenton's old commercial buildings are closed and mouldering, but Charles Brendle's 1898 **Harmonie Hall,** a combination dance hall and saloon, has been renovated. It stands a few dozen yards south of the Warrenton Store. The Baca Pavilion was moved to its present location from Fayetteville.

WARRENTON INN
SH 237 • 249-3074 • $ • W
The old Krause place, which originally was a grocery store and bar, is now a B&B. Five upstairs bedrooms share two bathrooms. The family room and dining room are downstairs. Country-style breakfast is included in the price. Country-style dinner is available at additional charge. Well-behaved children and pets OK. Write to P.O. Box 182, Warrenton 78961.

WARRENTON STORE
SH 237 • 249-3144
Stop here for local flavor, including yard eggs and barbecue on Saturday (brisket, chicken, and other meats). Come early or call ahead; it's very popular.

OLDENBURG

Fayette County • 54 • About 3.5 miles from Warrenton
Oldenburg was founded in 1836 by Johann Schmitt; it was named by Gus Stenken in honor of the German duchy from which he and many of his neighbors came. They felt very much at home in this alternately open and forested, well-watered, rolling countryside. Oldenburg's decline paralleled that of Texas agriculture.

Just south of Oldenburg, SH 237 ends at SH 159. Continue south toward La Grange on SH 159.

RUTERSVILLE

Fayette County • 72 • (409) • About 2 miles from Oldenburg
Rutersville is the next wide spot on the road to La Grange, but it was once the home of the first institute of higher education in Texas. Martin Ruter, who came to the state in 1837 as superintendent of the Methodist mission in Texas, dreamed of a university that would be the "Athens of the South." It would be located near the geographic center of Texas' already existing settlements and its reasonably antic-ipated settlements and accessible from all directions. Within 90 days of his arrival in Texas, Ruter had established 20 missions. He made public his dream in a sermon to the Congress of the Republic of Texas, whereupon several landowners made him offers of land. Ruter selected the name Bastrop University, wrote a charter, and rode

across Texas soliciting money and students. He died at Washington-on-the-Brazos in May 1838, his dream as yet unfulfilled.

Others carried on his dream. Anticipating the school's success, a group of men acquired title to a tract of land here in June 1838 and began the sale of town lots later that fall. They commenced a promotional campaign and by April 1839 had sold 100 lots.

Meanwhile, the newly organized Texas Conference of the Methodist Church appointed a president for the embryonic university and renamed it Rutersville College. Granted a charter in 1840, the school opened that same year with 63 students. The founders of Rutersville had given 52 acres for the college's male department and 24 for the female department.

As the college grew, so grew Rutersville. By 1841 the college had 100 students and four leagues of land at its disposal, courtesy of the Republic. Peak enrollment was 194, during the 1844–1845 term. Indian attacks, departure of students for the Mexican War, and the establishment of Baylor University caused a decline in enrollment. The school's decline was accelerated by questions of trustee impropriety, faculty misconduct, and the establishment of rival schools nearby.

By 1856 the school's properties had been merged with the Texas Monumental and Military Institute, which closed its doors forever at the outbreak of the Civil War. Rutersville followed the school in decline. Present-day Rutersville, located about a half-mile west of the college site, developed with the construction of modern highways.

Perhaps Rutersville's most famous resident was Asa Hill, the Paul Revere of the infamous Runaway Scrape. A member of the Republican Army in 1836, Hill was sent by General Sam Houston to warn all the people in Santa Anna's path. Hill and sons Jeffrey and John C. C. later joined the ill-fated Mier Expedition of 1842, which is detailed later in this chapter. Both Asa and Jeffrey were captured and imprisoned. But 14-year-old John was adopted by Mexican General Pedro Ampudia, who sent him to school in Matamoros and then to Santa Anna in Mexico City. There he was instrumental in gaining the release of his father and older brother from prison. Asa and Jeffrey returned to Texas immediately thereafter, but young John stayed in Mexico for nearly 40 more years, not returning to Texas until 1880. Asa Hill died here shortly after his return and is buried nearby.

There are quite a few "Three-Legged Willie" Williamson stories recorded in the annals of Texas history, and one of the best concerns an incident that occurred in Rutersville. It seems that a camp meeting was going on here at the time, and Williamson—being mistaken for a man of the cloth—was asked to pray. As a drought was then gripping the countryside, the day had been set aside for rain prayers.

Willie acquiesced to the worshippers' request and began praying: "Lord, we have met today to pray for rain. Lord thou knowest how much we need rain for man and beast. We need copious rains, real copious rains: rootsoakers, gully-washers. Lord we ask thee not to send us little sunshowers that will make our corn produce nubbins that all hell couldn't shuck." At this point his prayer was drowned out by a deafening sea of amens from the horrified congregation. It is not recorded how soon thereafter the next gully-washer fell.

Continue on SH 159 into La Grange.

LA GRANGE

Fayette County • 4,091 • (409) • About 5.5 miles from Rutersville

La Grange's first white settler was the legendary Aylett C. "Strap" Buckner, who built a trading post nearby in 1819. He had come to Texas as early as 1812 as a member of the Gutierrez-Magee Expedition. He was back again with Francisco Xavier Mina in 1816 and again in 1819 with Dr. James Long. Each of these expeditions had entered Texas for the purpose of carving out a republic. In a letter to Stephen F. Austin, Buckner claimed he had been the first person to build a cabin on the Colorado River, that he had kept an open house ever since he came, and that he had lost more property to Indian raiders than anyone else on the river. He became one of Austin's Old Three Hundred with the establishment of that colony. Austin sent him to make a treaty with the Waco and Tawakoni Indians near the present site of Waco in 1824.

Austin could not have sent a more imposing representative. Buckner had quite a reputation. Legend says he possessed the strength of 10 lions, and that he used it like 10 lions. Kind-natured, he had a pride in his strength that eventually became ungovernable. He had a queer penchant, the story goes, for good-naturedly knocking men down. He knocked down every man in Austin's colony at least thrice, including Austin himself. Strap would not hesitate to knock down anything; it was a merry pastime with him to knock a yearling bull stark dead with his fist. Once Strap confronted a great black bull who had been terrorizing the colonists. They had named him Noche. The bull charged Strap on the field of combat, and he met Noche with a blow to the frontlet from his bare fist, which sent the bull staggering back on his haunches and caused the blood to flow in rivers from his smoking nostrils. Recovering from his surprise, Noche turned tail and ran, never to be seen again.

After next impressing the Indians residing nearby with his strength, Buckner got gloriously drunk and declared himself "Champion of the World" and challenged anybody and everybody to fight him, even the Devil himself. At this point a terrible tempest arose, during which the air was filled with smoke and fire and brimstone, and The Devil himself appeared. He took Strap up on his challenge and the ensuing battle lasted a day and night. In the end, the Devil conquered and carried Strap away on a cloud of pale blue smoke.

So much for legend. In real life, Buckner quarreled openly with Austin, then settled down to become his fast friend and ally. Never one to pass up a good fight, Buckner was killed at the Battle of Velasco in 1832. A creek that empties into the Colorado on the western outskirts of La Grange bears his name.

The first building located within the present-day city limits was a twin blockhouse built by James Ross in 1826. John Moore killed Ross in 1826 and took possession of the fort, renaming it Moore's Fort. Neighboring settlers often came to the fort for refuge from Indian attacks.

La Grange had the semblance of a town by 1831, but was not surveyed and platted until 1837, when it became the county seat of the newly created Fayette County. The county was named for the Marquis de Lafayette, the city for Lafayette's estate in France. La Grange means "the meadow."

Moore was the dominant force in early La Grange. Persons who opposed Moore's dream of making La Grange the most important town in Fayette County founded the rival Colorado City, located at the La Bahia Rd. river-crossing, directly across the river from La Grange. The proposed Colorado City was unanimously selected by the Second Congress of the Republic for the capital of Texas, but the bill was vetoed by President Sam Houston. A Colorado River flood destroyed what there was of the city, and the Fayette County court abolished the city in 1841.

La Grange became a center for education in the 1840s and 1850s, with such schools as the La Grange Collegiate Institution, La Grange Female Institute, La Grange Male and Female Seminary, and La Grange Select School. Livestock and cotton, much of the latter grown under the plantation system, also sustained the county's economy before the Civil War.

The county voted against secession by a narrow margin in 1861, but 1,300 Fayette County men marched off to war under the Bonnie Blue Flag nonetheless. Special county war taxes provided relief for the families of soldiers off at the front. Freighters carried cotton stored at La Grange and Round Top down to Mexico, where the bales were exchanged for desperately needed supplies. La Grange's position on both the river and the La Bahia Rd. made it a prime shipping center. Teamsters often sang among themselves to make the long drives less boring, and one of their favorite songs went as follows:

> Hollered at the mule and the mule wouldn't mind: Well, I whopt him in the head with the leadin' line, And it's, "Go on, mule, you better stop saddlin." Hollered at the mule and the mule wouldn't gee: Well, I tuck him in the head with the singletree, And it's "Go on, mule, you better stop saddlin."

Supposedly no Klan organization existed in Fayette County after the Civil War, but violence indicative of Klan activity did exist. In one instance, a "big octoroon Negro from up north came to our county to preach equality to our colored citizens. This copper colored agitator was quietly taken out on the Fayetteville-Rutersville Road one night and hanged to a willow tree. A warning sign was left pinned on him." The teller of the above story also said that Colorado and Fayette County Klansmen reciprocated in their necktie parties (each group hung victims from the other group's county) so that their respective identities might better be kept secret.

By 1882, La Grange had attained increased importance as a regional shipping center. It was now the terminus of a Galveston, Harrisburg, and San Antonio branch line that joined the main GH&SA tracks at Glidden, west of Columbus. The Missouri-Kansas-Texas railroad came through on its way to Houston a couple of years later.

In 1996, La Grange became a Texas Main Street city, and embarked on an ambitious plan to revitalize its downtown by restoring and renovating old historical buildings and finding new uses and businesses for them. La Grange's courthouse square has a number of centenarian buildings; some are modernized, others have been restored or were never altered. The first building to be renovated and restored under the Main Street program was the Dyers Building at the corner of Main and Travis. Built about 1885, it has been a dry goods store, pharmacy/confectionary, and courthouse annex (in 1890, while the current courthouse was under construction). Much of downtown La Grange dates back to the prosperous times at the turn of the twentieth century.

To get downtown, turn right on SH 71-B at its intersection with SH 159. Proceed west on SH 71-B, which is called Travis St. A couple of blocks past the railroad tracks, you pass La Grange High School on your left. One block past the high school, turn right on Monroe and go 1 block to see St. James Episcopal Church.

ST. JAMES EPISCOPAL CHURCH
156 N. Monroe at Colorado • 968-3910

The circa 1885 St. James sanctuary is a good example of that period's American brand of Queen Anne Revival design. Queen Anne Revival as practiced in England was a style of half-timber work, brick, hung tile, and stucco. After its migration to America during the 1870s, the Queen Anne style was often executed in wood alone, the walls being covered with shingles. Richard Upjohn designed the church; his father was a renowned designer of churches and founder of the American Institute of Architects.

Shingles cover most of the walls and the steeply pitched roof of this wooden-framed building. The vastness of the roof is relieved by little gable "eyebrows." The square base of the bell tower is covered with horizontal boards, articulated with diagonal boards as if to simulate half-timbering. Just above are two bands of panels in a repeating quatrefoil design. Tudor spindles, also characteristic of the Queen Anne Revival style, support the porch roof.

Continue west toward downtown on Colorado. Three blocks west of the St. James church is the La Grange post office.

LA GRANGE POST OFFICE
113 E. Colorado at Jefferson

This muted example of Art Moderne architecture—Texas Centennial style—is lifted from anonymity by the bas-relief carvings that decorate the exterior; three separate panels depict the steamship, airplane, and railroad locomotive in their respective 1930s zenith forms.

While we're on the subject of post offices, did you know that the post office's rural free delivery system began right here in La Grange? Texas farmers began getting their mail delivered August 1, 1889, when the nation's first RFD route began operating out of La Grange. Prior to this, farmers had to trek to the nearest post office, which wasn't always very close, to pick up and drop off mail.

In another block, you're at the courthouse square. Park here and take a stroll around the square.

DAWSON OAK
Colorado and Washington

A centuries-old oak tree stands at the corner of Colorado and Washington, in front of the bank. The granite marker beside it tells the tragic, heroic story of Captain Nicholas Mosby Dawson and his company.

For almost a century and a half, this tree has served as a rallying point for Fayette County's war-bound volunteers. When, several days after the fact, news hit La Grange of the Mexican invasion of Texas and subsequent capture of San Antonio on September 11, 1842, Captain Dawson rallied a group of about 16 men here under the oak. Leaving La Grange on September 16, they marched toward San Antonio to reinforce the volunteer Texans who were attempting to recapture the city. Along the way, Dawson's force swelled to 54 strong. They pressed on toward San Antonio as fast as their fatigued horses could carry them.

On September 18, seven days after Mexican General Adrian Woll's capture of San Antonio, Colonel Mathew "Old Paint" Caldwell and his Texans lured the main force of the Mexican invaders into a trap at Salado Creek just north of San Antonio. There the Texans won a decisive victory, checking the Mexican advance and preventing the capture of the Republic capital at Austin.

But as this successful battle was being waged, a tragedy was being enacted just two miles away, unknown to Caldwell and his men. Dawson and his men were intercepted at this point by a force of Mexican cavalry, just minutes away from joining their Texan comrades in battle. Dawson's exhausted Texans took cover in a mesquite thicket and prepared to resist attack. But the Mexicans withdrew from rifle range and brought up two cannons, showering the Texans with death. Soon half the force lay dead or dying. Dawson raised a white flag of surrender, realizing the Texans' cause was hopeless against such odds. As the Texans lay down their arms, the Mexican cavalry charged. Of the 54 men, Dawson and 34 more were slain. Fifteen were captured, three escaped.

Colonel Caldwell and his troops arrived at the scene the next day, to discover a field littered with the stripped and mutilated bodies of their fellow Texans. Heavy rains overnight had bleached the nude corpses to a ghastly white. Caldwell's men buried the unidentifiable bodies of their less fortunate countrymen in a makeshift mass grave.

As news of the invasion and butchery spread across the Republic, there were demands for retaliation, which led to the ill-fated Mier Expedition of Christmas 1842. Again patriotic Fayette County residents rallied at the oak tree, joining the avenging march to Mexico. Under the command of General Alexander Somervell, the Texans had captured Laredo and Guerrero by mid-December, but had failed to engage the Mexican Army. Recognizing that the expedition was a failure, Somervell ordered his army to march home. But only 189 of the men obeyed his order. The remaining 308 troops elected a new commander and chose to attack the border town of Mier. They did so in the afternoon hours of Christmas Day 1842. Outnumbered ten to one, they nonetheless killed 600 Mexicans and wounded 200 more, while only 30 Texans were killed or wounded. But by the afternoon of December 26 the Texans were hungry, thirsty, and low on powder, and their discipline had begun to crack. The Mexican commander General Pedro Ampudia sent a white flag to the Texans and boldly demanded their surrender, saying that he had just been reinforced by a large Mexican contingent. This was a lie, but the Texans' commander fell for the ruse and ordered his troops to lay down their arms. They did so without agreeing on any terms of capitulation, which was a mistake; as soon as the Texans were in Mexican hands, orders for their mass execution were issued. Ampudia reversed these orders, though, and marched the able-bodied Texans over a tortuous route to Salado, Mexico. There the Texans escaped and headed for the Mexican mountains, where they became hopelessly lost. Many died of exposure and starvation, 176 were recaptured, and only 5 made it back to Texas.

The recaptured party was marched back to Salado, where Santa Anna decreed that every tenth man would be shot. The result was the Black Bean Episode, in which 159 white beans and 17 black beans were placed in a jar. Each Texan was blindfolded and ordered to draw a bean. Those drawing black beans were marched to the Salado prison's outer wall and shot in the back.

The remaining prisoners were marched to Mexico City, where Captain Ewen Cameron, mastermind of the Salado escape, was executed. Most of the Texans were placed in the Perote prison. Sixteen of these prisoners tunneled their way out; eight escaped to Texas, eight were recaptured. Over the next year, many died in prison and a few were released at the request of the U.S. government. The remaining prisoners were released by Santa Anna in September 1844, in accordance with the deathbed wish of his wife. The Dawson Oak stands as a living tribute to the indiscriminate bravery of these men.

Continue along Colorado, then take a left on Main.

LUKAS BAKERY
135 N. Main, on the square • 968-3052 • Monday through Friday 5:30–6:30, Saturday 5:30–2 • No Cr. • W
Lukas Bakery supplies many local restaurants with their "homemade" bread, and while bread is the bakery's bread-and-butter product, it also puts out a variety of tasty kolaches, cookies, and pastries guaranteed to do maximum damage to your waistline while inflicting minimum damage to your pocketbook.

Cross Travis/SH 71 and head east on Travis to continue your tour around the courthouse square.

OLD COUNTY JAIL/TOURIST INFORMATION AND CULTURE CENTER
171 S. Main, behind Prause's Market, 1 block south of the courthouse square • (800) 524-7264 • Open daily
This picturesque stone gothic castle dates to 1881. The stone was quarried in nearby Muldoon. The jailer and his family lived in an apartment downstairs. In 1995, the La Grange Chamber of Commerce moved in and the Tourist Information and Culture Center was established here as well. The Center features information about each community in Fayette County and displays of Fayette County Sheriff history, including Sheriff Jim Flourney, made famous by Marvin Zindler and *The Best Little Whorehouse in Texas.* You can take a tour of the cell block and look through the guards' peepholes. No gallows, but the official La Grange hanging rope is on display. It was used in the only two legal hangings in Fayette County, which took place in July 1899 and January 1909. Sheriff August Loessin, who served as Fayette County sheriff for 25 years, presided over both executions. The hangings took place outside on the jail grounds. An admission ticket to one of the hangings, signed by the sheriff, is also on view.

PRAUSE'S MARKET
W. Travis at Main, on the square • 968-3259
Open Monday through Saturday • W
This La Grange institution offers all-star pork and beef-pork sausage, smoked ham, Canadian bacon, and pork tenderloin, in addition to a complete line of fresh meats and larruping good barbecue. Many locals will go nowhere else for their meat.

FRANK'S PLACE CAFE
235 W. Travis • 968-3759 • Open Monday through Saturday, breakfast, lunch, and dinner • $ • W

This downtown mainstay serves big Texas breakfasts, steaks, chicken, quail, pork chops, fish and other seafood, stew, chili, and burgers, both regular and exotic (buffalo, emu). Or just stop for a Shiner and admire the old bar.

PASTIME CLUB
213 W. Travis • 968-5731 • Open daily • W

The trappings are a little plainer and the service friendlier here at the Pastime. The domino tables in the back sit empty most of the time now; all the old-timers are dying off laments Frieda, the part-time barkeep.

Turn left on Washington to complete your tour of the courthouse square.

CITY GROCERY
124 N. Washington, on the square • 968-3393
Open Monday through Saturday • No Cr. • W

The independent-grocery-store-on-the-square downtown is a dying breed. Its prices may be a little higher and its selection of goods may not be as expansive as the bigger chain supermarkets, but the downtown grocery is usually the only place you'll find custom-cut meat and local products such as yard eggs, noodles, and locally ground flour. You'll find these types of items at the City Grocery. One outstanding local product is Burton Dried Sausage from nearby Burton. The handwritten "specials" posted on the store's windows usually include lye, canning jars, and other products essential to soapmaking, home canning, and other of the "old ways" still practiced by area residents.

A few doors up from City Grocery is Texas' oldest still-operating drugstore, housed in one of Central Texas' more unique buildings.

HERMES DRUG STORE
148 N. Washington • 968-3357 • Open Monday through Saturday • W

Step inside Hermes Drug Store and you'll see that you've stepped inside Texas' most antiquely ornate drugstore, as well as its oldest drugstore. The elaborate patterned-tin ceiling is a riot of intricate lyre-and-rose-pattern squares. Wood-and-glass cabinets ornately carved in the Greek Revival style line the north and south walls, highlighted by Ionic columns and oval beveled mirrors.

Each set of cabinets rests atop a wall-length line of wooden drawers stacked three high. Each of the several dozen drawers has its own labeled square ceramic knob. "Sulphur," "Suppositor," "SODA Bibor P.V.," "Insect Guns," "Artists Brushes," "Rubber Bands," "Nux Vomica," "Sundries," "Lamp Black"—these are just a few of the graceful hand-painted inscriptions on the drawer knobs.

Of course, it's been years since some of the drawers have held the contents inscribed on their knobs. Hermes Drug Store has been in operation continuously since 1856, although there hasn't been a Hermes in La Grange for many years.

Built in 1907, this two-story Romanesque Revival structure appears at first to be constructed of rough-cut red sandstone or painted limestone blocks. But take a closer look, specifically at the southern-most second-story column, and you'll see that what appears to be stone is merely stucco over red brick, sculpted and dimpled to look like stone. The contrasting ivory-color window lintels, first-story columns and arches, and cornice trim are also painted stucco. H. W. Speckels was the architect responsible. The one other prominent example in Central Texas of this articulated stucco facade style is the castle-like Old General Land Office building (1857) on the state capital grounds in Austin.

Just around the corner from the Hermes building, at 135 W. Colorado, is another two-story building of similar stucco-over-brick construction, sculpted to look like limestone blocks. It now houses the Weber Insurance Agency. Although the modernized first-story facade has obliterated any cornerstone the building might once have had, the uniformly buff-color second story bears that unmistakable Speckels look.

FAYETTE COUNTY COURTHOUSE
Courthouse square, 151 N. Washington • 968-3251
Monday through Friday 8–5 • Free • W

The most visually arresting building on the square is, of course, the Fayette County Courthouse, built in 1891 to the tune of $96,000. The finished product was well worth the cost, don't you agree?

The exterior walls are Belton white limestone, complemented with blue sandstone quarried at nearby Muldoon. Red Pecos sandstone stringcourses (decorative horizontal mouldings) and pink Burnet granite columns and steps form rich accents. At the base of the clock tower is a large stone slab on which is carved a large American eagle. Above this, at the tower's four corners, are carved griffins. The roof is covered with slate and Spanish tile. The building originally had an open court in the center, but it was converted into a vault and offices during the 1940s.

Take Main north from the courthouse square to its dead end to see four of La Grange's best remaining Victorian gingerbread houses— some restored, some not. From the courthouse square, head east to Jefferson/ US 77 and proceed south. Eight and a half blocks south of the intersection of US 77 and SH 71, you see the Faison home on your right and the Fayette County Library and Museum on your left.

FAISON HOME
822 S. Jefferson • 968-5532 • Group tours by appointment April through August • Admission
This house started life in 1841 as a two-room structure made of local pine. It was acquired and enlarged in 1855 by S. S. Munger. Nathaniel Faison acquired the home in 1866. Faison had been a member of the ill-fated Dawson Expedition, one of the 15 men taken prisoner on the battlefield near San Antonio. Faison was pardoned by Santa Anna and returned to La Grange in 1843. Elected county clerk that year, he worked tirelessly to have the bones of his slain comrades returned to Fayette County. Faison passed away in 1870, but his family owned the house until 1961, when the La Grange Garden Club acquired it, restored it, and turned it into a museum.

Architecturally, the house's most interesting feature is its porch. It is decorated with rococo jigsaw details, the most unusual of which are the trailing brackets located at the base of each porch column, which form a sort of balustrade across the front of the porch.

FAYETTE COUNTY LIBRARY AND MUSEUM
855 S. Jefferson • 968-6418 • Tuesday 10–6:30, Wednesday through Friday 10–5, Saturday 10–1, Sunday 1–5 • Free W first floor only
Directly across Jefferson from the Faison home is the Fayette County library and museum. The museum houses a collection of Fayette County memorabilia and artifacts.

From the museum, continue south on US 77 out of town, across the Colorado River, to Monument Hill State Historical Site. A mile south

*of the river turn right on Spur 92, which leads to the park. The route
to the park is well documented.*

MONUMENT HILL AND KREISCHE BREWERY STATE HISTORICAL PARKS

**Take SH 77 south across the Colorado River, and then 0.4 mile
on Spur 92, west to the park entrance • 968-5658 • Open daily,
except Christmas Day • Admission • W variable**

Here rest the martyrs of the Battle of Salado and the victims of the
Black Bean Episode of the Mier Expedition. Monument Hill and
Kreische Brewery State Historical Parks (40.2 acres) were acquired
by the state over a lengthy period, beginning in 1907. A 0.36 acre
tract (monument and tomb area) was transferred from the Board of
Control in 1949 by legislative act. In 1956 the Archbishop of San
Antonio deeded 3.58 acres (funds for the acreage were donated by
the citizens of Fayette County). The adjacent 36-acre Kreische brewery and home site was acquired in 1977. The park was opened for
tours in 1983, after archaeological and structural work had been
completed and trails improved.

During the Mexican War in 1847, Texas Rangers, under the command of Major Walter P. Lane, detoured from a reconnaissance mission (with Captain John Duesenberry, a "white bean veteran" from
La Grange) and retrieved 16 of the 17 remains buried at Hacienda
Salado. After being carried around on packhorses until the end of the
war, the bones were brought to La Grange by Captain Duesenberry.
In that same year of 1848, citizens from La Grange and Fayette
County went to the Salado Creek burial site near San Antonio and
retrieved the remains of Captain Dawson and his men. The remains
of these two groups of Texas heroes were reburied with full military
honors on September 18, 1848 (the sixth anniversary of the Dawson
massacre), in the tomb on Monument Hill on a beautiful bluff overlooking the Colorado River and the City of La Grange. The site was
specially selected for its grandeur and to appease Fayette County for
the earlier failed attempt to locate the Republic's capital here. Sam
Houston and a host of other dignitaries and citizens from all over the
state attended the ceremonies.

A monument to these fallen men was erected by the state on the La
Grange courthouse square in 1884. A new gray granite vault was
built over the tomb in 1933, and the monument marking the site was
erected in 1936 by the State of Texas as a Texas Independence centennial project.

The Kreische Brewery and Kreische Home Complex

H. L. Kreische immigrated to Texas in 1846 through the port of Galveston. He moved from New Braunfels and purchased this property in 1849. A master stonemason, he lived on this bluff overlooking the Colorado River with his wife, Josepha Appelt Kreische, and six children. Kreische constructed his large three-story stone and wooden home in the hillside, finishing the first portion around 1855 and completing the rest of the home in 1857. Between 1860 and 1870, Kreische devoted most of his attention to brewing beer, and his brewery was one of the first commercial breweries in Texas. He could brew 700 barrels in a good year. By 1879, his brewery was the third-largest brewery in the state. Kreische died in 1882 after an accident. The brewery went out of business by 1884, largely due to increasing competition from mass-produced beers of the day. Today, the stabilized brewery ruins consist of two masonry levels; an original third story made of wood is missing. A barrel-arched vault is located on the lowest level, where Mr. Kreische produced a lager beer, during at least part of the year. Lager is made with a slower fermentation process than other beers, and requires lower temperatures. Kreische made his lager before artificial refrigeration made the practice more common in Texas. He did this by harnessing cold spring waters and channeling cooled air drafts into the fermentation area to keep it cool. The second floor is composed of levels, stairs, and rooms of varying sizes.

The Kreische house is a rectangular structure built into the side of a slope, with two stone stories and a large wooden attic. Kreische's sons and daughters lived in the house until the last daughter, Miss Julia Kreische, died in 1952. The house was still largely intact, with few modern modifications. A museum in the park's headquarters building interprets the Kreische family, the brewery, and the home.

Park activities include picnicking, nature study, and historical study. Arrangements can be made with the park staff to hold weddings, family reunions, or other group functions in the picnic area and/or the historical facilities. Group tours by staff and volunteer docents are available with advanced scheduling, and regularly scheduled tours of the brewery are available on the weekends. The Trail of Lights is held during the first half of December on selected evenings, where visitors can experience a beautifully decorated trail with Christmas lights that overlooks the lighted town of La Grange. It follows the bluff and proceeds through the Kreische home, which is decorated with Christmas trees, wreaths, lamps, and candles and offers entertainment and refreshments. The Monument Hill and

Kreische Brewery Docent Organization sponsors these and other events, with assistance from the park staff. Please call or correspond with the park staff for further information.

The brewery is open for guided tours on Saturday and Sunday afternoons, conducted by the park's trained docents. Tours of the Kreische house are scheduled on selected weekends when docent volunteers are available. This is typically on the first Sunday afternoon of each month. Special weekday group tours of Monument Hill, the Brewery, or the Kreische house can be arranged in advance through the park headquarters. Larger groups enjoy a special overview of the park on a historical, scenic guided tour along the park's interpretive trail (with kolaches and refreshments as an option).

Park facilities include picnic sites; the historical monument and tomb; Kreische house, smokehouse, and barn; interpretive exhibits; a bluff overlook; playground; restrooms without showers; and the Texas State Park Store at the park headquarters. The bluff at Monument Hill is the northern limit of the Oakville Escarpment of Miocene-era-bearing sandstone. This escarpment or "cuesta" marks the boundary between the Upland Post Oak Woodlands and the Fayette Prairie environments. Here, along the bluff, eastern plant and animal communities of the woodlands and prairie coexist with an isolated colony of western species. Numerous plants and animals common to the limestone-based soils of the Hill Country, 70 miles northwest, have been transported and deposited in this locale by the Colorado River, located at the base of the 200-foot bluff cliff. These species flourish in pockets of alkaline soils produced through erosion of the calcareous sandstone cap of the escarpment. The occurrence of such biological diversity at one location is not unique, but is uncommon, and makes this a beautiful place in Central Texas. Oak and cedar forests and predominately little blue stem prairie environments are intermixed throughout the park. Mr. Kreische's old roads, trails, retaining walls, and buildings add beauty and places of shelter to the environment. The park's nature trail has a list of more common plant and animal species and is available at the park headquarters for further study.

Write to 414 State Loop 92, La Grange 78945-5733. *Elevation:* 272 ft. Due to the hilly nature of the park's terrain, some areas are higher and lower than this average. *Weather:* average January minimum temperature 41 degrees; average July maximum temperature 95 degrees; average annual rainfall 37.4 in.

DINING

BON TON RESTAURANT
SH 71-B, at the intersection with SH 71 bypass, on the far west side of La Grange • 968-5863 • Open daily, breakfast, lunch, and dinner • MC, V • W

The Bon Ton is a La Grange eating institution, now at its third location in the last 70 years. The antique charm of the original downtown location has never been recovered here, but the food draws folks in anyway: as always, homestyle country cooking, with homemade bread and pies. There is a buffet for eaters of heroic proportions.

WEIKEL'S STORE AND BAKERY
2247 SH 71-B, across from McDonald's at the intersection with SH 71 bypass, on the far west side of La Grange • 968-9413 Open daily • W

Convenient gas stop on the far west side of town, but the real reason to stop is the baked goods: all sorts of kolaches, cinnamon rolls, pigs in blankets, homemade bread, and the like. An obligatory stop for many travelers.

OTHER AREA ATTRACTIONS

COOPER FARM NATURAL SCIENCE LABORATORY
12 miles northeast of La Grange on Waldeck Rd., off FM 1291

Owned and managed by the LCRA, Cooper Farm is a 180-acre natural science laboratory that tests planting and management techniques that will attract wildlife and contribute to soil conservation. The idea is to show local landowners that wildlife and agriculture are compatible in a region that is heavily agricultural. Several projects are underway or planned, including planting tree stands to give deer protective corridors and relocating deer from other LCRA lands where deer populations have grown too large. In response, neighboring landowners holding more than 20,000 acres have formed a wildlife management cooperative called the North Central Fayette County Wildlife Management Co-op.

Researchers are also studying ways to improve the soil, such as using gypsum as a soil enricher on some of the farm's coastal bermuda grass pastures in order to grow better hay with higher yields. Gypsum is a byproduct of burning coal at nearby Fayette Power Project. A greenhouse holds 2,000 trees and other plants that will be planted at LCRA parks and recreation areas. There is also a 1.3-mile trail that passes through various wildlife plantings and other experimental sites.

ANNUAL EVENT

SEPTEMBER • Fayette County Fair • Fayette County Fairgrounds, US 77 • Labor Day weekend • Admission • W
The fair features entertainment, horse racing, tractor pulls, livestock exhibitions, agricultural and home economics displays, a parade, and dances.

Leave La Grange on US 77 north. Seven miles north of La Grange, turn left on FM 153.

FM 153 winds its way to Winchester through thick stands of fragrant, tall pines.

WINCHESTER

Fayette County • 50 • About 16 miles from La Grange
Winchester was originally settled by John Ingram, who came to Texas at the tender age of 13. After he came of age, he was granted a one-fourth-league tract in Austin's second colony. A veteran of the Battle of Gonzales, the siege of Bexar, and the Battle of San Jacinto, he received a total of nearly 2,000 acres from the Republic and the State of Texas for his wartime services.

The town proper was laid out in 1851 by John Gromme and named for Winchester, Tennessee, birthplace of some of the early settlers. The SA&AP railroad had reached Winchester by 1890, turning the town into a regional shipping center. But with the decline of the railroad and the family farm system, and the growth of the modern highway system, Winchester found itself off the beaten track and has since slipped into a peaceful somnolence. Today, Winchester is a collection of mostly pre-World War I houses and abandoned, slowly decaying frame commercial buildings.

Winchester is also the southernmost tip of the tiny "Wendish Belt" in Central Texas. The Wends are a Slavic people who live in Lusatia in eastern Germany. In 1854, a congregation of nearly 600 Wendish Lutherans led by Rev. Johann Kilian sailed aboard the *Ben Nevis* to Galveston, seeking a better life and escape from Prussian oppression. They settled on a 4,254-acre tract of rather poor land in a German area southwest of Giddings in Lee County, about 11 miles north of Winchester. There they founded Serbin, meaning "Wendish Land." In search of better land, some Wends began to spread into the surrounding countryside, north to Fedor and Loebau in Lee County, and south to Warda and Winchester in Fayette County. The Wends comprise one of the smallest European ethnic communities in the U.S., having immigrated here en masse only once. (To get to Serbin and its wonderfully painted St. Paul Lutheran Church, take FM 448, which intersects FM 153 on the outskirts of Winchester just before you cross the railroad tracks, north to the intersection with FM 2239. Turn left on FM 2239 to reach Serbin.)

After crossing the railroad tracks, turn right on Front St., which parallels the railroad tracks, for a tour of old downtown Winchester. The long-closed Dew Drop Inn sits on the corner of FM 153 and Front. A block and a half later, you come to two old commercial wooden buildings.

The northside building of this pair of classic, turn-of-the-century, shotgun-style stores with rectangular false fronts started life as Winchester's bank. When the bank went bust in 1932, the **Post Office** moved in, and stayed over 50 years. A few yards to the south and west of the old post office (Nueces at Thomas, one block north of FM 153) is the old **Schmidt Store,** the only brick commercial building in town. C. H. Schmidt built this brick, one-story store in 1913, during Winchester's halcyon days. It was his third store here. He came from Germany in 1890 and built his first store in 1892. Outgrowing that wooden building, he built another, larger store in 1908, which he outgrew only four years later. Schmidt sold everything but coffins. At the time, Schmidt competed with half a dozen other general merchandise stores in town. He died in 1921, and his daughter and son-in-law took over the store. Grandson Calvin Harris took over the store in 1973 and ran it until 1989. It has changed owners and names several times since.

ST. MICHAEL'S LUTHERAN CHURCH
North edge of town • Sunday worship service 9 A.M.

Set on Winchester's "hill," St. Michael's Church with its whitewashed spire is easily visible. The congregation dates to 1876, but not by that name. On St. Michael's Day 1887, members gathered to choose a name for their congregation, and that's what they chose. The current wooden sanctuary dates to 1906. The spare interior reflects the attitudes of the church's founders; its most ornate features are the white altar imported from Germany and the baptismal built long ago by a congregation member. The pipe organ in the loft dates to the sanctuary's construction and is played every Sunday.

The big red house just west of the church is the old **Ramsey Hotel,** built by Mr. and Mrs. Alex Ramsey sometime during the 1890s in downtown Winchester. He was also postmaster. The hotel had six rooms downstairs and six more upstairs. After the Ramseys died, Ben Noack bought it. Several years later he had it torn down and reassembled as before at its current location. It has been remodeled several times since and is currently a private residence.

From Winchester, continue west on FM 153. In a little over 3 miles, you cross back into Bastrop County. Before you get to SH 71 and Smithville, there are two more points of interest along FM 153.

ROCKY HILL RANCH
Off FM 153 (north side), about 9 miles from Winchester
512-237-3112 • Open daily • Fee • W variable
Rocky Hill Ranch is a 1,200-acre ranch with over 30 miles of mountain bike trails over several different types of terrain; there are rocks, sand, dirt, pine forest, canyons, hills, and creek crossings. The trail system is graded according to the individual rider's skill level. Green trails have gentle slopes and limited technical riding. Blue trails have challenging slopes, stream crossings and technical riding. Black trails have very challenging slopes, crossings, and technical riding. The 3-mile Rocky Hill expert course features "the wall," a 60-degree canyon crossing that only a handful of riders have pedaled up. Several NORBA races are held here yearly; ex-world professional road champion Lance Armstrong has ridden and raced here during the off-season. Helmets are required. Families welcome. Hikers are also welcome. Other diversions include sand volleyball, fishing, horseshoe pitching, and washers. You can camp at a historic springfed waterhole where Indians and wagon trains once camped. The Rocky Hill Cafe and Saloon serves cold drinks, beer, burgers, and sandwiches and features rock and country bands on weekends. Sunsets from the saloon's front porch are great.

BUESCHER STATE PARK
Park Rd. 1, off FM 153, about 10 miles from Winchester
512-237-2241 • Open daily • Admission • W variable

A virtual twin to nearby Bastrop State Park, Buescher State Park measures 1,016 acres. Between the years 1933 and 1936, Mr. Emile Buescher deeded 318 acres of land to the state. After his death, his heirs donated 318 more acres, and the rest of the park land was acquired from the city of Smithville. The opening in 1940 of the original park totaled 1,738 acres, but approximately 700 acres were deeded to the M. D. Anderson and UT Cancer Center.

El Camino Real (King's Highway) once ran near the park, connecting San Antonio de Bexar with Spanish missions in East Texas. It generally followed present-day SH 21 and the Old San Antonio Road. The original park improvements were made by the Civilian Conservation Corps. A scenic road connects Buescher State Park with Bastrop State Park, traveling through a part of the Lost Pines, a remnant of what was probably once an extensive pine-oak forest that covered much of Central Texas during a time when Ice-Age glaciers reigned not too far to the north.

Activities include biking, boating, fishing in a stocked lake, lake swimming, nature study, and hiking. The 13-mile-long winding and hilly road between Buescher and Bastrop State Parks is ideal for biking, but should be used only by experienced cyclists.

Approximately 6 miles between the parks is private land; do not camp between parks or trespass on private land. The park's facilities include restrooms with and without showers; campsites with water; campsites with water and electricity; screened shelters; picnic sites; a dump station; a playground and group picnic pavilion (for day use only, capacity 75) with a fireplace, picnic tables, and a restroom with showers in the area. A recreational hall (for day and night use; capacity 150) with a full kitchen, heat, fans, a patio, a fireplace, and a restroom. There is a Texas State Park Store. The beautiful wooded setting, which includes a lake, makes for fruitful birding; some 250 species of birds spend time in or inhabit the park over the course of a year. Mammals include white-tailed deer, raccoons, opossums, bobcats, and armadillos, along with rabbits, squirrels and small rodents. Fish for catfish, bass, crappie, and perch, plus rainbow trout in the winter.

Write to P.O. Box 75, Smithville 78957-0075. *Elevation:* 324 ft. *Weather:* Average rainfall of 36.5 in. January minimum temperature 38 degrees and July maximum 96 degrees.

Not far away to the west is the old Alum Creek Settlement, where Andy Potter, the man who was to become known across Texas as the Fightin' Parson, got religion.

Potter, who once called himself "the ringleader in sin," at first found Alum Creek an ideal place to live, but later called it the worst community he had ever seen. On the Sabbath, he and his crowd would assemble at the grocery, get drunk, fight, and gamble. He and Noah Smithwick seemed to have a particular affinity for each other, never forsaking each other even in the direst of circumstances. But after a bloody fight that pitted the two of them against a dozen or more men, Smithwick told him, "Potter, it is time to stop; it is time to reform." He went to the camp meeting going on at the time and was converted. Potter's comment: "I had lost my strongest brother in sin."

Indignant over the conversion of his friend Smithwick, Potter attended the next meeting, with no good purpose. But instead of busting up the services, Potter was won over to the Lord by Brother John's sermon and was led to the altar by Smithwick.

Previously a leader in sin, Potter now felt he had to be a leader in the new life. So even though he could not write and had only read a few chapters from the Bible, he entered the itinerant ministry, a profession that took him all over Texas and the frontier.

Turn left on Loop 230 from FM 153 and travel the last 2 miles into Smithville to complete the trip.

INDEX